John Almon

The Remembrancer:

Or, Impartial Repository of Public Events. For the Year 1777

John Almon

The Remembrancer:
Or, Impartial Repository of Public Events. For the Year 1777

ISBN/EAN: 9783337903817

Printed in Europe, USA, Canada, Australia, Japan

Cover: Foto ©ninafisch / pixelio.de

More available books at **www.hansebooks.com**

Ubi Libertas, ibi patria

BENJAMIN FRANKLIN, LL.D. & F.R.S.

" *Those who would give up Essential Liberty to purchase
a little Temporary Safety, deserve neither Liberty nor
Safety.*" *Address of the Assembly of Pennsylvania, in 1755.*

Engraved from an Original Picture by Jn.° Lodge.

Printed according to Act of Parliament, for J. Almon in Piccadilly, London, 21st April 1777.

REMEMBRANCER;

OR

IMPARTIAL REPOSITORY

OF

PUBLIC EVENTS.

For the YEAR 1777.

REMEMBRANCER.

The Constitution of the Commonwealth of Pennsylvania, as established by the General Convention elected for that Purpose, and held at Philadelphia, July 15th, 1776, and continued by Adjournments to September 28, 1776. Published by Authority.

WHEREAS all government ought to be instituted and supported for the security and protection of the community as such, and to enable the individuals who compose it to enjoy their natural rights, and the other blessings which the author of existence has bestowed upon man ; and whenever these great ends of government are not obtained, the people have a right, by common consent, to change it, and take such measures as to them may appear necessary to promote their safety and happiness. And whereas the inhabitants of this common-wealth have, in consideration of protection only, heretofore acknowledged allegiance to the King of Great-Britain, and the said King has not only withdrawn that protection, but commenced and still continues to carry on, with unabated vengeance, a most cruel and unjust war against them, employing therein not only the troops of Great-Britain, but foreign mercenaries, savages and slaves, for the avowed purpose of reducing them to a total and abject submission to the despotic domination of the British parliament, with many other acts of tyranny, (more fully set forth in the Declaration of Congress) whereby all allegiance and fealty to the said King and his successors are dissolved and at an end, and all power and authority derived from him ceased in these colonies. And whereas it is absolutely necessary for the welfare and safety of the inhabitants of said colonies, that they be henceforth free and independent states, and that just, permanent

A   nent

nent and proper forms of government exist in every part of them, derived from, and founded on the authority of, the people only, agreeable to the directions of the Honourable American Congress. We, the Representatives of the Freemen of Pennsylvania in General Convention met, for the express purpose of framing such a government, confessing the goodness of the great Governor of the Universe (who alone knows to what degree of earthly happiness mankind may attain by perfecting the arts of government) in permitting the people of this state, by common consent, and without violence, deliberately to form for themselves such just rules as they shall think best, for governing their future society; and being fully convinced that it is our indispensable duty to establish such original principles of government as will best promote the general happiness of the people of this state and their posterity, and provide for future improvements, without partiality for or prejudice against any particular class, sect or denomination of men whatever, Do, by virtue of the authority vested in us by our constituents, ordain, declare and establish the following Declaration of Rights and Frame of Government to be The Constitution of the Common-wealth, and to remain in force therein for ever, unaltered, except in such articles as shall hereafter on experience be found to require improvement, and which shall by the same authority of the people, fairly delegated as this frame of government directs, be amended or improved for the more effectual obtaining and securing the great end and design of all government, herein before mentioned.

CHAPTER I.

A Declaration of the Rights of the Inhabitants of the State of Pennsylvania.

I. THAT all men are born equally free and independent, and have certain natural, inherent and unalienable rights, amongst which are the enjoying and defending life and liberty, acquiring, possessing and protecting property, and pursuing and obtaining happiness and safety.

II. That all men have a natural and unalienable right to worship Almighty God according to the dictates of their own consciences and understanding : And that no man ought or of right can be compelled to attend any religious worship, or erect or support any place of worship, or maintain any ministry, contrary to, or against, his own free will and consent : Nor can any man, who acknowledges the being of a God, be justly deprived or abridged of any civil right as a citizen, on account of his religious sentiments or peculiar mode of religious worship : And that no authority can or ought to be vested in, or assumed by, any power whatever, that shall in any case interfere with, or in any manner controul, the right of conscience in the free exercise of religious worship.

III. That the people of this state have the sole exclusive and inherent right of governing and regulating the internal police of the same.

IV. That all power being originally inherent in, and consequently derived from, the people ; therefore all officers of government, whether legislative or executive, are their trustees and servants, and at all times accountable to them.

V. That government is, or ought to be, instituted for the common benefit, protection and security of the people, nation or community ; and not for the particular emolument or advantage of any single man, family or set of men who are a part only of that community : And that the community hath an indubitable, unalienable and indefeasible right to reform, alter or abolish government in such manner as shall be by that community judged most conducive to the public weal.   VI.

VI. That those who are employed in the legislative and executive business of the state may be restrained from oppression, the people have a right, at such periods as they may think proper, to reduce their public officers to a private station, and supply the vacancies by certain and regular elections.

VII. That all elections ought to be free ; and that all free men having a sufficient evident common interest with, and attachment to the community, have a right to elect officers, or be elected into office.

VIII. That every member of society hath a right to be protected in the enjoyment of life, liberty and property, and therefore is bound to contribute his proportion towards the expence of that protection, and yield his personal service, when necessary, or an equivalent thereto : But no part of a man's property can be justly taken from him, or applied to public uses, without his own consent, or that of his legal representatives : Nor can any man who is conscientiously scrupulous of bearing arms, be justly compelled thereto, if he will pay such equivalent : Nor are the people bound by any laws, but such as they have in like manner assented to, for their common good.

IX. That in all prosecutions for criminal offences, a man hath a right to be heard by himself and his council, to demand the cause and nature of his accusation, to be confronted with the witnesses, to call for evidence in his favour, and a speedy public trial, by an impartial jury of the country, without the unanimous consent of which jury he cannot be found guilty : Nor can he be compelled to give evidence against himself: Nor can any man be justly deprived of his liberty, except by the laws of the land or the judgment of his peers.

X. That the people have a right to hold themselves, their houses; papers and possessions free from search or seizure ; and therefore warrants without oaths or affirmations first made, affording a sufficient foundation for them, and whereby any officer or messenger may be commanded or required to search suspected places, or to seize any person or persons, his or their property, not particularly described, are contrary to that right, and ought not to be granted.

XI. That in controversies respecting property, and in suits between man and man, the parties have a right to trial by jury, which ought to be held sacred,

XII. That the people have a right to freedom of speech, and of writing, and publishing their sentiments ; therefore the freedom of the press ought not to be restrained.

XIII. That the people have a right to bear arms for the defence of themselves and the state ; and as standing armies, in the time of peace, are dangerous to liberty, they ought not to be kept up : And that the military should be kept under strict subordination to, and governed by, the civil power.

XIV. That a frequent recurrence to fundamental principles, and a firm adherence to justice, moderation, temperance, industry and frugality, are absolutely necessary to preserve the blessings of liberty, and keep a government free : The people ought therefore to pay particular attention to these points in the choice of officers and representatives, and have a right to exact a due and constant regard to them, from their legislators and magistrates in the making and executing such laws as are necessary for the good government of the state.

XV. That all men have a natural inherent right to emigrate from one state to another that will receive them, or to form a new state in vacant countries, or in such countries as they can purchase, whenever they think that thereby they may promote their own happiness.

A 2   XVI.

XVI. That the people have a right to affemble together, to confult for their common good, to inftruct their reprefentatives, and to apply to the legiflature for redrefs of grievances, by addrefs, petition or remonftrance.

CHAPTER II.
Plan or Frame of Government.

Sect. 1. The common-wealth, or ftate of Pennfylvania fhall be governed hereafter by an affembly of the reprefentatives of the freemen of the fame, and a prefident and council, in manner and form following—

Sect. 2. The fupreme legiflative power fhall be vefted in a houfe of reprefentatives of the freemen of the common-wealth or ftate of Pennfylvania.

Sect. 3. The fupreme executive power fhall be vefted in a prefident and council.

Sect. 4. Courts of juftice fhall be eftablifhed in the city of Philadelphia and in every county of this ftate.

Sect. 5. The freemen of this common-wealth and their fons fhall be trained and armed for its defence, under fuch regulations, reftrictions and exceptions as the general affembly fhall by law direct, preferving always to the people the right of chufing their colonel and all commiffioned officers under that rank in fuch manner and as often as by the faid laws fhall be directed.

Sect. 6. Every freeman of the full age of twenty-one years, having refided in this ftate for the fpace of one whole year next before the day of election for reprefentatives, and paid public taxes during that time, fhall enjoy the right of an elector: provided always, that fons of freeholders of the age of twenty-one years fhall be entitled to vote although they have not paid taxes.

Sect. 7. The houfe of reprefentatives of the freemen of this common-wealth fhall confift of perfons moft noted for wifdom and virtue, to be chofen by the freemen of every city and county of this common-wealth refpectively. And no perfon fhall be elected unlefs he has refided in the city or county for which he fhall be chofen two years immediately before the faid election; nor fhall any member, while he continues fuch, hold any other office except in the militia.

Sect. 8. No perfon fhall be capable of being elected a member to ferve in the houfe of reprefentatives of the freemen of this common-wealth more than four years in feven.

Sect. 9. The members of the houfe of reprefentatives fhall be chofen annually by ballot by the freemen of the common-wealth, on the fecond Tuefday in October for ever, (except this prefent year) and fhall meet on the fourth Monday of the fame month, and fhall be ftiled, The General Affembly of Reprefentatives of the Freemen of Pennfylvania, and fhall have power to choofe their fpeaker, the treafurer of the ftate, and their other officers; fit on their own adjournments; prepare bills and enact them into laws; judge of the elections and qualifications of their own members; they may expel a member, but not a fecond time for the fame caufe; they may adminifter oaths or affirmations on examination of witneffes; redrefs grievances; impeach ftate criminals; grant charters of incorporation; conftitute towns, boroughs, cities and counties: and fhall have all other powers neceffary for the legiflature of a free ftate or common-wealth :—But they fhall have no power to add to, alter, abolifh, or infringe any part of this conftitution.

Sect. 10. A quorum of the houfe of reprefentatives fhall confift of two thirds of the whole number of members elected; and having met and chofen their fpeaker, fhall each of them before they proceed to bufinefs take and fubfcribe, as well the oath or affirmation of fidelity and allegiance herein after directed, as the following oath or affirmation, viz.

" I

"I ——— do swear (or affirm) "that as a member of this assembly, "I will not propose or assent to any "bill, vote, or resolution, which "shall appear to me injurious to the "people; nor do consent to any act "or thing whatever that shall have a "tendency to lessen or abridge their "rights and privileges, as declared "in the constitution of this state; but "will in all things conduct myself as "a faithful honest representative and "guardian of the people, according "to the best of my judgment and "abilities."

And each member, before he takes his seat, shall make and subscribe the following declaration, viz.

" I do believe in one God, the "Creator and Governor of the Uni- "verse, the rewarder of the good "and punisher of the wicked. And "I do acknowledge the Scriptures of "the Old and New Testament to be "given by Divine Inspiration."

And no further or other religious test shall ever hereafter be required of any civil officer or magistrate in this state.

Sect. 11. Delegates to represent this state in Congress shall be chosen by ballot by the future general assembly at their first meeting, and annually for ever afterwards, as long as such representation shall be necessary. Any delegate may be superseded at any time, by the general assembly appointing another in his stead. No man shall sit in Congress longer than two years successively, nor be capable of re-election for three years afterwards: and no person who holds any office in the gift of the Congress shall hereafter be elected to represent this common-wealth in Congress.

Sect. 12. If any city or cities, county or counties shall neglect or refuse to elect and send representatives to the general assembly, two thirds of the members from the cities or counties that do elect and send representatives, provided they be a majority of the cities and counties of the whole state when met, shall have all the powers of the general assembly as fully and amply as if the whole were present.

Sect. 13. The doors of the house in which the representatives of the freemen of this state shall sit in general assembly, shall be and remain open for the admission of all persons who behave decently, except when the welfare of this state may require the doors to be shut.

Sect. 14. The votes and proceedings of the general assembly shall be printed weekly during their sitting, with the yeas and nays on any question, vote or resolution, where any two members require it, except when the vote is taken by ballot; and when the yeas and nays are so taken, every member shall have a right to insert the reasons of his vote upon the minutes, if he desire it.

Sect. 15. To the end that laws before they are enacted may be more maturely considered, and the inconvenience of hasty determinations as much as possible prevented, all bills of a public nature shall be printed for the consideration of the people, before they are read in general assembly the last time for debate and amendment; and except on occasions of sudden necessity, shall not be passed into laws until the next session of assembly; and for the more perfect satisfaction of the public, the reasons and motives for making such laws shall be fully and clearly expressed in the preambles.

Sect. 16. The stile of the laws of this common-wealth shall be, " Be it enacted, and it is hereby enacted by the representatives of the freemen of the common-wealth of Pennsylvania, in general assembly met, and by the authority of the same." And the general assembly shall affix their seal to every bill, as soon as it is enacted into a law, which seal shall be kept by the assembly and shall be called, The Seal of the Laws of Pennsylvania, and

and shall not be used for any other purpose.

Sect. 17. The city of Philadelphia and each county in this commonwealth respectively, shall on the first Tuesday of November in this present year, and on the second Tuesday in October, annually for the two next succeeding years, to wit, the year one thousand seven hundred and seventy-seven, and the year one thousand seven hundred and seventy-eight, chuse six persons to represent them in general assembly. But as representation in proportion to the number of taxable inhabitants is the only principle which can at all times secure liberty and make the voice of the majority of the people the law of the land; therefore the general assembly shall cause compleat lists of the taxable inhabitants in the city and each county in the common-wealth respectively, to be taken and returned to them, on or before the last meeting of the assembly, elected in the year one thousand seven hundred and seventy-eight, who shall appoint a representation to each, in proportion to the number of taxables in such returns, which representation shall continue for the next seven years afterwards, at the end of which, a new return of the taxable inhabitants shall be made, and a representation agreeable thereto appointed by the said assembly, and so on septennially for ever. The wages of the representatives in general assembly, and all other state charges shall be paid out of the state treasury.

Sect. 18. In order that the freemen of this common-wealth may enjoy the benefit of election as equally as may be until the representation shall commence, as directed in the foregoing section, each county at its own choice may be divided into districts, hold elections therein, and elect their representatives in the county, and their other elective officers, as shall be hereafter regulated by the general as-

sembly of this state. And no inhabitant of this state shall have more than one annual vote at the general election for representatives in assembly.

Sect. 19. For the present, the supreme executive council of this state shall consist of twelve persons, chosen in the following manner: The freemen of the city of Philadelphia and of the counties of Philadelphia, Chester and Bucks respectively, shall choose by ballot one person for the city and one for each county aforesaid, to serve for three years, and no longer, at the time and place for electing representatives in general assembly. The freemen of the counties of Lancaster, York, Cumberland and Berks, shall in like manner, elect one person for each county respectively, to serve as counsellors for two years and no longer. And the counties of Northampton, Bedford, Northumberland and Westmoreland respectively, shall, in like manner, elect one person for each county, to serve as counsellors for one year and no longer. And at the expiration of the time for which each counsellor was chosen to serve, the freemen of the city of Philadelphia and of the several counties in this state respectively, shall elect one person to serve as counsellor for three years, and no longer; and so on every third year for ever. By this mode of election and continual rotation, more men will be trained to public business, there will in every subsequent year be found in the council, a number of persons acquainted with the proceedings of the foregoing years, whereby the business will be more consistently conducted, and moreover the danger of establishing an inconvenient aristocracy, will be effectually prevented. All vacancies in the council that may happen by death, resignation, or otherwise, shall be filled at the next general election for representatives in general assembly, unless a particular election

election for that purpose shall be sooner appointed by the president and council. No member of the general assembly or delegate in congress, shall be chosen a member of the council. The president and vice-president shall be chosen annually by the joint ballot of the general assembly and council, of the members of the council. Any person having served as a counsellor for three successive years, shall be incapable of holding that office for four years afterwards. Every member of the council shall be a justice of the peace for the whole commonwealth, by virtue of his office.

In case new additional counties shall hereafter be erected in this state, such county or counties shall elect a counsellor, and such county or counties shall be annexed to the next neighbouring counties, and shall take rotation with such counties.

The council shall meet annually, at the same time and place with the general assembly.

The treasurer of the state, trustees of the loan-office, naval officers, collectors of customs or excise, judge of the admiralty, attornies-general, sheriffs, and prothonotaries, shall not be capable of a seat in the general assembly, executive council, or continental congress.

Sect. 20. The president, and in his absence the vice-president, with the council, five of whom shall be a quorum, shall have power to appoint and commissionate judges, naval officers, judge of the admiralty, attorney-general and all other officers, civil and military, except such as are chosen by the general assembly, or the people, agreeable to this frame of government and the laws that may be made hereafter; and shall supply every vacancy, in any office, occasioned by death, resignation, removal or disqualification, until the office can be filled in the time and manner directed by law or this constitution. They are to correspond with other states, and

transact business with the officers of government, civil and military; and to prepare such business as may appear to them necessary, to lay before the general assembly. They shall sit as judges, to hear and determine on impeachments, taking to their assistance, for advice only, the justices of the supreme court. And shall have power to grant pardons, and remit fines, in all cases whatsoever, except in cases of impeachment; and in cases of treason and murder shall have power to grant reprieves, but not to pardon, until the end of the next sessions of assembly; but there shall be no remission or mitigation of punishment on impeachments, except by act of the legislature; they are also to take care that the laws be faithfully executed; they are to expedite the execution of such measures as may be resolved on by the general assembly; and they may draw upon the treasury for such sums as shall be appropriated by the house: they may also lay embargoes, or prohibit the exportation of any commodity, for any time, not exceeding thirty days, in the recess of the house only: they may grant such licences as shall be directed by law, and shall have power to call together the general assembly when necessary, before the day to which they shall stand adjourned. The president shall be commander in chief of the forces of the state, but shall not command in person, except advised thereto by the council, and then only so long as they shall approve thereof. The president and council shall have a secretary, and keep fair books of their proceedings, wherein any counsellor may enter his dissent, with his reasons in support of it.

Sect. 21. All commissions shall be in the name, and by the authority of the freemen of the common-wealth of Pennsylvania, sealed with the state seal, signed by the president or vice-president, and attested by the secretary; which seal shall be kept by the council.   Sect.

Sect. 22. Every officer of state, whether judicial or executive, shall be liable to be impeached by the General Assembly, either when in office, or after his resignation, or removal for mal-administration: All impeachments shall be before the president or vice-president and council, who shall hear and determine the same.

Sect. 23. The judges of the supreme court of judicature shall have fixed salaries, be commissioned for seven years only, though capable of re-appointment at the end of that term, but removable for misbehaviour at any time by the General Assembly; —they shall not be allowed to sit as members in the Continental Congress, Executive Council, or General Assembly, nor to hold any other office civil or military, nor to take or receive fees or perquisites of any kind.

Sect. 24. The Supreme Court and the several courts of Common Pleas of this common-wealth shall, besides the powers usually exercised by such courts, have the powers of a court of Chancery, so far as relates to the perpetuating testimony, obtaining evidence from places not within this state, and the care of the persons and estates of those who are *non compotes mentis*, and such other powers as may be found necessary by future General Assemblies, not inconsistent with this constitution.

Sect. 25. Trials shall be by jury as heretofore: And it is recommended to the legislature of this state to provide by law against every corruption or partiality in the choice, return, or appointment of juries.

Sect. 26. Courts of Sessions, Common Pleas, and Orphans Courts shall be held quarterly in each city and county; and the legislature shall have power to establish all such other courts as they may judge for the good of the inhabitants of the state. All courts shall be open, and justice shall be impartially administered without corruption or unnecessary delay: All

their officers shall be paid an adequate but moderate compensation for their services: And if any officer shall take greater or other fees than the laws allow him, either directly or indirectly, it shall ever after disqualify him from holding any office in this state.

Sect. 27. All prosecutions shall commence in the name and by the authority of the freemen of the common-wealth of Pennsylvania; and all indictments shall conclude with these words, " Against the peace and dignity of the same." The style of all process hereafter in this state shall be, The Common-Wealth of Pennsylvania.

Sect. 28. The person of a debtor, where there is not a strong presumption of fraud, shall not be continued in prison, after delivering up, *bona fide*, all his estate real and personal, for the use of his creditors, in such manner as shall be hereafter regulated by law. All prisoners shall be bailable by sufficient sureties, unless for capital offences, when the proof is evident or presumption great.

Sect. 29. Excessive bail shall not be exacted for bailable offences: And all fines shall be moderate.

Sect. 30. Justices of the peace shall be elected by the freeholders of each city and county respectively, that is to say, two or more persons may be chosen for each ward, township or district, as the law shall hereafter direct: And their names shall be returned to the president in council, who shall commissionate one or more of them for each ward, township or district so returning, for seven years, removable for misconduct by the General Assembly:—But if any city or county, ward, township or district in this common-wealth, shall hereafter incline to change the manner of appointing their justices of the peace as settled in this article, the General Assembly may make laws to regulate the same, agreeable to the desire of a majority of the freeholders of the city

or county, ward, townfhip, or diftrict fo applying. No juftice of the
peace fhall fit in the General Affembly unlefs he firft refign his commiffion, nor fhall he be allowed to take
any fees ; nor any falary or allowance
except fuch as the future legiflature
may grant.

Sect. 31. Sheriffs and coroners
fhall be elected annually in each city
and county, by the freemen ; that is
to fay, two perfons for each office,
one of whom for each, is to be commiffioned by the prefident in council.
No perfon fhall continue in the office
of fheriff more than three fucceffive
years, or be capable of being again
elected during four years afterwards.
The election fhall be held at the fame
time and place appointed for the election of reprefentatives : And the commiffioners and affeffors, and other
officers chofen by the people, fhall
alfo be then and there elected, as has
been ufual heretofore, until altered
or otherwife regulated by the future
legiflature of this ftate.

Sect. 32. All elections, whether
by the people or in General Affembly, fhall be by ballot, free and voluntary : And any elector, who fhall
receive any gift or reward for his
vote, in meat, drink, monies or
otherwife, fhall forfeit his right to
elect for that time, and fuffer fuch
other penalty as future laws fhall direct. And any perfon who fhall directly or indirectly give, promife or
beftow any fuch rewards to be elected,
fhall be thereby rendered incapable
to ferve for the enfuing year.

Sect. 33. All fees, licence money,
fines and forfeitures heretofore granted, or paid to the governor, or his
deputies for the fupport of government, fhall hereafter be paid into the
public treafury, unlefs altered or abo-
lifhed by the future legiflature.

Sect. 34. A regifter's office for the
probate of wills and granting letters

of adminiftration, and an office for
the recording of deeds, fhall be kept
in each city and county : the officers
to be appointed by the General Affembly, removeable at their pleafure,
and to be commiffioned by the prefident in council.

Sect. 35. The printing-preffes
fhall be free to every perfon who un-
dertakes to examine the proceedings
of the legiflature, or any part of government.

Sect. 36. As every freeman, to
preferve his independence, (if without a fufficient eftate) ought to have
fome profeffion, calling, trade or
farm, whereby he may honeftly fub-
fift, there can be no neceffity for,
nor ufe in eftablifhing offices of profit,
the ufual effects of which are dependence and fervility, unbecoming freemen, in the poffeffors and expect-
ants ; faction, contention, corruption,
and diforder among the people. But
if any man is called into public fervice, to the prejudice of his private
affairs, he has a right to a reafonable
compenfation : and whenever an
office, through increafe of fees, or
otherwife, becomes fo profitable as to
occafion many to apply for it, the
profits ought to be leffened by the
legiflature.

Sect. 37. The future legiflature of
this ftate, fhall regulate intails in
fuch a manner as to prevent perpe-
tuities.

Sect. 38. The penal laws as heretofore ufed, fhall be reformed by the
future legiflature of this ftate, as
foon as may be, and punifhments
made in fome cafes lefs fanguinary,
and in general more proportionate to
the crimes.

Sect. 39. To deter more effectually
from the commiffion of crimes, by
continued vifible punifhment of long
duration, and to make fanguinary
punifhments lefs neceffary, houfes
ought to be provided for punifhing

B
by

by hard labour, thofe who fhall be convicted of crimes not capital; wherein the criminals fhall be employed for the benefit of the public, or for reparation of injuries done to private perfons: and all perfons at proper times fhall be admitted to fee the prifoners at their labour.

Sect. 40. Every officer, whether judicial, executive or military, in authority under this common-wealth, fhall take the following oath or affirmation of allegiance, and general oath of office before he enter on the execution of his office: The oath or affirmation of allegiance: " I ——— " do fwear, (or affirm) that I will " be true and faithful to the com-" mon-wealth of Pennfylvania: and " that I will not directly or indirectly " do any act or thing prejudicial or " injurious to the conftitution or go-" vernment thereof as eftablifhed by " the convention." The oath or affirmation of office: " I ——— do " fwear (or affirm) that I will faith-" fully execute the office of ——— " for the ——— of ———, and " will do equal right and juftice to " all men to the beft of my judgment " and abilities, according to law."—

Sect. 41. No public tax, cuftom or contribution fhall be impofed upon, or paid by the people of this ftate, except by a law for that purpofe: and before any law be made for raifing it, the purpofe for which any tax is to be raifed ought to appear clearly to the legiflature to be of more fervice to the community than the money would be, if not collected, which being well obferved, taxes can never be burthens.

Sect. 42. Every foreigner of good character, who comes to fettle in this ftate, having firft taken an oath or affirmation of allegiance to the fame, may purchafe, or by other juft means acquire, hold and transfer land or other real eftate; and after one year's refidence, fhall be deemed a free denizen thereof, and entitled to all the rights of a natural born fubject of this ftate, except that he fhall not be capable of being elected a reprefentative until after two years refidence.

Sect. 43. The inhabitants of this ftate fhall have liberty to fowl and hunt in feafonable times on the lands they hold, and on all other lands therein not inclofed; and in like manner to fifh in all boatable waters and others not private property.

Sect. 44. A fchool or fchools fhall be eftablifhed in each county by the legiflature, for the convenient inftruction of youth, with fuch falaries to the mafters paid by the public as may enable them to inftruct youth at low prices: and all ufeful learning fhall be duly encouraged and promoted in one or more univerfities.

Sect. 45. Laws for the encouragement of virtue, and prevention of vice and immorality, fhall be made and conftantly kept in force, and provifion fhall be made for their due execution: and all religious focieties or bodies of men heretofore united or incorporated for the advancement of religion and learning, or for other pious and charitable purpofes, fhall be encouraged and protected in the enjoyment of the privileges, immunities and eftates which they were accuftomed to enjoy, or could of right have enjoyed under the laws and former conftitution of this ftate.

Sect. 46. The declaration of rights is hereby declared to be a part of the conftitution of this common-wealth, and ought never to be violated on any pretence whatever.

Sect. 47. In order that the freedom of this common-wealth may be preferved inviolate for ever, there fhall be chofen by ballot by the freemen in each city and county refpectively, on the fecond Tuefday in October, in the year one thoufand feven hundred and eighty three, and on the fecond Tuefday in October in every feventh year thereafter, two perfons in each city and county of this

this state, to be called the Council of Censors; who shall meet together on the second Monday of November, next ensuing their election; the majority of whom shall be a quorum in every case, except as to calling a convention, in which two thirds of the whole number elected shall agree; and whose duty it shall be to enquire whether the constitution has been preserved inviolate in every part? And whether the legislative and executive branches of government have performed their duty as guardians of the people, or assumed to themselves, or exercised other or greater powers than they are intitled to by the constitution: they are also to enquire whether the public taxes have been justly laid and collected in all parts of this common-wealth, in what manner the public monies have been disposed of, and whether the laws have been duly executed: for these purposes they shall have power to send for persons, papers and records; they shall have authority to pass public censures, to order impeachments, and to recommend to the legislature the repealing such laws as appear to them to have been enacted contrary to the principles of the constitution: these powers they shall continue to have, for and during the space of one year from the day of their election, and no longer: the said Council of Censors shall also have power to call a convention, to meet within two years after their sitting, if there appear to them an absolute necessity of amending any article of the constitution which may be defective, explaining such as may be thought not clearly expressed, and of adding such as are necessary for the preservation of the rights and happiness of the people: but the articles to be amended, and the amendments proposed, and such articles as are proposed to be added

or abolished, shall be promulgated at least six months before the day appointed for the election of such convention, for the previous consideration of the people, that they may have an opportunity of instructing their delegates on the subject.

The AMERICAN CRISIS.
Number I.
By the Author of Common Sense.

THESE are the times that try men's souls. The summer soldier and the sunshine patriot will, in this crisis, shrink from the service of his country; but he that stands it *now*, deserves the thanks of man and woman. Tyranny, like hell, is not easily conquered; yet we have this consolation with us, that the harder the conflict, the more glorious the triumph. What we obtain too cheap, we esteem too lightly:— 'Tis dearness only that gives every thing its value. Heaven knows how to set a proper price upon its goods; and it would be strange indeed, if so celestial an article as FREEDOM should not be highly rated. Britain, with an army to enforce her tyranny, has declared, that she has a right *(not only to* TAX*)* but " *to* BIND *us in* ALL CASES WHATSOEVER," and if being *bound in that manner* is not slavery, then is there not such a thing as slavery upon earth. Even the expression is impious, for so unlimited a power can belong only to GOD.

Whether the independance of the Continent was declared too soon, or delayed too long, I will not now enter into as an argument; my own simple opinion is, that had it been eight months earlier, it would have been much better. We did not make a proper use of last winter, neither could we, while we were in a dependant state. However, the fault, if it were one, was all our own; we have none to blame but ourselves*. But no great

---

* The present winter (meaning the last) is worth an age, if rightly employed, but if lost, or neglected, the whole continent will partake of the evil; and there is no punishment that man does not deserve, be he who, or what, or where he will, that may be the means of sacrificing a season so precious and useful. *Common Sense.*

deal

deal is loft yet; all that Howe has been doing for this month paft, is rather a ravage than a conqueft, which the fpirit of the Jerfies a year ago would have quickly repulfed, and which time and a little refolution will foon recover.

I have as little fuperftition in me as any man living, but my fecret opinion has ever been, and ftill is, that God Almighty will not give up a people to military deftruction, or leave them unfupportedly to perifh, who had fo earneftly and fo repeatedly fought to avoid the calamities of war, by every decent method which wifdom could invent. Neither have I fo much of the infidel in me, as to fuppofe, that He has relinquifhed the government of the world, and given us up to the care of devils; and as I do not, I cannot fee on what grounds the can look up to heaven for help againft us: A common murderer, a highwayman, or a houfe-breaker, has as good a pretence as he.

'Tis furprifing to fee how rapidly a panic will fometimes run through a country. All nations and ages have been fubject to them. Britain has trembled like an ague at the report of a French fleet of flat-bottomed boats; and in the fourteenth century, the whole Englifh army, after ravaging the kingdom of France, was driven back like men petrified with fear; and this brave exploit was performed by a few broken forces, collected and headed by a woman, Joan of Arc. Would that heaven might infpire fome Jerfey maid to fpirit up her countrymen, and fave her fair fellow fufferers from ravage and ravifhment! Yet panics, in fome cafes, have their ufes; they produce as much good as hurt. Their duration is always fhort; the mind foon grows through them, and acquires a firmer habit than before. But their peculiar advantage is, that they are the touchftones of fincerity and hypocrify, and bring things and men to light, which might otherwife

have lain for ever undifcovered. In fact, they have the fame effect on fecret traitors, which an imaginary apparition would upon a private murderer. They fift out the hidden thoughts of man, and hold them up in public to the world. Many a difguifed Tory has lately fhewn his head, that fhall penitentially folemnife with curfes the day on which Howe arrived upon the Delaware.

As I was with the troops at fort Lee, and marched with them to the edge of Pennfylvania, I am well acquainted with many circumftances, which thofe who lived at a diftance know but little or nothing of. Our fituation there was exceedingly cramped, the place being on a narrow neck of land, between the North river and the Hackenfack. Our force was inconfiderable, being not one fourth fo great as Howe could bring againft us. We had no army at hand to have relieved the garrifon, had we fhut ourfelves up and flood on the defence. Our ammunition, light artillery, and the beft part of our ftores, had been removed upon the apprehenfion that Howe would endeavour to penetrate the Jerfies, in which cafe fort Lee could be of no ufe to us; for it muft occur to every thinking man, whether in the army or not, that thefe kind of field forts are only for temporary purpofes, and laft in ufe no longer than the enemy directs his force againft the particular object which fuch forts are raifed to defend. Such was our fituation and condition at fort Lee on the morning of the 20th of November, when an officer arrived with information that the enemy with two hundred boats had landed about feven or eight miles above. Major General Green, who commanded the garrifon, immediately ordered them under arms, and fent exprefs to his Excellency General Wafhington, at the town of Hackenfack, diftant by way of the ferry, fix miles. Our firft object was to fecure the bridge over the Hackenfack,

fack, which laid up the river between the enemy and us, about fix miles from us and three from them. General Washington arrived in about three quarters of an hour, and marched at the head of the troops towards the bridge, which place I expected we fhould have a brufh for; however, they did not chufe to difpute it with us, and the greateft part of our troops went over the bridge, the reft over the ferry, except fome which paffed at a mill on a fmall creek, between the bridge and the ferry, and made their way through fome marfhy grounds up to the town of Hackenfack, and there paffed the river. We brought off as much baggage as the waggons could contain, the reft was left. The fimple object was to bring off the garrifon, and to march them on till they could be ftrengthened by the Jerfey or Pennfylvania militia, fo as to be enabled to make a ftand. We ftaid four days at Newark, collected in our outpofts, with fome of the Jerfey militia, and marched out twice to meet the enemy, on information of their being advancing, though our numbers were greatly inferior to theirs. General Howe, in my opinion, committed a great error in generalfhip, in not throwing a body of forces off from Statten-ifland through Amboy, by which means he might have feized all our ftores at Brunfwick, and intercepted our march into Pennfylvania. But if we believe the power of hell to be limited, we muft likewife believe that their agents are under fome providential controul.

I fhall not now attempt to give all the particulars of our retreat to the Delaware; fuffice it for the prefent to fay, that both officers and men, though greatly haraffed and fatigued, frequently without reft, covering, or provifion, the inevitable confequences of a long retreat, bore it with a manly and a martial fpirit. All their wifhes were one, which was that the country would turn out and help them to drive the enemy back. Voltaire has remarked, that King William never appeared to full advantage but in difficulties and in action; the fame remark may be made on General Wafhington, for the character fits him. There is a natural firmnefs in fome minds, which cannot be unlocked by trifles, but which, when unlocked, difcovers a cabinet of fortitude; and I reckon it among thofe kind of public bleffings which we do not immediately fee, that God had bleft him with uninterrupted health, and given him a mind that can even flourifh upon care.

I fhall conclude this paper with fome mifcellaneous remarks on the ftate of our affairs, and fhall begin with afking the following queftion, Why is it that the enemy hath left the New-England provinces, and made thefe middle ones the feat of war? The anfwer is eafy: New-England is not infefted with Tories, and we are. I have been tender in raifing the cry againft thefe men, and ufed numberlefs arguments to fhew them their danger, but it will not do to facrifice a world to either their folly or their bafenefs. The period is now arrived in which either they or we muft change our fentiments, or one or both muft fall. And what is a Tory? Good God! What is he? I fhould not be afraid to go with an hundred Whigs againft a thoufand Tories, were they to attempt to get into arms. Every Tory is a coward, for a fervile, flavifh, felf-interefted fear is the foundation of Toryifm; and a man under fuch influence, though he may be cruel, never can be brave.

But before the line of irrecoverable feparation be drawn between us, let us reafon the matter together: Your conduct is an invitation to the enemy, yet not one in a thoufand of you has heart enough to join him. Howe is as much deceived by you as the American caufe is injured by you. He expects you will all take up arms and flock to his ftandard with mufkets on

your

your shoulders. Your opinions are of no use to him unless you support him personally, for it is soldiers and not Tories that he wants.

I once felt all that kind of anger, which a man ought to feel, against the mean principles that are held by the Tories. A noted one, who kept a tavern at Amboy, was standing at his door, with as pretty a child in his hand, about eight or nine years old, as most I ever saw, and after speaking his mind as freely as he thought was prudent, finished with this unfatherly expression, " *Well! give me peace in my days.*" Not a man lives on the Continent but fully believes that separation must some time or other finally take place, and a generous parent would have said, " *If there must be trouble, let it be in my day, that my child may have peace ;*" and this single reflexion, well applied, is sufficient to awaken every man to duty. Not a place upon earth might be so happy as America. Her situation is remote from all the wrangling world, and she has nothing to do but to trade with them. A man may easily distinguish in himself between temper and principle, and I am as confident, as I am that God governs the world, that America will never be happy till she gets clear of foreign dominion. Wars, without ceasing, will break out till that period arrives, and the Continent must in the end be conqueror; for, though the flame of liberty may sometimes cease to shine, the coal never can expire.

America did not, nor does not want force ; but she wanted a proper application of that force. Wisdom is not the purchase of a day, and it is no wonder that we should err at first setting off. From an excess of tenderness, we were unwilling to raise an army, and trusted our cause to the temporary defence of a well meaning militia. A summer's experience has now taught us better ; yet with those troops, while they were collected, we

were able to set bounds to the progress of the enemy ; and, thank GOD ! they are again assembling. I always considered a militia as the best troops in the world for a sudden exertion, but they will not do for a long campaign. Howe, it is probable, will make an attempt on this city ; should he fail on this side the Delaware, he is ruined ; if he succeeds, our cause is not ruined. He stakes all on his side against a part on ours ; admitting he succeeds, the consequence will be, that armies from both ends of the continent will march to assist their suffering friends in the middle states ; for he cannot go every where, it is impossible. I consider Howe as the greatest enemy the Tories have ; he is bringing a war into their country, which, had it not been for him and partly for themselves, they had been clear of. Should he now be expelled, I wish with all the devotion of a Christian, that the names of Whig and Tory may never more be mentioned ; but should the Tories give him encouragement to come, or assistance if he come, I as sincerely wish that our next year's arms may expel them from the Continent, and the Congress appropriate their possessions to the relief of those who have suffered in well doing. A single successful battle next year will settle the whole. America could carry on a two years war by the confiscation of the property of disaffected persons, and be made happy by their expulsion. Say not that this is revenge, call it rather the soft resentment of a suffering people, who, having no object in view but the GOOD OF ALL, have staked their OWN ALL upon a seemingly doubtful event. Yet it is folly to argue against determined hardness ; eloquence may strike the ear, and the language of sorrow draw forth the tear of compassion, but nothing can reach the heart that is steeled with prejudice.

Quitting this class of men, I turn, with the warm ardour of a friend, to those thofe who have nobly ftood, and are yet determined to ftand the matter out. I call not upon a few, but upon all; not on THIS ftate or THAT ftate, but on every ftate; up and help us; lay your fhoulders to the wheel; better have too much force than too little, when fo great an object is at ftake. Let it be told to the future world, that in the depth of winter, when nothing but hope and virtue could furvive, that the city and the country, alarmed at one common danger, came forth to meet and to repulfe it. Say not that thoufands are gone, turn out your tens of thoufands; throw not the burthen of the day upon Providence, but *fhew your faith by your works*, that GOD may blefs you. It matters not where you live, or what rank of life you hold, the evil or the blefling will reach you all. The far and the near, the home counties and the back, the rich and the poor, fhall fuffer or rejoice alike. The heart that feels not now is dead. The blood of his children fhall curfe his cowardice, who fhrinks back at a time when a little might have faved the whole, and made *them* happy. I love the man that can fmile in trouble, that can gather ftrength from diftrefs, and grow brave by reflection. 'Tis the bufinefs of little minds to fhrink; but he, whofe heart is firm, and whofe confcience approves his conduct, will purfue his principles unto death. My own line of reafoning is to myfelf, as ftrait and clear as a ray of light. Not all the treafures of the world, fo far as I believe, could have induced me to fupport an offenfive war, for I think it murder; but if a thief break into my houfe, burn or deftroy my property, and kill or threaten to kill me or thofe that are in it, and to "*bind me in all cafes whatfoever*," to his abfolute will, am I to fuffer it? What fignifies it to me, whether he who does it, is a   or a common man; my countryman, or not my countryman; whether it is done by an individual villain, or an army of them?

If we reafon to the root of things we fhall find no difference; neither can any juft caufe be affigned why we fhould punifh in the one cafe and pardon in the other. Let them call me rebel, and welcome, I feel no concern from it; but I fhould fuffer the mifery of devils, were I to make a whore of my foul by   whofe   is of a ftupid, ftubborn, worthlefs, brutifh man. I conceive likewife a horrid idea in receiving   from   who at the laft day fhall be fhrieking to the rocks and mountains to cover him, and fleeing with terror from the orphan, the widow, and the flain of America.

There are cafes which cannot be overdone by language, and this is one. There are perfons too who fee not the full extent of the evil that threatens them; they folace themfelves with hopes that the enemy, if they fucceed, will be merciful. It is the madnefs of folly to expect mercy from thofe who have refufed to do juftice, and even mercy, where conqueft is the object, is only a trick of war. The cunning of the fox is as murderous as the violence of the wolf, and we ought to guard equally againft both. Howe's firft object is partly by threats and partly by promifes, to terrify or feduce the people to deliver up their arms, and receive mercy. The miniftry recommended the fame plan to Gage, and this is what the Tories call making their peace; " a " peace which paffeth all underftanding" indeed! A peace which would be the immediate forerunner of a worfe ruin than any we have yet thought of. Ye men of Pennfylvania, do reafon upon thofe things! Were the back counties to give up their arms, they would fall an eafy prey to the Indians, who are all armed. This perhaps is what fome Tories would not be forry for. Were the home counties to deliver up their arms, they would be expofed to the refentment of the back counties,

counties, who would then have it in their power to chastise their defection at pleasure. And were any one state to give up its arms, THAT state must be garrisoned by all Howe's army of Britons and Hessians, to preserve it from the anger of the rest. Mutual fear is a principal link in the chain of mutual love, and woe be to that state that breaks the compact. Howe is mercifully inviting you to barbarous destruction, and men must be either rogues or fools that will not see it. I dwell not upon the vapours of imagination, I bring reason to your ears, and in language as plain as A, B, C, hold up truth to your eyes.

I thank God that I fear not. I see no real cause for fear. I know our situation well, and can see the way out of it. While our army was collected, Howe dared not risk a battle, and it is no credit to him that he decamped from the White Plains, and waited a mean opportunity to ravage the defenceless Jersies; but it is great credit to us, that, with a handful of men, we sustained an orderly retreat for near an hundred miles, brought off our ammunition, all our field pieces, the greatest part of our stores, and had four rivers to pass. None can say that our retreat was precipitate, for we were near three weeks in performing it, that the country might have time to come in. Twice we marched back to meet the enemy, and remained out till dark. The sign of fear was not seen in our camp, and had not some of the cowardly and disaffected inhabitants spread false alarms through the country, the Jersies had never been ravaged. Once more we are again collected and collecting; our new army at both ends of the continent is recruiting fast, and we shall be able to open the next campaign with sixty thousand men, well armed and clothed. This is our situation, and who will may know it. By perseverance and fortitude we have the prospect of a glorious issue;

by cowardice and submission, the sad choice of a variety of evils, a ravaged country, a depopulated city, habitations without safety, and slavery without hope, our homes turned into barracks and bawdy-houses for Hessians, and a future race to provide for whose fathers we shall doubt of. Look on this picture, and weep over it!—And if there yet remains one thoughtless wretch who believes it not, let him suffer it unlamented.

THE AMERICAN CRISIS.
NUMBER II.
By the Author of Common Sense.
TO LORD HOWE.

I come now more particularly to your proclamation of the 30th Nov. last. Had you gained an entire conquest over the armies of America, and then put forth a proclamation, offering (what you call) mercy, your conduct would have had some specious show of humanity; but to creep by surprise into a province, and there endeavour to terrify and seduce the inhabitants from their allegiance to the rest, by promises which you neither meant nor were able to fulfil, is both cruel and unmanly: cruel in its effects; because, unless you can keep all the ground you have marched over, how are you, in the words of your proclamation, to secure to your proselytes " the enjoyment of their property?" What are to become either of your new-adopted subjects, or your old friends the Tories, in Burlington, Bordentown, Trenton, Montholly, and many other places, where you proudly lorded it for a few days, and then fled with the precipitation of a pursued thief? What, I say, are to become of those wretches? What are to become of those who went over to you from this city and state? What more can you say to them than " Shift for " yourselves:" Or what more can they then hope for than to wander like vagabonds over the face of the earth? You may now tell them to take their

leave

leave of America, and all that once was theirs. Recommend them, for confolation, to there perhaps they may make a fhift to live on the fcraps of fome dangling parafite, and chufe companions among thoufands like themfelves. A traitor is the fouleft fiend on earth.

In a political fenfe we ought to thank you for thus bequeathing eftates to the continent ; we fhall foon, at this rate, be able to carry on a war without expence, and grow rich by the ill policy of Lord Howe, and the generous defection of the Tories. Had you fet your foot into this city, you would have beftowed eftates upon us which we never thought of, by bringing forth traitors we were unwilling to fufpect. But thefe men, you will fay, " are his Majefty's moft " faithful fubjects ;" let that honour then be all their fortune, and let his Majefty take them to himfelf.

I am now thoroughly difgufted with them ; they live in ungrateful eafe, and bend their whole minds to mifchief. It feems as if God had given them over to a fpirit of infidelity, and that they are open to conviction in no other line but that of punifhment. It is time to have done with tarring, feathering, carting, and taking fecurities for their future good behaviour ; every fenfible man muft feel a confciencious fhame at feeing a poor fellow hawked about the ftreets for a fhew, when it is known that he is only the tool of fome principal villain, biaffed into his offence by the force of falfe reafoning, or bribed thereto through fad neceffity. We difhonour ourfelves by attacking fuch trifling characters, while greater ones are fuffered to efcape ; 'tis our duty to find *them* out, and their proper punifhment would be to exile them from the continent for ever. The circle of them is not fo great as fome imagine; the influence of a few has tainted many who are not naturally corrupt. A continual circulation of lies among thofe who are not much in the way of hearing them contradicted, will in time pafs for truth ; and the crime lies not in the believer but the inventor. I am not for declaring war againft every man that appears not fo warm as myfelf : difference of conftitution, temper, habit of fpeaking, and many other things, will go a great way in fixing the outward character of a man, yet fimple honefty may remain at bottom. Some men have naturally a military turn, and can brave hardfhips and the rifque of life with a chearful face ; others have not ; no flavery appears to them fo great as the fatigue of arms, and no terror fo powerful as that of perfonal danger : what can we fay ! we cannot alter nature, neither ought we to punifh the fons, becaufe the father begot them in a cowardly mood. However, I believe moft men have more courage than they know of, and that a little at firft is enough to begin with. I knew the time when I thought that the whiftling of a cannon-ball would almoft have frighten'd me to death ; but I have fince tried it, and find I can ftand it with as little difcompofure, and (I believe) with a much eafier confcience than your Lordfhip. The fame dread would return to me again were I in your fituation, for my folemn belief of your caufe is, that it is hellifh and damnable, and under that conviction every thinking man's heart *muft* fail him.

From a concern that a good caufe fhould be difhonoured by the leaft difunion among us, I faid in my former paper, No. I. " That fhould " the enemy now be expelled, I wifh, " with all the fincerity of a chriftian, " that the names of whig and tory " might never more be mentioned ;" but there is a knot of men among us of fuch a venomous caft, that they will not admit even one's good wifhes to act in their favour. Inftead of rejoicing that heaven had, as it were, providentially preferved this city from

C   plunder

plunder and destruction, by delivering so great a part of the enemy into our hands with so little effusion of blood, they stubbornly affected to disbelieve it till within an hour, nay half an hour of the prisoners arriving : and the quakers put forth a testimony dated the 20th December, signed, " John Pemberton" declaring their attachment to the British government*. These men are continually harping on the great sin of our bearing arms, but ———— may lay waste the world in blood and famine, and they, poor fallen souls, have nothing to say.

In some future paper I intend to distinguish between the different kind of persons who have been denominated *Tories* ; for, this I am clear in, that all are not so who have been called so ; and, as I mean not to conceal the name of any true friend, when there shall be occasion to mention him, neither will I that of an enemy, who ought to be known, let his rank, station, or religion be what it may. Much pains have been taken by some, to set your Lordship's private character in an amiable light, but as it has chiefly been done by men who know nothing about you, and who are no way remarkable for their attachment to us, we have no just authority for believing it. ———— was imposed on us by the same arts, but time at length, has done him justice, and the same fate may probably attend your lordship. Your avowed purpose here is to kill, conquer, plunder, pardon, and enslave ; and the ravages of your army through the Jerseys, have been marked with as much

barbarism, as if you had openly professed yourself the prince of Ruffians ; not even the appearance of humanity has been preserved, either on the march or the retreat of your troops ; no general order, that I could ever learn, has ever been issued to prevent, or even forbid your troops from robbery wherever they came, and the only instance of justice, if it can be called such, which has distinguished you for impartiality, is, that you treated and plundered all alike ; what could not be carried away have been destroyed, and mahogany furniture have been deliberately laid on the fire for fuel, rather than men should be fatigued with cutting wood†. There was a time when the whigs confided much in your supposed candour, and the tories rested themselves on your favour ; the experiments have now been made and failed ; and every town, nay, every cottage in the Jersies where your arms have been, is a testimony against you. How you may rest under this sacrifice of character I know not, but this I know, that you sleep and rise with the daily curses of thousands upon you ; perhaps the misery which the tories have suffered by your proffered mercy, give them some claim to their country's pity, and be in the end the best favour you could show them.

In a folio general order book belonging to Col. Rohl's battalion, taken at Trenton, and now in the possession of the Council of Safety for this state, the following barbarous order is frequently repeated, " His Excellency the Commander in Chief, orders, that all in-

---

* I have ever been careful of charging offences upon whole societies of men, but as the paper referred to is put forth by an unknown set of men, who claim to themselves the right of representing the whole ; and while the whole society of Quakers admit its validity by a silent acknowledgment, it is impossible that any distinction can be made ; and the more so, because the New-York Paper of the 30th December, printed by permission of our enemies, says that " the Quakers begin to speak openly of their attachment to the British Constitution." We are certain that we have many friends among them, and wish to know them.

† As some people may doubt the truth of such wanton destruction, I think it necessary to inform, that one of the people called Quakers, who lives at Trenton, gave me this information at the house of Mr. Michael Hutchinson (one of the same profession) who lives near to Trenton ferry, on the Pennsylvania side ; Mr. Hutchinson being present.

habitants

habitants which shall be found with arms, not having an officer with them, shall be immediately taken and hung up."—How many you may have thus privately sacrificed we know not, and the account can only be settled in another world. Your treatment of prisoners, in order to distress them to enlist into your infernal service, is not to be equalled by any instance in Europe. Yet this is the humane Lord Howe and his brother, whom the tories, and their three-quarter kindred the quakers, or some of them at least, have been holding up for patterns of justice and mercy!

A bad cause will ever be supported by bad means and bad men, and whoever will be at the pains of examining strictly into things, will find that one and the same spirit of oppression and impiety, more or less govern through your whole party in both countries. Not many days ago, I accidentally fell in company with a person of this city, noted for espousing your cause, and on my remarking to him " that it appeared clear to me, by the late providential turn of affairs, that God Almighty was visibly on our side," he replied, " we care nothing for that, you may have *him*, and welcome ; if we have but enough of the devil on our side, we shall do." However carelessly this might be spoken, matters not, 'tis still the insensible principle that directs all your conduct, and will at last most assuredly deceive and ruin you.

By what means, may I ask, do you expect to conquer America? If you could not effect it in the summer when our army was less than yours, nor in the winter when we had none, how are you to do it? In point of generalship you have been outwitted, and in point of fortitude, outdone ; your advantages turn out to your loss, and show us that it is in our power to ruin you by gifts. Like a game of drafts we can move out of *one* square to let you come in, in order that we may afterwards take two or three for one ; and as we can always keep a double corner for ourselves, we can always prevent a total defeat. You cannot be so insensible as not to see that we have two to one the advantage of you, because we conquer by a drawn game, and you lose by it. Burgoyne might have taught your Lordship this knowledge ; he has been long a student in the doctrine of chances.

I have no other idea of conquering countries than by subduing the armies which defend them : Have you done this, or can you do this? If you have not, it would be civil in you to let your proclamations alone for the present ; otherwise, you will ruin more Tories by your grace and favour than you will Whigs by your arms.

Were you to obtain possession of this city, you would not know what to do with it more than to plunder it. To hold it, in the manner you hold New-York, would be an additional dead weight upon your hands ; and if a general conquest is your object, you had better be without the city than with it. When you have defeated all our armies, the cities will fall into your hands of themselves ; but to creep into them in the manner you got into Princeton, Trenton, &c. is like robbing an orchard in the night before the fruit be ripe, and running away in the morning. Your experiment in the Jersies is sufficient to teach you that you have something more to do than barely to get into other people's houses ; and your new converts to whom you promised all manner of protection, and seduced into new guilt by pardoning them from their former virtues, must begin to have a very contemptible opinion both of your power and your policy. Your authority in the Jersies is now reduced to the small circle which your army occupies, and your proclamation is no where else seen unless it be to be laughed at. The mighty subduers of the continent are retreated into a nutshell,

C 2

and

and the proud forgivers of our fins are fled from thofe they came to pardon; and all this at a time when they were difpatching veffel after veffel to England with the great news of every day. In fhort, you have managed your Jerfey expedition fo very dexteroufly that the dead only are conquerors, becaufe none will difpute the ground with them.

In all the wars you have formerly been concerned in, you had only armies to contend with; in this cafe you have both an army and a country to combat with. In former wars, the countries followed the fate of their capitals; Canada fell with Quebec, and Minorca, with Port Mahon or St. Philips; by fubduing thofe, the conquerors opened a way into, and became mafters of the country: Here it is otherwife; if you get poffeffion of a city here, you are obliged to fhut yourfelves up in it, and can make no other ufe of it, than to fpend your country's money in. This is all the advantage you have drawn from New-York; and you would draw lefs from Philadelphia, becaufe it requires more force to keep it, and is much farther from the fea. A pretty figure you and the Tories would cut in this city, with a river full of ice, and a town full of fire; for the immediate confequence of your getting here would be, that you would be cannonaded out again, and the Tories be obliged to make good the damage; and this, fooner or later, will be the fate of New-York.

I wifh to fee the city faved, not fo much from military, as from natural motives. 'Tis the hiding-place of women and children, and Lord Howe's proper bufinefs is with our armies. When I put all the circumftances together which ought to be taken, I laugh at your notion of conquering America. Becaufe you lived in a little country where an army might run over the whole in a few days, and where a fingle company of foldiers might put a multitude to the route, you expect-

ed to find it the fame here. It is plain that you brought over with you all the narrow notions you were bred up with, and imagined that a proclamation in the king's name was to do great things, but Englifhmen always travel for knowledge, and your Lordfhip, I hope will return, if you return at all, much wifer than you came.

We may be furprifed by events we did not expect, and in that interval of recollection you may gain fome temporary advantage: Such was the cafe a few weeks ago, but we foon ripen again into reafon, collect our ftrength, and while you are preparing for a triumph, we came upon you with a defeat. Such it has been, and fuch it would be were you to try it an hundred times over. Were you to garrifon the places you might march over, in order to fecure their fubjection, (for remember you can do it by no other means) your army would be like a ftream of water running to nothing. By the time you reached from New-York to Virginia, you would be reduced to a ftring of drops not capable of hanging together; while we, by retreating from ftate to ftate, like a river turning back upon itfelf, would acquire ftrength in the fame proportion as you loft it, and in the end be capable of overwhelming you. The country in the mean time would fuffer, but 'tis a day of fuffering, and we ought to expect it. What we contend for is worthy the affliction we may go through. If we get but bread to eat, and any kind of raiment to put on, we ought, not only to be contented, but thankful. More than that we ought not to look for, and lefs than that heaven has not yet fuffered us to want. He that would fell his birthright for a little falt, is as worthlefs as he who fold it for porridge without falt. And he that would part with it for a gay coat, or a plain coat, ought for ever to be a flave in buff. What are falt, fugar and finery to the ineftimable bleffings of " liberty and fafety?"

safety?" Or what are the inconveniencies of a few months to the tributary bondage of ages? The meanest peasant in America, blessed with these sentiments, is a happy man compared with a New-York Tory; he can eat his morsel without repining, and when he has done, can sweeten it with a repast of wholesome air, he can take his child by the hand and bless it, without feeling the conscious shame of neglecting a parent's duty.

In publishing these remarks, I have several objects in view: On your part they are, to expose the folly of your pretended authority as a commissioner, the wickedness of your cause in general, and the impossibility of your conquering us at any rate. On the part of the public my meaning is, to show them their true and solid interest; to encourage them to their own good, to remove the fears and falsities which bad men had spread and weak men had encouraged; and to excite in all men a love for union and a chearfulness for duty.

I shall submit one more case to you respecting your conquest of this country, and then proceed to new observations:

Suppose our armies in every part of the continent were immediately to disperse, every man to his home, or where else he might be safe, and engage to re-assemble again on a certain future day; it is clear that you would then have no army to contend with, yet you would be as much at a loss in that case, as you are now; you would be afraid to send your troops in parties over the continent, either to disarm or prevent us from assembling, lest they should not return; and while you kept them together, having no army of ours to dispute with, you could not call it a conquest; you might furnish out a pompous page in the London Gazette, or the New-York paper, but when we returned at the appointed time, you would have the same work to do you had at first.

It has been the folly of Britain to suppose herself more powerful than she really is, and by that means to have arrogated to herself a rank in the world she is not entitled to; for more than this century past she has not been able to carry on a war without foreign assistance. In Marlborough's campaigns, and from that day to this, the number of German troops and officers assisting her have been about equal with her own; ten thousand Hessians were sent to England last war to protect her from a French invasion; and she would have cut but a poor figure in her Canadian and West-Indian expeditions, had not America been lavish of both her money and men to help her along. The only instance in which she was engaged singly, that I can recollect, was against the rebellion in Scotland in forty-five and forty-six, and in that, out of three battles, she was twice beaten, till by thus reducing their numbers (as we shall yours) and taking a supply ship that was coming to Scotland with cloaths, arms and money (as we have often done) she was at last enabled to defeat them. England was never famous by land; her officers have generally been suspected of cowardice; have more of the air of a dancing-master than a soldier, and by the sample we have taken prisoners we begin to give the preference to ourselves. Her strength of late has lain in her extravagance; but as her finances and her credit are now low, her sinews in that line begin to fail fast. As a nation she is the poorest in Europe; for were the whole kingdom, and all that is in it, to be put up to sale like the estate of a bankrupt, it would not fetch as much as she owes: yet this thoughtless wretch must go to war, and with the avowed design too of making us beasts of burthen, to support her in riot and debauchery, and to assist her afterwards in distressing those nations who are now our best friends. This ingratitude may suit a tory, or the unchristian

tian peevifhnefs of a fallen quaker, but none elfe.

'Tis the unhappy temper of the Englifh to be pleafed with any war, right or wrong, be it but fuccefsful; but they foon grow difcontented with ill fortune, and it is an even chance that they are as clamorous for peace next fummer, as were for war laft winter. In this natural view of things, your lordfhip ftands in a very ugly, critical fituation. Your whole character is ftaked upon your laurels; if they wither, you wither with them; if they flourifh, you cannot live long to look at them; and at any rate, the black account hereafter is not far off. What lately appeared to us misfortunes, were only bleffings in difguife; and the feeming advantages on your fide, have turned out to our profit. Even our lofs of this city, as far as we can fee, might be a principal gain to us: the more furface you fpread over, the thinner you will be, and the eafier wiped away; and our confolation under that apparent difafter would be, that the eftates of the Tories would become fecurities for the repairs. In fhort, there is no old ground we can fail upon, but fome new foundation rifes again to fupport us. " We have put, Sir, our hands to the plough, and curfed be he that looketh back."

Your king, in his fpeech to parliament laft fpring, declared to them, " That he had no doubt but the great force they had enabled him to fend to America, would effectually reduce the rebellious colonies." It has not, neither can it; but it has done juft enough to lay the foundation of its own next year's ruin. You are fenfible that you left England in a divided diftracted ftate of politics, and, by the command you had here, you became a principal prop in the court party; their fortunes reft on yours; by a fingle exprefs you can fix their value with the public, and the

degree to which their fpirits fhall rife or fall; they are in your hands as ftock, and you have the fecret of the alley with you. Thus fituated and connected, you become the unintentional mechanical inftrument of your own and their overthrow. The minifters put conqueft out of doubt, and the credit of both depended on the proof. To fupport them in the interim, it was neceffary you fhould make the moft of every thing; and we can tell by Hugh Gaine's New-York paper what the complexion of the London Gazette is. With fuch a lift of victories, the nation cannot expect you will afk new fupplies; and to confefs your want of them, would give the lie to your triumphs, and impeach the minifters of treafonable deception. If you make the neceffary demand at home, your party finks; if you make it not, you fink yourfelf; to afk it now, is too late, and to afk it before, was too foon, and unlefs it arrive quickly will be of no ufe. In fhort, the part you have to act, cannot be acted; and I am fully perfuaded that all you have to truft to, is to do the beft you can with what force you have got, or little more. Though we have greatly excelled you in point of generalfhip and bravery of men, yet, as a people, we have not entered into the full foul of enterprize; for I, who know England and the difpofition of the people well, am confident that it is eafier for us to effect a revolution there, than you a conqueft here: a few thoufand men landed in England with the declared defign

bringing his minifters to trial, and fetting up

ftead, would affuredly carry their point, while you were groveling here ignorant of the matter. As I fend all my papers to England, this, like Common Senfe, will find its way there; and though it may put one party on their guard, it will inform the

the other and the nation in general of our defign to help them.

Thus far, Sir, I have endeavoured to give you a picture of prefent affairs: you may draw from it what conclufions you pleafe. I wifh as well to the true profperity of England as you can, but I confider Independence as America's natural Right and Intereft, and never could fee any real difFervice it would be to Britain. If an Englifh merchant receives an order and is paid for it, it fignifies nothing to him who governs the country. This is my creed of politics. If I have any where expreffed myfelf over warmly, it is from a fixt immovable hatred I have, and ever had, to cruel men and cruel meafures. I have likewife an averfion to monarchy, as being too debafing to the dignity of man; but I never troubled others with my notions till very lately, nor ever publifhed a fyllable in England in my life. What I write is pure nature, and my pen and my foul have ever gone together. My writings I have always given away, referving only the expence of printing and paper, and fometimes not even that. I have never courted either fame or intereft, and my manner of life, to thofe who know it, will juftify what I fay. My ftudy is to be ufeful, and if your lordfhip loves mankind as well as I do, you would, feeing you cannot conquer us, caft about and lend your hand towards accomplifhing a peace. Our Independence, with God's blefling, we will maintain againft all the world; but as we wifh to avoid evil ourfelves, we wifh not to inflict it on others. I am never over inquifitive into the fecrets of the cabinet, but I have fome notion, that if you neglect the prefent opportunity, that it will not be in our power to make a feparate peace with you afterwards; for whatever treaties or alliances we form, we fhall moft faithfully abide by; wherefore you may be deceived, if you think you can make it with us

at any time. A lafting independent peace is my wifh, end, and aim; and to accomplifh that " I pray God the Americans may never be defeated, and I truft while they have good officers, and are well commanded, and willing to be commanded, that they never will." COMMON SENSE. *Philadelphia, Jan.* 13, 1777.

———

The following paper is copied from the Pennfylvania packet of February 4, 1777.
Tranflation of a letter written by a foreigner on his travels.
Dear Sir, *London, Dec.* 3, 1776
I Have now been fix months in England, and eight weeks of the time in or near this metropolis. You fhould have heard from me before, but my frequent excurfions and continual avocations, as well as the want of a proper opportunity, prevented. Agreeable to my promife, however, I now fit down to give you fome account of the character and politics of this ftrange people. So copious a fubject cannot be difcuffed in one letter, but you fhall hear from me again when further obfervation hath enabled me to be more particular.

The general character of the Englifh is certainly the moft abfurd and fantaftic that ever fell to the lot of human nature. As they are made up of contradictions, it would be unjuft to defcribe them by any uniform defignation. There is fcarce a virtue that adorns the mind, or a vice that difgraces mankind, but may be afcribed to them as a nation; but the former are often rendered ineffectual by mifapplication, and the latter qualified by a levity of manners that fhews them not to be conftitutional. An Englifhman will treat his enemy with great generofity, and his friend with ingratitude and inhumanity. He will lavifh his wealth when he has but little, and become a miferable wretch, when fortune pours her riches into his purfe. He will brave the utmoft hardfhips, and

and suffer the severest trials of life with heroic patience; and will drown himself, becaufe the wind is in the eaſt. He will lend large fums to a ſtranger on the flighteſt fecurity; and will go to law with his neareſt relation to wrong him out of his eſtate. To-day his heart expands with focial benevolence; to-morrow he is cold, fullen and reſerved. To day he poſſeſſes the wealth of a nabob; to-morrow he refuſes a groat to a beggar. —In ſhort, contradiction and abfurdity make an Engliſhman.

During the laſt century this people have riſen to a great height of wealth and power; but the inſtability of their temper will not ſuffer them to enjoy any bleſſing in poſſeſſion. At peace with all the world; feared and reſpected by their neighbours; daily enjoying the benefits of an extenſive and uninterrupted commerce; an eſtabliſhed policy, and a reformed religion, are circumſtances fufficient, one would ſuppoſe, to render any people happy and content. But the thirſt of lawleſs ambition can never be ſatisfied.—The Engliſh aſſume to themſelves the character of being the moſt *juſt, generous* and *humane* nation in the world; and yet they carry on the African trade: a trade attended with circumſtances of cruelty and horror that difgrace human nature; whereby they faſten for life the chains of miſery and fervitude on fome hundreds of their fellow creatures every year. They ſent one Clive to the Eaſt Indies to eſtabliſh a dominion there. A country which the Creator never defigned ſhould belong to the Engliſh, as is evident from his placing it on the oppoſite fide of the globe, and made the inhabitants of a different complexion. This Clive however arrived with his forces in the Eaſt-Indies; and under the fanction of his moſt *gracious* majeſty and a *free* parliament, put to death fome hundred thouſands of the inhabitants by the fword, famine, and by the moſt

atrocious cruelties—and ſo returned to England with immenfe riches, and a wife ſet in diamonds, and was made a lord; and then with great deliberation

to the ſatisfaction of the whole court.—You will be furprized at this; but the people here are not ſurprized at all. It is no unuſual thing to ſpend an evening with a great man in all the eaſy gaiety of focial life, and to hear next morning that he had hanged himſelf in a ſtable, or practiſed phlebotomy with a razor on his own jugular vein. The Engliſh now govern in the Eaſt-Indies with a ſupremacy of power, and a tyranny fo pure and unalloyed with any mixture of juſtice or humanity, as could not have been exceeded in the reigns of the twelve Cæfars.

This exploit being accompliſhed to the glory of God and honour of the nation; their *juſt, generous* and *humane* turned his attention to AMERICA. There he had three millions of who loved, honoured and obeyed him. He governed them by men of his own nomination; he had the whole regulation of their commerce, and the overflowings of their wealth were conducted by eaſy and natural channels to his coffers, and to the purſes of the merchants and manufacturers of kingdom. But he has quarrelled with people, becauſe they are fo ſtupid they cannot underſtand, or fo obſtinate that they will not acknowledge that *two and two make five.* Volumes have been written on this fubject, and all the force of reaſon and eloquence exerted to convince this wife that he is in an error. The Americans have moſt emphatically befeeched him to accept of the undiſguiſed loyalty of their hearts, declaring that they are ſatisfied that the fruits of their induſtry ſhould, as *heretofore*, center with him and people to enrich and aggrandize them; but humbly requeſt that they may not

be

be compelled to acknowledge that *two and two make five*, which would be a moſt diſtreſſing violation of truth; as they know and are fully convinced that they make only four.

But this humane ⸻ is far from giving up the point. He has rejected their petitions with ſcorn, and ſpurned at their offers of affection and fidelity. He declares he will even riſk the ⸻ of his anceſtors, but he will make the obſtinate Americans own this new doctrine.

To be as good as his word, he hath ſent over not only ⸻ fleets and armies, but hired a banditti of foreigners from a petty prince, who maintains himſelf and families by the merchandize of human blood, and has alſo employed Negroes and wild Indians to perſecute the poor Americans without mercy, until they ſhall own that *two and two make five*.

America is now a ſcene of deſolation and diſtreſs. A theatre whereon is acted a real tragedy, enriched with every ſpecies of cruelty and injuſtice. The royal army are raviſhing the women, murdering the men, and laying waſte that beautiful country under the conduct of Lord and General Howe, who are cajoling ſome and ruining others of theſe inoffenſive people, with all the compoſure in the world. His moſt gracious ⸻ receives from time to time ſuch accounts of their proceedings as they pleaſe to give him, and is as happy as ſuch a ⸻ can be. Who could have thought that ſo extenſive a country would be ravaged and plundered, becauſe the fooliſh inhabitants will not own that *two and two make five*, when their good and wiſe parliament deſire them to do ſo? eſpecially when the conſequence of ſo doing can be only the utter ruin of themſelves and their poſterity for ever.

But this is not all. The Americans, highly reſenting this treatment, have declared before God and the world, that they will be no longer penſioners of the ſmiles or frowns of ſuch a ⸻, or dependent on the juſtice or humanity of a ⸻ who pays no regard to either; but that they are determined to be from henceforth a free people; and will enjoy the ineſtimable privilege of believing and ſaying that *two and two* make only *four*, agreeable to the common ſenſe of mankind. How this affair will terminate is a matter of ſome uncertainty. But the chance is ten to one that ⸻

⸻ for this ridiculous whim, this *ignis fatuus* in politics.

You will ſay the ⸻ could not act upon ſuch abſurd principles, were he not countenanced and ſupported in his folly by the co-incident folly of the people.—True—But the folly of the people is of a different nature from that of the ⸻. The people ſee plainly with the Americans, that *two and two* can never make *five*, and yet they ſupport ⸻'s *dogma* with might and main. The truth is, they have by degrees reſigned ſo much power into the ⸻'s hands, that they dare not now contradict any thing ⸻ pleaſe to aſſert. And if ⸻ power ſhould be further increaſed by the ſubjection of America to ⸻ diſpoſal, the ruined people of England may bid adieu to their conſtitution for ever. Some of the wiſeſt among them ſay this, and have declared that the ſalvation of England depends on the ſucceſs of the Americans in the preſent war. This infatuated people have tired the world for theſe hundred years with loud eulogiums on liberty and their conſtitution, and yet they daily ſee that very conſtitution languiſhing in a deep conſumption without any efforts for its recovery. Inſtead of enjoying a frame of government beautiful in her proportions, and glowing with health and vigour, they are content to embrace a rotten proſtitute full of wounds

D   and

and bruifes and putrifying fores. Amufed with trifles, and long accuftomed to venality and corruption, they are not alarmed at the dreadful confequences. They love to talk of their beloved conftitution becaufe the idea is agreeable; and they honour their   becaufe it is the fashion. They worship the shadow of liberty with an idolatrous adoration, neglecting the fubftance as a thing of no value. Half the l   y of the nation is fupported by two popular fongs, viz. *God fave the king*, and *Britons strike home*. Thefe are vociferated at taverns, over porter, punch and wine, till the imagination is heated and the blood in a ferment, and then the worthy patriots ftagger forth and commit all manner of riots and excefs in honour of their king and country. There are fanatics in politics as well as religion, and perfecution is the confequence in both, when men refufe to attend to the cool dictates of common fenfe. The men in power know this weaknefs of the multitude; and whenever they find them grow uneafy under their encroachments, they get half a dozen court fcribblers to expatiate on the bleffings of the Britifh conftitution, and fing the fweet lullaby of liberty to the people to keep them quiet. Juft as a nurfe rattles three pieces of tin in a little rufh bafket to amufe her crying child. The poor infant thinks it has the world in poffeffion, and is fatisfied. The Englifh are not a people of an inventive genius. Moft of their able men are natives of other countries. The Scotch far exceed them in literature; and, in the arts, France and other nations invent for them, and they improve upon their inventions. Few ufeful arts owe their origin to native Englifh. The quadrant called Hadley's, was undoubtedly the contrivance of an American, though Hadley affumed the reputation of that difcovery. They were in high luck when a Shakefpeare and a Newton

happened to be born amongft them. The whole nation reft their credit upon thefe two men.

The extreme ignorance of the common people of this *civilized* and *polished* country is fcarcely to be credited. They know nothing but the particular branch of bufinefs to which their parents or the parish happened to put them apprentice. They are compelled to practice *that* with unremitting diligence, and beyond *that* they feldom extend their ideas. A manufacturer has been brought up a maker of pin-heads. He hath been at it forty years, and of courfe he makes them with great dexterity; but he cannot make a whole pin for his life. He thinks it is the perfection of human nature to make pin-heads. He leaves other matters to inferior abilities. It is enough for him that he believes in the Athanafian creed, reverences the fplendor of the court, and makes pin-heads. This he efteems the fum total of religion, politics and trade. He is fure that London is the fineft city in the world; Black-friars the moft magnificent of all poffible bridges, and the river Thames the largeft river in the univerfe.—It is in vain to tell him that there are many rivers in America in comparifon of which the Thames is but a ditch; that there are fingle provinces there larger than all England, and that the colonies formerly belonged to Great-Britain, now independent ftates, are vaftly more extenfive than England, Wales, Scotland and Ireland taken together. He cannot conceive this. He goes into his beft parlour and looks at a map of England five feet fquare; on the other fide of the room he fees a map of North and South America not four feet fquare, and cries *how can this be? It is altogether impoffible!* He has read the Arabian Nights entertainments, and he hears this wonderful account of America. He believes the one as much as the other. That a giant fhould should rise out of the sea, or that the Delaware should be a larger river than the Thames, are equally inconceivable to him. Talk to him of the British constitution, he will tell you it is a glorious one; he adores it. Ask him what it is, and he does not know even its first principles. Mention the freedom of elections, and he will tell you he has no business with these matters—that he lives in a borough, and that it is impossible but that 'Squire Goosecap must represent that borough in parliament; for his lady comes every Sunday to the parish church in a damask gown, and sits in a pew lined with green cloth—how then can it be otherwise?—Besides, 'Squire Goosecap is acquainted with the prime minister. These are things he is no way concerned in. He believes in the Athanasian creed, is astonished at the splendor of the court, and makes pin-heads—and what more can be expected of man?—

It is quite otherwise in America. The lowest of the people there are not without some degree of general knowledge. They turn their hands to every thing. Their situation obliges them to do so. A farmer cannot run to an artist upon every trifling occasion. He must make and mend and contrive for himself. This I observed in my travels through that country. In many towns and in every city they have public libraries. Not a shoemaker nor a taylor but will find time to read. He acquires knowledge imperceptibly and gets a love for books.—He reads voyages and travels, and becomes acquainted with the geography, customs and characters of other countries. He studies the first principles of government; he knows the great outlines of his rights as a free man, as a citizen, and is proud of the character; not as an empty name, but for its substantial benefits. He amuses himself a little with astronomy, and knows that the apparent motion of

the sun is occasioned by the real motion of the earth. In short, he knows that notwithstanding the determination of Lords and Commons to the contrary, *two and two can never make five*.

Such are the people of England, and such are the people of America. They are now at daggers drawn. At first the Americans knew little or nothing of warfare; but they improve daily. The British troops are teaching them the art of conquest, and they find them very apt scholars. The probable consequence is, that England will lose, and America gain an empire.

PHILADELPHIA.
December 19.
GENERAL ORDERS.
Head Quarters, Philadelphia, December 14, 1776.

Colonel Griffin is appointed Adjutant General to the troops in and about this city. All orders from the General, through him, either written or verbal, are to be strictly attended to, and punctually obeyed.

In case of an alarm of fire, the city guards and patroles are to suffer the inhabitants to pass unmolested at any hour of the night, and the good people of Philadelphia are earnestly requested and desired to give every assistance in their power, with engines and buckets, to extinguish the fire. And as the Congress, have ordered the city to be defended to the last extremity, the General hopes that no person will refuse to give every assistance possible to complete the fortifications that are to be erected in and about the city.

ISRAEL PUTNAM.

In CONGRESS, *November* 12, 1776.

Upon re-considering the resolution of the 16th of September last, for raising 88 battalions to serve during the present war with Great-Britain, Congress being of opinion that the readiness of the inhabitants of these states to enter into the service for limited times,

D 2

times, in defence of their invaluable privileges, on all former occasions, gives good ground to hope the same zeal for the public good will appear in future, when the necessity calls for their assistance, and the uncertain length of time which forces raised during the continuance of the war may be compelled to serve, may prevent many from inlisting, who would otherwise readily manifest their attachment to the common cause, by engaging for a limited time:

Therefore resolved, That all non-commissioned officers and soldiers who do not incline to engage their service during the continuance of the present war, and shall inlist to serve three years, unless sooner discharged by Congress, shall be intitled to and receive all such bounty and pay as are allowed to those who inlist during the present war, except the 100 acres of land, which land is to be granted those only who enlist without limitation of time. And each recruiting officer is required to provide two distinct enlisting rolls, one for such to sign who inlist during the continuance of the war, and the other of such as inlist for three years, if their service shall be so long required.

By order of Congress,
JOHN HANCOCK, Pref.

Journal of the American Army, from the taking of Fort Washington.
(Published in the Pennsylvania Journal.)

Fort Washington being obliged to surrender, by a violent attack made by the whole British army, on Saturday the 16th of November, the Generals determined to evacuate Fort Lee, which being principally intended to preserve the communication with Fort Washington, was become in a manner useless. The stores were ordered to be removed, and great part of them was immediately sent off. The enemy knowing the divided state of our army, and that the terms of the soldiers inlist-

ments would soon expire, conceived the design of penetrating into the Jerseys, and hoped, by pushing their successes, to be compleatly victorious. Accordingly, on Wednesday morning, the 20th of November, it was discovered that a large body of British and Hessian troops had crossed the North river, and landed about six miles above the fort. As our force was inferior to that of the enemy, the fort unfinished, and on a narrow neck of land; the garrison was ordered to march for Hackinsack bridge, which, though much nearer the enemy than the fort, they quietly suffered our troops to take possession of. The principal loss suffered at Fort Lee was that of the heavy cannon, the greatest part of which was left behind. Our troops continued at Hackinsack bridge and town that day and half of the next, when the inclemency of the weather, the want of quarters, and approach of the enemy, obliged them to proceed to Aquaconack, and from thence to Newark; a party being left at Aquaconack to observe the motions of the enemy. At Newark our little army was reinforced by Lord Sterling's and Col. Hand's brigades, which had been stationed at Brunswick. Three days after our troops left Hackinsack, a body of the enemy crossed the Passaic above Aquaconack, made their approaches slowly towards Newark, and seemed extremely desirous that we should leave the town without their being put to the trouble of fighting for it. The distance from Newark to Acquaconack is nine miles, and they were three days in marching that distance. From Newark our retreat was to Brunswick, and it was hoped the assistance of the Jersey Militia would enable General Washington to make the Banks of the Rariton the bounds of the enemy's progress; but on the 1st of Dec. the army was greatly weakened, by the expiration of the terms of the enlistments of the Maryland and Jersey Flying Camp; and the
militia

militia not coming in fo foon as was expected, another retreat was the neceffary confequence. Our army reached Trenton on the 4th of December, continued there till the 7th, and then, on the approach of the enemy, it was thought proper to pafs the Delaware.

This retreat was cenfured by fome as pufillanous and difgraceful; but, did they know that our army was at one time lefs than a thoufand effective men, and never more than 4000,—that the number of the enemy was at leaft 8000, exclufive of their artillery and light horfe,—that this handful of Americans retreated *flowly* above 80 miles without lofing a dozen men—and that fuffering themfelves to be forced to an action, would have been their intire deftruction—did they know this, they would never have cenfured it at all—they would have called it prudent—pofterity will call it glorious —and the names of Wafhington and Fabius will run parallel to eternity.

The enemy, intoxicated with fuccefs, refolved to enjoy the fruits of their conqueft. Fearlefs of an attack from this fide the river, they cantoned in parties at a diftance from each other, and fpread mifery and defolation wherever they went. Their rage and luft, their avarice and cruelty, knew no bounds; and murder, ravifhment, plunder, and the moft brutal treatment of every fex and age, were the firft acts that fignalized their conqueft. And if fuch were their outrages on the partial fubjection of a few villages--good God! what confummate wretchednefs is in ftore for that ftate over which their power fhall be fully eftablifhed.

While the enemy were in this fituation, their fecurity was increafed by the captivity of General Lee, who was unfortunately taken in the rear of his army, Dec. 13th, at Bafkinridge, by a party of light-horfe, commanded by Col. Harcourt. The fortune of our arms was now at its loweft ebb — but the tide was beginning to turn—

the militia of this city had joined General Wafhington—the junction of the two armies was foon after effected—and the back counties of this ftate, roufed by the diftreffes of America, poured out their yeomanry to the affiftance of the continental army. General Wafhington began now to have a refpectable force, and refolved not to be idle. On the 26th of December he croffed the Delaware, furprifed three regiments of Heffians, and with little or no lofs, took near a thoufand prifoners. [His letter, which is here inferted in the Journal, the reader will find in page 302, of laft volume.]

Soon after this manœuvre, and while the enemy were collecting their fcattered troops at Princeton and Brunfwick, Gen. Wafhington croffed the Delaware with all his army. On the 2d of January the enemy began to advance towards Trenton, which they entered in the afternoon, and there being nothing but a fmall creek between the two armies, a general engagement was expected next day— This it was manifeftly our advantage to avoid; and by a mafter-ftroke of generalfhip, Gen. Wafhington frees himfelf from his difagreeable fituation, and furprizes a party of the enemy in Princeton, which obliges their main body to return to Brunfwick, as is more particularly related in the following account.

Congrefs has received the following Intelligence from the Army at Pluckemin, in the State of New-Jerfey, Jan. 5.

" On the 2d inft. the enemy began to advance upon us at Trenton; and, after fome fkirmifhing, the head of their column reached that place about four of o'clock, whilft their rear was as far back as Maidenhead. They attempted to pafs Sanpinck creek, which runs through Trenton, at different places; but finding the forts guarded, they halted and kindled their fires. We were drawn up on the fouth fide of the creek. In this
fituation

fituation we remained till dark, cannonading the enemy, and receiving the fire of their field pieces, which did but little damage.

" At twelve o'clock, after renewing our fires, and leaving guards at the bridge in Trenton, and other paffes, on the fame ftream above, we marched by a round about road to Princeton. We found Princeton about fun-rife, with only three regiments, and three troops of light horfe in it, two of which were on their march to Trenton. Thefe three regiments, efpecially the two firft, made a gallant refiftance, and, in killed, wounded, and prifoners, muft have loft five hundred men. Upwards of one hundred of them were left dead on the field ; and with thofe carried on by the army, and fuch as were taken in the purfuit, and carried acrofs the Delaware, there are near three hundred prifoners, fourteen of whom are officers—all Britifh.

" Col, ——, Capt. Neal, of the artillery, Capt. Fleming, who commanded the firft Virginia regiment, and four or five other valuable officers, with about twenty-five or thirty privates, were flain in the field. Our whole lofs cannot be afcertained, as many who were in purfuit of the enemy, whom they chafed three or four miles, are not yet come in. We burnt the enemy's hay, and deftroyed fuch other things as the occafion would admit.

" From the beft intelligence we have been able to get, the enemy were fo much alarmed at the apprehenfion of lofing their ftores at Brunfwick, that they marched immediately thither from Trenton without halting, and got there before day.

" Soon after this affair, General Maxfield furprifed Elizabeth Town, took near an hundred prifouers and a quantity of baggage. By thefe repeated fuccefles the enemy have been obliged to relinquifh almoft all their poffeffions in the Jerfeys, and are now confined to the narrow compafs of Brunfwick and Amboy. On all fides by land they are furrounded by our troops. They cannot ftir out to forage but in large parties, which feldom return without lofs. Their continual apprehenfions of an attack, and our frequent fkirmifhes with them, harrafs them extremely ; and deferters, who come in daily, declare that their duty is heavy beyond conception. From this circumftance we hope in a week or two they will be obliged to retire to their old bounds, from whence, in a few months, they will, probably, be driven on board their fhips. The American arms can never be in the fituation they have been ; partial inliftments are now done away, and it is expected a large ftanding army will be able to take the field early in the fpring. And when our readers are told, that the American army has hitherto been inferior to the enemy in numbers, they may freely encourage the moft fanguine hopes of our future fuccefs."

The following letters are genuine.

Eagle, June the 20th, 1776.

I cannot, my worthy friend, permit the letters and parcels which I have fent (in the ftate I received them) to be landed, without adding a word upon the fubject of the injurious extremities in which our unhappy difputes have engaged us.

You will learn the nature of my miffion, from the official difpatches which I have recommended to be forwarded by the fame conveyance. Retaining all the earneftnefs I ever expreffed to fee our differences accommodated, I fhall conceive, if I meet with the difpofition in the Colonies which I was once taught to expect, the moft flattering hopes of proving ferviceable in the objects of the King's paternal folicitude, by promoting the eftablifhment of lafting peace and union with the Colonies. But if the deep-rooted prejudices of America,

America, and the necessity of preventing her trade from passing into foreign channels, must keep us still a divided people ; I shall, from every private as well as public motive, most heartily lament that this is not the moment wherein those great objects of my ambition are to be attained : and that I am to be longer deprived of an opportunity to assure you personally of the regard with which I am

Your sincere and faithful
humble servant,
HOWE.

P. S. I was disappointed of the opportunity I expected for sending this letter at the the time it was dated. And have been ever since prevented by calms and contrary winds, from getting here, to inform Gen. Howe of the commission with which I have the satisfaction to be charged, and of his being joined in it.

Off of Sandy Hook, 12th of July.
Superscribed HOWE.
To *B. Franklin, Esq; Philadelphia.*

Philadelphia, July 30, 1776.
My Lord,

I received safe the letters your Lordship so kindly forwarded to me, and beg you to accept my thanks.

The official dispatches to which you refer me, contain nothing more than what we had seen in the act of parliament, viz. " Offers of pardon upon submission ;" which I was sorry to find, as it must give your Lordship pain to be sent so far on so hopeless a business.

Directing pardons to be offered to the colonies, who are the very parties injured, expresses indeed that opinion of our ignorance, baseness, and insensibility, which your uninformed and proud nation has long been pleased to entertain of us ; but it can have no other effect than that of increasing our resentments.——It is impossible we should think of submission to a go-vernment, that has with the most wanton barbarity and cruelty burnt our defenceless towns in the midst of winter, excited the savages to massacre our [peaceful] farmers, and our slaves to murder their masters, and is even now * bringing foreign mercenaries to deluge our settlements with blood. These atrocious injuries have extinguished every spark of affection for that parent country we once held so dear :—but were it possible for *us* to forget and forgive them, it is not possible for *you* (I mean the British nation) to forgive the people you have so heavily injured ;—you can never confide again in those as fellow subjects, and permit them to enjoy equal freedom, to whom you know you have given such just causes of lasting enmity ; and this must impel you, were we again under your government, to endeavour the breaking our spirit by the severest tyranny, and obstructing by every means in your power our growing strength and prosperity.

But your Lordship mentions " the king's paternal solicitude for promoting the establishment of lasting peace and union with the colonies." If by peace is here meant, a peace to be entered into by distinct states, now at war, and his Majesty has given your Lordship powers to treat with us of such a peace, I may venture to say, though without authority, that I think a treaty for that purpose not quite impracticable, before we enter into foreign alliances. But I am persuaded you have no such powers. Your nation, tho' by punishing those American governors who have fomented the discord, rebuilding our burnt towns, and repairing as far as possible the mischiefs done us, she might recover a great share of our regard, and the greatest share of our growing commerce, with all the advantages of that additional strength,

to

---

* The reader must remember, that about this time the Hessians, &c. had just arrived from Europe at Staten Island in New-York.

to be derived from a friendship with us ;—I know too well her abounding pride and deficient wisdom, to believe she will ever take such salutary measures. Her fondness for conquest as a warlike nation ; her lust of dominion as an ambitious one ; and her thirst for a gainful monopoly as a commercial one (none of them legitimate causes of war) will all join to hide from her eyes every view of her true interest ; and continually goad her on in these ruinous distant expeditions, so destructive both of lives and of treasure, that they must prove as pernicious to her in the end, as the Croisades formerly were to most of the nations of Europe.

I have not the vanity, my Lord, to think of intimidating by thus predicting the effects of this war ; for I know it will in England have the fate of all my former predictions, not to be believed till the event shall verify it.

Long did I endeavour with unfeigned and unwearied zeal, to preserve from breaking that fine and noble china vase—the British empire ; for I knew that being once broken, the separate parts could not retain even their share of the strength and value that existed in the whole ; and that a perfect re-union of these parts could scarce ever be hoped for. Your Lordship may possibly remember the tears of joy that wet my cheek, when, at your good sister's in London, you once gave me expectations that a reconciliation might soon take place.— I had the misfortune to find these expectations disappointed, and to be treated as the cause of the mischief I was labouring to prevent. My consolation under that groundless and malevolent treatment was, that I retained the friendship of many wise and good men in that country, and among the rest some share in the regard of Lord Howe.

The well founded esteem, and permit me to say affection, which I shall always have for your Lordship, make it painful to me to see you engaged in conducting a war, the great ground of which, as described in your letter, is " the necessity of preventing the American trade from passing into foreign channels." To me it seems, that neither the obtaining or retaining any trade, how valuable soever, is an object for which men may justly spill each others blood ; that the true and sure means of extending and securing commerce, are the goodness and cheapness of commodities ; and that the profits of no trade can ever be equal to the expence of compelling it, and holding it by fleets and armies. I consider this war against us, therefore, as both unjust, and unwise ; and I am persuaded, that cool and dispassionate posterity will condemn to infamy those who advised it ; and that even success will not save from some degree of dishonour, those who have voluntarily engaged to conduct it.

I know your great motive in coming hither was the hope of being instrumental in a reconciliation ; and I believe, when you find that to be impossible, on any terms given you to propose, you will relinquish so odious a command, and return to a more honourable private station.

With the greatest and most sincere respect, I have the honour to be, My Lord, your Lordship's most obedient, humble servant,

B. FRANKLIN.

Directed to the Right Hon.
Lord Viscount Howe.

[It is necessary to mention that this correspondence was laid before the members of the continental congress, at the moment that it took place ; it being thought improper, that any member of that body should hold private intercourse with Lord Howe. It is to be presumed, that administration have likewise received copies of it through the hands of Lord Howe.]

In

In CONGRESS, Sept. 14, 1776.

Refolved, That all the Continental troops and militia, going home from fervice, reftore all Continental arms and other property, and alfo all ammunition remaining in their poffeffion at the time of their being about to return, their pay to be withheld unlefs they produce certificates from the Commiffary of Stores, or Quarter Mafter General, or their deputies in the department where fuch Continental troops or militia fhall ferve. And if any Continental property or ammunition be carried away by the militia before this refolve, ftoppages to be made from fuch as have not received their pay, and that meafures be taken with thofe (who have been paid) by the Councils of Safety or legiflatures of each ftate for the reftoration of fuch Continental property and ammunition.

Extract from the minutes,
CHARLES THOMSON, Secretary.

In CONGRESS, Nov. 4.

Refolved, That any perfon who fhall apprehend a deferter, and bring him to the regiment he belongs to, upon certificate thereof by the Colonel or Commanding Officer, fhall receive five dollars, aud all reafonable expences, which is to be deducted from the pay of fuch foldier.

That it be recommended to the feveral regiflatures, affemblies, or conventions of the colonies, to enact a law, or pafs an ordinance, inflicting the following punifhments upon fuch as harbour deferters, knowing them to be fuch, viz. a fine upon all fuch offenders, not lefs than 30, nor more than 50 dollars; and in cafe of inability to pay the fine, to be punifhed with whipping, not exceeding thirty-nine lafhes for each offence. Alfo, that they empower the Commander in Chief, or other officer commanding a detachment, or any out poft, to adminifter an oath, and fwear any perfon or perfons to the truth of any information or intelligence, or any other matter relative to the public fervice.

CHARLES THOMSON, Secretary.

United States LOTTERY, 1776.

The SCHEME is that this Lottery confifts of Four Claffes of One Hundred Thoufand Tickets each.

FIRST CLASS.

100,000 Tickets, at ten Dollars each, are	—		1,000,000
Deduction at *fifteen per cent.*	—		150,000
			850,000

No.		Prizes.		Dollars.
1	of	10,000	is	10,000
2		5,000		10,000
30		1,000		30,000
400		500		200,000
20,000		20		400,000

Carried to the fourth clafs	200,000
	850,000

SECOND CLASS.

100,000 Tickets at twenty Dollars each, are —— 2,000,000
Deduction at *fifteen per cent.* —— 300,000

1,700,000

No.		Prizes.		Dollars.
1	of	20,000	is	20,000
2		10,000		20,000
10		5,000		50,000
100		1,000		100,000
820		500		410,000
20,000		30		600,000

Carried to the fourth clafs 500,000

1,700,000

THIRD CLASS.

100,000 Tickets, at thirty Dollars each, are —— 3,000,000
Deduction at *fifteen per cent.* —— 450,000

2,550,000

No.		Prizes.		Dollars.
1	of	30,000	is	30,000
1		20,000		20,000
2		15,000		30,000
2		10,000		20,000
10		5,000		50,000
200		1,000		200,000
1000		500		500,000
20,000		40		800,000

Carried to the fourth clafs, 9,000,000

2,550,000

FOURTH CLASS.

100,000 Tickets, at forty Dollars each, are —— 4,000,000
Deduction at *fifteen per cent.* —— 600,000

3,400,000

Brought from the firft clafs, —— —— 200,000
Second ditto, —— —— 500,000
Third ditto, —— —— 900,000

5,000,000

No.		Prizes.		Dollars,
1	of	50,000	is	50,000
2		25,000		50,000
2		15,000		30,000
2		10,000		20,000
10		5,000		50,000
100		1,000		100,000
200		500		100,000
1,000		300		300,000
15,000		200		3,000,000
26,000		50		1,300,000
				5,000,000

42,317 Prizes.
57,683 Blanks.

100,000 Tickets.
Not near one and a half blanks to a prize.

This lottery is set on foot by a resolution of Congress, passed at Philadelphia, the 18th day of November, 1776, for the purpose of raising a sum of money on loan, bearing an annual interest of *four per cent.* which, with the sum arising from the deduction, is to be applied for carrying on the present most just and necessary war, in defence of the lives, liberties and property, of the inhabitants of these United States.

The fortunate adventurers in the first class, and so in the second and third, who draw more than forty dollars, shall, at their option, receive a treasury bank note for the prize or prizes drawn, payable at the end of five years, and an annual interest at the rate of *four per cent.* or the pre-emption of such tickets, in the next succeeding class, as shall not be renewed within the time limited.

Every adventurer in the first class shall have a right to go through the subsequent classes, but shall not be obliged to do it.

The drawers of twenty, thirty, and forty dollars, in the first, second, and third classes, who do not apply for their money within six weeks after the drawing is finished, shall be deemed adventurers in the next succeeding class, and have their tickets renewed, without any farther trouble.

If any other shall neglect or decline taking out and paying the price of their ticket for a subsequent class, within six weeks after the drawing is ended, their tickets shall be sold to the fortunate adventurers in the preceding class, or to such as shall apply for the same.

The fortunate adventurers in the last class, who draw fifty dollars, shall, upon application to the commissioners of the loan offices, in the respective states, where the drawers reside, receive their money without any deduction; and all who draw above fifty dollars, shall receive in like manner, without deduction, for the sums drawn, treasury bank notes, payable at the end of five years after the drawing, at the loan office of the state in which the drawers reside. The interest to commence from the last day of drawing, and to be paid annually at the said respective loan offices.

As this lottery is established for the sole purpose of raising a sum of money,

E 2

money, for carrying on the prefent juft war, undertaken in defence of the rights and liberties of America, in which every individual and pofterity will be fo deeply interefted; it is not doubted but every real friend to his country will moft chearfully become an adventurer, and that the fale of the tickets will be very rapid, efpecially as even the unfuccefsful adventurer will have the pleafing reflection of having contributed, in a degree, to the great and glorious American caufe.

The managers appointed by Congrefs are Sharp Delany, John Purviance, Owen Biddle, David Jackfon, Jacob Barge, Jonathan B. Smith, and James Searle, who are upon oath, and give bond for the faithful difcharge of their truft.

The drawing of the firft clafs will begin at Philadelphia, the 10th day of April next, or fooner, if fooner full.

The public will be advertifed as foon as the tickets are ready for fale.

The managers are inftructed to fell the tickets for ready money only.

Philad. Dec. 6, 1776.

In CONGRESS, Nov. 27, 1776.

Refolved, That it be recommended to the legiflatures of the United States refpectively, to pafs fuch laws as will moft effectually tend to prevent the COUNTERFEITING or FORGING the TICKETs of the public lottery.

Extract from the minutes,

CHARLES THOMSON, Sec.

In CONGRESS, Dec. 30, 1776.

It appearing to Congrefs that it will be extremely difficult, if not impracticable, to fupply the army of the United States with bacon, falted beef and pork, foap, tallow and candles, unlefs the exportation thereof be prohibited. Therefore,

Refolved, That none of the faid articles, except fuch as may be neceffary for the crew, be exported from any of the United States after the fifth day of January next, until the firft day of November next, or until Congrefs fhall make farther order therein.—And it is earneftly recommended to the executive powers of the feveral United States, to fee that this refolution be ftrictly complied with.

December 31. Refolved, That any reftriction heretofore impofed upon the exportation of ftaves or other lumber, except to Great-Britain, Ireland, and the Britifh iflands, or any place under the dominion of Great-Britain, ceafe.

By order of Congrefs,

JOHN HANCOCK, Prefident.

In CONGRESS, Dec. 27, 1776.

Refolved, That the Council of Safety of Pennfylvania be requefted to take the moft vigorous and fpeedy meafures for punifhing all fuch as fhall refufe Continental currency, and that the General be directed to give all neceffary aid to the Council of Safety for carrying their meafures on this fubject into effectual execution.

By order of Congrefs,

JOHN HANCOCK, Prefident.

Baltimore, December 27, 1776.

" Gentlemen,

" The great importance to the welfare of thefe United States of fupporting the credit of the Continental currency, will fuggeft the propriety of the above refolve, which I am commanded by Congrefs to tranfmit to you, and to requeft you will take meafures for an immediate compliance therewith.

" I have wrote to the General to give you every neceffary affiftance in carrying your determinations on this

this fubject into effectual execution. I have the honor to be, gentlemen, Your moft humble fervant,

JOHN HANCOCK, Prefident.

Hon. Council of Safety of Pennfylvania."

In COUNCIL of SAFETY, Philadelphia, January 1, 1777.

In confequence of the foregoing refolve of Congrefs, and the intelligence received from feveral parts of this ftate, that the difaffected and enemies to the United States of America are purfuing the moft dangerous fchemes to deftroy the credit of the money iffued under the authority of Congrefs, which wicked and mifchievous practices are likely to be attended with the moft pernicious confequences, unlefs immediately fuppreffed by a fpeedy and vigorous exertion of the powers invefted in this Council.— Therefore,

Refolved, That if any perfon or perfons, from and after the publication of this refolve, fhall refufe to take Continental currency in payment of any debt or contract whatfoever, or for any goods, merchandize, or commodity offered for fale, or fhall afk a greater price for any fuch commodity in Continental currency than in any other kind of money or fpecie, on full proof made thereof before any three members of any county Committee, or any three field officers of militia of this ftate, the perfon or perfons fo offending fhall, for the firft offence, be confidered as a dangerous member to fociety, and forfeit the goods offered for fale or bargained for, or debt contracted, to the perfon to whom the goods were offered for fale, or by whom they were bargained for, or from whom fuch debt is due. And fhall moreover pay a fine of five pounds to

the ftate, to be levied immediately by the perfons to whom forfeitures are directed to be paid by this refolve, provided fuch debt or contract do not exceed that fum. But if the debt due, or price of fuch goods bargained for, or offered to fale, exceed the fum of five pounds, then the perfon offending as aforefaid fhall, befides the debt due, goods contracted for or offered for fale, forfeit to the full amount of faid debt, contract or price agreed on or demanded, one third part of fuch forfeiture to be for the ufe of the informer, and the remaining two third parts to the ufe of this ftate, to be paid to the Committee of the county where the forfeiture is incurred, or, where no fuch Committee exifts, to the three field officers of the militia of the next neareft battalion, to be by them tranfmitted to the public treafury of this ftate, after deducting reafonable cofts; fuch forfeiture to be levied immediately by the direction and authority of the faid Committee or field officers. And every perfon fo offending fhall, for the fecond offence, be fubject to the aforementioned penalties, and be banifhed this ftate to fuch place, and in fuch manner, as this Council fhall direct. Neverthelefs, if any perfon fhall think him or herfelf aggrieved by the determination of the faid Committee or field officers, he or fhe fhall be allowed an appeal to this Council, provided the faid appeal be made within fix weeks after fuch determination made, and information thereof given, by the faid Committees or field officers, to the parties in writing.—A regular record of the proceedings in every cafe to be tranfmitted to this Board in four weeks after determination.

Refolved, That all perfons whofe fhops, ftores, or warehoufes have

been

been heretofore shut up, and have been restrained from carrying on a commercial intercourse with the inhabitants of this state for refusing Continental currency, shall be released from such restraint, and permitted to open their shops, stores, and warehouses, and that all persons who are in confinement for the same offence be immediately discharged from such confinement, to be subject nevertheless to the penalties described in the foregoing resolution for future offences.

By order of the Council,
THOMAS WHARTON, jun. President.

Philadelphia, Feb. 4. The assembly (who are entitled " The Representatives of the Freemen of the Commonwealth of Pennsylvania") have passed an act, making the Continental bills, and the bills emitted by the resolves of the late assemblies. a LEGAL TENDER in all payments whatsoever.

JOHN JACOBS, Speaker.

William Livingstone, Esq; Governor of Jersey, has issued a proclamation, dated the 17th of January, 1777, appointing the 6th of March to be observed throughout that state as a day of general fast, agreeable to a resolution of the Congress, appointing a general fast to be observed throughout the Colonies.

Philadelphia, Dec. 27, 1776. The Honourable Congress having appointed a Committee of their body to transact such Continental business in this city as may be proper and necessary, the said Committee give this public notice, that they meet every day, and sit from ten to three o'clock, at their office in Front-street, where Messrs. Barclay and Mitchell lately dwelt, opposite to Messrs. Conyngham, Nes-

bit and Company. All persons charged with public letters for the Congress, Board of War, Marine, or other Committees, are desired to take notice hereof, as such letters will be opened or forwarded by the Committee as the case may require. ROBERT MORRIS,
GEORGE CLYMER,
GEORGE WALTON.

PHILADELPHIA, Jan. 6, 1777.

In ASSEMBLY. Resolved, That the following address to the inhabitants of Pennsylvania be forthwith printed, and sent to the several counties of this state.

Friends and Countrymen,—It is much easier for you to conceive, than for us to describe, the evils consequent on the invasion of a country by a rapacious and plundering soldiery. Such is now the situation of the neighbouring state of New Jersey, and such soon will be ours, unless the enemy, who have taken advantage of the accidental weakness of our army, to make a winter campaign, are repelled by the strongest and most immediate exertions.

Every species of ravage and calamity have already marked the footsteps of our enemy, and they are now within a few miles of your metropolis, waiting to cross the Delaware, to glut their inordinate lust of rapine and desolation in the plunder of that rich and populous city. The most insensible cannot but perceive the shock our common cause must suffer, if this unfortunate event should take place—every one must be awake to the misery that must in this case attend every individual of this country. The love of ease, we hope, cannot so far prevail on you as to keep you from the field at this critical and alarming time.—We speak to a
peo-

people that a few months ago would with eagernefs have flown to arms at the firft appearance of their country's danger. We know the value you have ever fet on liberty, that beft gift of God ; with the maintenance of liberty is now connected your perfonal happinefs, and every dear and valuable blefling—the chaftity of the wives of your bofom, your daughters, which elfe may be violated by a brutal foldiery—But it is not a temporary evil only that is to be fuffered fhould our enemy prevail, the power of " binding us " in all cafes whatfoever," claimed by a Britifh Parliament, is to reach your pofterity, and to rivet chains upon them for ever. You once feemed fenfible of this, and were determined to die rather than fubmit—the fame grounds of difpute remain between Great-Britain and us, the fame fpirit and determination fhould alfo ftill remain.

We are not infenfible to the fatigues and hardfhips of thofe who engage in a winter's campaign, but we hope and believe this call on the militia will be the laft—the Continental army will fhortly be more formidable than ever, and as once before will again, by God's blefling, give a favourable turn to our affairs ; but if a fatal neceffity fhould again require your exertions, it is now, and will be, the bufinefs of your Reprefentatives in this Houfe to fix, as foon as poffible, the military eftablifhment of the ftate upon fuch juft and equitable principles, as will make the common duty of defence a common and equal burthen to all its inhabitants.

Extract from the minutes,

JOSIAH CRAWFORD,

Clerk, pro temp.

To the PEOPLE of MARYLAND.

THE very critical and alarming fituation of all America, the circumftances of this State, and what your incumbent duty requires in the prefent crifis, demand the moft ferious and attentive confideration of every wife and good man among you. At this hour the fate of America ftands fufpended. All your wifdom, integrity and virtue muft now be exerted to fave yourfelves and your pofterity from the horrors of flavery. The happinefs or mifery of prefent millions, and future miriads, depend on your fuceefs, in the prefent war with Great-Britain. I requeft your indulgence, while I offer to your confideration a few obfervations on thofe important fubjects : to your reafon and judgment only will I appeal.

Your caufe is juft, and the war with Great-Britain unavoidable and neceffary. The

and

have invariably, for a number of years, obftinately perfevered, in a fyftematical fcheme, to reduce the colonies to an unconditional fubmiffion to their will and pleafure. That fuch was their defign is manifeft. The many infidious, arbitrary and cruel acts of parliament, and the attempt by force to compel our obedience to them, indubitably evince it.

The facts ftated in the addrefs of the firft Congrefs to their conftituents, and the fubfequent conduct of the Britifh parliament, muft fatisfy the impartial world, that the cup of flavery was originally defigned for us, and that war, cruel and unnatural, fhould be waged againft us, if we refufed the bitter draught. The parliament of Great-Britain claimed a right to make laws in all cafes to affect our lives, liberty and property ; a claim fo extravagant

gant and wicked, that the civil liberty, the social happiness of us and all our posterity must cease the moment it is admitted. Reason and justice look down with indignation upon it. The claim by Great-Britain, to make laws for us, in all cases, or to tax us, or to alter or abolish our constitutions or forms of government, was inadmissible: an unlimited power to legislate for us, would constitute a complete and perfect system of slavery. If parliament can dispose of any *part* of our property, of consequence the *whole* must be subject to their will. If parliament can, in any manner, interfere in our internal *legislations*, a right will follow to alter or abolish them at pleasure. If parliament can tax us, we have no property. If parliament can abridge or destroy the securities, which our constitutions and forms of government give us for our liberties and our lives, then are we dependents, vassals and slaves.

The difference of conduct between the king and parliament of Britain, and the colonists and your Congress is worthy of observation. The king and parliament would not admit any bounds to their authority. They would admit no limitation to their power. Their object was to maintain an absolute unlimited supremacy of *legislation* over America: all your property, and the legislations of the colonies must be subject to their absolute discretion. To carry this claim into execution, every art and fraud, which the wit of man could invent, was practised to deceive and divide the unwary Americans. Volumes would scarce suffice to relate the various schemes and stratagems, the many injuries and oppressions to which recourse was had, to break their spirits, and to reduce them to submission. The

statutes, the instructions to, and the behaviour of their governors, must rise in judgment against the people of Britain. On our part, we petitioned, we remonstrated, from one end of the continent to the other. We stated our grievances, and humbly implored relief. Our repeated petitions were rejected, and treated with insult and contempt. Our oppressions were increased, and each rising sun beheld new miseries multiplied upon us. The Congress attempted to draw a line, by which to limit the authority of the parliament over the colonies. They were of opinion, that in all cases, in which our several legislatures were competent, the parliament ought not to interfere; that in such cases only where they were incompetent, parliament should have a legislative power. Congress only claimed an exemption from taxation, and that our charters and the essentials of our constitutions and governments should be preserved inviolate. Congress admitted a power in Great-Britain to regulate our external commerce, her great palladium and support, and from whence she draws immense wealth, as a compensation for the protection of her navy. The Congress offered, if our trade was placed on the same footing with the inhabitants in that kingdom, to contribute her proportion of expence for the defence of the whole empire. Could *less* be asked, or *more* be admitted, or required? Great-Britain rejected a peace and union with us on these terms.* From reason and justice she appealed

* *It may be remarked, that the line drawn and the above propositions made by Congress, were the same, in substance with the bill* proposed by the Earl of Chatham.

This is not the remark of the English editor: it is in the original, printed at Baltimore.

to the fword, and commenced the war. America refifted; but the Congrefs, anxious for peace and reconciliation, again petitioned. Actuated by a fpirit of avarice and defpotifm, and dead to all the feelings of humanity, the people of Britain profecuted the war againft us, with a cruelty and barbarity not practifed by any civilized nation. They wantonly burnt our towns, fpoiled our property, and carried wafte, deftruction and havock whereever they went. They incited and bribed the favages of the wildernefs to grant them their affiftance. The flaughter of your wives and children was the object of this diabolical meafure. To wreak her vengeance on her virtuous fons, Great-Britain thus infamoufly condefcended to what fhe fo loudly complained of, and execrated in the laft French war. The dagger was put into the hands of your flaves, with promifes of freedom, to murder their mafters. Defpairing by thefe means, and with her national forces, to fubjugate us, fhe meanly hired foreign mercenaries to affift her in our deftruction. To engage fuch wretches in her fervice, a liberty to plunder was granted, and many of them alledge a private promife of the monarch of Britain, to grant them the firft choice of our forfeited eftates. After thefe accumulated injuries, and after all reafonable hope of an accommodation had vanifhed, the Congrefs declared the Colonies *free* and *independent ftates.*

Thus have I endeavoured to fhew, that Great-Britain is the aggreffor, and that the prefent war is *honourable, juft* and *neceffary.* The declaration of independency was *expedient, wife* and *neceffary.* You have but this alternative, YOU MUST BE INDEPENDENT, or SLAVES.

Jan. 12, 1777.   An AMERICAN.

Vol. V.

STATE of MASSACHUSETTS BAY.

In the Houfe of REPRESENTATIVES, Dec. 28, 1777.

Refolved, That the following perfons be and hereby are appointed to mufter the men that have inlifted or fhall inlift into the Continental army, viz.

For the county of Suffolk, Nathaniel Barber, Efq; of Bofton.

For the county of Effex, John Cufhing, Efq; of Boxford.

For the county of Middlefex, Col. James Barrett, of Concord.

For the county of Hampfhire, Col. Benjamin Ruggles Woodbridge, of South Hadley.

For the county of Plymouth, Col. James Hatch, of Pembroke.

For the county of Barnftable, Jofeph Otis, Efq; of Barnftable.

For the county of Briftol, Capt. James Leonard, of Taunton.

For the county of Dukes-County, Ebenezer Smith, Efq;

For the county of Nantucket, Stephen Huffey, Efq;

For the county of Worcefter, Capt. Thomas Newhall, of Leicefter.

For the county of York, Nathaniel Wells, Efq; of Wells.

For the county of Cumberland, Major Daniel Ilfley, of Falmouth.

For the county of Lincoln, Dummer Sewall, Efq; of George-Town.

For the county of Berkfhire, Capt. Trueman Wheeler, of Great Barrington.

Refolved, That this ftate advance the Six Pounds bounty ordered by CONGRESS, to each non-commiffioned officer and private foldier that fhall inlift into the Continental army as the quota affigned this ftate, and that the fame be charged to the Continent.

F   Re-

Refolved, That the bounty of Twenty Pounds offered by this state to fuch non-commiffioned officers and foldiers as shall inlift into the Continental army during the war, or for three years, shall by warrant from the Council on the Treafurer, be paid to the feveral mufter-mafters appointed as aforefaid, in fuch proportion as the Council shall judge proper, each of them giving a receipt, and being accountable for fuch fum as he shall receive, to be by them paid to fuch men as they shall refpectively mufter, and alfo that the bounty of Six Pounds offered by Congrefs, be in like manner paid to faid mufter-mafters, to be paid to fuch non-commiffioned officers and foldiers as shall inlift as aforefaid, in all fuch cafes where the officer who inlifted them shall make oath, that the faid bounty of Six Pounds has not been otherwife received by him or paid to the faid non-commiffioned officers and foldiers offered to be muftered, which oath each of faid mufter-mafters is hereby impowered to adminifter.

Refolved, That each mufter-mafter shall have a right to mufter men inlifted in any county, and into any battalion belonging to this ftate. And that the mufter-mafters continue at or nigh their refpective counties, to perform the bufinefs to which they are hereby appointed, as they shall judge will beft promote the public fervice; and that they be allowed a reafonable reward for their fervices.

Refolved, That the refolve of Court of the eleventh of December current, appointing a Committee to tranfmit to the Committees of this Court, then at the camps, on the bufinefs of re-eftablishing the army, a number of Treafurer's Notes, &c. and appointing mufter-mafters for three battalions, be,

and it hereby is repealed, and made null and void.

Sent up for concurrence,
Sam. Freeman, Speak. Pro. Tem.
In Council, Dec. 28, 1776. Read and concurred.
John Avery, Dep. Sec'ry.
Confented to by the major part of the Council.
A true copy. Atteft,
John Avery, Dep. Sec'ry.

In Council, January 30, 1777.

Whereas it is reprefented to this Court, that fome perfons within this ftate are purchafing pork at an extravagant price, as well as other provifions, and are alfo employing perfons to do the fame within the ftate of Connecticut; and that they are caufing fuch provifions to be tranfported to fome fea-port towns within this ftate, which evil practice, if tolerated, muft prove very prejudicial to this and all the United States, and if carried on by perfons inimical to the rights of America, may be attended with fatal confequences.

Wherefore it is refolved, That the Board of War be directed to make the ftricteft enquiry poffible, from time to time, and if they shall obtain knowledge where quantities of pork or other provifions are depofited, that they have reafon to believe were procured in this manner, that they immediately fecure fuch provifions for the public ufe, agreeable to a late act of this government:—And all Selectmen and Committees of Correfpondence, Infpection and Safety of the feveral towns within this ftate, are alfo enjoined and directed to exercife the utmoft vigilance for the detection of fuch pernicious practices; and if they shall at any time learn where any fuch provifions are placed within their refpective towns, that they forth-

forthwith purfue fuch meafures by taking the fame into their own cuftody, or otherwife as they fhall judge neceffary, to prevent the purchafers or poffeffors thereof from fecreting them; and they are then forthwith to give information thereof to the Board of War, acquainting them of the names of the perfons concerned and other circumftances, and wait the inftructions of the Board of War refpecting the fame, which it is expected the Board of War will give without delay, and make returns to this Court from time to time, of their doings hereon.

Sent down for concurrence,

JOHN AVERY, Dep. Sec'ry.

In the Houfe of Reprefentatives, January 31, 1777.

Read and concurred, and the Board of War are directed to caufe this refolve to be publifhed in all the Bofton news-papers.

Sent up for concurrence,

J. WARREN, Speaker.

In Council, Jan. 31, 1777. Read and concurred.

JOHN AVERY, Dep. Sec'ry.

Confented to by the major part of the Council.

A true copy. Atteft.

JOHN AVERY, Dep. Sec'ry.

WAR-OFFICE, Feb. 11, 1777. Publifhed by order of the Board of War.

A true copy. Atteft.

J. LORING AUSTIN, Secretary.

STATE of MASSACHUSETT'S BAY.

In the Houfe of REPRESENTATIVES, Feb. 5, 1777.

Whereas the rum, molaffes, and fundry other articles herein after enumerated: now in this ftate, are all needed for the fupply of the army and the inhabitants of this ftate:

It is therefore Refolved, That all exportation of rum, molaffes, fugar, cotton wool, fheeps wool, flax, falt, coffee, cocoa, chocolate, linen, cotton and linen, woollen, and cotton goods of all kinds, provifions of all and every fort, fhoes, hides, deer fkins, fheep-fkins and leather of all kinds, as well by land as by water, from the counties of Suffolk and Middlefex, after the feventh day of February currant; and from the counties of Effex, Plymouth and Briftol, after the eighth; and from every other part of this ftate after the tenth, be ftopped, except to the different parts of this ftate.

And if any veffel fhall be found having any quantity of rum more than fixty gallons to a veffel of 80 tons, and for a three months voyage, and in that proportion for a larger or fmaller veffel, and on a longer or fhorter voyage, or having any other of the articles above enumerated on board more than is fufficient for the ufe of the crew of the faid veffel, fhe being outward bound therewith, or found at fea having failed from any port in this ftate, after the times fixed for this refolve's taking place in fuch port for any part of the world without this ftate; fuch veffel fhall be a lawful prize for any perfon or perfons who fhall take the fame, and fhall be libelled in fome maritime court within this ftate, within two months after having been found or brought in with fuch rum or other of faid articles on board, and fhall be condemned and fold in manner as is provided by the laws of this ftate for the condemnation and fale of veffels taken in carrying fupplies to the enemies of the united ftates of America; and the money fuch veffel and cargo may be fold for, fhall be difpofed of in the fame manner as veffels and cargoes are difpofed of

F 2   that

are taken as prizes. Provided nevertheless, That if it shall appear to the satisfaction of the court before whom such trial shall be had, that the owner or owners of such vessel did not knowingly transgress this Resolve, in that case such vessel shall not be liable to condemnation.

And it is further Resolved, If the committee of correspondence, inspection and safety, of any towns in this state, shall suspect that any team is loaded with any articles herein before enumerated, to be transported out of this state to any of the united states, that said committee be, and they are hereby empowered and directed to stop all such teams till such time as they can make proper enquiry, and by a certificate from the committee of correspondence of the town where such goods were taken or otherwise, shall obtain satisfaction that the same are not designed to be carried out of this state, as aforesaid : and if no such satisfaction shall be given within thirty days after detention thereof, and it shall not appear that such goods were removed from the town where they had been deposited before the times fixed for this Resolve's taking place, the committee so detaining the same is hereby impowered and directed to seize such articles, and having so done shall proceed to file an information against them, before the court of General Sessions of the peace in any county where said articles shall be stopped or seized, and the said court shall have full power to try the justice of said seizure by a jury, and no evidence shall be admitted upon such trial, but what was produced to the committee within the thirty days beforementioned, except in the judgment of the court before whom the trial is had, such evidence could not be obtained within that time. And in

case the said court shall adjudge and condemn the same as forfeited, after the necessary charges of condemnation, &c. are paid, one half shall be to the use of the committee who prosecuted as above, the other half to the use of this state.

Provided notwithstanding, That when any person shall transport any articles whatever to the American army, and can produce a certificate from the honourable the Council, the Board of War, or the Committee of Correspondence, Inspection and Safety of the town from whence such articles were taken, certifying that the goods he has in his custody belong either to the continent or to this state, or can by any other way give satisfaction hereof to any Committee of Correspondence, &c. enquiring concerning the same, in such case the person with such goods may proceed unmolested.

Provided also, That this resolve shall not be construed to extend to prevent the exportation of sugar in such quantities as are allowed by a resolve of this Court of the ninth day of January last, for the purpose of procuring flour and other provisions, and other articles for the use of the inhabitants of this state, and necessary supplies for the crews of such vessels as may be bound from this state, or to prohibit any exportations the Board of War may think proper to make for the public advantage, or to prevent the carrying any of the above enumerated articles from this to any neighbouring state, as purchased at any ordinary retail, either for the consumption of individuals or single families.

And it is hereby recommended to the good people of this state to afford all possible aid to the committees aforesaid, to enable them to

carry

carry thefe refolves into effectual execution.

And it is further refolved, That if it fhall hereafter appear, that any of the articles herein before enumerated had been tranfported by land or water out of this ftate, contrary to the true intent and meaning of this refolve, the owner or owners who fhall fend or carry the fame, fhall forfeit the value of fuch goods, to be recovered by action of debt, in any court proper to try the fame, and after paying the charges of profecution, one-half thereof fhall be to the perfon or perfons who fhall fue for the fame, the other half to the ufe of this ftate ; provided the action is commenced within three months after the goods are tranfported.

And further refolved, That Mr. Hofmer be, and hereby is directed, to procure one thoufand of thefe refolves to be printed, and that he immediately tranfmit to the feveral naval officers within this ftate, and the feveral Committees of Correfpondence, Infpection and Safety of the towns that border upon the neighbouring ftates, printed copies of the fame ; and that he caufe the fame to be printed in the Bofton news-papers.

J. WARREN, Speaker.

In Council, Feb. 7, 1777. Read and concurred.

JOHN AVERY, Dep. Sec'ry.

Confented to by the major part of the Council.

A true copy. Atteft.

JOHN AVERY, Dep. Sec'ry.

STATE OF MASSACHUSETT's BAY.

Council Chamber, Feb. 10, 1777. To the colonels appointed to the command of the continental battalions, to be raifed in this ftate.

The public fervice requiring that the feveral continental regiments raifed within this ftate fhould be immediately formed—you are hereby refpectively directed forthwith to make a return to the council of the number of men enlifted into your refpective battalions, and where you have ordered them to rendezvous.

A true copy.

Atteft. JOHN AVERY, Dep. Sec'y.

Captain Edward Rolland, arrived at Salem, a few days ago, after a fhort cruize, during which he has taken four fifh veffels, with 11,000 quintals, merchantable fifh, and a brig laden with wine ; three of the former are fafe in port.

ADDRESS *of the Convention of the Reprefentatives of the State of* New-York *to their Conftituents.*

At this important period, when the freedom and happinefs, or the flavery and mifery, of the prefent and future generation of Americans, is to be determined, on a folemn appeal to the Supreme Ruler of all events, to whom every individual muft one day anfwer for the part he now acts, it becomes the duty of the Reprefentatives of a free people, to call their attention to this moft ferious fubject. And the more fo, at a time when their enemies are induftrioufly endeavouring to delude, intimidate, and feduce them, by falfe fuggeftions, artful mifreprefentations, and infidious promifes of protection.

You and all men were created free, and authorized to eftablifh civil government, for the prefervation of your rights againft oppreffion, and the fecurity of that freedom which God hath given you, againft the rapacious hand of tyranny and lawlefs power. It is therefore not only neceffary to the well being of fociety, but the duty of of every man to oppose and repel all those, by whatever name or title distinguished, who prostitute the powers of government to destroy the happiness and freedom of the people over whom they may be appointed to rule.

Under the auspices and direction of Divine Providence, your forefathers removed to the wilds and wilderness of America. By their industry they made it a fruitful, and by their virtue a happy country. And we should still have enjoyed the blessings of peace and plenty, if we had not forgotten the source from which those blessings flowed, and permitted our country to be contaminated by the many shameful vices which have prevailed among us.

It is a well known truth that no virtuous people were ever oppressed; and it is also true that a scourge was never wanting to those of an opposite character. Even the Jews, those favourites of Heaven, met with the frowns, whenever they forgot the smiles of their benevolent Creator. Tyrants of Egypt, of Babylon, of Syria, and of Rome, they were severely chastized; and those tyrants themselves, when they had executed the vengeance of Almighty God, their own crimes bursting on their own heads, received the rewards justly due to their violation of the sacred rights of mankind.

You were born equally free with the Jews, and have as good right to be exempted from the arbitrary domination of Britain, as they had from the invasions of Egypt, Babylon, Syria or Rome. But they, for their wickedness, were permitted to be scourged by the latter, and we, for our wickedness, are scourged by tyrants as cruel and implacable as those.

Our case, however, is peculiarly distinguished from theirs. Their enemies were strangers, unenlightened, and bound to them by no ties of gratitude or consanguinity. Our enemies, on the contrary, call themselves Christians. They are of a nation and people bound to us by the strongest ties. A people by whose side we have fought and bled, whose power we have contributed to raise, who owe much of their wealth to our industry, and whose grandeur has been augmented by our exertions.

It is unnecessary to remind you, that during the space of between one and two hundred years, every man sat under his own vine and his own fig tree, and there was none to make him afraid. That the people of Britain never claimed a right to dispose of us, and every thing belonging to us, according to their will and pleasure, until the reign of the present King of that island. And that to enforce this abominable claim, they have invaded our country by sea and by land. From this extravagant and iniquitous claim, and from the unreasonable as well as cruel manner in which they would gain our submission, it seems as though Providence were determined to use them as instruments to punish the guilt of this country, and bring us back to a sense of duty to our Creator.

You may remember, that to obtain redress of the many grievances to which you had been subjected, the most dutiful petitions were presented, not only by the several assemblies, but by representatives of all America in General Congress. And you cannot have forgotten with what contempt they were rejected. Nay, the humblest of all petitions,

pray-

praying only to be heard, was answered by the sound of the trumpet and clashing of arms. This, however, is not the only occasion on which the hearts have been hardened; and in all probability it will add to the number of those instances, in which their oppression, injustice and hardness of heart have worked their destruction.

Being bound by the strongest obligations to defend the inheritance which God hath given us, to Him we referred our cause, and opposed the assaults of our task-masters, being determined rather to die free than live slaves, and entail bondage on our children.

By our vigorous efforts, and by the goodness of Divine Providence, those cruel invaders were driven from our country in the last campaign. We then flattered ourselves that the signal success of our arms, and the unanimity and spirit of our people, would have induced our foes to desist from the prosecution of their wicked designs, and disposed their hearts to peace. But peace we had not yet deserved. Exultation took place of thanksgiving, and we ascribed that to our own prowess, which was only to be attributed to the Great Guardian of the innocent.

The enemy, with greater strength, again invade us. Invade us not less by their arts than their arms. They tell you that if you submit, you shall have protection. That their king breathes nothing but peace. That he will revise (not repeal) all his acts and instructions, and will receive you into favor. But what are the terms on which you are promised peace? Have you heard of any, except *absolute unconditional obedience and servile submission?* If are honest, if not to cajole and deceive you, why are you not explicitly informed of the terms, and whether the parliament mean to tax you hereafter at their will and pleasure? Upon this and the like points, these military commissioners of peace are silent, and indeed are not authorized to say a word, unless a power to grant pardons implies a power to adjust claims and secure privileges, or unless the bare possession of life is the only privilege which Americans are to enjoy. For a power to grant pardons is the only one which their parliament or prince have thought proper to give them. And yet they speak of peace, but hold daggers in their hands. They invite you to accept of blessings, and stain your habitations with blood. Their voice resembles the voice of Jacob, but their hands are like the hands of Esau.

If their intends to repeal any of the acts we complain of, why are they not specially named? if he designs you shall be free, why does he not promise that the claim of to bind you in all cases whatsoever, shall be given up and relinquished? if a reasonable peace was intended, why not impower his commissioners to treat with the Congress, or with deputies from all the assemblies? or why was not some other mode devised, in which America might be heard? is it not highly ridiculous to pretend, that they are authorized to treat of a peace between Britain and America, with every man they meet? was such a treaty ever heard of before? is such an instance to be met with in the history of mankind? No! The truth is, peace is not meant, and their specious pretences and proclamations are calculated only to disunite and deceive.

If

If the   really defired peace, why   order all your veſſels to be ſeized and confiſcated ? why   command, that the men found on board ſuch veſſels ſhould be added to the crews of his ſhips of war, and compelled to fight againſt their own countrymen ; to ſpill the blood of their neighbours and friends, nay, of their fathers, their brothers and children : and all this before pretended ambaſſadors of peace had arrived on our ſhores ! Does any hiſtory, ſacred or prophane, record any thing more   more more execrably   ,   or

If there be one ſingle idea of peace   , why   order your cities to be burnt, your country defolated, your brethren to ſtarve and languiſh, and die in priſons ? If any thing was intended beſides deſtruction, devaſtation and bloodſhed, why are the mercenaries of Germany tranſported near four thouſand miles ; they plunder your houſes, raviſh your wives and daughters, ſtrip your infant children, expoſe whole families, naked, miſerable and forlorn, to want, to hunger, to inclement ſkies and wretched deaths ? If peace were not totally reprobated by   , why are thoſe puſilanimous, deluded, ſervile wretches among you, who for preſent eaſe or impious bribes would ſell their liberty, their children, and their ſouls ; who, like ſavages, worſhip every devil that promiſes not to hurt them, or obey any mandates, however cruel, for which they are paid : how is it, that theſe ſordid degenerate creatures, who bow the knee to   , and daily offer incenſe at   ſhrine, ſhould be denied the peace ſo repeatedly promiſed them ? Why are they indiſcriminately abuſed, robbed and

plundered with their more deſerving neighbours ? But in this world, as in the other, it is right and juſt that the wicked ſhould be puniſhed by their ſeducers.

In a word, if peace was the deſire of your enemies, and humanity their object, why do they thus trample under foot every right and every duty human and divine ? Why, like the demons of old, is their wrath to be expiated only by human ſacrifices ? Why do they excite the ſavages of the wilderneſs to murder our inhabitants, and exerciſe cruelties unheard of among civilized nations ? No regard for religion or virtue remains among them. Your very churches bear witneſs to their impiety. Your churches are uſed, without heſitation, as jails, as ſtables, and as houſes of ſport and theatrical exhibitions. What faith, what truſt, what confidence, can you repoſe in thoſe men, who are deaf to the calls of humanity, dead to every ſentiment of religion, and void of all regard for the temples of the Lord of Hoſts ?

And why all this deſolation, bloodſhed, and unparalleled cruelty ? They tell you to reduce you to obedience. Obedience ! To what ? To their ſovereign will and pleaſure. And what then ? Why then you ſhall be pardoned, becauſe you conſent to be ſlaves. And why ſhould you be ſlaves now, having been freemen ever ſince this country was ſettled ? Becauſe forfooth the   and   of an iſland, three thouſand miles off, chooſe that you ſhould be hewers of wood and drawers of water for them. And is this the people whoſe proud domination you are taught to ſolicit ? Is this the peace which ſome of you ſo ardently deſire ? For ſhame ! For ſhame !

But you are told that their armies are numerous, their fleet strong, their soldiers valiant, their resources great, that you will be conquered, that victory ever attends their standard, and therefore that your opposition is vain, your resistance fruitless. What then? You can but be slaves at last, if you think life worth holding on so base a tenure.

But who is it that gives victory? By whom is a nation exalted? Since what period hath the race been always to the swift, and the battle to the strong? Can you be persuaded that the merciful King of Kings hath surrendered his crown and sceptre to the merciless tyrant ? And committed the affairs of this lower world to his guidance, controul and direction? We learned otherwise from our fathers; and God himself hath told us, that strength and numbers avail not against him. Seek then to be at peace with him, solicit his alliance, and fear not the boasted strength and power of your foes.

You may be told that your forts have been taken, your country ravaged, and that your armies have retreated; and therefore God is not with you. It is true, that some forts have been taken, that our country hath been ravaged, and that our Maker is displeased with us. But it is also true, that the King of Heaven is not like   , implacable. If his assistance be sincerely implored, it will surely be obtained. If we turn from our sins, he will turn from his anger. Then will our arms be crowned with success, and the pride and power of our enemies, like the arrogance and pride of a Nebuchadnezzar, will vanish away. Let us do our duty, and victory will be our reward. Let a general reformation of manners take place. Let no more widows and orphans, compelled to fly from their peaceful abodes, complain that you make a market of their distress, and take cruel advan-

tage of their necessities. When your country is invaded, and cries aloud for your aid, fly not to some secure corner of a neighbouring state, and remain idle spectators of her distress, but share her fate, and manfully support her cause. Let universal charity, public spirit and private virtue, be inculcated, encouraged and practised. Unite in preparing for a vigorous defence of your country, as if all depended on your own exertions. And when you have done these things, then rely upon the good Providence of Almighty God for success; in full confidence that without his blessing, all our efforts will inevitably fail.

A people moving on these solid principles, never have been, and never will be subjugated by any whatever. Cease then to desire the flesh-pots of Egypt, and remember their task-masters and oppression. No longer hesitate about rejecting all dependence   , who will rule you only with a rod of iron. Tell those who blame you for declaring yourselves independent, that you have done no more than what
had done for you. That
declared you to be out of
protection. That   absolved
you from   . That
made war upon you, and instead of
became   destroyer. By
became independent of   .
If you are wise, you will always continue so. Freedom is now in your power. Value the heavenly gift. Remember, that if you dare to neglect or despise it, you offer an insult to the Divine Bestower. Nor despair of keeping it: despair and despondency mark a little mind, and indicate a groveling spirit.

After the armies of Rome had been repeatedly defeated by Hannibal, that imperial city was besieged by this brave and experienced General, at the head of a numerous and victorious army. But so far were her glorious citizens

citizens from being dismayed by the loss of so many battles, and of all their country; so confident in their own virtue, and the protection of Heaven; that the very land on which the Carthagenians were encamped, was sold at public auction for more than the usual price. These heroic citizens disdained to receive his protections, or to regard his proclamations. They remembered that their ancestors had left them free. Ancestors who had bled in rescuing their country from the tyranny of Kings. They invoked the protection of the Supreme Being, they bravely defended their city, with undaunted resolution they repelled the enemy, and recovered their country. Blush then, ye degenerate spirits! who give all over for lost, because your enemies have marched through three or four counties, in this and a neigbouring state. Ye, who basely fly to have the yoke of slavery fixed upon your necks, and to swear that you and your children after you shall be slaves for ever. Such men deserve to be slaves, and are fit only for beasts of burden to the rest of mankind. Happy would it be for America if they were removed away, instead of continuing in this country, to people it with a race of animals, who from their form must be classed with the human species, but possess none of those qualities which render man more respectable than the brutes.

There never yet was a war, in which victory and success did not sometimes change sides. In the present, nothing hath happened either singular or decisive. Inquire dispassionately, and be not deceived by those artful tales which emissaries from the enemy so industriously circulate.

A powerful and well disciplined army, supported by a respectable fleet, invade this country. They are opposed by an army, which though numerous and brave, is quite undisciplined. Notwithstanding this manifest disparity, they have never thought it prudent to give us battle, though they have often had the fairest opportunities. True it is, that taking advantage of that critical moment, when our forces were almost disbanded, they have penetrated into Jersey, and marched a considerable distance without being attacked. If any are alarmed at this circumstance, let them consider, that we do not fight for a few acres of land, but for freedom; for the freedom and happiness of millions yet unborn. Would it not be highly imprudent to risque such important events upon the issue of a general battle, when it is certain Great-Britain cannot long continue the war, and by protracting it, we cannot fail of success? The British Ministry, sensible of this truth, and convinced that the people of England are aware of it, have promised that the present campaign shall be the last. They are greatly and justly alarmed at their situation. A country drained of men and money; the necessity of supplying fleets and armies at so great a distance; the danger of domestic insurrections; the probability that France will take advantage of their defenceless condition; the ruin of their commerce by our privateers; these are circumstances at which the boldest are dismayed. They are convinced that the people will not remain long content in such a dangerous situation. Hence it is that they press so hard to make this campaign decisive; and hence it is that we should endeavour to avoid it. Even suppose that Philadelphia, which some believe to be of such great importance, suppose it was taken or abandoned, the conquest of America will still be at the same distance. Millions determined to be free, still remain to be subdued. Millions who disdain to part with their liberties, their consciences, and the happiness of their posterity in future ages, for infamous protections and dishonourable pardons.

But

But amidst all the terror and dismay which have taken hold upon some weak minds, let us consider the advantages under which we prosecute the present war. Our country supplies us with almost every commodity which is necessary for life or defence. Arms and ammunition are now abundantly manufactured in almost all the American states, and our armies will be amply supplied with all military stores. We have more fighting men in America than Britain can possibly send. Our trade is free, and every port of France and Spain affords protection to our ships. Other nations invited by the advantages of our commerce, will doubtless soon follow their example; and experience must convince the most incredulous, that the British navy cannot exclude us from the sea. If their armies have invaded, ravaged and plundered our dominions, and our people have not successfully attacked them on their boasted empire of the ocean, have not our privateers brought into the ports of America, British property to the amount of more than EIGHTEEN HUNDRED THOUSAND POUNDS sterling? And do we not daily receive the most valuable cargoes from foreign countries, in spite of those fleets whose colours have waved in triumph over the globe? The article of salt, about which some of you have been uneasy, will soon be fully supplied. The shores of America are washed by the ocean for more than 2000 miles; works for manufacturing salt have been erected, and proved successful, and many cargoes of it are expected, and have arrived in the neighbouring states. Provisions of every kind abound among us. From our plenteous stores Great-Britain hath heretofore supplied her necessities, though she now most wantonly and ungratefully abuses the kind hand which hath ministered to her wants, and alleviated her distress. As to cloathing, the rapid encrease of our manufac-

tures, and the supplies we obtain from abroad, quiet all fears upon that subject. By the most authentic intelligence from Europe, we are informed that the people of France are ripe for a war with Britain, and will not omit the present opportunity of extending their commerce, and humbling their rival. Every state in Europe beheld with a jealous eye, the growing power of the British Empire, and the additional strength she daily received from this amazing continent: for they could not but perceive, that their own security was diminished in proportion as her power to injure them increased. Whence is it then that some persons pretend to assure you, that France, Spain, and the other European states, are not disposed to favour you? The wise and virtuous of all nations have pronounced our cause to be just, and approved the manner in which our resistance hath been conducted.

Whoever, therefore, considers the natural strength and advantages of this country, the distance it lies from Britain, the obvious policy of many European powers, the great supplies of arms and ammunition chearfully afforded us by the French and Spaniards, and the feeble and destitute condition of Britain: that she is drained of men and money, obliged to hire foreign mercenaries for the execution of her wicked purposes; in arrears to her troops for a twelvemonth's pay, which she cannot or will not discharge; her credit sunk; her trade ruined; her inhabitants divided; her unpopular; and her Ministers execrated; that she is overwhelmed with a monstrous debt; cut off from the vast revenue heretofore obtained by taxes on American produce; her West-India Islands in a starving condition; her ships taken; her merchants involved in bankruptcy; her designs against us wicked, unjust, cruel, contrary to the laws of God and man, pursued with implacable,

unrelenting

unrelenting vengeance, and in a manner barbarous, and oppofed to the ufage of civilized nations: whoever confiders, that we have humbly fought peace, and been refufed; that we have been denied even a hearing; all petitions rejected; all our remonftrances difregarded; that we fight not for conqueft, but only for fecurity; that our caufe is the caufe of God, of human nature, and pofterity: whoever, we fay, ferioufly confiders thefe things, muft entertain very improper ideas of the Divine juftice, to which we have appealed, and be very little acquainted with the courfe of human affairs, to harbour the fmalleft doubt of our being fuccefsful.

Remember the long and glorious ftruggle of the United Netherlands, againft the power of Spain, to which they had once been fubjected. Their extent was fmall, their country poor, their people far from numerous, and unaccuftomed to arms, and in the neighbourhood of their enemies. Spain, at that time, the moft powerful kingdom in Europe; her fleet formidable; her armies great, inured to war, and led by the beft Generals of the age; and her treafury overflowing with the wealth of Mexico and Peru, endeavoured to enflave them. They dutifully remonftrated againft the defign; their petitions were treated with contempt, and fire and fword were carried into their country to compel fubmiffion. They nobly refolved to be free; they declared themfelves Independent States; and after an obftinate ftruggle, fruftrated the wicked intentions of Spain.

Switzerland prefents us with another inftance of magnanimity. That country was oppreffed by cruel tyrants, and left to their defencelefs portion of freedom.

Even England, whofe Genius now blufhes for the degeneracy of her fons, hath afforded examples of oppofition to tyranny, which are worthy to be imitated by all nations. His Sacred Majefty, Charles the Firft, loft his head and his crown, by attempting to enflave his fubjects; and his Sacred Majefty, James the Second, was for the fame reafon expelled the kingdom, with his whole family, and the Prince of Orange chofen King in his ftead. The Englifh were too wife to believe, that the perfon of any tyrant could be facred; and never fuffered any man to wear the crown, who attempted to exercife the powers of royalty to the deftruction of the people, from whom thofe powers were derived. This practice is not only confiftent with human reafon, but perfectly confonant to the will and practice of God himfelf: You know that the Jews were under his peculiar direction; and you need not be informed of the many inftances in which he took the crown from fuch of their Kings, as refufed to govern according to the laws of the Jews.

If then God hath given us freedom, are we not refponfible to him for that, as well as other talents? If it be our birthright, let us not fell it for a mefs of pottage, nor fuffer it to be torn from us by the hand of violence!—If the means of defence are in our power, and we do not make ufe of them, what excufe fhall we make to our children and our Creator? Thefe are queftions of the deepeft concern to us all. Thefe are queftions which materially affect our happinefs, not in this world but the world to come. And furely, " if ever a teft for the trial of fpirits can be neceffary, it is now. If ever thofe of liberty and faction ought to be diftinguifhed from each other, it is now. If ever it is incumbent on the people to know truth and to follow it, it is now."

Rouze, therefore, brave citizens! Do your duty like men! And be perfuaded, that Divine Providence will not permit this weftern world to be involved in the horrors of flavery. Confider! that from the earlieft ages of the world, religion, liberty, and reafon, reason, have been bending their course towards the setting sun. The Holy Gospels are yet to be preached to these western regions, and we have the highest reason to believe, that the Almighty will not suffer slavery and the Gospel to go hand in hand. It cannot! It will not be!

But if there be any among us, dead to all sense of honour and love of their country; if deaf to all the calls of liberty, virtue, and religion; if forgetful of the magnanimity of their ancestors, and the happiness of their children; if neither the examples nor the success of other nations, the dictates of reason and of nature, or the great duties they owe to their God, themselves, and their posterity, have any effect upon them; if neither the injuries they have received, the prize they are contending for, the future blessings or curses of their children, the applause or the reproach of all mankind, the approbation or displeasure of the great Judge, or the happiness or misery consequent upon their conduct, in this and a future state, can move them; then let them be assured, that they deserve to be slaves, and are entitled to nothing but anguish and tribulation. Let them banish from their remembrance, the reputation, the freedom, and happiness which they have inherited from their forefathers. Let them forget every duty, human and divine, remember not that they have children, and beware how they call to mind the justice of the Supreme Being: let them go into captivity like the idolatrous and disobedient Jews, and be a reproach and a bye-word among the nations.

But we think better things of you. We believe, and are persuaded, that you will do your duty like men, and chearfully refer your cause to the great and righteous Judge. If success crown your efforts, all the blessings of freedom will be your reward. If you fall in the contest, you will be happy with God and liberty in Heaven.

By the unanimous order of the Convention,
ABRAHAM TEN BROECK, President.
Fish-Kill, Dec. 23, 1776.

Fish-Kill, Feb. 3.

We learn that in New-York the inhabitants are greatly distressed. Every article of provision is scarce and dear. A person just from the city informs us, that the loaf which formerly sold for 8 coppers, sells for 24. No fresh butter to be had, only Irish butter, very strong, at three shillings per lb. oak wood at 5l. per cord. The Tories are very uneasy on account of General Heath's army being so near them: It is said they are moving some of their effects out of the city to Staten-Island. O fine times! who would not fly to New-York for protection?

A part of the troops under the command of General Heath, having been for some time employed in bringing off forage from that part of the county of Westchester which was most exposed; having effected their design without the least opposition, advanced as far as Morrisiania and Tippet Hill, where, in order to increase the consternation which their approach occasioned at New-York, and to amuse themselves with the fears of the enemy, they discharged a few shot at Fort Independence, and drew up at Morrisiania, as if with a design to cross Harlem river. From the great parade, and little appearance of real strength discovered by the enemy, as well as by the alarm which our approach gave, most people are satisfied that an expedition against New-York could not fail of success.

By a gentleman just arrived from head-quarters we are informed, that our scouting parties have had several successful skirmishes with the enemy, near Woodbridge; in one of which we took 11 prisoners, and killed the Colonel that commanded the enemy's party; in another which happened on Saturday last, we drove a party of the enemy

enemy for near two miles, and killed about 30 of them, when we unexpectedly fell in with their main body, and were forced to retreat with some loss.

He also informs us, that seldom less than 8, and sometimes 20 soldiers come over to us of a day, as they say, in quest of liberty.

He informs farther, that since the engagement at Princetown, we have taken at different times 120 baggage waggons, most of them loaded; and that the enemy's loss in New-Jersey, including desertions, is computed at about 4000 men.

A few days ago a Hessian Major and two Adjutants came over to General Washington, from the enemy; and every day more or less of their soldiers desert and come to us.

Three sailors were brought here yesterday, who were taken near Frog's Point, at a small distance from their vessel.

We are informed, that on Wednesday last week, his Excellency General Washington issued a proclamation desiring the whole army to be in readiness, with three days provision, whence it is conjectured we shall soon have important news from head-quarters.

We are well informed, that a party from our army have taken 40 waggons, loaded with stores, from the regulars.

Extract of a letter from Peeks-Kill, Jan. 29.

" Yesterday Daniel Strang of this county, a SPY from the enemy's army, was executed pursuant to a sentence of a General Court Martial; he was lurking about the army here, and had inlisting orders to recruit for the enemy, sewed in his breeches; which were found on him. It is to be hoped, his punishment will deter others from the horrid and unnatural act of conspiring against their country; and aiding her cruel enemies, in committing every kind of iniquity."

Feb. 9. We hear from the most un-doubted authority, that every man capable of bearing arms, without any distinction, was obliged to do military duty in New-York. Thus are those unhappy wretches whom fear prevented from supporting their country, driven to expose themselves to greater dangers, in maintaining the tyranny of their new masters.

Providence, February 15.

Extract of a letter from a Gentleman of Distinction in Connecticut, dated Feb. 10.

" At a town near Brunswick, on the 1st instant, 700 of General Washington's army had a skirmish with 1000 of the enemy. Our troops at first drove the enemy from their ground, and found 36 of them killed: but a reinforcement coming to the enemy, with some field-pieces (of which our troops had none) our detachment retreated, with the loss of 7 killed, and 14 wounded."

To the melancholy picture already exhibited of the brutal behaviour of Britons (who vainly boast of being " ever pre-eminent in mercy ") aided by Hessian and Waldeck mercenaries, in New-York and New-Jersey, it gives us pain to add, that they have not only outraged the feelings of humanity to many people, who were so unhappy as to fall into their hands, particularly the fair sex, but have degraded themselves beyond the power of language to express, by wantonly destroying the curious water-works at New-York, an elegant public library at Trenton, and the grand orrery, made by the celebrated Rittenhouse, which was placed in the college at Princetown,—a piece of mechanism, which the most untutored savage, staying the hand of violence, would have beheld with wonder, reverence and delight !——Thus are our cruel enemies warring against Liberty, Virtue, and the Arts and Sciences.

Extract of a letter from Paris, dated March 8.

" The King's troops burnt the Library at Trenton, and destroyed the

the College at Princetown, with the library and fine orrery made by Ritten-houfe, the beft in the world. They fhould not make way with the Sciences. I blame them for this. The Marfhal Duke de Richlieu, when the French army came to Gottingen (in Hanover) fent and pofted a fafe-guard at the Univerfity, writing at the fame time a polite letter to the Heads of the Colleges, affuring them of his protection, and that they might purfue their ftudies, with all confidence, in quiet; for neither the place nor the ftudents fhould receive from his troops the leaft injury or moleftation; it not being, he faid, the cuftom of the French nation to make war againft learning; they left that to barbarians. The Univerfity have his name to this day in the higheft veneration."

Newport, December 22.

A gentleman arrived in town on Saturday, from Bofton, informs that a privateer from the eaftward had lately taken a fhip with dry goods, &c. whofe cargo coft 37,000 fterling. *The following is the fubftance of a Declaration made before a Magiftrate at Jamaica.*

Captain Talmafh, late of Georgia, but laft from Auguftine, in the fchooner Peggy, on September 6, between Cape Nichola Mole and Cape Maize, was boarded by the Maidftone Englifh frigate, Captain Gardiner, who fired to bring them to; at the fame time a French frigate to windward bore down upon him, and fired a fhot to leeward, hoifted out their pinace, and fent their firft Lieutenant on board him, who very particularly inquired if his veffel was from the *United States of America*, and if he wanted protection; if fo he was willing to render him his fervices; being anfwered in the negative, he fheered off, but continued at a fmall diftance, during the time Capt. Gardiner was examining the papers of faid fchooner, of which protection

Mr. Talmafh informed Capt. Gardiner, while they were within hail of each other, upon which the Englifh frigate thought proper to difmifs the fchooner, who proceeded on her voyage to Jamaica; and the two fhips fteered one courfe.

New-London, January 30, 1777.

At the adjourned Superior Court held in this place laft week, the following perfons were convicted of the following crimes, viz.

Mofes Dunbar, of Waterbury, convicted of having a Captain's commiffion from General Howe, and inlifting men to ferve in the minifterial army—fentenced to fuffer death, but the time of his execution is not fixed upon.

The Rev. Roger Viets, of Salifbury, convicted of aiding and affifting Major French and a number of other prifoners in making their efcape, and holding a traiterous correfpondence with the enemy, fentenced to pay 20 pounds to this ftate, and fuffer one year's imprifonment.

Gurdon Whitmore, of Middletown, found guilty of high treafon by the jury: but an arreft of judgment being plead in his favour, a final determination of the trial was put off till March term.

Solomon Bill, laft from Middletown, convicted of counterfeiting the bills of credit of this State.—Sentenced to fuffer four years confinement in Newgate prifon.

Bofton, Feb. 16, 1777.

By a perfon lately from Halifax, we learn, that when the HOWES Proclamation was profer'd to the American prifoners to fign, (notwithftanding they were confined on board a guard-fhip, and told that General Howe had got poffeffion of Philadelphia,) they, like true Americans, to a man, nobly difdained to do it.

By an exprefs from Ticonderoga arrived here laft Tuefday, we hear is, that the lakes for 20 miles together were all open and free of ice.

We

We hear that a veſſel is arrived at Dartmouth from the Weſt-Indies, the maſter of which informs that an Engliſh cruizer had taken two American veſſels, which were French bottomed; in conſequence of which a French frigate from Martinico ſailed in queſt of her, took her, and carried her into ſaid port.

———————

Boſton, Dec. 20. Commodore Manly, in the continental ſhip Hancock, of 32 guns, is come round to Newbury Port.

Laſt Thurſday arrived in town, from the continental camps at New-York the Honourable Major General Lincoln, who commanded the militia of this State, which were ſent as a reinforcement for two months. His eſtabliſhed good character as a civilian at the Board of Council, actuated Colonel Crafts to meet him a few miles out of town, accompanied by many of his officers on horſeback, who eſcorted him into Congreſs-ſtreet, in imitation of the Romans, there to join the ſupreme Senate of the State.

Laſt Sunday a number of priſoners (marines and ſailors) arrived in town, from the interior parts of this State and Connecticut, and on Monday ſet off for Marblehead, in order to be exchanged for a number of our men, who lately arrived in the cartel veſſels there.

New-London, Dec. 20.

The State of Rhode-Iſland, by a Committee which came here laſt week, have agreed upon the exchange of priſoners in that State for a like number in the Britiſh fleet, which is to take place the 9th inſtant at this port. An exchange of priſoners in this State is poſtponed for the preſent.

Annapolis, (Maryland) Dec. 26.

The Hon. George Plater, William Paca, Daniel of St. Thomas Jenifer, Charles Carroll, barriſter, Thomas Johnſon, Charles Carroll of Carollton, Thomas Stone, Brice Thomas Beale Worthington, and Thomas Contee, Eſquires, of the weſtern ſhore; and the Hon. Matthew Tilgham, Joſeph Nicholſon, Robert Goldſborough, Turbutt Wright, James Tilgham, and Samuel Wilſon, Eſquires, of the eaſtern ſhore, are elected ſenators for this State.

On Saturday laſt the polls were cloſed for the election of delegates to repreſent Arne-Arnold county in General Aſſembly, when Thomas Tillard, Rezin Hammond, John Hall, and Benjamin Galloway, Eſquires, were elected.

Williamſburgh, Dec. 20.

Laſt Tueſday George Webb, Eſq. was choſen by the Legiſlature to be treaſurer of this Commonwealth, in the room of Robert C. Nicholas, Eſq. who has reſigned that important truſt (which he filled with much honour to himſelf, and applauſe from his country) rather than forego his beſt ſervices as a delegate in Aſſembly, at this critical conjuncture.

Beſides the ſix additional battalions on the continental eſtabliſhment, our Aſſembly have voted three other battalions for the defence of this State, with 1300 ſeamen and marines, and the principal rivers to be guarded with ſtrong forts. It is not doubted, therefore, that the free and independent people of Virginia will ſecond the patriotic views of their repreſentatives, by entering chearfully into their country's ſervice, and thereby bring matters to a proſperous and wiſhed for iſſue.

Amongſt the *Worthies* who have joined, or put themſelves under the protection of, Howe and Company, at Trenton, we find the names of the following *noted* perſonages, viz.

James Galloway, Eſq. late a Member of the Congreſs, Speaker of the Pennſylvania Senate, and printer of a public news-paper in Philadelphia.

John Allen, Eſq. (ſon of the *celebrated rhetorical, impartial, learned* Judge, whoſe memory will outlaſt the five mile ſtone) late a Member of the
Philadelphia

Philadelphia Committee of Observation, Inspection, &c.

Andrew Allen, Esq. (brother to Jack) late a Member of Congress, one of the Pennsylvania Committee of Safety, and, at the same time, a sworn advocate for George III. of Britain, and his creatures.

William Allen, Esq. (brother to Andrew) late a Lieutenant-Colonel in the continental service, which station he resigned—not because he was totally unfit for it, but because the Continental Congress *presumed* to declare the American States free and independent, without first asking the consent, and obtaining the approbation, of himself and *wise* family.

STATE of MASSACHUSETTS-BAY.
In the year of our Lord, one thousand seven hundred and seventy-seven.
An ACT to prevent Monoply and Oppression.

Whereas the avaricious conduct of many persons, by daily adding to the now exorbitant price of every necessary and convenient article of life; and encreasing the price of labour in general, unless a speedy and effectual stop be put thereto, will be attended with, the most fatal and pernicious consequences, as it not only disheartens and disaffects the soldiers, who have nobly entered into the service of their country, for the support of the best of causes, and distresses the poorer part of the community, by obliging them to give unreasonable prices for those things that are absolutely necessary to their very existence, but will be also very injurious to the State in general.—And whereas the Committee lately impowered by this State to proceed to Providence in Rhode-Island, and in behalf of this State there to meet with Committees from the other New-England States; and among other things to confer upon measures necessary to prevent monopoly and the high price of goods, and the necessaries of life, and for re-

gulation of vendues; have in conjunction with the said Committees, recommended that rates and prices be settled and affixed, by an act of this State, to the articles herein after enumerated:

Be it therefore enacted by the Council and House of Representatives in General Court assembled, and by the authority of the same, That from and after the 28th day of January, one thousand seven hundred and seventy-seven, the price of Farming Labour, in the summer season, shall not exceed 3s. by the day, and found as usual, and so in usual proportion at other seasons of the year, and the labour of mechanics and tradesmen, and other labour, beside what is herein hereafter especially enumerated in proportion thereunto, according to the usages and customs which have heretofore been adopted and practised in this State, when compared with farming labour.

And be it further enacted by the authority aforesaid, That the following articles shall not be sold for a higher price than is herein hereafter settled and affixed to them respectively, viz.

Wheat. Good merchantable wheat at 7s. 6d. per bushel.

Rye. Good merchantable rye or rye-meal at 5s. a bushel.

Indian Meal. Good Indian meal or corn at 4s. a bushel.

Sheeps Wool. Good merchantable sheeps wool at 2s. a lb.

Pork. Fresh pork well fatted and of a good quality at 4d. halfpenny a lb. and Salt Pork in usual proportion according to the price of salt.

Beef. Good well fatted grass-fed beef at 3d. a lb. and stall-fed beef well fated at 4d. a lb. and beef of an inferior quality in equal proportion.

Hides. Raw hides at 3d. a lb. Raw calf skins at 6d. a lb.

Salt. Good merchantable imported salt at 10s. a bushel. Salt manufactured from sea-water within this State at 12s. a bushel.

H   Rum.

Rum. Good merchantable West-India rum at 6s. 8d. a gallon by the hogshead, including the cask, and 6s. 10d. by the barrel, exclusive of the barrel, and 7s. 8d. by the single gallon, and 2s. by the quart, and so in proportion for a less quantity, according to the former custom and usages for retailing smaller quantities, saving an allowance of one penny a gallon for every ten miles the same shall be carried by land carriage from the first port of delivery.

New England Rum at 3s. 10d. a gallon by the hogshead or barrel, exclusive of 13s. 4d. for the hogshead, or 4s. for the barrel, and 4s. 6d. by the single gallon, at the town where the same is distilled, and so in like proportion for smaller quantities, according to the old and approved customs for retailing smaller quantities, allowing one penny each ten miles for every gallon that has been or shall be transported by land, from the place of distillery.

Sugar. Best Muscovado sugar at 54s. a hundred by the hogshead, and three pounds by the single hundred, and 8d. a lb. by the single pound at the place where it is first landed, and allowing 9d. for the transporting of every cwt. ten miles by land carriage. And sugars of an inferior quality in the usual proportion.

Molasses, of the best quality, at 3s. 4d. a gallon by the hogshead, including the cask, and 3s. 8d. by the barrel, exclusive of 3s. for the barrel, and 4s. by the single gallon at the place where it is first landed, from the West-Indies, and so in proportion in the country, allowing one penny a gallon for every ten miles transportation by land into the country, or from the place where it is so landed.

Cocoa. Best cocoa at six pounds ten shillings a cwt. American manufactured chocolate 1s. 8d. a lb.

Cheese manufactured in America 5d. a lb.

Butter at 10d. a lb. by the single lb. and 9d. the firkin.

Peas 8s. a bushel. Beans 6s. a bushel.

Potatoes. Potatoes, commonly called Spanish potatoes, of the best quality, at 1s. 4d. a bushel in the fall of the year, and not more than 2s. in any other season, and other potatoes in usual proportion.

Stockings. Men's best yarn stockings 6s. a pair, and in that proportion for an inferior quality.

Shoes. Men's shoes made of neat's leather, of the best common sort, 8s. a pair, and for others the like price according to their size and quality.

Salted Pork by the barrel 220 lb. in a barrel £.4 12s.

Beef. Beef by the barrel, 240 lb. in a barrel, £.3 14s. 6d.

Cotton. Cotton 3s. a lb. by the bag, and 3s. 8d. by the single pound, at the port where it is first landed from the West-Indies, and the like allowance for transportation as for other articles.

Oats. Oats 2s. a bushel.

Flax. Good well dressed merchantable flax, 1s. a lb.

Coffee. Good coffee 1s. 4d. a lb. by the single lb.

Good tried tallow 7d. halfpenny a lb. and rough tallow 5d. a lb.

Tow-Cloth. Good yard wide tow-cloth, 2s. 3d. a yard, and other tow-cloth in proportion, according to its width and quality, and the price of coarse linens to be computed after the same rate.

Flannel. Good yard wide striped flannel, 3s. 6d. a yard, and other flannels in proportion, according to their widths and qualities; and other woollen cloth, manufactured in America, according to their widths and qualities.

Wood. Green oak wood brought from the country, and delivered at the door of the buyer, 28s. a cord.

Good walnut wood, so delivered, 30s. a cord.

Good

Good walnut wood brought from the fouth fhore, and delivered at a wharf in Bofton, 28s. a cord.

Good oak wood, brought from the fouth fhore, and fo delivered, 24s. a cord.

Eaftern wood, in confideration of the rifque in bringing the fame, 22s. a cord, delivered at the wharf in Bofton.

Charcoal. Good charcoal, 1s. a bafket.

Tanned hides, at 1s. 3d. a lb. and curried leather in ufual proportion.

Homefpun yard wide cotton and linen cloth of the beft common fort, 3s. 6d. and other widths and qualities of cotton and linen in like proportion.

Mutton, lamb and veal, at 4d. a lb.

Flour, imported from the fouthern States, at 30s. a hundred.

Flour, manufactured in this State, at 25s.

Horfe-keeping, in Bofton, for a night, or twenty-four hours, with Englifh hay, 2s. and in other places in proportion. For keeping a yoke of oxen the fame as a horfe.

Teaming-work, 1s. 6d. for every ton weight a mile, excepting from Northampton to the northern army, for which may be taken 2s. a mile for each ton weight.

Turkeys, dunghill fowls, and ducks, to be fold only by the pound, at 5d. a pound.

Geefe, at 4d. a lb. Milk, at 2d. halfpenny a quart.

Good refined iron, at 50s. a hundred.

Bloomery iron, at 30s. a cwt. at the place of manufactory, and the fame allowance to be made for tranfporting of iron by land, as is allowed for other articles.

Liver oil, by the barrel, 4s. a gallon. Blubber refined, 30s. a barrel.

Englifh hay, of the beft quality, at 5s. a cwt. and fo in proportion for a meaner quality or fort of hay.

Good merchantable white pine boards, not to exceed 48s. a thoufand in Bofton, and other lumber in proportion, and the price in other parts of this State to be in proportion thereunto, according to ancient cuftoms and ufages.

And be it enacted by the authority aforefaid, That the prices of all the articles produced in America herein before enumerated, excepting thofe to which the prices of tranfportation are affixed, fhall be taken and deemed to be the prices of fuch goods and articles in the town of Bofton, and that the felectmen and committees of the feveral towns in this State fhall be, and hereby are impowered to affix and fettle in their refpective towns what fuch articles and goods fhall be fold for in their towns refpectively, according to the proportion the price fuch goods have borne in fuch towns, with the price they have been at in the town of Bofton, according to the ancient cuftoms and ufage of fuch towns. And the faid felectmen and committees are in like manner impowered and directed to fet and eftablifh the prices of goods herein not enumerated, according to the proportion the price of them have ufually borne in their refpective towns to thofe herein enumerated. And the faid fefelectmen and committees are alfo required to make out a fair lift of all the articles to which they fhall affix prices, and to poft the fame with the prices by them fo affixed, up in fome public place or places in the town where they live, and alfo to return a lift of fuch prices to the clerk of fuch town, there to remain upon record, and fuch prices by them affixed purfuant to the duty herein enjoined and power hereby given them, fhall be taken and deemed to be the price fet and affixed by this act in fuch town.

And be it alfo enacted, That in the plantations where there are no felectmen the committee fhall have fuch power, and be required to perform the fame duties as felectmen and com-

mittees

mittees have within their towns respectively.

And be it further enacted by the authority aforesaid, That the price of all European and East-India goods and merchandize of all kinds, which shall have been or shall be imported into this State, as also of all such goods which have been or shall be brought into this State in any prize vessel, shall not exceed the following rates, viz.

Woollen goods, coarse linens, duck, cordage, ticklenburgs and oznabrigs, shall not be sold by wholesale at a higher rate than in the proportion of £.275 sterling, for what usually cost £.100 sterling, in that part of Europe from whence they are imported; and any other goods, wares or merchandize, excepting hemp, warlike and military stores, imported from thence or brought, or which shall be brought into any port in this State in any prize vessel, shall not be sold at a higher rate from the prime cost as aforesaid, than in the proportion of £.250 sterling for what cost £.100 sterling in Europe; and the seller by wholesale shall make out a bill of parcels at the sterling cost of the articles sold, with his advance thereupon, and deliver the same to the bearer, under penalty of the sum at which such articles are so sold by him; and the retailers of such goods, wares and merchandize shall not sell them at a higher advance than 20 per cent. upon the wholesale price, and shall, if requested by the buyer, give a bill of parcels, with the sterling cost and the advance.

And be it further enacted by the authority aforesaid, That if any person having any article or articles necessary for the use of the American army or navy, shall with-hold or refuse to sell the same for a reasonable reward, in such case, upon complaint thereof made upon oath to the Council or Board of War of this State, or they knowing or suspecting the same, or either of them, are hereby authorized and empowered to issue their warrant to any sheriff, deputy sheriff or constable, to impress the same, and for that purpose in the day time, between sun-rise and sun-set, to break and enter any warehouses, stores or other places where such goods are deposited, or suspected to be deposited, and to take and apply the same to the use aforesaid, the owner thereof being paid the price at which such goods are fixed in this act, and in case the price of the goods so taken is not herein settled and fixed, the owner shall be paid for the same at a reasonable appraisement to be made of such goods, by three indifferent judicious men, under oath, for that purpose appointed, one of them by those who issued the said warrant, and one by the owner of the said goods, and one by the officer directed to execute said warrant; but if the owner shall decline to make such appointment, two of the said appraisers shall be appointed by the persons who shall execute such warrant, and the sum at which the said goods shall be appraised shall be immediately paid as aforesaid.

And be it further enacted by the authority aforesaid, That if any vendue master, or any one for, or under him, shall at any vendue or public sale, sell any article for a greater, or higher price than by this act is limited, he shall forfeit the sum equal to that for which such article shall be sold, and is hereby disqualified from acting at any time as an auctioneer or vendue master, and in case he, or any one in his behalf, should presume to act in that capacity, he shall forfeit the sum of £.50 for every offence.

And be it further enacted by the authority aforesaid, That every person who shall sell any of the articles abovementioned, at a greater price than is herein settled and fixed for the same, or others not enumerated in a manifest disproportion thereto, upon conviction, shall be fined for every article so sold of the price of twenty shillings, or under the sum of twenty shillings, and for every article of a

price

price above twenty shillings, a sum equal to that for which such article shall be sold—and every person who shall take, and receive for his service and labour, a greater sum than is settled, and fixed for the same in and by this act, shall forfeit and pay a like sum of money to that which he shall take and receive for such service and labour.

And be it further enacted, That whoever shall sell any goods, wares or merchandizes, or shall do any service or labour, at a greater price than is settled and fixed thereto, in and by this act upon credit, shall not maintain any action for the recovery thereof, but shall be barred therefrom, and the person against whom any action shall be brought for the recovery of such money, may plead the general issue thereto, and give the special matter in evidence to the jury.

And be it further enacted by the authority aforesaid, That all the fines and forfeitures mentioned in this act, shall and may be recovered in any court proper to try the same, within the county in which the offence shall have been committed, by action, presentment or indictment; one half thereof to the use of this State, and the residue to the prosecutor, together with the costs of prosecution. And all grand jurors are hereby strictly enjoined to take cognizance of, and to make due presentment of all offences against this act which shall come to their knowledge, or whereof they shall receive due information.

And be it further enacted by the authority aforesaid, That if any person shall engross, or have in his possession by purchase or otherwise, more of any article in this act enumerated or any other necessary of life than is necessary for the consumption of his own family and immediate dependants, and which he holds with an apparent design, in the judgment of the major part of the selectmen of the town where he lives, or where such article shall be to sell, trade upon, and not for his own consumption as aforesaid, and shall refuse to sell and dispose of the same for the common currency of this State or the United States of America, and at the price affixed and settled by this act, or by the selectmen and committee in pursuance of it, and complaint being thereof made to the major part of said selectmen, by or in behalf of any person who is in want of such article or articles for his own immediate support, the support of his family or immediate dependants; and the said selectmen or a major part of them, believing the same to be true, shall demand of such person so refusing, to sell such article or articles for such price as is affixed by this act, or by the selectmen and committee in pursuance of it; and if such person shall refuse to comply therewith, or cannot be found to have such demand made of him, the major part of said selectmen shall apply to some justice of the peace within the same county, for a warrant to open any store, warehouse or granary, in which such article or articles may be, or otherwise to take possession of the same: and the said justice shall, without delay, make out his warrant directed to some sheriff, deputy sheriff or constable, in form following, viz.

SUFFOLK, ß   To

Greeting.

(Seal.) WHEREAS complaint is this day made to me, by A, B, C, D and E. a major part of the selectmen of L, in the said county of S, that I K, of said L, (addition) hath now in his possession
with design to sell and trade upon the same, and which is not by him designed for the consumption of his family or immediate dependants; and that the said I K, does, though requested thereunto by the said selectmen, refuse to sell
thereof to N O, or R, within this
State,

State, who is in great neceffity therefore (for the fupport of his family and
immediate dependants) for the price
fet and affixed by a law of this State,
intitled, " An Act to prevent monoply and oppreffion." You are therefore hereby required, in the name of
the Government and people of the
Maffachufetts-Bay, in New-England,
taking with you a major part of the
felectmen of faid L, in the day time,
between the rifing and fetting of the
fun, to open the ftore of the faid I K,
or as the cafe may be, to take poffeffion of the faid
and the fame deliver to the faid felectmen, to the intent that the faid felectmen may fell and deliver to the faid
N O, the aforefaid
or fo much of that article as the faid
N O, has abfolutely neceffity for;
and you are to make true return of
this warrant to me as foon as may be,
w. your doings therein.
n under my hand and feal,
the   day of   in the
ye o. ur Lord, 177
And the faid felectmen, or the
major part of them, having poffeffion
of fuch article or articles in manner
aforefaid, fhall fell and deliver to fuch
re effitous perfons named in fuch warrant, fo much of the article therein
mentioned, as he ftands in need of
for the fupport of his family and immediate dependants, at the price affixed as aforefaid, and after deducting
out of the money received therefor,
the pay for their own fervice, at the
rate of four fhillings a day, the officers legal fees, and two fhillings for
the juftice's warrant, and fhall pay
the overplus, if any there be, to the
perfon who owned, or poffeffed fuch
goods. Provided neverthelefs, that
the faid felectmen fhall not be obliged
or impowered, in purfuance of this
act, to fupply any perfon as aforefaid,
who has by him, to their knowledge,
any of the articles in this act enumerated, or any other neceffary of life
more than he ftands in need of for his

own confumption, and refufes to expofe them to fale for the prices fet and
affixed in this act, or that fhall neglect, or refufe to bring them to market, according to his ufual cuftom.

And be it further enacted, That
when any action fhall be brought
againft any officer, who has a duty
affigned him by this act, he may
plead the general iffue, and give the
fpecial matter in evidence for his jufti-
fication.

STATE of MASSACHUSETTS-BAY.
In the year of our Lord, one thoufand
feven hundred and feventy-feven.
An ACT to prevent the attefting of
foldiers for fmall debts who have
inlifted or fhall inlift in the Continental army.

Whereas it is apprehended that divers perfons, either from inattention
to the public good, or a fpirit inimical to the liberties of America, will
arreft and imprifon for trifling debts,
many foldiers who have inlifted, or
are willing to inlift into the Continental army, which may greatly retard the bufinefs of raifing the faid
Continental army:

Be it therefore enacted by the
Council and Houfe of Reprefentatives
in General Court affembled, and by
the authority of the fame, That no
foldier who has inlifted, or fhall inlift
into the Continental army, fhall be
arrefted at the fuit of any creditor,
from and after the feventh day of February, in the year of our Lord, one
thoufand feven hundred and feventy-
feven, unlefs the faid creditor make
oath before fome magiftrate, that the
faid foldier is juftly indebted to him
in the fum of Ten Pounds Ten Shillings more than all difcounts; and
that the eftate of no fuch foldier be
liable to attachment at the fuit of, or
for the benefit of all his creditors, unlefs their debt in the whole, on being
afcertained by their oaths before fuch
magiftrate, fhall amount to more than
Forty-five pounds.

And

And be it further enacted by the authority aforesaid, That when any soldier shall be arrested contrary to the intent of this act, it shall and may be lawful for any justice of the peace within this State, upon complaint thereof made by the party himself, or by any his superior officers, to examine into the same by the oath of the parties or otherwise, and upon due proof made before him that such soldier so arrested, was legally inlisted as a soldier in the service of the United States, and arrested contrary to the intent of this act, he shall forthwith discharge such soldier so inlisted, by warrant under his hand and seal, without paying any fees; and the plaintiff or plaintiffs in any such civil suit or process, shall be at the whole cost and expence of every such suit or process brought against any inlisted soldier, contrary to the intent and meaning of this act: Provided this act shall not be construed to extend to prohibit the collectors of taxes from collecting such taxes as are or may be due from soldiers so inlisted.

STATE of MASSACHUSETTS-BAY.
In the year of our Lord, one thousand seven hundred and seventy-seven.
An ACT for preventing or punishing crimes that may be committed against the public safety, below the degree of treason and misprision of treason.

Whereas the Congress of the United Colonies of America, in order to preserve the inhabitants thereof from that ruin and misery to which they were destined by the avarice and cruelty of Great-Britain, did upon the fourth day of July, one thousand seven hundred and seventy-six, declare the said Colonies to be free States, independent of all people and nations; and whereas some evil minded persons within this State, have at divers times, by words and actions endeavoured to discourage the people thereof from supporting said declaration, as also in their opposition to those acts and measures of the King and Parliament of Great Britain, which induced the Congress to make such declaration:

Be it therefore enacted by the Council and House of Representatives in General Court assembled, and by the authority of the same, That if any person shall make use of any expressions in preaching or praying, or in public or private discourse or conversation, with an apparent design to discourage the people of this State, or any of them, from supporting said declaration, or that shall by words or actions, directly or indirectly, endeavour to support or justify the measures taken by the King and Parliament of Great-Britain against the American States, or shall dissuade the people of this State or any of them, from supporting their opposition to said measures, or shall endeavour by any ways or means to prevent the Continental army from being raised, or the Continental navy from being manned, or with an evident design to prevent the raising said army or manning said navy, shall dissuade or endeavour to prevent any person or persons from inlisting in the army or navy of the United States, or either of them, or shall use any means to hurt or destroy the credit of the public bills of the United States of America, or of this State; each person so offending, and being thereof convicted, shall pay a fine to the use of the town or plantation where such offence is committed, not exceeding Fifty Pounds, nor less than Twenty Shillings, at the discretion of the Court before whom the conviction shall be, and shall recognize for his good behaviour as such Court shall order, and stand committed until sentence be performed.

And be it further enacted by the authority aforesaid, That any justice of the peace, upon complaint made to him of such offence, and finding presumptive evidence that the same is true,

true, fhall order fuch offender to find fureties for his appearance at the next Court of General Seffions of the Peace, to be held in the county where fuch offence is committed, and in default thereof, to commit fuch offender to to the common gaol; and all fheriffs, conftables, grand-jurors, and tything-men, are directed and enjoined to make prefentment and complaint of all fuch offences as fhall come to their knowledge refpectively.

Bofton, Feb. 13, 1777.

At a full and refpectable meeting of the inhabitants of Bofton, at Faneuil-hall, on yefterday, they appeared unanimous in their refolutions to pro-mote the falutary intentions of the late act to prevent monopoly, &c. and earneftly recommended it to all the inhabitants that have any articles more than they want for their con-fumption, that they would difpofe of them agreeable to the prices fixed by the late regulating act, as they would regard the peace of the town, the di-ftreffes of the poor, fixing our me-dium to a certain value, and ftrength-ening the hands of Government at this important crifis. The committee of correfpondence were defired to in-form the committees of other towns, of the proceedings of faid meeting, in order to prevent any ill impreffions by falfe reports induftrioufly circulated from felfifh views, or in aid to the ene-mies of American freedom and inde-pendence.

Saturday laft the General Affembly of this State adjourned to Wednefday the fifth day of March next, having paffed the following Acts:

An Act for repealing a law of this State made and paffed by the Great and General Court at their prefent feffion, intitled, An Act to prohibit the exportation of lumber for a limit-ed time.

An Act for making and emitting bills of public credit for fifty thoufand and four pounds.

An Act for repealing an Act, in-titled, An Act for altering the place by law appointed for holding the fu-perior Court of Judicature, Court of Affize and General Gaol Delivery, and the Courts of General Seffions of the Peace, and inferior Courts of Common Pleas within and for the county of Suffolk, made and enacted by the Great and General Court or Af-fembly of this colony in February 1776.

An Act in addition to an Act paffed in the year 1694, for the relief of ideots and diftracted perfons.

An Act for incorporating the plan-tation called St. George's in the county of Lincoln, into a town, by the name of Warren.

An Act, intitled, An Act for dif-continuing the name of a town in the county of Worcefter, lately incorpo-rated by the name of *Hutchinfon* and calling the fame *Barré*.

An Act, intitled, An Act for eftab-lifhing a naval office, and for afcer-taining the fees.

An Act, intitled an Act to confirm the titles of Benjamin Titcomb and David Richardfon, to a certain 30 acre lot of land in Pearfontown, fo called, in the county of Cumberland, originally laid out for a fchool-lot, and to confirm to the inhabitants of faid Pearfontown, certain other lands voted and granted for the fupport of a fchool, by the proprietors of faid town-fhip in lieu of faid lot, and as an equivalent therefor.

An Act to fupply the treafury with the fum of two hundred thoufand pounds.

An Act for preventing the operation of an act made anno Domini, 1770, intitled, An Act for the reapealing the feveral laws now in force which relate to the limitation of perfonal ac-tions, and for the limitation of per-fonal actions for the future, and for avoiding fuits at law.

An Act to fupply the treafury with the fum of two hundred and fix thou-fand and four hundred pounds.

An

An Act for making and emitting bills of public credit, to the amount of seventy-five thousand pounds.

An Act for making and emitting bills of public credit to the amount of twenty thousand and thirty-four pounds.

. An Act for dividing and setting off the northerly half of the land in the east precinct in the town of Pownalborough, in the county of Lincoln, into a separate precinct, by the name of the North Precinct.

An Act for erecting a tract of land (called Fryburgh) of 2172 rods square, lying in the county of York, which was granted as a township to Joseph Fry, Esq. A. D. 1762, and confirmed 1763, into a town, by the name of Fryburgh.

An Act for apportioning and assessing a tax of one hundred and one thousand eight hundred and seventy-one pounds one shilling and two-pence halfpenny, upon the several towns and other places in this State; and also for assessing a tax of seven thousand three hundred and twenty pounds seventeen shillings, paid the representatives for their travel and attendance in the General Court in the year 1775. Also for assessing a tax of forty pounds one shilling on the town of Hancock, to pay a committee appointed by the General Court to go to said town.

An Act against treason and misprision of treason, and for regulating trials in such cases, and for directing the mode of executing judgments against persons attainted of felony.

An Act for preventing or punishing crimes that may be committed against the public safety, below the degree of treason and misprision of treason.

An Act for providing a reinforcement to the American army; wherein it is enacted, " That no rank or station in life, place, employment or office (except as is therein excepted) shall excuse or exempt any person from serving in arms for the defence of his country, either by himself or some able bodied effective man in his stead, or in case of his neglect or refusal, from paying the fine therein required.

Council-Chamber, Boston, Feb. 15, 1777.

Ordered, that the Selectmen and Committee of Correspondence, of the several towns and plantations of the counties of Berkshire, Hampshire, Worcester, Middlesex, Barnstable, Plimouth, Bristol, Essex, York, Cumberland and Lincoln, to whom it was recommended by a resolve of the General Court of the twentieth of January last, to purchase and collect the number of blankets allotted by said resolve to their respective towns and plantations, be and hereby are required and directed immediately to deliver said blankets to the muster masters of their respective counties, taking their receipts for the same. And the said muster masters are directed to deliver said blankets to such of the men that are or have been inlisted into the Continental army, who may stand in need of the same, upon their being applied to by any officer commanding said men for that purpose; they taking receipts of said men for what blankets they deliver them: and the muster masters are to make return to this Board, once in every ten days of the number of blankets they may receive, and also of the number they may have delivered out.

And the selectmen and committees of the several towns in the county of Suffolk, are hereby directed immediately to deliver what blankets they have collected, to the Board of War.

A true copy.

Attest.   JOHN AVERY, Dep. Sec.

STATE OF MASSACHUSETTS BAY.

Council-Chamber, Boston, Feb. 22, 1777.

Whereas it has been represented to this Board, that some of the officers lately appointed to enlist men for the fifteen Continental battalions to be raised in this State, have been offer-

I   ing

ing the bounty allowed by this State, to persons belonging to some of the other United States, to induce them to enter into the service, and to make up the proportion of this State, which is a practice in direct violation of the orders of this State, issued the 24th of November last.

Ordered, therefore, that all officers belonging to the fifteen battalions aforesaid, be and hereby are strictly forbidden to persist or continue in any such practice; and in case they should, they may depend upon being cashiered. And muster masters of the respective counties, are hereby directed not to suffer any such persons to pass muster; and to be extremely careful that the men they muster, are of sufficient stature, and able body.

A true copy.

Attest.   JOHN AVERY, Dep. Sec.

Boston, Feb. 15, 1777.

The Honourable Congress, having judged it necessary, for carrying on the present war, immediately to borrow a sum of money, upon the credit of the United States:

It is therefore expected, that every friend to his country, and the rights of mankind, will readily deposit in the public funds, what money he can spare from his necessary business, as he will thereby render eminent service to these States.

Loan certificates, or Bank notes, bearing annual interest, or 4 per cent. will be given for all monies so borrowed, signed by the Continental Treasurer, and counter-signed by one of the Commissioners of the Loan Office.

The universal credit of these certificates, and their convenience in carrying on commerce through the United States, must give them the preference to all other notes or bonds.

The following Monument was erected over the graves of the following heroes, who were inhumanly murdered by a body of savages, on the Isle aux Noix, in June last, by order of General Sullivan, then Commander there.

BENEATH this humble SOD,
Lie
Captain ADAMS,
Lieutenant CULBERTSON,
And 2 Privates of the 6th Pennsylvania battalions,
Not hirelings——but—Patriots.
They fell not in battle! but unarm'd,
Were basely murdered, and inhumanly scalp'd,
By the barbarous emissaries of the once just,
But now abandonn'd kingdom of Britain.
Sons of America! rest in quiet here!
Britannia blush! Burgoyne let fall a tear!
But tremble Europe's sons with savage race,
Death and revenge, await you with disgrace.
Isle aux Noix, June 21, 1776.

GENERAL ORDERS.

Head Quarters, Morris Town, January 22, 1777.

The General is sorry to find that the late general order, allowing the plunder taken from the enemy to be divided for the benefit of the captors, has been mistaken by some and abused by others. The indulgence was granted to the scouting parties *only*, as a reward for the extraordinary fatigue, hardship, and danger they were exposed to upon those parties. The General never meant, nor had an idea that any of our's, or the enemy's store, found at any evacuated post, were to be considered the property of those that first marched in. Neither did he mean that any public stores discovered by any of the scouting parties, should be appropriated to their use, unless they found the enemy in the actual possession and dispossessed them. Plunder taken under such circumstances, either by the militia or the Continental troops, to be reported

. by

by the commanding officer of the party to some of the Continental or Provincial Generals, who are directed to have all the provisions and military stores so taken, appraised by the Commissary and Quarter-Master General, or their deputies, and the party paid the value thereof. Such articles as are taken, not necessary for the use of the army, to be sold at public vendue, under the direction of the Quarter-Master General, or some of his deputies, for the benefit of the captors.

The General prohibits, in both the militia and Continental troops, in the most positive terms, the infamous practices of plundering the inhabitants, under the specious pretence of their being Tories. Let the persons of such as are known to be enemies to their country, be seized and confined, and their property disposed of as the law of the State directs.—It is our business to give protection and support to the poor distressed inhabitants, not to multiply and increase their calamities. After the publication of this Order, any officer, either militia or Continental, found attempting to conceal the public stores, plundering the inhabitants under the pretence of their being Tories, or selling at vendue plunder taken from the enemy, in any other manner than these orders direct, may expect to be punished in the severest manner, and be obliged to account for every thing so taken or sold. The Adjutant-General to furnish the commanding officer of each division with a copy of those orders, who is to circulate copies among his troops immediately.

A true copy of General Orders,

J. REED, Adjutant-General.

(General Washington's proclamation in last volume, page 308, should have been dated Jan. 25, 1777.)

GENERAL ORDERS.

Head Quarters, Morris Town, February, 1777.

The General informed that many frauds and abuses have been committed of late by sundry soldiers, who after inlisting in one regiment and receiving the bounty allowed by Congress, have deserted, inlisted in others and received new bounties: for prevention of such unjust and infamous practices, commands and strictly enjoins all officers of the Continental army to use their utmost endeavours to detect those who shall be guilty of such offences, and them having apprehended, they cause to be forthwith tried by a General Court-Martial, that they may be dealt with according to their crimes.

The General thinks proper to declare, that this offence is of the most enormous and flagrant nature, and not admitting of the least palliation or excuse; whoever are convicted thereof, and sentenced to die, may consider their execution certain and inevitable.

That such impositions may be less practicable, every officer engaged in the recruiting service, is required to have a piece of blue, red or yellow ribband, or tape, fixed in the hat of each soldier recruited, at the time of inlistment, which he shall constantly wear, under pain of receiving thirty-nine lashes, till the regiment or corps to which he belongs is assembled, and joins the army.

RECRUITING INSTRUCTIONS.

· You are immediately to inlist into the service of the United States of America all able-bodied men, who are willing to enter into the service, on the following terms, viz.

First, You are not to *inlist any but freemen*, able of body and under the age of fifty; carefully avoiding all persons labouring under lameness or other defects of body prejudicial to the service; if an such, or boys are brought in, the officer inlisting them will be chargeable with the expence they may be to the public.

Secondly, You are *not to inlist any deserters* from the army of the King of Great-Britain, or persons of disaffected

fected or fufpicious character, the American fervice having fuffered greatly by the *defertion of fuch perfons*.

Thirdly, You are to inlift to ferve three years, or during the continuance of the prefent war between Great-Britain and the American States, unlefs fooner difcharged by proper authority.

Fourthly, The men by you enlifted, are to be fubject to the rules and articles for the government of the army, publifhed by Congrefs the 20th of September, 1776, and are to fign thofe articles.

As an encouragement to fuch perfons as fhall inlift into the above fervice, you are authorifed to engage, befides the pay and provifions now allowed,

Firft, That every foldier fhall, upon being approved by a Major General, a Brigadier General, or Colonel Commandant of a Brigade, and fome Surgeon, be entitled to a bounty of twenty dollars and a fuit of cloaths, which fuit of cloaths fhall be given annually.

Second, He fhall alfo be entitled to one hundred acres of land at the expiration of the term of his inliftment, and in cafe of his death, in the fervice, his reprefentative fhall be entitled thereto.

When any perfon is inlifted, you are, as foon as convenient, to take him to fome perfon duly authorifed by the above articles, to adminifter the oath threin prefcribed.

To encourage the brave and fpirited to enter into the fervice, the General promifes them all the plunder they fhall take from the enemy, to be equally divided between the officers and men, according to their pay.

Given at Head Quarters, 17th day of December, 1776.

By his Excellency, G. Washington.

————

His Excellency General Wafhington ftrictly forbids all the officers and foldiers of the Continental army, of the militia, and all recruiting parties, plundering any perfon whatfoever, *whether Tories or others The effects of fuch perfons will be applied to public ufes in a regular manner* ; and it is expected that humanity and tendernefs to women and children, will diftinguifh brave Americans, contending for liberty, from infamous, mercenary ravagers, whether Britifh or Heffians. G. Washington.

Trenton, January 1, 1777.

Philadephia, November 27. The Honourable Congrefs have promoted Monfieur de Roche de Fermoy, a brave and experienced officer, and formerly a Colonel in the French fervice, to the rank of a Brigadier General.

Saturday laft the fhip Sam, lately commanded by Samuel Richardfon, was fent into this port ; fhe was taken on her paffage from Barbadoes to Liverpool, by the Continental floop Independence, Captain Young; was mounted with four guns, and had on board 20,000 dollars, two tons and a half of ivory, and 100 bars of iron.

On Thurfday laft arrived here the fhip King George, lately commanded by Edmund Williams, who was taken by the brig Montgomery, James Montgomery, mafter, bound from Jamaica for London.

Yefterday afternoon, at the review of the militia for the city and liberties, nothing could exceed the zeal and ardour of the men, who unanimoufly turned out volunteers, to ferve their country at this important juncture. So laudable an example, it is hoped, will be followed in the other parts.

At eleven o'clock this forenoon, a very large and general town meeting was held in the State Houfe Yard. The Members of the General Affembly, and Council of Safety, were prefent, Mr. Rittenhoufe, Vice Prefident of the Council, being in the Chair. The intelligence which has been received, of the probability of General

General Howe having it in contemplation to invade this State, was laid before the citizens, and they were informed that the Congress requested the militia of the city, and several of the counties, and part of the militia of each of the other counties, to march into New Jersey; the people expressed their chearful approbation of the measure by the most unanimous acclamations of joy ever observed on any occasion; and the militia are ordered to be reviewed to-morrow, at two o'clock in the afternoon. General Mifflin addressed his fellow citizens in a spirited, animating, and affectionate address, which was received by them with marks of approbation, which shewed their esteem for, and confidence in the General

Providence, Nov. 30, 1776. Captain Weit, in the privateer Joseph, has taken a transport ship, that left New-York in company with one hundred and thirty sail, all in ballast, bound to Europe, under convoy of three men of war. Captain Weit has also taken a Guineaman that had been captured by a Philadelphia privateer, and twice retaken by the enemy. The privateer that first took her, it is said, found a large sum of money on board, which was secured.

Newport, December 2. The sloop Providence, Captain Hecker, arrived in a certain port last Wednesday from a cruize, in company with the Alfred, having taken a rich ship, a brig and snow, the brig we mentioned in our last to have arrived safe; and it is said the Alfred, and the other two prizes, are safe in port at the Eastward.

A gentleman arrived in town on Saturday from Boston, informs, that a privateer from the Eastward, had lately taken a ship with dry goods, &c. whose cargo cost 37,000l. sterling.

Providence, December 28. Another prize taken by the Alfred is arrived, after having been re-taken by a British frigate, and again captured by an American cruizer.

The gentleman taken with General Lee was formerly a Colonel in the French service; the enemy drove *him before them on foot, and treated him with every other mark of indignity.* His name is Gayault.

Hartford, December 30. Last week the Honourable General Spencer passed through this town, in his way to Providence, being appointed to command on that station, in conjunction with the Honourable General Lincoln.

A letter from a gentleman at Peck's Hill, says, Our brigade have been to Hackinsack, taken 200 Tories, killed a number, and made prisoners of 30 regulars, who were stationed there as guard. We also took a bounty worth 6 or 7000l. consisting of wines, rum, &c.

Philadelphia, December 31. By the last advices from the Jerseys, we learn the enemy are every where flying before our army, who frequently take small parties of them. Since the affair at Trenton, it is said, we have taken four hundred, amongst whom are several officers.

Yesterday morning upwards of nine hundred Hessians, who were taken at Trenton, were brought to this city. The wretched condition of these unhappy men, most of whom, if not all, were dragged from their wives and families by a despotic and avaricious Prince, must sensibly affect every generous mind with the dreadful effects of arbitrary power.

Last Monday seven of the light horse belonging to this city, took nine light horsemen from the enemy, near Prince Town, without firing a gun.

Last Thursday afternoon Colonel Rohl died at Trenton, of the wounds he received that morning.

Boston, January 6. It must afford great

great fatisfaction to every lover of his country, to hear of the rapid fuccefs which the recruiting parties for the Continental army have met with in this and adjacent towns, as we can affure the public great numbers have voluntarily enlifted to ferve during the continuance of the war.

The beginning of laft week the privateer floop, commanded by William Dennis, fent into a fafe port at the fouthward, the Countefs of Eglington, a brigantine from Greenock in Glafgow, bound to Antigua. The following is a fchedule of the cargo on board the brigantine Countefs of Eglington, viz. 57 bales, 110 boxes, 34 cafks, 2 chefts, and 5 trunks of haberdafhery, 368 yards printed linen, 1223 pounds of wrought leather fhoes, 4513 pounds green glafs bottles, 39 barrels and two firkins ftrong ale, 6797 pounds tallow candles, 2420 refined fugar, 67,028 yards Britifh bounty linen, 7410 yards Irifh ditto, 4488 yards Britifh ftrip'd and check'd ditto, 207 firkins of butter, 126 gallons Portugal wine, and 210 bundles of iron hoops.

Philadelphia, January 7. This day an exprefs arrived from General Wafhington's army, at Pluckemin, Morris county, Eaft Jerfey, which he left laft Sunday night. By him we learn our army is in high fpirits, having had various engagements with the enemy, in which they have been victorious, and have taken feveral fieldpieces, a confiderable quantity of baggage, and *upwards of feven hundred prifoners,* amongft whom are many officers of rank and fortune.

Extract of a letter from a gentleman in the army to his friend in this city, dated Pluckemin, Jan. 5, 1777.

" We have a number of officers prifoners. I am juft called on to command the infantry at the funeral of Captain Leflie, a Britifh officer killed at Princetown. We bury him with military honours. On the field

I faw lying another Captain, of the name of Moftyn.

Philadelphia, January 11. We are informed that a body of Jerfey militia, under General Maxwell, attacked and defeated one regiment of Highlanders, and one of Heffian troops, at Spank Town, on Sunday laft. This accounts for a heavy firing heard on that day by different perfons towards Princetown.

Head Quarters, Philadelphia, January 11, 1777.

The General orders every officer and foldier, either in the Continental army, the troops of this ftate, or militia (Colonel Fleming's regiment excepted) now in this city, to affemble in the Barrack-yard to-morrow morning, at ten o'clock, with their arms and accoutrements, under pain of being feverely punifhed for any neglect.

Colonel Fleming's regiment is to parade, at the fame time, at the New Market in Second-ftreet, the South end of the city.

The troops are to draw three days provifions to-morrow morning, which are to be immediately cooked.

JOHN MITCHELL, Adjutant-General of this State.

Notice is hereby given, that four waggons will fhortly fet off from this city, to proceed to General Wafhington's head-quarters in New Jerfey, by order of the Council of Safety.— Such of the inhabitants of the city and liberties, as choofe to avail themfelves of this opportunity to fend cloathing and other neceffaries to their friends of the militia now in fervice, are defired to apply immediately to Jacob Schreiner, for the firft battalion; Alexander Todd, for the fecond; Wm. Davis, for the third; and Benjamin Armitage, for the artillery companies.

No more than twenty pounds weight will be received for any one perfon, person at the camp, nor any pay demanded for carriage.—Jan. 10.

Baltimore, January 14.
Extract of a letter from a General Officer in the Continental service, dated at Trenton, Jan. 9.

" A regiment of British troops at Spankton, six miles below Elizabeth Town, was attacked on Sunday by a party of Jersey militia ; the encounter continued about two hours.—— Two regiments marched up from Woodbridge and Amboy, to reinforce the enemy, which I suppose has saved them. The remains of the 17th, 40th, and 55th regiments, which had been engaged at Princetown, and now amount only to 250 men, are at Bonampton.

" Lord Howe lies ill, and the Hessian General scratched out one half of his hair, on hearing of the news at Trenton. *Fifty Hessians* were taken prisoners, and carried the other day to Morris Town.

" We lost a very good officer, Capt. Fleming, of the third Virginia battalion. Within ten yards of the enemy he called to his men, " Gentlemen, dress before you make ready." The British troops blackguarded our people, and damned them ; " they would dress them," and gave the first fire. Our men placed their fire so well, that the enemy screamed as if so many devils had got hold of them. They were encouraged by their officers, and advanced with their bayonets, but were forced out of the field by the braver Americans."

Jan. 22. Lately died in New Jersey, Colonel Ford, jun. of Morris county. This gentleman gallantly kept the field, at the head of a body of militia, and was an active partizan in his country's cause, until he was borne down by sickness and fatigue ; and his zeal for the freedom and happiness of the United States, was manifested, " in the evening hour of departing life."

The following is an extract from General Howe's orders to Colonel de Donop, commander of the Hessian cantonments along the Delaware, which fell into our hands upon the late route and flight of the enemy's troops.

" All salted and meal provisions, which may be judged to exceed the quantity necessary for the subsistence of *an ordinary family. shall be considered as a magazine of the enemy, and seized for the King, and given to the troops as a saving for the public.*"

In this authentic warrant, granted by the humane Mr. Howe to a Hessian plunderer, for ravaging the Jerseys, it is observable, that no reservation is made of Tory property ; which occasioned a Quaker, who had been pillaged, to exclaim, " Well, God made these men ; but I am sure the Devil governs them."

Jan. 16. Since our last fifty Hessian officers and soldiers, who were lately made prisoners at Trenton, arrived here from Philadelphia.

In one of the late actions in Jersey, Mr. Anthony Morris, an officer among the Philadelphia associators, a most worthy citizen, lost his life, bravely struggling for the freedom and independence of his country.

Intelligence received in CONGRESS.

Upon the evacuation of Elizabeth Town, General Maxwell fell upon the enemy's rear, and made 70 prisoners, and took a parcel of baggage.
CHARLES THOMSON, Sec.
Philadelphia, Jan. 14. It is said Gen. Heath has destroyed more than a hundred flat bottomed boats, which lay near Elizabeth Town.

Last night a party of Waldeckers arrived in this city, who were taken in the East Jerseys.

Extract of a letter from Major General Gates, to a gentleman in this city, dated Morristown, Jan. 9.

" Not a line have I received from you since you left us at Newtown—I am much obliged to you for the attention.—Were I not fully persuaded that

that you are anxious to know the success of our late manœuvres, I would not have wrote you a syllable this fortnight. I almost think the author of the Crisis a prophet, where he says the Tories will curse the day that Howe arrived on the Delaware. I verily believe the observation is coming true. The two late actions at Trenton and Princetown have put a very different face upon affairs. Within a fortnight past we have taken and killed of Howe's army *between two and three thousand men*—Our loss is trifling—we are daily picking up their parties—*yesterday we took seventy prisoners and thirty loads of baggage.*

" Great credit is due to the Philadelphia militia; their behaviour at Trenton in the cannonade, and at Princetown was brave, firm, and manly; they were broken at first in the action at Princetown, but soon formed in the face of grape-shot, and pushed on with a spirit that would do honour to veterans, besides which they have borne a winter's campaign with a soldier-like patience. General Cadwallader is a brave and gallant officer."

In COUNCIL *of* SAFETY, *Philadelphia, January* 14, 1777.

The officers of the militia are desired, as soon as they arrive in town, to make a report thereof to the Council of Safety, and at the same time to deliver in a return of the number their party consists of, and of what arms and necessaries they stand in need of, that the Council may furnish them as soon as possible, it being the intention of the Council of Safety, as well as the General commanding here, not to march the militia from this city, until they are equipped in the best manner the circumstances of the times will admit.

By order of Council,
THOMAS WHARTON, jun. President.

Philadelphia, Jan. 16. By letters from General Washington's army, of the 8th, 10th, and 11th instant, we have the following authentic intelligence, viz. That our army marched from Pluckemin, and arrived at Morristown on the 6th, that Gen. Maxwell, with a considerable body of Continental troops and militia, having marched towards Elizabeth town, sent back for a reinforcement, which having joined him, he advanced, and took possession of the town, and made prisoners *fifty* Waldeckers and *forty* Highlanders who were quartered there; and made prize of a schooner with baggage and some blankets on board. About the same time one thousand bushels of salt were secured by our troops at a place called Spank Town, about five miles from Woodbridge; when a party of our men attacked the enemy at that place, they sent for a reinforcement to Woodbridge, but the *Hessians absolutely refused to march*, having heard we were very numerous in that quarter. The English troops at Elizabeth Town would not suffer the Waldeckers to stand centry at the out-posts, several of them having deserted, and come over to us.

A person of character, who lately left New-York, informs that the inhabitants are greatly distressed for want of fuel, which was so scarce, that there was not tree, fence, or any piece of wood standing for several miles back of the town; and that they had appropriated certain houses to that use, at least fifty having been already destroyed.

Gen. Heath is on his march to New York, with a large army.

The main body of the enemy is at Brunswick; they have also some troops at Amboy, where some men of war and transports are collected, it is supposed, to take off the baggage.

Philadelphia, Jan. 18. The Hon. Council of Safety of Maryland have appointed Monday the third of February next, as a day of solemn fasting, humiliation and prayer, throughout

out that state, agreeable to a resolve of the Congress of the 11th ult.

This week four troops of the Virginia light-horse, commanded by Captains Lee, Nee, Nelson, Jameson, and Temple, arrived here.

Last Sunday evening died near Princetown, of the wounds he received in the engagement at that place, on the 3d instant, HUGH MERCER, Esq. Brigadier General in the Continental army. On Wednesday his body was brought to this city, and on Thursday buried on the south side of Christ-Church yard with military honours, attended by the Council of Safety, the Members of Assembly, gentlemen of the army, and a number of the most respectable inhabitants of this city. The uniform character, exalted abilities, and intrepidity of this illustrious officer, will render his name equally dear to America, with the liberty for which she is now contending, to the latest posterity.

Yesterday the remains of Capt. William Shippen, who was killed at Princetown the third instant, gloriously fighting for the liberty of his country, were interred in St. Peter's Church-yard. His funeral was attended by the Council of Safety, the Members of Assembly, officers of the army, a troop of Virginia light-horse, and a great number of inhabitants. This brave and unfortunate man was in his twenty-seventh year, and has left a widow and three young children to lament the death of an affectionate husband and tender parent, his servants a kind master, and his neighbours a sincere and obliging friend.

GENERAL ORDERS.

Every officer commanding battalions, detachments, or companies of the militia of this state, when they arrive at this city, are immediately to make written returns of their numbers to his Excellency Lord STERLING, at his quarters at the City tavern; then draw provisions, use their utmost diligence to be equipped; and, when ready to march, give notice to Colonel Bull, who will give his Lordship's farther commands.

Philadelphia, Jan. 16, 1777.

Baltimore, January 12.
In CONGRESS, *October* 21, 1776.

Resolved, That every officer who holds or shall hereafter hold a commission, or office from Congress, shall subscribe the following declaration, and take the following oath, viz.

† " I ———, do acknowledge the Thirteen United States of America, namely, New-Hampshire, Massachusetts-Bay, Rhode-Island, Connecticut, New-York, New-Jersey, Pennsylvania, Delaware, Maryland, Virginia, North-Carolina, South-Carolina, and Georgia, *to be Free, Independent, and Sovereign States,* and declare, that the people thereof owe no allegiance or obedience to

and I renounce, refuse, and abjure any allegiance or obedience to him. And I do swear, that I will, to the utmost of my power, support, maintain, and defend the said United States against the said

, and his heirs and successors, and his and their abettors, assistants and adherents; and will serve the said United States in the office of ———, which I now hold, and in any other office which I may hereafter hold, by their appointment, or under their authority, with fidelity and honour, and according to the best of my skill and understanding. So help me God. By order of Congress.

JOHN HANCOCK, President.
In CONGRESS, *January* 16, 1777.

Resolved, That a Committee of seven be appointed to inquire into the conduct of the British and Hessian General Officers, towards the officers, soldiers, and mariners, in the service of the United States, and any other persons

K

persons inhabitants of these States, in their possession as prisoners of war, or otherwise; and also into the conduct of the said Generals and Officers, and the troops under their command, towards the subjects of these States, and their property, more especially of the States of New-York and New-Jersey.

The Members chosen, Mr. Chase, Mr. Witherspoon, Mr. Clarke, Mr. Lewis, Mr. Ross, Mr. Heyward, and Mr. Smith.

Extract from the minutes,

Published by order of Congress,

CHARLES THOMSON, Sec.

CONGRESS has received the following intelligence from the army at Pluckemin, in the State of New Jersey, January 5. 1777.

" On the second instant the enemy began to advance upon us at Trenton; and, after some skirmishing, the head of their column reached that place about four o'clock, whilst their rear was as far back as Maidenhead. They attempted to pass Sanpinck-creek, which runs through Trenton, at different places; but finding the fords guarded, they halted and kindled their fires. We were drawn up on the south side of the creek. In this situation we remained till dark, cannonading the enemy, and receiving the fire of the field-pieces, which did but little damage.

" At twelve o'clock, after renewing our fires, and leaving guards at the bridge in Trenton, and other passes on the same stream above, we marched by a round about road to Princetown. We found Princetown, about sun-rise, with only three regiments, and three troops of light-horse in it, two of which were on their march to Trenton.—These three regiments, especially the two first, made a gallant resistance; and in killed, wounded, and prisoners, *must have lost five hundred men*. Upwards of one hundred of them were left dead on the field; and with those carried on by the army, and such as were taken in the pursuit, and carried across the Delaware, there are *near three hundred prisoners, fourteen of whom are officers—all British*.

" Colonels Haselet and Porter, Capt. Neal, of the artillery, Capt. Fleming, who commanded the first Virginia regiment, and four or five other valuable officers, with about twenty-five or thirty privates, were slain in the field. Our whole loss cannot be ascertained, as many who were in pursuit of the enemy, whom they chased three or four miles, are not yet come in. We burnt the enemy's hay, and destroyed such other things as the occasion would admit.

" From the best intelligence we have been able to get, the enemy were so much alarmed at the apprehension of losing their stores at Brunswick, that they marched immediately thither from Trenton, without halting, and got there before day.

" The militia of the Jerseys are taking spirit, and we hear, coming in fast."

Morris-Town, January 7, 1777.

" The enemy have totally evacuated Trenton and Princetown, and are now at Brunswick, and the several posts on the communication between that and Hudson's river, but chiefly at Brunswick. Their numbers and movements are variously reported; but all agree their force to be great. There have been two or three little skirmishes between their parties and some detachments of militia, in which the latter have been successful, and made a few prisoners; the most considerable was on Sunday morning, near Springfield, when eight or ten Waldeckers were killed and wounded, and the remainder of the party, thirty-nine or forty, made prisoners with two officers, by a force not superior in number, and without receiving the least damage."

Published by order of Congress,

CHARLES THOMSON, Sec.

Philadelphia,

Philadelphia, Jan. 18.

The following officers and volunteers,—viz.

Majors—Meigs, Bigelow,

Captains—Lamb, Topham, Thayer, Morgan, Ward, Goodrich, Hauchett,

Lieutenants—M'Dougall, Compton, Clarke, Webb, Christopher Febriger, Heth, Savage, Brown, Nichols, Bruin, Steel,

Ensign Tisdal,

Volunteers——Osborn, Duncan, Lockwood, M'Guire, Porterfield and Henry,

who were sent from Canada by General Carlton, are released from their parole, others of the same rank belonging to the British army having been exchanged for them.

I am, Sir,

Your humble servant,

ROBERT HARRISON,

Secretary to his Excellency General Washington.

Philadelphia, Jan. 23. Within these three or four days there have been several skirmishes in the East-Jersies, in which our troops have always beat the enemy. About three miles up the Rarition, from Brunswick, a party of our army attacked a large body of the enemy, and *took near six hundred head of cattle,* upwards *of fifty waggons,* and *a number of English horses,* of the *dray breed,* which were so excessively emaciated that they were scarce able to walk.

Philadelphia, Jan 25. This day the remains of Col. JOHN HASELET, of the Lower Counties, were interred in the Old Presbyterian Meeting yard, with military honours.

In COUNCIL *of* SAFETY, *Philadelphia, Jan.* 22, 1777.

Resolved, That Col. Melcher, Barrack Master General, be directed to quarter the militia upon the Non-Associators in this city and liberties, and on all Associators who have not served in this winter's campaign. The Council particularly recommend to him in quartering them, to proportion the numbers to the size of the houses and convenience of the families.

N. B. The Commanding Officers of the several battalions of Associators in this city and liberties, are requested to furnish the Barrack Master General with a return of the names of those that served this winter, for his government.

January 23, 1777.

Ordered, That the thanks of General Washington to the militia of Pennsylvania transmitted to this Board, be published in the public papers of this city.

" General Washington being informed that the time fixed by the Hon. Council of Safety of Pennsylvania for the service of part of the militia of that state is expired, and that some are desirous to return to Pennsylvania, agreeable to their engagements, the General takes the earliest opportunity of returning his most hearty thanks to those brave men, who in the most inclement season of the year nobly stepped forth in defence of their country.—The General acknowledges with pleasure the signal services done by the militia of Pennsylvania, and has the best reasons to expect the same spirit, zeal and activity, which lately brought them into field, will induce them to come forth on every future occasion, when the security and happiness of America, and their own state in particular, demand it.

" The General acknowledges with additional satisfaction the good services of those battalions who have determined to remain with him after the expiration of their times of service. He wishes not to detain them a minute longer than he thinks absolutely necessary to the security of their country, and will discharge them as soon as he finds his army in a condition to admit of it.

Philadelphia, Jan. 30. We are informed,

formed, from good authority, that many of the inhabitants of Monmouth county in New Jersey, who received written protections, are *now* determined to return them to his Britannic Majesty's Commissioners in *carriages*.

London, April 5. The Andrew Doria, one of the American armed vessels of 14 guns, had taken a King's sloop of war of 12 guns, after a smart engagement. By the American accounts, published by authority, it appears, that the West Indiamen taken by the American cruizers, to the 1st of February, 1777, amounted to 250 sail, valued at least at two millions sterling, exclusive of transports, European, and other vessels.

Notwithstanding the reports, that Mr. John Dickenson (the celebrated author of the Farmer's Letters, &c.) had raised for the King's service 2000 men in the Delaware counties, and had put himself at their head, the undoubted fact, upon the best authority, is, that he has retired with his family to his estate near Dover, about 70 miles from Philadelphia, where he now lives in perfect ease, and in acquiescence to the measures of the Congress. And his only brother, Colonel Dickenson, is with his regiment at Morris Town, under General Washington. And his first cousin, General Cadwallader, a gentleman of immense fortune, is also with General Washington, and commands the Pennsylvania forces. The same authority further says, that the people of Philadelphia were in the highest spirits, and every thing wore the most favourable aspect.

Extract of a letter from Bordentown, January 4, 1777.

" I am just arrived with Major Mifflin, from an expedition in the lower parts of the Jerseys, at a place called Monmouth Court House. We arrived there Thursday evening. We were informed of a party of men, consisting of about 200, under the command of Colonel Morris. We there formed our party (120 in number) in proper order, and intended to attack them in town about half an hour before night. Colonel Morris, it seems, got notice of our arrival, had his baggage loaded, and his men formed to draw off for Middle Town, about 18 miles from the Court House. They accordingly pushed off from the town, and got away about half a mile; we immediately pushed after them, and they halted. We came up about a quarter of an hour before night, and engaged them; a very heavy fire was kept up on both sides, and the enemy stood us about eight minutes, then gave way, and retreated precipitately. At this time it was quite dark, and we could not see what loss the enemy sustained. On our side we had none killed. We marched from the field to the town, and lodged there that night. The next morning we sent out a party to the field we had engaged in; they brought four dead bodies, which we buried. We took during the engagement twenty-three prisoners, and brought them to this place. We also took seven waggon-loads of stores, &c. and twelve horses."

A party from Colonel Humpton's regiment, who are stationed in West New-Jersey, about the middle of this month, went to Shrewsbury, in Monmouth county, where they took a large quantity of cloth and other stores, collected there by a set of Tories, who infest that country, many of which were obliged to make a precipitate retreat on board the English men of war.

Baltimore, Jan. 16, 1777. His Excellency Patrick Henry, Esq. Governor of the Commonwealth of Virginia, by the advice of his Privy Council, hath issued a proclamation, dated the third instant, strictly enjoining and requiring all the natives of Great Britain, who were partners with factors, agents, store-keepers, or clerks, in that Commonwealth, for any merchant,

chant, or merchants, in Great Britain, on the ift day of January, 1776, the time the act of the British Parliament for reftraining the trade of America, and feizing our property upon the water took place, *to depart the Commonwealth with their goods within forty days*, except fuch of the faid natives as have uniformly manifefted a friendly difpofition to the American caufe, or are attached to this country, by having wives or children here, agreeable to a refolution of the General Affembly, &c. In the mean time, fuch perfons are at liberty to difpofe of their goods and merchandize to any perfon or perfons who may be willing to purchafe the fame.

Morris Town, Jan. 19, 1777. General Howe has difcharged all the privates, who were prifoners in New-York; one half he fent to the World of Spirits for want of food—the other he hath fent to warn their countrymen of the danger of falling into his hands, and to convince them, by ocular demonftration, that it is infinitely better to be flain in battle, than to be taken prifoners by Britifh brutes, whofe tender mercies are cruelty. But it is not the prifoners alone, who have felt the effects of Britifh humanity. Every part of the country through which they have marched, has been plundered and ravaged. No difcrimination has been made with refpect to Whig or Tory, but all alike have been involed in one common fate. Their march through New Jerfey has been marked with the moft favage barbarity. But Weft-Chefter witneffeth more terrible things. The repofitories of the dead have ever been held facred by the moft barbarous and favage nations. But here, not being able to accomplifh their accurfed purpofes upon the living, they wreaked their vengeance on the dead. In many places, the graves in the church-yards were opened, and the bodies of the dead expofed upon the ground for feveral days. At Morif-

fania, the family vault was opened, the coffins broken, and the bones fcattered abroad. At Delancey's farm, the body of a beautiful young lady, which had been buried for two years, was taken out of the ground, and expofed for five days in a moft indecent manner; many more inftances could be mentioned, but my heart fickens at the recollection of fuch inhumanity. Some perfons try to believe, that it is only the Heffians who perpetrate thefe things, but I have good authority to fay, that the Britifh vie with, and even exceed the auxiliary troops in licentioufnefs. After fuch treatment, can it be poffible for any perfon ferioufly to wifh for a reconciliation with Great-Britain.

Extract of a letter from Rariton, (New Jerfey) Jan. 23.

" Laft Monday a party of Jerfey militia, confifting of about 400, and about 50 of the Pennfylvania riflemen, marched to attack a body of the enemy, confifting of about 600, who were pofted at a bridge at Millftone-river, near Abraham Vanneft's mill, which is two miles from Somerfet Court-houfe. In order more effectually to prevent our men from croffing, the enemy had placed three field pieces on a hill, about 50 yards from the bridge; when our men found it impoffible to crofs there, they went down the river, broke through the ice, waded acrofs the river up to their middles, flanked the enemy, routed them, and took 43 baggage-waggons, 104 horfes, 115 head of cattle, and about 60 or 70 fheep. We loft 4 or 5 men. We took 12 prifoners, and from the beft accounts, the enemy had 24 or 25 killed and wounded. A man who came from Brunfwick this afternoon, fays, the enemy allow that they loft 35 or 36 men, but fay the rebels left 300. There were not more than 400 of our men croffed the river: the enemy report, that they were attacked by 3000 of General Wafhington's troops there, and were abfolutely absolutely certain they were not militia, they were sure that no militia would fight in that way. There has been an engagement to day, the guns were heard beyond this, but we do not know where it was, nor the event. Our army, I believe, are drawing near Brunswick, with an intention to prevent the enemy from getting provisions; if they do so, the enemy will be obliged to leave Brunswick. They (the enemy) do not pretend to send as a foraging party less than 500 or 600 men."

Baltimore, Jan. 30, 1777.
Extract of a letter from Gen. Washington to Congress, dated Jan. 22, 1777.

" My last was on the 20th instant; since that, I have the pleasure to inform you, that General Dickinson, with about 400 militia, had defeated a foraging party of the enemy of an equal number, and have taken 40 waggons, and upwards of 100 horses, most of them of the English draft breed, and a number of sheep and cattle which they had collected.

" The enemy retreated with so much precipitation, that General Dickinson had only an opportunity of making 9 prisoners; they were observed to carry off a good many dead and wounded in light waggons."

This action opened near Somerset Court-house, on Millstone-river. General Dickinson's behaviour reflects the highest honour upon him, for though his troops were all raw, he led them through the river, middle deep, and gave the enemy so severe a charge, that altho' supported by three field-pieces, they gave way, and left their convoy.

Published by order of Congress,
CHARLES THOMSON, Sec.

Hartford, Jan. 27. The General Assembly, in their last Session, formed the militia of this State into six brigades. The Hon. David Wooster, and Jabez Huntington, of Norwich,

Esqrs. are appointed Major-Generals: the Hon. Eliphalet Dyer, Gurdon Saltonstall, Oliver Wolcott, Erastus Wolcott, James Wadsworth, and Gold Selleck Silliman, Esqrs. Brigadier-Generals. Lieut. Col. Hooker, of Farmington, is appointed Colonel and Jesse Root, Esq. of this town, Lieut. Col. of an independent regiment.

Extract of a letter from Philips's Manor, dated Feb. 1, 1777.

" Since our arrival here, have been in sight of the enemy every day at King's Bridge and Fort Independence.—At our first coming down, we encamped about half a mile from the fort, in an open field for six days, till there came a very heavy storm of snow, &c. and drove us back to the Manor again, and now have got a good house to live in; but how long we shall stay here is uncertain, for ever since our arrival we have been marching sometimes to the enemy and sometimes from them. We have had no proper engagement with them, but several small skirmishes, but have not lost one man out of our regiment; Col. Thatcher has lost several. Our regiment is on this side Fort Independence, and two regiments on the other side: this fort is about half a mile from King's Bridge, on York side. The Hessians have got a breast-work hove up, through much difficulty; at the beginning we beat them off with two field pieces, but the next day they came again, and we were obliged to retreat, by a cannonading from Fort Washington; since that we have been down several times, but cannot persuade them to come out to us, although their army is superior to ours: they have got almost all their troops out of New-York on the lines, and in the three forts, to prevent our going in; for in the morning we got down, as we were unexpected, put them in great surprize; at break of day their guards were all in confusion, some ran one way, some another,

ther, but could not take any of them prisoners, although in their hurry they left their baggage, which was very confiderable; *their guard-houfes are now ours*—fince our departure from Bofton, General Wafhington has been beating them, and has taken a great many prifoners, and a great deal of baggage, and continues fo to do.—General Putnam *has taken 96 waggons* with provifion which were going to Howe's army, and *Howe has fent in a flag, defiring a ceffation of arms* till April, but General Wafhington fent him word he would accomplish his defign, and then there would be a final one; and it feems very probable, for the day we were to crofs the river, he fent orders for us to march down and keep them in motion, whilft he was purfuing them. General Wafhington has got a fine army along with him, and plenty of provifions and all other ftores.—Our company are all in good health and fpirits, although we undergo the hardfhips of lying on the cold ground, fometimes have a houfe, and fometimes none; but think nothing of hardfhips, fo that we fubdue them, and have our LIBERTY."

Extract of a letter from a gentleman of rank in the Continental army, dated Morris Town, Feb 9.

" The enemy ftill remain at Brunfwick; a few days fince we brought off all the cattle, horfes and carriages round their lines.—Yefterday they fent out a large foraging party near Quibble-Town, they were foon drove in upon the run; their lofs is not known but it muft have been confiderable, as our people kept a conftant fire upon them for fome miles: they never got the leaft article of forage. The fpirit of defertion prevails in a great degree among the enemy's troops, both Britifh and Heffians, feveral ferjeants and corporals have come over. Their horfes are dying for want of forage, and we are well informed that they are fhort of pro-

vifions, and that their camp is filled with murmurs and diffenfions."

Hartford, Feb. 10. Laft Thurfday an exprefs came to town from General Wafhington's head quarters, in New Jerfey, who informs, that on Saturday the 1ft inft. a party of our men, about 700 in number, fell in with a body of the enemy, faid to be about 1000, with three field pieces, at Pifcataqua, about four miles from Brunfwick, when an engagement commenced, which lafted fome time; *but the enemy were at length obliged to retreat*, leaving about 36 of their men dead on the field. However, being joined by a confiderable reinforcement from their main body, with three additional field pieces, they returned and renewed the attack, when our people, being overpowered by numbers, were obliged to retreat; in both actions we had *nine men killed and* 14 *wounded*. The enemy were at the above place, procuring forage for their horfes.

Philadelphia, Feb. 13. The exprefs, who arrived here yefterday from head quarters, gives the following interefting intelligence, viz.

That when he came off with the difpatches from General Wafhington, General Green brought in the following account, that 300 of our troops were ftationed at Quibble-Town, under the command of Col. Scott, that 3000 of the enemy from Brunfwick attacked them, which obliged Col. Scott to retreat about a mile and a half, that being reinforced by a party of Lord Stirling's army, with four pieces of cannon, they renewed the engagement, obliged the *enemy to retreat with the lofs of* 300 *left dead on the field, and* 100 *taken prifoners*; and were in purfuit of them when General Green came away.

That deferters from the enemy inform, that their army are on half allowance, and their horfes dying for want of fodder.

Laft

Laſt Saturday ſix of the enemy's light horſe advancing towards Weſt Cheſter, three or four miles from Kingſbridge, a ſmall party of our militia attacked them, ſhot three of the riders, took one horſe, the other two ran off with the three remaining riders.

Boſton, February 20.

Extract of a letter from a gentleman of character at Morris Town, to his friend here.

" We had a very extraordinary ſkirmiſh with the enemy the 23d of January. A large number of waggons under an eſcort of 600 men, conſiſting of the 28th and 37th regiments, with two pieces of cannon, were proceeding from Brunſwick to Amboy, but were perceived by the 6th Virginia regiment, who were an out poſt, conſiſting of 400 men, commanded by Col. Buckner. The Lieut. Col. (Parker) was diſpatched with an advanced party of 600, who poſted themſelves moſt advantageouſly.—The enemy advanced in a column ten in front, when they came up within a 100 yards Parker gave them a well levelled fire, by which their Commandant Col. Preſton was killed. They kept an inceſſant blaze for twenty minutes, when Parker finding himſelf unſupported, retreated. The enemy had 25 killed on the ſpot, and about 40 wounded; they carried off their killed and wounded, except 13, who were left, and were afterwards dreſſed by a ſurgeon of ours; beſides the Colonel killed, the ſecond in command was ſhot through the body, and carried off ſpeechleſs; they had 1 Captain killed, and 1 wounded. Theſe particulars we have from the people living near the ſpot, and from a corporal, of the third regiment of guards, who deſerted from them two days ago. Col. Buckner, who got panic ſtruck, and left his Lieutenant Colonel unſupported, is under an arreſt, and will be tried for his life. What renders this little affair ſo extraordinary is, that we had not a ſingle man either killed or wounded; ſuch wretched *ſhooters* are Britiſh ſoldiers. The enemy are cloſely watched in Brunſwick. They have got to living, officers as well as men, on ſalt proviſions, and find it extremely difficult to get forage. That you may may judge what a clever way we are in, take a memorandum of five or ſix days.

Jan. 17. Three of the guards and one dragoon deſerted. Same day a large ſcouting party took 90 waggonloads of ſtores, in the county of Monmouth.

18th. 1 of 42d, 2 of light infantry, and 3 Yagers deſerted.

19th. 3 of 46th, and 2 of 71ſt deſerted.

20th. 4 Waldeckers were taken priſoners.

21ſt. 4 of 71ſt, 2 of 40th, 3 of 28th, 1 of 55th, and two marines were taken priſoners, with 47 waggons and 106 horſes; they were part of a large foraging party—who were attacked by an inferior number of our troops, and were ſoon ſet a ſcampering with the loſs of the greateſt part of their waggons.

22d. 4 of 3d regiment of guards were made priſoners.

A copy of a letter from a Gentleman in Albany to a Gentleman in Salem, dated the 15th of February, 1777.

Since I wrote the foregoing, an expreſs arrived from Ticonderoga, at which place a Captain in Livingſton's regiment is juſt got in from Canada, from whence he had juſt made his eſcape. He tells the commanding officer on oath, that a ſcouting and ſcalping party of ſavages, to the amount of 80, together with ſome Canadians and Regulars, to the amount of about 150, had ſet out from Canada; they were to have 20l. for every ſcalp they might bring in. That Colonel Frazer commanded at Montreal, had with him two hundred men, 150 men were at Saint

John's,

John's, and the like number at Chamblee ; all the foreigners were at Three Rivers, had mutinied twice or thrice in such manner *as obliged the commanding officer to turn out the British troops and what Canadians they have, in order to quell them.* That General Carleton was at Quebec, and that they were cutting wood on the lake for three veffels. He further fays, that people in general are much more affected to our caufe, than they were laft year; and that what Canadians have joined the Britifh army, are only the very loweft of the people ; the troops take whatever they ftand in need of from any perfon, juft give them a certificate of having taken it, without any other fatisfaction. Provifion is very difficult to be had, by even the troops.

Bofton, February 17.

Account of the exchange of prifoners at Rhode-Ifland, Feb. 11, 1777.

By account of Capt. Ayres,	123
To balance due to Britifh on laft account, — —	23
To delivered to Capt. Ayres,	46
Balance due to Americans,	54
	123

Newport, Feb 11. M. Read, Sec.

The General Affembly of Rhode-Ifland have appointed Henry Marchant, Efq. a Delegate of the Grand American Congrefs, for that ftate.

Albany, Committee Chamber, January 21, 1777.

Refolved, That every perfon who fhall offer any thing for fale, or fhall fell any thing for a lefs fum in gold or filver money, than in continental or other paper money, now paffing current in this county, fhall be confidered as a depreciator of the paper currency, and treated accordingly ; and that every perfon who fhall refufe to take the fame in payment, fhall be treated in like manner.

Ordered, That the above refolution be publifhed. Extract from the minutes, · Matthew Vifcher, Sec.

Williamfburgh, (Virginia) Dec 20.

In General Affembly, *Dec.* 19, 1776.

Whereas ————————— hath waged war againft this Commonwealth, and the United American States, and there are within this Commonwealth divers merchants and others, fubjects of ————, who while they remain here have frequent opportunities of feducing and corrupting the minds of the people, and are fufpected of holding correfpondence with, and giving intelligence to the enemy :

Refolved, nemine contradicente, That the Governor and Council be defired to caufe all fuch perfons to depart this Commonwealth, by immediately putting in execution the ftatute ftaple of the 27th of Edward III. chapter 17, againft all the natives of Great-Britain, who were partners with factors, agents, ftore-keepers, affiftant ftore-keepers, or clerks here, for any merchant or merchants in Great-Britain, at the time the act of the Britifh Parliament for reftraining the trade of America, and feizing our property upon the water, took place, except only fuch of them as have heretofore uniformly manifefted a friendly difpofition to the American caufe, or are attached to this country, by having wives or children here; and fuch ————, as fhall fatisfy the Governor and Council, that they have not been able to procure other means of departure, may have their paffage to any foreign port, in fuch veffels employed in the fervice of this Commonwealth, as the Governor and Council fhall direct. And that all, or any of them, who fhall be found here after the time refpectively allowed them to depart, fhall be confined as enemies and prifoners of war. And for furnifhing the Governor and Council with proper information, the Juftices of the

L   feveral

feveral county courts are impowered and required immediately to make enquiry for all fuch refiding within their refpective counties; and, after due examination had, to caufe a lift of their names to be entered upon record, and direct their clerk to tranfmit a copy thereof to the Governor. And that a copy of this refolve, together with a copy of the aforefaid ftatute ftaple, be forthwith printed in the Virginia Gazette.

A. CARY, Speaker of the Senate.
E. PENDLETON, Speaker of the H. D.

27th of Edward III. chapter xvii.

A merchant ftranger fhall not be impeached for another's debt, but upon good caufe. Merchants of enemies countries fell their goods in convenient time and depart.

Item. That no merchant ftranger be impeached for another's trefpafs, or for another's debt, whereof he is not debtor, pledge, or mainpernor. Provided always, that if our liege people, merchants, or others, be endamaged by any Lords of ftrange lands, or their fubjects, and the faid Lords (duly required) fail of right to our faid fubjects, we fhall have the law of marque, and of taking them again, as hath been ufed in times paft, without fraud or deceit; and in cafe that debate do rife (which God defend) betwixt us and any Lords of ftrange lands, we will not that the people and merchants of the faid lands be fuddenly fubdued in our faid realm and lands becaufe of fuch debate, but that they be warned, and proclamation thereof publifhed, that they fhall void the faid realm and lands, with their goods, freely, within forty days after the warning, and proclamation fo made; and that, in the mean time, they be not impeached, norder of their paffage, or of making their profit of the fame merchandizes, if they will fell them. And in cafe that for default of wind or of fhip, or for ficknefs, or for other evident caufe, they cannot avoid our faid realm and lands within fo fhort a time, then they fhall have other forty days, or more, if need be, within which they may pafs conveniently, with felling their merchandize as afore is faid.

A letter from an officer at New-York.

New-York, Feb. 14.

My dear Friend,

I am infinitely obliged to you for your letters. I got the three laft together. I can't tell you the fatisfaction they are of to me. I wifh I could make you a proper return by any letters of mine. As to the hiftory of the campaign, in truth I am not capable of it; and your public accounts will furnifh you with, I fancy, a jufter idea than any of us can give you. It may feem ftrange to you, but it will not to a fober military man, that the parties of a General's followers and the difcontented run fo high, that their reafonings upon events contaminate the facts themfelves.

I will however endeavour at a thing, that if I could effect anfwerable to my own idea of it, would be better information to your philofophical mind than any relations of battles and military operations; nay, in my opinion, would be better for the Minifter to have a clear fight of, than of the exacteft detail of every fkirmifh we have had with thefe perverfe raggamuffins, who plague us while they can't oppofe us, and whom we can't fubdue, though we beat them.

In a word then, the chapter of the Heffians is worth the attention of the Minifter, verfe by verfe. You will eafily imagine, that differing as we do in language, manners, and ideas, Englifh and Heffian did not coalefce into one corps; not but there was great communication and conftant vifiting, efpecially among the principal officers; but thefe were rather national civilities than perfonal kindnefles, wefses, and our younger people hardly kept up any communication with them. They rather affected to despise the thriftiness of the Heffian prudence, as a something bafe and fordid. The Heffian, naturally fierce, was not backward to return the difdain he met, and affected to confider the volatile fpirit with which our youngfters went to war, as unfoldierly, and talked of themfelves as the body on whom the fuccefs of the war was to depend. Whatever has fince been the effects, the prudence and good fenfe of Sir William turned thefe vanities at firft to good account. He indulged the forwardnefs of the foreigners; they were refufed no fervice, and they applied for almoft all; Kniphaufen had a fair claim to give his name to the fort, and Howe could not doubt that he had confirmed the good temper of the whole foreign army; but it excited pride and arrogance, inftead of gratitude in this boorifh fort of people. They began to complain that more than their fhare was put upon them, and in a manner claimed a fort of choice where, and when, and how, they fhould be employed. They had indeed, from the beginning, confidered themfelves pretty much as at free quarters in an enemy's country; nor were they much miftaken in the fact, for our new friends were little better than fpies upon us; but it is not eafy for you to conceive the quantity of plunder that the Heffian camp had collected early; their very men were fome of them as it were rich, and they took excellent care of what they got; the unthrifty manner of our people left them foon expofed to a thoufand inconveniencies that the Heffians were ftrangers to.

From the very outfet they had got a whim that they were to have allotments of land, in the very firft province that was conquered. Whether this was a recruiting tale, or whether a hope of lands was really fuggefted (as fome fay) to Heifter, I can't tell;

but that it fhould be in the firft province we got was abfurd : but you will not wonder that it made them eager to get into the Jerfeys.

They no fooner found themfelves difappointed of their immediate fettlements, than they confidered the country as an object of vengeance. The country was certainly ravaged at a high rate; it is inconceivable the terror they raifed in the Americans, who trembled at the very name of an Heffian. In a word, the rebellion feemed crufhed. There was no rebel army in the field; literally fpeaking, none. Wafhington was fled to Philadelphia, where he had a few hundreds, fcarce fufficient to awe his perfonal enemies; many of whom he imprudently put in prifon, while others fled to us, and their caufe fo hopelefs, that they had no pretence to claim more than their pardon, and that was all the proudeft of them met. They lived in our quarters hated by us as rebels, and defpifed by their countrymen as deferters.

Here you fee us in triumph, without an enemy, matters of a delightful country. And now we had leifure to fhew our ill humours, and they broke out without management. The general antipathy between us and the foreigners appeared without a mafk; they affumed the merit of all that was done. They confidered the country as their right. The increafe of their plunder, and the care of it, was their only care. In every corps of them, this was a common care, and was guarded as the proper baggage of the corps; they would not move without it. It was in vain that Howe exhaufted his temper in reafon and arguing: unluckily at the moment an irremediable mifchief fell out, juft at a bad nick, " want of pay." The regular pay of the Heffian had been, as in reafon one would think it might have been, left to their own mafter, who had however not provided for it: " but pay and good difcipline" are im-

poffible,

possible. Howe could do nothing, but shew the constancy of his nature in ordering what he could not remedy. The example of bad discipline naturally extended itself to the English. We began ourselves to feel the inconvenience of a desolated country, and in vain looked for the comforts we had found at first.

General Howe soon found that the submission of the country was all feigned; many who had sworn allegiance had fled, and those who remained had no better intentions. But it was not to be supposed, nor has it happened, that an unarmed reduced province could rise upon their conquerors. Howe distributed his army with a view to keeping the province under his long line, in that light was wise, and did answer its end; not an hand dared stir in the province. Means were concerted to provide the Hessians with their pay, and to reduce them to a proper temper. Arrangements were taken to establish a firmer discipline among our own people; in which, however, opinions differed widely: it was thought unreasonable to be over exact in an enemy's country: but the winter promised leisure to settle all this: when suddenly, Washington, with an hundred men, beat up the quarters at Trenton. The blockheads, whose heads are full of after-wisdom, now condemn Rhall for turning out his men: but take my word for it, the contempt the Hessians then had of the enemy was such, that he would have been branded for a coward had he done otherwise. Rhall was not an over-pleasant man, but he was a good and gallant officer; and it is scandalous to reproach him, as some have had the impudence to do, not only with rashness, but with the contradictory charge of want of spirit. By the same vile reasoning, an accidental shot might have stigmatized the hero Mawhood, and want of success might have displaced the never-enough-to-be-admired Harcourt.

Upon this adventure of Washington's, all our evil humours grew into rank disorders. My surprize is rather that we keep what we do, than that we have had some losses. Lord Cornwallis has done all that a good officer can do; but he has infinitely more than the enemy and the season to contend with. The British is now the only operative part of the army; and surely you see that they have more than enough to do for their number.

Among other mischiefs, we are pestered with stories of the wisdom and virtue of the rebels. I won't reckon perverseness and refractory spirit among virtues; and as to wisdom, which they tell us has created this army of Washington's by magic, the case is simply this: his first attempt was with an handful of men: it was, I own, a spirited thing. He happened to succeed. He came into a country of friends, and one success led to another. The march of a successful army always must encrease it. Philadelphia is rich, and her own danger made her liberal, and supplied an army that the circumstances of the times, not the wisdom of Washington, had created. After all, if we could now act with our whole force, they could not stand against us: but the experiment would be just now too dangerous. Would to God we were all British, and spoke the same language, and had the same heart; the rebels would soon listen to reason. But remember I tell you, our allies must be new modelled, or we must change them for British, and send them to take care of you, if we hope for success.

I'll mention a little circumstance of ten times the mischief of all Washington's success, and which proves our temper. Some Hessians who had strayed from their quarters, and possibly never found their way to the enemy's camp, came back to their colours after the affair of Trenton. These

Thefe fellows, to magnify their own merits, had their mouths full of the offers they had refufed of fettlements and eftablifhments in Pennfylvania; they tell wonderful ftories of the happy fituation of their comrades, who forfooth had not their virtue to withftand temptations. Thofe ftories, at firft either difregarded or laughed at, we have at laft in vain endeavoured to put a ftop to ; and Heifter has been very fincere an active in his behaviour; and fome who really had been prifoners, and efcaped, have formally declared how ill they were treated, and how much the Americans hate the Heffians; but the truth they tell us is not credited, while the flattering hopes, fuggefted by the lies of thofe rafcals, who meant no more than to make excufes for their abfence, operate monftroufly; and I do affure you, of my own knowledge, that there is fcarcely an inftance of an Heffian officer deferting, not one, of any one of the rank of Field Officer ; and perhaps after all, the Heffian brigades are as full as one ought to expect after fo much fervice. It is not the pofitive lofs, but the doubts and fears that are created which do the mifchief. If we could meet the enemy to-morrow in fair campaign and pitched battle, I have no doubt the Heffians would behave nobly. In the mean time, it is common-fenfe that obliges Howe not to have a frontier in their hands, as things now ftand ; perhaps diftinct fervices may be found for them and for the Britifh, which would fave the making bickerings and upbraidings that always happened when they were employed together.

I have really given you a fair ftate of the mind of the army: if you find fatisfaction yourfelf, or think it will give any light to ———, you will naturally let his Lordfhip fee : but I beg my name may not be given till you firft found him how he relifhes my notions.

Another copy of the American Crisis *having come to hand, fince the publication in page 11, by which it appears that the firft was an imperfect copy, the feven firft paragraphs of the fecond number being entirely omitted. They are as follows:*

The American Crisis. No. II.

By the Author of Common-Senfe.

To LORD HOWE.

What's in the name of Lord *that I fhould fear.*
To bring my grievance to the public ear.
CHURCHILL.

Universal empire is the prerogative of a writer. His concerns are with all mankind, and though he cannot command their obedience, he can affign them their duty. The republic of letters is more ancient than monarchy, and of far higher character in the world, than the vaffal Court of Britain ; he that rebels againft reafon is a real rebel ; but he that in defence of reafon, rebels againft tyranny, has a better title to " Defender of the " than

As a military man, your Lordfhip may hold out the fword of war, and call it the " Ultima Ratio Regum," *The laft reafon of Kings* ; we in return can fhow you the fword of juftice, and call it, " The beft fcourge of tyrants." The firft of thefe two may threaten, or even frighten, for awhile, and caft a fickly languor over an infulted people ; but reafon will foon recover the debauch, and reftore them again to tranquil fortitude. Your Lordfhip, I find, has now commenced author, and publifhed a Proclamation ; I too have publifhed a Crifis ; as they ftand, they are the antipodes of each other ; both cannot rife at once, and one of them muft defcend : and fo quick is the revolution of things, that your Lordfhip's performance, I fee, has already fallen many degrees from its firft place, and is now juft vifible on the edge of the political horizon.

It

It is aftonishing to what pitch of infatuation blind folly and obftinacy will carry mankind; and your Lordfhip's drowfy proclamation is a proof that it does not even quit them in their fleep. Perhaps you thought America too was taking a nap, and therefore, chofe, like Satan to Eve, to whifper the delufion foftly, left you fhould awaken her. This Continent, Sir, is too extenfive to fleep all at once, and too watchful, even in its flumbers, not to ftartle at the unhallowed foot of an invader. You may iffue your Proclamation, and welcome, for we have learned to *" reverence ourfelves,"* and fcorn the infulting that employs you. America, for your deceafed brother's fake, would gladly have fhewn you refpect, and it is a new aggravation to her feelings, that *Howe* fhould be forgetful, and raife his fword againft thofe, who at their own charge raifed a monument to his brother. But your has commanded, and you have not enough of nature left to refufe. Surely! there muft be fomething ftrangely degenerating in the love of monarchy, that can fo completely wear a man down to an ingrate, and make him proud to lick the duft that Kings have trod upon. A few more years, fhould you furvive them, will beftow on you the title of an old man, and in fome hour of future reflection you may probably find the fitnefs of Wolfey's defpairing penitence, *" Had I ferved my God as faithfully as I have ferved my King, he would not thus have forfaken me in my old age."*

The character you appear to us in is truly ridiculous. Your friends, the Tories, announced your coming with high defcriptions of your unlimited powers; but your Proclamation has given them the lie, by fhowing you to be a commiffioner without authority. Had your powers been ever fo great, they were nothing to us, farther than we pleafed; becaufe we had the fame right which other

nations had, to do what we thought was beft. " THE UNITED STATES OF AMERICA," will found as pompoufly in the world, or in hiftory, as " *The Kingdom of Great-Britain."* The character of *General Wafhington* will fill a page with as much luftre as that of *Lord Howe;* and the *Congrefs* have as much right to command the *King and Parliament* of England, to defift from Legiflation, as *they* or *you* have to command the . Only fuppofe how laughable fuch an edict would appear from us, and then, in that merry mood, do but turn the tables upon yourfelf, and you will fee how your Proclamation is received here. Having thus placed you in a proper pofition, in which you may have a full view of folly, and learn to defpife it, I hold up to you, for that purpofe, the following quotation from your own lunarian Proclamation, " And we (Lord Howe and General Howe) do command, (and in his Majefty's name forfooth) all fuch perfons as are affembled together under the name of General or Provincial Congreffes, Committees, Conventions, or other affociations, by whatever name or names known or diftinguifhed, to defift and ceafe from all fuch treafonable actings and doings."

You introduce your Proclamation by referring to your declaration of the 14th of July and the 19th of September. In the laft of thefe you funk yourfelf below the character of a private gentleman. That I may not feem to accufe you unjuftly, I fhall ftate the circumftance: by a verbal invitation of your's, communicated to Congrefs by General Sullivan, then a prifoner on his parole, you fignified your defire of conferring with fome members of that body as private gentlemen. It was beneath the dignity of the American Congrefs to pay any regard to a meffage that at beft was but a genteel affront, and had too much of the minifterial complexion of tampering with private perfons; and which might probably have been the cafe,

cafe, had the gentlemen who were deputed on that bufinefs, poffeffed that eafy kind of virtue which an Englifh courtier is fo truly diftinguifhed by. Your requeft, however, was complied with; for honeft men are naturally more tender of their civil than their political fame. The interview ended as every fenfible man thought it would; for your Lordfhip knows, as well as the writer of the Crifis, that it is impoffible for the King of England to promife the repeal, or even the revifal, of any acts of Parliament; wherefore, on your part, you had nothing to fay, more than to requeft, in the room of demanding, the entire furrender of the Continent; and then, if that was complied with, to promife that the inhabitants fhould efcape with their lives. This was the upfhot of the conference. You informed the Conferees that you were two months in foliciting thefe powers. We afk, what powers? for as Commiffioner you have none. If you mean the power of pardoning, it is an oblique proof that your was determined to facrifice all before him; and that you were two months in diffuading him from his purpofe. Another evidence of his favage obftinacy! From your own account of the matter, we may juftly draw thefe two conclufions; firft, that you ferve a ; and fecondly, that never was a Commiffioner fent on a more foolifh errand than yourfelf. This plain language may, perhaps, found uncouthly to an ear vitiated by courtly refinements; but words were made for ufe, and the fault lies in deferving them, or the abufe in applying them unfairly.

Soon after your return to New-York, you publifhed a very illiberal and unmanly hand-bill againft the Congrefs; for it was certainly ftepping out of the line of common civility; firft, to fcreen your national pride by foliciting an interview with them as private gentlemen, and in the conclufion to endeavour to deceive the multitude by making an hand-bill attack on the whole body of the Congrefs; you got them together under one name, and abufe them under another. But the and the caufe you fupport, afford you fo few inftances of acting the gentleman, that out of pity to your fituation the Congrefs pardoned the infult by taking no notice of it.

You fay in that hand-bill, "that they, the Congrefs, difavowed every purpofe for reconciliation not confonant with their extravagant and inadmiffible claim of independence." Why, God blefs me! what have you to do with our independence? We afk no leave of yours to fet it up; we afk no money of yours to fupport it; we can do better without your fleets and armies than with them; you may foon have enough to do to protect yourfelves without being burthened with us. We are very willing to be at peace with you, to buy of you and fell to you, and, like young beginners in the world, to work for our own living; therefore, why do you put yourfelves out of cafh, when we know you cannot fpare it, and we do not defire you to run into debt? I am willing, Sir, you fhould fee your folly in every view I can place it, and for that reafon defcend fometimes to tell you in jeft what I wifh you to fee in earneft. But to be more ferious with you, why do you fay, "their" independency? To fet you right, Sir, we tell you, that the independency is ours not theirs. The Congrefs were authorized by every State on the Continent to publifh it to all the world, and in fo doing are not to be confidered as the inventors, but only as the heralds that proclaimed it, or the office from which the fenfe of the people received a legal form; and it was as much as any or all their heads were worth, to have treated with you on the fubject of fubmiffion under any name whatever. But we know the men
in

in whom we have trufted. Can England fay the fame of her parliament?

I come now more particularly, &c. *as in page* 16.

And go on to the end of the fecond paragraph in page 19, *ending with the words,* " deceive and ruin you." *After which comes in the following* :

If ever a nation was mad and foolifh, blind to its own intereft, and bent on its own deftruction, it is Britain. There are fuch things as national fins, and though the punifhment of individuals may be referved to *another* world, national punifhment can only be inflicted in *this* world. Britain, as a nation, is in my inmoft belief the greateft and moft ungrateful offender againft God on the face of the whole earth : bleffed with all the commerce fhe could wifh for, and furnifhed by a vaft extenfion of dominion with the means of civilizing both the Eaftern and Weftern World, fhe has made no other ufe of both than proudly to idolize her own " thunder," and rip up the bowels of whole countries for what fhe could get ;—like Alexander, fhe has made war her fport, and inflicted mifery for prodigality fake. The blood of India is not yet repaid, nor the wretehednefs of Africa yet requitted. Of late fhe has enlarged her lift of national cruelties by her butcherly deftruction of the Caribbs of St. Vincent's, and in returning an anfwer by the fword to the meck prayer for " *Peace, Liberty, and Safety.*" Thefe are ferious things ; and whatever a foolifh , a debauched court, a trafficking Legiflature, or a blinded people may think, the national account with Heaven muft fome day or other be fettled : all countries have fooner or later been called to their reckoning ; the proudeft empires have funk when the balance was ftruck ; and Britain, like an individual penitent, muft undergo her day of forrow, and the fooner it happens to her the better. As I wifh it over, I wifh it to come,

but withal, wifh that it may be as light as poffible.

Perhaps your Lordfhip has no tafte for ferious things ; by your connexion in England I fhould fuppofe not ; therefore I fhall drop this part of the fubject, and take it up in a line in which you will better underftand me.

By what means, may I afk, &c. *as in page* 19, *to the end ; all the reft being right.*

—————

Philadelphia, March 5.

SPEECH of his Excellency WILLIAM LIVINGSTONE, Efq. Governor, Captain-General, and Commander in Chief, of the State of New-Jerfey, and the territories thereunto belonging, Chancellor and Ordinary in the fame.
To the Right Honourable the Council, and General Affembly of the faid State.

Gentlemen,

Having already laid before the Affembly, by meffages, the feveral matters that have occurred to me, as more particularly demanding their attention during the prefent feffion, it may feem lefs neceffary to addrefs you, in the more ceremonious form of a fpeech. But conceiving it my duty to the State, to deliver my fentiments on the prefent fituation of affairs, and the eventful conteft between Great Britain and America, which could not, with any propriety, be conveyed in occafional meffages, you will excufe my giving you the trouble of attending for that purpofe.

After deploring with you the defolation fpread through part of this State, by an unrelenting enemy, who have indeed marked their progrefs with a devaftation unknown to civilized nations ; and evincive of the moft implacable vengeance, I heartily congratulate you, on that fubfequent feries of fuccefs, wherewith it has pleafed the Almighty to crown the American arms ; and particularly on the important enterprize againft the enemy

enemy at Trenton; and the *fignal victory* obtained over them at Prince-town, by the gallant troops under the command of his Excellency General Wafhington.

Confidering the contemptible figure they make at prefent, and the difguft they have given to their own confede-rates amongft us; by their more than Gothic ravages; (for thus doth the Great Difpofer of events often deduce good out of evil) their irruption into our dominion will redound to the public benefit. It has certainly en-abled us the more effectually to diftin-guifh our friends from our enemies. It has winnowed the chaff from the grain. It has diferiminated the tem-porizing politician, who, on the firft appearance of danger, was determined to fecure his idol—property, at the hazard of the general weal; from the perfevering patriot, who having em-barked all in the common caufe, choofes rather to rifque, rather to loofe that all, for the prefervation of the more eftimable treafure, Liberty, than to poffefs it (enjoy it he could not) upon ignominious terms of tamely refigning his country and po-fterity to infamy and flavery. It has, however opened the eyes of thofe, who were made to believe that their impious merit, in abetting our profe-cutors, would exempt them from being involved in the common cala-mity. But as the rapacity of the ene-my was boundlefs, their rapine was indiferiminate, and their barbarity unparallelled. They have plundered friends and foes. Effects capable of divifion, they have divided; fuch as were not, they have deftroyed. They have warred upon decrepid age; war-red upon defencelefs youth. They have committed hoftilities againft the profeffors of literature, and the mi-niflers of religion; againft public re-cords, and private monuments; againft books of improvement, and papers of curiofity; and againft the *aits and fciences*. They have butchered the wounded afking for quarter; mangled the dying weltering in their blood; refufed the dead the rites of fepulture; fuffered prifoners to perifh for want of fuftenance; violated the chaftity of women; disfigured private dwellings of tafte and elegance; and, in the rage of impiety and barbarifm, *pro-faned edifices dedicated to Almighty God!*

Yet there are amongft us, who either from ambitious or lucrative motives, or intimidated by the terror of their arms; or from a partial fond-nefs for the Britifh conftitution; or deluded by infidious propofitions, are fecretly abetting, or openly aiding, their machinations, to deprive us of that liberty,—without which, man is a beaft, and government a curfe.

Befides the inexpreffible bafenefs of wifhing to rife on the ruin of our country; or to acquire riches at the expence of the liberties and fortunes of our fellow-citizens; how foon would thofe delufive dreams upon the conqueft of America be turned into difappointment. Where is the fund to recompence thofe retainers to the Britifh army; thofe intentional pen-fioners of a bankrupt nation? Was every ftate in America to be confif-cated, and converted into cafh, the product would not fatiate the avidity of their own creatures, nor furnifh an adequate repaft for the keen appetites of their own *minifterial beneficiaries.* Inftead of gratuities and promotion, thefe unhappy accomplices in their tyranny, would meet with fuperci-lious looks and cold difdain; and after tedious attendance be finally told, by their haughty mafters, that *they indeed* approved of the *treafon*, but defpifed the *traitor.* Infulted in fine by their pretended protectors, but real betrayers; and goaded with the flings of their own confciences, they would remain the frightful monu-ments of human contempt and Divine indignation; and linger out the reft of their days in felf-condemnation.

and

and remorse; and in weeping over the ruins of their country, which themselves had been instrumental in reducing to desolation and bondage. Others there are, who terrified at the power of Britain, have been persuaded that she is not only formidable, but irresistible. That her power is great, is beyond question; that it is not to be despised, is the dictate of common prudence. But then we ought also to consider her as weak in council; and groaning with debt; reduced in her trade, reduced in her revenues, immersed in pleasure, enervated with luxury, and in dissipation and venality surpassing all Europe. We ought to consider her as hated by a potent rival, her natural enemy, and particularly exasperated at her imperious conduct in the last war, as well as her provoking manner of commencing it; and then inflamed with resentment, and only watching a favourable juncture for open hostilities. We ought to consider the amazing expence and difficulty of transporting troops and provisions above three thousand miles, with the impossibility of recruiting their army at a less distance; save only, with such recreants, whose conscious guilt must on the first approach of danger appal the stoutest heart. These insuperable obstacles are known and acknowledged by every virtuous and impartial man in the nation. Even the   of this horrid war is incapable of concealing his own confusion and distress. Too great to be wholly suppressed, it frequently discovers itself in the course of his speech. A speech terrible in word, and fraught with contradiction; breathing threatenings and betraying terror; a motley mixture of magnanimity and consternation; of grandeur and abasement; with troops invincible he dreads a defeat, and wants reinforcements. Victorious in America, and triumphant on the ocean, he is an humble dependent on a *petty Prince*; and with full confidence in the friendship and alliance of France, he trembles at her *secret* designs and *open* preparations.

With all this, we ought to contrast the numerous and hardy sons of America, enured to toil; seasoned alike to heat and cold; hale, robust, patient of fatigue; and from an ardent love of liberty, ready to face danger and death. The immense extent of continent, which our infatuated enemies have undertaken to subjugate. The remarkable unanimity of its inhabitants, notwithstanding the exception of a few apostates and deserters; their unshaken resolution to maintain their freedom, or perish in the attempt; the fertility of our soil in all kinds of provision necessary for the support of war; our inexhaustible internal resources for military stores and naval armaments; our comparative œconomy in public expences, and the millions we save by reprobating the farther exchange of our valuable staples for the worthless baubles and finery of English manufacture; add to this, that in a cause so just and righteous on our part, we have the highest reason to expect the blessing of Heaven upon our glorious conflict. For who can doubt the interposition of the SUPREMELY JUST, in favour of a people forced to recur to arms, in defence of every thing dear and precious, against a nation deaf to our complaints, rejoicing in our misery, wantonly aggravating our oppressions, determined to divide our substance, and by fire and sword to compel us into submission.

Respecting the constitution of Great-Britain, being certain prerogatives of dangerous tendency, it has indeed been applauded by the best judges, and displays in its original structure, illustrious proofs of wisdom and the knowledge of mankind. But what avails the *best* constitution, with the *worst administration*? For what is their present government, and what has

has it been for years past, but a *pensioned confederacy* against reason, and virtue, and honour, and patriotism, and the rights of man! What their governors, but a set of political craftsmen, flagitiously conspiring to erect the babel of DESPOTISM, on the ruins of the antient and beautiful fabric of LAW? A shameless cabal, notoriously employed in deceiving the Prince, corrupting the parliament, debasing the people, depressing the most virtuous, and exalting the most profligate! In short, an insatiable junto of public spoilers, lavishing the national wealth, and by peculation and plunder, daily accumulating a debt already enormous! And what is the majority of their parliament, formerly the most august assembly in the world, but venal pensioners on the crown, a perfect mockery on all representation, and at the absolute devotion of every minister! What were the characteristics of their administration of the provinces? The substitution of instructions in the room of the law; the multiplication of offices to strengthen the court interest; perpetually extending the prerogatives of the King, and retrenching the rights of the subject; advancing to the most eminent stations, men without education, and of dissolute manners; employing, with the peoples money, a band of emissaries to misrepresent and traduce the people; sporting with our persons and estates, by filling the highest seats of justice with bankrupts, bullies, and blockheads.

From such a nation (though all this we bare, and should probably have borne for a century, had they not avowedly claimed the unconditional disposal of life and property) it is evidently our interest to be detached. To remain happy or safe in our connection with her, became henceforth utterly impossible. *She is moreover precipitating her own fall, or the age of miracles is returned*; and

Britain, a phænomenon in the political world, without a parallel!

The proclamations to ensnare the timid and credulous, are beyond expression disingenuous and tantalizing. In a gilded pill they conceal real poison. They add insult to injury. After repeated intimations of *comissioners* to *treat* with America, we are presented, instead of the peaceful olive-branch, with the devouring sword; instead of being visited by plenipotentiaries, to bring matters to an accommodation, we are invaded with an army, in *their* opinion, able to subdue us; and upon discovering their error, the terms propounded amount to this: " *If you will submit* " *without resistance, we are content* " *to take your property, and spare* " *your lives*; and then (the consum-" mation of arrogance!) *we will* " *graciously pardon you for having hi-*" *therto defended both.*"

Consider then their bewildered councils, their blundering ministers, their want of men and money, their impaired credit, and declining commerce, their lost revenues, and starving islands, the corruption of their parliament, with the effeminacy of the nation, and the success of their enterprise is against all probability. Considering farther, the horrid enormity of waging war against their own brethren, expostulating for an audience, complaining of injuries, and supplicating for redress, and waging it with a ferocity and vengeance unknown to modern ages, and contrary to all laws, human and divine; and we can neither question the justice of our opposition, nor the assistance of Heaven to crown it with victory.

Let us, however, not presumptuously rely on the interposition of Providence, without exerting those efforts which it is our duty to exert, and which our bountiful Creator has enabled us to exert. Let us do our part to open the next campaign with

redoubled

redoubled vigour; and until the UNITED STATES have humbled the pride of BRITAIN, and obtained an honourable peace, chearfully furnish our proportion for continuing the war—A war on our fide founded on the immutable obligation of felf-defence, and in fupport of freedom, of virtue, and every thing tending to ennoble our nature, and render our people happy. On their part, prompted by boundlefs avarice, and a thirft for abfolute fway, and built on a claim repugnant to every principle of reafon and equity—*A claim fubverfive of all liberty, natural, civil, moral, and religious; incompatible with human happinefs, and ufurping the attributes of* DEITY, *degrading man, and* BLASPHEMING GOD.

Let us all, therefore, of every rank and degree, remember our plighted faith and honour to maintain the caufe with our lives and fortunes. Let us inflexibly perfevere in profecuting to a happy period, what has been fo glorioufly begun, and hitherto fo profperoufly conducted.— And let thofe in more diftinguifhed ftations ufe all their influence and authority to roufe the fupine; to animate the irrefolute; to confirm the wavering; and to draw from his lurking hole, the fkulking neutral, who leaving to others the heat and and burden of the day, means in the final refult to reap the fruits of that victory, for which he will not contend. Let us be peculiarly affiduous in bringing to condign punifhment, thofe deteftable parricides who have been openly active againft their native country. And may we, in all our deliberations and proceedings, be influenced and directed by the great arbiter of the fate of nations, by whom empires rife and fall, and who will not always fuffer *the fceptre of the wicked to reft on the lot of the righteous,* but in due time avenge an injured people on their UNFEELING

OPPRESSOR, *and his bloody inftruments.*

WILLIAM LIVINGSTONE.
Hadderfie'd, Feb. 25, 1777.

Tranflation of a Memorial prefented by Sir Jofeph Yorke to the States General, on the twenty-firft day of February, 1777.

" Since the commencement of the unnatural rebellion, which has broke out in the Englifh colonies againft the legal conftitution of the Mother Country, the underfigned Ambaffador Extraordinary and Plenipotentiary of the King of Great Britain, has had frequent occafions to addrefs himfelf to your High Mightineffes, in the name of his Mafter, to engage them by all motives of national intereft, of good neighbourhood, of friendfhip, and finally of treaties, to put a ftop to the clandeftine commerce which is carried on between their fubjects and the rebels. If the meafures which your High Mightineffes have thought proper to take had been as efficacious as your affurances have been amicable, the underfigned would not now have been under the difagreeable neceffity of bringing to the cognizance of your High Mightineffes, facts of the moft ferious nature.

" The King hath hitherto borne, with unexampled patience, the irregular conduct of your fubjects in their interefted commerce at St. Euftatia, as alfo in America. His Majefty has always flattered himfelf, that in giving time to your High Mightineffes to examine to the bottom this conduct, fo irregular and fo infufferable, they would have taken meafures neceffary to reprefs the abufe, to reftrain their fubjects within bounds, and to make them refpect the rights and friendfhip of Great-Britain.

" The complaints which I have orders to make to their High Mightineffes, are founded upon authentic documents annexed to this Memorial,
where

where their High Mightinesses will see with astonishment, and I doubt not at the same time with displeasure, that their new Governor, M. Van Graaf, after having permitted an illicit commerce at St. Euftatia, hath passed his forgetfulness of his duty to the point of conniving at the Americans in their hostile equipments, and the permitting the seizure of an English vessel, by an American pirate, within cannon shot of that island. And in aggravation to the affront given to the English nation, and to all the powers of Europe, to return from the fortress of his government the salute of a rebel flag. In return to the amicable representations made by the president of the neighbouring island of St. Christopher, on these facts of notoriety, M. Van Graaf has answered in a manner the most vague and unsatisfactory, refusing to enter at all into the subject, or into an explanation of the matter with a Member of his Majesty's Council of St. Christopher's, dispatched by the President for that purpose to St. Euftatia.

"After exhibiting the documents annexed, nothing remains with me but to add, that the King who had read them, not with less surprize than indignation, hath ordered me to expressly demand of your High Mightinesses, a formal disavowal of the salute by Fort Orange, at St. Euftatia, to the rebel ship, the dismission and immediate recall of Governor Van Graaf, and to declare further, on the part of his Majesty, that until that satisfaction is given, they are not to expect that his Majesty will suffer himself to be amused by mere assurances, or that he will delay one instant to take such mea-

sures as he shall think due to the interests and dignity of his Crown.

(Signed)   JOS. YORKE.

Given at the Hague, Feb. 21, 1777."

Copy of a memorial delivered under the orders of the States General, to the King of Great Britain, by the Envoy Extraordinary and Plenipotentiary from their High Mightinesses *.

SIRE,

"It is with the most profound respect, that the under-signed Envoy Extraordinary and Plenipotentiary of their High Mightinesses, in consequence of the orders which he hath received, hath the honour to represent to your Majesty, that the memorial which your Ambassador hath presented to their High Mightinesses on the 21st of last month, hath touched them very sensibly; and that they find themselves obliged to make complaint of the reproaches which are contained in it, as if their High Mightinesses were to be suspected of a will and intention of amusing your Majesty by amicable assurances, which they have falsified by their acts; also of the menacing tone which reigns in that memorial, and appears to their High Mightinesses too highly strained, beyond that which is the accorded and accustomed manner, and that ought to take place between two sovereign and independent powers, and especially between two neighbouring powers, which have been of so many years continuance, united by the ties of good harmony and mutual friendship.

"Their High Mightinesses trust that on all occasions, and particularly in respect to the unfortunate troubles of your Majesty's colonies in America, they have held a conduct towards

* This is the answer to his Majesty's complaints made to the States in the preceding memorial. Disdaining the spirit and manner of the complaint, they passed by the Ambassador (Sir Joseph Yorke), and also the Secretary of State (Lord Suffolk), and come under their Minister at London to address himself directly to the King, and to deliver their answer into his own hands.

your

your Majesty, which has been expected from a good neighbour, and a friendly and affectionate power.

"Their High Mightinesses, Sire, hold your Majesty's friendship in the highest estimation, and wish to do every thing in their power (as far as the honour and dignity of their state will permit them to go) to cultivate it still more and more; but they cannot at the same time so far restrain themselves, as to disguise the very poignant sensation, with which that memorial hath impressed them.

"It is alone from the motive of demonstrating to your Majesty every possible regard, and to prove that their High Mightinesses will not neglect any thing, which may serve to investigate properly the truth of the facts, from whence the complaints made to them seem to have arisen, that they have resolved to institute an enquiry in a manner the most summary, and cut off all trainings of delay.

"To this end their High Mightinesses, passing by the ordinary and usual form in like cases, requiring a report in writing from their officers and others employed in their colonies, have already dispatched their orders to the Commandant of St. Eustatia, to render himself within the Republic without delay, and as soon as possible, to give the necessary information of all that has passed within the island of St. Eustatia, and that which hath come to his knowledge relative to the American Colonies and their vessels, during the period of his command, and to lay his conduct, touching that matter, before the eyes of their High Mightinesses.

"The under-signed is charged by his orders to bring the information of this resolution to your Majesty, as also that their High Mightinesses make no difficulty of disavowing, in the most express manner, every act or mark of honour which may have been given by their officers, or by

any of their servants, to the vessels of your Majesty's colonies of North-America, or that they may give hereafter, so far as those acts or marks of honour may be of such a nature, as that any can conclude from them that it is intended thereby, in the least degree, to recognize the independence of those colonies.

"The under-signed is also further charged to inform your Majesty, that their High Mightinesses have, in consequence, given their orders to their Governors and Councils in the West-Indies, and have enjoined them afresh, in the strongest terms, to observe exactly the placards and orders against the exportation of military stores to the American colonies of your Majesty, and to see them executed most rigorously.

(Signed)   WELDEREN."

Dated London, March 26, 1777.

Copy of a letter from Lord Suffolk to the Count de Welderen, the Dutch Minister at London, dated the 10th of April, 1777.

St. *James's, April* 10, 1777.

"The King having taken cognizance of the memorial you addressed to his Majesty on the 26th ult. in consequence of the orders you have received from their High Mightinesses, orders me to assure you, that his Majesty accepts it with satisfaction—at the same time that he cannot perceive that the memorial presented by his Ambassador to the States General of the United Provinces, the 21st of February, contained any thing contrary to what ought to take place between sovereigns and independent powers in the weighty circumstances in question.

"His Majesty was the more sensibly affected with the affair which constituted the principal subject of the complaint, because it was occasioned by the indecent proceedings of a Governor in the service of a neighbour, who has been united for so long a time with his Majesty by the bands of good harmony and mutual affection.

"His Majesty has heard with pleasure,

fure, that their High Mightinesses have fulfilled his expectation; that they have recalled their Governor; that the insult is disavowed, and that orders are dispatched to the governors and commanders of the colonies of their High Mightinesses in the West-Indies, to observe strictly the placarts and orders against the exportation of military stores to his Majesty's colonies in America, actually in rebellion; and being persuaded that their High Mightinesses will watch over the punctual execution of their ordinances, with pleasure puts an end to all cause of vexation that the consequences of the offensive conduct of the Governor of St. Eustatia may have given them.

I have the honour to be,
(Signed) SUFFOLK."

———————

Brussels, April 18. An ordinance has been published here, for prolonging, during the term of one year, the ordinance of the 27th of April, 1776, prohibiting the supplying the British colonies in America with warlike stores. *Gazette.*

Paris, April 21. His Imperial Majesty arrived here on Friday last in the evening, under the title of Count Falkenstein. *Ibid.*

St. James's, April 26. In pursuance of an Act of Parliament made in the present year of his Majesty's reign, intitled, " An Act to im-
" power his Majesty to secure and
" detain persons charged with or suf-
" pected of the crime of high trea-
" son committed in any of his Ma-
" jesty's colonies or plantations in
" America, or on the high seas, or
" the crime of piracy;" the King has been pleased, by warrants under his Royal sign manual, to appoint a certain messuage or building called Forton, on the Gosport side of Portsmouth harbour, in the parish of Alverstoke in the county of Southampton, and also a certain messuage or building called Old Mill Prison, situ-

ated in the borough of Plymouth in the county of Devon, to be places of confinement for such prisoners. *Ibid.*

———————

London, April 23. The Lexington, an American sloop of war, Captain Johnson, arrived a few days since at Bourdeaux in France, with dispatches from Baltimore in Maryland. She left it the beginning of March, and on her passage took two prizes; one an empty transport, which she burnt at sea, and the other she carried to Bourdeaux. Part of her advices are, that there had been an insurrection in favour of Government on the Eastern shore of Maryland: about 500 persons appeared in arms, but they were immediately dispersed by a Continental Virginia regiment, their leaders imprisoned, and the rest implored and received mercy. That Lord and General Howe, had in the month of February, attempted to open a negociation with the Congress, through General Lee, who wrote a letter to them for that purpose, but the proposal was rejected with disdain, the Congress declaring, " *They would treat with no power on earth, which did not first acknowledge their independency.*" That all the colonies had fully compleated their levies, and the troops were marching from all quarters to join General Washington's army. That it was expected General Howe would attempt, early in the Spring, before (he supposed) Washington's army would be compleated, to march towards Philadelphia, and that he might make some progress that way. But this was rather *hoped* than feared, it being evident, from the superior strength of General Washington, that General Howe could easily be stopped on his march, and his *retreat* rendered almost impossible.

———————

The following are extracts of a genuine letter from Nantz, in France; received in London, April 23.
" An express packet is just arrived here,

here, which failed from Baltimore, about the middle of February. She brings an account, that the beating up of the cantonments of the British troops in Jersey, brought on several skirmishes, in which the regulars lost since the 26th of December, upwards of 2000 men, killed, wounded, and taken prisoners, 12 brass field pieces, almost the entire baggage of two brigades, several pairs of colours, ammunition waggons, drums, &c. that there was no cordiality between the English and Hessian Generals, the latter of whom were much dissatisfied, and many of the Hessians had, and were daily deserting to the American army; that General Washington was drawing lines round the British army in the Jerseys, and had reduced it to very great distress, and made the communication with the ships extremely difficult and hazardous; that the Congress had resolved to augment their army to 110 battalions (82,560 men) and which they expected would be ready to take the field early in the spring, all their former levies being nearly compleated, the people having been stimulated to enter through the great disorders which the British, as well as the Hessians, had committed in the Jerseys, many authentic cases of rapes, murders, and other brutalities, having been published, which had excited the greatest rage; that the late successes had quite altered the face of affairs; and that the arrangements throughout all the provinces were carried on with confidence and the greatest harmony. About 10,000 men were assembled at Rye in Connecticut, and preparations made to receive the troops from Rhode Island, had they attempted to land. Many valuable captures had been made by the American privateers, among others a vessel with 12,000 suits of cloathing, and 4000 stand of arms.

" The last letters from the West-Indies mention, that an American vessel, under French colours, from Maryland and Martinico, had been taken and carried into Dominica. The French Governor was so much exasperated at this step, that he immediately gave orders to seize every English vessel within his power. Six were seized at Martinico, their sails taken away, and their rudders unhung. An aid-de-camp, and an interpreter, were gone from Dominica to Martinique on this business.

" The prizes which the American frigates now here (Nantz) have taken, have been sold in the Bay of Quiberon, which has foreign privileges, and which makes it seem, that Government is not acquainted with what passes; for as L'Orient is a King's port, the Commissary of Marine was not willing to permit the the sale *there*, and he has since received an order from Court, to cause the frigate and her prizes to quit the port, which had been executed in *form only*, as the American frigate is now actually careening in our port (Nantz) and two of her prizes, with wine and fish, discharged here."

The American Plenipotentiaries at Paris (so they are stiled in France) have taken up their residence at the house kept by a relation of M. de Maurepas, the Minister, who when he visits his relation, which he does frequently, fails not to visit his lodgers also.

Other intelligence brought from America to France, is,

In South-Carolina every thing perfectly quiet; trade in a very flourishing way; manufactures of cloaths, &c. making for the Negroes with great rapidity; some planters had already made more than sufficient for themselves. In Charles Town harbour, above thirty sail of foreign vessels. Had four privateers at sea, which had taken several prizes.

We

Every thing perfectly quiet in Virginia and Maryland. The little mutiny in Maryland entirely put an end to, and the chiefs confined in prison:

The Congress at Philadelphia.

On the 14th of March, General Washington's army at Morris Town confisted of fourteen thousand men; effective.

By the middle of May, the Congress expected the Continental army to be entirely completed.

About one hundred and twenty *additional* privateers, from the different ports in America, were to be ready for sea by the middle of April.

Eleven thousand men, well accoutred, under the command of General Arnold, were near Providence.—This circumstance prevented Lord Percy's sending to New-York the remainder of the light infantry, which General Howe had wrote for. Lord Percy's answer, in substance, was this, " That if ordered, he must obey; but thought it his duty to represent his situation first, that the enemy having collected a large force in his neighbourhood, &c. &c. such diminution of the troops under his command, would greatly endanger the public service, in that quarter."

The fact respecting Lord Percy is stated to be as follows :

After the affair at Trenton, General Howe wrote to Lord Percy for a second reinforcement of 1500 men. Lord Percy did not immediately comply with this order; but returned for answer, that the enemy were collecting a large force near Providence, of which circumstance he supposed General Howe unacquainted, that he thought it his duty to represent this matter, and to add, that he apprehended it would be dangerous to the service in that part, to send away so large a corps.

General Howe replied, that Lord Percy knew the consequence of disobedience of orders, that he would be tried by a Court Martial, and would certainly be broke; that he (General Howe, was inclined to shew his Lordship all the indulgence that his services deserved, at the same time he insisted upon his orders being punctually obeyed.

The troops were sent.

Lord Percy wrote an account of the whole affair, and sent it (by the the last vessel from Rhode-Island) to his father, the Duke of Northumberland; at the same time beseeching his Grace, to lay him with all humility at his Majesty's feet, and to solicit his immediate recal.

The Duke complied with his son's request. The King was greatly surprised. Lord George Germaine was sent for, his Lordship was surprised also, not having had the least information of such difference.

———— ————

Philadelphia, February 6, 1777.

Last Friday the following gentlemen were elected at the Statehouse, viz. Thomas Wharton, jun; Counsellor, and Col. Bull, Col. Moor, Major Lollar, and Col. Coats, Members of Assembly for the county of Philadelphia.

The Hon. John M'Kinley, Esq. is appointed Governor and Commander in Chief of the Delaware State.

When Governor Trumbull of Connecticut recommended it to the housholders in that State, who are not obliged to do military duty, to form themselves into companies, choose their own officers, and equip themselves for the defence of these States, a number of *aged* gentlemen in the first society in the town of Warterbury, embodied themselves, and nominated their own officers, who were honoured with commissions, and when the regiment of militia to which they belong were ordered to New-York, agreeable to a late resolve of General Assembly, this company was the first in the regiment that marched and reached the place of rendezvous: it

is

is now at this place, and confifts of twenty-four men, their ages, added together, *are a thoufand years*; they are all married men, and when they came from home, left behind them their wives, *with a hundred and forty-nine children and grand-children.* One of them is fifty-eight years of age, has had *nineteen children*, and *twelve* grand-children; fourteen of his own children are now living.—A worthy example of patriotifm—let others go and do likewife.

Extract of a letter from an Officer of Diftinction, dated at Chatham, between Morris-Town, and Elizabeth-Town, New-Jerfey, Feb. 3, 1777.

" We have hemmed the enemy in, and begin to pinch them. On the 23d ult. we trimmed two regiments near to Woodbridge, killed 30 privates, and feveral officers. Had Col. Buckner, who commanded, behaved well, we fhould have deftroyed one regiment. He is now under an arreft. We loft no men that day.

" On the 1ft inft. 3000 of the enemy, under command of Sir William Erfkine, came out of Brunfwick to forage. They had eight pieces of cannon. Several of our fcouting parties joined, to the amount of 600 men, under the command of Col. Scot, of the 5th Virginia regiment. A difpofition was made to attack the enemy. Col. Scot, with 90 Virginians on the right, attacked 200 Britifh grenadiers, and drove them to their cannon. The other parties not marching fo brifkly up to the attack, the Colonel was engaged ten minutes by himfelf, and 300 frefh men being fent againft him, was obliged to give way, and formed again within 300 yards of the enemy. By this time, two other divifions had got up with the enemy; but fuperior numbers at laft prevailed. Our troops retreated about a quarter of a mile, formed again and looked the enemy in the face until

they retreated. The enemy had 36 killed, that the country people faw, and upwards of 100 wounded. *We have loft 3 officers, and 12 privates killea, and about as many wounded.* Lieut. Gregory, from Elizabeth City County, Virginia, a brave officer, and Adjutant Kelly, of the 5th Virginia regiment, one of the braveft men in the army; he was carried off the field with a flefh wound only, and 5 more Virginians; but the enemy coming on that ground, *murdered them, by beating out their brains, with a barbarity exceeding that of the favages.*"

Extract of a letter from General PUT-NAM, to the Council of Safety of Pennfylvania, received at Philadelphia by exprefs, dated at Prince-Town, Feb. 18, 1777.

" Yefterday evening Col. Nelfon, with 150 men, at Lawrence' Neck, attacked 60 men of Cortland Skinner's brigade, commanded by the enemy's *renowned* Land Pilot, Major Richard Stockton—routed them, and took the whole prifoners —among them the Major, a Captain, and three fubalterns, with 70 ftand of arms. Fifty of the Bedford Pennfylvania riflemen behaved like veterans."

The following are promoted to the rank of Majors General in the army of the United States—Lord Sterling, Thomas Mifflin, Arthur St, Clair, Adam Stephen, and Benjamin Lincoln, Efqrs.

Col. Enoch Poor, Col. Glover, Col. Patterfon, Colonel Anthony Wayne, Col. James Mitchel Varnum, Col. John Phillip Dehaas, Col. George Weedon, Col. Muhlenburg, Col. John Cadwallader, and Col. William Woodford, are alfo promoted to the rank of Brigadiers General.

Extract of a letter from Prince-Town, March 5.

" On the 25th ult. a party of our troops

troops took poſſeſſion of an advantageous piece of ground, on the ſouth ſide of the Rariton, near Brunſwick ; upon which, they, that night, erected a battery of ſix 32 pounders. The firſt notice Lord Cornwallis, and the ſtarving army in Brunſwick, had of it, was on the 27th in the morning, when the battery fired upon a number of boats coming from Amboy with proviſions. Four or five of the boats were ſunk, and the reſt driven back to Amboy, who from thence carried the account to New-York. Upon which General Howe came himſelf into Jerſey, and tried to open the communication with Brunſwick, for all communication with Brunſwick, except by the Rariton, was cut off ſome time before, and remains ſo ſtill. He failed in his attempt, and narrowly eſcaped being killed, or made priſoner. Brunſwick continues blockaded on every ſide ; and the army and inhabitants are in the greateſt diſtreſs for proviſions. Even at New-York, beef is 1s. 2d. per pound, and mutton is 2s. 7d. The Heſſians are very ſickly. General Waſhington's army is full 20,000 men, and more are daily coming in.''

New-York, March 17.
By his Excellency Sir WILLIAM HOWE,
Knight of the moſt Honourable Order of the Bath, one of his Majeſty's Commiſſioners for reſtoring peace to the colonies, General and Commander in Chief of all his Majeſty's forces within the colonies lying on the Atlantic Ocean, from Nova Scotia to Weſt Florida incluſive, &c. &c.

PROCLAMATION.

'' Whereas it has been repreſented to me that many of his Majeſty's European and American ſubjects are compelled by force, or otherwiſe induced, to bear arms in oppoſition to the re-eſtabliſhment of the conſtitutional authority of government in America, and are diſcouraged from returning to their allegiance by ill founded doubts of the reception ſuch tender of their duty may meet with : I therefore declare, and do hereby promiſe and engage, That all perſons bearing arms as aforeſaid, who ſhall ſurrender themſelves to any officer commanding any part of his Majeſty's forces, on or before the firſt day of May next, ſhall be entitled to pardon for all offences heretofore committed againſt his crown and dignity, and their eſtates and effects be ſecured from ſeizure, forfeiture, or confiſcation.—That every non-commiſſioned officer and private man who ſhall come in *with his arms*, ſhall alſo receive the *full value for them.*— That the American born ſubjects ſhall be permitted to enter into any of the Provincial corps in his Majeſty's ſervice, or to return home as they think fit.—And that the Britiſh and Iriſh born ſubjects ſhall either be taken into his Majeſty's ſervice, or conveyed to the place of their nativity, at their own option.

'' Given under my hand, at Head Quarters in New-York, the 15th day of March, 1777.
W. HOWE.''
By his Excellency's command,
ROBERT M'KENZIE, Sec.

Whitehall, March 20.
Extract of a letter from the Honourable General Sir William Howe to Lord George Germain, dated New-York, Feb. 12, 1777.
The diſpoſition of the troops in this quarter having undergone little alteration ſince my laſt diſpatch, I have only to adviſe your Lordſhip of the return of a brigade of Britiſh, and ſome companies of Grenadiers and Light Infantry, from Rhode Iſland, to ſtrengthen Lord Cornwallis's corps in Jerſey, in order to enable his Lordſhip, with more ſecurity to the poſts of Branſwick and Amboy, to make a movement, when the

weather

weather proves favourable, againſt the enemy ſtill remaining at Morris-Town.

Lieutenant-General Clinton being gone to England, Lord Percy has ſucceeded to the command at Rhode-Iſland, and has with him Major-General Preſcot, one troop of the 17th Light Dragoons, one brigade of Britiſh, and two of Heſſians.

His Excellency Governor Tryon has offered his ſervice in the command of a corps of Provincials for the enſuing campaign, and preſuming this meaſure will be approved by his Majeſty, I ſhall endeavour to place ſuch a corps under his command as may be of eſſential ſervice in the proſecution of the war.

Major-General Robertſon, who will have the honour to deliver this diſpatch, can give your Lordſhip the beſt information reſpecting the preſent ſtate of this country.

Major-General Robertſon, who left New-York the 18th of February, and by whom the letter, of which the above is an extract, has been received, gives an account of ſeveral advantages gained by parties compoſed of Britiſh and Heſſian troops, employed in eſcorting convoys in the Jerſeys, over large bodies of the rebels, by which they had been attacked: particularly that a party of the 42d, which was eſcorting ſome forage waggons from Brunſwick, having been attacked by a great number of the rebels, Sir William Erſkine marched out with a detachment to their relief, and taking a poſition which placed the rebels between two fires, obliged them to retreat in great confuſion, leaving between three and four hundred dead upon the ſpot.

That a conſiderable number of the rebels having appeared on the heights above the Light-Houſe at Sandy Hook, Major Gordon, with 200 men, landed behind them, attacked and defeated them, killing ſeveral,

and taking 74 priſoners, which had occaſioned the rebels to abandon all that part of Monmouth county.

That the Heſſian ſoldiers, that had fought their way through the rebels at Trenton, and come to New-York, had requeſted General Howe to ſend them back into the Jerſeys, that they might have a ſhare in any ſervice that the ſeaſon would admit of; with which the General had complied, and they were ſent back accordingly.

That the rebels on the Weſt Cheſter ſide, had collected all the militia they could draw together from the New England Provinces and the Weſtern parts of New-York, bringing with them a number of empty waggons, in expectation of plundering the inhabitants of New York Iſland, and had appeared before Fort Independence, near King's Bridge, which they ſummoned to ſurrender; but upon receiving ſome cannon ſhot from the place, and perceiving the diſpoſition making by General Knyphauſen, who commands at King's Bridge, for attacking them, they withdrew with their waggons, and diſperſed.

That General Howe propoſed paſſing over from New-York into the Jerſeys on the 18th of February, having ordered the troops which were returned from Rhode-Iſland to diſembark at Amboy.

That all his Majeſty's ſhips fit for ſea were kept out cruizing, notwithſtanding the rigour of the ſeaſon, and had taken and ſent into New-York near two hundred ſail of prizes.

That although when the King's troops took poſſeſſion of the city of New-York, it was found almoſt without inhabitants, the eagerneſs of the people to return under his Majeſty's government was ſuch, that the number of inhabitants on the 17th of February amounted to upwards of 11,000. That they kept conſtant watch,

watch, and patroled the city night and day, to guard againſt any further attempts of rebel incendiaries, and that their zeal and alertneſs had prevented any late material injury to the city or ſhipping from fire.

That the Congreſs, after declaring General Waſhington Dictator of the American States for ſix months, had withdrawn to Baltimore in Maryland, leaving a Committee at Philadelphia to aſſiſt him with their advice.

Copy of a letter from Governor Tryon to Lord George Germain.

New York, Feb. 11, 1777.

MY LORD,

The ſucceſs that accompanied my endeavours to unite the inhabitants of this city, by an oath of allegiance and fidelity to his Majeſty and his government, has met my warmeſt wiſhes, 2970 of the inhabitants having qualified thereto in my preſence. The Mayor, Recorder, and Alderman Waddle, were employed in adminiſtering the oath.

I have the ſatisfaction to aſſure your Lordſhip, as the invitation to the people to give this voluntary teſtimony of their loyalty to his Majeſty and his government was made even without a ſhadow of compulſion, it gave me peculiar ſatisfaction to ſee the chearfulneſs with which they attended the ſummons. I verily believe there are not one hundred citizens who have not availed themſelves of the opportunity of thus teſtifying their attachment to government. The Mayor, ſince I went through the ſeveral wards, has atteſted 50 more men, (and is daily adding to the number) which makes the whole ſworn in the city 3020, which added to thoſe atteſted on Staten Iſland, in the three counties in Long Iſland, and in Weſt Cheſter county, (all which amounted to upwards of 2600) makes the whole amount to 5600 men.

Thus, my Lord, I have uſed my beſt endeavours to ſecure the fidelity of the inhabitants of this government, within thoſe diſtricts through which the King's troops have moved. I have aſſured the General that, ſhould he remove all his troops from this city, there would not be the leaſt riſk of a revolt from the inhabitants; but, on the contrary, was confident large numbers would take a ſhare in the defence of the town againſt the rebels.

The loyal inhabitants of Queen's county received the 800 ſtand of arms, diſtributed by the General's permiſſion, with demonſtrations of joy, and with a profeſſed reſolution to uſe them in defence of the iſland.

I am anxious that ſome grace from government may ſpeedily be extended to this loyal quarter of the province.

I have the honour to be, &c.

London Gazette.] W. TRYON.

Spithead, April 18. His Majeſty's ſhip the St. Albans ſailed on the 16th inſtant from St. Helen's, and this morning the Blonde, and Porpoiſe, with their ſeveral convoys for America, having on board the Anſpach troops and Hanau Chaſſeurs, and the Brunſwick and Hanau recruits. *Ibid.*

Spithead, April 19. Yeſterday and this morning arrived the Reſolution and Royal Britain tranſports from Willemſtadt, with Heſſian and Hanau recruits, for their reſpective corps in America. *Ibid.*

Spithead, May 9. This morning his Majeſty's ſhip the Proteus, with the Royal Britain, Reſolution, and Chriſtian tranſports, having on board the Hanau Chaſſeurs, and the St. St. Andrew Ordnance ſtore-ſhip, failed from hence for Quebec. *Ibid.*

General Burgoyne ſailed from Plymouth for Quebec in the Apollo, 32 guns, on the ſecond of April. And General Clinton ſailed from Plymouth for New-York in the Liverpool, 28 guns, on the 9th of May.

Whitehall,

Whitehall, May 10, 1777.
Extract of a letter from the Honourable General Sir William Howe to Lord George Germain, dated New-York, April 1, 1777.

There have not been any occurrences since my last worthy your Lordship's notice, except the success of a detachment of five hundred men that I sent up the North River in transports on the 22d of March, convoyed by the Brune Frigate, to destroy a considerable deposit of provisions and stores, which the enemy had made at Peek's Kill, near fifty miles distant from New-York. Lieut. Colonel Bird of the 15th regiment commanded the party. The rebels stationed there, retiring upon his approach, he got easy possession of the post. Before their retreat they set fire to the principal store-houses, and thereby rendered useless the only wharf where it was practicable to embark the remaining stores in convenient time, which made it expedient to destroy the greater part. This was completely effected to the amount specified in the inclosed return; and the detachment reimbarking without interruption, returned here the 26th.

Return of Provisions, stores, &c. (for the use of the rebel army) taken and destroyed by a detachment of the King's troops, commanded by Lieut. Colonel Bird, of the 15th infantry, at Peek's Kill upon the North River, the 23d and 24th of March, 1777.

Destroyed and burnt by the King's troops: 310 hogsheads of rum, 150 hogsheads of molasses, 800 barrels of flour, 150 barrels of biscuit, 170 barrels of pork, 30 barrels of beef, 17 barrels of pitch and tar, 800 bushels of oats, 2500 bushels of wheat, 800 bushels of buck wheat, 12 casks of coffee, 9 cases of chocolate, 50 casks of tallow, 30 chests of candles, 15 barrels of salt, 200 iron pots and camp kettles, 500 canteens of wood and bowls, &c. 400 intrenching tools, 30 casks of nails, 150 waggons and carts with harness, 1 iron twelve pounder on a field carriage.

Destroyed and burnt by the rebels: 100 hogsheads of rum, 500 barrels of flour, 500 bundles of straw, 1 magazine of hay, 2030 bushels of wheat, 1 ammunition waggon loaded.

Total: 410 hogsheads of rum, 150 hogsheads of molasses, 1300 barrels of flour, 150 barrels of biscuit, 170 barrels of pork, 30 barrels of beef, 17 barrels of pitch and tar, 500 bundles of straw, 1 magazine of hay, 800 bushels of oats, 4500 bushels of wheat, 800 bushels of buck wheat, 12 casks of coffee, 9 cases of chocolate, 50 casks of tallow, 30 chests of candles, 15 barrels of salt, 200 iron pots and camp kettles, 500 canteens of wood and bowls, &c. 400 intrenching tools, 30 casks of nails, 150 waggons and carts with harness, 1 iron twelve pounder on a carriage, 1 ammunition waggon loaded.

N. B. Two piles of barracks for 1200 men, and seven store-houses containing the above stores, with many other articles that cannot be justly ascertained, were burnt; also several sloops and petiaugers destroyed, loaded with provisions.

(Signed)   JOHN BIRD,
Lieutenant-Colonel 15th regiment of foot.

Admiralty Office, May 10, 1777.
Extract of a letter from Lord Viscount Howe, Vice Admiral of the White, and Commander in Chief of his Majesty's ships and vessels in North America, to Mr. Stephens, dated at New-York, the 31st of March, 1777.

Commodore Hotham anchored the 19th of January in Chesepeak Bay, where, by his unexpected appearance, an opportunity offered for seizing a ship laden with about 550 hogsheads of tobacco intended for Nantz. He sailed from Chesepeak Bay, on the 11th of February, and, arriving off the Delaware, on the 17th, was forced away from that station by strong northerly winds, which prevented

vented his return until the 11th inftant; and an opportunity was thereby afforded for an armed frigate fitted by the rebels, with feveral trading veffels, to put to fea from that river. The Commodore had the good fortune to take an American fhip, laden with ammunition and military ftores from Nantz, after his return, and fent her under convoy of the Daphne to this port. Several other captures have been made by the fhips of this fouthern fquadron, in number from twenty-five to thirty, which have been moftly funk or otherwife deftroyed. I have reafon, from different relations, to believe, that the fmall fquadrons under Captain Hammond and Captain Davis have made as many more; but the particulars not having been yet tranfmitted, none of thefe captures are added to the general lift herewith inclofed.

The General meditating an attempt by furprize to take or deftroy a confiderable magazine which the rebels had formed at Peek's Kill, about fifty miles up the North river, a corps of troops, commanded by Colonel Bird, embarked in four tranfports; and proceeding up the North river the 22d inftant, under the conduct of Captain Fergufon, in the Brune, with the Dependence, and another galley, fitted for the occafion; the enemy, upon the fudden difcovery and approach of the armament next day, fet fire to a part of their magazines and barracks, before they retreated. The troops, after they landed, did the fame to the reft; whereby this plentiful depofit of provifions, ftores, and other neceffaries of various kinds, was totally deftroyed, with no other lofs than two feamen, who were miffing when the troops re-embarked the fucceeding day.　　　*London Gazette.*

Eagle, off New-York, March 31, 1777.
Lift of veffels feized as prizes, and of re-captures made, by the American fquadron, between the 10th of March and the 31ft of December, 1776, according to the returns received by the Vice Admiral, the Vifcount Howe.

P R I Z E S.

Taken by the Orpheus.

Ranger, David Wran, mafter, from Nantucket, Fifhing, in ballaft. A floop from the Weft-Indies, driven on fhore, and burnt. Betfy, Thomas Willy, mafter, from Philadelphia to the Weft-Indies, laden with flour, driven on fhore and blown up. —— —— from the Weft-Indies, with ammunition, merchandize, &c. Fidelity, William Willis, mafter, from Philadelphia to the Weft-Indies, with flour. Polly, Philip Lacy, mafter, belonging to the Congrefs, from Philadelphia to France, with oil, flour, and fpermaceti candles. Peggy, Thomas Patten, mafter, belonging to the Congrefs, from Philadelphia to the Weft-Indies, with flour. Martin, James Neal, mafter, from Philadelphia to the Weft-Indies, with flour. Sarah and Elizabeth, John Connor, mafter, from Philadelphia to the Weft-Indies, with flour. Fancy, Jofeph Titcomb, mafter, from Philadelphia to New-England, with flour. Delaware, James M'Knight, mafter, from Philadelphia to the Weft-Indies, with flour. Endeavour, A. Bartlet, mafter, from Philadelphia to the Weft-Indies, with flour. Mary Ann, Guil, de Grave, mafter, from Philadelphia to the Weft-Indies, with flour. Difpatch, Peter Parker, mafter, belonging to the Congrefs, from Philadelphia to France, with flour.

By the Orpheus *and* Daphne.

Two Brothers, James Gillet, mafter, Mayne and Co. owners, from Philadelphia to St. Euftatia, with bread, flour, and fpermaceti candles. Colonel Parry, Wm. Gamble, mafter, Leaming and co. owners, from Philadelphia to South Carolina, with flour, &c. Fanny, Don M'Kay, mafter, Wm. Bell, owner, from St. Euftatia

Euſtatia to Philadelphia, with ofnaburgs, linen, rum, molaſſes, &c. Schylkill, Benjamin Camby, maſter, Harbutſon and co. owners, from Philadelphia to Cape Nichola Mole, with flour and bread. Greenwich Packet, James Glaſcow, maſter, James Young, owner, from Philadelphia to Winyew, Carolina, with rum, flour, and porter. Nancy, James Kinney, maſter, David Bevin, owner, from Martinico to Philadelphia, with bale and caſe goods, medicines, and claret. Samuel, John Hutchins, maſter, Skinner and co. owners, from Bourdeaux to New-York, with ſaltpetre, ſulphur, ſalt, canvaſs, and coarſe linen. St. Patrick, Frederick Lyhme, maſter, Joſ. Carſun, owner, from St. Euſtatia to Philadelphia, with dry goods. The cargo taken out. Royal Scob, Eber Merrick, maſter, S. C. Merrick, owner, from Cape Nichola Mole to Rhode Iſland, with molaſſes. Thomas, Robert Standley, maſter, T. Stephens, owner, from Beverly to Baltimore, with ſugar and rum. Reſource, Raymond Lafon, maſter, Vidau and co. owners, from Philadelphia to Port au Prince, with flour and lumber.

By the Orpheus *and* King's Fiſher.

Adrian, from Philadelphia to France, with tobacco, flour, bread, and ſtaves.

By the Perſeus.

Viper, B. Wornwell, maſter, Martin and co. owners, from Boſton, on a cruize; fitted as a privateer. Betſey, Alexander Wilſon maſter, john Pain, owner, from Boſton to Bourdeaux, with dye-wood, pot-aſh, &c. Roby, William Howland, maſter, J. Howland and co. owners, from Dartmouth, New-England, to Surinam, with fiſh, horſes, ſpermaceti candles, and ſtaves. Adventure, Job Prince, maſter, Prince and co. owners, from Boſton to Hiſpaniola, with fiſh, ſtaves, ſpermaceti candles and pine plank. Hawke, S. Williams, maſter,

Ruſſel and co. owners, from Hiſpaniola to Rhode-Iſland. Harlequin, Nathaniel Phillips, maſter, Jer. Ingram, owner, from Hiſpaniola to Rhode-Iſland, both with molaſſes, had been taken by the William and Mary tranſport. Seahorſe, Thomas Coffin maſter, Marſhall and co. owners, from Turk's Iſland to Martha's vineyard, with ſalt.

By the Solebay.

Hope, from Egg Harbour to Surinam, with flour, tar, pitch and lumber. Nancy, from North Carolina to St. Euſtatia; Peggy, from ditto to ditto; both with tobacco, tar, turpentine and lumber.

By the Cerberus, *and ſhips ſtationed with her, off* Block Iſland.

Lyon, M. Barlow, belonging to the Congreſs, bound from Cape Francois to Dartmouth, with powder, arms, ſalt and molaſſes. Polly, Robert Croſby, maſter, —— Franklin owner, from New-York to Damaraza, with flour and lumber. Leviathan, B. Woodcock maſter, B. Woodcock, owner, from Milford to St. Croix, with lumber. Betſey, J. Arthur maſter, —— Shaw, owner, from New London to Cape Francois, with flour, fiſh, &c. Annabella, William Cook maſter, William Cook, owner, from Amboy to St. Croix, with flour, fiſh, and lumber. Elizabeth, Joſeph Lippet, maſter, John Brown owner, from St. Euſtatia to Providence, with powder, arms and linen. Hawke, John Clarkſon, maſter, from Newberry to Surinam, with flour, beef, pork and fiſh. William, John Tucker, maſter, from St. Euſtatia to Salem, with wine, rum and linen. Catherine, the people took the boat and left her. Mercury, George Bunker, maſter, from the coaſt of Brazil to Nantucket, with oil. Mermaid, Joſ. Coffin, maſter, from ditto to ditto, with oil, put on board the Mercury. Betſey and Polly, —— Hilton, maſter, —— Hilton, owner, from New-York to Sandykook, with proviſions for Governor

vernor Tryon. Run on fhore, a fhip from the Weft-Indies, prize to the Andrew Doria privateer. Felicité, —— Gouace, mafter, from Rhode-Ifland to Cape Francois, with fifh, flour, and fpermaceti candles. Succefs, E. Hathaway, mafter, J. Otis, owner, from Cape Francois to Dartmouth, with molaffes. Jofeph, Elias Coffin, mafter, from Cape Francois to Nantucket, with molaffes. Batchelor, —— Shaw, owner, (the people took the boat, and left the veffel off Montock point) with molaffes. Succefs, J. Coffin mafter, Jackfon and co. owners, from Cape Nicola to New-berry, with molaffes. Betfey Vaffal, E. Bacon, mafter, Solomon Davis, owner, from Cape Francois to Barn-ftable, with molaffes.

By the Unicorn.

Katy, Edward Dillingham, mafter, N. Green, owner, from Rhode-Ifland to Curacoa, with flour, tobacco, and fpermaceti candles. Dolphin, John Campbel, mafter, J. Campbel, owner, from Falmouth to Hifpaniola, with fifh and lumber. Lively, John Parfons, mafter, Jackfon and co. owners, from Philadelphia to Newberry, with flour and iron.

By the Camilla.

Independence, John Gill, mafter, from Bofton, on a cruize, armed with 6 carriage-guns and 8 fwivels. Admiral Montague, John Hay, mafter, from Hifpaniola to Rhode-Ifland, with molaffes and coffee. Chance, Thomas Bell, mafter, to Georgia, with flour and rum. Polly, William Thomfon, mafter, to Surinam, in ballaft.

By the Raven.

Friendfhip, William Townfhend, mafter, M. Kelfall, owner, from Georgia to foreign Weft-India iflands, with rice. Hope, Jean Louis, mafter, — Moncreau, owner, from Philadelphia to Charles Town, with flour and lumber. *By the* Roebuck, *and fhips under Captain* Hammond's *orders.*

Maria, —— Stockholm, mafter,

Dennis, owner, from St. Euftatia to Egg Harbour, with bale goods and powder. Grace, ——, from Philadelphia to Baltimore, in ballaft. A fmall floop, nobody on board, in ballaft, deftroyed. A pilot boat, ditto, loft. Polly, William Bowen, mafter, William Bowen, owner, from Philadelphia to North Carolina, with nine pound fhot, iron, and groceries. A fmall floop, in ballaft. Dove, T. Atkins, mafter, M. Dence, owner, from Plymouth in New-England to Philadelphia, in ballaft, deftroyed off Cape Hinlopen. Dolphin, T. Burgefs, mafter, J. Simpfon, owner, from Dartmouth in New-England to Philadelphia, in ballaft, deftroyed off Cape Hinlopen. Betfey, C. Wey, mafter, W. Shepherd, owner, from Chinkateaque to Philadelphia, with oats and tobacco, deftroyed off Cape Hinlopen. Sally, Seymour Hood, mafter, E. Batchelor, owner, from Ocnifock, North-Carolina, to Philadelphia, with tar and turpentine, deftroyed off Cape Hinlopen. Chance, Thomas Rofe, mafter, Meff. Curfon, of Philadelphia, owners, from Philadelphia to Cork, with flax feed and ftaves. Dove, nobody on board her, floop cut out off Egg harbour, in ballaft. Cazia, —— from Cape Francois to Philadelphia, with molaffes and coffee, Dolphin, William Knox, mafter, — Pringle, owner, from Philadelphia to St. Euftatia, with hams and bread. Ranger, nobody on board her, from St. Euftatia to Philadelphia, with bale goods and arms. Little John, J. Darrel, mafter, Davenport and co. owners, from Bermuda to Philadelphia, with falt and limes. Dolphin, T. Woodhoufe, mafter, Henry Cowper, owner, from Philadelphia to St. Croix, with flour, bread and flaves. Sufannah, P. Rimington, mafter, P. Rimington owner, from Rhode-Ifland to South-Carolina, with cyder and chocolate.

By the Liverpool.

St. Barbara, D. R. Gomales, mafter,

O

ter, belonging to the Spanish Assiento. from the Havannah to Dominica, with 2500 dollars.

By the Fowey.

Sally, Ar. Crawford, master, Z. Allen, owner, from Providence to Hispaniola, with lumber and flour. Polly, W. Gardner, master, N. Shaw, jun. owner, from Saltatude to Philadelphia, with salt.

By the Otter.

A schooner, nobody on board her. A sloop, ditto. Jenny, ditto, and and run on shore. Philadelphia Packet, nobody on board her, from the river Elke to Baltimore, with different goods. Vulcan, S. French, master, R. Ewers, owner, from the river Elke to Patuxent, with stone and iron. Nancy, J. Robinson, master, E. Carr, owner, from the Eastern shore to the river Elke, with tobacco and feathers. Nancy, L. Gallcheugh master, J. Taylor, owner, from Neabscoe to Baltimore, with Indian corn.

By the Roebuck.

Pigeon, —— Smith, master, —— Simpson, owner, from Philadelphia to Charles-Town, with bread and flour. Success, J. Burrows, master, Mercer and co. owners, from Hispaniola to Philadelphia, with molasses and rum.

By the Perseus.

Connecticut, Benjamin Jones, master, S. White owner, from Boston to Baltimore, with 14 casks of sugar. Le Joli Cœur, B. Ervan, master, from St. Domingo to Marseilles, with rum, sugar and coffee.

By the Camilla.

Le Fonbenne, W. De Gallet, master, W. Gallet, owner, from Cape Francois to Miquelon, with wine, molasses, &c.

By the Falcon.

Sloop, nobody found on board, with oil.

By the Roebuck.

Two Friends, J. Vickery, master, Mead and co. owners, from Cape Francois to Philadelphia, with powder arms, molasses, &c. Adventure,

W. Pile, master, Townsend and co. owners, from St. Croix to Philadelphia, with salt and dry goods, removed the cargo on board. Delight, William Church, master, Cartwright and co. owners, from Boston to Philadelphia, with sugar, wine and rum. New-York, J. Walker, master, T. Pennington, owner, from Curacoa to New-York, with salt.

By the Pearl.

Lexington, W. Hallock, master, belonging to the Congress, from Cape Francois to Philadelphia, with powder and dry goods. Read, J. Bennet, master, J. Bennett and co. owners, from St. Eustatia to Wilmington, with salt and dry goods. Betsey, J. Hayman, master, J. Hayman and co. owners, from St. Martin's to Baltimore, with salt. Schooner, no person found on board, with sugar, &c.

By the Falcon.

Kitty, S. Nichols, master, D. Beveridge, owner, from Cape Francois to Philadelphia, with molasses, rum, and dry goods.

By the Galatea.

Dolphin, John Parker, master, from Philadelphia to Bermuda, with flour and Indian corn. William, Joseph Bunker, master, from Bourdeaux to Rhode-Island, with gunpowder and small arms. Sword Fish, S. Kingsley, master, from Cape Nicola to Halifax, with rum and molasses. Hearts of Oak, F. Howell, master, from Cape Francois to Philadelphia, with rum, linens, turpentine and dry goods.

By the Nautilus.

New-York Packet, E. Pringle, master, E. Pringle, owner, from Philadelphia to St. Croix, with flour.

By the Lively.

Mary, J. Morgan, master, J. Wilson, owner, from Bourdeaux to Philadelphia, with small arms, wine, oil, &c.

By the Merlin.

Joseph, B. Hewes, master, Smith and

and co. owners, from Cadiz to North Carolina, with wine, salt, and Jesuits bark.

By the Scorpion.

Morning Star, James Club, master, Lisle and co. owners, from Philadelphia to the West-Indies, with flour, bread and onions.

By the Viper.

May Flower, S. Crofman, master, S. Crofman owner, from Piscataqua, on a fishing voyage. Dover, A. Fumald, master, A. Fumald, owner, from Piscataqua, on a fishing voyage, with fish. Endeavour, J. Batson, master, J. Batson, owner, from Piscataqua, on a fishing voyage, with fish. Two Brothers, J. Bowden, master, J. Bowden, owner, from Piscataqua, on a fishing voyage, with fish. —— No person found on board, with fire-wood. —— Ditto, with empty casks. Polly, on a fishing voyage, with fish. Louisa, J. Colston, master, St. New, owner, from Macchias to Tortola, with lumber, shingles, &c. Unity, J. Lord, master, — Jones, owner, from Macchias to Newberry, with lumber, shingles, &c. Nancy, R. Adams, belonging to the Congress, from Macchias to Newbery, with lumber, shingles, &c.

By the Milford. Tryon. Sloop. Retrieve. William. George. Globe.

By the Juno. Joseph.

By the Liverpool. Victory.

By the Hope. General Gates. Hope.

By the Lizard. Putnam.

By the Albany. Providence.

By the Province Armed Schooner. Friendship.

By the Liverpool.

Sally, John Williams, master, J. and A. Stuart, owners, from Hamburgh to New-York, with linens, canvas, &c.

By the Phœnix, Roebuck, *and* Tartar, *in the North River.*

Independence, Crane, armed for war.

RECAPTURES.

By the Orpheus *and* Daphne.

Britannia, B. T. Hughes, master, B. T. Hughes, owner, from Jamaica, to Liverpool, ballast, and one ton of ivory.

By the Perseus.

Layton, —— Johnson, master, a transport. A transport, part of the Flora's convoy, retaken, the soldiers had been taken out at New-York, taken again. Peggy, William Cook, master, Morfield and son, owners, from Virginia to St. Augustine, with rum, molasses and linen.

By the Cerberus, *and ships stationed with her off* Block Island.

Agnes, William Mather, master, John Mather, owner, from Antigua to London, with sugar. Jenny, William M'Neilly master, from Barbadoes to Belfast, with rum. Carron, J. Montgomery, master, from the Bay of Honduras to Cork, with mahogany and logwood.

By the Unicorn.

Thomas and William, James Smith, master, John Watkinson, owner, from New-York to Cork, a transport in ballast. Hetty, Charles Ross, master, C. Ross and co. owners, from Gaspee to Barbadoes, with fish and oil.

By the Camilla.

George, James Cordray, master, to Maryland, ballast, and some old guns.

By the Otter.

—— Mr. Nason, owner, from Barbadoes to the fleet at Virginia, with 320 puncheons of rum.

By the Galatea.

Favourite, —— Davis, master, from Antigua to Liverpool, with sugar. Alice. Dispatch, N. Sergent, master, from the Grenades to Cork, in ballast.

By the Milford.

John. Diana. Halifax. Lively. Venus. Carolina.

By the Juno. Dinah.

By the Liverpool. Either. Bee.

By the Hope. Betsey. Lord Stanley.

By the Lizard. Hope.

Total number of captures - 140
Recaptures - - - 26

HOWE.

An

An authentic Lift of Britifh Ships and Veffels taken by American Privateers, fince the Publication of the laft Lift. See Page 312 of laft Volume.

Ships Names and Mafters.	From and to	
A large brig,	for Guernfey,	worth 7000l.
A large veffel,	from Africa,	with 350 flaves.
Amelia, M'Neal,	Africa to St. Kitt's.	
Ann, Kennedy,	Jamaica to New-York.	
Apollo, Smith,	Africa to the Iflands,	with flaves.
Athol, Wadie,	Quebec to Dominica.	
Aurora, Pocock,	Briftol to Tortola.	
Barbary.		tranfp. retaken.
Batchelor, Dyfart,	Grenada to London,	retaken.
Betfey, Martindale.		
Betfey, Cully,	London to Plymouth,	with provifions.
		retaken.
Britannia, Wickers,	Exeter to Newfoundland.	
Brothers, Morgan,	Nevis to Dublin.	
Cæfar, O'Brien,	Loo to the Weft-Indies.	
Chalkely, Fuze,	Honduras to Briftol.	
Champion,	for Briftol,	with fugar, &c.
Champion, Fellows,	Rocley Bay to Courland Bay.	
Chopthank frigate, Lenox,	Penfacola to Grenada.	
Clementia, Rogers,	Challeur Bay to Weft-Indies.	
Countefs of Eglington.		
Cromwell, Bruce,	Jamaica to Briftol.	
Duke of Leinfter, North,	Dublin to Jamaica.	
Elizabeth, Hope,	London to Leeward Iflands,	retaken.
Elizabeth, Edwards.		
Elizabeth, Snowball,	Corke to New-York.	
Elizabeth, Gornes,	Liverpoole to Antigua.	
Falmouth, Bogg,	Glafgow to Quebec.	
Fame, Bound,	—— to London.	
Fanny, Bell,	Whitehaven to New-York.	
Fanny, Steel,	Belfaft to the Leeward Iflands.	
Fleece, Fortune,	Lifbon to Dingle.	
Fly, Harvey,	Alicant to Newfoundland.	
Friends Adventure, Cummings,	London to St. Kitt's.	
Friendfhip, Wellicot,	London to Newfoundland.	
Gerney, Doyle,	Corke to Bourdeaux,	burnt.
Goodwill, Richardfon,	Whitehaven to Grenada.	
Hannah, Wilkinfon,	—— to London.	
Hawke, Price,	from Africa,	with 450 flaves.
Helen, Fofter,	Lifbon to Southampton.	
Hope, Prince,	Newfoundland to Weft-Indies.	
Hope.		
Induftry,	Africa to Weft-Indies.	
Ifabell, Hewfon,	Orkneys to Oporto.	
John, Walker,	Ireland to Antigua.	
Jofeph, Kelly,	belonging to Poole,	reftored by the French.
Jofeph, Kelly,	Meffina to Hamburg, reftored by the French.	
Lark, Smith.		
Little John,	Miffifippi to Leeward Iflands, retaken.	

Liverly,

Ships Names and Masters.	From and to	
Lively, Ray,		
Liverpoole, Baird,	Gibraltar to London.	
Lonsdale, Gragson,	Whitehaven to Quebec.	
Lord North, Martin,	for Corke.	
Lovely Lass, Polluck,	Glasgow to Jamaica.	
Marq. of Rockingham, Pocock,		retaken.
Maria, Walsh,	Leeward Isl. to St. Augustine.	
Maria,	St. Vincent's,	with rum.
Mary, Jones,	St. Kitt's to Liverpool.	
Mary, Maundell,	Poole to Cadiz,	retaken.
Mary, Harrison,	Africa to the Grenades,	with slaves.
Mary Ann, Gilchrist,	Honduras to London.	
Mary and Joseph, Walsh,	Newfoundland to a market.	
Mercury, Seaton,	London to Nevis,	retaken.
Mercury, Griffiths,	Africa to the West-Indies.	
Mercury, Hindley,	Glasgow to Jamaica.	
Minerva, Winning,	Honduras to London.	
Newman, Smith,	Newfoundland to West-Indies,	
Noble, Addir,	Corke to New-York.	
Northam, Westcot,	London to Rhode-Island.	
Penelope, Booth,	Liverpool to Africa.	
Penguin,	Newfoundland to a market,	retaken.
Percy, Bell,	London to New-York.	transport.
Percy, Rogerson,	Corke to New-York.	
Perseverance, Lauder,	Halifax to West-Indies.	
Peter and John, M'Cartney,	Oporto to London.	
Phenix, Davis,	Tinmouth to the Islands.	
Polly, Denny,	West-Indies to Liverpool,	transport.
Poplar, Cleveland.		
Prince George, Ponsonby,	Whitehaven to Jamaica.	
Prince of Orange, Storer,	Harwich to Helvoetsluys,	a packet-boat, restored, but not the mail.
Providence, Penlerick,	Corke to Lisbon,	retaken.
Providence and Mary, Glynn,	Corke to New-York.	
Resolution, Burnet,	Newfoundland to West-Indies, sunk.	
Royal Charlotte, Fenwick,	London to Antigua.	
Sally, Burrows.		
Sally, Hartwell,	London to Tobago.	
Sally, Jones,	London to Quebec,	transp. worth 12,000l.
Sally, Hawson,	Jamaica to Liverpool.	
St. George,	Africa to West-Indies,	with 450 slaves.
Sukey, Whitewood,	Newfoundland to West-Indies, retaken.	
Surprize,	London to New-York,	transp. retaken.
Swallow, Hindman,	Africa to Grenada,	with slaves.
Swift, Clark,	London to West-Indies.	
Teresa, Rackwell,	Exon to Newfoundland,	with soldiers.
Thomas,	Liverpool to Barbadoes.	retaken.
Thomas, Read,	Liverpool to Dominica,	
Thomas, Nicholson,	Jamaica to Bristol.	
Three Friends, Chivers.		
Three Sisters, Spicers,	St. Ubes to Corke.	

Trepessey,

Ships Names and Masters.	From and to	
Trepeffey, Combes,	London to Newfoundland.	
Trial, Brown.		
Triton, Fairbank.		
Triton, Hookey,	Newfoundland to a market.	
True Love, Moulton,	Grenada to London.	
True Briton, Babb,	London to Newfoundland.	
Twite, Lanning,	Corke to St. Croix,	with fix others, names not yet come to hand.
Two Brothers, Salter,	Corke to West-Indies.	
Two Betties, Batfon,	Gibraltar to London,	retaken.
Two transports going to New-York with German chaffeurs.		
Venus, Peacock,	Jamaica to London,	afterwards loft.
Venus, Brown,	London to Newfoundland.	
Venus, Sharp,	Whitehaven to Grenada.	
Unice, Anderson,	London to Nevis.	
Weatherhall, Cox,	London to West-Indies.	
William and Mary, Howe,	Oporto to Holland.	
——— ———,	Halifax to New-York,	worth 2030l. fterl.
William, ftorefbip.		

Total 119; of which 17 retaken and reftored.

Mr. HUTCHINSON'S LETTERS continued [*].

Mr. Hutchinfon's Letters, lately publifhed, muft convince every unprejudiced perfon, that the Colonies had fufficient reafon to be alarmed at the proceedings of the Britifh Parliament, and that it was high time for them to be jealous for their liberties: and yet in his letter to the Honourable John Hely Hutchinfon of Palmerfton, near Dublin, of February 14, 1772, he concludes,

" IS not an unwarrantable defire of independence at the bottom of all the difcontent both in Ireland and in the Colonies? In a government which has any thing popular in its form or conftitution, the remote parts will grow more diffatisfied with any unfavourable diftinctions in proportion as thofe parts increafe and become confiderable. A doubt or fcruple in the fupreme authority of its abfolute uncontroulable power, and a relaxation in confequence will encreafe the diffatisfaction, and endanger a dif-

union or total feparation. Six words of Mr. Pitt, when he faid, " I am glad America has refifted," gave a deeper wound to the peace of America, than all the tumultuous, riotons, and rebellious acts which preceded. For thirty years before that, I had been concerned in government, and never knew the authority of an act of Parliament called in queftion. All, which had any refpect to us, we printed immediately and made a part of our code. Since that time, the members of the affembly grumble and mutter, and afk by what authority acts of Parliament are mixed with our provincial laws? And the Houfe of Reprefentatives have repeatedly refolved, that it is unconftitutional for the people to be governed by laws made by any power in which they are not reprefented. The Miniftry have been conftantly advifed of thefe irregularities to fay the leaft of them, and they have fometimes come before Parliament, but no cenfure has yet been paffed. A late explicit denial of the authority of the Commiffioners

[*] Thefe Letters, together with the remarks, are literally taken from the Bofton Gazette. For the former Letters, fee the indexes to the four preceding volumes.

of

of the cuftoms is now before the King, and I have not thought myfelf at liberty to fuffer the Affembly which denied that authority, and confequently the authority of Parliament, to eftablifh the Board, to fit again until I know his Majefty's pleafure upon it.

" It is not likely that the American Colonies will remain a part of the dominions of Great-Britain another century; but whilft they do remain, I cannot conceive of any line to be drawn. The fupreme abfolute legiflative power muft remain entire, to be exercifed over the Colonies, fo far as is neceffary, for the maintenance of its own authority, and the general weal of the whole Empire, and no farther. In the 27th and 29th books of Livy, we find an inftance of refractorinefs in the Roman Colonies, not altogether unlike to that of the Britifh Colonies, and of the fpirited and fuccefsful doings of the Roman Senate upon that cccafion. I have often wondered, that in all the publications in the late controverfy, no notice has been taken of fo pertinent a piece of hiftory."

[Good ufage on the part of the Britifh Adminiftration, might, perhaps, have retained the Colonies another century; but that they have loft them fo early, the inhabitants of Great-Britain may thank Mr. Hutchinfon, the Miniftry, and themfelves—in patiently' fuffering Government to purfue its bloody plan of dragooning us, into the abfurd opinion of Parliament's having a right to make laws binding us in all cafes whatfoever.]

Bofton, 18th January, 1765.
" Rev. Sir, [Unknown.]
" I was aftonifhed, after reading Robinfon's * Hiftory of Scotland, and having fettled Mary Stewart's character in my own mind, as one of the moft infamous in hiftory, to find him drawing her with fcarce a blemifh."

Bofton, September, 1765.
" Dear Sir, [Mr. Jackfon.]
" I am fure you will defire to hear from America by every opportunity. After the date of my laft letter, I covered a news-paper to you which gave an account of the riots at Rhode-Ifland. In Connecticut they refrain hitherto from violence upon the lives or eftates of obnoxious perfons; but hang and burn in effigy, and do it, as they do, every thing elfe, with *great formality.* We have no advices of any thing further at New-York than their obliging the Stamp Officer to declare his refignation. To the northward of Philadelphia every where, and to the fouthward of it in fome places, the people are abfolutely without the ufe of reafon; but in fome places more raving than in others."

" Dear Sir, *26th March,* 1763.
" The Governor never has been fo grofsly abufed as in a late libel in Edes and Gill. I never gave any *offence* to the Grand Jury with more zeal than I did this; and I told them almoft in plain words, that they might depend upon being d —— if they did not find a bill; but they were willing to run the rifque of it. This has convinced me as much as any thing which has happened among us, that the laws have loft all their force."

Bofton, 20th Sept. 1769.
" My dear Sir, [SirF. Bernard.]
" I have had fome hints given me, as if fome part of my correfpondence in England might prove of differvice to me. You are fenfible that in America we have no intereft at all in parties in England; for my part, I know but little of the connexions. I have no views from correfponding in England, but to promote meafures for reftoring America to its former ftate. Whilft you was here there was no room to confider me as a public perfon. Whilft I am in command I fhall never mention any thing relative to my adminiftration but to the Miniftry, or to you as ftill Governor

* So fpelt in the letter book through miftake.

in

in Chief to be communicated to them. But if you think it necessary, *I will forbear all correspondence*, except to the Minitry."

Boston, 4th October, 1769.

" Dear Sir, [*Mr. Jackson.*]

" In one of your letters you acquaint me, that you have a set or two of my books left, and was uncertain to whom they were designed. I suppose they must be of the last eight which Mr. Rogers sent you. I find they were intended for Lord North, Sir Edward Hawke, Sir Jeffry Amherst, Lord Ad. Gordon, Col. Barre, Mr. Whately, Mr. Huske, and Mr. Jackson: they were all persons to whom I have been known at one time or other. Their connexions in England we in America know nothing of, and have no other interest in your party disputes than to wish that the powers which be may continue, and that those may be one uniform meafure of administration, so far as respects us until government is restored among us. *However, if at any time I should mention any person whose connexions may be such as that exception may be taken to me shewing any mark of respect, I beg your friendship so far as to suspend it.*

" I will desire Mr. Harrison's care of another box of books, intended as an appendix to the first volume of my history, being a collection of original papers relative to it.

" To the eight I have named, please to add Duke of Grafton, Marquis of Rockingham, Lord Dartmouth, Lord Shelburne, Lord Mansfield, Lord Camden, Lord Clare, Gen. Conway, Mr. G. Grenville, Mr. York, Mr. De Grey, Mr. Touchett, Mr. Cooper, and Dr. Franklin, to each of whom I sent the history, and add besides, Lord Hillsborough, Gov. Pownall, Mr. John Pownall, Gen. Mackay."

Boston, 20th Oct. 1769.

" Dear Sir, [*Mr. Jackson.*]

" I shall send by Capt. Hyde the ten books which were not ready for Harrison. To give you as little trouble as possible, I have desired Mr. William Palmer to receive them, and send them to your house; and *if in the list of persons named, you think it more proper for me to omit any*, I shall esteem it as an additional favour, *if you will, dispose of the book intended for them to such other persons as may be without exception*; for I have not mentioned to any one my having intended a book to them. I am ashamed of giving you this trouble, and do not sign to repeat it."

Boston, 27th Oct. 1769.

" Dear Sir, [*Mr. Manduit.*]

" I take it for granted the last duties will be taken off. Assurances have been given to all the Colonies, and several of them have behaved decently; but we shall not think you were induced to it by any other motive than the fears you were under from our combinations, unless you convince us you are able to dissolve them."

Boston, 19th May, 1770.

" My dear Sir, [Sir F. Bernard.]

" I am told by one of the ministers of the town, that Dr. Cooper has a letter from a Member of Parliament, and he told me from whom, a gentleman who you know used to correspond with him, in which it is said, that shipping back 10,000l. worth of goods will do more than storing 100,000l. and it is said that this letter has done much to turn the scale when it was upon a balance, whether the goods should go back or not. Good God! can the people of America ever return to a due subordination to Great-Britain whilst Members of the House of Commons there publicly or privately justify them in their revolt. I could not help mentioning this to you; but must intreat you to let no person know that this intelligence comes from me. I am, with the greatest respect, &c."

Boston, 26th Jun , 1770.

" My Lord, [Lord Hillsborough.]

" I have never asked the advice of

the

the Council in form, upon the expediency of applying for more ships or troops, because I was sure they would advise me to apply for the removal of those which remain; and yet without their advice, considering the restrictions I am under by the charter, I did not think I could answer expressly applying for them, especially as I knew that Governor Bernard's caution in not applying without advice of Council had been approved of by his Majesty. I however constantly advised General Gage and Commodore Hood of every transaction of any moment, that I might enable them to judge what ships and troops are necessary to be kept here."

[This is the proper place for the following anecdote. General Gage having received from Gov. Hutchinson a letter containing such a representation of the state of affairs at Boston, as might probably have induced him to have ordered more troops this way, he shewed it to a certain officer then with him at New-York, who upon leaving his house informed a friend of the writers, what a representation Hutchinson had given, what was the evident design of it, and then calling the Governor for his craft by some hard name, added, I have prevented the General's being caught in the snare, or words to that purpose; and have advised him to write back in answer to it, that he was ordered by the Ministry to send what troops the Governor might require, and that whenever the requisition was made he would forward them.

Had Gen. Gage sent the troops without a requisition, and any evil had arose, he must have borne the blame, and the Governor would have excused himself because of his not having required them. Had any evil arose for want of the troops, Hutchinson would have pleaded in his excuse, that he had sent the General a fair representation of affairs; and in the preceding letter to Lord Hillsborough, he assigns a reason why he did not make a direct application.]

A NEW CATECHISM.

[*From the* BOSTON GAZETTE.]

Question. What is WAR?

Answer. It is the curse of mankind, the mother of pestilence and famine, and the undistinguishing destroyer of the human species.

Q. How is WAR divided?

A. Into offensive and defensive.

Q. What is the chief end of offensive war?

A. Sometimes it is to regain by the sword what had been unjustly taken away from the rightful possessor: and sometimes, it is to gratify the ambition of a tyrannic Prince, by subjecting to his arbitrary will a people whom God had created free, and giving their hard earned possessions to support him in luxury, idleness, and sensuality.

Q. Are there any instances of such?

A. Yes, many, both in ancient and modern times: history is filled with the wicked lives and miserable deaths of tyrants. The of , whose history is not yet compleated, is . He carried an *offensive war* into the East-Indies,

He is now carrying an *offensive war* into ; aiming at the absolute disposal of that extensive country and all its numerous inhabitants;

Q. What is a *defensive war?*

A. It is the taking up arms to resist tyrannic power, and bravely suffering present hardships and encountering present dangers, to secure lasting liberty, property and life, to future generations.

Q. Is a *defensive war* justifiable in a religious view?

A. The foundation of war is laid in the wickedness of mankind. Were

P   all

all men virtuous, juſt and good, there would be no contention, or cauſe of contention amongſt them; but as the caſe is far otherwiſe, war is become *abſolute'y neceſſary*; as many other things are, which are only the product of the weakneſſes or iniquity of men. Even the invaluable bleſſings of a conſtitutional government would be unneceſſary incumbrances, were there no open violence or ſecret treachery to be guarded againſt. God has given to men wit to contrive, power to execute, and freedom of will to direct his conduct. It cannot be therefore, but that ſome will abuſe theſe great privileges, and exert theſe powers to the ruin of others. The oppreſſed will then have no way to ſcreen themſelves from injury, but by exerting the ſame powers in their defence; and it is their duty ſo to do. If it were otherwiſe, a few miſcreants would tyranniſe over the reſt of mankind, and make them abject ſlaves of oppreſſion and penſioners of their will. Thus it is that a *juſt defenſive war* is not only neceſſary, but an indiſpenſible duty, and conſiſtent with religion accommodated, as it muſt be, to our preſent ſtate of imperfect ſtate of exiſtence.

Q. Is it upon theſe principles that the people of America are now reſiſting the arms of England, and oppoſing force to force?

A. Strictly ſo. The Americans had nothing in view but to live peaceably and dutifully in a conſtitutional ſubmiſſion to Great-Britain. They ſuffered patiently for a long time, many unjuſt encroachments of power; being loth to offend their rulers by a too ſtrict attention to every right, till at laſt the deſigns of the Court became too evident to be miſtaken; and they were puſhed to the diſtreſſing neceſſity of chooſing one of two great evils, viz. either to enliſt themſelves and their unborn poſterity the avowed, unconditional ſlaves of a corrupt and wicked adminiſtration, or to brave

the horrors of war in a noble conteſt for liberty and life. They have wiſely determined on the latter; and, after ſolemnly appealing to God and the world for the juſtice of their cauſe, they are proſecuting the war under the favour of Heaven, and with the moſt promiſing hopes of ſucceſs. Supported by the equity of their principles, they have ſurmounted the greateſt difficulties, and exhibited inſtances of bravery not exceeded by the heroes of antiquity—and may Heaven proſper their virtuous undertaking!

Q. But it has often been ſaid that America is in a ſtate of rebellion :—tell me therefore what is *rebellion?*

A. It is when a great number of people, headed by one or more factious leaders, aim at depoſing their lawful Prince, without any juſt cauſe of complaint againſt him, in order to place another on his throne.

Q. Is this the caſe of America?

A. By no means. They have repeatedly declared, with all ſincerity, that they were ever ready to ſupport with their lives and fortunes the preſent King of Great Britain, on the throne of his anceſtors, and only requeſted in return, the enjoyment of thoſe ineſtimable rights which the Britiſh conſtitution confirms to all its ſubjects; and, without which, the boaſted freedom of that conſtitution is but a ſolemn mockery, and an empty name.

Q. To whom has the Britiſh Court committed the conduct of the preſent war?

A. To Lord and General Howe.

Q. Who are thoſe gentlemen?

A. They are the brothers of a Colonel Howe, who fought bravely by the ſide of the Americans in a former war, and fell in battle; who, by his amiable character, endeared himſelf to thoſe people ſo much, that they lamented his fate with unfeigned ſorrow, and erected at their own expence, fence, a coftly monument to his memory. But thefe gentlemen, with unrelenting hearts and facriligeous hands, have defiled their brother's monument with the blood of thofe whofe affection reared it to his honour, and plunged their murderous weapons in bofoms glowing with love and efteem for their mother's fon.

Q. What progrefs have the Engliſh made in fubduing America?

A. Very little. They got poffeffeffion of Bofton by the tacit confent of its inhabitants, but could not hold it long. They were but tenants at will, ftrictly fpeaking, for their landlords turned them out without any warning, and deftrained upon certain military ftores, &c. although they had fat there at a rent of above 500l. per day.

Q. What did they next?

A. They took Staten-Ifland, where there was nothing to oppofe them, and a part of Long-Ifland, by an exertion of almoft their whole force againft a fmall part of the American army, and then ferried themfelves over to the city of NEW-YORK, from thence they crept into the Jerfeys, and taking advantage of a critical period, when the American army was difbanded by the terms of their enliftment, and before a new force could be raifed, they heroically advanced to the banks of the Delaware, well knowing, there was nothing to oppofe their progrefs. On the banks of the Delaware they fet them down, fettled, as they thought, for the winter feafon; and plundered the adjacent country. In the mean time, thefe extraordinary conductors of the war publiſhed a wonderful and gracious proclamation; offering fuch protection as they could afford, to all thofe who would accept of it, upon the eafy terms of abfolute unconditional fubmiffion. But the Americans, whofe refources are endlefs, foon found a fpirited militia to fup-

ply the place of the difbanded troops, until a new army could be raifed. This militia croffed the Delaware in a fnow ftorm at midnight, and after marching ten miles, very uncivilly attacked the enemy before they had breakfafted, and drove them from the banks of the Delaware in the utmoft confternation, and with the lofs of twelve hundred men. The American army then re-croffed the Delaware, and fuffered the enemy to return to their poft, where they anxioufly waited the arrival of an expected reinforcement. But the American General, by a ftroke of policy above their comprehenfion, once more paffed the river with his army, and kindled a few fires in the night near their ftation; and whilft they were foolifhly gazing at the beauty of the curling flames, he marched on, attacked, routed, and entirely defeated the faid reinforcements. The fhattered remains of General Howe's army, are now clofe confined in Brunfwick; where they are doing penance on falt meat and mufty bifcuit.

Q. Where is injuftice, obftinacy and folly united in one character in an eminent degree?

A. In ‚ He is unjuft, becaufe he endeavours to gain by force what is denied him by the laws of the

he is obftinate, becaufe he refufes to hear the humble petitions and modeft reafonings of an oppreffed people, and will not yield to the forcible convictions of truth, and his folly is confpicuous in quarrelling with a people who loved and honoured him, who were the chief fupporters of his and dignity, and a never failing fource of encreafing wealth.

Q. Who is the fnuggeft man in the world?

A. Lord Howe.

Q. Who is the weakeft?

P 2   A. General

A. General Howe.

Q. Who is the greateſt liar upon earth?

A. Hugh Gaine, of New-York, Printer.

Q. Who is the moſt *ungrateful* man in the world?

A. Governor S——.

Q. Why do you call him *Governor?*

A. Becauſe when Lord and General Howe thought they had conquered the Jerſeys, they appointed him Lieutenant-Governor of that State. S—— aſſumed that title over one-tenth part of the ſaid State, and continued his uſurpation for ſix weeks, five days, thirty-ſix minutes, ten ſeconds, and thirty hundred parts of a ſecond, and then was depoſed.

Q. Why is he called ungrateful?

A. Becauſe he has joined the enemies of his country, and enliſted men to fight againſt his neighbours, his friends and his kinsfolk; becauſe he has endeavoured to transfer the ſoil that gave him bread from the rightful poſſeſſors to a foreign hand; becauſe he is doing all he can to defraud the fruit of his body of their juſt inheritance, and becauſe, to gain preſent eaſe and tranſitory honours, he would faſten the chains of ſlavery on three millions of people and their offspring for ever.

Q. Who is the beſt man living?

A. *His Excellency General Waſhington;* to whom the title of *Excellency* is applied with the greateſt propriety. He has left a peaceful habitation and an affluent fortune to encounter all the dangers and hardſhips of war; nobly ſtepping forth in defence of truth, juſtice and his country. In private life he wins the heart and wears the love of all who are ſo happy as to live within the ſphere of his action. In his public character, he commands univerſal reſpect and admiration: conſcious that the principles on which he acts are indeed founded in virtue, he ſteadily and coolly purſues thoſe principles, with a mind neither depreſſed by diſappointments, nor elated by ſucceſs, he gives full exerciſe to that diſcretion and wiſdom which he ſo eminently poſſeſſes. He retreats like a General, and attacks like a Hero. If there are ſpots in his character, they are like the ſpots in the Sun; only diſcernable by the magnifying powers of a teleſcope. Had he lived in the days of idolatry, he had been worſhipped as a God. One age cannot do juſtice to his merit; but the united voices of a grateful poſterity ſhall pay a chearful tribute of undiſſembled praiſe to the great aſſertor of their country's freedom.

BOSTON, MARCH 13, 1777.

At a Meeting of the Freeholders and other Inhabitants of this Town, at Faneuil-Hall, on Monday laſt, the Honourable THOMAS CUSHING, *was choſen Moderator, and the following Town-Officers for the Year enſuing, viz*

Town-Clerk. William Cooper, Eſq.

Selectmen. John Scolley, Eſq. Samuel Auſtin, Eſq. Oliver Wendell, Eſq. John Pitts, Eſq. Capt. Guſtavus Fellows, Mr. Harbottle Dorr, Deacon Thomas Greenough, Jonathan Williams, Eſq. and Capt. Thomas Preſton.

Town-Treaſurer. David Jefferies, Eſq.

Overſeers of the Poor. William Phillips, Eſq. Iſaac Smith, Eſq. Mr. Jonathan Maſon, Capt. Samuel Partridge, Mr. Samuel Whitwell, Mr. John White, Edward Proctor, Eſq. William Powell, Eſq. Mr. John Sweetſer, Mr. Edward Payne, Samuel Barrat, Eſq. and Mr. Samuel Hewes.

Committee of Correſpondence, Inſpection and Safety. Capt. William Mackay, Nathaniel Barber, Eſq. Perez Morton, Eſq. Benjamin Hitchborn, Eſq. Mr. William Davis, Mr. Herman Brimmer, Mr. Ebenezer Dorr, Francis Shaw, Eſq. Capt. John

John Simkins, Mr. Moses Grant, Mr. Benjamin Burt, Dr. Peter Roberts, Mr. Henry Bass, Capt. Amasa Davis, and John Winthrop, Esq.

Fire Wards. John Scolley, Esq. William Cooper, Esq. Edward Proctor, Esq. Caleb Davis, Esq. Capt. John Pulling, Thomas Crafts, Esq. Ebenezer Hancock, Esq. Paul Revere, Esq. Mr. Thomas Tileston, Major Andrew Symmes, John Winthrop, Esq. Capt. Joseph Webb, Capt. Gustavus Fellows, Mr. John Dillard, Mr. Thomas Trieston, Francis Shaw, Esq.

Committee for purchasing grain. Deacon Timothy Newell, Mr. John Sweetser, Jonathan Williams, Esq.

Surveyors of wheat. Mr. John White, and Mr. John Lucas.

Surveyor of hemp. Benjamin Austin, Esq.

Assessors. Deacon Benjamin Church, Mr. Jonathan Brown, Mr. Samuel Davis, Giles Harris, Esq. Mr. William Lowder, Mr. George B. Gedney, and Mr. Thomas Foster.

Informer of Deer. Mr. Adam Colson.

Assay Masters. Mr. Thomas Green, and Mr. John Skinner.

Fence Viewers. Messieurs William Crafts, John Lambert, jun. Nathaniel Wales, Stephen Wales, and Nathan Hancock.

Surveyors of Boards. Messieurs Clement Collins, Abraham Howard, Andrew Symmes, Joseph Butler, Benjamin Page, Joseph Ford, John Rogers, Thomas Urann, Edward Ranger, John Bulfinch, jun. Joseph Ballard, James Blake, John Lambert, jun. Nathan Hancock, Ebenezer Freeland, John Champney, Henry Blaisdel. [*Boston Gazette.*]

———

To the FREEMEN of Massachusetts.
[*From the same.*]
Gentlemen,

The man who calmly sits down to frame a Civil Constitution and Form of Government, so as to be permanent and produce the greatest possible good to the people, will not only study natural law, the origin of civil society and history, but will also well weigh and consider the general bent and inclination, the dislike and aversion of the people, to this or that: he will adopt that Form of Government that is *practicable*, though it may not be in theory the *best possible*. Whether the following Essay is, in general, well adapted to the end, the reader may judge. The author, or rather compiler (for some articles are mere copies) has not vanity enough to suppose it perfect, or to think himself capable of making it so; but had his capacity been more extensive, he has not had leisure for the purpose; and this Essay is only the hasty production of a few hours, now and then at distant periods of time: but being conscious of the most upright intentions, and confiding in the reader's candour, he ventures it to the public eye; and hopes it may stir up others of greater abilities and more leisure, to exhibit a more perfect system. If what is here offered to the public, with a single view to their good, should in any way be remarked upon, the writer, who wishes to be unnoticed, will not think himself obliged to make any reply, he having neither ability, leisure or inclination for controversy; and as several of his particular friends, for whom he has the most sincere esteem, and who are by nature and education vastly his superiors, are of very different sentiments, he would choose, on that account, as well as for other reasons, to be unknown. The reader may, perhaps, more readily form a judgment upon the following Essay, by having a sketch of some of the leading principles, upon which it was built, laid before him. It is therein supposed—That by nature all men are equally FREE—That no one has a right to govern others without their consent—That all civil government is derived from the people, and

is

is rightfully formed by them, and them only, for their own good——That in small societies, *the people at large*, and they only, have not only a right to, but may conveniently meet together *personally*, and make laws for their own government—That in larger societies it may be very inconvenient, perhaps impossible, for the people at large, to assemble together *personally*, and legislate for themselves; in which case, a vicarious body of the people, chosen and deputed by them to legislate in their place and stead, are the *only proper Legislators*—That this Representative Body ought to be frequently chosen; each one to be resident in the particular district choosing, and all to be as equally chosen from among the whole, as the circumstances of the whole, and its several parts, will admit—That this deputed Body in their vicarious capacity, ought to be distinct from their executive and judicial parts of government; and the executive and judicial officers excluded, as far as may be, from acting in the Legislative Department—That every parish, town, corporation, and county, may choose their respective officers; and that any of those officers, being otherwise legally qualified, may be eligible to any of the legislative, executive or judicial parts of government, but only to *one place*, in some one of these departments, at one and the same time.——It also supposes, That the rights and liberties of the people are easier and better preserved in small societies than in large ones; and that when Common-wealths, or States, are so large, that the most distant parts of the government are too remote from the seat thereof, to obtain easy and frequent intelligence of its various movements, they are then in great danger from aspiring and designing men, of having the free exercise of their rights and liberties abridged, and of degenerating into monarchical government, which

generally ends in despotism and the most abject slavery, from which they seldom emerge without deluging the world with blood; and therefore it is better that large States should be divided, than small ones joined.—— And it also supposes, That Representation and Taxation are so intimately connected with each other, that the latter cannot, with any propriety, be imposed, without supposing the Subject taxed, to have had a right of choice in the election of the Representative body taxing; and therefore, that all persons taxable, ought to be admitted to vote for Deputies to the GENERAL COURT, and to be considered as FREEMEN.—That representation, especially as it respects the number of DELEGATES, ought to be grounded principally upon *freehold*, rather than upon *personal estate*; because the former *will* remain always within the State, although it may change Masters; but the latter *may* be removed to Britain, or to some other State.—Also, That a rotation in office, when practicable, will be the means of training up many persons to the knowledge of public business, more than without such rotation; and will make them competent to many offices in the State, without which, they would be wholly incompetent. And also, That all men have a right to worship GOD, according to the dictates of their own consciences.

These are some of the leading principles upon which the Writer has built the following Essay, without much regard to their order; if the public should attend to the subject matter, the arrangement of the parts may easily be adjusted by some abler politicians, who, by altering, diminishing, or adding (as the subject may require) may form such a perfect System of Government, as will effect a greater degree of happiness, and more steady and permanent, than this Colony has ever yet enjoyed. To this end, he is of opinion, that there

is

is greater propriety in having Government formed by a GENERAL CONVENTION, chosen for that special purpose, than by a GENERAL COURT, who may possibly think themselves bound to adhere, in some degree, to old forms and customs; and probably will not feel themselves quite so *free* in this momentous affair, as such a CONVENTION. That you may be directed by the ALL-WISE GOVERNOR OF THE UNIVERSE, into the wisest and best measures for obtaining this great and invaluable blessing, is the sincere and ardent prayer of, Gentlemen,

Your real Friend and Servant,
PHILELEUTHERUS.

Boston, February 27, 1777.

In the year of our Lord, 1777.

An ACT of the General-Convention of the Common-Wealth, or State of Massachusetts, declaring the same to be a free STATE, and independent of Great-Britain, and establishing a new Constitution and Form of Civil Government; which General-Convention was elected by the whole People for this sole purpose, and was held at, &c.

Whereas Great-Britain has, by a long series of arbitrary and despotic measures, enforced by large fleets and armies, intolerably oppressed this Colony, laying waste by fire and sword whole towns and villages, killing many of its inhabitants, captivating others, and ruining thousands—has treated their petitions, their repeated petitions, with neglect and contempt —has deprived them of the free exercise of their chartered rights, and destroyed their ancient Constitution and Form of Civil Government—has (by act of Parliament) put them out of protection of the crown of Great-Britain, and declared them to be in a state of rebellion: all which, and much more, will particularly appear, by the following *declaration of the United States of America*, to be the distressed case of the American Colonies, viz.

[*Here read the Declaration of Independency, of July* 4, 1776, *published by order of the Congress.*]

The ancient Government of this Colony being thus *totally dissolved*, and the people driven into a state of nature, it becomes their indispensible duty, and what self-preservation requires, to declare themselves independent of Great Britain, and to establish such a Constitution and Form of Civil Government, as to them appears best calculated to promote their greatest possible happiness: and being fully persuaded, that the most plain and simple and good Form of Government is, the less expensive it will prove, the easier any people will comprehend it, the sooner will they discover any attempts to alter or destroy it, and consequently, the more vigorous that Government will be, and the more likely to continue permanent; especially when to this is added, the consideration of as equal, full, free and frequent choice of a Representative Body of the whole People, for the sole purpose of Legislation, as their circumstances will admit: in which case, in such a Government, ambitious men will have but little ground to hope for building up their own particular greatness, upon their country's ruin.

And whereas it is absolutely necessary for the welfare and safety of the inhabitants of this Common-Wealth, that a just and permanent Constitution and Form of Civil Government should be established as soon as possible, derived from and founded on the authority of the People only, in whom is the origin of all governmental power, and who have at all times a right, by common consent (whenever the great end of Government, the general good is not obtained) to alter and change their Constitution and Form of Government, in such a manner as may best

best promote the safety and happiness of the whole.

We, therefore, the Representatives of the Freemen of Massachusetts, in General Convention met, for the express purpose of framing such a Constitution and Form of Government; gratefully acknowledging the goodness of the Supreme Governor of all, in permitting us peaceably, and by common consent, deliberately to form such rules, as we shall judge best adapted for governing this Common-Wealth in justice and righteousness; and being fully convinced that it is our indispensible duty to establish, to the utmost of our power, such original principles of Civil Government, as will best promote the general happiness of the people, do, by virtue of the authority vested in us by our Constituents, declare, enact and establish the following Constitution and Form of Civil Government for this Common-Wealth, to be and remain in full force therein, from and after the second Wednesday in   , and for ever thereafter to remain unaltered, except in such articles as shall hereafter, on new circumstances arising, or on experience, be found to require alteration, and which shall, by the like authority of the people, convened for that sole purpose, be altered for the more effectual obtaining and securing *the great end and design of all good Government*, The Good of the People.

Be it therefore declared and enacted by the General Convention of this Common-Wealth, assembled for the sole purpose of declaring and enacting Independency, and establishing a new Constitution and Form of Civil Government, and by the authority of the same, it hereby is declared and enacted, as in the following general articles, viz.

1. That this Colony is, and of right ought to be, and for ever hereafter shall, by the favour of all-gracious Heaven, be a free State,

and absolutely independent of the Crown and Government of Great-Britain; and shall be stiled, The Common-Wealth, or State of Massachusetts.

2. That the present system of Colony Laws shall be and remain in full force, for and during   year, from and after the date hereof, and no longer, unless sooner repealed, in the whole, or in part, or otherwise ordered by this State.

3. That all Letters-Patent, Charter and Charters, called Letters-Patent, or Royal Charters, and said to have been heretofore *granted* to this Province, or any part thereof, that now is part of this Common-Wealth, by any Royal, or other authority of Great-Britain, shall, from and after   year next after the date hereof, be absolutely null and void, and shall have no further effect, so far only as it may respect private property and governmental powers, but not otherwise: and in the mean time, a good and sufficient law or laws shall be made and enacted for the quieting possessions.

4. That all and every law, and part of a law, heretofore made, and which any way respected the Constitution of the General Court of this Common-Wealth, that now is, or any part of said Court, or any of its powers, members or privileges, or which had any respect to the election of any of its members, shall, and hereby are repealed, and rendered absolutely null and void, and shall have no further effect from and after the said second Wednesday of

5. That this declaration of the general, fundamental and essential rights of the people of this Common-Wealth, shall, for ever hereafter, be considered as the general fundamental of the said new Constitution and Form of Government; and every order, law and statute, that shall hereafter be made by the General Court of this Common-Wealth, shall conform to the

the spirit, and plain and simple meaning and intention of these general fundamentals; and all and every order, law and statute, that may hereafter happen to be made, and shall be found contrary thereto, shall be null and void, and have no effect, and be immediately repealed: and no alteration in these general fundamentals shall hereafter be made, but only by the *immediate* consent of the good people of this Common-Wealth, *at large*, or their *Deputies chosen for that special purpose.*

6. That all men are born equally free and independent, and their Maker has left them free liberty to set up such governments as best please themselves. " That magistrates were set up for the good of nations, not nations for the honour or glory of magistrates." " That the right and power of magistrates in every country, was that which the laws of that country made it to be." And, " That usurpation gives no right to govern."

7. That all men have a natural and unalienable right to worship GOD according to the dictates of their own consciences, and to enjoy a full and free liberty therein; provided that they, under pretence of religion, do not attempt to subvert the Constitution and Form of Government of this State: for the more full establishment whereof, and that this Constitution and Form of Government may, at all times hereafter, be fully known and understood, the minister, or public teacher of religion in each and every town and parish within this Government, shall, in the afternoon of every first Lord's-day in   , for ever hereafter, openly and distinctly read this Constitution and Form of Government, together with its preamble and introduction, to the congregation of such town or parish. And every public teacher of religion shall, before he officiates as such, subscribe this Constitution and Form of Government, or be debarred the benefit

of any contract or agreement he may have made with the people of any town or parish, respecting his salary as a teacher of religion.

8. That no person shall, under any pretence whatever, maliciously and advisedly, by acting, doing, writing, printing, preaching, praying or speaking; act, do, write, print, preach, utter, express, or declare any words, sentences, act or thing, to stir up the good people of this State to hatred or dislike of the Constitution and Form of Government thereof. But this shall not be construed to restrain the freedom of debates in the General Court, or in the Council of Safety. Neither shall it be construed so as to restrain the FREEDOM OF THE PRESS, or of speaking, writing or publishing any matter or thing not manifestly injurious to the public, or to any private person.

9. That the freedom of speech, and debates or proceedings of the General Court or Assembly, and also of the Council of Safety, shall not be called in question in any other Court.

10. That no act, imposition, order, law, or statute, shall hereafter be made, or imposed upon the good people of this Common-Wealth, but only such as shall be made or imposed by their own personal consent, or by the consent of their Representatives in General Court assembled.

11. That the supreme Legislative Power shall be vested in a House of Representatives, which shall be annually chosen for the sole purpose of Legislation; which Representatives, when formed into a General Court, shall sit and act, as one single Body, upon the legislative business of this State, once, or oftener, every year; and shall not continue, or exist as a Court, for any longer time than one year.

12. That there shall be annually, at least, a general and free election of Deputies, or Representatives, for Members to serve in said General Court,

Q

Court, to be chosen by the whole people, as is herein-after expressed; which election shall be absolutely FREE.

13. That there shall be annually, one General Court or Assembly of the Representative Body of the whole people, for the sole purpose of Legislation; and which shall be called the GENERAL COURT, or ASSEMBLY of the COMMON-WEALTH, or STATE of MASSACHUSETTS; to be convened, held and kept at Boston, (or such other place as said General Court may at any time order) upon every second Wednesday in , yearly, and every year for ever hereafter, with power of adjournment; which said General Court, shall consist of such freeholders as shall be annually elected, or deputed by the several towns within this State, agreeable to the following rule of choice, viz. each and every town having *sixty*, and not so many as *ninety* resident freeholders, each of whom having an estate of freehold in land, within the town wherein he resides, to the value of Four Pounds per year, at the least, *may*, if they see fit, by a major vote of its inhabitants (as is hereinafter described) elect or depute, by written ballot, in such manner as has been the usual custom in this Colony, one of their resident freeholders, such as aforesaid, and no more than one, to sit and act from time to time, in said General Court, until the second Wednesday in next following such election, and no longer: and each and every town in this State, having *ninety* such freeholders as aforesaid, and not more than Two Hundred, *shall* annually elect and depute one, and no more than one such resident freeholder as aforesaid, in like manner, and for like purposes as aforesaid: and each and every town *may*, if they see fit, for each and every 150 such freeholders as aforesaid, above the said first 200, elect

or depute one other such freeholder as aforesaid, in like manner, and for like purpose as aforesaid: and each and every town, not having so many as 90 freeholders, such as aforesaid, *may*, if they see fit, join in election with any other adjoining town within this State; and the number of such freeholders in such towns so joining in election, shall regulate, in manner as aforesaid, the number of Deputies which they *shall*, or *may* send (as the case may be) to the General Court: and each and every plantation, whose bounds, when ascertained, *shall* contain, within the same, so many as 90 such freeholders as aforesaid, *shall* then be incorporated into towns, and each and every such town *shall* elect and depute, in the manner and for the purpose aforesaid, *one* such freeholder as aforesaid, to represent them in the General Court. Provided nevertheless, That in every town, every male resident of 21 years of age and upwards, whether a freeholder or not, but being liable to taxation, and belonging to such town, shall have a *right* to vote in the choice of Representatives, in common with the freeholders and other members of such town; but the number of Deputies shall not be thereby increased, but shall be wholly regulated by the number of freeholders, in manner as aforesaid. Which said General Court, when first assembled, *shall* by written ballot, on the first or second day of their sitting, choose one of their Members to preside as Speaker, to regulate the debates of said Court, and to sign in their behalf, all the orders, laws and statutes, and all other public papers that are to be authenticated: and they shall in like manner, choose some suitable person to serve as Secretary, and another to serve as Clerk to said Court. The said Court shall then, by written ballot, choose of their Members to serve as a Council of Safety, which Council shall be the Supreme Executive

tive power of this State, and shall be assistants to the General Court by their advice only; which said Council shall continue until the second Wednesday in   , next following such choice, and no longer. And all vacancies in the General Court, occasioned by the choice of said Council, or otherwise, *may* be filled up, by the respective towns whose Representatives have been thus removed, by new elections of Deputies, in manner as aforesaid. And all vacancies, at any time, or by any means happening in the said Council, *shall* be filled up by said General Court, in manner as aforesaid. And the said Council shall immediately choose, on the first or second day of their sitting, by written ballot, one of their Members for their President, to regulate their debates, and to authenticate all such papers as they may have occasion to give authenticity to: and they shall, in like manner, choose some other fit person for their Secretary. Which General Court, when constituted as aforesaid, and the Council of Safety and assistants chosen as aforesaid, shall have full power to ordain, make and establish all, and all manner of good and wholesome orders, laws and statutes, for the well ordering and governing the good people of this Common-Wealth, and for the support, comfort and defence of the same. And the said General Court shall, from time to time, and at all times, constitute and appoint all such Executive and Judicial Courts, and all such civil and military officers (excepting parish, town, corporation and county officers) as to them may appear to be of public utility. And all orders, laws, and statutes, ordained, made and enacted by the said General Court, shall be signed by their Speaker for the time being, in their behalf, and published, before obedience thereto be exacted from the people. And every person who shall be elected to serve as a Member

in the said General Court, shall, before he fit or act therein, subscribe the following declaration, which shall be kept among the records of said Court, viz.

STATE OF MASSACHUSETTS.
[Place and date.]

We the subscribers, do solemnly and severally declare, That we will do every thing in our power to promote the prosperity and happiness of this Common-Wealth; and will oppose and prevent, to the utmost of our abilities, every attempt to hurt or destroy the same; and this we will do, by a firm and steady adherence to, and support of, that Constitution and Form of Civil Government, adopted and established in this State, in the year 1777.   A. B.
                                C. D. &c.

14. That the Legislative, Executive and Judiciary Departments, shall be as separate and distinct as possible; so that neither shall, without necessity, exercise the powers belonging to the other; nor shall any person exercise the powers of more than one of them at the same time; except that the Justices of the County Courts shall be eligible to either the General Court, or Council of Safety; and excepting also, That the Council of Safety, shall sit as Justices in cases of impeachment, and in cases of appeal from the Probate Court.

15. That the General Court, and the Council of Safety, shall each choose their own officers, and settle their own orders and rules of proceeding in their respective Bodies.

16. That all Governmental matters, whether orders, laws or statutes, shall originate in, and be compleated by the General Assembly; but when they have read any Bill, or other matter twice, they shall then send it to the Council of Safety for their advice, who shall also read it twice, and then return it to the General Court, with their proposed amendments and remarks, if any, in writing; and the

General Court shall then read it a third time, and finally pass upon it. This will give the advantage of examination by two separate and distinct bodies; and will be still more safe, if the several readings are upon as many several days; which may, and ought to be done, excepting in extraordinary cases.

17. That every town shall pay their own Delegates for their *attendance* at the General Court, but their *travel* shall be paid by the Government. And every Delegate shall constantly attend said Court, or assign reasonable excuse, to the satisfaction of the Court, or abide such judgment as they may order.

18. That the General Court shall appoint all civil and military officers (excepting as is excepted in the 13th article) the Justices and Judges, during good behaviour; and other officers, during pleasure: which officers, and all other persons, shall be impeachable for misbehaviour in office, or otherwise, by the said Court, before and by the Council of Safety; excepting only, that if a Member of said Council shall be impeached by the General Court, the trial shall be before said Court, by their own Members.

19. That all cases, whether capital, criminal, or between man and man, or respecting any property, whether real, personal or mixed, shall be tried by a jury of *fifteen* freeholders of the vicinity, who shall be judges of law as well as fact, any *twelve* of whom, agreeing in their judgment, it shall be declared to be their verdict. Excepting cases of impeachment, mentioned in the last foregoing article. And excepting appeals from the Probate Court; and also cases where some express law refers the same to be tried otherwise, in some inferior Court; in which last cases also, any party aggrieved, may appeal to some superior Court, and have trial by a jury. And any party

may challenge jurors, in manner as has been customary in this Colony heretofore.

20. That excessive bail shall not be required, nor excessive fines imposed, nor cruel and unusual punishments inflicted, in any cases.

21. That all grants, and promises of fines and forfeitures, of particular persons before conviction, are and shall be illegal and void.

22. That levying money, by any person or persons, under pretence of its being for the use of the State, without grant of the General Court, is and shall be illegal.

23. That the raising or keeping a standing army within the Commonwealth, without consent of the General Assembly, is and shall be illegal.

24. That it is, and for ever shall be, the right of any of the good people of this Government, either individually or in collective bodies, to petition the General Court.

25. That the laws of this Commonwealth shall, in all cases, be construed in favour of life and liberty; so that neither shall be taken away or abridged, but from necessity and the best evidence.

26. That all due encouragement shall be given to schools and colleges, for promoting arts, agriculture, manufactures, and all useful science and good learning. This will support the State, and preserve liberty.

27. That no person shall be taken, or imprisoned, but by the written law of this Common-Wealth: or by natural law, as grounded upon right reason; and these shall be the only laws by which the good people thereof shall be judged and governed: and this, without any reference being had to the laws or customs of Great-Britain, or any other State.

28. That no person shall be put out of, or dispossessed of his freehold, lands, livelihood, liberties or free customs, unless it may be by the lawful judgment, or verdict of his equals,

men

men of his own condition, by due course of law.—Nor shall any person be deprived of the benefit of the law, unless he be outlawed by the law of the land.

29. That no person shall be exiled, or banished out of the Common-Wealth, unless he be exiled or banished according to the law thereof. Nor shall any person be, in any sort or degree destroyed, unless it be by the verdict of his equals, according to the law of the State. And justice, right or law, shall not be sold, nor denied, nor deferred, or delayed to any person, but shall be equally and impartially administered to all.

30. That the Delegates, or Representatives for this Common-Wealth, to the Continental Congress of the United States of America, shall be chosen annually, at least, by written ballot, by the General Court.

31. That there shall always be a well regulated militia kept up within this Government, well provided with arms and accoutrements.

32. That there shall be annually, at least, a County Convention in each county, for transacting county business, and for the choice of all county officers: and all parish and town-officers shall be chosen by their respective parishes and towns.

33. That a rotation of officers, in many offices from the lowest to the highest, is very desireable, when the circumstances of the Common-Wealth will admit thereof; as thereby many more persons will obtain a competent knowledge of public business, than without such rotation.

34. That all Courts of Justice and Equity shall be open to all persons: and the debates in the General Assembly shall, when the safety of the State permits, be open to all.

35. That a power of reprieving persons under sentence of death, shall be lodged in the Supreme Executive, in such manner as the Legislative may order; but no power of granting pardon shall be in any but the Legislative.

36. That the person of a debtor, where there is not a strong presumption of fraud, shall not be continued in prison, after delivering up all his estate, for the use of his creditors.

37. That appeals shall be had, when required, from the Probate Courts, to the Council of Safety, before and by whom trial shall be had.

38. That the people have a right to hold themselves, their houses, papers and possessions, free from search or seizure; and therefore warrants, without oaths or affirmations first made, affording sufficient foundation for them, and whereby any officer or messenger may be commanded or required to search suspected places, or to seize any person or persons, or any property, not particularly described, are contrary to common right and liberty, and are illegal.

39. That as all men have a right, by common consent, when in society, to form such kind of government for themselves, as they please, so they have a right, by common consent, to alter the same, and adopt such other mode of Government as may best please themselves: and they have also a like right, as a body, or individually, to emigrate to any other State, or to vacant countries, if they please, or to divide their Government into two, or more, distinct States, as may best suit themselves.

40. That the Council of Safety shall sit at the same time and place with the General Assembly; and at all such other times as the General Court may order, and may do business with a major part of their whole number, which shall be considered as a Council for all purposes.

41. That sumptuary laws against luxury, plays, &c. and extravagant expences in dress, diet, and the like, suited to the circumstances of the Common-Wealth, and the spirit of the Constitution, shall be established with

with all convenient fpeed.—Luxury, as Baron Montefquieu fays, is neceffary in Monarchies, but ruinous to Democracies.

42. That, in order to preferve Liberty,—to diftribute the burdens and favours attending the feveral offices, in the feveral parts of this Government—and to prevent, as far as poffible, any one man—family—or their connections, from engroffing many places of honour and profit; no man holding any office or place, in the fervice of the UNITED STATES, by commiffion or otherwife, fhall, at the fame time, hold any office or place in the fervice of this State, whether by commiffion or otherwife. Nor fhall any one man hold more than one office or place in the fervice of this State, at one and the fame time, whether by commiffion or otherwife, excepting only through neceffity, or as is herein before in this Act excepted.

43. And that a new fyftem of laws for this Common-Wealth grounded upon the general principles of this Act, fhall be made and eftablifhed within   year from and after the date hereof; and that a Committee for that purpofe, fhall be appointed by the next General Court (as early in their fitting as may be) to continue one year, if found neceffary, from and after their appointment, and no longer; whofe duty it fhall be, to prepare and report to the General Court, from time to time, all fuch laws for the faid new fyftem, as to them may appear beft adapted to promote the lafting peace and happinefs of this COMMON-WEALTH.

PHILADELPHIA.

An Act for making the Continental Bills of Credit, and the Bills of Credit emitted by Refolves of the late Affemblies, legal tender, and for other purpofes therein mentioned.

Whereas it is highly neceffary that the bills of credit emitted and made current by the Continental Congrefs, and the bills of credit emitted and made current by the late Affemblies of Pennfylvania, ought to be made legal tender in all payments, and to be alike taken by every perfon in this State, in the difcharge of debts, and for the purchafing the neceffaries of life, and materials of defence; and it is evidently neceffary that the counterfeiting of the faid bills of credit made current by public authority, fhould be prevented.

Be it therefore enacted, and it is hereby enacted by the Reprefentatives of the Freemen of the Commonwealth of Pennfylvania, in General Affembly met, and by the authority of the fame, That, from and after the fixth day of February next, the bills of credit emitted and made current by the Continental Congrefs fhall pafs current in this State, and be received in payments and difcharge of all manner of debts, rents, fum and fums of money whatfoever, due, or hereafter to become due, payable, or accruing upon or by reafon of any mortgage, bond, fpecialty, bills, note, book account, promife, affumption, or any other contract whatfoever, according to the fum which the faid bills refpectively entitles the bearer thereof to receive, each dollar therein expreffed to be taken and efteemed at the rate or value of Seven Shillings and Sixpence, and of equal value in the payment of fuch debts with a Spanifh milled filver dollar, weighing feventeen penny-weights and fix grains, any claufe, provifo or device, in any bond, note, or other inftrument of writing, to the contrary thereof in any wife notwithftanding.

And be it further enacted by the authority aforefaid, That the bills of credit emitted and made current by the refolves of the late Affemblies of Pennfylvania, and the bills of credit emitted on loan by an act of Affembly of the 26th of February, 1773, fhall, in like manner be, and is hereby declared to be a legal tender, and fhall be be taken and received in payment and discharge of all manner of debts whatsoever as aforesaid, according to the sums specified in said bills; and if any person or persons, from and after the said sixth day of February next, shall refuse to receive any of the said bills of credit when properly tendered in payment of any debt or demand whatsoever, provided the whole of such debt or demand be tendered, he, she, or they so refusing, shall be for ever barred from suing for, or recovering the same in any court of this State, and if any suit or suits shall be commenced for such debt or demand, after tender and refusal as aforesaid, the defendant may plead payment, and give this act and the special matter in evidence.

Provided nevertheless, and be it further enacted by the authority aforesaid, That after any such tender as aforesaid being made, if the creditor to whom such money is tendered, shall within four days next thereafter, make demand of the said debt before two creditable witnesses, it shall and may be lawful for such creditor to sue for and recover such debt; but shall recover no interest on said debt after such tender, or costs on his action.

And be it further enacted by the authority aforesaid, That where any such tender shall, as aforesaid, be made, in order to pay any debt or demand of money due and payable of any kind whatsoever and refused, and not demanded within four days after such tender as aforesaid, then, and in such case, the said debt or money due or payable, mentioned in any mortgage, bond, specialty, bill, or note, book account, or any other debt whatsoever, is hereby declared to be forfeited, the one third part thereof to the debtor, and the other two third parts to this State: and every such debtor who shall make such tender is hereby directed and required to pay the two third parts of every debt so forfeited, into the hands of the Treasurer of the County, appointed to receive the State tax, (whose receipt shall be a sufficient discharge to such debtor for the monies by this act forfeited) retaining the one third part in his, her, or their own hands.

And whereas divers persons in this State (taking advantage of the necessitous) when they put money on loan, or in other contracts, have bargained with, and bound the borrower or purchaser, to pay the debt in sterling money of Great-Britain, according as the exchange might be between the cities of Philadelphia and London. And as the intercourse between the said cities is now so far obstructed that no such exchange can be ascertained, and except some rule is settled by law, the debtor cannot pay his debt, though he be so disposed and has in his possession bills of credit for that purpose, for remedy whereof, Be it enacted, That where any person stands bound to pay any debt in sterling money aforesaid, according to the exchange as aforesaid, such creditor shall receive Continental bills of credit, or bills of credit of this State in payment and discharge of any such debt, at the rate of One Hundred and Fifty-five Pounds Pennsylvania currency, for One Hundred Pounds sterling, if tendered as aforesaid, and on refusal thereof shall be deemed and taken to be within the meaning of this Act, in cases of refusal of the bills of credit in tender as aforesaid.

And whereas bonds or other writings may have been given for money, to be paid in Half Johannes's weighing nine penny-weights, or as much in bills of credit as will purchase the same. It is hereby declared and enacted, That eight Continental dollars in bills of credit aforesaid, or Three Pounds in bills of credit of this State afore-mentioned, or of any of the bills of credit of Pennsylvania, shall be deemed and taken to be
worth

worth one gold Portugal Half Johannes, weighing as aforesaid, and in the same proportion for all other gold coin.—And all persons whomsoever, refusing to take and receive such bills of credit in payment and discharge of such debt, and redemption of such bond, or other writing as aforesaid, shall be deemed and taken to be within the meaning of this Act, and shall forfeit such debt, and be in all things dealt with as in this Act is directed in cases of refusal on tender.

And be it further enacted by the authority aforesaid, That every such debtor who shall make tender of any debt or demand as aforesaid, which shall be refused and not again demanded as aforesaid, is hereby directed and required, under the penalty of Two Shillings out of the Pound of such debt, within the space of six days, to inform one or more of the Commissioners of the county for the time being, elected or appointed to levy the public taxes, of the sum so tendered, and to whom, and the time when, and the names of the witnesses present at such tender—and the Commissioners of every county shall keep fair books of entries of all such sums of money forfeited by this Act, and lay the same before the Committees of Assembly, appointed to settle the public accounts for the time being, and in case any debtor neglect to give such information, then any other person who gives the first information shall be entitled to the aforesaid Two Shillings in the Pound, and Three-pence per mile travelling charges for his trouble.

And be it further enacted by the authority aforesaid, That the Commissioners for the time being, of every county of this State, are hereby authorized and required to ask, demand, sue for and recover, two third parts of every debt or sum of money, so as aforesaid tendered and refused, and not afterwards demanded as aforesaid, which action or actions, suit or suits, shall be brought or commenced and prosecuted by the said Commissioners, by name and stile of the Commissioners of such county; and the process shall be the same, and as effectual in law, as if such mortgage, bond, specialty or note, was given to such Commissioners *bona fide*, for a valuable consideration, or as if such other debt was contracted with said Commissioner or Commissioners; and after receiving the same, some one of them shall enter satisfaction in the records of such mortgage, as is required by an Act of General Assembly of Pennsylvania, in cases of discharging mortgages.

And if any person or persons, having so as aforesaid tendered any money in payment of any debt, and the same being refused and sued for and recovered by the Commissioners, or paid without any suit commenced, it shall and may be lawful for every such debtor to ask for, and demand his, her, or their mortgage, bond, specialty, bill or note, or a discharge of his, her, or their debt, if it shall be of any other kind or denomination; every such demand being made before two creditable witnesses, and such creditor refusing or neglecting to deliver up to such debtor such writing, or give such discharge as aforesaid, it shall and may be lawful for every such debtor to sue for and recover, of and from such creditor, his or her heirs, executors or administrators, a sum of money equal to the sum for which such mortgage, bond, specialty, bill or note was given, together with interest and costs of suit.

And be it further enacted by the authority aforesaid, That in every case where any title, deed or deeds have been, or shall be, lodged or deposited in the hands of any person or persons, to whom any mortgage has been, or may be made, and the money mentioned herein forfeited, as by this Act declared, and such mortgager,

gager, his or her heirs, executors, or administrators, or the owner of the lands and tenements mentioned in such deeds, shall demand the same and be refused, it shall and may be lawful for such mortgager, his or her heirs, executors, or administrators, or such owner of the lands, to sue for and recover of such mortgagee, his or her heirs, executors, administrators or assigns, a sum of money not exceeding double the value of the lands and tenements mentioned in such deeds ; and if any such person or persons as aforesaid, being sued, shall, at any time before the determination of such suit, deliver up to the plaintiff, or lodge such deed or deeds, whole and undefaced in the Prothonotary's office of the court wherein such action shall be, and pay the costs of suit, and a sum as the court shall order, not exceeding Twenty Pounds, to the prosecutor for his trouble, in that case such action shall cease.

And in all cases where tender shall be made as aforesaid, and the person to whom such tender may be made, shall afterwards assign, transfer, or set over any mortgage, bond, specialty, bill or note, every such person shall be, and is hereby declared to be, guilty of fraud, and forfeit and pay to the person to whom such assignment as aforesaid may be made, or to his or her heirs, executors or administrators, a sum equal to double the sum mentioned in such mortgage, bond, specialty, bill or note, so assigned or transferred, to be recovered by an action of debt in any court of record in this State.

And be it further enacted by the authority aforesaid, That if any person whatsoever shall, after the sixth day of February next aforesaid, refuse to take and receive any of the bills of credit aforesaid, in payment for any live stock, necessary of life, commo-

dity, manufacture, article or goods whatsoever, which he or she shall sell, or expose to sale, and offer the same for a less price, or smaller sum of money, to be paid in gold or silver, or in any one sort of the bills of credit, or other current money passing in payment of debts in this State, than in the bills of credit emitted by the Continental Congress, or in bills of credit emitted by Resolves of Assembly aforesaid, every such person shall forfeit to the use of the State a sum of money equal to, or as much as, the sum he or she had refused to take for the commodity so sold, or that he or she had asked for or rated such stock, necessary of life, commodity, manufacture, article or goods at ; and on proof thereof being made by two creditable witnesses before any one of the Justices of the peace of the county, such Justice shall (if such sum of money as aforesaid forfeited shall not exceed Five Pounds) issue his precept in the name of the State, in the nature of a summons, or capias, as the case may be, and prosecute and recover the sum so proved to be forfeited, in the manner prescribed and directed by the laws for recovery of debts not exceeding Five Pounds, together with cost of suit—And if any such forfeiture, as aforesaid, shall exceed Five Pounds, the Justice before whom any such proof shall be made, shall, within six weeks, send an account in writing to the Commissioners of the county, or one of them, containing the names of the witnesses proving the same, and the person who, and the sum that he or she has so forfeited— And the said Commissioners are hereby enjoined and required, as soon as may be, to sue for and recover such sum or sums of money in the same manner, and when so recovered, pay the same to the same persons as is in this act directed in

R   cases

cafes of refufal on tender. And when any Juftice fhall recover any money, fo as aforefaid forfeited, he fhall pay the fame to the Treafurer aforefaid, who fhall give his receipt for the fame. And every Juftice of the Peace in this State fhall, once in each year, fend an account to the faid Commiffioners of the fum or fums of money he fhall have recovered, fo as aforefaid forfeited, which the Commiffioners fhall make fair entries of, and report the fame to the Committee of Affembly aforefaid for the time being. And the fees or allowance to the faid Commiffioners, for the fervices and duties by this act required, fhall be the fame as they have a right by law to take and receive in other cafes. And if any of the faid Commiffioners fhall refufe or neglect to do and perform his or their duty, by this Act directed and required, fuch Commiffioners refpectively fhall be fined in a fum of money not exceeding Ten Pounds, by the next Court of Quarter Seffions, and another or others appointed in his or their ftead, by the faid Court. Every fuch fine to be for the ufe of the State, and be recovered as fines are directed to be recovered, by the Act for raifing county rates and levies.

And be it further enacted by the authority aforefaid, That if any perfon or perfons, from and after the publication of this Act, fhall counterfeit or alter any of the aforefaid bills of credit, with defign to increafe the value of fuch bill, by this Act made a legal tender, or any of the bills of credit made current by any of the Affemblies, Conventions, or Congreffes of any of the United States of North-America, or utter any of faid Bills of Credit, fo counterfeited or altered, knowing them to be fuch, and being duly convicted thereof, fhall fuffer all the pains and penalties, fines and forfeitures which by the late laws of Pennfylvania could or might have been inflicted

on any perfon or perfons fo offending.

(Signed) JOHN JACOBS, Speaker.

Baltimore, February 11. Colonel Rohl, the Heffian Commandant, who lately died of the wounds he received at Trenton, declared upon his death-bed, that although the Englifh had endeavoured to throw all the odium of the many rapes, murders, &c. upon his countrymen, yet, that to his certain knowledge, they were chiefly, if not altogether, perpetrated by their own officers and foldiers.

The General Affembly of the State of Connecticut met at Norwich in February, 1777, and fixed the following prices, *viz.* Labour in the Summer not to exceed 3s. *per* day; Wheat 6s. *per* Bufhel; Rye 3s. 6d.; Indian Corn 3s.; Wool 2s. *per lib*; Flax 10d.; Pork from 5s. to 7s. *per* fcore, 3d. ¼ *per* lib. from 7s. to 10s. 3d. ¼, from 10s. and upwards, 3d. ¼; Grafs-fed Beef not to exceed 24s. *per* hundred—fo in proportion according to its quality; Raw Hides 3d. *per* lib; Salt 10s. *per* bufhel; Weft India Rum 6s. *per* gallon, *per* hogfhead; Beft Mufcovado Sugar 60s. *per* hundred; New England Rum 3s. 6d. *per* gallon, *per* hogfhead; Molaffes 3s. *per* gallon, *per* hogfhead; Tea 4s. 6d. *per* lib. Butter 10d.; Cheefe 6d.

The above prices are in Continental Currency.

The Virginia Gazette, from which the following extracts are made, is decorated in the front, with the Figure of a Snake, under which is a Scroll, with this infcription, " Don't tread on me," and the Motto, " High Heaven to gracious Ends direct the Storm "!

Williamfburgh, Virginia, April 11. A Letter from a Gentleman of Diftinction, dated Head Quarters, Morris-Town, March 29, 1777, to his Excellency the Governor—" Sir, Brigadier General Knox does me the

the favour of transcribing part of a letter which he this moment received from Col. Jackson, commanding one of the 16 additional battalions."
—"Boston, March 20, 1777. Last Tuesday a large ship arrived at Portsmouth from France; she has on board 1000 barrels of powder, 12,000 stand of arms (I say 12,000 stand of arms) a compleat set of cannon for the frigate at Portsmouth, and a very large quantity of linnens, woollens, &c. with a French General, Colonel, and Major. These gentlemen come well recommended by Dr. Franklin. She brings an account, that at the same time, and from the same port, a French fifty-gun ship failed for this place, with fifty brass field pieces, and other war-like stores. All and every part of this may be depended on as a fact.—Yesterday arrived here two very fine prize ships from London, loaded with dry goods, worth 50,000 l. sterling.

Philadelphia, March 25. Yesterday arrived here the Brig Sally, Captain Stucker, in 11 weeks from Nantz in France, with 10,000 stand of arms and a large number of gun-locks.

Williamsburgh, April 13. A very extensive trade is carrying on betwixt France and the United States. Virginia has compleated all her levies (ordered by the Congress), which are on their march to join General Washington.

The accounts published of the fire in Portsmouth Dock Yard in England are true. General Burgoyne arrived in England the 10th of December in a very bad state of health, but he had the honour of a long conference with his sovereign, and probably kissed his hand, which may possibly restore him. Our old acquaintance Lord Dunmore had likewise the good fortune to get to St. James's the 20th of the same month from New York, who likewise had the honour of a conference, and no doubt kissed his king all over.

Philadelphia, February 6. Yesterday the Assembly elected Dr. Franklin, Robert Morris, William Moore, and Jonathan B. Smith, Esquires, and General Roberdeau, Delegates in the Continental Congress.

New Haven, February 26. Two privateers of considerable force have been lately fitted out at Martinico, and manned with Frenchmen, but officered with the subjects of the United States, who are commissioned by Congress.

PHILADELPHIA, *March 5.*
Extract of a letter from Morris-Town, dated March 1.
" Since the action of the 23d several deserters have come here, who say, that they heard Major French tell General Vaughan, that their loss, in killed and wounded, amounted to 509: that it was impossible for them, with 1500 or 2000 men and 6 field pieces, to do any thing against an innumerable number of rebels, who attacked them in front, rear, and flank at the same time; it is true they were attacked in that manner, but not by more than 600. The enemy were extremely cruel in their retreat; they seeing a poor countryman standing at his own door, laid hold of him; he shewed a protection signed by Gen. Howe's secretary; they damned him and his protection, and said those who had taken protections were as damned rebels as those who had not, and immediately sent a ball through his body, which not proving instant death, they stabbed him with bayonets. After such an instance, it is not to be wondered at their beating the brains out of their wounded, one of whom they served in that manner last Sunday."

Gen. Howe arrived at Brunswick on Friday night, the 21st ult. being sent for to settle a difference between the British and Hessian troops, which had nearly terminated in blows.

R 2   *Phila-*

Philadelphia, March 6. Yesterday at noon his Excellency THOMAS WHARTON, jun. Efq. Prefident of the Supreme Executive Council of the Commonwealth of Pennfylvania, Captain General and Commander in Chief in and over the fame, was proclaimed at the Court Houfe, in the prefence of a vaft concourfe of people, who expreffed the higheft fatisfaction on the occafion, by unanimous fhouts of acclamation.

The proceffion began at the State Houfe, and was conducted in the following order, viz.

Conftables with their ftaves,
Sub Sheriffs,
High Sheriffs and Coroner,
Serjeant at Arms,
The Hon. Speaker of the Houfe—
Clerk of the Houfe on his right hand,
Members of General Affembly,
PRESIDENT and VICE PRESIDENT,
Members of the Supreme Executive Council,
Gentlemen, Members of the Council of Safety, and the Navy Board.

Proclamation being made by the High Sheriff, commanding filence on pain of imprifonment, the PRESIDENT and the Hon. Speaker of the Houfe of Affembly came forward. The Clerk of the Houfe then publifhed the election of the PRESIDENT and VICE-PRESIDENT, as made and declared by the General Affembly and Supreme Executive Council, and proclaimed the Prefident.

On the fignal from the acclamations of the people, 13 cannons were fired from the brafs field pieces taken from the Heffians at Trenton.

The proceffion then returned;
Conftables with their ftaves,
Sub Sheriffs,
High Sheriffs and Coroner,
His Excellency the PRESIDENT and VICE-PRESIDENT,
Members of the Supreme Executive Council,
Serjeant at Arms,
The Hon. Speaker of the Houfe—
Clerk of the Houfe on his left hand,
Members of the General Affembly, Gentlemen, Members of the Council of Safety, and the Navy Board,

And dined together at the City Tavern, where an entertainment was provided by order of the Houfe. The Members of Congrefs then in the city, and the General officers of the army of the United States of America being alfo prefent.

After dinner, the following toafts were drank, under the difcharge of cannon, viz.

1. The United States of America. 2. The Congrefs. 3. The Commonwealth of Pennfylvania. 4. General Wafhington, and the Army of the United States of America. 5. The Navy of the United States. 6. The Friends of Liberty in all parts of the world. 7. Perpetual Union and ftrict Friendfhip among the States of America. 8. The Arts and Sciences. 9. Agriculture. 10. Trade and Navigation. 11. The Memory of the brave Patriots of all ranks, who have glorioufly fallen in their Country's Caufe. 12. May every American know his true intereft. 13. May Juftice, Firmnefs and Humanity ever characterize Americans. 14. May Human Knowledge, Virtue and Happinefs receive their laft perfection in America. 15. May every private Confideration give way to the Means of our public Defence. 16. General Lee and all our Friends in Captivity. 17. Doctor Franklin.

The bells of the city were rang, and the whole was conducted with the utmoft decency, and no accident happened of any kind.

Philadelphia, April 16. The following intelligence was received on Monday, afferted by Heny Fifher, and exprefs fent to Bombay Hook, to Benjamin Brooks, and from him to James Cameron at Port Penn, certifying, that there are more of the enemies fhips of war in Delaware, viz. Three in Whore Kiln

Kiln Road, three at the Middle, and three at the Narrows. Signed Benj. Brooks, James Cameron. April 14, 1777.

In Congrefs, April 14, 1777.

Whereas the ftate of Pennfylvania is threatened with an immediate invafion; and, from the adjournment of the legiflative and executive authorities of the Commonwealth, it is impracticable to carry into immediate execution many meafures of the utmoft importance, not only to the fafety of this Commonwealth, but likewife to the general welfare of the United States,

Refolved, That it is the indifpenfible duty of Congrefs to watch over all matters (the neglect of which may, in its confequences, deeply affect the welfare of the United States) till fuch time as the legiflative and executive authorities of the Commonwealth of Pennfylvania can refume the regular exercife of their different functions.

Refolved, That his Excellency the Prefident of the Supreme Executive Council of the Commonwealth of Pennfylvania be requefted forthwith to convene the legiflative and executive authorities of this ftate, in order that proper meafures may be purfued for the defence of the fame.

Refolved, That a committee of three be appointed to confer with the Prefident of the Supreme Executive Council, with fuch other Members of the faid Council as can be convened with the Board of War for the State of Pennfylvania, and with the Delegates of the faid State in Congrefs, concerning the mode of authority which they fhall conceive moft eligible to be exercifed during the recefs of the Houfe of Affembly, and the Council, in order that if the fame be approved by Congrefs may be immediately adopted.

The Members chofen, Mr. S. Adams, Mr. Dewer, and Mr. R. H. Lee.

In Congrefs, April 15.

The Committee appointed by Congrefs on the 14th day of April, to confer with the Prefident and Members of the Supreme Executive Council of the Commonwealth of Pennfylvania, the Board of War of faid State, and the Delegates reprefenting the fame in Congrefs, concerning the authority which fhould be deemed eligible to be exercifed during the recefs of the Council and Affembly, report

That a conference, agreeable to the order of Congrefs, has been held, when the following gentlemen were prefent:

His Excellency Thomas Wharton, jun. Efq; Prefident of the Supreme Executive Council.

Board of War. Owen Biddle, Efq; Chairman, Jofeph Dean, Richard Bache, John Shee.

Delegates for the State of Pennfylvania in Congrefs. Robert Morris, James Wilfon, Dan. Roberdeau, George Clymer, Efqrs.

Committee of Congrefs. Mr. Samuel Adams, Mr. Richard H. Lee, Mr. Duer.

That it appears clearly to the members in conference, that the executive authority of the Commonwealth of Pennfylvania is incapable of any exertion, adequate to the prefent crifis, and that it is of the greateft importance, that every power fhould be called forth into action, which may conduce to the fafety of this ftate, with which the liberties and profperity of the whole are fo intimately connected. From this confideration, and at the particular inftance and requeft of the Prefident of the Supreme Executive Council and Board of War of the ftate of Pennfylvania, we beg leave to recommend the following refolutions to be adopted by Congrefs:

Refolved, That the Prefident of the Supreme Executive Council, of the Commonwealth of Pennfylvania, together

together with as many members of said Council as can be convened, the Board of War, and (in such cases as relate to the marine) the Navy Board of said State, should, in the present critical exigency of affairs, exercise every authority to promote the safety of the State, till such time as the legislative and executive authorities of the Commonwealth of Pennsylvania can be convened.

Resolved, That it be, and it is hereby earnestly recommended by Congress, to the good people of Pennsylvania, chearfully to submit to the exertion of an authority which is indispensibly essential to the preservation of the lives, liberties, and property of themselves, their families, and posterity.

Resolved, That the commanding officer of the Continental forces in this city, afford every possible assistance in carrying into execution all such measures as may be recommended to him by the authority above-mentioned.

Resolved, That Congress will chearfully co-operate with the authority above-mentioned, in facilitating every measure which may be deemed conducive to the safety of the State.

Congress taking into consideration the foregoing report,

Resolved, That the same be concurred in, and that the resolutions proposed be agreed to.

Extract from the minutes,

CHARLES THOMSON, Sec.

———————

Pennsylvania War-Office, Philadelphia, April 17, 1777.

I. Resolved, That a Committee of Fifty be appointed to have the direction and superintendance of the removal of all the provisions and other stores now in this city, or near the river Delaware in this State, below the Falls of Trenton, that will be useful to our enemies, should they get possession of them, or that may be necessary to the army of the United States.

II. That the inhabitants of this city and liberties be allowed to retain as much provisions of all kinds as is usual and customary for families to be possessed of at this season, it being the intention of this Board to remove the extraordinary stores only of those who have been returned, as having greater quantities than is usually laid up by families of similar circumstances in common times.

III. That all provisions, the property of private persons, so returned to this Board, over and above what is customary as aforesaid, be removed into the country to such place or places as this Board may direct.

Extract of a letter from Lewis-Town to the Congress at Philadelphia, April 12.

" Yesterday morning the ship Morris, Capt. Anderson, was chaced into the mouth of our bay by a frigate; the Roebuck made sail after her. Capt. Anderson run his ship ashore about half a mile from the light-house, the two ships continually firing at him, and he returned the fire for near three hours in the most brave and gallant manner. The ships sent three boats, which were beat off by the Morris. Capt. Anderson landed his packet for the Congress, which I have sent up by two French gentlemen. When finding he could defend her no longer, he laid a train, and blew the ship up, and I am sorry to tell you, that so brave a man has fell in the attempt. The scene was horrid to behold. The cargo is in part blown on shore— viz. guns, cloaths, gun-locks, &c. We have a number of men employed in saving the cargo. The Roebuck is now in the road, and two frigates at anchor upon the lower part of the Brown. There has been a flag from the Roebuck. The officer says, they

expect

expect their whole squadron in shortly; and should they arrive, I will give you the earliest advice in my power.

I am, Gentlemen,
Your humble servant,
HENRY FISHER."

Philadelphia, April 19.

" *In sight of the Capes of Virginia, April* 12, *on board the Continental ship of war Trumbull.*

" Gentlemen,

" I have the pleasure to acquaint you, that at one P. M. I fell in with two transports from England, one of eight, the other of ten guns. They engaged us three glasses, when they struck their colours. They killed seven of our men, and wounded eight more. We shattered them in a terrible manner, and killed and wounded numbers of their crews. I have the pleasure to inform you, that our people behaved well, and with much courage. I am, Gentlemen,

Your humble servant,
DUDLEY SALTONSTALL.

" P. S. I shall give you an account of the powder, military stores and arms on board them, and of my proceedings in general."

[*To the Hon.* JOHN HANCOCK, *Esq. or any of the* MARINE COMMITTEE *jointly.*]

Boston, April 4. By an officer of distinction, who arrived in this metropolis last Monday from the American army near Peek's-Kill, we have the following authentic accounts of the landing of the enemy at that place, viz. On Sunday the 23d of March, about eleven o'clock in the morning, the Brune frigate, with the two gallies taken from us last campaign, a small one built by the enemy, and four transports, anchored in the Bay of Peek's-Kill: at one o'clock, P. M. they landed under cover of the gallies, the 5th, 23d, 44th, and 64th regiments, under the command of Colonel Bird, with

four pieces of artillery, and 50 of the train, at Lent's Cove, South side of the Bay, a mile and a half from the town: they advanced to Cronk's Hill, South-East side of the town, and formed on it: before this, boats with men rowed towards the North landing, as if they intended to land there, on our flank, or to get in our rear. From the number of boats which landed the troops, General M'Dougall, and every discerning officer who saw them, were clearly of opinion, that the enemy's force far exceeded ours: but he determined to have full evidence of it before he quitted the post, and therefore waited for the enemy, in a position from which his retreat was secured till they came within musket-shot: at this distance he had a full view of the enemy formed on the hill, and they were treble his force. The rum and provisions *there being destroyed*, and the heavy artillery sent off, (except one iron 12 pounder, which for want of horses was lost) the General ordered the troops to retire, which they did, in good order, to Barrack No. 2, two miles and a half from the town. The enemy cannonaded us, and wounded one of our men mortally: there he took post to secure the pass of the mountains, and some mills which contained a quantity of flour and grain, belonging to the Continent: the enemy placed a picket guard of 100 men a mile from our post. The next day, about four o'clock in the afternoon, Lieutenant-Colonel Willet, with about 60 men of Colonel Granscott's regiment, got undiscovered on the right flank of the enemy's picket, while a small party was sent on their left, to draw their attention: it had the desired effect, for Colonel Willet got near them undiscovered, when a skirmish ensued for 15 minutes. The Colonel ordered his men to fix bayonets, and rush upon them; and the enemy fled with great precipitation. We had two

men

men wounded; the enemy had nine killed and wounded. The enemy embarked that day, on hearing a reinforcement was expected that evening: the next morning we took poffeffion of the town. The enemy in the afternoon went down the river, below Croton, in purfuit of ftock and provifions. Our principal lofs is the rum, molaffes, and flour, ordered to be deftroyed, and the fugar burnt by the enemy, in the Commiffary's ftore.

Fifh-Kill, March 6.
Extract of a letter from Morris-Town, March 2.

" Laft Sunday the enemy came out from Woodbridge with 1,900 men, and 6 field pieces; the action commenced about half paft 9 in the morning, and continued with intermiffion, all the day; we killed, wounded, and took prifoners fix hundred; fome fay feven hundred; however, the firft I had from Dr. ——, who was on the field, during the whole affair : we have a farther confirmation of it fince by a deferter. The day before yefterday four deferters came over to us; fcarce a day paffes without fome deferters or prifoners coming in. The Quakers and Tories are coming in daily, with and for protections."

Bofton, March 13. By a gentleman from Head-Quarters, which he left the 3d inftant, we are informed, that on Sunday the 23d of February, about 2000 of the enemy, who went on a foraging party, from Amboy, attacked our guards, and drove them five or fix miles; when our troops were reinforced, by General Maxwell, with about 1400 men, chiefly militia; when they, in their turn, were obliged to retreat, with fo much precipitation, as not to be able to return but two fires.—We took fix prifoners, and found two of their dead; but, by deferters, who have come off fince, we are told, their lofs was about 500 killed and wound-

ed. Our lofs was 3 killed and 11 wounded.

The enemy came out with a large number of waggons, with intent to draw in their plunder; but, miftaken fools! returned, to their great mortification, with their waggons loaded with killed and wounded.

We are informed, from undoubted authority, that the town of Falmouth, in the county of Cumberland, have, to their honour, raifed, for the Continental fervice, inftead of one feventh of their inhabitants, near one fifth part, and the other towns, in that county, in like proportion.

Bofton March 16, 1777. Captain Pinkham, in a brig, from London, bound to St. Auguftine, on his paffage put into St. Martin's, on fome bufinefs; fhe had on board *cloathing for a regiment of foldiers,* military ftores and dry goods; alfo, the whole furniture, plate, &c. of the Governor of St. Auguftine, and feveral gentlemen, paffengers; who, being afhore one evening, Capt. Pinkham weighed anchor, and ftood to fea, and is fafe arrived at North Carolina.

Extract of a letter from Morris-Town, March 20.

" A Corporal and 4 privates of the Britifh grenadiers came over a few days ago, alfo a private of the 71ft regiment, and fince that another grenadier; by information from them, and other concurrent teftimony from New-York, General Howe's plan is, to march to Philadelphia by land, and, to facilitate the expedition, he has got a parcel of boats ready (to ferve for pontoons) to lay a bridge acrofs the Delaware; in confequence thereof it is conjectured General Wafhington will remove head quarters foon.

A letter from New York, dated April 20, fays, " Provifions are extremely dear at New York, beef at 14d fterling per pound by the quarter; mutton and veal at 18d. butter at 4s. 1d. a fcant two pound roll; milk

milk 7d. sterling *per* quart; bread very dear, and all sorts of poultry, which is now very scarce; cabbages, small, from. 7d to 2od. a piece; spinage at 10d. and 12d. for half a peck; three, four, and five eggs, for 7d. and every thing else in proportion; fire wood, the common sort of oak, at 4l. currency, 45s. sterling *per* cord; coals three guineas and an half *per* chaldron, and before got in, half a guinea for carting, &c. more.

The Indians have scalped and killed about 50 of the rebels at a place called Sabbath Day Point on Lake George; and we hear that the six nations are assembling to make an expedition, in order to cure the New Englanders, who have caught the itch of rambling towards their country. Great bodies of Indians are likewise expected to come over the Lakes with General Carleton from Canada. General Carleton has found means to send advices, across the country, to General Howe; they are dated the second of April. He says, that the Americans have no force upon Lake Champlain, in consequence of which he will embark on the 20th of May; that they have 2000 men at Ticonderoga, under General Wayne; that they have fortified the islands upon Lake George, where they have made themselves very strong; and that as they have made South Bay totally impracticable to pass, he does not expect to be at Albany till late in the season. But he has sent General Frafer with the light infantry, Canadians and Indians, by the Mohawk river, to make a diversion in the rear of the Americans; from which he expects great advantages.

By his Excellency Sir WILLIAM HOWE, Knight of the Most Honourable order of the Bath, one of His Majesty's Commissioners for restoring peace to the Colonies, General and Commander in Chief of all his Majesty's forces within the Colonies lying on the Atlantic Ocean, from Nova-Scotia to West Florida, inclusive, &c. &c.

PROCLAMATION.

" Whereas for the more speedy and effectual suppression of the unnatural rebellion subsisting in North-America, it has been thought proper to levy a number of Provincial troops, thereby affording to His Majesty's faithful and well-disposed subjects, inhabitants of the Colonies, an opportunity to co-operate in relieving themselves from the miseries attendant on anarchy and tyranny, and restoring the blessings of peace and order with just and lawful government: as a reward for the promptitude and zeal wherewith his Majesty's faithful subjects have entered into the corps now raising, and as a further encouragement to others to follow their laudable example, I do hereby, in consequence of authority to me given by his Majesty, promise and engage, That all persons who have, or do hereafter, inlist into any of the said Provincial corps, to serve for two years, or during the present war in North-America, and shall continue faithfully to serve in any of the said corps agreeable to such their engagements, shall, after being reduced or disbanded, obtain, according to their respective stations, grants of the following quantities of vacant lands in the Colonies wherein their corps have been or shall be raised, or in such other Colony as his Majesty shall think fit——Every non-commissioned-officer, 200 acres; every private soldier, 50 acres.

" The same to be granted to such of the said non-commissioned officers and soldiers as shall personally apply for the same, by the Governor of the respective Colonies, without fee or reward, subject at the expiration of ten years to the same quit rents as other lands are subject to in the province within which they shall be granted, and subject to the same

S   conditions

conditions of cultivation and improvement.

" Given under my Hand, at Head Quarters in New York, this 21ſt day of April, 1777.
W. HOWE."

By His Excellency's Command,
ROBERT MACKENSIE, Sec.

Copy of a letter wrote to Sir William Howe by Lieutenant Colonel Archibald Campbell, and by him forwarded through the hands of the Council at Boſton.

" Sir, Concord Gaol, 14 Feb. 1777.

" After the ſubjeɛt of my firſt epiſtle to your Excellency, when the fortune of war had placed me in the hands of the Americans, you will think it ſtrange that at this period I ſhould be compelled to exhibit ſentiments ſo diametrically oppoſite, and yet equally conſiſtent with truth.

" Your Excellency was informed on that occaſion, that I had received from thoſe who took me, and from the controuling power at Boſton, every mark of humanity, and treatment ſuitable to my rank ; but I am perſuaded you are yet a ſtranger to the return, which at this hour I experience, after a well meant endeavour to ſuppreſs, what but too often happens in civil controverſy—the chance of ill-grounded repreſentation.

" Scarce eight days had elapſed after the period of my firſt addreſs, when I found myſelf ſtripped of half my private property, the very neceſſaries of life ; and I have been lately informed, that the ſide arms of my officers have actually been diſpoſed of, notwithſtanding they were honourably reſtored to them by the captors : I was however ſent upon my parole of honour to Reading as an Officer, where I reſided till the firſt of this month ; during which time it was even beyond the power of malevolent aſperſion to charge my conduct juſtly with impropriety.

" On the 1ſt of February I was committed by an order of Congreſs, through the Council of Boſton, to the common gaol of Concord, intimating for a reaſon, that your Excellency had refuſed to exchange General Lee for ſix Field Officers (of whom I happened to be one) and that your Excellency had put that officer under cuſtody of the Provoſt.

" How far it may be confiſtent to ill-treat an officer, becauſe his commander does not chooſe to accept of a proffered barter of that nature, is left to reaſon, and future conſequences to decide, eſpecially when it is conſidered that there is no perſonal charge againſt that officer, and the public faith and honour of America was pledged for his being treated as a gentleman.

" With reſpect to your Excellency's treatment of General Lee, I can ſcarcely think it ſimilar to mine ; but that you may be able with the more preciſion to decide on that point, I ſhall briefly ſtate my preſent unmerited condition.

" I am lodged in a dungeon of twelve or thirteen feet ſquare, whoſe ſides are black with the greaſe and litter of ſucceſſive criminals. Two doors, with double locks and bolts, ſhut me up from the yard, with an expreſs prohibition to enter it, either for my health, or the neceſſary calls of nature.

" Two ſmall windows, ſtrongly grated with iron, introduce a gloomy light to the apartment, and theſe are at this hour without a ſingle pane of glaſs, although the ſeaſon for froſt and ſnew is actually in the extreme. In the corner of the cell, boxed up with the partition, ſtands a neceſſary houſe, which does not ſeem to have been emptied ſince its firſt appropriation to this convenience of malefactors. A loathſome black hole, decorated with a pair of fixed chains, is granted me for my inner apartment ; from whence a felon was but the moment before removed, to make way for your humble ſervant, and in which his litter and excrement to this hour remains.

" The

" The attendance of a fingle fervant on my perfon is alfo denied me, and every vifit from a friend pofitively refufed. In fhort, Sir, was a fire to take place in any chamber of the gaol. which is all of wood, the chimney ftacks excepted, I might perifh in the flames before the gaoler could go through the ceremony of unbolting doors; although, to do him juftice in his ftation, I really think him a man of humanity. His houfe is fo remote from the gaol, that any call from within, efpecially if the wind is high, might be long of reaching him effectually.

" Thus have I ftated to your Excellency the particulars of my fituation. How far I had a claim to expect it, reafon and propriety will dictate.

" I have the honour to be with great refpect,   SIR,
" Your Excellency's moft faithful,
" And moft obedient
" Humble fervant,
(Signed)   ARCH. CAMPBELL,
Lieut. Col. of the 71ft regiment." *
His Excellency General Howe, &c.

Extract of a letter from Bofton, Jan. 5.

" I am forry to inform you that we have been compelled, contrary to our inclinations, to deprive Colonel Campbell of that liberty with which he has been indulged ever fince his captivity. If he feels a melancholy change in his fituation, he muft thank his friends for it. We have at all times fhewn the ftrongeft difpofition to foften the miferies of war. Humanity will, I truft, mark the character of an American as ftrongly as a determined and virtuous oppofition to tyranny. But humanity carried beyond a certain point, degenerates into weaknefs. The conduct of our enemies not only juftifies feverity, but makes it fometimes abfolutely neceffary. Their behaviour to Colonel Ethan Allen, their conduct at the Cedars, the murders committed by the Indians, at their inftigation, upon defencelefs women and children on our frontiers, with innumerable other inftances of their barbarity which could be produced, exhibit fufficient proofs of the malignity of their hearts. Long experience has taught us, that the moft powerful arguments make no impreffion on them. What then muft be done? Muft we fuffer their cruelties to be wantonly and repeatedly exercifed with impunity? As they have fhewn themfelves deaf to the voice of reafon, retaliation is the only means of redrefs left in our power: this may perhaps bring them to a proper fenfe of their duty, and reftrain them from future violence. The Congrefs, as foon as they were informed of the capture of General Lee, offered, according to the laws of war, to exchange fix Field Officers for him: Colonel Campbell was one of the number. This propofal was rejected by Gen. Howe, and General Lee was put into clofe confinement. It was faid likewife, that on account of the King's perfonal diflike to him, he was to be tried and executed as a deferter. The Congrefs immediately ordered the fix Field Officers to be put into confinement. They have informed themfelves minutely of the nature of General Lee's imprifonment, and thefe officers are kept precifely in the fame ftate. If any violence is offered to the American General, whatever may be the pretence, their lives muft be anfwerable for it. The following refolution of the Congrefs will fhew Colonel Campbell's friends what they are to expect, if the Miniftry dare to put their threats againft General Lee into execution:

Refolved, That if the enemy fhall commit any violences, by putting to death, or otherwife ill-treating the prifoners retained by them, recourfe be had to retaliation, as the fole means of ftopping the progrefs of human butchery; and for that purpofe, that punifhments of the fame kind and degree be inflicted on the prifoners

---

* Alfo Member for Dumferline, &c. in Scotland.

prisoners in our possession, till the enemy shall be taught the respect due to the violated rights of nations. By order of the Congress,

Signed,   JOHN HANCOCK.

Newbern, (North Carolina) Jan. 14.

On Friday last his Excellency Richard Caswell, Esq. Governor of this State, arrived here. He was met about six miles from town by about thirty gentlemen on horseback, who accompanied him to Newbern, the bells ringing as soon as he entered the town. Being conducted to Mr. Edward Wrenford's tavern, where a handsome collation was prepared, he received from the Continental officers and soldiers (drawn up for the purpose) a salute with small arms; the fort, Pennsylvania Farmer, and the other vessels in the harbour, fired many guns, under a display of the colours of the United States, and in the evening the town was handsomely illuminated.

On Monday the 13th instant the inhabitants of the town assembled, and waited upon his Excellency with a congratulatory address.

WILLIAMSBURG, January 31.

Extract of a letter from Sir John Peyton of Gloucester county, to the Hon. John Page, Esq. President of the Council, dated Jan. 28, 1777.

" I have seen Mr. Edward Hughes, who was taken by the enemy last Wednesday. He informs me there are three ships in the bay, a 60, 50, and a 36 gun frigate, under the command of Commodore Hotham. He brought with him the inclosed; and if it is proper that an exchange should be made, shall be much obliged to you for your interest in bringing it about as soon as possible. Mr. Hughes gives great praise to the Commodore for his generous and humane behaviour, who, after being informed of the circumstances of Hughes's family, &c. gave him his boat, with almost every thing in her, detaining a Negro, which he said he understood was a tolerable pilot, but assured him, at the

same time, he should be returned as soon as he got a better; that he did not mean to distress individuals, who industriously were going from river to river to support their families.— Hughes understood they were to cruize here, and expect 7 or 8 sail more every day."

To Sir JOHN PEYTON, North River.

On board the ship Preston,

" Sir,   Jan. 22, 1777.

" This will inform you, that I had the misfortune to be taken by the above-mentioned ship on Monday the 20th instant; and as I understand there are a great many prisoners in in Baltimore, beg your interest for an exchange, which I believe the Commodore will agree to. There are several other prisoners on board who join me in this request.

     I am, Sir,

     Your most obedient servant,

       WILLIAM SEON."

To the above letter the Commodore subjoined the following lines.

" Having on board the squadron under my command a number of prisoners, I shall be ready to exchange them, if any person be duly authorized to treat with me for such exchange.   W. HOTHAM."

By command of the Commodore,

     TITUS LIVIE, Sec.

Preston, in Chesapeak Bay,

    Jan. 25, 1777.

Narrative of the proceedings of Commodore Hotham, in the Preston man of war, since his departure from Rhode-Island, in January last, in a letter from an officer on board to his relation in London

     New-York, April 15.

" We sailed from Rhode-Island the 13th of January, and arrived the 26th ditto, in Lynn Haven Bay, near St. James's River, Virginia, and on running into the Bay, we fell in with a sloop, fired a gun at her, sent our boats on board, and took her. She was from St. Eustatia, laden with 40 hogsheads of rum, and ballasted with salt.

falt. We then ran further up the Bay, to Point Comfort, where we perceived a rebel privateer and several floops: on feeing us they got on their ways, ran the ship on fhore, and pufhed the reft on into fhoal water. We then came to an anchor, and not hoifting any colours, they could not tell what to make of us, but fent a privateer floop to reconnoitre; at whom, after firing fome fhot, we fent our boats on board and took her. The Commodore fent a Lieutenant, with 40 feamen, and a Lieutenant with 24 marines on board her, with orders to attack the privateer and fhip. On our approach the former made off, but the fhip we boarded, took 15 prifoners, and found her to be laden with 600 hogfheads of tobacco. She is a new fhip, called the Farmer, bound from Baltimore for Nantz. Next day our boats boarded and took a fmall boat of the enemy's, having on board 10 barrels of flour, and 150l. of their paper currency.

" The Farmer, our rich prize, went under the fame convoy, commanded by Lieutenant Graves of the navy. On the 14th of March we took a fmall veffel, with a quantity of limes on board; and next day we failed for the Delaware, but on our arrival at the mouth of that river, a violent gale of wind came on, and drove us to fea, where we were rolling for three weeks, during which time we took three fmall prizes, which we funk, and a fecond time attempted the Delaware, and finally came to an anchor in that river: next morning we perceived a large fhip ftanding in; on feeing us fhe fteered up another channel, where the water being fhoal, could not follow her, we therefore fent our tender to attack her; upon which all the people abandoned the fhip, after endeavouring to run her afhore, but our men got on board juft time to fave her. She proved to be laden with gunpowder, arms, lead, &c.

from France; to the rebels fhe was computed to be 40,000l. but to us fhe is not worth more than 3000l.

" The 15th of March we fell in with two fchooners, one French, the other an American, both of which we made prizes of; and the fame day fent the Daphne to convoy the fhip and two fchooners to New-York; they were both laden with rum and molaffes; immediately upon parting we defcried another fail, gave chace, and took her, which proved to be a brig from Philadelphia to Cape François, belonging to a Frenchman, having on board 707 barrels of flour, which we fent immediately to New-York; two days after we chaced another brig, and took her, bound from Nantucket with only 10 hogfheads of fugar and 50 barrels of oil; the former were took out, but the latter with the veffel we funk.

" The day after we funk a rebel fchooner laden with flour, which we were obliged to do, it blowing fo hard a gale that we could not get poffeffion of her, and taking advantage of the wind, we in a few days reached New-York, which was a very defirable object, as you may judge when I tell you that we fent to the hofpital about 100 feamen, and 45 marines, all very ill of the fcurvy."

Extract of a letter from an English Gentleman at Martinico, dated March 21, to one of the owners of Venus, bound to Grenada, which was taken and carried into Martinico

" The French enjoy all the advantages of a war, without any of the inconveniences; prizes are brought in here every day by privateers, who call themfelves Americans, but are in reality French property, manned by French, Spaniards, &c. Guineamen are their principal objects, which they frequently fall in with. Above a dozen have been already brought in here and fold, with their cargoes, from ten to twelve Jees a head. I have been here this week paft, endeavouring

deavouring to recover a sloop of mine, with fifty-four new Negroes, taken by a sloop belonging to this island, under American colours; she had French papers, and notwithstanding I have proved her to be French property, the General absolutely refused to give her up, merely because he supposed her having cleared out at Grenada for Tobago: such injustice never was heard of; for suppose her English property, and the sloop an American, this is a neutral port, and can afford no Court of Admiralty for the condemnation of their prizes; in short, nothing but a war can stop their iniquitous proceedings.

" Your brig, the Venus, Capt. Sharp, was taken the 18th inst. close in with St. Vincent, on her way to Grenada, by a sloop belonging to Mr. Pregent, of this island, but under American colours, named the Retaliation, Capt. Ord, (the only American on board her.) The Venus made a noble defence, and had it not been for boarding, would not have surrendered; she fought the sloop three hours, and even when boarded, would not strike. Mr. Wilson, the supercargo, was shot through the body by a pistol, of which wound it is thought he will die; three others were terribly wounded with cutlasses. I have done all in my power to serve them, and made Mr. Pregent promise, that when they can be removed, they shall be sent to some of the English islands. The Venus is lying in a bay about a league from hence; I should claim her as English property, did I think it would avail any thing, but I know it would not. The Governor, on my too peremptorily demanding the sloop and Negroes to be restored, told me, that had I not brought him a letter from Lord M'Cartney, (our Governor at Grenada) he would lodge me twenty-four hours in the common gaol for my temerity."

Boston, New England, April 24. A few days ago arrived in this city, a number of troops from the Westward, which makes our army here amount to 10,327 effective men. This morning the Provincial brig of War, Hibernia, Moses Foster, commander, arrived from Curacoa, with a cargo of muskets, pistols, cannon-balls, powder, &c. She was chaced to the mouth of the harbour by an English ship of war of 20 guns.

Charles-Town, April 28. Yesterday morning arrived the Orilhune, of 40 guns, and a Xebeque of 18 guns: they both came from St. Maloes, are laden with cloathing for the Provincial army, saltpetre, pole-axes, and a quantity of grape-shot. They were both purchased by some American gentlemen now in France, for the service of the Congress.

Extract of a letter from Barbadoes, April 4.

" In England you will scarcely believe that the French and Dutch Islands now supply the English Islands in the West-Indies with many articles, and particularly provisions. It is thus accounted for: the Americans carry goods to those foreign markets, from whence we are glad to purchase them at an advanced price."

The following letter was sent to the master of the Merchants-Hall in Bristol, from the Chamber of Commerce in Liverpool:

Chamber of Commerce, Liverpool, May 28.

" Sir,

" By various accounts from different persons and places, undoubted intelligence has been received here, of some illegal and dangerous practices carried on by the French in the West-Indies.

" A vessel belonging to this place with slaves, cane-wood and ivory, has been carried into St. Lucia by a French sloop of 10 guns and 50 men, said to be owned by Mr. Bligera, a merchant in Martinico. The sloop had only one Englishman on board, who

who was honoured with the ftile of Captain, but the actual commander and his officers, were French, and the crew all French, or other foreigners.

"The Venus, Captain Sharpe, of and from Whitehaven for Grenada, was taken after a gallant defence of three hours, by a privateer belonging to Martinico, manned with French, Portuguefe, and Spaniards, having only an American for mafter. Many others are fitting out on this plan, both at Martinico and Guadaloupe; the Congrefs agents have blank commiffions, which they fill up there, and are very liberal of them. Thefe proceedings appear to us fo very ruinous to the trade of Great-Britain, that it has been determined to bring the bufinefs before Parliament by petition. We fhall efteem ourfelves happy, if honoured with the concurrence of the merchants of Briftol in our intended application.

"I have the honour to be, &c.

JOHN DOBSON, Prefident.
To Henry Garnett, Efq.
Mafter of the Merchants-hall, Briftol.

Extract of a letter from Nantz, May 27,

"The Concord, from Charles-Town, which arrived here about a fortnight fince with a loading of rice, indigo, &c. yefterday had a public fale, when every thing fold remarkably cheap; indigo went at two fhillings and two-pence, Englifh, per lb. which in London would fetch four fhillings and fixpence, or five fhillings. Rice, and every thing elfe, fold very badly, but then it muft be remembered, that they went for ready money only, confequently few only could be buyers, and they indeed will make more than cent. per cent. by their bargains; the quantity of goods by this channel overftocks the market, and were it not for orders from England, and other parts, they would not find a fufficient vent for their goods.

Extract of a letter from Guernfey, June 5.

"An American privateer of twelve guns came into this road yefterday morning; tacked about on the firing of the guns from the Caftle, and juft off the Ifland took a large brig bound for this port, which they have fince carried into Cherburgh. She had the impudence to fend her boat in the dufk of the evening to a little ifland off here, called Jetto, and unluckily carried off the Lieutenant of Northey's Independent Company here, with the garrifon Adjutant, who were fhooting rabbits for their diverfion. Two gentlemen of confequence are gone to Cherburgh to demand them. The poor pilferers got nothing but fix or feven little Guinea pigs made into a pye for the gentlemen's dinner, and a few bottles of claret, though the brig they took is valued at 7000l. belonging to 'Squire Tupper?

The following letter was fent to Mefl. Wakefield, Pratt, and Myers, Merchants, in the city of London:

Admiralty Office, May 20.

"Gentlemen, Having laid before my Lords Commiffioners of the Admiralty the Memorial of the Merchants importers of Linen from Ireland, defiring that they will give protection to the linen fhips bound from Newry to England, and that the convoy may likewife call at Dublin for fuch fhips as may be there, I am commanded by their Lordfhips to acquaint you, that they have ordered his Majefty's cutter the Either to proceed immediately to Belfaft and Newry, to convoy the trade to England from thofe ports to Dublin, where the Wafp floop is ordered to be in readinefs to convoy, in conjunction with the faid cutter, fuch trade, and any other, which may be there bound to England, and ready to fail, which they are to fee fafe into the Englifh Channel, to the eaftward of the Lizard, good, and then to return to Dublin, ... to convoy the linen ... ... further or... ... ... inform you, that ... ... off... ... to cruize, till further ... ... between the Land's-End and the coast of Ireland, in the track of the trade passing that way, for their greater security and protection. I am, Gentlemen, your humble servant,

GEORGE JACKSON, D. S."

[In no former war, not even in any of the wars with France and Spain, the linen vessels from Ireland were ever convoyed.]

The following is a copy of a Letter which the Lord Mayor of Dublin received from the Right Hon. Richard Heron, secretary to his Excellency the Lord Lieutenant of Ireland. His Lordship directed the same to be published in the Papers, and posted in the Coffee-House for the information of the Merchants and Traders.

Dublin-Castle, May 24, 1777.

" My Lord,

" His Excellency, my Lord Lieutenant having this day received a letter, dated the 19th instant, from Lord Weymouth, His Majesty's Principal Secretary of State, acquainting his Excellency that his Majesty's Ships Boyne and Belleisle, both third rates, are now cruizing between Cape Clear and Ushant ; and that two cutters are ordered to cruize between the Land's End and the coast of Ireland ; and that another sloop and cutter are appointed a standing convoy for the Linen Ships, and other Trade, from Dublin to England ; besides which, several of his Majesty's ships and vessels are cruizing to the Westward: I am commanded by his Excellency to give your Lordship this early information thereof, and to desire that your Lordship will be pleased cause the same to be communicated to the Merchants and Traders of this city,

in such manner as your Lordship shall think proper. I have the honour to be, my Lord, your Lordship's most obedient, humble servant,

RICHARD HERON."

Extract of a letter from Waterford, May 25.

" We have advices here from Sligo, Ballyshannon, and Killybeggs, that three stout American privateers were seen last week about eight leagues West and by North from the island called Rosses, off the coast of Donegall, to pick up the ships bound from Greenock or Glasgow to America or the West-Indies. A fisherman of West-port, in the county of Mayo, saw them ; they wanted to have spoke with him, but the poor fellow supposed they wanted his fish, and not thinking they would pay him for it, the wind being right on shore, he pushed for it, and left them."

Extract of a letter from Bantry, May 26.

" We have just had a messenger here from Beerhaven, with an account that an American privateer of 16 guns, and full of men, put in their for water and fresh provisions ; she staid near ten hours, and paid for every thing."

Whitehaven, in England, May 22. Yesterday evening arrived here, under the command of Mr. Stuart, a large ship, formerly belonging to London, but, being taken by an American privateer, was sold to Mercer and Schenk, Merchants in Philadelphia, who (as will appear particularly by the following letter) sent her to Virginia, agreeable to a charter of the Continental Congress.

The Mercer, at that time commanded by Nathaniel Dowse, left Cape Henry the 14th of April last, having on board 290 hogsheads of tobacco, the property of the Continental Congress, 16 hogsheads belonging to the owners, a quantity of fustick, flour, and some other articles, with which Captain Dowse

was

was ordered to proceed on his voyage to Bourdeaux, in France. They were in all 18 persons on board, 16 of whom were English, Scotch, or Irish (four of them belonged to Whitehaven, two to Workington, and one to Harrington) who had been prisoners in America.

Such a superiority in number soon suggested the thought of taking the charge of the vessel from Capt. Dowse and his mate; the scheme was concerted, and on the 5th of May inst. at ten P. M. in Lat. 46. 10. Long. 25. 53 while the Captain was in bed, they informed the mate (who had the watch) of their intention, seized the Captain's papers, altered the course from E. by S. to N. E. by N. declared Mr. Stuart their commander, Whitehaven the port of their destination, where they arrived (as before mentioned) amidst the joyful acclamations of numbers.

An express was immediately sent off to London; the Officers of the Customs have taken the vessel into their possession, and this morning the English flag was hoisted above the Thirteen Stripes of the Colonies.

Captain Nicholas de Moulpied, of the Betty, of Guernsey, is come passenger in the above vessel; his ship was taken by the Americans the 12th of August, 1776, and carried into Dartmouth.

Capt. Dowse is 63 years of age, had four fine houses destroyed at Charles-Town, near Boston, and had the remainder of his property (except Bunker's Hill, which belonged to him) in this ship.

*To Mess. Samuel and J. H. Delap,
Merchants in Bourdeaux.
Philadelphia, March 14, 1777.*

" This will be delivered to you by Capt. Nathaniel Dowse, Commander of our ship Mercer. She brings you a load of tobacco for account of the Honourable Continental Congress, for which you are to receive 13l. 10s. sterling per ton of four hogsheads.

" We have also ordered our friend Benjamin Harrison, jun. Esq. of Virginia, to ship in her, on our account, a few hogsheads of tobacco, with some flour and lumber to be stowed in the vacancies of the hogsheads, which be pleased to make the most of. Also sell the ship, if you can get for her what you think her value. We gave 1700l. sterling for her, and thought her cheap, being well found, a new vessel, and neatly finished. If you cannot sell her, employ her on freight, and in the best manner you can cover in the property.

" Our instructions to Capt. Dowse are to leave the ship in your care, and make the best of his way home, with all the crew on board: in which you will be pleased to assist him, as they are all in high wages.

" But in case France has declared war against Great Britain, or if there is any certainty of such an event taking place, than purchase for us a small fast-sailing vessel, of about 30 tons, to carry four three pounders, six or eight swivels, and a few good small arms, and put in her to the value of 600l. sterling of the articles hereafter mentioned, and give the command either to Capt. Dowse, of the Mercer; Capt. Mercrie, of the Polly; Capt. Peter Callas, of the Moor; or Capt. Thomas Chartwright, of the Two Friends; whichever may arrive with you first. They all sailed for Virginia much at one time, from Boston, to take in their cargoes.

" What money after this remains in your hands for the freight, nett proceeds of the vessel, the fustick and other goods, on our account, retain in your hands until further orders, except one seventh, which pay to Mess. Pye, Richard, and Wilkinson, Merchants in Amsterdam, for account of Archibald and John Blair, subject to the order of Archibald Blair.

" Do not advance Capt. Dowse, or any of our captains or crews, any

T money,

money, but what is abfolutely neceffary for the prefent fupport, as it
is more advantage to us to pay them
in Bofton.

" We had like to have forgot to
defire you to fend the veffel, and
goods ordered, back to Bofton or
Portfmouth, which be pleafed to attend to. It will give us pleafure to
hear from you, and to render you
any fervice in our power. If you
meet with an opportunity to the eaftward, direct our letters to the care
of Mr. Thomas Ruffel, Merchant
in Bofton, Mr. John Duffield in Virginia, or to any of your friends in
that quarter.

" We are, Gentlemen, your very
humble fervants,

" MERCER & SCHENK."

Return of the cargo. 100l. fterling
jefuits bark, 300l. in good bohea
tea, beft quality, 100l. in pins, 100l.
in gold and filver lace for the military.

With as much fine white falt in
barrels as will put her in a good fet
of ballaft.

P. S. While Capt. Dowfe is difcharging, get the fmall veffel and
goods in readinefs, as difpatch is the
life of bufinefs; and as the other veffels arrive, purchafe a fmall veffel for
each of the captains and crews, and
put in each to the fame amount, viz.
600l fterling in goods forted agreeable to the above.

MERCER & SCHENK

[This veffel was formerly called
The Earl of Errol.]

The Prince of Orange packet,
mentioned in the lift of veffels taken
in page 109, was carried into Dunkirk. The fmugglers at Dunkirk
were exceedingly offended with the
bringing the packet into that port.
They faid it would occafion fome
Englifh frigates, or armed veffels, to
be ftationed off that port, which
would greatly obftruct their trade;
and a defperate quarrel enfued between them and the crew of the Ame-

rican privateer, which had taken and
brought in the packet. Upon this,
the Commandant of Dunkirk put
put them all in prifon, together with
Cunningham, the Captain of the
privateer. As foon as advice of the
capture reached London, Lord Stormont, the Englifh minifter at Paris,
prefented to the French miniftry a
memorial, in which he affirmed that
the pretended privateer was no other
than a pirate, and requefted upon
that ground the reftoration of the
prize. Cunningham being in confinement, no anfwer was immediately given. The privateer had
been fitted out at Dunkirk, but it
was not known for what purpofe;
which, and fome other irregularities
in Cunningham's conduct, were fuppofed to be the caufe of complying
with the ambaffador's requeft. However, upon nicer and further examination, the French court were fo
well fatisfied, that Cunningham and
his crew were in a fhort time after
releafed from their confinement.

Bruffels, June 9. We are well in-
formed that Mr. Cunningham, Cap-
tain of the American privateer the
Surprife, fent the mail (with the
letters from London of the 29th of
April laft) which he took in the
Prince of Orange Packet, to Dr.
Franklin at Paris

*Extract of a letter from the Poftmafter
at Harwich, June 14, to the Poftmafter General, at London.*

" The mafter of a fifhing-fmack,
arrived here laft night from Dunkirk, acquaints me, that he faw
Cunningham and his crew at large
on Thurfday laft, and they were proving carriage guns, in order to be
put on board a large cutter of 130
tons; that fhe was to be navigated by
French failors to Havre, and that
Cunningham and the crew were going over land, in order to fit her
for fea. He alfo declared, that he
faw a brig in Dunkirk road, that
had got on board the powder, fmall
arms,

arms, ammunition, &c. for the said cutter, which is painted blue and yellow, which was built for the smuggling trade, and reported to be a fast sailer; that Cunningham told him the guns proving were for his use on board the said vessel; that he said he would soon have another Harwich boat, which he did not in the least fear but he should make a legal prize, which also was confirmed by the crew the same evening at a publick house. I thought proper to give you this intelligence, and make no doubt of necessary steps being taken to put a stop to the proceedings of this daring pirate. She is to mount 20 carriage guns, and to have 50 or 60 men.

"I am, Sir, your's,
"JAMES CLEMENTS."
[This letter was sent to Llyod's Coffee-House by A. TODD, Esq. Secretary to the Post-master General.]

Whitehall, June 5, 1777.
Extract of a letter from General Sir William Howe to Lord George Germaine, dated at New-York the 24th of April, received by the Mercury Packet.

"Though no material occurrence has passed since the departure of the Le Despencer Packet on the 11th instant; yet, being desirous your Lordship should early receive the duplicates of my last dispatches, in case of an accident happening to the originals, I send them by the Mercury Packet, with orders to stop at Rhode-Island for Lord Percy, which will cause very little delay to her passage.

"Lord Cornwallis, ever watchful to take advantages of the enemy's situation, surprized and defeated, on the 13th inst. at break of day, a corps of the Rebels at Bound Brook, killed 30, and took between 80 and 90 prisoners, including officers, with 3 brass field pieces. The General Officer commanding there very narrowly escaped being of the number. The loss on our part was only 3 yagers,

and 4 soldiers of the light infantry slightly wounded.

"A detached corps of troops, consisting of 1800 rank and file, having embarked in transports, proceeded from hence yesterday, with 6 field pieces, under the command of Governor Tryon, who has accepted of the rank of Major-General of Provincials. The design is to destroy a large magazine of provisions and military stores formed by the enemy at Danbury, in Connecticut. Brigadier-General Agnew and Sir William Erskine are upon this service, the naval part of which is under the conduct of Captain Duncan, commander of his Majesty's ship Eagle. It is supposed that the debarkation should be made at or near Norwalk, which is 20 miles to the Southward of Danbury; and I hope to have the honour of reporting to your Lordship the success of this expedition in my next dispatch."

Earl Percy, who arrived in the above Packet, from Rhode-Island, has communicated to Lord George Germaine the following copy of a letter to his Lordship from Captain Hutchinson, his Aid de Camp:

On board the Mercury Packet, Long-Island Sound, April 30, 1777.
"My Lord,
"Having on Monday evening last, on my way through the Sound, fallen in with Major-General Tryon's detachment, which he was then re-embarking at Norwalk Bay, I was induced to go on board the Senegal to receive the General's commands, and if possible to learn, for your Lordship's information, the success of so important an expedition. The fleet being under way by the time I got on board, the General had just time to desire me to inform your Lordship that he had succeeded beyond his expectations, having compleatly destroyed two principal magazines belonging to the Rebels at Danbury

T 2

and

and Ridgefield, confifting of provifions and other military ftores, fuch as rum, tents, waggons, harnefs, made-up ammunition, hofpital medicines, and cloathing; and that with the lofs of very few men. That he had met with little oppofition on his way to Danbury, but on his return was attacked by Arnold, at the head of a large body of Rebels from Peek's-Kill, who harraffed his march exceedingly almoft the whole way from Ridgefield to near the water-fide; but that he at laft made a fuccefsful charge with his bayonets on their main body, by which he deftroyed a confiderable number, and drove the reft into the utmoft confufion, which enabled him to refume his march, and to re-embark his troops, horfes, artillery, and wounded men, without further moleftation. That he had not then been able to collect the different returns, but from the beft accounts he could get, believed his lofs did not exceed 50 men killed and wounded; that he had no officers killed and only a few wounded. He added, that he was much indebted to the fpirit and bravery of his troops, and particularly fo to Major Stewart, who had diftinguifhed himfelf in a moft confpicuous manner on the occafion. This too I had afterwards explained by General Agnew and his Major of Brigade, Leflie, who informed me that Stewart, with about ten or twelve men only, rufhed forward into the enemy's line, and by his example, animated the reft of our troops to make a general charge, which by that time was become abfolutely neceffary from a want of ammunition, &c.

The Rebels, it feems, had contrived in the fpace of half an hour, with their ufual induftry, to cover themfelves with a kind of breaft work, on the ground over which our troops muft pafs. Leflie faid that there could not be lefs than 4000 barrels of beef and pork, 3000 bar-

rels of flour, and above 50 puncheons of rum, deftroyed in the whole, befides the other articles of camp ftores and cloathing above-mentioned. That a great part of thefe were found in the churches at Danbury and Ridgefield, fome in houfes, and fome in the woods; but that the whole was difcovered, and either ftaved or burnt, together with the above-mentioned towns. Major Leflie likewife faid, that he thought there was above 300 of the Rebels deftroyed, which indeed feemed to be the general opinion. General Woofter, he faid, was certainly mortally wounded; that Arnold efcaped very narrowly with the lofs of his horfe, which was killed. Every body faid, he behaved that day with uncommon refolution, as to perfonal bravery, but did not give him much credit for his judgment as a General. I heard that about 170 prifoners were brought on board, but do not recollect at what place, or in what manner they were taken, being only about ten minutes on board, I could not poffibly collect fo many particulars as I wifhed.

General Agnew had got a flight wound on the fhoulder, and I was told that Major Hope, Capt. Thorne, and Lieut. Haftings, were flightly wounded, and a Captain in Brown's corps, who was faid to be the only one in danger. I was told that General Tryon had returned that corps public thanks for their very gallant behaviour.

General Tryon's detachment confifted of about 2000 men from the 4th, 15th, 23d, 27th, 44th, and 64th regiments, and Brigadier General Brown's corps, with 12 of the 17th light dragoons, and fix light field pieces. They landed on Friday the 25th of April at Norwalk Bay, and proceeded firft to Danbury, from which they returned by way of Ridgefield, and re-embarked on Monday afternoon, the 28th. And it being General Tryon's orders to return as foon as this fervice was performed, they failed immediately for New-York.

Captain Duncan, of the Eagle, had the command of the naval department, having with him the Senegal and Swan floops of war. No accident of any kind happened to any of the fhipping.

This, my Lord, is the fubftance of the information I had time to collect.

G. HUTCHINSON, Aid de Camp.
[*London Gazette.*]

Extract of a letter from the Hon. Sir William Howe to Lord George Germaine, dated New-York, May 22, 1777.

My Lord,

Your Lordfhip's difpatches by Major Balfour, in the Augufta, arrived on the 8th inftant; but as the prefent conveyance is by a private merchant fhip, I fhall defer anfwering them particularly until the failing of the packet, which will be in a fhort time.

In my letter of the 24th of April I mentioned an embarkation of troops detached under the command of Major General Tryon, for the deftruction of one of the enemy's magazines of provifions and ftores, collected at Danbury in Connecticut. I have now the honour of reporting to your Lordfhip the fuccefs of that expedition, and to inclofe a return of the ftores deftroyed.

The troops landed without oppofition in the afternoon of the 25th of April, about four miles to the Eaftward of Norwalk, and 20 from Danbury.

In the afternoon of the 26th the detachment reached Danbury, meeting only fmall parties of the enemy on the march; but General Tryon having intelligence that the whole force of the country was collecting, to take every advantage of the ftrong ground he was to pafs on his return to the fhipping, and finding it impoffible to procure carriages to bring off any part of the ftores, they were effectually deftroyed; in the execution of which the village was unavoidably burnt.

On the 27th in the morning the troops quitted Danbury, and met with little oppofition until they came near to Ridgefield, which was occupied by General Arnold, who had thrown up entrenchments to difpute the paffage, while General Wooller hung upon the rear with a feparate corps. The village was forced, and the enemy drove back on all fides.

General Tryon lay that night at Ridgefield, and renewed his march on the morning of the 28th. The enemy having been reinforced with troops and cannon, difputed every advantageous fituation, keeping at the fame time fmall parties to harrafs the rear, until the General had formed his detachment upon a height, within cannon fhot of the fhipping, when the enemy advancing, feemingly with an intention to attack him, he ordered the troops to charge with their bayonets, which was executed with fuch impetuofity that the rebels were totally put to flight, and the detachment embarked without further moleftation.

The inclofed return fet forth the lofs fuftained by the King's troops, and that of the enemy from the beft information; but I have the fatisfaction to inform your Lordfhip our wounded officers are in the faireft way of recovery.

The enemy's army in Jerfey has been encamped fome days near to Boundbrook. Lord Cornwallis is alfo encamped at Brunfwick on each fide of the Rariton, and upon the communication between that place and Amboy; Major General Vaughan's corps being encamped at the latter place, making ufe of the tents of laft year, the camp equipage of the prefent not being yet arrived. His Lordfhip has alfo thrown a bridge

over

over the Rariton at the town of Brunſwick.

By various accounts received from the neighbourhood of Albany, there is reaſon to believe ſome advanced parties from the Northern army have appeared at Crown Point, and that Sir Guy Carleton will be upon the Lake early in June.

Return of the ſtores, ordnance, proviſions, &c. as nearly as could be aſcertained, found at the rebels ſtores, and deſtroyed by the King's troops at Danbury, &c. in Connecticut, April 27, 1777.

A quantity of ordnance ſtores, with iron, &c.

4000 barrels of beef and pork.
1000 barrels of flour.
100 large tierces of biſket.
89 barrels of rice.
120 puncheons of rum.

Several large ſtores of wheat, oats, and Indian corn, in bulk; the quantity thereof could not poſſibly be aſcertained.

30 pipes of wine.
100 hogſheads of ſugar.
50 ditto of molaſſes.
20 caſks of coffee.
15 large caſks filled with medicines of all kinds.
10 barrels of ſaltpetre.
1020 tents and marquees.
A number of iron boilers.
A large quantity of hoſpital bedding, &c.
Engineers, pioneers, and carpenters tools.
A printing-preſs complete.
Tar, tallow, &c.
5000 pairs of ſhoes and ſtockings.

At a mill between Ridgeberry and Ridgefield 100 barrels of flour, and a quantity of Indian corn.

At the bridge at the Weſt Brace of Norwalk river, and in the woods contiguous.

100 hogſheads of rum.
Several cheſts of arms.
Paper cartridges.
Field forges.
500 tents.

Return of the killed, wounded, and miſſing of the following corps on the 27th and 28th of April, upon the expedition under the command of Major-General Tryon.

4th regiment, 1 captain, 1 ſerjeant, 15 rank and file, wounded; 2 rank and file miſſing.

15th ditto, 8 rank and file killed; 1 captain, 1 ſerjeant, 15 rank and file wounded; 2 rank and file miſſing.

23d ditto, 5 rank and file killed; 1 ſubaltern, 1 ſerjeant, 18 rank and file wounded; 10 rank and file miſſing.

27th ditto, 1 rank and file killed; 1 field officer, 1 captain, 1 ſubaltern, 10 rank and file wounded; 6 rank and file miſſing.

44th ditto, 3 rank and file killed; 1 field officer, 3 ſerjeants, 12 rank and file wounded; 1 drummer and fifer, 4 rank and file miſſing.

64th ditto, 1 captain, 1 ſubaltern, 11 rank and file wounded.

Prince of Wales's American Volunteers, 1 drummer and fifer, 6 rank and file killed; 1 field officer, 2 captains, 3 ſerjeants, 11 rank and file wounded; 3 rank and file miſſing.

Total, 1 drummer and fifer, 23 rank and file killed; 3 field officers, 6 captains, 3 ſubalterns, 9 ſerjeants, 92 rank and file wounded; 1 drummer and fifer, 27 rank and file miſſing.

Royal Artillery, 2 additionals killed; 3 matroſſes, 1 wheeler wounded; 1 matroſs miſſing.

(Signed)   W. HOWE.

4th regiment, Capt. Thorne wounded.
15th, Captain Dirmas, Lieutenant Haſtings, of 12th regiment, acting as a volunteer, wounded.
27th, Major Conran, Captain Rutherford, Enſign Minchin wounded.
23d, Second Lieutenant Price, Volunteer Vale wounded.
44th, Major Hope wounded.

64th,

64th, Captain Calder, Enfign Mercer wounded.

Prince of Wales's American Volunteer's, Colonel Browne, Captain Lyman, Captain Seon wounded.

71ft regiment, Captain Simon Frazer, a Volunteer, wounded.

Return of the Rebels killed and wounded on the 27th and 28th of April, 1777, in Connecticut, by the detachment under the command of Major General Tryon.

K I L L E D.

General Woofter, Colonel Goold, Colonel Lamb of the Artillery, Colonel Henman, Dr. Atwater, a man of confiderable influence, Captain Cooe, Lieutenant Thompfon, 100 privates.

W O U N D E D.

Colonel Whiting, Capt. Benjamin, Lieut. Cooe, 250 privates.

T A K E N.

50 privates, including feveral committee men.

Admiralty Office, June 24, 1777. Vice-Admiral Gayton, Commander in Chief of his Majefty's fhips on the Jamaica ftation, writes, in his letter of the 2d of laft month, that the whole number of rebel veffels which had been taken by the fhips under his command, amounted to 124 fail.

[*London Gazette.*]

An American account of the preceding action (from the Connecticut Journal.)

On Friday the 25th of April, twenty-fix fail of the enemy's fhips appeared off Norwalk Iflands, ftanding in for Cedar Point, where they anchored at four o'clock P. M. and foon began landing troops; by ten o'clock they had landed two brigades, confifting of upwards of two thoufand men, and marched immediately for Danbury, where they arrived the next day at two o'clock P. M. The handful of Continental troops there, were obliged to evacuate the town, having previoufly fecured a part of the ftores, provifions, &c. The enemy, on their arrival, began burning and deftroying the ftores, houfes, provifions, &c. On the appearance of the enemy, the country was alarmed: early the next morning, Brigadier Gen. Silliman, with about 500 militia, (all that were collected) purfued the enemy; at Reading he was joined by Major General Woofter, and Brigadier General Arnold. The heavy rain all the afternoon retarded the march of our troops fo much, that they did not reach Bethel (a village two miles from Danbury) till eleven o'clock at night, much fatigued, and their arms rendered ufelefs by being wet. It was thought prudent to refrefh the men, and attack the enemy on their return. Early the next morning, (which proved rainy) the whole were in motion; 200 men remained with Gen. Woofter, and about 400 were detached under Gen. Arnold and Gen. Silliman, on the road leading to Norwalk. At 9 o'clock A. M. intelligence was received that the enemy had taken the road leading to Norwalk, of which Gen. Woofter was advifed, and purfued them, with whom he came up about eleven o'clock, when a fmart fkirmifh enfued, in which Gen. Woofter, who behaved with great intrepidity, unfortunately received a wound by a mufket ball, through the groin, which it is feared will prove mortal. General Arnold, by a forced march acrofs the country, reached Ridgefield at 11 o'clock, and having pofted his fmall party (being joined by about 100 men) of 500 men, waited the approach of the army, who were foon difcovered advancing in a column, with three field pieces in front, and three in rear, and large fiank guards of near 200 men in each. At noon they began difcharging their artillery, and were foon within mufket fhot, when a fmart action enfued between the whole, which continued

about

about an hour, in which our men behaved with great spirit, but being overpowered by numbers, were obliged to give way, though not until the enemy were raising a small breastwork, thrown across the way, at which General Arnold had taken post with about two hundred men (the rest of our small body were posted on the flanks) who acted with great spirit; the General had his horse shot under him when the enemy were within ten yards of him, but luckily received no hurt; recovering himself, he drew his pistols and shot the soldier, who was advancing with his fixed bayonet. He then ordered his troops to retreat through a shower of small and grape shot. In this action the enemy suffered very considerably, leaving about 30 dead and wounded on the ground, and besides a number unknown, buried. Here we had the misfortune of losing Lieutenant Colonel Goold, one subaltern, and several privates killed and wounded. It was found impossible to rally our troops, and General Arnold ordered a stand to be made at Sagatuck Bridge, where it was expected the enemy would pass.

At nine o'clock A. M. the 28th, about 500 men were collected at Sagatuck Bridge, including part of two companies of Col. Lamb's battalion of artillery, with three field pieces, under command of Lieut. Col. Oswald, one field piece, with part of the artillery from Fairfield, sixty Continental troops, and three companies of volunteers from New Haven, with whom Generals Arnold and Silliman took post about two miles above the bridge. Soon after the enemy appeared in sight, their rear was attacked by Col. Huntington, (commanding a party of 500 men) who sent to Gen. Arnold for instructions and for some officer to assist him.—Gen. Silliman was ordered to his assistance; the enemy finding our troops advantageously posted, made

a halt, and after some little time wheeled off to the left, and forded Sagatuck river, three miles above the bridge. Gen. Arnold observing this motion, ordered the whole to march directly to the bridge to attack the enemy in flank, Gen. Silliman at the same time to attack their rear; the enemy by running full speed had passed the bridge on Fairfield side with their main body, before our troops could pass it. Gen. Silliman finding it impossible to overtake the enemy in their rout, proceeded to the bridge. When the whole were formed, they marched in two columns with two field pieces on the right, the other on the left of the enemy, when a smart skirmish and firing of field pieces ensued, which continued about three hours. The enemy having gained the high hill of Compo, several attempts were made to dislodge them, but without effect. The enemy landed a number of fresh troops to cover their embarkation, which they effected a little before sun-set, weighed anchor immediately, and stood across the Sound for Huntingdon on Long-Island.

Our loss cannot be exactly ascertained, no return being made. It is judged to be about sixty killed and wounded. We made about twenty prisoners.

OTHER PARTICULARS, *brought by a transport, which arrived in England three or four days after the Packet, which brought the first account, in pages 147 and 148.*

General Howe had been informed, that Mr. Washington had some very considerable magazines in Croatlandt's Manor: he wanted to destroy them, as the most effectual mode of distressing the enemy at the opening of the campaign. The object was important, but the execution proved abortive. He first sent the party up the North River, but they did nothing. He next sent General Tryon, with

with two thousand men, 500 of whom were Scotch and Irish, who had come in and joined General Howe, since his arrival at New-York, up the East River. They landed at Norwalk, and proceeded, without hindrance, to Ridgefield and Danbury, at which places, as General Howe had been informed, the Americans had formed one or two confiderable magazines, from their principal stores, in Croatlandt Manor. This information proved *falſe*; for when General Tryon advanced to Ridgefield and Danbury, he could not find any magazine, unless a quantity of rum concealed in a wood can be called a magazine. The hogſheads were ſtaved. In ſeveral of the houſes, in both Danbury and Ridgefield, they were informed there were rum, ſugar, ſhoes, &c. In order to deſtroy theſe, in the quickeſt manner poſſible, all ſuch houſes were immediately ſet on fire. The Americans having no troops at either place, both towns were nearly conſumed. When this was effected, it was reſolved to return to the ſhips; but the American militia, who were watching the motions of the King's troops up the North River, hearing of the operations at Danbury and Ridgefield, haſtened to the relief of thoſe places, but came too late to be of any ſervice in ſaving them, and, therefore, by a quick march, got on both ſides the road, by which the King's troops were to march in their return to the ſhips. A ſort of running fight began; in which both ſides ſuffered confiderably. Of the firing, ſome judgment may be formed, when, it is certain, the King's troops landed with *ſixty* rounds each man, had not any occaſion to fire their pieces once until this attack began, and that when they had got to their boats, they had not *one* round left. The men were ſo exceedingly tired and fatigued with this long and harraſſing march, that when they reached the water-

ſide, the ſailors were obliged to lift moſt of them into the boats. Had any accident happened to the boats or veſſels, ſuch as a ſtorm, &c. the troops muſt inevitably, every man, have been made priſoners, or cut to pieces. The loſs of the King's troops is between 360 and 380 in killed, wounded, and miſſing, beſides all the waggons which they took with them, not one of which they brought back; they were intended for forage. The whole was a ſilly expedition; has anſwered no purpoſe whatever, except to give further provocation. There was no magazine for the ſervice of the enemy's army: what there was, may in ſome degree be called a ſtore of country goods; though it hardly deſerves that name. There are a hundred ſuch in different places. General Tryon was ſelected for this buſineſs, in hopes, his appearance in the country would draw numbers to join him. But it had not that effect. He made no doubt of four or five thouſand men joining him when he got into the country! But he has no influence beyond New York. General Howe is in great diſtreſs for forage. In the judgment of every ſenſible man at New York, the conqueſt of America appears every day more and more impracticable.

The King's army, in general, and particularly the troops at New-York and Amboy, are exceeding ſickly of a dyſentry, which carries off numbers of them daily. The country round Amboy is a perfect deſart for ſeveral miles, owing to a proclamation iſſued by General Waſhington, in March, ordering all the proviſions and forage in Jerſey to be removed out of the province; and all that was not, to be deſtroyed. Had this been done at the beginning of winter, General Howe would not have had a horſe alive. General Howe cannot take the field till the end

end of May. Very few Americans have joined General Howe: at the utmost they are not five hundred; the people who have joined him are refugees from Boston, people who have been driven out of Virginia, &c. chiefly Scotch and Irish, and some English. They are formed into 13 regiments of 300 men each. During the months of March and April, the King's army are reckoned to have lost near three thousand men in Jersey. There are imprisoned at Lancaster and that neighbourhood fourteen hundred Hessians. Many of the Hessians have lately deserted; scarce a day passes without some of them going off. By deserters from General Washington his army (including what was with General Putnam at Prince-town) was said to be forty thousand men on the 29th of April. They are chiefly Southern troops. The Virginia corps is reckoned the best, and consists of 8000 effective. Lord Howe is informed, that the thirteen frigates lately built in different ports by the Congress are all compleatly manned, and out at sea. General Grant is far from being in high favour with either Lord Cornwallis or General Howe. A difference has broke out between General Howe and General Tryon; the latter wanted a provincial staff, which the former refused to grant.

What gives disgust is the partiality General Howe shews to Lord Cornwallis. It was this and this only that occasioned Lord Percy to leave the army: he had the post that was fit for a brigadier general, though he was a lieutenant general; and Lord Cornwallis has the post that is proper for a lieutenant general.

Lord Cornwallis surprised a little post at Boundbrook, but did not think proper to stay; he returned as fast as he could to Brunswick. And the Provincials in turn surprised his post at Bonum town. These circumstances afford a very unpromising prospect of conquest; as they shew, that whenever any parties of the King's troops are sent out, they can stay but a few minutes; they are obliged to make the best of their way back as soon as possible, lest the country should be alarmed, and their retreat be cut off.

The Congress (since the arrival of the stores from France) have ordered six seventy-four gun ships to be built as fast as possible. The timbers have been cut for them some time. The keels of two of them were laid about the middle of April.

The infamous manner of plundering, begun first by the Hessians, and now practised by the whole army, is mentioned in every letter from America. The constant and innumerable ravishments of the farmers wives and daughters are truly shocking; and some of the circumstances are so affecting, so brutal and cruel, that decency will not permit them to be related. As to the plundering, there is nothing so common as to see the soldiers wives, and other women, who follow the army, carrying each three or four silk gowns, fine linen, &c. &c. which have been stolen by the soldiers from the different houses in their march, or where they last slept; many of the soldiers have got watches, which they have stolen in the same manner. The officers, at least several of them, are not free from these practices; and the considerable remittances which they have made to England, are urged as proofs of the gain they have made by plunder. These cruelties and robberies have irritated the Americans beyond the possibility of expression, and have put peace totally out of sight. And as to conquest, it is ridiculous, unless the army was at least three times larger than it is, to be stationed in every place it conquers, and thereby to hold every place by military power;

the

the whole army to be paid, recruited, and fed from England.

Hertford, May 7. Governor Tryon having collected a gang of starved wretches from among the British troops and Tories, came over from Long-Island the 26th ult. and landed at Campo, between Norwalk and Fairfield, from thence they beat through the woods to Danbury, where they found a quantity of provision, some of which they eat, and some they destroyed, and some they attempted to carry off; but a number of people collecting, alarmed their guilty fears, and caused them to flee back with precipitation, through thick and thin, wet and dry, rough and smooth, leaving bag and baggage, about 50 killed, and 20 taken prisoners, 18 or 20 of whom are now in gaol in this place. Thus ended the glorious expedition of Tryon. He found such good picking while Governor of New-York, that his head aches beyond conception to get possession of that government again: but he must gnaw his trencher a great while before that time arrives. We expect another visit from these hungry bellies in a short time, that it may be proper enough to keep a good look-out. [*Connecticut Journal.*

Newhaven, April 30. A Member of Congress, in a letter dated April 15, 1777, writes to his friend in this town (Newhaven) *That an extract of a letter from England to the Commissioners* (Dr. Franklin, &c. in France) *mentions, that the British Ministry intended totally to destroy the New England States, and make slaves of the Southern.* [*Ibid.*

New-York, May 12, 1777.

Majors Balfour and Gardiner arrived in the Augusta, of 64 guns, from Plymouth. The ship sailed from Portsmouth the 28th of March.

Came passengers in the Augusta also, Daniel Wier, Esq. Commissary

General to the army, under the command of Sir William Howe; Daniel Chamier, Esq. being promoted to the place of Auditor General, &c. &c.

The Americans say that the King's troops, employed in destroying the magazines at Danbury, "behaved with great barbarity, wantonly and cruelly murdering the wounded prisoners who fell into their hands, and plundering the inhabitants, burning and destroying every thing in their way."

New-York, May 19. Last Saturday sevennight, about four in the afternoon, a body of about 2000 rebels, which had been collected from the neighbouring posts of Quibbletown, Samptown, Westfield, Chatham, &c. commanded by Brigadier Generals Stevens and Maxwell, attacked the picquet of the 42d or Royal Highland regiment at Piscataway, commanded by Lieutenant Colonel Stirling. The picquet, which was in a short time supported by two companies, advanced into the wood, where, notwithstanding the very superior number of the rebels, they maintained their ground, until they were joined by the rest of the regiment, when a very heavy fire commenced, which obliged the rebels to retreat in the greatest confusion towards their left, where they fell in with the light infantry, quartered between Piscataway and Bonham Town, who were advancing to support the 42d. The whole of the rebels now gave way, and fled with the utmost precipitation, our troops pursuing them close to their encampment (on the heights near Motuchen meeting-house) which they began to strike with the greatest terror.

The ardour of the troops was so great, that it was with difficulty they could be restrained from storming the encampment; but night coming on, they were ordered to return to their cantonments. In this affair we had

U 2

two

two officers and 26 men killed and wounded.

Yesterday sevennight a sloop with a flag of truce arrived here from Albany, by whom we are informed, that previous to her departure an express arrived from Ticonderoga with intelligence, that sixteen sail of vessels, and a number of boats, with part of General Sir Guy Carleton's army, were in sight of Crown Point, and that the whole army were supposed to be upon their passage: that the garrison of Ticonderoga consists of only 1500 men, sick included; that the rebels were persecuting the friends of Government with unremitting industry: that John Monro, Esq. Major Hogan, Lieutenant Hughston, and Mr. Charity French, were sentenced to suffer death: that one Mr. Mawbie, and two other gentlemen, were hanged last week at Peck's Kill; and that thirteen others were to have been executed at Fort Montgommery on Friday last: that in consequence of those cruelties 100 loyalists assembled to the eastward of Albany, in order to relieve their friends: that a body of 400 of the rebels were sent against them, when a skirmish ensued, in which eight rebels and three loyalists were killed upon the spot: the loyalists then struck into the woods, and got safe to Gen. Carleton's army.

Last Monday afternoon a detachment of his Majesty's provincial troops, consisting of 300 men, under the command of Lieutenant Colonels Barton and Dongan, marched from Bergen Town, in order to attack General Heard, who lay at Pennoton with a party of rebels of 350. The various impediments occasioned by morasses, &c rendered it impossible for the troops to reach the place by the time intended. Col. Barton, who commanded, held a consultation, wherein it was determined to take the road to Paramus, and to destroy some stores said to be deposited there, under a guard of 80 or 100 men: Col. Dongan was previously detached with a small party to Saddle River and Slotterdam, in order to surprize a party of rebels, under the command of Capt. Marinus and two others: the Colonel arrived at the place at the dawn of day, made the attack, carried his point, took the Captain, his Lieutenant, and three others, together with a small cask of powder, some ball, eight or nine stand of arms, a drum, and some other articles. In this skirmish the Colonel had the misfortune to have Capt. Hardnut, a worthy officer, wounded in the groin by a bayonet, but not mortally. Col. Barton marched on to Paramus, drove the rebels from their strong holds, and obliged them to retreat to the woods. The bravery of the provincial troops on this occasion does them honour.

By a gentleman arrived here last Tuesday from Albany, which place he left on Wednesday the 7th instant, we learn, that a party of Indians had attacked the picquet guard at Fort Stanwix, scalped four, and taken the rest prisoners; that the Committee of the city of Albany inflict great hardships on the friends of Government; that a number of their emissaries in conducting some friends of Government, whom they had taken prisoners, through Levingston's Manor, were attacked by a number of loyalists, who rescued their friends; but the rebels being reinforced next day, they attacked the loyalists, who were obliged to surrender prisoners of war. The rebels have sunk a number of chevaux de frize opposite New Windsor, but are not very sanguine in their expectations that they will obstruct the navigation.

The rebels, we are assured, are again busy at Danbury, in collecting provisions, &c. and intend to erect some fortifications at that place, in order to secure their stores.

The

The fleet from this port for Quebec arrived at Halifax on the 27th of April. [New-York Gazette.

Extract of a letter from Lord George Germaine to Governor Tryon, dated Whitehall, March 3, 1777.

" When I had the honour to lay your dispatches before the King, his Majesty observed, with great satisfaction, the effusions of loyalty and affection which break forth in the addresses of his faithful subjects upon their deliverance from the tyranny and oppression of the rebel Committees; and the proof given by the inhabitants of King's county, of their zeal for the success of his Majesty's measures, by so generously contributing towards the expence of raising Colonel Fanning's battalion, was highly pleasing to the King, and cannot fail of recommending them to his Majesty's favour.

" Should their example be followed by the King's other loyal subjects, it must be productive of the best effects, and not only remove all reproach of lukewarmness in the cause of the constitution, but have a great tendency to dash the hopes of the rebels, by convincing them, that Government has resources even in America for crushing their rebellion. And, for the greater encouragement of the King's faithful subjects to stand forth upon this great occasion, his Majesty is graciously pleased to authorize you to give assurances of grants of like portions of lands to the non-commissioned officers and private soldiers of the corps which shall be raised in your province, and continue in his Majesty's service during the war, as were given to his Majesty's troops of the same rank by the proclamation of 1763."

By his Excellency Sir WILLIAM HOWE, Knight of the most noble Order of the Bath.

PROCLAMATION.

Whereas a plentiful supply of vegetables, and of fresh provisions of all kinds, will greatly tend to the preservation of the health of his Majesty's troops and others; and the raising large quantities of hay, and other forage, will very much conduce to his Majesty's service, as well as be of general use: in order therefore to give all due encouragement to all his Majesty's liege subjects, so that they may chearfully exert themselves in raising such supplies, under a full assurance of enjoying all possible protection in so doing, I have thought fit to issue this Proclamation, strictly charging and commanding, that no person or persons whomsoever, under any colour or pretence whatsoever, presume to trespass upon any inclosure, or fences whatsoever, now standing, or hereafter to be erected, as they will answer for the same at their peril. And to the end that this Proclamation may be more strictly observed, I do hereby further charge, require and command all officers, soldiers and others, to seize and deliver over to any officer commanding any part of his Majesty's forces, or to the Provost Marshal, all such persons as they shall find acting in disobedience hereto, in order that such offenders may be brought to condign punishment for the same; hereby declaring that any neglect herein shall be considered and punished as a breach of orders. And I do further charge and require the commanding officers of any of his Majesty's officers, and Provost Marshal, from time to time, to receive into custody all such offenders as shall be brought to them as aforesaid, and duly to make report thereof.

Given under my hand at Head Quarters, in New-York, the twentieth day of March 1777.

W. HOWE.

By his Excellency's command, Robert Mackenzie, Sec.

By

By Major General ROBERT PIGOT, *Commandant in New-York.*

PROCLAMATION.

Whereas great numbers of the citizens and soldiers make it a constant practice to throw the dirt and filth out of their houses and yards, into the streets and lanes of this city; which not only renders some of the streets almost impassable, but may tend greatly to injure the health of the inhabitants,

I have therefore thought fit to issue this Proclamation, hereby strictly charging and commanding all and every person within this city, who have already thrown any dirt or filth into the streets, immediately to cause the same to be removed: and I do hereby strictly forbid all persons for the future placing any dirt or filth in the streets or lanes of this city; of which all persons are to take notice, and govern themselves accordingly, under pain of military execution.

Given under my hand at New-York, the 10th day of May, in the 17th year of his Majesty's reign,

R. PIGOT, M. G.
And Commandant in New-York.

The following papers were received too late to be inserted in their proper places.

STATE of MASSACHUSETTS BAY.
In the House of Representatives.

Jan. 26, 1777.

Ordered.—That the following addresses be printed, and a copy thereof sent to each Minister of the Gospel within this State; to whom it is recommended to read the same, the next Lord's-day after he shall receive it, to his people, immediately after the religious exercises of the day are over: And also that a copy thereof be sent to the Commanding Officer of each company of the militia, in each town in this State, to be read to the companies of militia, while they are under arms, for the purpose of recruiting the army:

To the PEOPLE *of the* MASSACHUSETTS BAY.

" Friends and Countrymen!

" When a people within the reach of the highest temporal happiness human nature is capable of, are in danger of having it wrested from them, by an enemy whose paths are marked with blood, and an insupportable load of misery, which succeeding generations must bear through centuries of time, is offered instead of it; to rouse the brave, invite the generous, quicken the flow, and awaken all to a sense of their danger, is a measure as friendly as it is important. The danger of having your towns, your families, your fruitful fields, and all the riches and blessings derived from the industry and wisdom of your venerable ancestors, who may be ranked among the most virtuous and brave men the world ever produced, ravished from you, and possessed by a banditti, whom no laws can controul, and whose aim is to trample upon all the rights of humanity, would be sufficient to give the coward courage, and animate to the greatest feats in arms, the most supine and indolent. Surely then, while America, the asylum of happiness and freedom, is invested with a foe, whose sole aim is to rifle her sons of every enjoyment that renders life desireable, you will be ready in arms, to defend your country, your liberty, your wives, your children, and possessions, from rapine, abuse, and destruction.

" For this grand and noble purpose, so worthy of the virtuous and brave, and we humbly trust so pleasing to Almighty God, you have by your delegates, assembled in Council for several years past;—for this in April 1775, you arrayed yourselves in arms,—defeated and put to flight that band of Britons, who uninjured, and unoffended, like robbers and murderers, dared to assault your
peaceful

peaceful manfions;—and for this we truit you will be at all times ready to fpend your blood and treafure. In addreffing you upon the important fubject of your own defence, fhould we attempt a narration of the caufes of your danger, the many petitions you have prefented, praying for peace, liberty and fafety, and to avoid fhedding the blood of your fellow men, and the unexampled indignity and contempt with which thofe petitions were treated—it would be undefervedly to impeach you of inattention to your own fafety.

" Let it fuffice then to fay, that when every other method taken by you, was productive of nothing but infults,—and that flames in your houfes, murders on your perfons, and robberies on your property were returned, in anfwer to your peaceable, humble, and dutiful petitions, when the force of Britain, with that of her allies, were collected, and drawn into exertion, to reduce you from eafe and affluence, to flavery, and vaffalage;—the Congrefs of the United States, defpairing otherwife to eftablifh your fafety, upon principles which would render it durable, made that declaration, by which you become independent of Great Britain,—and in which character alone, you can be fecure and happy.

" But as the increafing power and opulence of the United States, are the dread and envy of thofe avaricious and ambitious minds, who had laid a plan for the monopoly and enjoyment of them, a large army is neceffary for your defence; and the Congrefs themfelves have determined upon eighty-eight battalions, of which 15 are to be raifed by this State.—The militia, who have been marched to aid the army under the conduct of that man, whofe fortitude, virtue, and patience, is perhaps without example, (and who hourly, without reward, but the approbation of his own mind) is rifquing his All, in

your caufe, will foon be on their return; —the enemy, angry at the chaftifement juftly given them, for their unprovoked cruelties to our brethren in the Jerfeys, are watching an opportunity to return the blow.—A farther draft from the militia would fo much burthen the people of this State, that this Court cannot think of it without pain and anxiety. We have therefore, being certain that you need no other ftimulous to your duty than having the line of it drawn for you, directed that the number of men, amounting to one-feventh part of all the male perfons of fixteen and upwards, fhould be immediately engaged in the Continental army, upon the encouragement given by Government; this encouragement we conceive to be greater than any ever given,—even to the greateft mercenaries.—Surely then, a people called to fight, not to fupport crowns, and principalities, but for their own freedom and happinefs, will readily engage.

" That the encouragement given might fully anfwer the defigns of Government, and the expectation of the foldiery, this Court have fettled the price of every neceffary and convenient article of life, produced in this country, and alfo the price of foreign goods, in a juft proportion to their price in the place from which they are imported, confidering the rifque of importation. And nothing is now wanting to give value to the foldiers wages, and ftability to our currency, but the vigorous and punctual execution and obfervance of that act; which we hope to fee fpeedily effected, by the public virtue, and zeal of this people, in the caufe of their country.

" But left fome of you fhould be deceived by the mifreprefentations of defigning men, we muft remind you, that all the pretenfions to peace and reconciliation, fo pompoufly dealt out in the infidious Proclamations of the
Commiffioners

Commiffioners of the King of Great-Britain, amount to nothing more than an invitation to give up your country, and fubmit unconditionally to the government of the Britifh Parliament. They tell you that their is gracioufly difpofed to revife all acts, which he fhall deem incompatible with your fafety;—but your good fenfe will lead you to determine, that if he is

he would long ago have determined as to the juftice of thofe acts, and muft have feen them founded on defpotifm, and replete with flavery;—but they do not tell you that their Sovereign has the leaft intention to repeal any one of thofe acts;—furely then, a revifion of them can never eafe your minds, or in the leaft alleviate your burthens.

" But thofe Commiffioners, although they offer themfelves as the Ambaffadors of Peace, and invite you to what they call the mild and gentle government of Britain, mark their footfteps with blood, rapine, and the moft unexampled barbarities, diftributing their dreadful, and favage feverity, as well to the fubmiffive as the obftinate, while neither rank, fex, or age, exempts any from the effects of their brutal paffions.

" Should America be overcome by, or fubmit to Britain, the needy and almoft perifhing tenant in Ireland, difarmed, and having but little property in the production of his toil and labour, foiling the bread for which his tender infants are fuffering to pay the haughty landlord's rent, or infulting collector's tax, would be but a faint refemblance of your calamity.

" Society, where no man is bound by other laws than thofe to which he gives his own confent, is the greateft ornament, and tends moft of all things to the felicity of human nature, and is a privilege which can never be given up by a people, with-

out their being exceedingly guilty before him who is the Beftower of every good and perfect gift.

" We therefore, for the fake of that religion, for the enjoyment whereof your anceftors fled to this country;—for the fake of your laws, and future felicity, intreat and urge you to act vigoroufly, and firmly, in this critical fituation of your country; and we doubt not but that your noble exertions under the fmiles of Heaven, will infure you that fuccefs and freedom, due to the wife man and the patriot.

" Above all, we earneftly exhort you to contribute all within your power to the encouragement of thofe virtues—for which the Supreme Being has declared that he will beftow his bleffings upon a nation, and to the difcouragement of thofe vices, for which he overturns kingdoms in his wrath; and that all proper times and feafons you feek to him by prayer and fupplication, for deliverance from the calamities of war, duly confidering, that without his powerful aid, and gracious interpofition, all your endeavours muft prove abortive and vain.

Sent up for concurrence.
Samuel Freeman, Speaker, P. T.
In Council, January 28, 1777.
Read and concurred.
John Avery, Dep. Sec.

———

To his Excellency HENRY CLINTON, Efq; Lieutenant General, commanding his Majefty's forces, in the colony of Rhode-Ifland, &c. &c.

" May it pleafe your Excellency,
" WE the freeholders and inhabitants of the town of Newport, penetrated with a truly grateful fenfe of his Majefty's paternal affection and tendernefs for his unhappy deluded American fubjects, exhibited in the Proclamation of November laft, made by the King's Commiffioners for reftoring peace to his colonies in
America,

America, humbly presume to address your Excellency; most heartily congratulating you upon your arrival amongst us, sincerely praying that your endeavours for the re-establishment of peace and good government to this once flourishing, but now distressed town, may be crowned with success.

" We have long beheld, with the deepest concern and anxiety, the baleful influence of factious and designing men, throughout his Majesty's American colonies, who by their evil counsels have effected an unnatural separation from the parent state, renounced their allegiance to the best of sovereigns, and upon the ruins of an unhappy constitution established a system, totally subversive of every idea of civil and religious liberty.

" The many instances of humanity and benignity displayed by your Excellency since your arrival embolden us to look up, and entreat that your Excellency would be pleased to interpose in our behalf, and so use your influence, with the King's Commissioners, that, through your intercession, this town may once more enjoy the King's most gracious protection, together with the blessings resulting from a constitutional dependance upon the supreme authority of Great Britain.

" We beg leave to represent to your Excellency, that we bear all loyal and dutiful allegiance to his Majesty King George the Third, his sacred person, crown, and dignity; and humbly pray to be declared at his peace, and obedient to the supremacy of Great-Britain; being convinced, that to be a subject of the British Empire, with all its consequences, is to be the freest member of any civil society in the known world."

Signed by 444 of the principal inhabitants of that town.

To which his Excellency was pleased to return the following answer:

" It gives me singular pleasure to receive this public testimony of your loyalty to the King, and attachment to the British constitution.

" Wishing to promote the prosperity of the town of Newport, I shall not fail to signify to the King's Commissioners your request.

" I return you thanks for the good opinion you are pleased to entertain of me; and can assure you, I shall be happy in being instrumental to restore peace and good order to this colony."

To his Excellency the Right Honourable HUGH EARL PERCY, *Lieutenant General, commanding his Majesty's forces within the colony of* Rhode Island, &c. &c.

" May it please your Excellency,

" We the subscribers, freeholders, and other inhabitants of the town of James Town, on the island of Connecticut, beg leave to congratulate your Excellency upon your arrival among us; as it affords the pleasing prospect of a speedy restoration of his Majesty's authority and government within this part of the colony; where many of the inhabitants have long suffered the severest evils, from the wanton exercise of lawless power.

" We are so sensible of the blessings resulting from a constitutional connection with the parent state, that your Excellency may be assured it is our ardent wish, once more to enjoy the King's most gracious protection, and that we may be declared at his peace.

" The many instances of clemency manifested by your immediate predecessor, his Excellency General Clinton, towards the inhabitants of Rhode Island and Connecticut, upon his taking possession of those islands, demands our warmest acknowledgements; and from your Lordship's known character for benevolence and humanity, we are fully persuaded

X　　　　　　　　　fuaded

fuaded that we fhall be admitted to the enjoyment of our liberties and properties, upon the true principles of the conftitution.

" We humbly prefume to repeat to your lordfhip, that we bear true and faithful allegiance to his Majefty King George, his facred perfon, crown and dignity, and feverally promife and declare, that we will remain in a peaceful obedience to his Majefty, and will not take up arms in oppofition to his authority "

Signed by all the inhabitants of the town.

To which his Excellency was pleafed to return the following anfwer:

" Gentlemen,

" It gives me the greateft fatis-faction, to find fuch expreffions of loyalty to his Majefty, and attachment to the Britifh conftitution, contained in your addrefs.

" You may be affured, that I fhall not fail to communicate to his Majefty's Commiffioners your wifh once more to enjoy the King's moft gracious protection, and to be de-clared at his peace.

" The compliments which you are pleafed to pay my immediate predeceffor General Clinton, for his behaviour during the time of his command here, are juftly his due; and I flatter myfelf, that, by en-deavouring to follow his example, I fhall merit your good opinion; for, be affured, it is my wifh, equally with every other Britifh officer, to protect the loyal and peaceable in-habitants of America, in the full enjoyment of their liberties and properties, upon the principles of the conftitution."

To his Excellency HUGH, EARL PERCY, Lieutenant - General, commanding his Majefty's forces on Rhode Ifland, &c. &c. &c.

May it pleafe your Excellency,

We, the fubfcribers, inhabitants of the town of Newport, hearing,

with the utmoft concern, that your Excellency intends foon to leave us, beg permiffion to approach your Ex-cellency with thofe fentiments which a deep fenfe of the great happinefs we have enjoyed under your Excel-lency's protection naturally excites on fuch an occafion.

We cannot help looking on your Excellency's departure as a great pub-lic lofs, when we reflect upon that extraordinary activity and vigilance wherewith your Excellency has pro-tected us from furrounding dangers, and on that juftice and impartiality, that humanity and tendernefs with which you have moderated the exer-cife of unlimited power.

With gratitude we acknowledge that in your Excellency's hands mi-litary government has uniformly worn the fair form of parental authority, that no unneceffary vigour hath been ufed, no oppreffion tolerated, and that, during the noife and tumults of a civil war, the troops under your Excellency's command have been kept under fuch order and difcipline as would have done honour to them-felves and their Commanders in times of public peace and fettled govern-ment.

The fear of offending (not infen-fibility) prevents us at prefent from attempting to exprefs how much we are affected with your Excellency's great and amiable private virtues; with that fpotlefs integrity of man-ners, and uniform regard to religion and decency, which would add dig-nity to the meaneft ftation; with that condefcending affability, which ftoops without any view to private advan-tage, and, above all, with that un-bounded and well-directed generofity which has fo often procured for your Excellency the bleffings of thofe who were ready to perifh.

Great virtues, my Lord, in an elevated ftation are like the fun; there is nothing hid from the heat of them: they have neceffarily endeared

your

your character to all the inhabitants of this place; and it is but justice to say, that during your residence among us, you have never given any cause for uneasiness or sorrow, but when you declared your intention of departing from us.

With great reluctance we submit to the painful necessity, which deprives us of your Excellency's benign patronage; and sincerely wish you a safe and pleasant passage to your native land, and a long continuance of perfect health. Your Excellency's illustrious rank and character renders it unnecessary to wish you any other blessings of life. Particularly we reflect with pleasure, that your Excellency's early and great public services have gone home long before you, and have there secured you that great reward peculiarly reserved for British Worthies, and highly suitable to your Excellency's generous principles, the warmest approbation of the best of princes, and of a brave and free people.

His EXCELLENCY's Answer.

Gentlemen,

Allow me to return you many thanks for your very affectionate address.

This public testimony of your approbation of my conduct since I have had the honour to command here, at the same time that it reflects the highest honour upon me, is more particularly pleasing to me, as it is a proof that I have been fortunate enough to fulfil the intentions of our gracious Sovereign in sending his troops to this island.

The compliments you are pleased to pay those troops for their regularity and good conduct since they have been amongst you, are justly their due. As it is the duty, so it is the wish of every British and Hessian soldier to protect all peaceable and innocent inhabitants.

Permit me, Gentlemen, to assure you, that I shall not without regret quit this Island, whose inhabitants I shall ever remember with gratitude and esteem: and be assured, that when I have the honour to return into the Royal presence, I shall not fail to do them that justice, which their behaviour has highly merited at my hands.

PHILADELPHIA, *Jan.* 4, 1777.

In COUNCIL *of* SAFETY.

Friends and Countrymen,

The present exigency of the times induces us once more to address you, while we can deplore the calamities of our country without restraint, and before the voice of truth and the exertions of tyranny are forced back into the bosom of the wretched sufferer. On your vigorous exertions alone at this time will depend the privilege of ever addressing you in the stile of freemen. Should the enemy be encouraged by further success, devastation and ruin must mark their footsteps.

We call upon you, we entreat and beseech you, to come forth to the assistance of our worthy General WASHINGTON and our invaded brethren in the Jerseys—If you wish to secure your property from being plundered, and to protect the innocence of our wives and children—If you wish to live in freedom, and are determined to maintain that best boon of Heaven, you have no time to deliberate—A manly resistance will secure every blessing—Inactivity and sloth will bring horror and destruction—Step forth like men—Feed not yourselves with the vain expectation of peace and security, should the enemy succeed in reducing this country; such hopes will vanish like the dreams of the night, and plunge you into an irretrievable abyss of unspeakable misery.

Shall we, Heaven and justice on our side, (unless we could impiously suppose

X 2

suppose that the Almighty has devoted mankind to slavery) shall we hesitate to meet our enemies in the hostile field? The sons of America have not drawn their swords to invade the rights of others, nor to reduce populous countries to a state of desolation---It was not to plunder the wealthy, nor to wrest from the laborious farmer or industrious mechanic his hard earned blessings, that America had recourse to arms---No ---Whilst our most humble petitions and pathetic expostulations yet rung in the ears of our enemies, they wantonly attacked us on our own peaceful shores.

May Heaven, who bestowed the blessings of liberty upon you, awaken you to a sense of your danger, and rouse that manly spirit of virtuous resolution which has ever bid defiance to the efforts of tyranny.----May you ever have the glorious prize of liberty in view, and bear with a becoming fortitude the fatigues and severities of a winter-campaign.----That, and that only, will entitle you to the superlative distinction of being deemed, under God, the deliverers of your country.

Many are the artifices of our enemies to delude and deceive. False tales of every kind are invented and propagated to amuse and delay you. For this purpose, among others, they have spread a report that your services are not wanted. Believe no such reports; they are propagated by traitors. Let all able bodied men, whether associates or not, step forth at this crisis, under the officers of the district where they reside, and march without delay to Philadelphia, except those of Berks and Northampton, who are to join Gen. Washington at Head Quarters.

We conclude with intreating all committees of inspection, officers of the militia, and every friend to his country, to exert their influence on the present occasion, and we have not the least doubt but their virtuous endeavours will be crowned with the most happy success.

By order of Council,

Tho. Wharton, jun. President.

For the REMEMBRANCER.

*—Of all the projects which men form, none are more uncertain than those, which depend upon the fortune of war.—*Answer of the Grand Master of *Rhodes* to the Sultan *Soliman.*

The genius of the nation has stepped forth to lift the veil from the precipice; and bids us pause upon our danger, and look backwards for retreat. Our allies are attacked without, a frantic war rages within, and armed foes stand umpires of the contest. This then is our danger. We cannot be safe when our enemies gladden at our condition, we cannot be wise when we waste the most improveable portion of our empire, we cannot be wealthy when our burthens increase fast upon a withering revenue.—Where then is our retreat? But yesterday, and a roll of waste parchment seemed the purchase: to-day, nothing is before us but devastation and blood.---But though we have let go the narrow moment left for magnanimity and concession, proud and senseless as we are, time must at last bring us to negotiation. What our condition may be at that period, is lost in dread and uncertainty. At all events the changing disease must have changing applications; and all that can now be done is to point out the constitution of the subject, and the blessings of a cure.

To balance a judgment formed in moments of superiority and pride, let me begin by a pointed question. *—Should America now, for the first time, be raised out of the deep, ready-planted and peopled by Almighty Power, and a new Columbus make it known unto us; let me ask, by what policy ought*

ought our measures towards it to be guided ?---I put humanity as much out of the question as it seems to be put at present; I forget all our useless rights, and think of nothing but our *interests*. Upon this basis, which is really worth a just contention, I affirm that we should rush into the alliance and trade of this rising people : it would be held as madness to reject them; and still a double madness to force them into connection with our enemies. To oppress, to slaughter them, because at some distant time and in some possible manner they may peradventure injure us, is a principle which would thrust us into war with all mankind, and which certainly ought to check our fond aggrandizement of Russia?--- America, *if left to herself*, will pursue her interests.

Now it is certainly *not* the present interest of America to manufacture. It would be easy to prove that their *Land*, the gift of nature, and unburthened with rent, affords the most profitable of all employments for their wealth.---But, to set policy out of the question, I say they cannot, they will not manufacture.---A system of manufacture requires close population; and never can resist competition without low wages, a subdivision of employments, and the sisterhood of the arts. While America therefore has such profusion of land and such scarcity of labor, all rivalship with Europe is at once forbidden. And what American will grovel at a mechanic loom, when he can walk the lord of his soil, and say, Here have I planted, here watered; when he can communicate a solid growing heritage to his posterity; and become that character which his every connection has taught him

to respect? If pride, if pleasure or profit, are motives that can have any share in the heart of man, they surely combine to cast this period of general manufacture at a distance. It would be easy to improve this reasoning : but I shall only guard it from misrepresentation.---I will not deny then that some *districts* may hereafter enter upon manufactures; I will not affirm, that the European workman upon his first emigration will always forget his cunning; perhaps too some articles of easy supply and difficult importation may be generally wrought among them ; and good policy also may at some expence preserve the seeds of necessary manufactures, that at critical moments they may be quickened into instant life ;---but what is there alarming in this? Is not *enough* still left to content us? In Europe, for instance, among nations most professing arts, would not an open trade (such as America means to give) fill their ports with British articles? I know those avaritious fears, which from the existence of one failure expect a thousand; I know that none but large minds which grasp the whole of things, can measure the disproportion between the exception and the compliance, and calmnly acquiesce in those petty deviations which always occur in great concerns. But I rest upon plain appeals to fact. Has America even yet, though goaded on by necessity and fury, furnished her home supplies; has not the rate of labor and profit most exorbitantly risen from the new demands; and do not their wisest men conceive that manufactures must chiefly reside in the colonies possessing slaves, because slaves only can be confined to their employments? *

* It seems the suggestion of Sir James Stewart, that to prevent American manufacture, it might be expedient to encourage slavery; and surely granting slavery its usual dullness and expence, Britain can have little to fear from its competition.

If

If America then has demands upon Europe, the next queftion is, *Who fhall be the fupplier?*---If there be a nation holding unity with them in language and laws, having common religion and common bl od, whofe manners and fafhions fprung from one ftock, and whom habit (for fo the fact is) and a thoufand namelefs links have already bound together; ---if there be fuch a nation, with flourifhing arts, extended credits, and a potent marine, that is the connection marked out to them from all mankind,—there can be no hefitation : I fpeak of Britain. America demands a counterpart, and Britain is that counterpart : fhe wants it, were it only for defence, and Britain is that defence. In fhort, looking over the whole circle of commerce, and taking in the ftate of our iflands, of America and of Europe, I no where fee fuch ties of union. So much of nature is there in the connection; and fo impoffible is it to weave a ftronger band than intereft joined to inclination, that, *phrenzy excepted*, it might have fubfifted while America wanted protection, or Britain wanted trade.

But there are, who boaft that our play has a double refource;---that we may *firft* aim at conqueft, and *that failing*, at pleafure accept of trade. This is the language of a giddy, thoughtlefs, hardened fpirit, which has fcattered more mifchiefs among mankind than the whole train of bafer paffions.---Let me

queftion it a little.---After outraging thefe haughty freemen with infults, and deluging them with blood, can we bid them *follow our fafhions*; predilection being the foul of fafhion, and influencing even our ideas of ufe * ?---In inftituting a foreign commerce, ought a war to preface it, that muft introduce frugality, poverty, manufacture and hoftile connections among the confumers? Is it for inftance that they may buy the more, that we make them frugal; or that they may pay the better, that we impoverifh them? And do we ferioufly mean to throw them upon home fupplies or French correfpondence; or to eftablifh among them the ill-judged policy of interdicting Britifh trade? ---Or laftly, do we wifh to excite a people, devoted to agriculture and abounding in territory, to profefs ambition and war?---If this be our *trading* fyftem, the bayonet will devour our profits, and we muft keep our accounts in blood. Madnefs, wicked madnefs!---The trade with this people that is *profitable*, muft be left to nature : and, " while their " good-will is their *own*," the fword cannot conquer their affections.

But the fecret is out. France fays, you fhall not conquer; you fhall not conftrain their trade. fhe fays it, and ratifies it with a fleet that infults us.---A vain, mortified power, arming at a period fo critical, gave juft alarms of inftant war. Perhaps they remained quiet from policy, perhaps from indecifion, or

---

* The man who is not ferioufly and habitually convinced in thefe points is young in commercial reafonings; and I would very particularly recommend his profiting by an entertaining fet of facts produced by Jofhua Gee (fee Gee on Trade chap. 22. and the conclufion.) —But furely every ftudent in fafhions muft have witneffed averfions and attachments to different goods, the moft fudden and capricious; fpeculatifts too muft have feen a thoufand ufeful things banifhed, to make room for others more expenfive and inconvenient; Englifhmen may have obferved this in their own country, to the prejudice of their own beft manufactures; and are not traders daily telling us that they find their demands go and come nobody knows how ?—America doubtlefs will fell according to intereft, in the beft markets; but excepting neceffaries and raw produce, we fhall buy—according to whim. And real neceffaries we find, by Jofhua Gee and the tea-act, include neither Englifh cloth nor Englifh tea.

perhaps

perhaps the unexpected vigor of America persuaded them that an open part was superfluous. But still an instant war *was* to be dreaded; and the minister avowed his fears of it by a press.----And who is hardy enough to say that we are now relieved from it? Such an armament, amidst every possible security for peace on *our* part, upon the gentlest interpretation, fixes these conclusions: first, that France will resist all enquiry into her late measures; next, that, should America be pressed, she will restore the balance by declaring war; and lastly, that she is prepared to profit by all events that may arise: and let me add, that while the enemy is armed and can begin war with such apparent advantages, disputes with her necessarily become less subject to accommodation.----In this situation shall I feel either triumph or comfort, because a captured packet-boat has been released? " Yes; France " is wondrously civil: she will give " you packet-boats for provinces, " as many as you please *."---And when the rupture takes place in Europe, not only *men* appear likely to fail us, but *money*. During the last war our subscriptions filled with sufficient ease; because the bankruptcy of France † so shocked her credit, that the money-holders of Europe had almost no safe depositary left but in our funds: but at present, when the credit of France seems rising with her trade, œconomy, and prospects of success, and the credit of England is suffering under contrary operations, France may divide the market with us, and share largely in our privilege of borrowing.----And do we ask why the Dutch so desert us in our need? Look at near eleven hundred pounds failure in our *net*

receipt of customs ‡; look at the threatening state of Europe; look at the war that divides us; look at the trade and strength we have lost, and *think who has gained them*;---look at these things, and (without throwing in our *rash memorial* ‖) let each man decide our situation.

What is to extricate us from this scene of difficulty, the power above us only knows: I am sure those who have led us into it know not.----Events are working on too rapidly to be long within our reach. Yet *one* circumstance there is, that may in *part* relieve us: I mean the speedy conviction of the impossibility and inutility of a conquest over America, and of the hazards of attempting it. God send then, that we may *soon* find all encouragement wanting to us! Under my convictions, who shall upbraid the prayer; unless it be prudent to wish that *ruinous* projects may be confirmed by flattering beginnings.

To expect that our *ministers* will accommodate these troubles, is hopeless anxiety.----Their blunders are too egregious for confession. Besides a change of measures must imply a change of men; since neither can *they* enough respect the Americans, nor the Americans enough respect *them*, for re-union: such a change too might produce a retrospect towards themselves. They will therefore go on in their conduct; thinking that a want of *power to suppress* the rebellion would be more easily forgiven, than the confessed want of discretion that provoked it. It is under these impressions that I expect a French war to be made the cover of their retreat from America; and it is hence too that I fully understand Lord Mansfield, when he says,

---

* The comment of Lord Chatham, delivered with that vigour of expression which accompanied every thing that fell from him when in support of his motion, May 30, 1777.
† In 1759, during the middle of the war, which she still pursued.
‡ Net receipt, 1,075,960l. lower than the last year, and the gross receipt 1,419,930l.
‖ See the Remembrancer, vol. v. p. 92.

" This

" *This* is not the period for negociation, and the *struggle* muſt go on *.---Where generoſity and honour are the beſt policy, a narrow illiberal heart commits more errors than the ſubtleſt underſtanding can correct?---With reſpect to *Lord Chatham's motion*, doubtleſs had health permitted, it ought to have appeared earlier : but it never can be out of ſeaſon to ſtop *ſhort* of ruin, and ſtay the hand that is *ſtill* to ſpill blood; it never can be out of ſeaſon to call back the affections of America, and make her become leſs diſpoſed for co-operating with France. And ſhould our army in the mean time have been ſucceſsful, conceſſion might give *effect* to that ſucceſs; or ſhould a defeat have intervened, it would become ſoftened in proportion as it was leſs deſerved.---Certainly there was a time when accommodation might have taken place in defiance of France: we had only to throw away certain fruitleſs blunders, that now coſt us 10 millions a year and our ſafety to perſiſt in.---Perhaps the moment is approaching, when the nation may inquire why this has *not* been done. It is not a new thing for a great and wiſe people to be deceived concerning diſtant countries; ---it is not a new thing for them to recover from that deception. And let thoſe whom it behoves beware of their reſentments.

---Whoever wiſhes to prove the ſtrength of his vanity and the weakneſs of his reaſon, let him publicly propheſy concerning near events. I have propheſied, and may be miſtaken ; but ſtill I have reaſoned from principles, and obſerved caution in my concluſions.---I am not fond of dark colouring, and if I have uſed it, it belongs rather to the ſubject than to the painter. While others have raiſed the ſtorm, and launched forth the ſhip of ſtate to be baffled by its fury, I picture the ſhip-wreck only that we may avoid it.

June 19. A BY-STANDER.

Admiralty-Office, June 28. Vice-Admiral Young, Commander in Chief of his Majeſty's ſhips and veſſels at the Leeward Iſlands, has, in his letter of the 2d of May laſt, tranſmitted to Mr. Stephens, Secretary of the Admiralty, the following liſt of prizes taken by the ſquadron under his command, between the 10th of March and the 30th of April, 1777:

The Fanny ſloop, Thomas Ridley, maſter, from Cape François, bound to America, laden with rum and molaſſes, taken by the Camilla.

The Mermaid ſloop, John Biſhop, maſter, from Cape François, bound to Rhode Iſland, laden with molaſſes and gunpowder, taken by the Galatea.

The Matyce ſchooner, John Baptiſt, maſter, from St. Euſtatia, bound to St. Kitts, laden with butter, taken by the Hind.

The Ranger ſchooner, William Davis, maſter, from Martinico, laden with ballaſt, taken by the Camilla.

The Betſey ſloop, Thomas Baker, maſter, from North Carolina, bound to St. Euſtatia, laden with tar, turpentine, and lumber, taken by the Hind.

The Champion ſchooner, Joſeph Haſkell, maſter, from America, bound to St. Euſtatia, laden with

---

* His declaration, May 30, 1777: in the following June however, to aſſiſt a labouring loan, every body is made to talk about the appearance of a ſpeedy pacification with America ! There are reaſons ſtill more binding than the forms of the conſtitution, which will induce the miniſter to ſurrender our acts of parliament through the medium of the parliament. Has parliament been forbid to agitate the repeal—then there can be no aſſurance of pacification. Were there any real defection in the colonies, it would be thundered out to us in a thouſand ways : it would tell itſelf; and would not need the wearied tongues and pens of hirelings for propagation.

lumber

lumber and fish, taken by the Perseus.

The Betfy schooner, John Holmes, master, from Surinam, bound to Ipswich, laden with molasses, taken by the Portland.

The Betfey sloop, James Howland, master, from Demaran, bound to Dartmouth, laden with rum, taken by the Portland.

The Catherine schooner, from Boston, bound to St. Pierre, Miquelon, laden with corn and lumber, taken by the Pelican.

The Bite sloop, George Dames, master, from North Carolina, bound to St. Martin's, laden with lumber and corn, taken by the Hind.

The Adriana sloop, George Codwife, master, from Virginia, bound to St. Thomas, laden with tobacco and lumber, taken by the Antigua.

The Spry schooner, William Yardsley, master, from St. Martin's, bound to Maryland, laden with salt, taken by the Antigua.

The Polly sloop, Thomas Dickinson, master, no papers on board, laden with ballast, taken by the Beaver.

The Rose schooner, Solomon Bunker, master, from Nantucket, bound to St. Martin's, laden with lumber and fish, taken by the Antigua.

A schooner, from Martinico, bound to America, laden with molasses, rum, wine, &c. taken by the Seaford.

The Ranger sloop, Daniel Bizelow, master, from Philadelphia, bound to St. Eustatia, laden with tobacco and flour, taken by the Antigua.

The ship La Seine, —— Morain, master, from Martinico, bound to America, laden with arms and warlike stores, taken by the Seaford.

The Dolphin schooner, Andrew M'Kenzie, master, from Philadelphia, bound to St. Eustatia, laden with flour and tar, taken by the Portland. [London Gazette.

Extract of a letter from Jamaica by the Grenville Packet, May 2.

" I arrived here on Friday last, after a pleasant passage of eight weeks.

This country has undergone a variety of changes since I left it, and is now in a bad state, owing to a long spell of dry weather, and the want of an American trade, provisions of all sorts fetching an exorbitant price, to the hurt of many ; and unless a speedy alteration, the consequences will be fatal to the planting business. We touched at Barbadoes, where they are in a starving condition, proceeding from the same causes. We had one of our fleet taken from us almost in sight of Barbadoes. They are now fitting out at Martinico a great number of privateers, and have carried into that port, within the space of one week, upwards of 14 sail of our ships. We have no privateers out of this place, and few prizes taken. This you may depend on as truth."

By his Excellency WILLIAM MATTHEW BURT, *Captain General and Governor in Chief, in and over all his Majesty's Leeward Charibbee Islands in America, Chancellor, Vice Admiral and Ordinary of the same, &c. &c. &c.*

" His Majesty having been informed, that during the present rebellion in America, his Majesty's rebellious subjects have frequently got intelligence of the state of his Majesty's plantations, and other matters which might be injurious to his service, by letters from private persons to their correspondents in Great-Britain and elsewhere, taken from on board ships coming from the plantations : it is his Majesty's pleasure, that I do hereby signify, and I do hereby to all Merchants, Planters, and others, That they be very cautious, during the present rebellion in America, in giving any account by letters, of the public state and condition of his Majesty's Leeward Islands, or any other accounts whatever, which might be (if intercepted) advantageous to his rebellious subjects : and that I do further give directions, and I do hereby direct accordingly,

all

all masters of ships, or other persons, that they put such letters as they may be entrusted with into a bag, with a sufficient weight to sink the same immediately, in case of imminent danger from vessels armed and fitted out by the said rebellious subjects.

Given under my hand this twenty-ninth day of April, 1777, and in the seventeenth year of his Majesty's reign.

WILLIAM MATTHEW BURT.

Published this thirtieth day of April, one thousand seven hundred and seventy-seven.

SAMUEL H. WARNER,
Dep. Pro. Marf.

ANTIGUA.

The Speech of his Excellency WILLIAM MATTHEW BURT, *Esq. to the Council and Assembly of this Island.*

Mr. President, Gentlemen of the Council,

Mr. Speaker, Gentlemen of the Assembly,

His Majesty having been most graciously pleased to appoint me his Commander in Chief of the Leeward Islands, duty and inclination unitedly prompted me to seize the earliest opportunity of repairing to the government committed to my care, to participate with you those distresses and inconveniencies, we were told the Leeward Islands laboured under, but submitted to with that loyalty, and zeal, which ever has, and, I trust, ever will, distinguish his Majesty's faithful subjects residing within this government.

The unnatural and wanton rebellion, which, through the industry of artful and designing men, was raised in North America, after every lenient measure, which his Majesty's parental anxiety for recovering them from their delusion, had been tried; at last drew on them the armed resentment of our mother country; it is with infinite concern, I find, some within these Islands have felt the baneful effects of this rebellion, which, I trust, through the blessing of God, our Sovereign's wisdom, the strength of his arms, and above all, that mercy which is always ready to be extended to those, who will return to their allegiance, will speedily be extinguished with honour to our mother country, and restore its commerce to Great Britain and her colonies.

It is a sensible felicity to us all, there never was a period when Great Britain had a Sovereign who consulted more the true interest, not only of those subjects near, but also the most remote from his royal presence, and had more at heart their protection, constitutional happiness, the maintenance and free enjoyment of all their franchises.

The present prudential armaments making in England to support, if necessary, our allies, the honour and dignity of the crown and nation, will, I flatter myself, be an example for us to put ourselves in the best posture of defence, in case any unforeseen accidents should interrupt the present amity which subsists between Great Britain, and the European powers.

Mr. Speaker, Gentlemen of the Assembly,

In pursuance with his Majesty's instructions, I am under the necessity of mentioning to you, a settlement to be made on me immediately on my arrival, to support the dignity and character of Captain General.

Your own wisdom will point out the properest mode in which this is to be done.—I flatter myself you will find this settlement not misapplied, and I shall approve of it and be contented.

Whenever his Majesty's service shall require any supplies to be raised by your house, for any purposes which may from time to time arise, in which I shall ever consider the honour and interest of this Island, I will direct proper estimates to be laid before

before you ; and will moſt ſtudiouſly avoid recommending any unneceſſary expence.

Mr. Preſident, Gentlemen of the Council,

Mr. Speaker, Gentlemen of the Aſſembly,

While his Majeſty ſhall be graciouſly pleaſed to continue this diſtant part of his dominions under my care, an unwearied attention to promote the worſhip of God, and our pure religion as eſtabliſhed by law, to diſtribute ſpeedy and impartial juſtice, to forward every matter which can ſupport and ſtrengthen your civil and commercial intereſts, to maintain our moſt excellent conſtitution, to eſtabliſh and cement univerſal harmony ſhall animate me ; thoroughly convinced, while engaged in theſe purſuits, I ſhall receive my Sovereign's approbation, your ſupport, and that of this whole government.

Extract of a letter from Grenada, April 18.

" Every thing continues exceſſive dear here, and we are happy if we can get any thing for money, by reaſon of the quantity of veſſels that are taken by the American privateers. A fleet of veſſels came from Ireland a few days ago ; from ſixty veſſels that departed from Ireland not above twenty-five arrived in this and the neighbouring iſlands ; the others (as it is thought) being all taken by the American privateers. God knows, if this American war continues much longer, we ſhall all die with hunger.

" There was a guineaman that came from Africa with 450 Negroes, ſome thouſand weight of gold duſt, and a great many elephants teeth ; the whole cargo being computed to be worth 20,000l. ſterling, taken by an American privateer, a brig, mounting fourteen cannon, a few days ago. The name of the guineaman was the St. George, Capt. Moore ; ſhe was bound for this iſland."

Extract of a letter from Charles Town, South Carolina, May 17.

" A chief of the Oneida Indians is arrived here from the Cherokee country, attended by ſeveral of his countrymen, and a number of Cherokees. He has been on an embaſſy of importance to the ſeveral tribes on the Ohio, as far as the Chickeſaws. He ſays hundreds of Indians are on their march for Philadelphia, in order to join the provincial army."

Extract of a letter from Charles Town, South Carolina, May 20.

" The French have ſtationed a number of their men of war, frigates, and armed veſſels, to cruize round their Weſt-India iſlands, to protect the trade they carry on with the Americans, who now drive a very great traffick with the people of Martinico, Guadaloupe, &c.

" A general amneſty to all French deſerters is publiſhed at Martinico. A veſſel from Turk's-Iſland brings us a copy of the French commandant's inſtructions reſpecting the protection of all American veſſels, and informs, that he requeſted it might be made known to all America as ſoon as poſſible."

Extract of a letter from Philadelphia, May 26.

" The inhabitants of North and South Carolina all the winter carried on almoſt a free trade, on account that there were no ports near their coaſts, therefore the Engliſh men of war could not well cruize upon them, conſequently buſineſs has gone on there very rapidly between the Carolineans and the French and Dutch."

Some private letters received from Charles-Town, South-Carolina, mention, that a brigadier-general and a knight of the order of St. Louis arrived there the 14th of May laſt in a provincial privateer from St. Maloes, with an intent to ſerve in the army of the United States of America. With the above officer ſeveral young gentlemen of good families in

France

France arrived also for the same purpose.

SOUTH CAROLINA.

At a General Assembly begun and holden at Charles-Town, on Friday the 6th day of December, in the year of our Lord one thousand seven hundred and seventy-six, and from thence continued by divers adjournments to the 13th day of February, in the year of our Lord one thousand seven hundred and seventy-seven.

An ORDINANCE, *For establishing an* OATH *of* ABJURATION *and* ALLEGIANCE.

WHEREAS in all states protection and allegiance are, or ought to be, reciprocal, and those who will not bear the latter are not entitled to the benefits of the former:

Be it therefore ordained, by his Excellency John Rutledge, Esq; President and Commander in chief in and over the state of South Carolina, by the Honourable the Legislative Council and General Assembly of the said state, and by the authority of the same, That the President and Commander in Chief for the time being, with the advice of the Privy Council, shall appoint proper persons to administer the following oath to all the late officers of the King of Great Britain; and to all other persons (other than prisoners of war) who now are or hereafter may come into this state, as they the said President and Privy Council shall suspect of holding principles injurious to the rights of the state:

" I A. B. do acknowledge, that the state of South Carolina is, and of right ought to be, a free, independent, and sovereign state, and that the people thereof owe no allegiance or obedience to George the Third of Great-Britain; and I do renounce, refuse, and abjure, any allegiance or obedience to him. And I do also swear (or affirm, as the case may be) that I will, to the utmost of my power, support, maintain, and defend the said state against the said King George the Third, his heirs and successors, and his or their abettors, assistants, and adherents. And I further swear, that I will bear faithful and true allegiance to the said state, and to the utmost of my power will support, maintain, and defend the freedom and independence thereof."

And be it further ordained, by the authority aforesaid, That if any person or persons to whom the said oath shall be tendered, shall refuse to take the same, then he or they shall, within sixty days after such refusal, or as soon as may be hereafter, be sent off from this state, taking his or their families with them, if he or they shall think fit so to do, to Europe or the West-Indies, at the public expence, except such persons as in the opinion of the President and Privy Council are able to pay their own expences; provided, nevertheless, That all and every such person or persons shall be at liberty to sell and dispose of his or their estates or interests in this state, and (after satisfying all just and equitable claims and demands which shall be brought against him or them) to carry the amount and produce thereof with him or them; and also to nominate an attorney or attornies (to be approved of by the President and Privy Council) to sell and dispose of his or their estate or estates; and in like manner with the subjects of this state, to demand security, or sue for, as the case may be; and to recover, in his or their hand or hands, all such debts and sums of money as are or shall be due, owing, or payable to him or them respectively, and to remit the same to him or them respectively, in such way and manner as they shall think fit, provided it be not repugnant to the resolutions of the Congress, or the laws of this state.

And be it further ordained by the authority aforesaid, That if any person or persons, so sent off from the state, shall return to the same,

then

then he or they shall be adjudged guilty of treason against the state, and shall, upon conviction thereof, suffer death as a traitor.

And be it further ordained, by the authority aforesaid, That all and every such person or persons in this state, who shall hereafter accept or take any office or plan of trust or emolument under the authority thereof, shall, before he enter upon the execution of such office, or plan of trust, take the oath before-mentioned.

JOHN MATTHEWS, Speaker of the General Assembly.

In the Council Chamber, the 13th day of February, 1777.

Assented to, J. RUTLEDGE.

HUGH RUTLEDGE, Speaker of the Legislative Council,

W. NESBIT, Dep. Sec.

South-Carolina, Secretary Office.

(A true copy.)

Several letters received by merchants in London from their correspondents in France, confirm the daily reports of the great partiality shewn to the Americans by all ranks of people there, particularly the merchants and traders, some of whom are making great fortunes by their new correspondents and good friends (as they call them) the Americans; and though the French Ministry do not *publicly* encourage such a commerce, yet it is universally believed they *connive* at it, as it is well known they dare not so openly pursue such a traffic without the assent of the Court. One letter in particular from a gentleman in Bourdeaux, dated the 14th of June, says, " I wonder at the supineness of the British adm —— n, in suffering the French publicly to carry on a trade with North-America; such conduct in a kingdom, professing amicable dispositions towards Great Britain, surely deserves not only the censure, but the resentment of the British arms."

Extract of a letter from Mr. Neale, late commander of his Majesty's schooner Prince William, of eight guns, dated Boston Prison, May 13.

" In my last I acquainted you of my success in taking American prizes; but my fortune now is quite the reverse: on the 2d of this month, falling in with the Spy, an American privateer snow of 12 guns, my vessel was taken after an engagement of three glasses, and brought into this port, where myself and crew are prisoners. Boston harbour swarms with privateers and their prizes: this is a great place of rendezvous with them; the privateers men come on shore here full of money, and enjoy themselves much after the same manner the English seamen at Portsmouth and Plymouth, &c. did in the late war; and by the best information I can get, there are no less than fifteen foreign vessels lately arrived in the harbour with cargoes of various articles."

Extract of a letter from Dunkirk, June 26.

" This morning, between eight and nine o'clock, Capt. Cunningham and Capt. Roberts sailed from this place in two ships, built, armed, and manned here; these ships belong to some person in M. de S————'s favour, and are to cruize against the English and Portuguese ships, chiefly, as it is represented, against the mails: Cunningham pledged his honour to his employers on sailing, that they should soon hear of him; the ship on board which he is, is one of the best sailers known; the crew is composed of all the most desperate fellows which could be procured in so blessed a port as Dunkirk."

A letter from St. Maloes says, that a French ship of 28 guns, called the Diadem, which was a privateer in the late war, has been purchased at that port for the Americans, whose use she is fitting for, and is almost ready for sea. The Captain of her

is

is a perfon from Nantucket; fhe is to carry 28 guns, 22 nine pounders, and fix fours, befides a number of fwivels, and is provided with clofe quarters, and every requifite to compleat her for a fhip of war. She is manned with a few Americans; the others are Englifh, Irifh, and French. *Extract of a letter from Nantucket, May* 15.

" The 11th inft. Capt. Simpkins, commander of the Fortune Provincial fhip of war, of 22 guns, 4 cohorns, and 18 fwivels, fell in with the Englifh brig Bofcawen, of 18 fix-pounders, near this port, and after an engagement of upwards of an hour, the latter was taken, and carried for Bofton. We faw the action, which was continued a confiderable time very refolute, by both parties, and feemed to us rather doubtful. The Captain of the brig was wounded, and the officer that was fecond in command was killed."

Extract of a letter from Kinfale, June 24.

" Two fifhing-boats, who came in here yefterday, brought on fhore the crew of a fhip taken by an American privateer off Briftol Channel; the privateer made a fignal to the fifhing-boats, which they thought fignified their want of a pilot for Corke or Kinfale, and accordingly went on board, when they put the crew on board them, having fent the veffel the day before for France. The privateer's people behaved very well to the fifhermen, paid them for what fifh they took, and the Captain gave them a cafk of brandy for their trouble in coming on board. She was called the Refolution, mounted fourteen guns, and had one hundred and ten men when fhe left New-England, but at that time not above eighty, on account of the number they had put on board their prizes, having taken five already. We have received advices from the Weftward, that two privateers had appeared off there, in wait-ing, as fuppofed, for the homeward-bound fhips for Liverpool and Briftol."

Whitehaven, (in England) Thurfday, June 26.

The brig Crawford, formerly of Glafgow, arrived here this morning with one hundred and ten feamen, befides five women and fome children, which had been taken by the Americans from different veffels, all in this channel.

The following authentic account will beft explain this difagreeable affair, which our duty to the public obliges us, however, unwilling, to relate :

The Expedition, Braithwaite, failed from hence on Sunday the 15th inft. bound for Norway ; the Wednefday following, being then about two miles from the Mull of Cantire, fhe fell in with three American privateers, viz. the Reprifal, Commodore Wickes, of 18 guns and 130 men, with eight cohorns in her tops, and a number of fwivels; her carriage guns all fix pounders, double fortified: the Lexington, Johnfon, of 16 guns and 110 men, with 4 cohorns in her tops, and a great number of fwivels; her carriages fame weight of metal as the Reprifal's, and fortified in the fame manner; and the Dolphin, Nicholfon, of 10 guns and 64 men, with a number of fwivels and fmall arms.

The following is an account of all the veffels taken by the faid privateers from the 19th inftant to the 23d inclufive.

June 19th. Sloop Merrin of Greenock, Neal Taylor, from Greenock to Suna, ballaft, funk.

19th. Brig Expedition of Whitehaven, William Braithwaite, from Whitehaven to Norway, ballaft, funk.

19th. Ship ——, Ribble M'Gomrey, ballaft, fent to France.

21ft. Brig Jenny and Sally of Glafgow, Wm. Drummond, from Glafgow

Glasgow to Norway, ballast, sent to France.

20th. Sloop Jason, of Whitehaven, Isaac Hutchinson, from Whitehaven to Petersburgh, ballast, sent to France.

20th. Jenny and Peggy of Irvin, William Howe, from —— to Irvin, ballast, sunk.

20th. Sloop Edward and Ann of Queensferry, Edward Brown, from Koningsburg to Liverpool, wheat, sent to France.

21st. Bark John and Thomas of Whitehaven, John Yowart, from Norway to Dublin, deals, sent to France.

22d. Brig Grayftock of Workington, James Clarke, from Workington to Dublin, coals, sunk.

22d. Brig Richard of Whitehaven, Thomas Ledger, from Whitehaven to Dublin, coals, sunk.

22d. Brig Favourite of Maryport, Caleb Grave, from Maryport to Dublin, coals, sunk.

23d. Ship Grace of Liverpool, John Wardley, from Jamaica to Liverpool, rum, fugar, and tobacco, sent to France.

23d. Brig Peggy of Killabeg, Thomas Atridge, from Corke to Liverpool, butter and hides, sent to France.

23d. Brig Crawford of Greenock, Alexander Alexander, from Greenock to St. Ubes, ballast, given to the masters and crews to brig them to Whitehaven.

Sunk also a small boat off the Mull of Cantire, Thomas Mac Dugan, master.

On Tuesday last, Johnson, (by permission of his Commodore, Wickes,) put 110 of the prisoners on board the Crawford, with leave for them to depart, and make the best of their way to any port in England. They were put on board said vessel about one league from Tufcar, but under a promise of reaching Whitehaven, if possible, without putting into any port, or landing any of the paffengers. The reason of this caution is obvious; Whitehaven being at the greatest distance, the alarm would be so much longer in reaching the ears of Government, which they could not doubt would immediately take the most hasty steps to prevent any future depredations, especially so near home.

Another account says, they left the privateers on Monday last, five leagues N. E. from Tufcar.

The above privateers, the first of which is frigate built, the second a brig, and the third a cutter, sailed from Nantz about five weeks ago, went round Ireland, and up the North Channel; they detained the Crawford till they had reached Tufcar, when, having a free wind, they stood out of the channel, and the Crawford, under the command of Captain John Yowart, directed her course for Whitehaven, where she arrived as above-mentioned.

Copy of the Original Letter.

On board the Reprifal, the 3d of June, 1777.

" These are to certify, that the brig Crawford, Alexander Alexander, formerly master, who was taken by one of the squadron (yesterday) under my command: that I give the said brig to each of the under written men, who have been taken by me and my squadron, to carry them to Whitehaven, and there to dispose of her upon their joint accounts, and to be disposed of, as they think most proper after their arrival at the said port of Whitehaven. Given under my hand the day and date above written.

Witness, LAMBERT WICKES.
Henry Johnson.

Alexander Alexander, master of the brig Crawford.

John Yowart, master of the John and Thomas.

Joseph Hutchinson, master of the Jason.

Thomas

Thomas Attridge, mafter of the fhip Peggy.

John Wardley, of the fhip Grace, Liverpool.

Caleb Grave, mafter of the Favourite, of Maryport.

William Drummond, mafter of the Jenny and Sally."

London, July 4. The following advertifement appeared in all the daily news-papers :

" New Lloyd's Coffee-houfe,
" July 3, 1777.

" THE merchants, owners of
" fhips, and infurers, obferving that
" the French, in violation of the
" law of nations, have permitted
" American privateers not only to
" bring in Britifh fhips and cargoes,
" but alfo to fell the fame in their
" ports in Europe and the Weft-
" Indies, many of which privateers,
" it is well known, are the property
" of, and manned by, Frenchmen ;
" and whereas a continuance of fuch
" practice muft prove ruinous to the
" commercial interefts of this king-
" dom, the owners of all fuch fhips
" and cargoes as have been, or may
" be, taken, and fold in any of the
" ports of France or the Weft-Indies,
" are earneftly intreated to fend the
" particulars thereof to Lord Vif-
" count Weymouth, his Majefty's
" Secretary of State for the fouthern
" department, and alfo to the Lords
" of the Admiralty, in order that
" Adminiftration may be fully ap-
" prifed of the alarming extent of
" this growing and deftructive evil."

For the REMEMBRANCER.

The number of our fhips taken by the American and French privateers is truly alarming ; and what appears more furprizing is, that we fcarcely ever hear of any of thofe privateers being taken, but frequently a number of their trading fhips. —This circumftance, to the intelligent Englifh merchant, accounts for the myftery, viz. In former wars, the firft object of adminiftration was, to protect our own commerce, then to annoy the enemy's ; for which purpofe, befides the proper convoys, a number of our men of war were ordered to cruize in the various tracts and latitudes of *our trade*, which effectually fecured it. The refidue of our fleet was either employed in fquadrons againft the enemy, or in fingle fhips in the latitudes of *their trade*, to deftroy it. But this wife and fafe fyftem has been reverfed, for the fake of encouraging a few naval commanders, at the expence of the merchants ; for our officers are now at liberty, without any regard to the protection of our trade, to cruize in the latitudes of the enemy's, where they joyfully fucceed in taking fome prizes.

The American and French privateers more fuccefsfully and joyfully cruize in the latitudes of ours, where it is left open and uncontrouled to their range. And who can now be furprized at their depredations ? fince, as long as we have more fhipping and trade than they, they muft have the advantage of us in this foolifh warfare.

We heard of inroads fome time fince made by the Georgians into the northern diftricts of Eaft Florida. It originated from a defire in the commanders in Florida to get plunder of the Georgians, as it was well known how incapable we were to carry on an honourable and regular war with them, from fuch an infant colony. Accordingly, plunder was obtained, which anfwered a military purpofe very well, who had all to get, and nothing to lofe. But what was the confequence ? the Georgians (before not hoftile towards their neighbours) make an invafion into the province, and retaliate upon the unfufpecting, unguarded Florida planter, to his great grief and ruin, and fully compenfate

penfate themfelves for the injury and ravages they received from our fuppofed military protectors.

When the mifchief was done by the Georgians, a fhip or two were ftationed in St. Mary's and St. John's rivers, near the fences. Had this been done at firft, before our governors commenced hoftilities againft their neighbours, it would have fe cured the colony.

I have lately been informed, that even thefe two or three veffels in St. John's and St. Mary's rivers have left their ftations, and are gone out to the more profitable employ of cruizing in the enemy's trading latitudes. What a pleafing reflection muft this be to the naked Floridans!

Extract of a letter from Rotterdam, March 30, 1777.

" Yefterday the Prince of Anfpach arrived here with a regiment of chaffeurs to guard the recruits going to America, and prevent mutiny and defertion. Never was there exhibited in any age or country a more fhocking fpectacle ; the poor wretches were many of them bound hands and feet, and tranfported in waggons and carts : but notwithftanding this precaution, many of them found means to defert, and others were fhot by the chaffeurs, in attempting to do it. No words can exprefs the indignation which I felt from the barbarous treatment of thefe poor peafants, (*none of them were foldiers*) thus torn from every attachment of country, of confanguinity, and of friendfhip, and fold to fuffer and perifh by the fatigues, difeafes, and dangers of a long voyage, and diftant, cruel war. Their Prince too difcovered fome emotions ; but they were from vexation for the lofs he was likely to fuftain by thofe of his recruits, who were either deferted or fhot before their actual delivery to the purchafers. At length, however, the greateft part of thefe wretches

were embarked ; and the Prince, like a true father of his people, returned to enjoy the price of their blood.

PHILADELPHIA.

War-Office, February 11, 1777.

The Board of War having received information of the good fuccefs the recruiting officers meet with in raifing the new levies ; but that from a defire in the officers to have their battalions and companies entirely compleated, before they join the army, great numbers of ufeful foldiers are idle in quarters, when their fervices are wanted at camp : I have it in direction to order and ftrictly enjoin all recruiting officers, in the fervice of the United States, on the weftern fide of the North River, and in the Middle States, forthwith to march their men to the feveral places of rendezvous, appointed for affembling the regiments, as foon as thirty privates are raifed in any company, leaving proper officers to compleat the refpective regiments and companies at the places of recruiting. And all officers, commanding regiments, who have recruiting parties out on fervice, in the faid Middle States, are directed to attend diligently to the equipping and fending off the companies to join General Wafhington, as fpeedily as poffible, after their arrival at the places of rendezvous. RICHARD PETERS, Sec.

Philadelphia, February 19. Laft Friday the following gentlemen were elected at the ftatehoufe, viz. Thomas Wharton, jun. counfellor, and Col. Bull, Col. Moor, Major Lollar, and Col. Coats, members of affembly for the county of Philadelphia.

The Hon. John M'Kinly, Efq. is appointed Governor and Commander in Chief of the Delaware ftate.

PHILADELPHIA.

Extract of a letter from Haddonfield, March 17, 1777.

" I have juft feen a letter from

Z   Ge

Gen. Maxwell, dated at Weftfield, on the 14th inftant, in which he mentions a fkirmifh of fome importance with the enemy, on Saturday the 8th inftant: as it is new to me, I tranfmit it to you, though you may probably have had a better account of it. He mentions that the enemy had brought out all their troops from Amboy, &c. fuppofed to be about 3000, and pofted themfelves on Punk-hill: They brought artillery and a number of waggons, as if to forage, though there was none left in that neighbourhood worth notice. General Maxwell, with the troops under his command, was on a rifing ground to the northward, in plain view, though at a good diftance. The enemy were too well fituated to be attacked: he fent a party to the left to amufe them, but his real defign was to the right on the heights towards Bonamtown: he fent a ftrong party that way to examine their lines, if they had any, and to fall in near the end of them, that he might fall on their flank; this was performed by part of Col. Potter's battalion of Pennfylvania militia, and part of Col. Thatcher's of N. E. Col. Cook of the Pennfylvanians had been ordered from Matuching to come down on Carman's-Hill, and keep along the heights till he met the enemy. About half a mile lower down, between Carman's Hill and Woodbridge, the two parties being lined, met a ftrong advanced party of the enemy. On the firft firing Col. Martin and Lieut. Col. Lindley were fent to fupport them; they all behaved well, and kept their ground till they were fupported from the main body, which immediately marched that way. The enemy alfo fent out a reinforcement; but on another regiment of ours being fent on the left to cut them off from their main body, the party gave way in great confufion; the flame catched their main body, and all went together. Our people purfued them, and took a prifoner and a baggage waggon clofe in their rear, a good way down in the plain ground. Bonamtown lay too near on the right, and a plain open ground towards Amboy, to purfue far. They left four dead in the field, and we took three prifoners. By the quantity the enemy carried off in fleds and waggons, it is fuppofed they had near twenty killed, and twice that number wounded. Gen. Maxwell alfo mentions, that by a foldier taken about the 11th inftant he learns, that Gen. Howe was at Bonam-town during the engagement, till he faw his troops make the beft of their way home, and then he thought it was time for him to go. That the enemy's real defign in coming out that day was to fecure the General a fafe paffage to Amboy, and that he is fince gone to New-York. The foldier further fays, they talk no more of going to Morris Town. Gen. Maxwell adds, that by every account from prifoners, deferters, and inhabitants, the killed, wounded and miffing of the enemy, in the action of the 23d of February, was upwards of 500."

Philadelphia, March 18. 1777. The following articles are handing about in this city, and were the firft night figned by upwards of fifty, and fince then by a confiderable number of the friends of liberty:

Whereas by the fteady perfeverance of many true friends to liberty, and the public welfare, a happy coalition has been effected between different parties equally folicitous for the welfare of their country, though differing in opinion as to fome means not effentially neceffary for obtaining it, and there is a fair profpect of the reftoration of order and the due eftablifhment of civil and legal authority, under which the ftrength of the State may be collected and exerted, and the inhabitants in every ftate of life be fecured secured in the possession of peace and property. And whereas it appears that there is nevertheless a scheme now forming to overturn all present order and authority, and to deprive us of the advantages of a militia law for our defence, and to throw our public affairs again into confusion, we, whose names are underwritten, in order to prevent the irreparable mischiefs, which must ensue, should the enemies to our peace succeed, do solemnly engage ourselves to each other, and to the public, that we will most firmly adhere to and abide by the following articles:

First, That we will, to the utmost of our abilities, support the just and necessary authority of Congress, and the union and independence of the American States, against all foreign power and domestic machinations whatever.

Secondly, That we will, as far as in us lies, promote peace and good order in the State, and endeavour to bring to justice those who shall attempt to disturb either.

Thirdly, That we will not, by force or violence, or by false representations, endeavour either to confirm or overturn any part of the present constitution, contrary to the general sense of the State, but will refer the proof of every part thereof either to a candid reasoning or a fair experiment.

Fourthly, That in the mean time we will, to the utmost of our power, support the civil magistrate in the execution of such wholesome laws as are or shall be enacted by the present Assembly.

GENERAL ORDERS.
Philadelphia, March 20, 1777.
Complaint being made of the irregular behaviour of certain of the British deserters, to the great annoyance of the peaceable inhabitants of this city, it is therefore ordered, that all deserters from the enemy's army, at

present in Philadelphia, who have not written licences from proper authority to remain in town, do immediately repair to some other part of the continent. They will be furnished with proper passes by giving their names, and the name of the places to which they are desirous to remove, to the Town-Major. Such as are found in this city after three days, may expect to be sent to jail.

HORATIO GATES, Major Gen.

Boston, February 6. Saturday last set off for Newport, under a strong guard, commanded by Captain Ayres, a number of prisoners from the inland parts of this state, in order to be exchanged for an equal number of ours now with the enemy.

And on Monday another pack of those vermin passed through Cambridge from the state of New-Hampshire, on their way to Newport, to be exchanged; among whom were several of Rogers's rangers, who were taken in the battle of White-Plains, near New-York.

Several companies of soldiers who have inlisted during the continuance of the war have marched from this state within these few days past for Ticonderoga, and numbers more will set off shortly.

We hear that a general exchange of prisoners is soon to take place over the whole Continent; those taken in Quebec are already exchanged.

We are well assured from good authority, that General Howe was by his successes in the Jerseys, so sure of reducing the Americans to a submission, that he had wrote leases of their lands, and had actually given them to a number that had submitted. Is this a term of peace which some would solicit, to have their lands leased to them!

Boston, Feb. 26. The Honourable General Assembly of the State of Rhode-Island, have appointed Henry Marchant, Esq. a Delegate for that

Z 2. State.

State in the Grand American Congrefs.

We learn from Providence, that on Friday laft, a fchooner, one of the enemy's tenders, from Newport, going round Warwick-Point, near that place, ran a-ground; on difcovery of which, Admiral Hopkins, fent down the river a veffel of force, to take poffeffion of her, and when fhe had got within about a mile of her, the enemy blew her up.

Providence. March 1. Friday fe'nnight a party of our troops landed on Rhode-Ifland, and brought off a quantity of hay and oats. Capt. Tyler, in the Spitfire galley, attended the landing, and gallantly fuftained the enemy's fire from a battery of fix guns for feveral hours, which was brifkly returned, but with what effect we have not yet learnt. When the troops had compleated the fervice affigned them, the Spitfire drew off; fhe was confiderably damaged in her hull and rigging, and had feven men wounded, one of them mortally.

In Congrefs, January 16, 1777. *Refolved,* That a committee of feven be appointed to enquire into the conduct of the Britifh and Heffian general officers towards the officers, foldiers, and mariners in the fervice of the United States, and any other perfons inhabitants of thefe ftates, in their poffeffion as prifoners of war, or otherwife; and alfo into the conduct of the faid generals and officers, and the troops under their command, towards the fubjects of thefe ftates, and their property, more efpecially of the ftates of New-York and New-Jerfey.

The members chofen, Mr. Chafe, Mr. Witherfpoon, Mr. Clarke, Mr. Lewis, Mr. Rofs, Mr. Heyward, and Mr. Smith. *Extract from the Minutes.*

Publifhed by order of Congrefs,
CHARLES THOMPSON, Sec.

In Congrefs, February 26, 1777.
Refolved, That an intereft of fix per cent. per annum be allowed on all fums of money already borrowed, and directed to be borrowed on Loan Office certificates, although fuch certificates mention only an intereft of four per cent. per annum.

Refolved, That the intereft on the prizes drawn in the Continental lottery, fhall remain at Four per cent.

Refolved, That it be recommended to the legiflatures of the feveral States, not to offer or to give more than at the rate of fix per cent. per annum upon any monies to be borrowed in their refpective loan offices.

Extract from the Minutes,
CHARLES THOMSON, Sec.

Philadelphia, March 20. The Congrefs having generoufly offered the large intereft of fix per cent. per annum on their certificates, it is to be hoped that a laudable zeal for the public welfare, as well as their own intereft, will induce thofe who have money, to lend it to their country. The States of America are their fecurity, and the intereft will be paid in the moft punctual manner, without any of the trouble, expence or delay, which frequently attends collecting it from individuals, on private fecurity.

In Council of Safety, Feb. 15, 1777. *Refolved,* That applications for offices in the Pennfylvania regiments, now raifing for the Continental fervice, will be received until Monday the 24th inftant, when this Board will certainly proceed to fill up the vacancies ftill remaining.

All officers already appointed in the above regiments, who are not on command, are required forthwith, to repair to their duty. *By order of Council,*
THOMAS WHARTON, jun. Prefident.

In Council of Safety, Feb. 15.
Whereas the Honourable Congres has authorized and directed this Council to erect a fortification at Billingfport for the defence and fecurity of the city and harbour of Philadelphia,

part

part of which work has already been carried on under the direction of this Board, and, as it is necessary that some proper person be appointed, not only to superintend the said works, but to command such parties, whether regular soldiers, militia, or others, as may be employed to complete and defend them, therefore,

Resolved, That JOHN BULL, Esq. be appointed Colonel Commandant of the fortifications at Billingsport, and Superintendant of the works, and that all officers and others, employed in erecting or defending the same, do pay due obedience to his commands, until the works are completed, or farther orders given by this Board, or other proper authority.

Resolved, That BRATHWAITE JONES, Esq, be appointed chief engineer at Billingsport, with the rank, pay, and rations of Lieutenant Colonel ; and all officers and soldiers under his command, as well as workmen employed there, are to obey him as such, until the fortifications at that place are completed, or until it shall be otherwise ordered by proper authority. *Extract from the Minutes*,
JACOB. S HOWELL, Sec

To Major John Davis, *of the third battalion of* Cumberland *County Militia.*

I am much obliged to you for your activity, vigour and diligence, since you have been under my command ; you will therefore march your men immediately to Philadelphia, and there discharge them ; returning into the store all the ammunition, arms and accoutrements, you received at that place.

I am Sir, your humble servant,
ISRAEL PUTNAM.

Princetown, Feb. 5, 1777.

To Major JOHN DAVIS, *of the third battalion of* Cumberland *County Militia.*

Dear Sir,

I am happy in an opportunity of presenting my compliments to you and your corps of officers, on their return from Monmouth county, and, in behalf of the inhabitants of said county, in expressing my gratitude to Col. Guerney, yourself, and the other gentlemen, for the great pains that have been taken to support a regular discipline, and to correct and make amends to the utmost of your powers for those irregularities and errors which are the unavoidable consequences of the march of a detachment of militia in such haste as your's did, through a country where no regular provision had been made for their subsistence, and where so many of the inhabitants were inimical to the cause.

It is with pleasure I can declare, that I have the greatest reason to think the salvation of the property and the security of the persons of many friends to freedom owing, under God, to the spirited exertions of the two detachments which marched into Monmouth ; the first under the command of Col. Guerney, and the second under your command.

In short, those detachments have rescued the county from the tyranny of the Tories, and put it in the power of their own militia to recover and embody themselves in such manner as to be able to stand on their own defence. —I wish you, dear Sir, a safe return with your detachment to your and their houses and connections, and a long and happy enjoyment of those domestic blessings, which you have taken so much pains to restore and secure to others in a neighbouring state ; and that you may never find those under your command less ready to turn out for the public good, than they have been in this excursion. I am, dear Sir, with the most unfeigned respect, your friend and humble servant,

NATHAN SCUDDER, Col. 1st bat.
Monmouth County, New-Jersey.

GENERAL ORDERS.

Head Quarters, Morris-Town, Feb. 6, 1777. The General, informed that

that many frauds and abuses had been committed of late by sundry soldiers, who, after inlisting in one regiment, and receiving the bounty allowed by Congress, have deserted, inlisted in others, and received new bounties; for prevention of such unjust and infamous practices, commands and strictly enjoins all officers of the Continental army, to use their utmost endeavours to detect those who shall be guilty of such offences; and them having apprehended, they cause to be forthwith tried by a general court martial, that they may be dealt with according to their crimes.

The General thinks proper to declare, that this offence is of the most enormous and flagrant nature, and not admitting of the least palliation or excuse; whosoever are convicted thereof, and SENTENCED TO DIE, may consider their EXECUTION CERTAIN and INEVITABLE.

That such impositions may be less practicable, every officer engaged in the recruiting service is required to have a piece of blue, red, or yellow ribband or tape, fixed in the hat of each soldier recruited, at the time of inlistment; which he shall constantly wear, under pain of receiving thirty-nine lashes, till the regiment or corps to which he belongs is assembled, and joins the army.

A true copy taken from General Orders.

G. WEEDON, Adj. Gen.

Head Quarters, Morris-Town, March 11, 1777. The regiment of Pennsylvania militia, commanded by Col. Potter, having fulfilled the time to which they stood engaged, are honourably discharged, and his Excellency General Washington returns his thanks to Col. Potter, and the officers and soldiers of the regiment, for their distinguished behaviour whilst in service, a behaviour that reflects honour upon themselves, and has been of service to their country.

ARTHUR ST. CLAIR, *Major General.*

Barbadoes, December 7, 1776.

At a meeting of the General Assembly, at the Town-Hall, on Tuesday, the twenty-sixth day of November, 1776, pursuant to adjournment.

The Hon. Sir JOHN GAY ALLEYNE, Bart. Speaker.

The Minutes of the last meeting were read and committed. Mr. Secretary being at the door, was admitted, and presented to Mr. Speaker, a paper, sealed, directed ' To the Hon. the Speaker, and to the Members of the General Assembly," and signed Edward Hay, and Mr. Secretary then withdrew.

Mr. Speaker broke the seal, and put the letter into the hands of the Clerk, who, by order read the contents in these words:

" Mr. Speaker and Gentlemen of the Assembly,

" I have received your address to me, and have laid it before the King.
                              'EDWARD HAY."

Pilgrim House, 29th October, 1776.

Ordered, That the same be entered in the Journals, and published in the Minutes.

Mr. Speaker informed the House, that since their last meeting he received two letters from the agent of the island, addressed to him as Speaker of the Assembly, and that the first letter was accompanied with a memorial in the Agent's own name, to the Right Hon. Lord George Sackville Germain, one of his Majesty's principal Secretaries of State, and the letters and memorial being delivered by Mr. Speaker to the clerk, he was ordered to read the same, and they were accordingly by him read as follows:

Cavendish square, Sept. 11, 1776.

" Sir,

" I have had the honour of your letter of the 15th of July, inclosing an address to the King, from the Honourable the House of Assembly. You, Sir, have signified, as Speaker, their commands, to lay it before his Majesty.

Majesty in the same official manner, as the former; and I am now to inform you of my exact and immediate obedience. On the 8th, I delivered the address, and a memorial with it, into the office of the Secretary of State for America. Lord George Germain was not in town; but I gave them open to his Secretary, Mr. Knox, who assured me they should be dispatched to his Lordship that day; adding, that Lord George would be in town on the 10th, and that I might then see him at his own house at 11 o'clock.

" As I expected that Lord George would not be in the way, or, that he might not be at leisure to hear all that I had in my mind to say, my own memory might have been treacherous, or, the Minister's might have failed, through a multiplicity of great affairs, I had thought it right to accompany the Assembly's address to the King, with the memorial from myself to the Secretary of State. It was fortunate I took the step; for I was again disappointed in meeting with his Lordship yesterday. I was punctual to the hour; but Lord George, nor Mr. Knox, were at home. Returning in an hour, they were both gone out, and supposed to be at the office. At the office they had not been that day. I went back, and then his Lordship was just gone to the King. I had left a card at the office to tell I had been there, and another at the house, to say I had been there also, three times that morning, to know his Lordship's commands.

" I have no doubt but Lord George laid the address yesterday before the King; perhaps it was thought any further information, at that juncture, unnecessary: I shall in proper time attend him to learn his Majesty's pleasure.

" Inclosed is a copy of the memorial. You will observe, in the conclusion, a proposal for relief. To be silent on that point was, perhaps, a decent respect, which the Assembly might think right to observe towards the Sovereign; but it was a hint, which became your agent humbly to suggest to the Minister: the matter was of too much moment to be dissembled with.

" The Hon. the Assembly have my best wishes for success, and my utmost endeavours, in every shape, shall not be wanting.

I remain with great esteem
and regard,
S I R,
Your most obedient,
And faithful humble servant,
GEORGE WALKER.

To Sir John Gay Alleyne, Bart. Speaker of the Assembly of Barbadoes.

[See the Petition, and other Papers, in Vol. iii. page 274.]

[C O P Y.]

To the Hon. Sir John Gay Alleyne, Baronet, Speaker of the Assembly of Barbadoes.

By Captain Leech,
Q. D. C.

Cavendish-square, Sept. 20, 1776.

" Sir,

" I take the first opportunity of forwarding a duplicate of the letter, which I had the honour of writing to you on the 11th instant.

" Being desirous of a personal conference with Lord George Germain, I took the liberty of sending him a note, of which the inclosed is a copy: in consequence of the answer, which also accompanies the note, I had the satisfaction of an interview at the appointed time.

" Lord George acquainted me, that he had immediately presented the Assembly's address to the King; who had been graciously pleased to order it to be laid before the Lords of the Treasury for their consideration, together with the memorial. I observed to his Lordship, that the two papers were distinct: the address was
the

the public act of the Assembly; the memorial was of a more private nature, containing my own sentiments to himself, in case I should not have had the good fortune to have met with his Lordship. He said, he was always glad to see every gentleman, who could give him information upon any public matter; that he did consider the two papers as distinct, but thought they should go together, as the one was a commentary upon the other; that they were referred to the Treasury, because the manner of the relief was complicated with the business of that office. I added, that I looked upon the Secretary of State for America, as the patron of the Colonies; and although the business might come within the bounds of another department, I hoped his Lordship would become an advocate upon the occasion. He answered, that he should see Lord North that day, and would certainly recommend it to him. In the course of the conversation, in which he was pleased to indulge me, Lord George did me the honour to approve much the idea in the memorial of an exchange of rum for provisions.

" From Lord George's, I went directly to Lord North's. Finding Mr. Robinson, his principal Secretary there, I told him that Lord George Germain, had just informed me, that the King had ordered the address from the Assembly of Barbadoes to be referred to the Treasury, and that I was come to bespeak his good offices. He said, the papers had not come to the office; when they did, he would take proper care of them. To get to the speech of Mr. Robinson upon so very busy a day, Lord North being just come to town from Worcester and to attend his Majesty at the levee, which was begun, I had promised not to detain him two minutes; without therefore entering upon the subject matter, I said, that being unwilling to trouble Lord North, before he had made

himself acquainted with the business, yet, anxious to lose no time, I should be glad of his instructions what to do. Mr. Robinson politely acquiesced in the hint, and assured me, he would speak to Lord North, and send me a note as soon as a time could be fixed.

" Having thus related, Sir, the circumstances, the honourable the House of Assembly will form their own opinion. So far it looks well, that the King should have referred the matter to the Treasury and not to the Board of Trade. The business of the latter would have been to have examined into the merits of the case; by forbearing this preliminary step, his Majesty appears to have been satisfied with the representations of the state of his people as made by this Assembly. The part belonging to the Treasury, is, to examine the nature of the relief, whether pecuniary or commercial; to what degree to be extended, and in what manner to carry it into execution? With these, other considerations will be combined, which properly belong to the province of the Secretary for America, and he has promised to recommend it.

" I will not repeat assurances of my zeal, but endeavour to multiply instances. I have the honour to remain with great regard and respect,

S I R,

Your most obedient,
And faithful humble servant,
GEORGE WALKER."

[C O P Y.]
To the Right Honourable Lord George Germain.

Cavendish-square, Sept. 13, 1776.

" My Lord,

" Having delivered into your Lordship's office, an address from the Assembly of the island of Barbadoes to the King, and accompanied it with a memorial to yourself, I beg the favour of knowing a time, when I may have the honour of attending your
Lordship

Lordſhip upon that ſubject. I remain,
with reſpect, my Lord,

Your Lordſhip's moſt obedient
Humble ſervant,
GEORGE WALKER. '

[C O P Y.]

To George Walker, Eſq.
Cavendiſh-Square.

" Lord George Germain preſents
his compliments to Mr. Walker, and
will be glad to ſee him at his houſe
in Pall-Mall to-morrow, at twelve
at noon."

Pall-Mall, Tueſday, Sept. 11.

Cavendiſh Square, Oct. 1, 1776.

" Sir,

" On the foregoing pages is a
copy of a letter I had the honour of
writing to you by Captain Leech,
who was to have ſailed immediately,
but as he is now to wait for the Weſt-
India convoy, which from the firſt
was not to have been ready till the
middle of this month ; and is now ſaid
to be deferred till the beginning of the
next, I thought it right to forward
you a duplicate by the preſent packet.
Not that the packet is always the
moſt ſpeedy conveyance, for in theſe
critical times, their motions are governed rather by the occaſions of government, than regulated by ſtated
times and ſeaſons.

" Nothing farther has been done
ſince that letter. Lord North has had
the misfortune to break his arm by
a fall from his horſe, which accident
unavoidably delays the progreſs of
all buſineſs at the Treaſury Board.
I am therefore obliged to content
myſelf with compliments of enquiry
after his health ; which I find with
pleaſure to be as well as poſſible.

I remain with great regard,
S I R,

Your moſt obedient,
And faithful humble ſervant,
GEORGE WALKER."

BARBADOS.

At a meeting of the General Aſſembly
at the Town-Hall, on Tueſday the
21ſt day of January, 1777, pur-
ſuant to an adjournment, preſent;

The Honourable Sir JOHN GAY
ALLEYNE, Bart. Speaker.
William Gibbes Alleyne,
Hon. Hillary Rowe, jun.
Thomas Alleyne,
John Wheeler Ridgway,
Joſhua Gittens,
Hon. Samuel Walcott,
John Stewart,
Joſeph Wood,
John Burke,
Samuel Hinds,
Valentine Jones,
Eyre Walcott, and
Thomas Burton, Eſquires.

A verbal meſſage from his Excellency to the Houſe, delivered by Mr.
Secretary to the Clerk this morning,
and by the Clerk communicated to
the Houſe. " That the Agent's
bill was read the laſt Council day before the Board three times, and has
had the unanimous conſent of the Honourable the Members. His Excellency refuſed his aſſent to this bill,
but will be ready to give his aſſent to
any other bill, appointing any other
perſon Agent for this iſland, in Great
Britain, except the Honourable
George Walker, Eſq.

On the motion of Mr. Thomas
Alleyne, ſeconded by Mr. Stewart,
Reſolved, nem. con.

That an humble addreſs be preſented to the Governor, praying his
Excellency to communicate to the
Houſe, his reaſons for refuſing his
aſſent to the bill lately paſſed the
Council and Aſſembly, for continuing the Hon. George Walker, Eſq.
the Agent of this Iſland, in Great-
Britain.

Ordered, That ſuch addreſs be immediately prepared, which being accordingly done, the ſame was read
by order.

A 2   Reſolved,

Refolved, nem. con. That the addrefs do pafs.

Ordered, That Mr. Jones and Mr. Maycock do prefent the faid addrefs to his Excellency.

Ordered, That the faid addrefs be entered in the Journals, and publifhed in the Minutes, and the fame is as follows, viz.

To his Excellency the Honourable EDWARD HAY, his Majefty's Captain General, Governor and Commander in Chief of this ifland, Chancellor, Ordinary, and Vice Admiral of the fame.

The humble addrefs of the General Affembly.

May it pleafe your Excellency,

The important affairs of the ifland in the year 1763, requiring an Agent of an extenfive knowledge in the various branches of the public intereft, the Hon. George Walker, Efq. a Member of his Majefty's Council, was unanimoufly appointed to that office by the Legiflature, as a perfon in whofe fuperior conduct and unqueftionable zeal, the ifland repofed the utmoft confidence. That the important fervices rendered by that Gentleman to this community fince he has been nominated to the Agency, having well juftified the firft appointment, he has been every year fince appointed to the faid office, and an annual act paffed for that purpofe, by the general voice of the Legiflative body. With the utmoft concern then, We have received your Excellency's meffage, importing, that you had refufed your affent to the bill that has lately had the unanimous confent of two branches of the Legiflature, both Council and Affembly, for the continuance of the faid George Walker, to be the Agent of this ifland for the current year.

We the Reprefentatives of the people, in their General Affembly, do therefore humbly pray, that your Excellency will be pleafed to communicate to this Houfe your reafons for refufing your affent to the faid bill.

BARBADOS.

At a meeting of the General Affembly, on Tuefday the 18th day of February, 1777, at the Town-Hall, purfuant to adjournment; prefent,

The Honourable Sir JOHN GAY ALLEYNE, Bart. Speaker.
George Sanders,
William Gibbet Alleyne,
Thomas Alleyne,
Jofhua Gittens,
Hon. Samuel Walcott,
John Stewart,
Samuel Hinds,
Valentine Jones,
Richard Haynes,
Eyre Walcott,
James Marfhall,
Thomas Burton,
And Dotin Maycock, Efquires.

The Minutes of the laft meeting were read and confirmed.

The Houfe being informed Mr. Secretary was at the door, he was admitted, and delivered to Mr. Speaker his Excellency's anfwer to the addrefs of the Houfe at their laft meeting.

Ordered, That the fame be read, which was done in thefe words, viz.

" Mr. Speaker, and Gentlemen of the Affembly,

" By the meffage delivered to you by the Deputy Secretary, you have been informed what part of the Agent's bill I objected to.

" My reafons for refufing my affent to that bill have been laid before his Majefty.

EDWARD HAY.

Pilgrim-Houfe, Tuefday, Feb. 18, 1777.

Mr. Thomas Alleyne then got up and moved the Houfe to come to the two following refolutions, viz.

1ft, Refolved, That after the fulleft experience, which, in the courfe of a long fervice, this country has had of the uncommon zeal and fuperior ability of the Hon. George Walker, Efq. in the office of Agent for the ifland, island, in Great Britain; joined to that unreserved testimony, which has been so conspicuously given of his recent, as well as former, merit with the public, by the unanimous suffrages both of Council and Assembly, in the bill that was passed by their respective bodies, for continuing this gentleman in the same office for the current year, this Assembly cannot; under such circumstances, renounce their first nomination of the said George Walker to that department, and proceed to the choice of any other person in his place, without an act of injustice to so worthy a servant of the public, an injury to our country, and a dishonour to ourselves.

2d, Resolved, That the thanks of this House be transmitted by the Speaker to the said George Walker, for his many laudable and successful services to Barbados, in Great-Britain, lamenting the loss of so valuable an Agent, and at so critical a juncture; and requesting withal his generous attention still to the important interests of this community, as far as he can properly exert his friendly cares under the present sanction, assuring him of our earnest desires to restore him to the full enjoyment of that office, to which he has done honour to his talents, and reflected no less upon the judgment of his country that had distinguished them.

Mr. Alleyne's motion being seconded by Mr. Hinde, the question was ordered to be separately put, on each of the resolutions, and the question on the first resolution being about to be put, Mr. Maycock expressed himself as follows:

" Mr. Speaker,

" I cannot agree to this motion in the latitude in which I think it must be understood; the design of it is, that we should come to a resolution (by which, if any effect is intended, it ought to be that of its being binding on us) that we cannot appoint any other Agent than Mr. Walker, under the *circumstances* expressed in the motion, without *an injury to our country*, and *a dishonour to ourselves*. Now, I know of no circumstances that ought to prevent us from the discharge of our duty to the public, and therefore if occurrences should happen (and in the present situation of affairs, I think, such are very likely to happen) under which it might be absolutely necessary, for the good of the country, that we should appoint some other Agent; if Mr. Walker cannot be replaced, in that case we must either appoint such other Agent, and violate the resolution intended to be binding on us; that is to say, we must act with inconsistency, or we must adhere to our resolution and appoint no other Agent, and then we should indeed (to use the language of the motion) *do injury to our country* and *dishonour to ourselves*. I wish to be understood, that my reasons for opposing this motion, arise from a consideration for the public and ourselves; for, in respect to the Gentleman who is the subject of it, I can chearfully concur in every honourable mention that is made of him, can readily agree to every acknowledgment which is due to him for his services, and can sincerely regret the several occurrences which have contributed to interrupt the continuance of them.

To which Mr. Speaker answered, " that he thought the resolution moved for was to be justified in its full extent; for if the extraordinary merit of Mr. Walker in the course of a long service was so readily acknowledged, and no reason had been vouchsafed to the request humbly made to the Governor for his Excellency's refusing his assent to the bill, after it had passed the Council as unanimously as it had done the House of Assembly, then surely the House were bound in justice to Mr. Walker, in duty to their country, and in ho-

nour

hour to their own body, not to make a sacrifice of this old and valuable servant of the public, to no one apparent consideration of a *public* nature whatsoever; especially, when, besides the disgrace of too ready a submission in their body to so great a loss as that of the best Agent ever employed by this colony, and at such a crisis, the House would appear to make a virtual surrender by it, of that indispensable constitutional right vested in them, of choosing their own Agent; or utterly destroy all the salutary effects of such a right of choosing, in matters of the most interesting consequence to this community, in which their Agent might be called to act —That if any very particular occurrences should, notwithstanding, arise to make it absolutely necessary for the *good of the country*, (of which that House, however, were to be themselves the judges) to give up the point; then, indeed, to that *first and great principle of duty* in all *governments*, every other consideration must give way; and then too an unbiassed regard for that principle would with ease be able to reconcile any seeming inconsistency of the measure with a former equally disinterested determination to the contrary: but for the House to find themselves deprived, in the manner that would appear upon the face of their proceedings, of so very able a servant of his country, acting in so important an office; and yet to sit down calmly with the loss, or to forbear expressing themselves in the degree of warmth proposed under the pain of it, what would this be, but to give the public an occasion to suspect that the House were indifferent to the event, and only waited the result of his Excellency's reasons, laid before his Majesty, to direct them tamely to another choice: whereas, it was their duty to follow those reasons, whatever they were, with proper declarations of their own; in order that

the Assembly might make known at large their real sentiments under the dilemma, as well as give some pledge to their constituents of their firmness in so just a cause; for if the House should *passively* consent to name any other Agent than the faithful one, who has been so long devoted to their service, and so frequently honoured with testimonies of their esteem; if they should be the least inclinable to concur in thus requiting the services of a man, whose fidelity to their interest may have been his only fault; what hope remained to them of being ever faithfully served again in that department? Nay, what other return could reasonably be expected by them from a successor so unworthily promoted, but that he should betray his trust, encouraged by the treacherous example of their own weakness in his promotion! Mr. Speaker declared, therefore, in favour of the first resolution, as being equally necessary for the honour of the House, as the last was for the satisfaction of the Gentleman who was the subject of it."

The question being then put the House divided, the members voting as follows:

Yea 10, viz.
Mr. Marshall,
Mr. Eyre Walton,
Colonel Haynes,
Mr. Jones,
Mr. Hinds,
Mr. Stewart,
Mr. Thomas Alleyne,
Mr. Will. Gibbes Alleyne,
Mr. Sanders,
And Mr. Speaker.
Nay 4, viz.
Mr. Maycock,
Mr. Burton,
Judge Walcott,
And Mr. Gittens.

The question being carried in the affirmative, the House accordingly came to the first resolution proposed.

The

The second resolution was unanimously agreed to.

Ordered, That Mr. Speaker do transmit the thanks of this House to Mr. Walker, agreeable to the said resolution.

PHILADELPHIA.

An ACT directing the mode of collecting the fines imposed on persons who did not meet and exercise, in order to learn the Art Military, according to the resolves of the late Assembly of Pennsylvania.

WHEREAS by a resolve of the late House of Assembly, dated the 5th day of April, 1776, imposing a fine on all able bodied effective male white persons, capable of bearing arms, not associators, between the ages of sixteen and fifty years (Ministers of the Gospel, of all denominations, School-masters, in actual employ, and servants, purchased *bona fide*, and for a valuable consideration only excepted). And whereas (to the great discouragement and dissatisfaction of the spirited and virtuous associators in this state) the fines have not yet been collected, therefore, for making effectual the said resolve, *Be it enacted, and it is hereby enacted*, by the representatives of the freemen of the Commonwealth of Pennsylvania, in General Assembly met, and by the authority of the same, That the three Commissioners, which, at the time of their meeting, shall then have been last elected in each county respectively, in this Commonwealth, or any two of them, be required and enjoined, and they are hereby required and enjoined, to meet together, at the Court-House in their respective counties, on the twenty-eighth day of February instant, and appoint a proper person in each ward, township, and district, under their hands and seals, to make a return to them in writing, of the names and firnames of every male white person capable

of bearing arms, at the time of passing the said resolves by the said late Assembly, between the ages of sixteen and fifty years (Ministers of the Gospel of all denominations, School-masters, in actual employ, and servants purchased *bona fide*, and for valuable consideration only excepted) where such returns have not already been made.

And be it further enacted by the authority aforesaid, That if any person or persons, appointed as aforesaid, shall neglect or refuse to perform the duty aforesaid, the Commissioners aforesaid of the respective counties, or any two of them, are hereby required and enjoined to fine him or them, in any sum not exceeding twenty pounds, and such fine shall be levied and recovered in the same manner as hath been heretofore directed by the laws of Pennsylvania, for levying and recovering fines imposed on assessors refusing or neglecting to perform the duties therein required of them, which fines shall be paid into the hands of the respective County Treasurers, to be by them applied to the same use as other monies directed to be levied by this Act. And the Commissioners aforesaid, or any two of them, are hereby enjoined and required to appoint some proper person to make out the lists aforesaid, in the place of the person first appointed, who shall make out such lists, and return them to the Commissioners on or before the twenty-seventh day of March next ensuing.

And be it further enacted by the authority aforesaid, That every person appointed as aforesaid, shall, before he enters upon the duty of his office, take an oath or affirmation, which any Justice, Commissioner or County assessor, is hereby authorized and required to administer, without fee or reward, (if a person of the first appointment) that he will make a faithful and diligent enquiry, and endeavour by proper and lawful ways and means,

to

to procure a true and exact account and list of the names and surnames of all male white persons capable of bearing arms, who were between the ages of sixteen and fifty years before the last Monday in February last past, residing within his township, borough, ward or district, and will make a just and true return of such account or list to the Commissioners aforesaid, on or before the eleventh day of March next ensuing, or (if a person not of the first appointment) on or before the twenty-seventh day of March next ensuing; and every person appointed and acting as aforesaid, shall receive for his trouble in making out and returning such lists, the sum of five shillings for every day he shall be employed in that service. And if any dispute shall arise concerning the age of any non-associator, the same shall be determined by the Commissioners aforesaid, who shall be judges of the evidence produced in favour of such non-associator.

And be it further enacted by the authority aforesaid, That the Captain or Commanding Officer of each company is hereby required and enjoined, on or before the twentieth day of March next ensuing, to deliver, under his hand, to the Colonel or Commanding Officer of the battalion to which he belongs, a list of all the persons belonging to his company, who have at any time signed the articles of association, therein mentioning the time of their first signing the said articles, the county and township, borough, ward or district, in which each of the said associaters resides, which the Colonel or Commanding Officer shall carefully keep, and therefrom shall immediately make out and return, on or before the twenty-seventh day of March, a fair duplicate to the Commissioners aforesaid, except the same be already done.

And be it further enacted by the authority aforesaid, That the Com-

missioners aforesaid respectively, or any two of them, are hereby required and enjoined to cause their clerks to make out fair lists of the names and surnames of all persons mentioned in the duplicates returned to them as aforesaid, with the places of abode of those who appeared by the duplicates returned by the Colonels or Commanding Officers, not to have signed the articles of association. And thereupon the said Commissioners are required to charge every such person not associating, the sum of three pounds ten shillings, on the lists made out on their order as aforesaid; and every person who hath signed the articles of association, after the last Monday of February last, three shillings and six-pence for each and every parade-day appointed by the aforesaid Resolves, before his signing as aforesaid; all which lists as aforesaid, to be made out on or before the tenth day of April next, on which day the assessors of the city, and the assessors of the counties respectively, or any four of them, and one or more of the Commissioners, shall meet together at the County Court-house, or such convenient place as the said Commissioners shall appoint, and appoint a proper person in each township, ward, and district, in the same manner as directed in the county levy Act of Pennsylvania for collecting the county taxes, to collect the fines aforesaid; which Collectors, so appointed, shall have the same powers and authorities as the Collectors appointed by virtue of the county levy Act as aforesaid, for collecting county taxes, have had and exercised, or ought to have and exercise.

And be it further enacted by the authority aforesaid, That if any Collector, appointed as aforesaid, shall refuse or neglect to do and perform his several and respective duties, as required by this Act, he shall forfeit and pay the sum of twenty pounds, to be recovered in the same manner as
fines

fines are directed to be recovered from the Collectors appointed by virtue of the county levy Act aforesaid, upon their neglect or refusal, and be paid into the same hands, and applied to the same uses, as other money raised by virtue of this Act. And, in such case, the Commissioners of the counties respectively, or any two of them, shall appoint another Collector in his stead, who shall have the same power and authority as the other Collector aforesaid, and be subject to the same fines and forfeitures as aforesaid.

And be it further enacted by the authority aforesaid, That if any apprentice was willing to associate, and his master or mistress did not permit him so to do, and detained him from going to the parade on any of the days of exercise appointed by the Resolve of the late Assembly, such master or mistress shall be liable to the payment of three shillings and six-pence for each time he or she did hinder or so detain his or her said apprentice: and if such apprentice shall have neglected or refused to appear on any of the said days of exercise, not being detained by his said master or mistress, he, if of estate, shall, by his guardian, pay such fine. And the father or mother of any minor or minors, associators, and non-associators, being in the service of his father or mother, shall be accountable to the Collector for his or their fines charged as aforesaid.

And be it further enacted by the authority aforesaid, That if any Commissioner, or City or County Assessor, shall neglect or refuse to perform any of the duties required of him by this Act, such Commissioner or Assessor shall forfeit and pay the sum of thirty pounds for every such offence; such fine to be levied and recovered in the county levy Act aforesaid, and paid and appropriated in the same manner, and for the same purposes, as the other monies raised by virtue of this Act; and in such case,

the Commissioner or Commissioners and Assessors, who shall proceed agreeable to the directions of this Act, or a majority of them, are hereby enjoined to appoint another suitable and proper person to act in his stead, so refusing or neglecting as aforesaid; which person so appointed shall have the same power and authority, and perform the several duties hereby required of the said Commissioners and Assessors; and on failure thereof shall forfeit and pay the sum of thirty pounds, to be applied as aforesaid.

Provided nevertheless, and it is hereby enacted by the authority aforesaid, That those who have formed themselves into regular companies, and signed written articles of association, agreeable to the intentions of the resolves of the late Assembly, and have attended the parade, and mustered the number of twenty days within the time limited by the said Assembly (unless having marched into the Jersies on actual service) shall be considered in the same light, and dealt with in the same manner, as those who have signed the articles of association framed by the late House of Assembly. And that such as have not signed any association whatever, nor attended to any particular muster-days, yet, on the first call of the associators last summer, did chearfully turn out to camp, and serve the time then required of the associators in defence of the American States, shall be deemed as associators from the time of their engaging in the said service.

And be it further enacted by the authority aforesaid, That if any non-associator, or the parent, guardian, master or mistress, of any non-associator, between the ages of sixteen and twenty-one years, or any other non-associator, shall think him or herself aggrieved by the assessment aforesaid, he or she may appeal to the County Commissioners where he or she resides, who, or any two of them, shall meet together on or before the twelfth day

of

of May next enfuing, and fo from day to day, as long as may be neceffary, and at fuch place or places as the Commiffioners, or any two of them, fhall appoint; of which days and places of meeting they fhall caufe the Collectors to give due notice to the perfons fo charged, or by this Act made liable to the fines as aforefaid: and alfo return the names of all perfons omitted or not charged in their duplicates refpectively, who are made fineable by this Act; and then, and there, the faid Commiffioners, or any two of them, fhall hear fu ' appeals as may be made to them; and may difcharge fuch offen cor, or lower the fame, as to them, on confideration of inability of perfon or eftate, (only) fhall appear juft and equitable.

And be it further enacted by the authority aforefaid, That the faid Commiffioners of the counties refpectively, or any two of them, within ten days after hearing and determining the appeal made to them, fhall rectify and adjuft the lifts returned to them as aforefaid, and the affeffments thereon, and deliver to the Treafurers of the counties refpectively a true account of the fum total which every Collector fhall be charged with in purfuance of this Act; and fhall caufe their clerks to make out and deliver fair duplicates thereof to the refpective Collectors of the townfhips, boroughs, wards, and diftricts, within the faid city and counties refpectively, who fhall collect the faid fums, and fhall pay the fame into the hands of the County Treafurers refpectively, who fhall pay the fame into the hands of the State-Treafurer for the time being, to be applied in fuch manner as this or any future Houfe of Affembly fhall direct; and the Commiffioners and Affeffors fhall be allowed feven fhillings and fix-pence per diem for their fervice aforefaid. And all perfons fhall be liable to the payment of the faid fums in the fame manner, and the Collectors fhall have the fame

powers, and fhall proceed in collecting and levying the faid fums, and fhall be accountable in the fame manner as is directed by the Act of General Affembly of the province of Pennfylvania, entituled, " An Act for raifing county rates and levies, for collecting the county taxes," and the Collectors fhall have for their care and trouble in collecting the faid fines, one fhilling in the pound for all fuch monies collected as aforfaid; and the Treafurer fhall have for his care and trouble in receiving from the Collectors, delivering to the State-Treafurer, and paying the Commiffioners orders, one per cent. and the State-Treafurer fhall have for his trouble one fourth per cent.

And be it further enacted by the authority aforefaid, That the Treafurers of the counties refpectively, before they enter on the duties hereby required of them, fhall give fecurity to the Commiffioners, for the faithful difcharge of their office, in the fum of fifteen hundred pounds.

JOHN JACOBS, *Speaker*.
Paffed Friday, Feb. 14, 1777.

An ACT authorifing the Collectors of the Excife due and to become due on fpirituous liquors, to collect the fame, and directing the mode of obtaining tavern and other licences; and for other purpofes therein mentioned.

WHEREAS, by the ceafing of the powers of government in the province of Pennfylvania, the feveral and refpective Collectors of Excife impofed on fpirituous liquors, by the laws late of the faid province, could not collect the fame as by the faid laws they are directed and required, although the fame was and ftill is abfolutely neceffary for the purpofes of defraying the expences of government, and finking the bills of credit emitted by Refolves of the late Affembly for the public defence: and although it is evident that dealers in

liquors

liquors have received greater profits on such liquors than was customary theretofore, or than is just and reasonable, to the encreasing their own estates and the injury of many of the good people of the State. And as it is also just and reasonable, that all persons who make great profits and advantage by the public, should contribute to the public expence accordingly, Be it therefore enacted by the Representatives of the Freemen of the Commonwealth in Pennsylvania, in General Assembly met, and by the authority of the same, That the Collector of Excise on spirituous liquors in each county in this State, who was appointed to that office by the last Assembly of the said province, shall be, and continue, Collector of the Excise, on spirituous liquors in the county for which he was so appointed, if living, until another shall be appointed in his stead: and the said Collectors, and every of them, and such others as may be hereafter appointed, shall have, use and exercise all the powers and authority which Collectors of the Excise might, could or ought to have had, used and exercised, under or by virtue of the said laws, and shall in all things respecting the duties of the said office be governed by the laws aforesaid. And all persons whomsoever that, by the laws aforesaid, ought to have paid excise, if the force and effect of the said laws had not ceased, shall be, and are hereby declared to be within the meaning and intention of this Act, and shall pay the duty or excise, on all liquors they and each of them have purchased and not paid excise for according to the said laws, as far as can be known and discovered: and all retailers of spirituous liquors, and every other person coming under, or within the notice of the said laws, are hereby declared to be, and to have been subject to all the duties of excise, fines and forfeitures, pains and penalties by the

said laws inflicted, or directed to be collected, paid, taken and received, as fully and amply as the same could or might have been done at any time before the fourteenth day of May last.

And whereas it is represented to this House, that divers tavern-keepers, public-house-keepers, beer-house-keepers, and keepers of dram-shops, have not taken out licences, or paid licence-fees, as the laws of the said province directed and required, although they have continued their respective businesses as before, and received as great profits and emoluments therefrom as those who have taken and paid for such licences. Now, in order that equal justice may be done to all, and the licence-fees applied to the use of the State according to the true intent and meaning of the constitution thereof, Be it enacted by the authority aforesaid, That where any person had kept a tavern, inn, public house of entertainment, ale-house, beer-house or dram-shop, by the Governor's licence, in the year 1775, and did not take out a licence for the year 1776, although they continued to keep such tavern, inn, public-house, ale-house or dram-shop; every such person is hereby declared indebted to this State a sum of money equal to the sum he, or she, had last paid, or ought to have paid for such licence, agreeable to the laws aforesaid: and every person who has (without licence) set up and kept a tavern, public house of entertainment, inn, ale-house, beer-house or dram-shop, and continued the same for the space of three months in the year 1776, or in the years 1776 and 1777, as hereby declared to be indebted to this State a sum of money equal to the fees or sum of money directed by the laws aforesaid, to be paid for a licence for keeping such house or tavern, or dram-shop, which shall be recovered by the Collector

B b

of

of Excise for the respective counties in the same manner as fines and forfeitures are directed to be recovered by the laws aforesaid : and when recovered, shall be considered as fines or forfeitures, and paid into the Treasury with the other fines and excise monies; and the Collectors shall have the same allowance or pay, for collecting, as by the said laws he ought to have for collecting fines and forfeitures.

And be it further enacted by the authority aforesaid, That no person or persons whatsoever within this State, shall set up, or keep a tavern, inn, public house of entertainment, ale-house, beer-house or dram-shop, unless such person or persons be first recommended by the Justices in the respective County Courts of Quarter-Sessions for the said county, to the President and Council of this State for the time being, for a licence for so doing, who shall (on such person having given bond, and paid to the Clerk of such Court respectively, the whole of the fees as directed by the laws aforesaid to be paid for such licence) grant the same, and the Secretary of the Council of this State shall have for making out each licence the sum of six shillings. And if any person or persons shall keep any tavern, inn, public house of entertainment, ale-house, beer-house, or dram-shop, by virtue of a licence from the President aforesaid, he, she or they, shall be in all things subject to the rules, regulations and restrictions of the said laws in such cases made and provided, where the licence was to be granted by the Governors of Pennsylvania. And if any person or persons shall keep any tavern, public house of entertainment, inn, ale-house, beer-house or dram-shop, without first obtaining a licence for each respective year, all and every such person and persons shall, for every such offence, be dealt with as the said laws in such case direct.

And be it further enacted by the authority aforesaid, That the Clerk of the Court of such respective county shall pay all such monies as he shall so receive (his own lawful fees only excepted) into the State Treasury forthwith after the term at which such recommendations were granted, and transmit an account of the number such licences and the sum of money so received and paid into the hands of the Treasurer, to the Committee appointed by the Assembly to settle the public accounts for the time being, which monies shall be subject to the draughts and orders of the House of Assembly.

And be it further enacted by the authority aforesaid, That the President, and in his absence the Vice-President of the State, shall grant licences in all cases where the Governors of Pennsylvania have heretofore granted licences, and the fees shall be the same as have heretofore usually been in like cases, and shall be paid into the hands of the State Secretary (except in the case aforesaid)—And the said Secretary shall make fair entries of all such monies he shall so receive, and shall once in three months, or oftner, pay the same into the hands of the Treasurer aforesaid, for the use of the State, retaining in his hands the sum of five shillings for his trouble in making out each of the said licences, and affixing the seal to the same, and shall transmit an account thereof, on oath or affirmation, to the Committee of Accounts for the time being, appointed by the General Assembly to settle the public accounts.

And be it further enacted by the authority aforesaid, That all pedlars, hawkers and petty chapmen, shall be, and are hereby declared to be, within the meaning and intention of this Act.

JOHN JACOBS, *Speaker.*

Passed Tuesday, Feb. 18, 1777.

An

An ACT to difcourage defertion, and to punifh all fuch perfons as fhall harbour or conceal deferters.

WHEREAS many foldiers, being duly inlifted or employed in the fervice of the United States of America, and others in the fervice of this State, defert and abfent themfelves illegally from their refpective duties, to the great prejudice of the fervice and the ill example of others: in order therefore, that an evil fo dangerous in its confequences may be properly difcouraged, and (if poffible) finally prevented, and the encouragers and abettors thereof duly punifhed, Be it enacted by the Reprefentatives of the Freemen of the Commonwealth of Pennfylvania in General Affembly met, and by the authority of the fame, That it fhall and may be lawful to and for the Conftable of the township, ward, or borough, where any perfon who fhall be fufpected to be a deferter fhall be found, who is hereby authorifed and required to apprehend, or caufe him to be apprehended, and brought before any Juftice of the Peace of this State living in or near fuch place, who is hereby authorifed and required to examine fuch fufpected perfon ; and if, by his confeffion, or the teftimony of one or more witnefs or witneffes, upon oath or affirmation, or by the knowledge of fuch Juftice of the Peace, it fhall appear that fuch fufpected perfon is an inlifted foldier, and ought to be with the troop or company to which he belongs, fuch Juftice of the Peace fhall forthwith caufe him to be conveyed to the gaol of the county where he fhall be found ; and the Sheriff of the county fhall forthwith tranfmit an account thereof to the Colonel or commanding officer of the battalion to which faid deferter fhall belong, or of the neareft battalion, to the end that fuch perfon may be proceeded againft according to the martial law of the United States: and the keeper of fuch gaol or houfe of correction fhall receive the full fubfiftence of fuch deferter or deferters, but fhall not be intitled to any fee or reward on account of the imprifonment of fuch deferter or deferters, any law, ufage or cuftom, to the contrary notwithftanding. And for the better encouragement of every Conftable to fecure or apprehend fuch deferters as aforefaid, Be it further enacted by the authority aforefaid, That the officer, to whom faid deferter fhall be delivered, fhall be paid into the hands of the gaoler or fheriff, where fuch deferter fhall be apprehended and detained, over and befide the reward ordered to be paid by Congrefs for each deferter he fhall fo deliver, the fum of three dollars for the ufe of the Conftable or Conftables who hath or have apprehended the faid deferter or deferters.

And be it further enacted by the authority aforefaid, That if any perfon fhall harbour or entertain, for the fpace of fix hours by day, or twelve hours by night, any deferter or deferters, knowing him or them to be fuch, without apprehending him or them, or giving notice thereof to the next Juftice of the Peace, or to fome Conftable, every fuch perfon fo offending fhall forfeit and pay for every fuch offence the fum of five pounds: or if any perfon fhall knowingly detain, buy or exchange, or otherwife receive any arms, caps, cloaths, or other furniture or accoutrements belonging to the United States of America, or either of them, from any foldier or deferter, upon any account or pretence whatfoever, or caufe the colour of fuch cloaths to be changed, the perfon or perfons fo offending, on being thereof legally convicted, fhall forfeit and pay, over and above the value thereof, the fum of five pounds ; one moiety thereof, and of the laft mentioned fine, to the overfeers of the poor of the townfhip, for

the

the use of the poor thereof, and the other moiety to the informer : and in case any such offender, who shall be convicted as aforesaid, of harbouring or assisting any such deserter or deserters, or having knowingly received any arms, cloaths, caps, or other furniture belonging to the said United States, or either of them, or of having caused the colour of such cloaths to be changed, contrary to the intent of this Act, and shall not have sufficient goods or chattels whereon distress may be made to the value of the penalties and forfeitures incurred by him, her or them, for such offence, or give sufficient sureties for the payment of such penalties within sixty days after such conviction ; then, and in such case, any two Justices of the Peace shall and may, by warrant under their hands and seals, either commit such offender to the common gaol, there to remain without bail or mainprize, for the space of six weeks, or cause such offender to be publicly whipped on his or her back with any number of lashes, not exceeding twenty-one. Provided always, That no Commissioned Officer, or any other person, shall break open any house to search for deserters without a warrant from a Justice of the Peace ; and every Commissioned Officer, or any other person, who shall, without warrant from one or more Justice or Justices of the Peace of this State (which said warrant the said Justice or Justices are hereby impowered to grant) forcibly enter into, or break open, the dwelling-house or out house of any person whatsoever, under pretence of searching for deserters, shall, upon due proof thereof, forfeit and pay the sum of thirty pounds to the owner of such house, and make good all damages, he, she or they may sustain by such breaking.

And be it further enacted by the authority aforesaid, That the constables of each ward in the city of Philadelphia, the district of Southwark, and of every township in this State, respectively, are hereby enjoined and required, under the penalty of twenty shillings for every neglect, to go as often as the case may require, to every suspected place or house in his township, or the adjacent townships, that he shall suspect or be informed of, and apprehend every suspected person, and take him or them before the next Justice, and if on examination it shall appear probable that he or they is or are a deserter or deserters, such Justice shall commit him or them to the county gaol, until it shall be known whether he or they be a deserter or deserters, or not. And if any able-bodied man shall travel, or come into any part of this State, without a pass from some Justice of the county, or some other Justice of the Peace, from whence he may have come ; or, if a soldier, from his Commanding Officer ; every such person so travelling, or coming into the State as aforesaid, shall be deemed and taken to be a deserter, and within the meaning of this Act, except the contrary be made appear : and every constable is hereby authorised (if need be) to call to his aid sufficient assistance (men of the neighbourhood) to apprehend any deserter or deserters ; and if any person or persons so called or commanded to assist the constable, shall disobey or refuse such assistance, on complaint thereof made to the next Justice, every person so refusing shall, if convicted, forfeit and pay to the said Justice the sum of twenty shillings ; one moiety to the use of the poor of the township where such refusal shall be, and the other for the use of such constable, to be recovered as debts under forty shillings.

And in order to encourage the apprehending deserters, every person not a constable, who shall apprehend any deserter, and deliver him to some constable, shall be entitled to receive for every such deserter the sum of twenty shillings, to be paid out of the State-

State-Treasury; or if he conveys such deserter to the county gaol, he shall be entitled to the same reward as constables by this act are entitled to receive. JOHN JACOBS, *Speaker.*

Passed Thursday, Feb. 20, 1777.

An ACT to impower the Justices of Peace for the city of Philadelphia to do and perform certain matters and things formerly directed to be done and performed by the Mayor, Recorder, and Aldermen of the said city.

Whereas by an Act of the General Assembly of the province of Pensylvania, passed on the seventh day of June, in the year of our Lord one thousand seven hundred and twelve, intitled " An Act for raising money on the inhabitants of the city of Philadelphia, for the public use and benefit thereof;" and by one other Act, intitled " An Act for regulating party walls, buildings, and partition fences in the city of Philadelphia;" and by one other Act passed the twenty-first day of October, in the year of our Lord one thousand seven hundred and sixty-one, intitled " An Act for the better employment, relief, and support of the poor, within the city of Philadelphia, the district of Southwark, and the township of Moyamensing, Passyunk, and the Northern Liberties;" and by one other Act passed the eighteenth day of February, in the year of our Lord one thousand seven hundred and sixtynine, intitled " An Act for regulating, pitching, paving, and cleaning the highways, streets, lanes and alleys, and for regulating, making, and amending the water courses and common sewers within the inhabited and settled parts of the city of Philadelphia, for raising money for defraying the expences thereof, and for other purposes therein mentioned;" and by one other Act passed the ninth day of March, in the year of our

Lord one thousand seven hundred and seventy-one, intitled " An Act for the relief of the poor ;" and by one other Act passed the same day, intitled " An Act for regulating and continuing the nightly watch, and enlightening the streets, lanes and alleys in the city of Philadelphia, and for other purposes therein mentioned;" the aid and assistance of the Mayor, Recorder, and Aldermen of the city of Philadelphia, or some or one of them, were necessary to enable the proper officers elected or appointed in pursuance of the above recited Acts of Assembly, or any of them, to put such an Act or Acts in force. And whereas, by the change of the government of the said province, the powers of the Mayor, Recorder, and Aldermen, have ceased and become void, whereby the aforesaid Acts of Assembly cannot be put in force, according to the true intent and meaning thereof, to the great inconvenience and injury of the good people of the said city, district and townships, for remedy whereof, be it enacted, and it is hereby enacted by the Representatives of the Freemen of the Commonwealth of Pennsylvania in General Assembly met, and by the authority of the same, That in all cases whereby any or either of the afore-mentioned Acts of General Assembly, the Mayor or Recorder, and one or more of the Aldermen of the city of Philadelphia, are, or is made necessary for the execution of, or in any ways putting in force such Act respectively, or to enable any officer or officers mentioned therein, to do and perform the duties and services of him or them required, the Justices of the Peace of the said city of Philadelphia, or any three of them, shall be, and are hereby declared to be able and capable in law to do and perform all and singular the duties and services that are in and by the said several and respective Acts

of

of Assembly required of and from the Mayor, Recorder, or Aldermen of the said city. And in all cases where the said Justices, or any three of them, shall act, do, and perform any duty, service, or business that is in any of the said Acts required to be done and performed by the Mayor, Recorder and Aldermen, the same shall be, and is hereby declared to be, of the same force and effect, and as sufficient and binding in all cases on all persons that shall be within the meaning and intention of this Act, as the same could or ought to have been heretofore when such service and duty were done and performed by the Mayor, Recorder and Aldermen, agreeable to the intent and meaning of the several and respective Acts aforesaid.

JOHN JACOBS, Speaker.

Passed March 14, 1777.

Admiralty-Office, August 2, 1777.

Vice-Admiral Young, Commander in Chief of his Majesty's ships and vessels at the Leeward Islands, has, in his letter of the 12th of June, transmitted to Mr. Stephens a list of prizes taken by the squadron under his command since the capture of those mentioned in the Gazette of the 28th of June, a copy of which list is as follows:

The Peggy schooner, Jacob Evans, master, from North Carolina to St. Eustatia, with corn and staves—by the Hind.

The Nancy sloop, Samuel Dunwall, master, from St. Kitt's to America, with salt and ironmongery—by the Otter.

The Juno brig, Isaac Coleman, master, from Surinam to Boston, with molasses—by the Otter.

The Oliver Cromwell privateer, Herman Courter, master, 24 guns, 150 men—by the Beaver.

The First Attempt schooner, Nicholas Johnson, master, from New-

bery Port to Guadaloupe, with fish and lumber—by the Seaford.

The Sophia schooner, Lazarus Sillia, master, from St. Eustatia to Martinico, with indigo and rice—by the the Seaford.

The Jenny privateer, George Ralls, master, by the Seaford.

The Betsey sloop, William Richardson, master, from Virginia to St. Eustatia, with tobacco, corn, &c. by the Cygnet.

The De Water Guise, Archibald Chatelain, master, from St. Eustatia to Middleburg, with indigo, tobacco, rum, rice, &c.—by the Seaford.

The De Hoog, Al. B. Hoop Zeal, master, from St. Eustatia to Flushing—by the Seaford.

The Dolly sloop, from Casco Bay to Eustatia, with fish and lumber—by the Portland.

The Betsy sloop, from New London to St. Eustatia, with fish and lumber—by the Portland.

The Relief sloop, from South Carolina to St. Eustatia, with corn and turpentine—by the Portland.

The Mosketo privateer, John Harris, master, 14 guns, 71 men—by the Ariadne.

Admiralty-Office, August 2, 1777. *The following is an extract of a letter from Captain Jones, of his Majesty's sloop the Beaver, of 14 six pounders, and 125 men, to Mr. Stephens. Dated at St. Kitt's the 12th of June, 1777.*

I beg you will be pleased to acquaint their Lordships, that on the 18th ult. near the Island St. Lucia, and then going to Tobago for the homeward-bound trade, I fell in with and engaged a privateer of the rebels, and that in less than three quarters of an hour, under a very close fire, she yielded to the superior valour and good order of my officers and men.

She proved to be their capital ship in these seas, and the second best fitted
ted

ted out for America, carries 24 guns, of which 14 are nine pounders, 10 swivels, 10 coherns, and 150 men; has ports to all her guns, and fights her men under cover, and is named the Oliver Cromwell, Herman Courter, Commander.

We had the good fortune not to lose a man, and had only 3 wounded, with little or no damage to the rigging, &c.

On the rebels side 20 men were killed, and 20 wounded; her rigging, masts, and sails much cut and hurt. [London Gazette
Extract of a Letter from Grenada, April 29.

" A gentleman who went to Martinico to claim two vessels, which had been carried in there by the rebels, returned there a few days ago, and reported, with much accuracy, to Lord Macartney, the reception he met with from the French Governor; who, saying it was a neutral port, would give no redress. He then applied to Mr. Bingham, the agent for the Congress, who is treated with as much respect as the British Ambassador at Paris; and from him making purchase of the vessels, dispatched them with French papers and French masters. He saw 16 sail of privateers at anchor, mounting from 10 to 20 guns, and they had opened several rendezvouses for entering seamen. The merchants make no secret of being concerned in this piratical business, and every encouragement is given to promote it, by the principal person The mischief done to the West-India Islands by them is amazing."

London, July 3. An officer just arrived from Martinico, from whence, for the better security, he took his passage to France in a French ship, assures us, that during his abode on the afore-mentioned island, he saw nothing but American colours parading in every part, with drummers beating up for volunteers, for the

service of the American Congress; and that on his entering several of the houses of rendezvous, to see who presided at those places, he was astonished to find them all Frenchmen, and scarcely one person among them who could even so much as speak English.

In the Leeward Island fleet came home passengers the Captain and Surgeon of a large Guineaman, that was taken by a privateer, by whom the following particulars are received:

The Guineaman was fitted out from the Thames, and intended to send her cargo from Africa to Jamaica, but was taken within three days sail of that island, by a large privateer of 14 guns, and 120 men, who sent her into Martinico. There were only three Englishmen on board the privateer, the Captain and two more, the rest of the crew were all French, or various nations picked up at Martinico, where the privateer was fitted out. Five or six prizes had been carried into Martinico before them, and all had come to a very bad market except the first. When they arrived at that place, English silk stockings, such as are sold daily at 10 or 12 shillings, were currently sold for a dollar, or 4s. 6d. and the sailors were hawking, from door to door, pieces of Irish linen, and the most they could get were two dollars or nine shillings for the piece.

The slaves they had on board never fetched the original cost paid for them in Africa: and every sort and kind of prize goods were sold in the same proportion.

London, July 7. A correspondent says, that the fact upon which the Harwich Packet was obtained, is now come out;—it was not done out of any complaisance to our Court; nor in consequence of any demand made by our Ambassador; but purely, because somebody *bought her.* Somebody *paid* for her; no matter who. Mr. Cunningham received the value of of his prize ; and it was quite indifferent to him, whether the buyer was an Englishman, a Scot, or a Frenchman. The credulous people of England were told the packet was restored,—and the privateer's crew sent to prison. The imprisonment was a farce, a mere ostensible trick to cover the fraud. And thus are the people of England duped. No man hereafter need be surprized at the enormous sum in the Civil List-accounts, charged to *secret service* ; but every man of penetration and judgment, is surprized, at the patience of this country, in not resenting, in a becoming manner, the infinite number of tricks, frauds, and impositions, daily practised upon them, by the present Ministers.

So long since as the month of May last, our Court very confidently gave out, "That all was peace and quietness (their own words) between the French Court and them ; for that each side had agreed to disarm a certain number of ships." But in June the *ton* was changed ; it was confessed the French had raised some objections ; and in July the pretended agreement was totally abandoned by the ministerialists.

AMERICAN COMMERCE CLAIMED, AND AMERICAN INDEPENDENCE ACKNOWLEDGED.

Monsieur de Sartine, Minister of the French marine department, has sent the following letter to the principal Chambers of Commerce in France:

Versailles, le 4 Juillet, 1777.

"Je viens d'être informé, Messieurs, par des lettres venues de la Martinique, qu'on y debitoit, que le Commandant General de cette colonie avoit declaré aux negocians & armateurs, qu'il est convenu entre la Cour de France et celle de Londres, que les Anglois pourroient saisir sur les navires François toutes les denrées du cru de la nouvelle Angleterre qu'ils pourroient y trouver, & que les denrées & les batimens seront de bonne prise.

"Je m'empresse de prevenir les allarmes que cette assertion sans fondement pourroit repandre dans les esprits. Si le Commandant General de la Martinique a parlé de la saisie des batimens en cas pareil, il n'a pu qu'annoncer une pretention de la part des Anglois qu'on a peutre et interpreté l'effet d'une convention entre les Cours de France et de Londres. Mais le Roi me charge de vous faire sçavoir que cette convention entre les deux cours n'existe pas, & que sa Majesté est determinée à reclamer tout batiment François qui auroit été arreté sous ce pretexte, & à proteger le commerce.

(Signé) " DE SARTINE."

TRANSLATION.

Versailles, the 4th July, 1777.

" Gentlemen,

"I have just been informed, by letters received from Martinico, that it was given out there, that the Governor of that colony had declared to the merchants and owners of ships, that it was agreed between the Courts of France and London, that the English may seize all commodities of the growth of New-England *, which they may find on board of French ships, and that the goods and vessels shall be lawful prize. I am solicitous to prevent the alarm, which may be spread in people's minds by this groundless assertion. If the Governor of Martinico has spoken of the seizure of vessels, in such case, he can only have mentioned a pretention on the part of the English, which, perhaps, has been interpreted as the effect of an agreement between the Courts of France and London : but the King charges me to acquaint you, that no such agreement exists, between the two Courts, and that his Majesty

---

* A common term in France for the British American Colonies.

Majesty is determined to reclaim every French vessel, which might be seized under the pretext, and to protect the trade.

(Signed) " De SARTINE."

Thus do the French publicly claim, and determine to assert, a right of trading with the revolted Colonies, and of bringing the produce of our late American dominions, in their own vessels, directly to France; a privilege totally subversive of the acts of navigation and trade, which have been the source of our naval and national strength for more than one hundred years, and which till the present time, no nation in Europe has avowedly dared to violate. This the French have now ventured to do; and the example given by them, will be followed by Spain, by Portugal (the new ally of those kingdoms) and by every other power, who from situation can partake in the benefits of that invaluable commerce; a commerce which, till within these few years, was exclusively our own, and which is now for ever lost; even the idea of recovering it, is become ridiculous. The trade is now free and open to all, and till we are able to contend with, and prevail over many nations (the strongest in the world) united against us, we shall not regain it. But what hope can we have from arms? We now wage war with those, who lived with us as brothers, and whom we despised as foes, and find in them an enemy mightier than ourselves.

On the important matter of Monsieur de Sartine, Minister of the French Marine Department's circular letter to the Chamber Commerce in France, we cannot help citing the following clauses from the statutes of the 12th and 15th of Charles the Second:

" That for the increase of shipping, and encouragement of the navigation of this nation, wherein, under the good providence and protection of God, and the wealth, safety, and strength of this kingdom is so much concerned; Be it enacted by the King's Most Excellent Majesty, and by the Lords and Commons in this present Parliament assembled, and by the authority thereof, that from and after the first day of December, one thousand six hundred and sixty, and from thenceforward, no goods or commodities whatsoever shall be imported into, or exported out, of any lands, islands, plantations or territories to his Majesty belonging, or in his possession, or which may hereafter belong unto, or be in the possession of his Majesty, his heirs and successors, in Asia, Africa, or America, in any other ship or ships, vessel or vessels whatsoever, but in such ships or vessels as do truly, and without fraud, belong only to the people of England or Ireland, dominion of Wales, or town of Berwick upon Tweed, or are of the built of and belonging to any the said lands, islands, plantations or territories, as the proprietors and right owners thereof, and whereof the master and three-fourths of the mariners at least are English; under the penalty of the forfeiture and loss of all the goods and commodities which shall be imported into, or exported, out of any the aforesaid places in any other ship or vessel; as also of the ship or vessel, with all its guns, furniture, tackle, ammunition and apparel; one third part thereof to his Majesty, his heirs and successors; one third part to the Governor of such land, plantation, island or territory, where such default shall be committed, in case the said ship or goods be there seized; or otherwise, that third part also to his Majesty, his heirs and successors; and the other third part to him or them who shall seize, inform, or sue for the same in any Court of Record, by bill, information, plaint, or other

C c

action,

action, wherein no effoin, protection, or wager of law shall be allowed; and all Admirals, and other commanders at sea, of any of the ships of war, or other ship, having commission from his Majesty, or from his heirs or successors, are hereby authorized, and strictly required, *to seize and bring in as prize*, all such ships or vessels as shall have offended contrary hereunto, and deliver them to the Court of Admiralty, there to be proceeded against; and in case of condemnation, one moiety of such forfeitures shall be to the use of such Admirals or Commanders, and their companies, to be divided and proportioned amongst them, according to the rules and orders of the sea, in case of ships taken prize; and the other moiety to the use of his Majesty, his heirs and successors. And that in regard his Majesty's plantations beyond the seas are inhabited and peopled by his subjects of this his kingdom of England, for the maintaining a greater correspondence and kindness between them, and keeping them in firmer dependence upon it, and rendering them yet more beneficial and advantageous unto it, in the further employment and increase of English shipping and seamen, vent of English woollen and other manufactures and commodities, rendering the navigation to and from the same more safe and cheap, making this kingdom a staple, not only of the commodities of those plantations, but also of the commodities of other countries and places, for the supplying of them; and it being the usage of other nations to keep their plantations trade to themselves; and be it enacted, and it is hereby enacted, that from and after the five and twentieth day of March, one thousand six hundred sixty-four, no commodity of the growth, production, or manufacture of Europe, shall be imported into any land, island, plantation, colony, territory, or place to

his Majesty belonging, or which shall hereafter belong unto, or be in the possession of his Majesty, his heirs, and successors, in Asia, Africa, or America, (Tangier only excepted) but what shall be *bona fide*, and without fraud, laden and shipped in England, Wales, or the town of Berwick upon Tweed, and in English built shipping; or which were, *bona fide*, bought before the first day of October, one thousand six hundred sixty and two, and such certificate thereof had, as is directed in one act passed the last sessions of this present Parliament, intituled, "An Act for preventing frauds, and regulating abuses in his Majesty's customs;" and whereof the masters and three-fourths of the mariners at least are English, and which shall be carried directly thence to the said lands, plantations, colonies, territories, or places, and from no other place or places whatsoever, any law, statute, or usage to the contrary notwithstanding, under the penalty of the loss of all such commodities of the growth, production, or manufacture of Europe, as shall be imported into any of them, from any other place whatsoever, by land or water; and if by water, of the ship or vessel also in which they were imported, with all her guns, tackle, furniture, ammunition, and apparel; one third part to his Majesty, his heirs, and successors; one third part to the Governor of such land, island, plantation, colony, territory, or place, into which such goods were imported, if the said ship, vessel, or goods be there seized or informed against and sued for; or otherwise, that third part also to his Majesty, his heirs, and successors; and the other third part to him or them who shall seize, inform, or sue for the same in any of his Majesty's Courts in such of the said lands, islands, colonies, plantations, territories, or places where the offence was committed, or in any Court of Record,

Record in England, by bill, information, plaint, or other action, wherein no essoin, protection, or wager of law shall be allowed."

When the considerate reader compares these clauses with the foregoing letter from the Minister of the French Marine Department, must he not be convinced, that our affairs are at last brought to the mournful alternative, either of suffering France to engross the trade of America, in direct violation of the above statutes, or of seizing her vessels, and immediately running into a war, which must be fatal to our best interests? In either case, France will be the *carrier* of American produce, through the whole extent of that trade, and by such means rise to a degree of naval power, to which this country has never attained. It must be obvious also, to common observation, that the claim of France to the American trade can only be founded on the idea of Americans being no longer colonists of Great-Britain, but the subjects of Independent States. War therefore with France is as indispensibly necessary, as it now is with America; since, to prevent the establishment of that independence the present unnatural and self-destroying war is continued.

Copy of a letter from an English Gentleman at Paris, dated July 28, 1777.

" You will, no doubt, have heard long ere this, and with great eclat on the part of Lord Stormont, and exultation on that of your Ministers, that the Court of Versailles, in answer to the boasted remonstrance of the English Ministry, had knocked under, and faithfully promised to shut their ports against the American privateers and their prizes. Be it so; let these purblind politicians exult, and deluded England go to sleep; I promise you that a short time will awaken both from their lethargy. In addition to Mr. Sartine's letter,

which you have already got, I send you the following striking proof of the sincerity with which the French adhere to their own interest, and their natural, unconquerable enmity to England. The fact is undoubted, as you will venture from my authority to affirm, and will soon receive a fuller confirmation :

" The General Mifflin privateer, which has lately committed such depredations upon your coasts, and in the very mouths of your harbours, is just arrived at Brest, where she found the French squadron under the command of Monsieur de Chaffault. The privateer saluted the French Admiral, who was at a loss how to conduct himself. A council of war was held therefore immediately, when, after an hour and a half's consultation, it was agreed to return the salute, which was done in form, as to the vessel of a Sovereign Independent State. This is known and approved of by the Court. It is but the other day that the Governor of St. Eustatia was ordered home by the States General of Holland, for returning the salute of the American flag, in consequence of a strong, decisive memorial from Sir Joseph Yorke. Eustatia is at a distance; Brest is at home. The fact will not admit of shuffling. Now is the time, therefore, for the spunk of Lord Weymouth, and the firmness of Lord George Sackville (Germaine); I beg his Lordship's pardon. You may safely defy the Courtiers to deny, or palliate a single circumstance of this. I see the papers say, that Cunningham is chained up in Dunkirk harbour; but I will whisper you, that he has broke his chains, and is now prowling at large for prey, as the beasts in that foul den at Llyod's will soon discover. The General Mifflin is preparing for sea again; yet the French ports are shut, as the Scotch will tell you in the City."

Copy

Copy of a letter from Philip Stephens, Esq. Secretary of the Admiralty, to the Worshipful William Crosbie, Esq. Mayor of Liverpool, dated Admiralty-Office, July 11, 1777.

" My Lords Commissioners of the Admiralty having stationed the Albion, Exeter, Arethusa, and Ceres, between the coasts of Great Britain and Ireland, in quest of the American privateers, and for the protection of trade in those parts, I am commanded by their Lordships to acquaint you thereof, for the information of the merchants of Liverpool ; and that the commanders of those ships have directions to enquire for intelligence respecting such privateers at the following places, viz.

At Dublin and Cambletown,
The Albion of 74 guns, and Ceres sloop.

At Milford and Corke alternately,
The Exeter of 64 guns.

At Whitehaven, and afterwards at Cambletown and Carrickfergus,
The Arethusa of 32 guns.

Other cruizers between Milford Haven and Ireland."

The Admiralty have been obliged to appoint convoys for all the British and Irish coasts.

———————

The Spanish relation of taking of the island of St. Catharine, by the Spanish army, under the command of the Captain General Don Pedro de Cevallos, extracted from authentic letters from Madrid, dated June 6 :

" Our fleet, consisting of 116 sail, left Cadiz the 13th of November, 1776, and after a most happy passage found themselves on the 8th of February in 26d. 36m. lat. and 337d. 24m. long. when they took a Portugueze merchant ship, called the Lucia a Fortunada, bound from Rio Janeiro to Lisbon, on board which they found letters which informed them, that four ships of war and five frigates were placed in the Bay of Garupa to observe and attack us, if we should enter the port of St. Catharine ; in consequence of which we resolved to sail for that place in order to attack them.

" No sooner had we discovered the island of St. Catharine on February 10, and had doubled the Cape of the Bay of Garrupas, than our frigate the St. Margaret informed us, that she had seen the enemy's squadron, consisting of 12 sail, for two days. On this information, our General Don Cevallos, and the Marquis of Casa-Tilly, commander of the squadron, having deliberated, they judged it more proper to enter the port of the island than to pursue their squadron, which they accordingly entered on February 20, excepting a few transport vessels, on board of which there were 1400 men, which we supposed had made for Monte Video, the place of general rendezvous.

" The Portugueze forces in garrison on the island were much more considerable than usual ; independent of four battalions of troops, and 200 artillery, they had regimented the militia, so that the force was not less than 4000 men, exclusive of what they called auxiliaries, and the inhabitants of the island, who were to assist in defending the castle and the strong forts of Saint Croix and Punta Grosa, very strongly situated by nature and art, and well provided with provisions and ammunition.

When the place had been reconnoitred, the army was debarked the 22d at night. Next day we occupied the camp near within cannon-shot of Punta Grosa, while the Septentrion and two bomb vessels approached the castle. In the night a body of troops was dispatched towards the left, and dispositions were made for our army to take possession
of

of the Heights, which the Governor feeing, and the Portugueze being intimidated at our movements, they abandoned the caftle without firing a gun, and retired to a ftrong advanced work, but with fuch precipitation, that they left all their cannon and ftores, and every provifion for a long fiege.

" The Portugueze troops in the caftle of St. Croix, feeing the caftle abandoned, and a body of Spaniards marching towards them, took a like refolution with the other Portugueze troops, and abandoned it, with their other intrenchments and batteries, fo that the whole ifland was evacuated on the 25th. And having paffed over to the Continent, and croffed the river Catabon, about feven or eight leagues from the ifland, their Commander in Chief, Don Antonio Carlos Hartado de Mendoza, fent Brigadier Don Jofeph Cuftodio de Sa-y Faria, with orders to propofe to our commander, Don Cevallos, to grant them fhips to tranfport them to Rio Janeiro; but this he refufed to confent to, and infifted they fhould furrender themfelves prifoners of war; which, after fome meffages paffing, they agreed to, and fhips were to be allowed to tranfport the officers only to Rio Janeiro, on promife of not ferving in any manner againft his Catholic Majefty, and to furrender themfelves to any other place, when called on by the Spanifh General. Since which all the Portugueze foldiers have been fent to Buenos Ayres, and nothing remains on the ifland belonging to the Crown of Portugal.

Paris, June 27. Our laft accounts from Madrid mention, that Don Cevallos, Commander of the Spanifh fleet at Brazil, after taking the ifland of St. Catherine, fet fail from thence, and arrived at San Pedro the 7th of March; and, it is faid, he purpofes to take poffeffion of all the Portu-

gueze Settlements on the Rio Grande, which it is thought will not require a long time. After this, the fquadron army will unite in Buenos Ayres, and proceed from thence to befiege the fortrefs of St. Sacrament, which is a very ftrong place, and has a confiderable garrifon well provided with every thing neceffary for a long and obftinate refiftance.

Extract of a letter from the Hague, July 1.

" We have accounts from Paris, that news have been received there from Madrid, that peace was concluded between Spain and Portugal in that laft-mentioned capital on the 10th of laft month; but that the conditions of this accommodation are not yet known. It is only faid, that things are to remain in *ftatu quo*; but this feems rather an equivocal determination, as it makes a very great difference whether it means to leave things as they were previous to conquefts made by the Spaniards in America, or whether they are to remain as they are now, and leave Spain in the poffeffion of the ifland of St. Catharine, &c. it is imagined the Court of Madrid will endeavour to detach the Queen of Portugal from her alliance with Great Britain, in which, if they fucceed, a rupture is thought inevitable.

London, July 8. Authentic advice is received, that preliminaries of peace, between Spain and Portugal, are abfolutely figned. As our Court have had no concern in this matter, the firft confequence is, that Portugal will be loft to this country. Every man who knows any thing of Portugal, knows that our trade with Portugal has been highly advantageous to us; particularly in her taking our woollens, ftuffs, &c. &c. in return for which, we have had her gold, &c. The beft, and only apology, for the conduct of our Minifters, during the laft feven years, feems to be *infanity*.

The

The Court and Council have been so immersed in, and infatuated with, the rage of making war upon ourselves, in North America, that nothing else has been attended to. To this wildness and madness, we owe the loss of Portugal. By these preliminary articles, it is said to be agreed, That all hostilities shall cease between Spain and Portugal in South America; and that each party shall, for the present only, keep whatever she is in possession of at the signing of these preliminaries, which are to be understood as laying the foundation of, and as opening a treaty of peace and alliance between Spain and Portugal. Signed the 10th of June, 1777.

Extract of a Letter from Gibraltar, dated May 1, 1777.

" Yesterday a schooner coming in from Cadiz, with money on board (about 12,000 dollars) wine, and other articles, for the garrison, was boarded and taken by a Spanish guardship. The English Commodore (Captain Hay, of the Alarm) on seeing Spanish colours hoisted on board the schooner, sent boats from our fleet to retake her. She was so closely chaced by them, as to oblige her to run ashore on the coast of Spain, within reach of their guns. A barge, with 12 men armed with muskets, and commanded by the master of the Alarm, came up with her. Many shots were fired by the Spaniards, some of which took place in the boat. They were returned by our sailors, who boarded the vessel, and took out the money. The Spanish battery then opened on them, firing two or three shots among them, without doing any damage. On a signal made by the Commodore, they returned, and brought with them the money. It remains to see, whether the vessel, or any satisfaction, will be demanded for an English subject, who was killed by the Spaniards on their first boarding her.

For the Remembrancer.

The following Paper was drawn up in a Committee of Congress, June 25, 1775, but does not appear on their Minutes, a severe Act of Parliament which arrived about that time having determined them not to give the sum proposed in it. It is supposed to have been written by Dr. Franklin.

Forasmuch as the enemies of America in the Parliament of Great Britain, to render us odious to the nation, and give an ill impression of us in the minds of other European powers, have represented us as unjust and ungrateful in the highest degree; asserting on every occasion, that the Colonies were settled at the expence of Britain; that they were at the expence of the same protected in their infancy; that they now ungratefully and unjustly refuse to contribute to their own protection and the common defence of the nation; that they aim at independence; that they intend an abolition of the Navigation Acts; and that they are fraudulent in their commercial dealings, and purpose to cheat their creditors in Britain, by avoiding the payment of their just debts : —

As by frequent repetition these groundless assertions and malicious calumnies may, if not contradicted and refuted, obtain farther credit, and be injurious throughout Europe to the reputation and interest of the Confederate Colonies, it seems proper and necessary to examine them in our own just vindication.

With regard to the first, *that the Colonies were settled at the expence of Britain*, it is a known fact, that none of the Twelve United Colonies were settled, or even discovered at the expence of England. Henry the Seventh, indeed granted a commission to Sebastian Cabot, a Venetian, and his sons, to sail into the western seas for the discovery of new countries; but it was to be *suis eorum propriis*

propriis sumptibus et expensis, at their own costs and charges*. They discovered, but soon slighted and neglected, these northern territories, which were after more than a hundred years dereliction purchased of the natives, and settled at the charge and by the labour of private men and bodies of men, our ancestors, who came over hither for that purpose. But our adversaries have never been able to produce any record, that ever the Parliament or Government of England was at the smallest expence on these accounts; on the contrary, there exists on the Journals of Parliament, a solemn declaration in 1642, only 22 years after the first settlement of the Massachusetts, when if such an expence had ever been incurred, some of the Members must have known and remembered it, " That these Colonies had been planted and established *without any expence to the State* †." New-York is the only Colony in the founding of which England can pretend to have been at any expence; and that was only the charge of a small armament to take it from the Dutch, who planted it. But to retain this Colony at the peace, another at that time, full as valuable, planted by private countrymen of ours, was given up by the Crown to the Dutch in exchange, viz. Surinam, now a wealthy sugar colony in Guiana, and which but for that cession might still have remained in our possession. Of late, indeed, Britain, has been at some expence in planting two Colonies, Georgia ‡ and Nova Scotia, but those are not in our confederacy; and the expence she has been at in their name

has chiefly been in grants of sums unnecessarily large, by way of salaries to officers sent from England, and in jobs to friends, whereby dependants might be provided for; those excessive grants not being requisite to the welfare and good government of the Colonies; which good government (as experience in many instances of other Colonies has taught us) may be much more frugally, and full as effectually, provided for and supported.

With regard to the second assertion, *That these Colonies were protected in their infant state by England,* it is a notorious fact, that in none of the many wars with the Indian natives, sustained by our infant settlements for a century after our first arrival, were ever any troops or forces of any kind sent from England to assist us; nor were any forts built at her expence to secure our sea-ports from foreign invaders; nor any ships of war sent to protect our trade till many years after our first settlement, when our commerce became an object of revenue, or of advantage to British merchants; and then it was thought necessary to have a frigate in some of our ports, during peace, to give weight to the authority of Custom-house Officers, who were to restrain that commerce for the benefit of England. Our own arms with our poverty, and the care of a kind Providence, were all this time our only protection; while we were neglected by the English Government, which either thought us not worth its care, or having no good-will to some of us, on account of our different sentiments in religion and po-

---

* See the Commission in the Appendix to Pownall's Administration of the Colonies. Edit. 1775.

† " Veneris, 10 March, 1642. Whereas the Plantations in New-England have, by the " blessing of the Almighty, had good and prosperous success, without any public charge to " this State, and are now likely to prove very happy for the propagation of the Gospel in " those parts, and very beneficial and commodious to this kingdom and nation : The Com- " mons now assembled in Parliament, &c. &c. &c."

‡ Georgia has since acceded, July 1775.

litics,

litics, was indifferent what became of us. On the other hand, the Colonies have not been wanting to do what they could in every war for annoying the enemies of Britain. They formerly affifted her in the conqueft of Nova Scotia. In the war before laft they took Louifbourg, and put it into her hands. She made her peace with that ftrong fortrefs, by reftoring it to France, greatly to their detriment. In the laft war, it is true, Britain fent a fleet and an army, who acted with an equal army of our's in the reduction of Canada, and perhaps thereby did more for us than we in the preceding wars had done for her. Let it be remembered, however, that fhe rejected the plan we formed in the Congrefs at Albany, in 1754, for our own defence, by an union of the Colonies; an union fhe was jealous of, and therefore chofe to fend her own forces; otherwife her aid, to protect us, was not wanted. And from our firft fettlement to that time, her military operations in our favour were fmall, compared with the advantages fhe drew from her exclufive commerce with us. We are, however, willing to give full weight to this obligation; and as we are daily growing ftronger, and our affiftance to her becomes of more importance, we fhould with pleafure embrace the firft opportunity of fhewing our gratitude by returning the favour in kind. But when Britain values herfelf as affording us protection, we defire it may be confidered that we have followed her in all her wars, and joined with her at our own expence againft all fhe thought fit to quarrel with. This fhe has required of us; and would never permit us to keep peace with any power fhe declared her enemy; though by feparate treaties we might

well have done it. Under fuch circumftances, when at her inftance we made nations our enemies, whom we might otherwife have retained our friends, we fubmit it to the common fenfe of mankind, whether her protection of us in thefe wars was not our *juft due*, and to be claimed of *right*, inftead of being received as a *favour?* And whether, when all the parts of an empire exert themfelves to the utmoft in their common defence, and in annoying the common enemy, it is not as well the *parts* that protect the *whole*, as the *whole* that protects the *parts*. The protection then has been proportionably mutual. And whenever the time fhall come, that our abilities may as far exceed hers, as hers have exceeded ours, we hope we fhall be reafonable enough to reft fatisfied with her proportionable exertions, and not think we do too much for a part of the empire, when that part does as much as it can for the whole.

The charge againft us, *that we refufe to contribute to our own protection*, appears from the above to be groundlefs; but we farther declare it to be abfolutely falfe; for it is well known that we ever held it as our duty to grant aids to the Crown upon requifition, towards carrying on its wars; which duty we have chearfully complied with to the utmoft of our abilities, infomuch that frequent and grateful acknowlodgments thereof by King and Parliament appear on their records *. But as Britain has enjoyed a moft gainful monopoly of our commerce, the fame with our maintaining the dignity of the King's reprefentative in each colony, and all our own feparate eftablifhments of government, civil and military, has ever hitherto been deemed an equivalent for fuch aids as might other-

* Suppofed to allude to certain paffages in the Journals of the Houfe of Commons on the 4th of April 1748, 28th January 1756, 3d February 1756, 16th and 19th of May 1757, 1ft of June 1758, 26th and 30th of April 1759, 26th and 31ft of March and 28th of April 1760, 9th and 20th January 1761, 22d and 26th January 1762, and 14th and 17th March 1763.

wife

wife be expected from us in time of peace. And we hereby declare, that on a reconciliation with Britain, we shall not only continue to grant aids in time of war as aforesaid, but, whenever she shall think fit to abolish her monopoly, and give us the same privileges of trade as Scotland received at the Union, and allow us a free commerce with all the rest of the world, we shall willingly agree (and we doubt not it will be ratified by our constituents) to give and pay into the Sinking Fund [100,000l.] sterling per annum for the term of one hundred years; which duly, faithfully, and inviolably applied to that purpose, is demonstrably more than sufficient to extinguish all her present national debt, since it will in that time amount, at legal British interest, to more than 230,000,000l.

But if Britain does not think fit to accept this proposition, we, in order to remove her groundless jealousies, *that we aim at independence, and an abolition of the Navigation Act*, (which hath in truth never been our intention) and to avoid all future disputes about the right of making that and other acts for regulating our commerce, do hereby declare ourselves ready and willing to enter into a covenant with Britain, that she shall fully possess, enjoy, and exercise that right for an hundred years to come, the same being *bona fide* used for the common benefit; and in case of such agreement, that every assembly be advised by us to confirm it solemnly by laws of their own, which once made cannot be repealed without the assent of the Crown.

The last charge, *that we are dishonest traders, and aim at defrauding our creditors in Britain*, is sufficiently and authentically refuted by the solemn declarations of the British merchants to Parliament, (both at the time of the Stamp Act, and in the last session) who bore ample testimony to the general good faith and fair dealing of the Americans, and declared their confidence in our integrity; for which we refer to our petitions on the Journals of the House of Commons. And we presume we may safely call on the body of the British tradesmen, who have had experience of both, to say, whether they have not received much more punctual payment from us than they generally have from the Members of their own two Houses of Parliament.

On the whole of the above it appears, that the charge of *ingratitude* towards the Mother Country, brought with so much confidence against the Colonies, is totally without foundation; and that there is much more reason for retorting that charge on Britain, who not only never contributes any aid, nor affords by an exclusive commerce any advantages to Saxony, *her* Mother Country; but no longer since than in the last war, without the least provocation, subsidized the King of Prussia while he ravaged that Mother Country, and carried fire and sword into its capital, the fine city of Dresden. An example we hope no provocation will induce us to imitate.

———————

Bristol (England) July 2. Last Thursday a vessel arrived at Cork from Quebec in nineteen days. She brings an account of Gen. Burgoyne's arrival in the Apollo frigate; that he had taken the command, and was gone to Trois Rivieres; that General Carleton would return to Quebec—that the snow was not off the ground the 4th of June, and that the troops were beginning to move.

London, July 3. The Sally, Henderson, a transport, is arrived at Dover from Quebec; she left that place the 4th of June, and brings an account that General Burgoyne arrived at Quebec on the 6th of May, and that twenty-eight sail of different sorts of transports were also arrived.

D d By

By a private letter from an officer in Sir Guy Carleton's army, dated May 16, we have the following abridged detail of general facts during the winter encampments:

" The winter set in so soon after our taking possession of Crown Point, that for want of timber, &c. we could not make it tenable, the evacuation of it therefore closed the campaign.

" Winter quarters was our next object, and by the happy disposal of the troops, spent six months of a winter less severe than we sometimes meet in England. Amusements took the lead of business, and the clangor of war gave place to balls, assemblies, &c. The inhabitants readily accepted the soldiers as lodgers, and seemed happy to give every assistance to those who came so far to protect them. The following has been the disposition of the troops:

" The 20th regiment quartered on the Isle aux Noix, with artillery, &c. composed the advanced post. The 21st regiment, under the command of Brigadier General Hamilton, occupied St. John's; and here all our vessels and batteaux were arranged, when fortunately not the least accident happened to them. At Chamblee Fort, the 53d regiment, commanded by Brigadier General Powel, and the Sorrell river, to the village, commanded by the 31st regiment.

" Longueil, La Prairie, and all down to Sorrell, on the river St. Lawrence side, occupied by the grenadiers, light infantry, and 24th regiment, under the command of Brigadier General Fraser. Montreal has in the garrison the artillery and 29th regiment, and there Major General Philips took up his quarters. The Island of Montreal is occupied by the 9th and 47th, Colonel Maclean and Sir John Johnston's corps. From Repentigny (the end of the island) to Cape Sante, about 13

leagues from Quebec, on the North; and from Sorrell Down, on the South of the river St. Lawrence, occupied by the Germans. Trois Rivieres is their head quarters, and commanded by Major General Riedesel.

" General Carleton remained at Quebec, with his family; the 34th regiment were in garrison; and the 62d regiment at Point Levi, almost opposite the town.

" Thus has our army been distributed in their winter quarters. We are now preparing to advance, as soon as the weather will permit; it will be three weeks at least, though we shall be in motion in a few days.

" It is imagined the rebels will not meet us on the Lakes, having no force competent to our's; their defence will be at Ticonderoga, which they have fortified greatly, having made a bridge to communicate with their works, and fixed a boom to prevent our vessels getting up. They have now 2000 men there, and by the first of next month are to have 20,000.

London, August 5. Sunday arrived at Dover the Harmony, Capt. Stancliff, the Devonshire, Penlington, and the Ann, Russel, from Quebec. They left Quebec on the fifth of July. In them came passengers, Major Gordon, chief engineer to the army in Canada, and Colonel Christie, intended to have been Quarter-master to the army. On the 22d of June part of the army were on Bouqet River, on the west side of Lake Champlain, about 50 miles north of Crown Point. The army was under the command of General Burgoyne. General Carleton was at Quebec, waiting for leave, (which he had wrote for upon the arrival of General Burgoyne) to return to England.

A letter from an officer in the army, dated June 25, which says, the advanced guard were at Putnam's Creek, about twelve miles from Ticonderoga. This letter further says,
that

that they shall invest that place by the first or second of July, that the garrison confists of 4500 men, and that General Burgoyne has sent all the Indians (in number about 500) to intercept a convoy of provisions for the garrison. On the 27th of June, General Carleton arrived at Quebec from Montreal, anxioufly expecting the leave he wrote for, to return to England.

Another letter from an officer, dated June 22, says, General Burgoyne having orders to take the command of the army to crofs the Lakes, to leave a fufficient number of men for the protection of the province, and make a detachment under the command of Lieut. Col. St. Leger, of the 34th regiment, obliges General Carleton to leave the army, and return to his government, with the 29th, 31ft, and 34th regiments, 650 of the Brunfwickers, Col. Maclean's corps, and a detachment of 50 men from each of the Britifh regiments for its safety. General Burgoyne proceeds to the Lakes with the grenadiers, light infantry, seven Britifh regiments, the artillery, the Germans, and the Savages.

Our army are partly advanced on Lake Champlain, the others coming up, &c. while our veffels are advanced on the Lake, under the command of Captain Lutwidge, of the Triton frigate, who acts as Commodore. Our naval ftrength is very great. All the veffels, as well of the rebels as our own, are enlarged and ftrongly equipped, befides a new 20 gun fhip built this fpring. We fhall have but little ufe for them, nor fhall we meet with any obftruction till we get to Ticonderoga. Gen. Burgoyne fays, in a few days he fhall be againft Ticonderoga: he and all the Generals are at St. John's; he goes on board the Maria, I believe, tomorrow. Col. St. Leger is to fet off in a few days, by way of Ofwego and the Mohawk river, with orders to land upon the German flats. He is to have fome chaffeurs, 120 of the 3.th regiment, 100 of the 8th, fome Canadians, Sir John Johnfon's corps, and a party of Indians. The Canadians are fulky.

General Wafhington, in a letter to Congrefs, dated in May, 1777, acquaints them, he had received information from Ticonderoga, of 3000 of the Northern troops being arrived in good health and fpirits, at that garrifon, the beginning of May; and that the remainder of the reinforcements (12,000 men) deftined for that garrifon, were on their march from the Maffachufets Bay, &c. and expected there, the latter end of May at fartheft. This Northern army is to be commanded by General Gates, General Coudrey, and feveral French Generals. It would be at leaft 17,000 ftrong, and be well provided with engineers, artillery, mortars, &c.

PROCLAMATION.
By JOHN BURGOYNE, *Efq. &c &c.*
Camp at Putnam Creek,
June 29, 1777.

"The forces entrufted to my command are defigned to act in concert, and upon a common principle with the numerous armies and fleets which already difplay, in every quarter of America, the power, the juftice, and, when properly fought, the mercy of the King.

"The caufe in which the Britifh arms are thus exerted, applies to the moft affecting interefts of the human heart; and the military fervants of the Crown, at firft called forth for the fole purpofe of reftoring the rights of the conftitution, now combine with love of their country, and duty to their Sovereign, the other extenfive incitements which fpring from a due fenfe of the general privileges of mankind.

"To the eyes and ears of the temperate

perate part of the public, and to the breafts of fuffering thoufands in the provinces, be the melancholy appeal, whether the prefent unnatural rebellion has not been made a foundation for the compleateft fyftem of tyranny, that ever God in his difpleafure fuffered for a time to be exercifed over a froward and ftubborn generation. Arbitrary imprifonment, confifcation of property, perfecution and torture, unprecedented in the inquifitions of the Romifh Church, are among the palpable enormities which verify the affirmative. Thefe are inflicted by affemblies and committees, who dare to profefs themfelves friends to liberty, upon the moft quiet fubjects, without diftinction of age or fex, for the fole crime, often for the fole fufpicion, of having adhered in principle to the government under which they were born, and to which, by every tie divine and human, they owe allegiance. To confummate thefe fhocking proceedings, the profanation of religion is added to the moft profligate proftitution of common reafon; the confciences of men are fet at nought, and multitudes are compelled not only to bear arms, but alfo to fwear fubjection to an ufurpation they abhor.

" Animated by thefe confiderations, at the head of troops in the full powers of health, difcipline, and valour, determined to ftrike where neceffary, and anxious to fpare where poffible, I, by thefe prefents, invite and exhort all perfons, in all places where the progrefs of this army may point, and, by the bleffing of God, I will extend it far, to maintain fuch a conduct as may juftify me in protecting their lands, habitations, and families; the intention of this addrefs is to hold forth fecurity, not depredation, to the country.

" To thofe whom fpirit and principle may induce to partake the glorious tafk of redeeming their countrymen from dungeons, and re-eftablifh-ing the bleffings of legal government, I offer encouragement and employment; and, upon the firft intelligence of their affociations, I will find means to affift their undertakings.

" The domeftic, the induftrious, the infirm, and even the timid inhabitants, I am defirous to protect, provided they remain quietly at their houfes; that they do not fuffer their cattle to be removed, nor their corn or forage to be fecreted or deftroyed; that they do not break up their bridges or roads, nor by any other acts, directly or indirectly, endeavour to obftruct the operations of the King's troops, or fupply or affift thofe of the enemy.

" Every fpecies of provifion brought to my camp will be paid for at an equitable rate, and in folid coin. In confcioufnefs of Chriftianity, my Royal Mafter's clemency, and the honour of foldierfhip, I have dwelt upon this invitation, and wifhed for more perfuafive terms to give it impreffion; and let not people be led to difregard it by confidering their diftance from the immediate fituation of my camp. I have but to give ftretch to the Indian forces under my direction, and they amount to thoufands, to overtake the hardened enemies of Great Britain and America. I confider them the fame wherever they may lurk.

" If, notwithftanding thefe endeavours, and fincere inclination to effect them, the phrenzy of hoftility fhould remain, I truft I fhall ftand acquitted in the eyes of God and man, in denouncing and executing the vengeance of the ftate againft the wilful outcafts.

" The meffengers of juftice and of wrath wait them in the field; and devaftation, famine, and every concomitant horror that a reluctant, but indifpenfible profecution of military duty muft occafion, will bar the way to their return."

From

From the QUEBEC GAZETTE.
Extract of a letter from New-York.

" The design of the Indians joining the rebels has greatly alarmed us. The Ohio and Western Indians, it is now no longer a doubt, have sent belts of friendship to the Congress, as have the Five Nations, the Shawanese, and Delawares."

Extract of a letter from Shippersburgh, in Pennsylvania, to a Gentleman in Baltimore, in Maryland, May 15.

" I received a letter last night from Mr. Jonas Bingham, at the Lower Shawanese town, advising me that the trade in the woods seems to be at an end. A body of Indians, of the Mingoe tribe, are certainly in arms, and on their march for Philadelphia. I am sorry to observe the savages seem determined to sacrifice themselves to the will of the Congress."

From the VIRGINIA GAZETTE.
To Messrs. DIXON *and* HUNTER.
Chatham (N. Jersey) Feb. 15, 1777.
" Gentlemen,

" General Stephen's brigade has engaged the enemy's strong foraging parties three several times lately, and, with sustaining but little loss, did them very considerable damage. On the first inst. they treated some of our wounded, who had the misfortune to fall into their hands, with the most savage barbarity: in consequence of that, the General wrote a letter to Sir William Erskine, a copy of which, and Sir William's answer, have done myself the pleasure to enclose you. We lost that day two gallant officers, Adjutant Kelly, of the 5th Virginia regiment, and Lieutenant Gregory of the 6th. Our hickory hearts, as usual, behaved like heroes ; ninety of them, under the command of the brave Colonel Scott, beat, at fair cutting, 230 of their best troops.

I am, very respectfully,
Your obedient servant,
ROBERT FORSYTH,
B. Major to Gen. Stephen."

Copy of a letter sent to Sir WILLIAM ERSKINE, complaining of the cruelty of the British troops.

" Sir,
" It is told us, that Sir William Erskine commanded the British troops covering the foraging party at Drake's Farm, on Saturday the 1st instant.

" Is it possible that a gentleman, an officer so eminently distinguished for his bravery and experience ! should allow the troops under his command to murder the wounded after the manner of savages ! until this time, it was universally allowed, that humanity was a certain concomitant of valour. It now appears, that Britains, unhappily divested of many excellent qualities peculiar to their ancestors, are become strangers to humanity, and deaf to the entreaties of the brave, after the misfortune of having fallen into their power. Mr. Kelly, a brave officer in my brigade, and five other Virginians, slightly wounded in the muscular parts, were murdered, and their bodies mangled, and their brains beat out, by the troops of his Britannic Majesty, on Saturday the first instant.

" The cruelties exercised on the worthy General Mercer, near to Princetown, on the 3d of January, were equally barbarous. It gives pain to a generous mind, Sir William, to see you tarnish the laurels so honourably obtained last war, by permitting such savage barbarity in the troops under your command. Such conduct, Sir, will inspire the Americans with a hatred to Britons, so inveterate and insurmountable, that they never will form an alliance, or the least connection with them.

" I can assure you, Sir, that the savages after General Braddock's defeat, notwithstanding the great influence of the French over them, could not be prevailed on to butcher the wounded in the manner your troops have done, until they were first made drunk. I do not know,
Sir

Sir William, that your troops gave you that trouble. So far does British cruelty, now a days, surpass that of the savages.

"In spite of all the British agents sent amongst the different nations, we have beat the Indians into good humour, and they offer their service. It is their custom, in war, to scalp, take out the hearts, and mangle the bodies of their enemies. This is shocking to the humanity natural to the white inhabitants of America. However, if the British officers do not restrain their soldiers from glutting their cruelties with the wanton destruction of the wounded, the United States, contrary to their natural disposition, will be compelled to employ a body of ferocious savages, who can, with an unrelenting heart, eat the flesh, and drink the blood of their enemies. I well remember, that in the year 1763, Lieutenant Gordon, of the Royal Americans, and eight more of the the British soldiers, were roasted alive, and eaten up by the fierce savages that now offer their services.

"The Americans have hitherto treated the wounded and prisoners of the British troops with that civility and tenderness natural to a brave and generous people; but should the inhuman cruelty of your men compel the American army to retaliate, let it be remembered, that the British officers stand answerable to the world, and to posterity, for the many dreadful consequences.

I am, Sir, with due respect,

Your most humble servant,

ADAM STEPHEN,
B. G. United States."

The ANSWER.

Brunswick, Feb. 10, 1777.

"Sir,

"I received your letter of the 4th instant, and am extremely obliged to you for the good opinion you seem to have had of my past character, but as much hurt at the unmerited charge you lay against me at present.

"It is unnecessary for me to answer minutely every paragraph of your letter, which is wrote in a style and language I have not been accustomed to. I only beg leave to inform you, that I never countenanced an act of barbarity in my life time, nor can I think any gentleman in the British service equal to it. We, on the contrary, wish to treat prisoners with lenity, and to take all possible care of the wounded that fall into our hands, as humanity will always meet with the approbation of every officer in the army.

"However, I may mention, that it is not to be wondered at if our soldiers are a little exasperated, considering the many cruelties that have been of late committed on them and their * officers, *even unarmed,* passing single from quarter to quarter.

I am, Sir, with respect,

Your most obedient humble servant,

WILLIAM ERSKINE,
Brigadier and Q. M. G.

Copy of a letter from Lord CORNWALLIS to General WASHINGTON, dated Brunswick, April 3, 1777.

"Sir,

"I inclose you a letter which Lieutenant Colonel Walcott delivered yesterday to Lieutenant Col. Harrison, and which Lieutenant Col.

---

* Several officers in the rear of an escort were surprized by a party of the militia, and surrendered to them, but soon after clapped spurs to their horses and fled; upon which the militia fired immediately, and killed three of them, amongst whom was Major Philips.—This is the cruelty alluded to in Sir William's letter.

Harrison,

Harrison did not then think proper to receive.

I am, Sir, with due refpect,
Your moft obedient humble fervant,
CORNWALLIS."
General Wafhington, &c. &c. &c.

(C O P Y.)

Demand, &c. by Lieutenant Colonel WALCOTT, April 2, 1777, of Return of Prifoners.

" Whereas General Wafhington did, in his letter to General Howe, bearing date the 30th day of June, 1776, declare that he was authorifed to propofe, and he did in faid letter accordingly propofe, a general exchange of all prifoners of war, in the manner and upon the terms following, viz. " officers for officers of equal rank, foldier for foldier, and citizen for citizen." To which propofal his Excellency General Sir William Howe did, in his anfwer of the firft of Auguft following, accede and agree. And whereas, in purfuance of this agreement, General Sir William Howe, relying upon the honour and good faith of Gen. Wafhington, for the due and punctual performance thereof on his part, hath, at feveral times, fent and delivered over to Gen. Wafhington, as will fully appear from the lifts with them tranfmitted, a number of officers on their parole, and upwards of two thoufand two hundred privates, of the enemy his prifoners; and who, as well officers as privates, are ftill to be confidered as fuch until they fhall be regularly exchanged, officers for officers of equal rank, and the privates by a like number of thofe now in the poffeffion of General Wafhington; fome of whom, having been taken before, or about the time of concluding the agreement, have, in direct violation thereof, been detained as prifoners for full eight months, and others, taken in the latter end of December and in the beginning of January laft, have been in the like condition of prifoners for three months; none, or very few of whom, have hitherto been fent in, in return or exchange of the number of prifoners fent by Gen. Howe to Gen. Wafhington. I, Lieut. Col. William Walcott, vefted with full powers for this among other purpofes, do therefore in the moft pofitive and peremptory manner, require and demand of General Wafhington, the full and due performance of the agreement above recited; and confequently the fpeedy and immediate releafe of all prifoners of war, whether Britifh, Heffians, Waldeckers, Provincials or Canadians, as well officers as foldiers, now in his poffeffion, or fo far as they fhall go or may go towards the exchange of thofe fent and delivered over to Gen. Wafhington. And whereas there are ftill in the poffeffion of Gen. Sir William Howe'a very confiderable number of officers, and a number of privates of the enemy, prifoners unexchanged; I do farther require and demand of Gen. Wafhington, that fo foon as he fhall have completed the exchange of thofe already delivered over to him, agreeable to my requifition and demand for that purpofe, he fhall proceed to the exchange of thefe laft mentioned officers and privates, in conformity to the agreement of the 30th of July and 1ft of Auguft, 1776; to the execution of which the groundlefs and unprecedented objections offered on the part of Gen. Wafhington, by Lieut. Col. Harrifon, cannot with any degree of reafon, or confiftently with common fenfe, be allowed or admitted as obftacles. The one, that " the whole of the prifoners contained in the Commiffary's lifts, and delivered over to General Wafhington, fhould not be accounted for, becaufe many of them died on their return to the place of their arrival." Pofterior therefore confeffedly, from the objection itfelf as ftated, to their

being

being delivered over to Gen. Washington, all of whom therefore muit be, and all of whom, this objection notwithstanding, I do again require and demand to be exchanged, according to the express terms of the agreement, " soldier for soldier," for every man delivered to the person who received them for and in the behalf of Gen. Washington: The other. " The case of Lieut. Col. Lee," whose release Gen. Washington might with greater propriety demand, whenever, within the terms of the said agreement, " officers for officers of equal rank," he shall have in his possession an officer of rank equal to the reputed rank of the gentleman in question; but until that appear, the demand and objection upon this subject are at least premature. I do moreover expect and demand, that an immediate and categorical answer shall be given to these just and reasonable requisitions and demands. Given at the house of the Rev. Mr. Beech, in the township of Hillsborough, the second day of April, one thousand seven hundred seventy and seven.

W. WALCOTT, Lieut. Col.
To General Washington, &c. &c.

(C O P Y.)
General WASHINGTON's Answer to the foregoing letter.

Morristown, April 9, 1777.
" Sir,

" I take the liberty of transmitting you a copy of a paper addressed to me by Lieut. Col. Walcott of your army, which came inclosed in a letter from Lieut. Gen. Lord Cornwallis. It is with peculiar regret I am constrained to observe, that this illiberal performance of Col. Walcott is obviously calculated to answer a less generous purpose than that of merely effecting an exchange, contains a gross misrepresentation of facts, and is a palpable deviation from that delicate line, which I expected would mark his conduct as a man of candour and ingenuity.

" That gentleman has censured two articles infifted on by me through Lieut. Col. Harrison, at their meeting on the 10th ult, as groundless, unprecedented, and inconsistent with any degree of reason or common sense, though founded, as I conceive, in the clearest principles of equity and justice—Not contenting himself with this, which would have given me no concern, he has assumed the privilege of mutilating and mistating these articles, in such a manner as to change their meaning, and to adopt them to the unfair conclusions he wished to establish.

Having premised these things, and being charged in direct and positive terms by Col. Walcott, who acted under your authority, with a violation of the agreement made between us for the exchange of prisoners, and called upon for a performance of the same, I think it necessary to explain the motives of my conduct, and the grounds on which those articles or objections stand.

By respect to the first, I freely repeat, that I do not hold myself bound either by the spirit of the agreement, or by the principles of justice, to account for those prisoners, who, from the rigour and severity of their treatment, were in so emaciated and languishing state at the time they came out, as to render their death almost certain and inevitable, and which, in many instances, happened while they were returning to their homes, and in many others after their arrival. You must be sensible that our engagement, as well as all others of the kind, though in letter it expresses only an equality of rank and number, as the rule of exchange, yet it necessarily implies a regard to the general principles of mutual compensation and advantage. This is inherent in its nature, is the voice of reason, and no stipulation, as to the condition in
which

which prifoners fhould be returned, was requifite. Humanity dictated, that their treatment fhould be fuch as their health and comfort demanded; and where her laws have been duly refpected, their condition has been generally good.—Nor is this the language of humanity alone—juftice declares the fame. The object of every cartel, or fimilar agreement, is the benefit of the prifoners themfelves, and that of the contending powers —— on this footing, it equally exacts, that they fhould be well treated, as that they fhould be exchanged: the reverfe is therefore an evident infraction, and ought to fubject the party, on whom it is chargeable, to all the damage and ill confequences refulting from it. Nor can it be expected, that thofe unfitted for future fervice by acts of feverity, in direct violation of a compact, are proper fubjects for an exchange. In fuch a cafe, to return others not in the fame predicament, would be to give without receiving an equivalent, and would afford the greateft encouragement to cruelty and inhumanity. The argument drawn from the mere circumftance of the prifoners having been received, is of no validity. Though from their wretched fituation, they could not at that time be deemed proper for an exchange, our humanity required that they fhould be permitted to return amongft us. It may perhaps be fairly doubted, whether an apprehenfion of their death, or that of a great part of them, did not contribute fomewhat to their being fent out when they were. Such an event, whilft they remained with you, would have been truly interefting, becaufe it would have *deftroyed* every fhadow of claim for the return of the prifoners in your hands, and therefore policy, concurring with humanity, dictated that the meafure fhould be adopted. Happy had it been, if the expedient had been thought of before thefe ill-fated men were reduced to fuch extremity.

It is confeffed, however, on all fides, that after their delivery they ftill continued your prifoners, and would be fo, till regularly exchanged. I acknowledge that I fhould be, and I have been, always willing, notwithftanding this confeffion, to account for every man who was in a proper condition, and fit to be exchanged at the time they came out, fo far as the proportion of prifoners with us would extend. With what propriety, or upon what foundation of juftice, can more be demanded? This has been propofed, or what is the fame, was moft clearly implied in the firft article, or objection, made by Lieut. Col. Harrifon, and illiberally rejected fince, inconfiftent with any degree of reafon or common fenfe. Painful as it is, I am compelled to confider it as a fact not to be queftioned, that the ufage of our prifoners whilft in your poffeffion, the privates at leaft, was fuch as could not be juftified. This was proclaimed by the concurrent teftimony of all who came out, their appearance fanctified the affertion,—and melancholy experience, in the fpeedy death of a large part of them, ftamped it with infallible certainty.

In refpect to the fecond article infifted on,—your difcriminating Major Gen. Lee from other captive officers belonging to the American army, demanded my particular attention. I was authorifed to conclude from your laying him under particular reftraints, and from your letter of the 23d of January laft, that you confidered him in a fingular point of view, and meant to exclude him from the common right of exchange, ftipulated for all officers in general terms. This diftinction, the more injurious and unwarrantable as you never excepted him, though you knew him to be an officer in our army at the time, and long before, the agreement was entered into, made it my duty to affert his right in an explicit manner, and to endeavour to put the matter on fo

E e

unequivocal

unequivocal a footing as to enfure his enlargement whenever an officer of equal rank, belonging to your army, fhould be in our power. This was attempted by the article, and nothing more—nor is any other inference to be drawn from it. It is true a propofition was made fince his captivity, to give a certain number of officers of inferior rank in exchange for him, but it was not claimed as a matter of right. What name then does that proceeding merit, by which it is fuggefted that the immediate releafe of Gen. Lee had been demanded, without having an officer of equal rank to give for him ? The fuggeftion cannot be fupported by the moft tortured expofition, nor will it have credit where candour is deemed a virtue, and words preferve their form and meaning.

As to the charge of delay in not returning the prifoners in our hands—the difperfed fituation of thofe taken at a more early period of the war, through the different States, arifing from the circumftances of their captivity, and a regard to their better accommodation, made their detention for a confiderable time unavoidable. When the agreement fubfifting between us took place, the fpeedieft directions were given to have them collected, that an exchange might be effected. This was done in part, and at a juncture when motives of policy oppofed the meafure, but were made to yield to rigid maxims of good faith. We were purfuing the exchange, and continued our exertions to accomplifh it, till the miferable appearance indicating an approaching cataftrophe, of thofe fent out by you, made it improper. For feeing that a difficulty might arife, and that it might be expected that I fhould account for the whole of them, which I by no means thought equitable, it became neceffary that the matter fhould be adjufted, and the due proportion fettled, for which I ought to be refponfible, before any

thing farther could be done on my part. Upon this ground ftands alfo the detention of thofe who have been fince captured.

Added to thefe confiderations—the difcrimination fet up in the inftance of General Lee, is to be regarded as utterly irreconcileable to the tenor of our agreement, and an infurmountable obftacle to a compliance with your demands.

Thus, Sir, have I explained the motives of my conduct, and, I truft, vindicated myfelf in the eye of impartiality, from the improper and groundlefs charge which you, and the gentleman acting by your authority, have been pleafed to alledge againft me—If in doing this I have departed in the fmalleft degree from that delicacy, which I always wifhed fhould form a part of my character, you will remember I have been forced into recrimination, and that it has become an act of neceffary juftice.

I fhall now declare it to be my ardent wifh, that a general exchange may take place on generous and liberal principles, as far as it can be effected, and that the agreement fubfifting between us for that purpofe fhould be inviolably obferved, and I call upon you, by every obligation of good faith, to remove all impediments on your part to the accomplifhment of it. If, however, you do not, I confole myfelf with a hope that thofe unfortunate men, whofe lot it is to be your prifoners, will bear their fufferings with becoming fortitude and magnanimity.

I am, Sir, with due refpect,
Your moft obedient
Humble fervant,
G. WASHINGTON.

His Excellency General Sir WILLIAM HOWE.

Publifhed by order of CONGRESS,
CHARLES THOMPSON, *Secretary.*
General

General Howe to General Washington.

New-York, 21st April, 1777.

Sir,

I have received your letter of the ninth inst. concerning the requisition of Lieutenant Colonel Walcott, a copy of which came inclosed.

Though I observe that officer has meant to insist very strongly on the justice of the claim for the return of prisoners in your possession, which was one of the objects of his appointment, I do not see reason to suspect that any personal incivility was intended by the terms in which his opinion is expressed.

Without entering into a needless discussion of the candour or illiberality on the sentiments on which your arguments are founded, yet since you are pleased to assert, that — " the usage of your prisoners was such as could not be justified, — that this was proclaimed by the concurrent testimony of all who came out, — that their appearance sanctified the assertion, and that melancholy experience, in the speedy death of a large part of them, stamped it with infallible certainty," these, I say, being what you are pleased to assume as facts, I cannot omit making some observations upon them.

It might, perhaps, suit with the policy of those who persist in every expedient to cherish the popular delusion, that the released prisoners should complain of ill usage, or their captivity might really form a grievous comparison with the state they were in before they were persuaded to encounter the vicissitudes of war. But if their sufferings were as great as you think yourself authorised to assert, a dispassionate consideration of the following indisputable and notorious facts will point out the cause to which they are to be, in a great measure, ascribed:

All the prisoners were confined in the most airy buildings, and on board the largest transports in the fleet, which were the very healthiest places of reception that could possibly be provided for them.

They were supplied with the same provisions, both in quantity and quality, as were allowed to the King's troops not on service, some accidental instances excepted, wherein however the omission, when known, was immediately remedied.

Near one half of the whole number of prisoners, whose diseases appeared to require peculiar care, as well as separation from the rest, were at different times received into the British hospitals, and their own surgeons, without restriction, supplied with medicines for the remaining sick, until it was discovered that they disputed not to dispose of large quantities by private sale.

From this short state of facts, it is evident that your prisoners were provided with proper habitations, sufficient and wholesome food, and medicines. Nor do I know of any comfort or assistance compatible with their situation as prisoners, of which they were in want, excepting cloathing; the relief to their distress in this, and the article of money, of which you were repeatedly advised, and they had claim to receive from your care, was neglected or refused, while they were furnished with every necessary I was in a situation to supply.

To what cause a speedy death of a large part of them is to be attributed, I cannot determine, but your own experience will suggest to you, whether the army under your command, in the course of last campaign, was free from such calamitous mortality, though assisted with refreshments from all parts of the surrounding provinces.

It is insinuated, that I might have released the prisoners before any of the ill consequences had taken place. I am obliged to say, the event at least appears to have proved the caution with which I ought to have adopted that expedient. The

E e 2

prisoners

prisoners were ready to be delivered up, waiting only for your proceeding in the exchange, which you had proposed, and I agreed to.

I admit that able men are not to be required by the party who, contrary to the laws of humanity, through design, or even neglect of reasonable and practicable care, should have caused the debility of the prisoners he shall have to offer for exchange ; but the argument is not applicable to me in the present instance.

I might finally put this question: How is the cause of debility in prisoners to be ascertained ? But as we differ so much in the principle upon which your objections are framed ; as I think those objections are unsupported by precedent or equity, and that your adherence to them would be a direct and determined violation of the agreement, it becomes unnecessary for me to add more, than to call upon you to fulfil your agreement for returning the prisoners demanded by Lieut. Col. Walcott.

With respect to the care of Mr. Lee, now professed to be a principal motive for your refusal to continue the exchange of prisoners, it is comprehended, I must insist, under my general and original exception to persons in his circumstances.

With due respect,
I am, Sir,
Your most obedient servant,
W. HOWE.
To General George Washington, &c.

General Howe to General Washington.
New-York, May 22, 1777.
Sir,

Not having received an answer to my letter of the 21st of April, I am to request your final decision, upon the demand I then made of the prisoners in your possession, both officers and soldiers, in exchange for those I have returned, and for your determination respecting the prisoners

now here, that I may make my arrangements accordingly

It is with concern, I receive frequent accounts of the ill treatment of Lieut. Col. Campbell, which I had reason to flatter myself you would have prevented. He has, it is true, been taken out of a common dungeon, where he had been confined with a degree of rigour, that the most atrocious crimes would not have justified ; but he is still kept in the jailor's house, exposed to daily insults from the deluded populace. This usage being repugnant to every sentiment of humanity, and highly unworthy of the character you profess, I am compelled to repeat my complaint against it, and to claim immediate redress to this much injured gentleman.

With due respect,
I am, Sir,
Your most obedient humble servant,
W. HOWE.
General Washington, &c &c.

General Howe to General Washington.
New-York, June 5, 1777.
Sir,

So many days have elapsed since my letter to you of the 22d of May was dispatched, without an answer, and lest, by any accident, it should not have gotten to your hands, I am induced to send you a duplicate thereof, and to press my request for your final decision, upon the demands therein contained.

With due respect,
I am, Sir,
Your most obedient servant,
W. HOWE.
General Washington, &c. &c.

Philadelphia, March 18.
Extract of a letter from an Officer in New-Jersey.

" The officer who commanded the two thousand British troops, going as a reinforcement from Amboy to Brunswick, we hear, is under an arrest great for undertaking, like Don Quixote, to do impossibilities. He, instead of marching directly to Brunswick, which he might have done, must needs go fourteen miles out of the direct road to take prisoners General Maxwell and his party at Sparktown, and to make his triumphant entry into Brunswick, leading his captives in chains like an old Roman General, in which he found his fatal mistake, when too late to remedy it, for he found that he had surrounded a nest of American hornets, who soon put his whole body to flight, pursued them to Amboy, and obliged them to get on board their ships again, since which they have never ventured a second time to reinforce their cooped up brethren in Brunswick."

Philadelphia, March 18. On Tuesday the 5th instant five hundred men attacked the Hessian picquet guard near Brunswick, drove them in, took eleven milch cows, two horses, and brought off fifteen or twenty loads of hay, which those mercenaries had stacked up within their lines. After the Hessians ran, a number of the light horse came out, drew their swords, and cut a few capers, but did not choose to disturb our men, whom they saw very leisurely take away the hay.

Extract of a letter from Morris-Town, March 10.

" General Maxwell attacked the enemy on Saturday last, near Quibble, or Squabble-Town, as they were penetrating into the country for provender, most kinds of which are much wanted among them. We had three men slightly wounded, none killed or taken. The enemy left four dead on the field, and carried off numbers, as usual, which, by accounts from the prisoners, were twenty, and numbers wounded. Their rear was so closely pursued, that they left one waggon behind; the three prisoners taken are just arrived, and say, the 42d, or

Highland Watch, suffered greatly in the action.

" Yesterday Major Butler, whose station is near this town, had a brush with the enemy, drove in their picquet guard, took four slain off the field, and seven horses. The express waits, or would be more particular."

Extract of a letter from a Gentleman at the Camp at Morris-Town, May 16, 1777.

" Our army has been so small, and the posts we have to defend are so many, that we could not carry on those offensive operations against the enemy which every good man wishes for; but our army now increases fast, and I trust, by the blessing of Heaven, we shall give the *Tyrant Murderers* a knock before very long. Our troops have frequent skirmishes with them, and generally drive them. Last week a party from General Maxwell's division attacked the enemy, and killed a Scotch Major and 40 or 50 Highlanders; also a party from General Lincoln's division attacked them and killed a number. The enemy keep very close in their lines. A number of Tory traitors have been hanged in these States southward of New-England."

Extracts from the several American Papers.

Fish-Kill, May 22.

Extract of a letter from Morris-Town, May 18, 1777.

" Last week we had a smart engagement with the enemy, near Piscataway, we drove them in, and killed some, when immediately they were reinforced, and advanced a second time, but were again repulsed. In the two actions, we killed, wounded and took prisoners, *one hundred*; our loss was about twenty-five. Three deserters came over to us the next day, and all say the above account is what they left."

Hartford, April 21. The Hon. the

the Continental Congress, have promoted Col. ——— Learned, of the Maſſachuſett's Bay, Col. George Clinton, of New-York, Col. Edward Hand of Pennſylvania, and Col. Scott of Virginia, to the rank of Brigadiers General.

Providence, April 19. On Wedneſday laſt Col. Jackſon's Independent Company, belonging to Boſton, arrived here from thence. They were dreſſed in neat uniforms, and made a very martial appearance.

A gentleman from the Weſtward informs, that the enemy at New-York continue to treat the American priſoners with great barbarity. Their allowance to each man for three days is 1lb of beef, 3 worm-eaten muſty biſcuits, and a quart of ſalt water; the meat they are obliged to eat raw, as they have not the ſmalleſt allowance of fuel. Owing to this more than ſavage cruelty, the priſoners die faſt, and in the ſmall ſpace of three weeks (during the winter) no leſs than 700 brave men periſhed.—Nothing ſhort of RETALIATION will compel theſe Britiſh barbarians to reſpect the law of nations.

New-Haven, May 7. Friday laſt died at Danbury, of the wound he received on the 26th ult. that brave and experienced ſoldier, the Hon. Major General DAVID WOOSTER, of this town.

Laſt Monday, Daniel Griſwould, a traitor and ſpy, was executed in purſuance of the ſentence of a general court martial.

Charles-Town (S. C.) April 9. We have the pleaſure to inform our readers, that the levies for the Continental army, which no longer conſiſts of militia, occaſionally called out, and diſmiſſed at certain ſhort periods, but of men who engage to ſerve to the end of the preſent conteſt, have been made with amazing rapidity; that it is now amply provided (which was far from being the caſe laſt year) with cloathing, good arms and ammuni-

tion, Eight braſs field-pieces, and almoſt every other requiſite: and that, the ſoldiery have ſuch confidence in, and ſo great an affection for General Waſhington, that it is the common opinion, " He was born for the ſalvation of America," ſo that, it is not unlikely, the preſent year's campaign may be opened in May, and that the ſtrength and courage of both parties fairly tried before the enſuing winter.

Philadelphia, April 16. The Honourable the Congreſs have ordered a monument to be erected in Boſton, in honour of Major General WARREN; and another in Virginia, in honour of Brigadier General MERCER, as a teſtimony of their illuſtrious virtues, and of the gratitude of their country. They have likewiſe ordered the eldeſt ſon of the former of thoſe gentleman, and the youngeſt ſon of the latter, to be educated at the expence of the United States.

Hartford, May 12.
Extract of a letter from Fiſh-Kill, dated May 8, 1777.

" By the Albany poſt I am informed as follows : " Seven ſtores of the enemy are conſumed by fire at St. John's, in which were the rigging of their veſſels.—News very favourable from the Northward, but cannot now be made public."

The notorious Richard Steel, alias Williams, who is univerſally known in this State, and who broke out of Newgate about three years ſince, has lately made his appearance at the Eaſtward, cloathed with a commiſſion from General Howe. He was laſt week taken up and committed to the gaol at Boſton. He was three times tried for his life for burglary in this Colony.——Is this the alternative, Oh, Howe! to be reduced to the neceſſity of recruiting your abandoned army by ſuch gallows marked inſtruments as the above.

Monday, 20th ult. two ſoldiers were ſhot at Peek's-Kill for deſertion. Laſt evening, 15 of the enemy's
ſhips

ships passed to this place, standing to the Eastward.

New-London, May 9. A privateer from a neighbouring port has, in the course of a few days, taken two sloops and one schooner, said to be of considerable value. A letter, wrote in New-York (said to be by an officer) was found on board the schooner, directed to a person at Newport, which says they lost 100 men in the Danbury affair. The same letter adds, that the Hessians are a set of d——d poltroons, and that he (the writer) had much rather have dealings with the rebels than with them.

About 100 of the enemy's horses, and a number of waggons, were left by them on the shore, when they embarked after their expedition to Danbury.

Boston, April 28. Sunday last arrived a French ship of 20 guns from Bourdeaux, laden with dry goods, hard-ware, wine, &c. &c. Also a State sloop from Martinico, with powder, arms, salt, &c.

Our last advices from Philadelphia, and from the best authority assure us, that agreeable prospects of trade are opening with foreign powers; and a vessel lately arrived from Sweden with powder, flints, lead, sulphur, &c. &c. and that the States were now able to negotiate loans abroad—that Britain cannot procure any great reinforcement for her army here, without involving herself in a French and Spanish war, and that her credit in Holland is very low—That we have now arms and military stores in abundance; Quarter-masters, and Commissaries stores in plenty; a considerable quantity of blankets, and cloathing; and what is a capital article indeed, tents of the best quality, sufficient to cover thirty thousand men.

Extract of a letter from Morris-Town, April 26.

" On Tuesday the 22d inst. at night, a party of our men, under the command of Capt. Combe, went within the enemy's lines, and took two centinels, from whom he extorted the countersign. He then went to attack the picquet guard, but one of his men deserting, the enemy were informed of his intention, and, having prepared themselves, gave our people a very warm reception. But Combe, who is not to be surprised by trifles, advanced upon them with such spirit, that he drove them into the guard-house, from whence they fired through the door and windows. However, Combe ordered his men before the door, which they instantly obeyed, and rushed upon the enemy with charged bayonets, who received us in the same manner, but were soon obliged to call for quarter, upon which they were all taken prisoners. The picquet guard consisted of two subalterns and thirty men; both the officers and 14 men were killed, and 16 were brought in prisoners. In the attack, Combe was wounded in the foot, and both his subalterns in the body, but are like to do well. It is very remarkable he had not a man in the whole action killed and only three wounded, none of them mortal."

Extract of a letter from a Gentleman in Connecticut, dated May 24, 1777.

" A ship is arrived at Chesapeak Bay, with 10,000 stand of arms, and a large quantity of cloathing made up. From the enemy's motions, they more probably intend to the Southward, than up the river. At Albany are three or four hundred Indians of the Six Nations, some from every tribe, even the Senecas, and some from Cagnawaga; all of them assure their friendly dispositions and intentions towards the United States.

" The fleet of 27 sail, principally large ships, from Newport, are passed up Sound yesterday and day before."

Major Andrew Brown is appointed Deputy Master-Master for the Eastern department of the army of the United States of America.

Tuesday last 17 ships, 7 schooners, and

and two floops, with a number of troops on board, left Rhode-Island, and went up the Sound, where it is faid by a deferter, they were to be joined by others from Long-Island, when, it was conjectured, they were going to make another attack upon fome part of Connecticut.

Hartford, May 26.

Extract of a letter from Brigadier General Parfons, to his honour Governor Trumbull, dated Newhaven, May 25, 1777.

" I fincerely congratulate your honour on the fuccefs of our arms on Long-Island. Colonel Meigs left Sachem's Head on Friday, at one o'clock in the afternoon, with a detachment of 160 men, officers included, and landed within three miles of Sagg Harbour, at about one the night following ; and having made the proper difpofitions for attacking the enemy in five different places, proceeded with the greateft order and filence till within twenty rods of the enemy, when they rufhed on with fixed bayonets upon the different barracks, guards, and quarters of the enemy ; whilft Captain Throop, with a party under his command, at the fame time took poffeffion of the wharfs and veffels lying there. The alarm foon became general, and an inceffant fire of grape and round fhot was kept up from an armed fchooner of 12 guns, which lay within 150 yards of the wharfs, for near an hour ; notwithftanding which, the party burnt all the veffels at the wharf, killed and captivated all the men belonging to them, deftroyed about 100 tons of hay, large quantities of grain, ten hogfheads of rum, and other Weft-India goods, and fecured all the foldiers who were there ftationed. The prifoners are about 90 in number, among which are, one Captain, two Commiffaries, Mr. Chew and Mr. Bell.

" I have the fatisfaction to be informed, that the officers and men,

without exception, behaved with the greateft order and bravery, and had not a man either killed or wounded on our fide."

Philadelphia, June 1.

Extract of a letter from his Excellency General Washington to Congrefs, dated Head-Quarters, Middle Brook Camp, 31ft May, 1777.

" —— I have the pleafure to communicate a very agreeable piece of intelligence, which I received from General Parfons, of the deftruction of twelve of the enemy's veffels in Sagg Harbour, upon the Eaft end of Long-Island. I give you this letter at length, which I think reflects high honour upon the conduct and bravery of Colonel Meigs, his officers and men."

New Haven, May 25, 1777.

" Dear General,

" Having received information that the enemy were collecting forage, horfes, &c. on the Eaft end of Long-Ifland, I ordered a detachment from the feveral regiments then at this place, confifting of 1 Major, 4 Captains, viz. Throop, Pond, Mansfield, and Savage, 9 fubalterns, and 220 non-commiffioned officers and privates, under the command of Lieut. Col. Meigs, to attack their different pofts on that part of the ifland, deftroy the forage, &c. which they had collected. Col. Meigs embarked his men here in 13 whaleboats the 21ft inftant, and proceeded to Guildford ; but the wind proving high, and the fea rough, could not pafs the Sound until Friday the 23d : he left Guildford at one o'clock in the afternoon of the 23d, with 170 of his detachment, under convoy of two armed floops, and in company with another unarmed (to bring off prifoners) acrofs the Sound to the North branch of the ifland near Southhold, where he arrived about fix o'clock in the evening. The enemy's troops on this branch of the ifland had marched from New-York two days before ;

but

but about 60 of the enemy remaining at a place called Sagg Harbour, near 15 miles distant on the South branch of the island, he ordered the whaleboats, with as many men as could be transported, across the bay, over land to the bay, where they re-embarked to the number of 130, and at about 12 o'clock arrived safe across the bay, within about four miles of the harbour; where having secured the boats in the wood, under the care of a a guard, Col. Meigs formed his little remaining detachment in proper order for attacking the different posts and quarters of the enemy, and securing the vessels and forage at the same time. They marched in the greatest order and silence, and at two o'clock arrived at the harbour. The several divisions, with fixed bayonets, attacked the guards and post assigned them; whilst Capt. Throop, with the detachment under his command, secured the vessels and forage lying at the wharf. The alarm soon became general, when an armed schooner of 12 guns and 70 men, lying 150 yards off the wharf, began a fire upon our troops (which continued without cessation for about three quarters of an hour) with grape and round shot; but the troops, with the greatest intrepidity, returned the fire upon the schooner, and set fire to the vessels and forage, and killed and captivated all the soldiers and sailors, except about six, who made their escape under cover of the night.

" Twelve brigs and sloops (one an armed vessel with 12 guns) about 120 tons of pressed hay, oats, corn, and other forage, 10 hogsheads of rum, and a large quantity of other merchandize, were entirely consumed. It gives me great satisfaction to hear the officers and soldiers, without exception, behaved with the greatest bravery, order, and intrepidity. Colonel Meigs having finished the business on which he was sent, returned safe with all his men to Guilford by two o'clock P. M. yesterday, with 90 prisoners, having in 25 hours, by land and water, transported his men full 90 miles, and succeeded in his attempt beyond my most sanguine expectations, without having a single man killed or wounded. It gives me singular pleasure to hear no disposition appeared in any one soldier to plunder the inhabitants, or violate private property, in the smallest degree; and that, even the cloathing, and other articles, belonging to the prisoners, the soldiers, with a generosity (not learned from British troops) have, with great chearfulness, restored to them where they have fallen into their hands.

" Major Humphry, who waits on your Excellency with the account, was in the action with Colonel Meigs, and will be able to give any further information. A list of the prisoners is inclosed. I am your Excellency's

Most obedient humble servant,

SAM. H. PARSONS."

His Excellency General Washington.

A list of prisoners taken at the East end of Long-Island, by Colonel Meigs.

1 Captain, —— Raymond.
2 Commissaries, Chew and Bell.
10 Masters of vessels.
3 Serjeants.
1 Corporal.
45 Privates.
27 Seamen.
1 Soldier sick, whose parole was taken.
—
90 Prisoners.
6 Killed.
—
96

Published by order of Congress,

CHARLES THOMSON, Sec.

June 2, 1777.

Philadelphia, June 4. We hear the enemy at Brunswick have been lately reinforced with three brigades from Rhode-Island and New-York.

On

On Wednesday last the Hon. Major General Schuyler left this city, to repair to his command in the Northern department. The President and several members of Congress accompanied him some miles out of town.

From New-York we are informed, that the Hessians continue very sickly and die fast.——That those persons who are friends to American Independence, are severely treated, especially by the renegado Americans (alias Tories)—That the Frenchmen, taken at sea, in French or American vessels, are treated with great cruelty; and that they now sell the cargoes of the French vessels heretofore taken.

We can with pleasure inform our readers, that General Washington has now received such supplies of men, &c. that he has moved his headquarters from Morris-Town to Middle-Brook, on the east side of the Rariton, within seven miles and a half of Brunswick, where his army (which is not composed of soldiers whose times are continually expiring, but of those inlisted for the war) are now encamped, and make a show that must please every person who is not a Tory.

From our posts, near Middle-Brook, we are able to see and watch the movements of the enemy, who are encamped on Brunswick hills, the West side of Rariton.

Williamsburgh, May 30, 1777.

Forty of the Cherokee nation are now here on a negociation of peace, which it is hoped will be lasting, and to request a boundary line may be drawn, to prevent encroachments on their lands. They have had an audience, and it is expected a compact will be settled with them in a few days. Among them are Oconostoto, the Little Carpenter, the Pigeon, and other headmen and warriors. After the talk was concluded, they favoured the public with a dance on the green in front of the palace, where a considerable number of spectators, both male and female, were agreeably entertained.

The capes are now blocked up by the Phœnix, Capt. Parker, the Senegal, the Raleigh armed brig of 12 guns, and a sloop of 10. They are so situated, that it is impossible for vessels bound in or out to escape them. Capt. Parker has determined not to send or receive any more flags.

Wednesday Thomas Davis (late Adjutant Davis) and six other Tories and traitors, mounted in a waggon, under a proper guard, making a very *decent* appearance, passed down the street on their way to the public gaol, from Alexandria, where they are to remain for trial.

Albany (Province of New-York) May 26, 1777.

About 300 Indians, of the different tribes of the Six Nations, are now in town holding a conference with the Commissioners. They have just opened the treaty; therefore we cannot give a particular detail of their business. But this, from what we can learn, is their determined resolution, *to maintain a strict neutrality — all we want.*

The week before last Captain Roosa and his Lieutenant, two noted Tories, lately taken in arms as they were marching towards the enemy, were hanged at Esopus (in this State) as a suitable reward for their treasonable practices.

They had deluded a number of other poor wretches (who were taken along with them, and are now in confinement) to go with them to New-York, assuring them, that when they had shewn themselves there, they would be suffered to return immediately to their farms; that in a fortnight General Howe and army would penetrate Ulster county, and reward their loyalty, by giving them possession of their Whig neighbours farms.

Williamsburg, May 30. Yesterday, by joint ballot of both Houses of Assembly, fembly, his Excellency Patrick Henry, Efq, was unanimoufly re-elected Governor of this Commonwealth, as was Edmund Ralph, Efq. to be Attorney-General.

The following Gentlemen were alfo chofen of the Hon. Council of this State, viz. John Page, Dudley Digges, John Blair, Bartholomew Danbridge, Thomas Walker, Nathaniel Harrifon, David Jamefon, and Thomas Nelfon, jun. Efquires.

Charles-Town, June 23. On Tuefday laft Capt Richard Wells, as Prize-Mafter, brought into fafe port, the Induftry, from Jamaica, taken on the 8th of May, by the privateer floop St. Louis, of Georgia, commanded by Captain Samuel Spencer.

Capt. Wells put into the Havanna on the 6th inftant, where he met *with a moft hofpitable reception,* and was readily fupplied with every thing he wanted. Captain Surton, in a letter of marque brig, belonging to Philadelphia, put into the fame port on the 7th, and Captain Spencer on the 8th, who both met with the like reception and treatment.

About three weeks fince, a French General Officer went from Cape François in a 36 gun f.igate, to claim reftitution, or remonftrate on the illegal capture of feveral French veffels—Admiral Gayton having ordered a former veffel fent on that errand to depart immediately on pain of being funk.

The French veffel, from which a number of officers were landed laft Monday, has fince arrived in a fafe port. She is arrived from Bourdeaux, and left it the 20th of March. On the 20th of that month, a veffel arrived there with difpatches from Congrefs, to the Hon. Dr. Franklin, and other Agents of the United States, refident in France.

On Wednefday laft, a number of ufeful brafs ordnance, with their appurtenances, a large quantity of gunpowder, &c. were received here.

There was a miftake in the account inferted in our laft, of officers landed from a French fnow, to enter into the Continental fervice : the Marquis de Montcalm is not among them ; but there are the Marquis de la Fayette, Baron de Kalb, and the Vifcount de Mauroiy, all Major Generals, an engineer, and eleven other officers of interior rank. [*Carolina Gazette.*

Providence, May 10. We learn that two floops were taken a few days fince in the Eaftern Sound, and carried into a fafe harbour in Connecticut. They were bound from New-York to Newport, laden with flour, dry goods, &c. A certain John Freebody, of the refpectable order of Newport Tories, was taken in one of the above floops ; alfo (which will be judged more valuable) a large fum of money, faid to be about 20,000 dollars.

Bofton, May 12. The laft accounts from New-York are, that the enemy appeared to be in motion, but their deftination a profound fecret. It is fuppofed Philadelphia and Bofton are at leaft on their guard, efpecially the latter, where it is apprehended the Tories now refiding will be taken proper care of.

Extract of a letter, dated Middleton,
May 3.

" Laft Monday I fet out for New-Haven with the militia, on the news of the enemy's going to Danbury to deftroy the ftores we had there. The following is a copy of the Quartermafter's return to Gen. Arnold, of what ftores were deftroyed, viz. 1700 barrels pork, 50 of beef, 7 hogfheads rum, 11 tierces claret, 3 quarter cafks Madeira wine, 12 to 1700 bufhels wheat, rye and corn, 12 coils rope, a fmall quantity coal, and fmiths tools, 10 waggons, 1600 tents, not good for much."

P. S. Since the letter was inclofed, I have received the following account ; 62 regulars taken up dead, which our people buried, 100 and upwards were

F f 2   killed,

killed, which we took up scattered about the road, three houses were burnt, in which were found a number of human bones, supposed to be regulars tossed in, that our people might not know what was killed. Between 30 and 40 of our people were killed, and 7 or 80 wounded. The enemy, consisting of about three or four thousand men, were attacked by 500 men only. Gen. Arnold's horse was shot under him. The General, after being dismounted, killed the soldier who shot his horse.

Boston, May 15. A Continental frigate is arrived at St. Pierre's, Martinico.

Twelve Tories are condemned to the gallows, by the convention of the State of New-York, several more are confined, and it is thought will have the same salutary medicine.

Boston, May 19. Last week arrived at a safe port, a prize ship, taken by a privateer commanded by Captain Wigglesworth. She was bound from London to the West-Indies, *has a cargo of dry goods, &c.* to a very large amount, one invoice amounts to 4600l. sterling.

A gentleman arrived in town yesterday from Albany, informs, that Gen. Gates's army at Ticonderoga consists of between five and 6000 troops, who are all in health and high spirits; that the Canadians were disaffected with the British troops, *and burnt most of their stores at St John's.*

Boston, May 22. We have the pleasure to inform our readers, that the Honourable Major General Gates sent a small party of his troops to disperse a large body of those troublesome vermin, called Tories, who had collected themselves in an advantageous part of the country, in Albany county, in order, as is imagined, to oppose a few of the free Sons of Columbia, who, as they foolishly thought, were obliged to pass that way, to a certain quarter, when a skirmish ensued, in which the abject wretches (the Tories)

had 6 killed, many wounded, and upwards of 50 taken prisoners.

Boston, May 27. On Thursday last very favourable accounts were received from the Creek Nation of Indians— a nation that has been long and assiduously tampered with, and stirred up, by British agents, to commit those barbarities upon us which the English nation formerly could not even bear to hear of without being struck with horror.

Providence, May 3. A few days ago a Serjeant, belonging to the British forces on Rhode-Island, deserted from thence, and arrived here. An Ensign of the 43d regiment, was taken prisoner at the same time.

On Tuesday last three soldiers belonging to the Continental army, viz. Robert Key, Peter Nagle, and Richard Querry, under sentence of death for attempting to desert to the enemy, were conducted from hence under guard, to Coventry, where, on Wednesday, the first mentioned person, was shot. He appeared to be truly sensible of the enormity of his crime, and hoped that the ignominious death he was about to suffer, would prevent others from deserting. Nagle and Querry were reprieved.

Philadelphia, May 3. By advices this day from East Jersies, we learn that the enemy are abandoning Brunswick, having sent some of their cannon and stores to Staten-Island; and that Cortland Skinner had sent all his furniture from Amboy to New-York. Sickness amongst the Hessian soldiers, and the excessive fatigue of the British, is said to be the occasion of this manœuvre; however that may be, we have another instance of Howe's declining a general engagement with Washington.

Extract of a letter from Gen. Washington, to Congress, dated May 5, 1777.

" By Major Throop, one of General Gates's Aids de Camp, and who left Albany on Tuesday last, I am informed,

formed, the accounts of Gen. Carleton's approach towards Ticonderoga were premature. He says General Gates received a letter before he came away from Brigadier Gen. Wayne, of the 24th ult. in which he mentioned nothing of it. That three thousand troops had arrived there all in high spirits and health, except nine ; and that that post could never be carried without the loss of much blood."

The Honourable the Congress have promoted Brigadier General Arnold, to the rank of Major General.

Philadelphia, May 14. Yesterday arrived the brig Sally, Capt. Stocker, in eleven weeks upon Nantz in France, with ten thousand stands of small arms, and a large number of gun locks.

Boston, April 3. General Sir William Howe (vain man!) on the 15th ult. issued another *infidious Proclamation* lengthening out *the day of grace to the rebellious Americans, &c.* for six weeks longer.

Brigadier General de Coudray, an engineer of reputation in the French army, and a Major General in the American army are arrived here from St. Domingo, in a ship laden with cloathing, arms, ammunition, &c. and immediately, in company with several other French officers (who were passengers in the same vessel) proceeded to General Washington's camp in New Jersey.

Boston, May 29. On the 5th of May, five large vessels arrived at Charles-Town, South-Carolina, *from France,* laden with all sorts of cloathing, arms, and ammunition.

The Randolph, an American frigate of 32 guns, and six large privateer brigantines, were the middle of May cruizing on the coast of Carolina for the protection of its trade. A very considerable and uninterrupted commerce had been carried on for many months from the several ports of South and North Carolina.

The Mercury, a large French ship dispatched from Nantz to New-England the beginning of February, safely landed her cargo, of arms, ammunition, and cloathing, at Portsmouth in New Hampshire. [*She left Portsmouth the* 5th *of June, and arrived at Nantz the beginning of July.*]

The Amphitrite, another large French ship, after a passage of 90 days, of which time she was a month beating about the coast of America, without seeing any of the enemy's cruizers, arrived the 20th of April at Portsmouth in New Hampshire. The Amphitrite affords a most encouraging and important supply of arms, &c. to the Americans. Her cargo consists of

60 pieces of brass artillery, **with** carriages, and every other necessary compleat.
10 tons of gunpowder.
10,000 muskets and bayonets.
Tents and camp equipage for 15,000 men.
And a very large quantity of blankets, lead, ball, &c.

Twenty-four experienced French officers of the *Train,* and Colonel Conway (from the French service) came passengers in the Amphitrite.

Boston, May 31. Last Tuesday se'ennight, 18 ships, 2 schooners and sloops, having on board, it is said, 2000 troops, left Rhode-Island, and stood up the Sound. Next day they were seen passing Montauk, standing to the Southward.

Last Sunday se'ennight, a large number of men of war and transports, with a number of flat-bottom boats, were seen off Huntingdon and Oyster-Bay. In the afternoon they went into Huntingdon, to anchor. On Tuesday following three boats left the above fleet, and stood off Westerly shore. From which movements, it is conjectured, they intend making another attack upon some part of Connecticut.

An intercepted letter from a Tory at New-York, to his wife in the Jersies, fies, fays, " You muft not expect to fee me this fummer, as the plan of going to Philadelphia is laid afide for this campaign."

The Congrefs have promoted Col. Jedidiah Huntingdon, and Col. Jofeph Reed to the rank of Brigadiers General in the Continental army.

Alfo Thomas Conway, Efq. Knight of the order of St. Louis and Colonel in the Irifh brigades, in the fervice of the King of France, is appointed to the fame rank.

A perfon was lately executed at Philadelphia, for attempting to feduce from their duty, three of the Chevaux de Frize Pilots. They got fifty half Johannes from him, before they lodged an information againft him. It is alledged, that he was employed in this bufinefs by Mr. Galloway, formerly Speaker of the Affembly of Pennfylvania.

Whitehall, *July* 12, 1777
Extract of a letter from General Sir William Howe to Lord George Germain, dated at New-York, the 3d of June, 1777.

YOUR Lordfhip's numbers 3, 4, and 5, of the 3d of March, and No. 6, of the 5th following, I had the honour to receive by Major Balfour on the arrival of his Majefty's fhip Augufta the 8th of May, the duplicates of which have fince arrived by the Sandwich packet. The earlieft opportunity was taken of fignifying his Majefty's moft gracious approbation of the behaviour of the officers, whofe names are particularized by your Lordfhip.

The arrival of the camp equipage on the 24th of May, both for the army and provincials, has relieved me from much anxiety, being articles greatly wanted for the opening of the campaign, which will now immediately take place in Jerfey, where the enemy's principal ftrength ftill remains; and I fhall proceed, as occurrences may arife, according to the plan made known to your Lordfhip in my former difpatches.

The remount horfes for the 16th and 17th dragoons are arrived in good order, with the lofs of ten horfes on the paffage. The officers of the guards and Britifh recruits alfo arrived on the 24th of May the Anfpach troops, 432 German recruits, and 51 German chaffeurs, on the 3d inftant, convoyed by the Somerfet. Thefe troops appear to be in very good health, and have difembarked upon Staten Ifland to refrefh for a fhort time.

I have the pleafure to inform your Lordfhip of the arrival of Major General Gray in the Somerfet.

Major Dixon, of the corps of engineers, who has his Majefty's leave to return to Britain, will have the honour of delivering my difpatches to your Lordfhip by the Halifax packet; and I prefume upon the acknowledged abilities of this gentleman, and his thorough knowledge of the fituation of the country, to juftify me in referring your Lordfhip to him, for the moft particular as well as general information.

Admiralty Office, *July* 10, 1777.
Extract of a letter from Vice Admiral Lord Vifcount Howe to Mr. Stephens, dated off New York, the 8th of June, 1777.

THE Nonfuch arrived here the 25th paft, and the Camel and Bute the 28th, with all the tranfports; three excepted, of the convoy that failed at the fame time from Portfmouth. They had continued under the conduct of Capt. Finch of the Camelion, fince the 6th of May, the Ifis and Swift having been feparated on the paffage. Two of the miffing tranfports came in a few days before, and the third a few days after Captain Finch. But the Ifis and Swift did not arrive till the 7th inftant.

On the 3d inftant Captain Ourry arrived in the Somerfet, with the tranfports transports he had in charge ; but the Mercury parted company the third day after they left the British coast. The troops by both these convoys are in good health.

Capt. Mason arrived here on the 7th instant in the Dispatch with the Springfield and two more transports, part of the convoy that sailed from England under the charge of Capt. Onslow. As the separation happened when they were not more than 150 leagues from this port, the arrival of the St. Albans, with the rest or the transports, may be daily expected.

As there was reason to believe it might be soon requisite to embark a considerable part of the army, timely preparation has been made for that purpose : and as my attendance would be necessary with the transports in consequence, I have recalled Commodore Hotham from the Delaware to direct the naval operations, and carry on the current service of the port.

Sir George Collier, who commands the detachment of the squadron at Halifax, will be attentive to afford all possible protection to the fisheries at Canso and Isle Madame.

The following is a list of vessels seized as prizes, and of re-captures made by the American squadron, between the 1st of January, 1777, and the 22d of May following, according to the returns received by the vice-admiral Lord Viscount Howe.

Prizes taken by the Daphne.

January 31. Moore, George Collis, master, from Boston ; in ballast. March 8. Mary, Joseph Hatch, master, from Boston ; in ballast. 9, Juno, George Eldridge, master, from St. Eustatia ; with salt. 12. Sally, deserted by the people, from Nantz ; with gunpowder, lead, &c. 14 Adventure, William Young, master, from St. Croix ; with rum, salt, bales, &c. 28. Cronelia and Molly, John

Lockhart, master, from Martinique ; with powder, molasses, and sailcloth. April 3. Nancy, Joseph Bennet, master, from St. Eustatia ; with rum, salt, and dry goods. Ditto. Ann, Charles Buikley, from Martinique. April 5. Bolton, William Stevens, master, from Philadelphia ; with tobacco, flour, bread, lumber, tar, and turpentine.

By the Emerald.

Feb. 12. Two Friends, Thomas Cartwright, master, from Boston ; in ballast. 14. Phenix, from St. Thomas ; with 38 guns and salt. Ditto. Betsey, Joseph Frith, master, from St. Croix, with salt and powder. 15. Hope, Ephraim Bartlett, master, from New England ; with rum, sugar and molasses. Feb. 19. Either, John Gordon, master, from Providence in Rhode Island ; with casks and sugar. March 3. Edward, Samuel Arnold, master, from Baltimore, with bread and flour. 5. Hannah, Lot Price, master, from New England ; in ballast. 8. Judith, Mark Burnam, master, from Virginia ; with flour 13. Delphin, Jonathan Clark, master, from Madeira ; with wine. 17. Charming Nancy, Peter Bathel, master, from Philadelphia ; with flour. 19. Two Sisters, Renic. Davis, master, from Cape Ann ; in ballast. 23. Mifflin, Henry Marshal, master, from Portsmouth, New England ; in ballast. Ditto General Mercer, William Lewis, master from Surinam ; with molasses. powder and sugar. April 3. Industry, John Jaques, master, from Martinique ; with salt, medicines, &c. 4. Friendship, John Gibbons, master, from Curacoa ; in ballast Ditto. Friendship, Nicholas Houtvat, master, from Virginia ; with bread, flour and tobacco. 15. Ann, Francis Robins, master, from Baltimore ; with tobacco, flour and staves. Ditto. Susannah, William Horn, master, from Virginia ; with tobacco and flour. 20. Revenge. Henry Lawslaw,

Lawglew, master, from Guadaloupe; with rum, brady, &c.

Recapture by the Brune.

Jan. 6. Duntreath, James Creighton, master, from St. Augustine; with lumber.

Prizes by the Brune.

Jan. 18. Lovely Moriam, Seth Ewill, master, from St. Eustatia; with salt, and bale goods. 20. Farmer, Benjamin Datheil, master, from Baltimore; with tobacco, staves, &c. 30. William, William Russel, master, from Newbury; with blubber and salt. Feb. 3. Le Jason,—Bayonne, master, from Martinique; with salt and merchandise. 4. Dispatch, Nathaniel Fair, master, from Boston; in ballast. 9. La Tempete, Jean Baptiste, master, from Cayenne; with wine, spirits, canvas, &c. April 14. Winyaw, Samuel Barlow, master, from Boston; in ballast. 15. Swiftsure, John Monro, master, from St. Thomas; with rum and dry goods. Ditto. Le Bien Heureux, Gasp. Giurlavi, master, from Martinique; with wine and dry goods. 21. York, from Cape Fear; with pitch and tar. 30. Gratitude, Frederick Lykmes, from Cape Fear; with turpentine. Ditto. Liberty, Abraham Jones, master, from Wilmington; in ballast. May 6. La Marie Françoise, Pascal Ferbon, master, from Cape François; with salt, brandy and rum

Recapture by the Phœnix.

Jan. 2. Ranger, James Renown, master, from St. Croix.

Prizes by Ditto.

Jan. 8. Fly James Wilson, master, from Martinique; with arms and ammunition. 12. Royal George, Jere. Burrows, master, from Bermuda; with salt. 27. Three Friends, Samuel Robins, master, from Boston; with 10 hogsheads of sugar. Ditto. Adventure, William Jones, master, from Hispaniola; with salt. Feb. 17. Molly, Uriah Atkins, master, from Boston; in ballast. 18. Alex-

andria, Barnabas Gardner, master, from Bedford; with 30 hogsheads of sugar. 27. Nancy, Isaac Taylor, master, from Senepuxen; with nine hogsheads of tobacco. March 2. Ninety-two, Jere. Rogers, master, from Hispaniola; with salt and dry goods. 8. Betsey, John Churchward, master, from North Carolina; with naval stores. 10. Wolf, Simon Elliott, master, from St. Thomas; with salt, guns and dry goods. April 13 Olive Branch, Aaron Andrews, master, from Boston; in ballast. 22. Esther, from Dartmouth; with sugar and rum. 23. Betsey, George Shockley, master, from Dartmouth; in ballast. 28. Billy and Mary, John Burrows, master, from Maryland; with tobacco. May 5. Hetty, Francis Saltus, master, from Charles Town; with salt, rice, &c. Ditto. Two Schooners chaced on shore about five miles to the southward of Cape Henry. 9. Les Graces, Jean B. Dussaut, master, from Port au Prince; with salt, spirits and molasses. 19. Unknown, deserted by the people; with rum and salt. 26. A privateer of ten guns, chaced on shore to the southward of Cape Henry.

B. the Preston.

Jan. 20. Batchelor, William Scon, master, from St. Eustatia; with rum, salt and dry goods. 24. Good Intent, John Finlayson, master, from Cape François; with rum, salt and dry goods. 27. Runfast, Nem. Semes, master, from Marblehead; with salt, rum and sugar. Ditto. Content, Samuel Gale, master, from Marblehead; with salt, rum and sugar. 31. Molly, — Humphrey, master, from Elk river; in ballast. Feb. 5. Supposed to be the Ranger, John Sandford, master, from Cape François; with molasses, rum and salt. March 15. La Rose, Augustin Coulter, master, from Philadelphia; with flour. 17. Hanover, Uriah Gardner, master, from Nantucket; with molasses and sugar. 29. Polly

29. Polly, William Gallop, mafter, from Philadelphia; with flour.

By the Roebuck.

Jan. 1. Friendfhip, Daniel Rhods, from Cape Nicholas; with molaffes and fugar. 10. Peggy, Alexander Thompfon, from Savannah; with rice, indigo and hides. 11. Adventure, Lawrence Sandford, mafter, from Cape Nicholas; with powder and fail cloth. 13. Rofe, Jofeph Coftin, mafter, from Hifpaniola; with molaffes and wine. April 2. Defence, Thomas Pickering, mafter, from Charles-town, South Carolina; armed for war. 20. Turtle, Nathaniel Robinfon, mafter, from Eaft Creek; with fence rails.

Prize by the Pearl.

Jan. 3. A veffel from Cape François; with molaffes and coffee.

Recapture by Ditto.

Jan. 6. Little John, from Miffifippi; with lumber and ftaves.

Prizes by the Pearl.

March 19. Speedwell, John Brynen, mafter, from Charles-town; with rice, &c. 24. Anna-Maria, Francis Royland, mafter, from Georgia; with rice and indigo. April 6. Willing Maid, Roger Pye, mafter, from St. Thomas's; with falt, rum, &c. Ditto. Harmony, James Briggs, mafter, from Surinam; with rum and fugar. Ditto. Mary, (French) from Cape François; with rum, fugar and molaffes. March 21. Batchelor, — on fufpicion of piracy; one gun, befides fwivels and cohorns. April 21. A veffel, name unknown. 25. Small floop, — Shaw, mafter; with Indian corn and wheat. May 29. Chance, John Verder, mafter, from Philadelphia; with flour and bread.—Whaleboat, John M'Kenny, mafter, from Lewis, to look out, being an advice boat. --A veffel with flax and flax-feed.

By the Perfeus.

Jan. 7. Speedwell, John Hazard, mafter, from Georgia; with rice, indigo and fkins.

Recapture by Ditto.

Jan. 12. Thomas, Thomas Nicholfon, mafter, from Jamaica; with logwood, fuftic and mahogany.

Prizes by Ditto.

Jan. 25. Adventure, Thomas Nevell, mafter, from St. Thomas's; with wine and dry goods. Ditto. Union, (French) Jean Collineux, mafter, from Martinique; with bale goods.

Recaptures by Ditto.

Feb. 8. Macarel, from Cork; with provifions for the army. 13. Marquifs of Rockingham, Ifaac Pocock, mafter, from Briftol; with dry goods.

Prizes by Ditto.

Feb. 20. Adventure, William Coffin, mafter, from Newberry; with lumber. March 1. Champion, Jofeph Hafkil, mafter, from Manchefter; with lumber. April 5. Neptune, Daniel Van Vorhus, mafter, from Philadelphia; with flour, hoops and ftaves. Ditto. Sachem, James Robinfon, mafter, from the Congrefs; floop on a cruize; armed for war.

By the Thames.

April 12. Raven, Charles Jenkins, mafter, from Philadelphia. 24. Jemmy, John Lippitt, mafter, from Demarrata; with rum and falt. 25. Raleigh privateer, John Barratt, from Virginia. 28. Induftry, Gabriel Sund, mafter, from Baltimore; with flour.

By the Camilla.

Feb. 28. Ranger, William Davis, mafter, from St. Lucia; in ballaft. April 15. A veffel unknown; with rum, molaffes and fugar. 20. A veffel from Cape Nichola; with molaffes. 21. Perfect, Etienne Connet, mafter, from Cape Nichola; with molaffes. 25. A veffel unknown, from South Carolina; with rum and rice. 26. A veffel unknown; with rum and rice.

By the Chatham.

Jan. 14. Lucretia, Jacob Serley,

G g   mafter,

mafter, from Bourdeaux; with salt-petre and fulphur.

By the Orpheus.

Feb. 16. Three Friends, Benjamin Cliffon, mafter, from South Carolina; with rice, indigo and dry goods.

By the Amazon.

Feb. 3. Fortune, Andrew Palmer, mafter, from St. Thomas's; with arms, ammunition and dry goods. March 13. A veffel, Samuel Bube, mafter, from Stonington; with falt, fugar and rum. 14. Oliver, John Buikley, mafter, from St. Thomas's; with fugar and rum. April 7. Tryal, Jof. Bafs, mafter, from Philadelphia; wich flour, iron, fteel and ftarch.

By the Juno.

Feb. 19. Chance (mafter dead) from Hifpaniola; with mohaffes, coffee and rum. March 11. Hero, James Latham, mafter, from New London; with horfes and lumber. Ditto. A veffel, laden with rum and molaffes.

By the Unicorn.

Jan. 11. Othello, George Dunbar Sweet, mafter, from Havannah; in ballaft 15. Savage, Nath. Atkin, mafter, from Bofton; with fugar, rum and mahogany. Ditto. Smack, John Leighton, mafter, from Bofton; with fugar, rum, fifh, &c. 16. Naby, Stephen Atwood, mafter, from Chatham; in ballaft. 19. William, Peter Bontacon, from New Haven; with flax feed.

Recapture by Ditto.

Feb. 14. Thomas, Oliver Read, mafter, from Liverpool; with provifions.

Prizes by Ditto.

Feb. 16. Sally, John Sandford, mafter, from Dyton; with onions, potatoes, cheefe and fugar. March 4. Happy Couple, David Lawrence, mafter, from South Carolina; with rice and indigo. 7. Olive, Johial Tinker, mafter, from Cape François; with falt and molaffes. 14.

Betfey, Jonathan Tucker, mafter, from Salem; with fugar and earthen ware. 15. Betfey, John Moody, mafter, from Bofton; with oil and fugar. May 11. Mariamne, Mark Towel, mafter, from Virginia; with tobacco and flour.

By the Mermaid.

Jan. 9. Dartmouth, James Littlefield, mafter, from Bofton; with lumber. April 1. Clariffa, Noah Millar, mafter, from St Euftatia; with falt. 15. Efcape Benjamin Weeks, mafter, from Maryland; with flour.

Recapture by Ditto.

April 19. Experiment, taken by the Lyon privateer of Egg Harbour; with coals.

Prizes by Ditto.

April 19. Hazard, run afhore and deftroyed by the above privateer; laden with oats. Ditto. Lyon privateer.

By the Merlin.

April 19. Difpatch, R. Collings Harding, mafter, from Bofton; with lumber, fugar and oil. 23. Induftry, Jacob Allen, mafter, from Winyaw; with rice and pitch. 25. Polly, Alexander Englifh, mafter, from Newberry; with lumber.

By the Senegal.

May 22. General Mercer, R. M. Richardfon, mafter, from Raphannock; with tobacco.

By the Lark.

April 5. Sophia, Jofeph Caney, mafter, from Mariegalante; with piece goods, wine and coffee. 17. Lady Wafhington, William Prefton, mafter, from Newberry; in ballaft.

Recapture by Ditto.

April 23. Friendfhip, a Quartermafter from the Emerald floop, mafter, (being a prize to the faid fhip, and retaken by the Rebels) from Virginia; with tobacco and flour.

Prizes by the Diamond.

Ditto. Succefs, John Langden, mafter, from Salem; with fugar.

Prizes

Prizes by the Diamond *and Greyhound.*

April 5. Polly, Charles Colehan, mafter, from St. Euftatia; with molaffes, falt, coffee and cordage. 12. Timoleon, Jofeph Blaid, mafter, from Bourdeaux; with lead and bale goods. 18. Polly, from St. Lucia; with molaffes, coffee, &c. 22. Succefs, from Bofton; with potatoes, Indian corn, &c. 28. Paris, from Guadalupe; with arms, ammunition and warlike ftores. Ditto. A veffel from Newberry; with fugar. Ditto. Ditto, with lumber and fifh. Ditto. Juno, from Old York; with lumber. Ditto. Savage, from Marblehead; with fifh. Ditto. Betfy, from South Carolina; with rice, tar and indigo. 30. Tayron, from South Carolina; with rice, pitch, &c. May 2. Berfheba, from Bofton; with lumber, pitch, tar, &c. 11. Hannah; with molaffes, falt, linen and cordage.

Prizes by the Diamond *and* Unicorn.

May 13. Tryal, H. Archer, mafter; with flour.

By the Falcon.

Jan. 19. A veffel; in ballaft. 22. Seaflower, Thomas Cocker, mafter; with falt, molaffes, &c. May 8. Induftry, Jacob Godwin, mafter, from New London; with lumber and horfes. 12. Charter Street, Andrew Rogers, mafter, from St. Euftatia; with falt and dry goods. April— A veffel from St. Lucia; with coffee, molaffes, &c.

By the Galatea.

Jan. 6. Good Intent, David Burch, from Baltimore; with flour, bread, &c. 13. Bold Defiance, William Taylor, mafter, from Virginia; with flour, bread, &c. Feb. 3. Sufannah, Tef. M'Kenfie, from South Carolina; with rice. Ditto. Baker, Zeb. Bapfon, mafter, from Newberry; with molaffes and cordage. 6. Revenge privateer, Samuel Fowlis, mafter, from Martinique; with canvas and woollens. 13. Family Fader, B. Wainwright, mafter, from South Carolina; with rice, indigo and corn. Ditto. Eagle, George

Johnfon, mafter, from St. Euftatia; with gunpowder, falt and dry goods. 14. Mermaid, George Bifhop, mafter, from Cape François; with molaffes, fugar and dry goods. 23. A veffel, Thomas Yates, mafter, from Virginia. March 12. Difpatch, John Hutchins, mafter, from Maryland; with Indian corn. 19. Good Intent. Nath. Bethel, mafter, from North Carolina; with Indian corn. 25. Wafhington, D. Livingfton, mafter, from Philadelphia; with flour and lumber. Ditto. Peggy, Jonn Cockran, mafter, from North Carolina; with Indian Corn. April 2. Friendfhip, William Bateman, mafter, from Salem; with lumber and fpars. 18. Alfton, William Thompfon, mafter, from South Carolina; with rice, rum, tea and falt. 21. François, (letter of marque) Thomas Baker, mafter, from St. Euftatia; with falt.

By the Galatea.

April 24. Molly, Benjamin Cox, mafter, from South Carolina; with rice, pitch, &c. Ditto. Proteus, William Proby, mafter, from St. Croix; with rum, fugar and molaffes. 25. Dove, Abraham Toppen, mafter, from Winyaw; with rice, pitch and turpentine. 26. John, Chriftopher Worth, mafter, from Nantucket; with fugar. 28. Phœnix, Elifha Coffin, mafter, from Nantucket; with fugar and oil.

By the Sphynx.

March 27. Minerva, Jof. Dean, mafter, from Surinam; with molaffes, coffee, &c.

Recapture by the Milford.

Feb. 23. Elizabeth, from Liverpool; with dry goods.

Prizes by Ditto.

March 9. Two Sifters, from the Weft Indies; with molaffes. 26. Cabot privateer, — Olney, mafter, from New England. Bella, from Nova Scotia; with lumber.

Recapture by the Liverpool.

Jan. 2. Providence, William Penterick, mafter, from Cork; with provifions.

Veffels

*Veſſels ſeized or deſtroyed in the laſt
year, but not included in the return of
31ſt of December, 1776, no account
of them being then received.*

1776. *Prizes by the* Phœnix.

December 31. York, Samuel
Talman, maſter, from Demarara;
with rum.

By the Experiment.

December 7. Polly, Robert Nel-
ſon, maſter, from North Carolina;
with bees wax and ſtaves.

By the Chatham.

December 18. Betty, James Sutton, maſter, from Cape Breton; in
ballaſt.

By the Cerberus.

December 29. Succeſs, Giles
Pierce, maſter, from Charles-town;
with rice, indigo and leather.

Recapture by Ditto.

Dec. 29. Ditto. Betty, J. Brice,
maſter, from Jamaica; with rum.

Prizes by Ditto.

December 11. Lyon, Ladwick
Champlain, maſter, from New London; with horſes, &c. 12. Lyon,
Iſaac Harlow, maſter, from Dartmouth; with ſugar, rum and molaſſes.

By the Falcon.

Dec. 18. A veſſel unknown; down
the Delaware. 19. Ditto; with oil.
31. Kitty, Samuel Nichols, maſter,
from Cape François; with molaſſes,
rum and dry goods.

By the Liverpool.

Auguſt 12. Swan; with Indian
corn. 13. Charming Sally, deſerted
by the people; with molaſſes and
rum.

1776. *Recaptures by* Ditto.

Aug. 13. Nevs, Edward Coffin,
maſter, from Nevis; with rum and
ſugar. Ditto. Devonſhire, William Fiſher, maſter, from Antigua;
with rum and ſugar.

Prize by Ditto.

Sept. 12. Warren, William Burke,
maſter, from Marblehead.

By the Hope *and* Diligence.

Oct. 3. General Gates, Joſhua
Stone, maſter.

By the Galatea.

Dec. 12. Neptune, Thomas Mun-
ro, maſter, from Surinam; with molaſſes, cocoa and ſugar. 15. Fame,
Nathaniel Bernard, maſter, from
Harbour Iſland; with ſalt. 16.
Lovely, Benjamin Jenkins, maſter,
from Cape Nichola; with molaſſes.
20. Peggy, Edward North, maſter,
from South Carolina; with indigo.
25. Betſy, James Lampheer, maſter,
from New London; with lumber and
proviſions. Ditto. Buckſkin privateer, Joſeph Handy, maſter, from
Maryland. 30. Union, Eba Waters, maſter, from New London;
with lumber and ſtock.

By the Brune.

July. Harlem; with powder,
arms, &c.

Total number of captures   203
Recaptures   15

H O W E.

Plymouth, July 8. This afternoon
the Experiment, with the ſhips and
veſſels under her convoy, ſailed out of
the Sound.

Portſmouth, July 9. Yeſterday the
Briſtol, with her convoy, ſailed from
St. Helen's for New-York.

[*London Gazette.*

———————

*Subſtance of private letters brought by
the Halifax packet, which brought
the preceding letters from Lord and
Gen. Howe, and left New-York on
the 9th of June.*

*Extract of a letter from an Officer of
the 17th regiment, dated Amboy,
May* 14.

" The men of war and frigates on
the American ſtation have had ſur-
priſing ſucceſs. The officers of the
navy have all the profit, but we have
the trouble. Several of the Captains
of the men of war have, it is ſaid,
cleared upwards of 10,000l.

" His Majeſty has been pleaſed,
in a letter from Lord George Germaine to Sir William Howe, to return
his thanks to Lord Cornwallis, and
the troops under his command, for
their good behaviour on the march

after

after the rebels through the Jerseys; to Col. Harcourt for his spirited behaviour in taking Lee; to our gallant Col. Mawhood for his bravery and good conduct on the 3d of January, and to all the regiments under his command, but in a particular manner to the 17th.

"Mr. Washington has declared, he will not give up any more prisoners, although an exchange was agreed upon; and Gen. Howe, relying on his word, gave up 2200 more of his people than he had of ours, expecting he would return that number, if he should chance to take any of our men; but now he positively refuses to exchange any private men."

Extract of a letter from a Gentleman at Perth Amboy, dated June 5.

"No movement has yet been made. General Howe is drawing most of the troops into the Jerseys. The rebels seem determined to dispute every point with us, so that we shall have warm work of it. This part of the army has been encamped here for a fortnight."

Other letters say, that on the 9th of June Sir William Howe was still at New-York; but that the next day (the 10th) part of the army were to embark; and it was thought that the whole army would be in motion in the field by the 14th. Mr. Washington seems preparing to leave Jersey, in order to cover Philadelphia; which General Howe is informed the Americans mean to defend. He does not know the number of Mr. Washington's army, but apprehends it to be confiderable.

There are private letters by the packet, which say, that an embarkation of about 1000 men was made the 2d of June, and sailed, but it is not known where. That the grand expedition was preparing when the packet failed. That there are disagreements and factions in the army; that the reports concerning ————, and the opinions entertained of him

by the several officers, render the present state, as well as future prospect of affairs, extremely disagreeable, distressing, and perplexing; insomuch, that some persons say, they wish *any other* officer had the ————. It is further said, that the subaltern officers have no confidence in his judgment; the general officers say he is indolent, attends to pleasure more than business, &c. &c. and a thousand such rumours, and opinions are in constant circulation throughout the army.

A letter from New-York of the 27th of May, says, General Howe is gone into Jersey, and has taken the greatest part of his army with him. His motive is supposed to be, to bring off Lord Cornwallis, who begins to be closely pressed by Mr. Washington on all sides.

Another letter from New York, dated June 1, says, it is given out, that Major Dixon is going home on his private affairs. But this is only the ostensible reason: the true reason is, it is to make room for Mr. Montresor; General Howe likes Mr. Montresor better; and he is to be Chief Engineer in the room of Mr. Dixon.

[When the last officer who came from New-York, had the honour of a conference with the King, his Majesty asked, "How happened it, that General Washington seemed always to have intelligence of what General Howe was about, and General Howe to know so little of General Washington?" "Sir, said the officer, it is not owing to any neglect in General Howe, but to every man in America being General Howe's enemy. This answer, is said to have made a greater impression upon his Majesty's mind, than any other circumstance whatever.]

Another letter brought by the packet says, That Philadelphia is too strong to be attempted on any side. That Mr. Washington has removed

from

from Morris-Town to Boundbrook. Mr. Howe does not know with what intention; but says, he is posted in so strong a manner, and so strongly entrenched, he does not chuse to attack him. Mr. Washington is, by his new position, between eight and nine miles nearer to New-York. That Lord Cornwallis is acting upon the *defensive* in Jersey; it is true, he has got possession of some of the heights near Brunswick, but the enemy are so strong in that neighbourhood, Mr. Howe must do something to afford a seasonable relief to Lord Cornwallis.

Extract of a letter from New-York, by the Salisbury, Mason, arrived at Corke, dated June 18.

"General Howe is gone to Brunswick, where the army are now encamped, except those left for the defence of the city and island, which have taken post between King's-bridge and Fort Kniphausen, and consist of two brigades of Hessians, two brigades of British, and two thousand Provincials, under command of General Kniphausen. But General Pigot has the command in New-York city. The Connecticut rebels under Arnold, lie in the White Plains, at the distance of about ten or twelve miles.

So great a scarcity is there of fresh provisions at New-York, that a milch cow was on the 14th of June purchased by an officer of distinction in the army there, at the *moderate* price of thirty guineas. An egg is sold for one shilling.

By the Pole, which arrived at Liverpool, July 20, from New-York, which she left on the 24th of June, advice was received, that eleven thousand men under General Washington were entrenched at Bound Brook, and had forty pieces of cannon, with twelve boats on carriages, for passing the rivers; and that three thousand men under General Putnam, were posted nearer Prince-Town. These

posts General Howe reconnoitred: he left Brunswick on the 15th of June, and marched within four miles of General Washington's camp; he remained in that situation four days. On the 20th, he ordered the tents to be struck, and to the surprize of every one, ordered the army to wheel and march back to Brunswick. And immediately every thing was prepared to embark. [The plan was to gain some advantage over Mr. Washington before the attempt was made upon Philadelphia; but Mr. W. being stronger than was expected, that part of the plan has miscarried, and General Howe obliged to proceed to his next operation, leaving Mr. W. in full force.]

The following is an Ordinance of the Convention of New-York, for settling the new Form of Government of that State.

Kingston, May 8, 1777.

Whereas, until such time as the Constitution and Government of this State shall be fully organized, it is necessary that some persons be vested with *power* to provide for the safety of the same:

Therefore resolved, That John Morin Scott, Robert R. Livingston, Christopher Tappen, Abraham Yates, jun. Governor Morris, Zephaniah Platt, John Jay, Charles De Witt, Robert Harpur, Jacob Cuyler, Thomas Tredwell, Pierre Van Cortlandt, Matthew Cantine, John Sloss Hobert, and Jonathan G. Tompkins, or the major part of them, be, and they hereby are appointed a Council of Safety, and invested with all the powers necessary for the safety and preservation of the State, until a meeting of the Legislature: Provided that the executive powers of the State shall be vested in the Governor, as soon as he shall be chosen and admitted into office; previous to which admission, such Governor shall appear before the said Council, and take the oath of allegiance,

legiance, and also the following oath of office, to be taken by the Governors and Lieutenant Governors of this State, to wit,

" I by the suffrage of the freeholders of the State of New-York, according to the laws and constitution of the said State, elected to serve the good people thereof, as their do here, solemnly, in the presence of that almighty and eternal God, before whom I shall one day answer for my conduct, covenant and promise to and with the good people of the State of New-York, that I will in all things, to the best of my knowledge and ability, faithfully perform the trust, so as aforesaid reposed in me, by executing the laws, and maintaining the peace, freedom, honour, and independence of the said State, in conformity to the powers unto me delegated by the Constitution; and I pray God so to preserve and help me, when in my extremest necessity I shall invoke his holy name, as I do keep this my sacred oath and declaration."

And whereas the appointment of officers in this State, is by the Constitution thereof vested in the Governor, by and with the advice and consent of a Council of Appointment, which doth not, and cannot exist, until after an election of Representatives in the Senate and Assembly.

And whereas many of the said officers are necessary, not only for the immediate execution of the laws of this State, and the distribution of justice, but also for the holding of such elections aforesaid.

Therefore resolved, That the following persons be, and they hereby are appointed within this State, by authority of the same, to wit, That Robert R. Livingston be Chancellor; John Jay, Chief Justice; Robert Yates and John Sloss Hobart, Puisne Judges; and Egbert Benson, Attorney General of this State. That

Volkert P. Douw be First Judge; and Jacob C. Ten Eyck, Abraham Ten Broeck, Henry Bleecker, Walter Livingston, and John H. Ten Eyck, the other Judges for the county of Albany; and that Henry J. Wendell be Sheriff, and Leonard Gansevoort, Clerk of the said county. That Ephraim Paine be first Judge, and Zephaniah Platt, and Anthony Hoffman, the other Judges, for the county of Dutchess; and that Melancton Smith be Sheriff, and Henry Livingston, Clerk of the said county. That Lewis Morris be First Judge; Stephen Ward, Joseph Strang, and Jonathan G. Tompkins, the other Judges for the county of West-Chester; and John Thomas be Sheriff; and John Bartow, Clerk of the said county. That Levi Pawling be First Judge, and Dirck Wynckhoop, jun. the other Judge for the county of Ulster; and that Egbert Dumond be Sheriff, and George Clinton, Clerk of the said county. That be First Judge, and the other Judges of the county of Tryon; and that Anthony Van Veghton be Sheriff, and Clerk of the said county. That be First Judge, , the other Judges of the county of Orange; and that Jesse Woodhull be Sheriff, and , Clerk of the said county. That William Duer be First Judge; John Williams and William Marsh, the other Judges for the county of Charlotte; and that Edward Savage be Sheriff, and Ebenezer Clarke, Clerk of the said county. That be First Judge; the other Judges of the county of Cumberland; and that Paul Spooner be Sheriff, and , Clerk of the said county. And that be the First Judge, and the other Judges for the county of Gloucester; and that Nathaniel

thaniel Merril be Sheriff, and Clerk of the said county *.

And further resolved, That each and every of the persons herein before appointed, do, before the Council of Safety aforesaid, or such persons as shall be by them appointed, take and subscribe the following oath of allegiance, to wit,

" I do solemnly swear and declare, in the presence of Almighty God, that I will bear true faith and allegiance to the State of New-York, as a good subject of the said State ; and will do my duty as such a subject ought to do."

And further, That every of the judicial officers above-mentioned, do, before he take upon him the exercise of his office, make the following oath, in manner above-mentioned :

" I do solemnly swear and declare, in the presence of Almighty God, that I will, to the best of my knowledge and abilities, execute the office of within the State of New-York, according to the Laws and Constitution of the said State, in defence of the freedom and independence thereof, and for the maintenance of liberty, and the distribution of justice among the subjects of the said State, without fear, favour, partiality, affection or hope of ward."

And also that every of the Sheriffs herein before named, do, before he exercise his said office, take in like manner, the following oath, to wit,

" I Sheriff of the county of do solemnly swear and declare, in the presence of Almighty God, that I will in all things, to the best of my knowledge and ability, do my duty as Sheriff of the said county, according to the Laws

and Constitution of this State of New-York, for the furtherance of justice, and in support of the rights and liberties of the said State, and of the subjects thereof."

And that every of the Clerks herein before named, do in like manner, take the following oath, to wit,

" I Clerk of do solemnly swear and declare, in the presence of Almighty God, that I will justly and honestly keep the records and papers by virtue of my said office of Clerk committed unto me, and in all other things to the best of my knowledge and understanding, faithfully perform the duty of my said office of Clerk, without favour or partiality."

And whereas it will be proper that all officers within this State, be, as soon as possible, appointed, in the mode for that purpose prescribed by the Constitution :

Therefore resolved, that all and singular the officers herein before appointed, shall respectively hold their offices, according to the tenure of such officers respectively specified in the said Constitution, if respectively approved of, by the Council for the appointment of officers, at their first session ; at which session, such of the said officers as shall be approved of by the said Council, as aforesaid, shall receive their commissions in proper form. It is nevertheless provided, that every of the persons herein before named, who held the like office with that so as aforesaid conferred upon him, under authority derived from the King of Great-Britain, during good behaviour, shall continue to hold the said office, so long as he shall well and faithfully perform the duties of such office.

And whereas no permanent provi-

* The blanks for inserting the names of Judges and Clerks, of the counties of Tryon and Orange were, at the request of the Deputies from those counties, not filled up; the said Deputies engaging to be answerable to their Constituents for the same ; and the blanks for Judges and Clerks of the counties of Cumberland and Gloucester, were not filled up for want of a representation of, and sufficient information from the said counties.

sion

fion could with propriety, be made in the Conftitution of this State, for the mode of holding elections within the fame, fuch provifions being properly within the power of the Legiflature, and depending, from time to time, upon the fituation and circumftances of the State. And whereas it is neceffary to point out fome mode, by which elections for a Governor, Lieutenant-Governor, and members of the Legiflature, may be held within this State:

Therefore refolved, That the Sheriffs of the feveral counties, herein before-mentioned, upon public notice for that purpofe, by them given, at leaft ten days before the day of election, do direct that elections be held for Governor, Lieutenant-Governor and Senators in each county, by the freeholders thereof, qualified as is by the Conftitution prefcribed, and for members of Affembly, by the people at large, at the following places, to wit,

In the county of Albany, at the City-Hall in the city of Albany,—at the houfe of William White, in Schenectady,—at the houfe of George Man, in Schohary,—at the houfe of Lambert Van Valckenburgh, at Cockfackie Flatts,—at the houfe of Cornelius Miller, at Claverack,—at the houfe of Solomon Demming, in King's diftrict,—at the houfe of Ifaac Becker in Tamhanick,—and at the houfe of Abraham Bloodgood, at Stillwater.

In the county of Ulfter, at the Court-Houfe, in the town of Kingfton,—at the houfe of Ann Du Bois, in New-Paltz,—at the houfe of Sarah Hill, in Hanover precinct,—at the houfe of Martin Wygant, in the precinct of Newburgh.

In the county of Orange, at the Court-Houfe, in Gofhen,—at or near the Prefbyterian Church, in Warwick,—at the houfe of John Brewfter, in the precinct of Cornwall,—at the Court-Houfe, at the New City, in

the precinct of Kakiat,—at the houfe of Paulus Vandervort, in Haverftraw,—and at the houfe of Jofeph Maybee, in the precinct of Tappan.

In the county of Weft-Chefter, at the houfe of Elijah Hunter, in Bedford,—and at the houfe of Captain Abraham Thiel, in the manor of Cortlandt.

In the county of Dutchefs, at the houfe of the widow of Simon Weftfall, deceafed, in Rhinebeck precinct, at the houfe of John Stoutenburgh, in Charlotte precinct,—at the houfe of Captain Jonathan Dennis, in Beckman's precinct,—at or near New-Hachenfack church, in Rumbout precinct,—and at Matthew Patterfon's, in Fredericfburgh precinct.

In the county of Tryon, at the houfe of Johannis Veder, in the Mohack diftrict,—at the houfe of John Dunn, in Conajohary diftrict,—at the church in Stone Arabia, in Palatine diftrict,—at the houfe of Frederick Bellinger, in the German Flatts diftrict,—at Smith's Hall, in Old England diftrict,—and at the houfe of Alexander Harper, in the townfhip of Harpers-field.

In the county of Cumberland, at the houfe of Seth Smith in Brattleborough,—at the houfe of Luke Znoulton, in New-Fain,—at the Court-Houfe in Weftminfter,—at the houfe of —— Tarbell, in Chefter,—at the Town-Houfe, in Windfor,—and at the houfe of Colonel Marfh, in Hertford.

In the county of Charlotte, at the new Prefbyterian Church, in New Perth—at the houfe of Anthony Hoffnagle, in Kingfbury,—at the houfe of Nathaniel Spring, in Granville,—and at fome convenient place in each of the towns of Manchefter, Danby and Caftle-Town.

And in the county of Gloucefter, at fuch places as the Sheriff of the faid county, by the advice of the County Committee fhall appoint, for the convenience of electors within the fame.

H h   And

And that the Sheriff of every county, shall order the elections to be held in each place above-mentioned, in his county, on the same day, under the direction of two reputable freeholders; one to be appointed by the County Committee, the other by the Sheriff, to attend at each of the places where the elections are, as aforesaid, directed to be held in every county, who shall jointly superintend the said elections, and return to the Sheriff of the county in which such elections are held, true poll lists of the elections in the several places, for Governor, Lieutenant-Governor, Senators and Representatives in authority; which list the Sheriff shall transmit under his oath of office, to the Council of Safety, as far as the same shall relate to Governor, Lieutenant-Governor, and Senators, and shall cast up the greatest number of votes for the Representatives in Assembly, and make return of the names of such of them as are duly elected, in the manner that has heretofore been usual and customary; and the Council of Safety shall, upon receipt of the poll lists of the election for Governor, Lieutenant-Governor and Senators, examine the same, and declare who is the Governor, who the Lieutenant-Governor, and who the Senators so chosen, and shall administer to the said Governor and Lieutenant-Governor, the oaths of allegiance and of office. The said elections within the several counties to be so held, as that the persons thereby chosen may be assembled at Kingston, in the county of Ulster, or such other place as the said Council of Safety shall appoint, on the first day of July next; Provided, if by any unforeseen accident, such elections cannot be held, then the said Council shall order election at such other time or times, as shall, in their opinion, be most conducive to the general interest of the State.

And it is further resolved, That

such freeholders as have fled from the southern parts of this State, and are now actually resident in any of the other counties of this State, shall be entitled to vote within such counties, for Governor and Lieutenant-Governor, as if they had actually possessed freeholds within the same. And that in case an election in any county should be held, by reason of the death or resignation of the Sheriff, or for any other cause, that the Council of Safety, or the Governor, in case he shall be sworn into his office, issue orders for an election for Representatives in Assembly, in such county, and appoint a returning officer to hold the same. And where no County Committee shall be in being, or such Committee shall neglect to appoint returning officers for the places above-named in such county, that the person for that purpose appointed by the Sheriff, shall alone hold the election, and make return to the Sheriff in like manner, as is above directed.

And whereas it is impracticable for the inhabitants of the southern district of this State, to choose Senators to represent them in the Senate thereof, or for the counties of the said district, Westchester excepted, to elect Representatives in Assembly; and it is reasonable and right to give to the said district and counties, a proportionable share in the legislation of the whole State, as far is possible in its present circumstances; therefore

Resolved, That Lewis Morris, Pierre Van Cortlandt, John Morin Scott, Jonathan Lawrence, William Floyd, William Smith, of Suffolk, Isaac Roosevelt, Doctor John Jones and Philip Livingston, be, and they hereby are appointed Senators for the southern district of this State; and in case of vacancy, such vacancy to be filled up by the choice of the Assembly: and that Abraham Brasher, Daniel Dunscomb, Evert Bancker, Peter P. Van Zandt, Robert Harpur, Abraham P. Lott, Jacobus Van Zandt,

Zandt, Henry Rutgers, jun. and Frederick Jay, be, and they hereby are appointed Representatives in Assembly of the city and county of New-York; Philip Edsall, Daniel Lawrence, Benjamin Coe and Benjamin Birdsall, of the county of Queen's; Burnet Miller, David Gelston, Ezra L'Homme-dieu, Thomas Tredwell and Thomas Wickes, of the county of Suffolk; William Boerum and Henry Williams, of the county of King's; and Joshua Mercereau and Abraham Jones of the county of Richmond; and in case of vacancy, such vacancy to be filled up by the choice of the Senate. Provided always, that none of the said Senators or Representatives in Assembly so appointed, or hereafter to be appointed as aforesaid, shall continue longer in office, than until the electors they represent, shall respectively be in a capacity of electing.

By order of Convention,

ABM. TEN BROECK, President.

Attest. JOHN M'KEESON, Sec.

———————

For the REMEMBRANCER.

The following paper is taken from Holt's NEW-YORK PAPER, *printed a few days before General Howe took possession of New-York.*

Mr. Holt,

As the following extract from an old Act of Assembly is seasonable at this time, I doubt not your willingness to communicate it to the public. AMERICANUS.

" Be it enacted by the Governor, Council, and Representatives met in General Assembly, and it is hereby enacted and declared by the authority of the same, That the supreme legislative power and authority, under their Majesties William and Mary, King and Queen of England, &c. shall for ever be and reside in a Governor in Chief, and Council, appointed by their Majesties, their heirs and successors, and the people by their Representatives, met and convened in General Assembly."

" That no aid, tax, talliage or custom, loan, benevolence, gift, excise, duty, or imposition whatsoever, shall be laid, assessed, imposed, levied or required, of, or on any of their Majesties subjects within this province, &c. or their estates, upon any manner of colour or pretence whatsoever, but by the act and covenant of the Governor and Council, and Representatives of the people in General Assembly met and convened."

The act from which this extract is made, was passed in the year 169:, and *disallowed* by the King six years afterwards; it will, however, serve to shew what were the sentiments of the legislature of the province at that early period, respecting the right of *legislation* and *taxation*; which the British Parliament has since claimed and attempted to exercise: and will also prove that our claim (made in a legal form) of independence of the Parliament in these two capital articles, is above half a century older than their new fangled claim of right to make laws, *binding upon us in all cases whatever.*

———————

At a meeting of the freeholders and other inhabitants of the town of Boston, on the 26th of May, 1777, *the following* INSTRUCTIONS *to their Representatives were reported, by Thomas Crafts, Esq. Mr. John Winthrop, Mr. Joseph Barrel, Perez Morton, and Benjamin Kent, Esqrs. a Committee appointed for that purpose, which were accepted by the town, and are now published by their order:*

To the Honourable John Hancock, Esq. David Jefferies, Caleb Davis, Oliver Wendell, John Brown, John Pitts, and Ellis Gray, Esquires, Representatives for the town of Boston.

Gentlemen,

You being chosen by the voice of the town of Boston, to represent them in the Great and General Court, and as it muft be agreeable to you to know the minds of your conftituents in all important matters, we think fit to give you the following INSTRUCTIONS:

With refpect to the General Courts forming a new Conftitution, you are directed by a unanimous vote of a full meeting, on no terms to confent to it, but to ufe your influence, and oppofe it heartily, if fuch an attempt fhould be made ; for we apprehend this matter *(at a fuitable time)* will properly come before the people at large, to delegate *a felect number for that purpofe, and that alone* ; when fome things which we efteem *abfolutely neceffary* to a good form, may be viewed by a General Court, in the light *of felf-denying ordinances,* which it is natural to conclude, are always difagreeable to human nature, among other things we have *particularly in view, making the Council entirely independent of the Houfe, and to prevent the lately too prevalent cuftom of accumulating offices in one perfon* ; we could wifh to eftablifh it, as a certain rule, that no perfon whatever be entrufted with more than *one* office at a time, (*and for the difcharge of it, let there be honourable allowance* ;) and to keep the *members of the General Court from accepting any :* this we apprehend will have a happy effect upon the State at large, and is agreeable to the cuftom of all States, until corruption and bribery deftroy the principles of virtue.

You are alfo directed to move for and exert yourfelves to get an immediate and total repeal of the *acts* commonly called the *regulating acts.* Our reafons for defiring this repeal are, becaufe we have done our utmoft to carry them into execution, and find them fo formed, that it is impoffible to accomplifh it: *they are,* (however well defigned) a growing fource of animofity and ill will, tending to raife a difference between town and country at this important crifis,

an event ardently wifhed for by our enemies, but ought to be guarded againft with the utmoft caution by every friend to his country ; for we are fure that our *intereft and happinefs* is intimately interwoven with the *intereft and happinefs of our brethren in the country* ; and if ever the trial is made, we fhall affuredly find that a difunion and feparation of fuch intereft will be *the ruin of both.*

Becaufe we apprehend the faid acts have very greatly raifed the price of almoft every neceffary of life, and we have great reafon to fear the evil will be growing fo long as they are in being, though we are firmly of opinion, if the *acts are repealed, and our trade freed from the cruel fhackles with which it has been lately injudicioufly bound,* that a *plentiful import will as affuredly lower the prices, as a fcarcity has raifed them* ; for it has been a known and acknowledged truth, by all nations *which were wife enough to encourage commerce,* that trade muft regulate itfelf ; can never be clogged but to its ruin, and always flourifhes when left alone : it is juftly compared to a coy miftrefs ; fhe muft be courted by delicacy, and ruined by force.

Becaufe it has the greateft tendency to deftroy our currency, and render money of little value ; it has thrown many of the *honeft and fair traders* (who wifh to retain a good confcience) out of bufinefs, and fet up in their room *mufhroom pedlars,* who adulterate their commodities, and take every advantage, thereby bringing a difgrace upon commerce, without which, town nor country are not worth defending.

Becaufe we are fure, that very large and much wanted fupplies, the property of this State, and expected here are now ordered into fome of the fifter States, until thefe acts are repealed.

In fhort, becaufe we have experienced every ill we could poffibly fear

fear from thefe acts, and have not felt the leaft advantage from them; we cannot therefore but view them, replete with innumerable evils, directly oppofite to the idea of liberty, and without a poffibility of doing any good, the *firft act* in its confequences, introducing *all kind of knavery*, and the *fecond* clofes *the horrid fcene with perjury*. If thefe acts fhould be repealed, we conclude the land embargo will fall of courfe.

If there fhould be an attempt to have the pay of the Reprefentatives taken out of the public cheft, you are directed ftrenuoufly to oppofe it, as the only juft method that we can conceive of, is, *for each town to pay their own members.*

You are to move, that immediate application be made to Congrefs, that *all the States money* might be redeemed with *continental currency*, and each State charged by the Continent for what they receive? If this could be accomplifhed, and the money redeemed by *lean certificates*, it would operate doubly in favour of the State; for as *they* carry intereft, *they* would be fpeedily hoarded, and being taken out of circulating, would give the remaining currency a proportionably *greater value*, and in that cafe would be nearly equal to a tax, befides, the *currency* being all of the *fame fpecies*, a counterfeit would be more eafily difcovered, than when a great variety of money is paffing, and it would then be the joint intereft of *all the States to keep the credit good*, and might be a further means of ftrengthening the *union*.

Thefe matters, with all others that may come before the General Court, we leave to your firmnefs and prudence, and truft your exertions in the common caufe, will be fuch, as fhall recommend you to your fellow citizens, *and what is more*, gain you the approbation of God, and your confciences.

Bofton, May 29. Yefterday the General Affembly of this State convened at the State-Houfe in this town, when they unanimoufly made choice of the Hon. James Warren, Efq. for their Speaker, and the Hon. Robert Treat Pain, Efq. Speaker, pro tem. They likewife unanimoufly made choice of Samel Freemen, Efq. for their Clerk. Mr. Webfter, of Salifbury, delivered an excellent difcourfe from Ezek. 45, 8th and 9th verfes.

The following gentlemen were chofen Counfellors out of the firft eighteen, and the Houfe adjurned.

Hon. James Baldwin, Efq.
  Artemis Ward, Efq.
  Benjamin Greenleaf, Efq.
  Caleb Cufhing, Efq.
  Richard Darby, Efq.
  John Whetcomb, Efq.
  Samuel Holten, Efq.
  John Fifher, Efq.
  Mofes Gill, Efq.
  Benjamin White, Efq.
  Jofeph Palmer, Efq.
  Benjamin Auftin, Efq.
  Daniel Hopkins, Efq.

The CONSTITUTION *and* FORM *of* GOVERNMENT *agreed to by the Delegates of* MARYLAND *in free and full Convention affembled.*

1. That the Legiflature confift of two diftinct branches, a Senate, and a Houfe of Delegates, which fhall be ftiled the General Affembly of Maryland.

2. That the Houfe of Delegates fhall be chofen in the following manner: all freemen above twenty-one years of age, having a freehold of fifty acres of land in the county in which they offer to vote, and refiding therein, and all freemen having property in this State above the value of thirty pounds current money, and having refided in the county in which they offer to vote one whole year next preceding the election, fhall have a right of fuffrage in the election of De-

legates

legates for such county; and all free-men so qualified shall, on the first Monday of October seventeen hundred and seventy-seven, and on the same day in every year thereafter, assemble in the counties in which they are respectively qualified to vote, at the Court-house in the said counties, or at such other place as the Legislature shall direct, and when assembled they shall proceed to elect, *viva voce*, four Delegates for their respective counties, of the most wise, sensible, and discreet of the people, residents in the county where they are to be chosen one whole year next preceding the election, above twenty-one years of age, and having in the State real or personal property above the value of five hundred pounds current money, and upon the final casting of the polls, the four persons who shall appear to have the greatest number of legal votes, shall be declared and returned duly elected for their respective county.

3. That the Sheriff of each county, or in case of sickness, his deputy (summoning two Justices of the county; who are required to attend for the preservation of the peace) shall be Judge of the election, and may adjourn from day to day, if necessary, till the same be finished, so that the whole election shall be concluded in four days; and shall make his return thereof, under his hand, to the Chancellor of this State for the time being.

4. That all persons, qualified by the charter of the city of Annapolis to vote for Burgesses, shall, on the same first Monday of October, seventeen hundred and seventy-seven, and on the same day in every year for ever thereafter, elect, *viva voce*, by a majority of votes, two Delegates, qualified agreeable to the said charter; that the Mayor, Recorder and Aldermen, of the said city, or any three of them, be judges of the election, appoint the place in the said city for holding the same, and may

adjourn from day to day as aforesaid, and shall make return thereof as aforesaid; but the inhabitants of the said city shall not be entitled to vote for Delegates for Anne-Arundel county, unless they have a freehold of fifty acres of land in the county, distinct from the city.

5. That all persons, inhabitants of Baltimore-town, and having the same qualifications as electors in the county, shall, on the same first Monday of October, seventeen hundred and seventy-seven, and on the same day in every year for ever thereafter, at such place in the said town as the Judges shall appoint, elect, *viva voce*, by a majority of votes, two Delegates, qualified as aforesaid; but if the said inhabitants of the town shall so decrease, as that the number of persons having right of suffrage therein shall have been for the space of seven years successively less than one half the number of voters in some one county in this State, such town thenceforward shall cease to send two Delegates or Representatives to the House of Delegates, until the said town shall have one half of the number of voters in some one county in this State.

6. That the Commissioners of the said town, or any three or more of them, for the time being shall be judges of the said election, and may adjourn as aforesaid, and shall make return thereof as aforesaid; but the inhabitants of the said town shall not be entitled to vote for, or be elected Delegates for, Baltimore county, neither shall the inhabitants of Baltimore county, out of the limits of Baltimore town, be entitled to vote for, or be elected Delegates for, the said town.

1. That on refusal, death, disqualification, resignation, or removal out of this State, of any Delegate, or on his becoming Governor, or a member of the Council, a warrant of election shall issue by the Speaker, for the election of another in his place,

of

of which ten days notice at the leaft, excluding the day of notice and the day of election, fhall be given.

8. That not lefs than a majority of the Delegates, with their Speaker (to be chofen by them by ballot) conftitute an houfe for the tranfacting any bufinefs, other than that of adjourning.

9. That the Houfe of Delegates fhall judge of the elections and qualifications of Delegates.

10. That the Houfe of Delegates may originate all money bills, propofe bills to the Senate, or receive thofe offered by that body, and affent, diffent or propofe amendments; that they may enquire, on the oath of witneffes, into all complaints, grievances and offences, as the grand inqueft of this State, and may commit any perfon for any crime to the public gaol, there to remain till he be difcharged by due courfe of law; they may expel any member for a great mifdemeanor, but not a fecond time for the fame caufe; they may examine and pafs all accounts of the State, relating either to the collection or expenditure of the revenue, or appoint auditors to ftate and adjuft the fame: they may call for all public or official papers and records, and fend for perfons, whom they judge neceffary, in the courfe of their enquiries, concerning affairs relating to the public intereft, and may direct all office bonds (which fhall be made payable to the State) to be fued for any breach of duty.

11. That the Senate may be at full and perfect liberty to exercife their judgment in paffing laws, and that they may not be compelled by the Houfe of Delegates either to reject a money bill which the emergency of affairs may require, or to affent to fome other act of legiflation, in their confcience and judgment injurious to the public welfare; the Houfe of Delegates fhall not on any occafion, or under any pretence, annex to or blend with a money bill, any matter, claufe or thing, not immediately relating to and neceffary for the impofing, affeffing, levying or applying the taxes or fupplies, to be raifed for the fupport of government, or the current expences of the State; and to prevent altercation about fuch bills, it is declared, that no bill impofing duties or cuftoms for the mere regulation of commerce, or inflicting fines for the reformation of morals, or to enforce the execution of the laws, by which an incidental revenue may arife, fhall be accounted a money bill; but every bill affeffing, levying or applying taxes or fupplies for the fupport of government, or the current expences of the State, or appropriating money in the Treafury, fhall be deemed a money bill.

12. That the Houfe of Delegates may punifh, by imprifonment, any perfon who fhall be guilty of a contempt in their view, by any diforderly or riotous behaviour, or by threats to or abufe of their members, or by any obftruction to their proceedings; they may alfo punifh, by imprifonment, any perfon who fhall be guilty of a breach of privilege, by arrefting on civil procefs, or by affaulting, any of their members, during their fitting, or on their way to or return from the Houfe of Delegates, or by any affault of, or obftruction to their officers, in the execution of any order or procefs, or by affaulting or obftructing any witnefs, or any other perfon, attending on, or on their way to or from the Houfe, or by refcuing any perfon committed by the Houfe; and the Senate may exercife the fame power in fimilar cafes.

13. That the Treafurers (one for the weftern and another for the eaftern fhore) and the Commiffioners of the Loan-office, may be appointed by the Houfe of Delegates during their pleafure, and in cafe of refufal, death, refignations, difqualifications, or removal out of the State of any of the said

said Commissioners or Treasurers, in the recess of the General Assembly, the Governor, with the advice of the Council, may appoint and commission a fit and proper person to such vacant office, to hold the same until the meeting of the next General Assembly.

14. That the Senate be chosen in the following manner: all persons, qualified as aforesaid to vote for county Delegates, shall, on the first Monday of September seventeen hundred and eighty-one, and on the same day in every fifth year for ever thereafter, elect, *viva voce*, by a majority of votes, two persons for their respective counties, qualified as aforesaid to be elected county Delegates, to be electors of the Senate; and the Sheriff of each county, or in case of sickness his deputy (summoning two Justices of the county, who are required to attend for the preservation of the peace) shall hold and be judge of the said election, and make return thereof as aforesaid. And all persons qualified as aforesaid to vote for Delegates for the city of Annapolis and Baltimore-town shall, on the same first Monday of September seventeen hundred and eighty-one, and on the same day in every fifth year for ever thereafter, elect, *viva voce*, by a majority of votes, one person for the said city and town respectively, qualified as aforesaid to be elected a Delegate for the said city and town respectively; the said election to be held in the same manner as the election of Delegates for the said city and town, the right to elect the said elector with respect to Baltimore-town to continue as long as the right to elect Delegates for the said town.

15. That the said electors of the Senate meet at the city of Annapolis, or such other place as shall be appointed for convening the Legislature, on the third Monday in September, seventeen hundred and eighty-one, and on the same day in every fifth year for ever thereafter, and they, or any twenty-four of them so met, shall

proceed to elect, by ballot, either out of their own body, or the people at large, fifteen Senators (nine of whom to be residents on the western, and six to be residents on the eastern shore) men of the most wisdom, experience and virtue, above twenty-five years of age, residents of the State above three whole years next preceding the election, and having therein real and personal property above the value of one thousand pounds current money.

16. That the Senators shall be balloted for at one and the same time, and out of the gentlemen residents of western shore, who shall be proposed as Senators, the nine who shall, on striking the ballots, appear to have the greatest numbers in their favour, shall be accordingly declared and returned duly elected; and out of the gentlemen, residents of the eastern shore, who shall be proposed as Senators, the six who shall, on striking the ballots, appear to have the greatest numbers in their favour, shall be accordingly declared and returned duly elected; and if two or more, on the same shore, shall have an equal number of ballots in their favour, by which the choice shall not be determined on the first ballot, then the electors shall again ballot before they separate, in which they shall be confined to the persons who, on the first ballot, shall have had an equal number; and they who shall have the greatest number in their favour on the second ballot, shall be accordingly declared and returned duly elected; and if the whole number should not thus be made up, because of an equal number on the second ballot still being in favour of two or more persons, then the election shall be determined by lot, between those who have equal numbers; which proceedings of the electors shall be certified under their hands, and returned to the Chancellor for the time being.

17. That the electors or Senators shall

shall judge of the qualifications and elections of members of their body, and on a contested election shall admit to a feat, as an elector, such qualified person as shall appear to them to have the greatest number of legal votes in his favour.

18. That the electors immediately on their meeting, and before they proceed to the election of Senators, take such oath of support and fidelity to this State, as this Convention of the Legislature shall direct, and also an oath " to elect, without favour, affection, partiality, or prejudice, such persons for Senators, as they, in their judgment and conscience, believe best qualified for the office."

19. That in case of refusal, death, resignation, disqualification, or removal out of this State, of any Senator, or on his becoming Governor, or a member of the Council, the Senate shall immediately thereupon, or at their next meeting thereafter, elect by ballot, in the same manner as the electors are above directed to chuse Senators, another person in his place, for the residue of the said term of five years.

20. That not less than a majority of the Senate, with their President, (to be chosen by them by ballot) shall constitute an house for the transacting any business, other than that of adjourning.

21. That the Senate shall judge of the elections and qualifications of Senators.

22. That the Senate may originate any other, except money bills, to which their assent or dissent only shall be given, and may receive any other bills from the House of Delegates, and assent, dissent, or propose amendments.

23. That the General Assembly meet annually, on the first Monday of November, and if necessary oftener.

24. That each House shall appoint its own officers, and settle its own rules of proceeding.

25. That a person of wisdom, experience, and virtue, shall be chosen Governor, on the second Monday of November, 1777, and on the second Monday in every year for ever thereafter, by the joint ballot of both Houses, to be taken in each House respectively, deposited in a conference room, the boxes to be examined by a joint committee of both Houses, and the numbers severally reported, that the appointment may be entered ; which mode of taking the joint ballot of both Houses shall be adopted in all cases. But if two or more shall have an equal number of ballots in their favour, by which the choice shall not be determined on the first ballot, then a second ballot shall be taken, which shall be confined to the persons who, on the first ballot, shall have had an equal number; and if the ballot should again be equal between two or more persons, then the election of the Governor shall be determined by lot, between those who have equal numbers; and if the person chosen Governor shall die, resign, remove out of the State, or refuse to act (sitting the General Assembly) the Senate and House of Delegates shall immediately thereupon proceed to a new choice in manner aforesaid.

26. That the Senators and Delegates, on the second Tuesday of November, seventeen hundred and seventy-seven, and annually on the second Tuesday of November for ever thereafter, elect by joint ballot, in the same manner as Senators are directed to be chosen, five of the most sensible, discreet and experienced men, above twenty-five years of age, residents in the State above three years next preceding the election, and having therein a freehold of lands and tenements, above the value of of one thousand pounds current money, to be the Council to the Governor, whose proceedings shall be always entered on record, to any part whereof any member may enter his

I i   dissent,

diffent, and their advice, if fo required by the Governor or any member of the Council, fhall be given in writing, and figned by the members giving the fame refpectively; which proceedings of the Council fhall be laid before the Senate, or Houfe of Delegates, when called for by them, or either of them. The Council may appoint their own clerk, who fhall take fuch oath of fupport and fidelity to this State as this Convention or the Legiflature fhall direct, and of fecrecy, in fuch matters as he fhall be directed by the Board to keep fecret.

27. That the Delegates to Congrefs from this State fhall be chofen annnally, or fuperfeded in the mean time, by the joint ballot of both Houfes of Aflemby, and that there be a rotation in fuch manner that at leaft two of the number be annually changed, and no perfon fhall be capable of being a Delegate to Congrefs for more than three in any term of fix years; and no perfon who holds any office of profit in the gift of Congrefs fhall be eligible to fit in Congrefs, but if appointed to any fuch office his feat fhall be thereby vacated: that no perfon, unlefs above twenty-five years of age, and refident in the State more than five years next preceding the election, and having real and perfonal eftate in this State above the value of one thoufand pounds current money, fhall be eligible to fit in Congrefs.

General WASHINGTON *to General* Sir WILLIAM HOWE, (*in Anfwer to* Sir W. HOWE's *Letters. See page* 219.)

Middle-Brook, June 10, 1777.

Sir,

Your feveral letters of the 21ft of April, 22d of May, and 5th inftant, have been received.

Having ftated my fentiments in an explicit manner, in my letter of the 9th of April, upon the fubject of your demand, and the difagreement between us, I thought it unneceffary to trouble you with a repetition of them. From the complexion of your's of the 21ft of April, we appeared to differ fo widely, that I could entertain no hopes of a compromife being effected, or that an anfwer would produce any good end.

But as you have called on me again for my final determination upon the matter, I fhall freely give it, after making fome obfervations upon what you have faid, with intention to obviate the objections, on my part, to a compliance with your demand through Lieut. Col. Walcott.

You admit the principle upon which my objection, to account for the whole number of prifoners fent out by you, is founded, but deny the application, by delicately infinuating, in the firft inftance, that the ill treatment complained of was an "expedient to cherifh popular delufion," and by afferting, in the fecond, that fuppofing their fufferings to have been real, they were to be afcribed to other caufes than thofe affigned by me.

I fhall not undertake to determine on whom the charge of endeavouring to excite popular delufion falls with moft propriety; but I cannot forbear intimating, that however fuccefsful ingenious mifcolourings may be in fome inftances, to perplex the underftanding in matters of fpeculation, yet it is difficult to perfuade mankind to doubt the evidence of their fenfes, and the reality of thofe facts for which they can appeal to them. Unlefs this can be done, permit me to affure you, it will always be believed, whatever may be fuggefted to the contrary, that men could not be in a more deplorable fituation than thofe unhappy fufferers were, who are the fubject of our difference. Did I imagine that you, Sir, had any ferious fcruples on the occafion, I might produce, in fupport of what I have alledged, the ftrongeft proofs that human teftimony can afford.

To

To prove that the prifoners did not fuffer from any ill treatment, or neglect of your's, you fay, " they were confined in the moft airy buildings, and on board the largeft tranfports in the fleet.—That they were fupplied with the fame provifions, both in quantity and quality, as were allowed, to your troops not on fervice.—That the fick, fuch of them as required peculiar care, were received into the Britifh hofpitals, and the reft attended by their own furgeons, who were fupplied with medicines without reftrictions, till it was difcovered that they difpofed of large quantities by private fale."

That airy buildings were chofen to confine our men in, is a fact I fhall not difpute; but whether this was an advantage or not, in the winter feafon, I leave you to decide. I am inclined to think it was not, efpecially as there was a general complaint that they were deftitute of fire the greater part of the time, and were only prevented from feeling the inclemency of the weather, in its extremeft rigour, by their crouded fituation. This I muft believe was not very conducive to their health; and, if we may judge by comparifons, we muft conclude they endured fimilar inconveniences on board the tranfports.

As to the fupplies of provifion, I know not what they were. My ideas of the matter were drawn from their united teftimony, confirmed by their appearance, which reprefented the allowance as infufficient in quantity, bad in quality, and irregularly ferved. You yourfelf mention fome " accidental circumftances of omiffion." I apprehend they were much more frequent than you were apprized of. It may not be improper to obferve, that there is a material difference between perfons confined and deprived of every means of fubfiftence in aid of their allowance, and thofe who are at large, and have other refources, as is the

cafe with your troops not on fervice, who have the benefit of their pay, and what they can occafionally gain by their labour. You might alfo find from enquiry, that we made no diftinction in our fupplies between your foldiers, prifoners with us, and our own in the field. They were not ftinted to a fcanty pittance, but had full as much as they could ufe, and of the beft kind.

In refpect to the attention paid to the fick, I am forry their accommodation was injured in any degree by the mifconduct of the furgeons. I heartily join with you in reprobating their proceeding, and fhall efteem it a favour if you point out the perfons, and furnifh me with fuch proofs of their guilt as you may be poffeffed of.

The more effectually to exonerate yourfelf from the confequences imputed to the neglect or ill treatment of the prifoners, you affert they had every comfort and affiftance from you that your fituation would admit; and that they wanted nothing but money and cloathing, which ought to have been furnifhed by me.

Had we left your prifoners with us to depend entirely upon the fupplies they drew immediately from you, their condition would have been little better than that of ours, in your hands. Your officers and foldiers can both inform you, that they experienced every mark of public and private generofity that could be fhewn them; frequent inftances might be adduced, that on notice of your men being in want, orders were immediately given that neceffaries fhould be procured for them. Every thing was done on our part to facilitate any fteps you took for the fame end. You were permitted to have an agent among us, countenanced by public authority; and allowed every latitude he could wifh to enable him to execute his office. I am forry to fay, the fame conduct has not been obferved towards us, and that there are inftances to

I i 2

fhow

show, that far from endeavouring to remove the difficulties that necessarily lay in our way to making such ample supplies as we could wish, obstacles have been made, that might very well have been waved. A late instance of this is to be found in your refusing to let us have a procuring agent with you, who might purchase what was necessary to supply the wants of our men. You must be sensible, that for want of a regular mode being adjusted, for mutually conveying supplies, there was a necessity for an exercise of generosity on both sides. This was done by us, and we supposed would have been done by you, which made us less anxious in providing than we should have been, had we foreseen what has really happened. We ascribed every deficiency on your part to the intermediate situation of affairs in this respect; and, looking forward to a more provident arrangement of the matter, we thought it our duty not to let the prisoners with us be destitute of any thing requisite for their preservation: and imagined that your reasonings and feelings would have been the same. Your saying we were frequently advised of their distress, is of little avail. It was not done until it was too late to remedy the ill consequences of the past neglect, and till our prisoners were already reduced to a miserable extremity. I wish the sufferings may not have been encreased, in the article of cloathing, by their being deprived of what they had, through the rapacity of too many of their captors; reports of this kind have not been wanting.

You farther observe, that my own experience would suggest, whether our army, in the course of the last campaign, was not subject to the same calamitous mortality with the prisoners in your possession. I cannot but confess, that there was a great degree of sickness amongst us; but I can assure you, that the mortality bore no kind of resemblance to that which was experienced by the prisoners with you, and that the disorders in the camp had nearly ceased, before the captivity of a large proportion of them. The garrison that fell into your hands on the 16th of November, was found, I am convinced, in good health.

In reply to my intimation, that it would have been happy if the expedient of sending out our men had been earlier thought of, you are pleased to say that the event has proved the caution with which you ought to have adopted the measure. What inference can be drawn from my refusing to account for prisoners scarcely alive, and by no means in an exchangeable condition, to warrant an insinuation that I should have done the same, had they been released under different circumstances, let your own candour determine.

But then you ask, " How is the cause of debility in prisoners to be ascertained?" This seems to be considered as a perplexing question. For my part, I cannot view it as involving any great difficulty. There is no more familiar mode of reasoning than from effects to causes, even in matters of the most interesting importance. In the subject before us, the appearance of the prisoners, and what eventually happened, proved that they had been hardly dealt with; but their joint asseverations, aided by the information of others, not interested in the distress more than as they regarded the rights of humanity, established the fact too firmly for incredulity itself to doubt it.

I should hardly believe you to be serious in your application of the exception, to which you allude, to the case of Major-general Lee, if you had not persisted in a discrimination respecting him. I did not entertain the most distant idea, that he could have been supposed to come under the description contained in it; and to force such a construction upon that gentleman's circumstances, however it may be an evidence of ingenuity, is but an indifferent specimen of candour. I still adhere to what I have already advanced on this head, and can by no means think of departing from it.

I am now to give you my final decision on the subject of your demands. In doing this, I can little more than repeat what I have already said. I am extremely desirous of a general exchange on liberal and impartial principles, and it is with great concern I find that a matter so mutually interesting is impeded by unnecessary obstacles. But I cannot consent to its taking place on terms so disadvantageous, as those you propose, and which appear to me so contrary to justice and the spirit of the agreement.

I think it proper to declare, that I wish the difference between us to be adjusted on a generous and equitable plan, and mean not to avail myself of the releasement of the prisoners, to extort any thing from you, not compatible with the strictest justice. Let a reasonable proportion of prisoners to be accounted for, be settled, and General Lee declared exchangeable, when we shall have an officer of your's of equal rank in our possession; I ask no more. These being done, I shall be happy to proceed to a general exchange. But in the mean time I am willing that a partial one should take place for the prisoners now in your hands, as far as those in ours will extend, except with regard to Lieutenant-colonel Campbell and the Hessian field officers, who will be detained till you recognize General Lee a prisoner of war, and place him on the footing I claim.

This latter proposition I am induced to make from the distinction which your letter of the 22d of May, seems to hold forth, and I think it

necessary to add, that your conduct towards prisoners will govern mine.

The situation of Lieut. Col. Campbell, as represented to you, is such as I neither wished nor approve. Upon the first intimation of his complaints, I wrote upon the subject, and hoped there would have been no further cause of uneasiness. That gentleman, I am persuaded, will do me the justice to say, he has received no ill treatment at my instance. Unnecessary severity, and every species of insult I despise, and I trust, none will ever have just reason to censure me in this respect. I have written again on your remonstrance, and have no doubt such a line of conduct will be adopted, as will be consistent with the dictates of humanity, and agreeable to both his and your wishes.

I am, Sir, with due respect,
Your most obedient servant,
GEORGE WASHINGTON.
His Excellency General Sir William Howe.

For the REMEMBRANCER.

In a speech you some time ago printed, addressed by Governor Livingston to the Council and Assembly of New-Jersey, were many general censures on the conduct of our army. Their ravages were stiled *more than Gothic;* and their *barbarity* more than *savage.* These accusations were well founded, as the inclosed recital, taken from the *New London Gazette,* will prove. Private letters give the most shocking accounts of a continuance of the same inhuman policy. These, for the present, are withheld, as the Congress have appointed a Committee, of which Dr. Witherspoon is Chairman, to prepare an authenticated history of what in our day is stiled, *British humanity!*

Gracious Heaven! how is the English national character and glory degraded and fallen!

From

From the NEW LONDON GAZETTE.

I have been waiting for some time in expectation that some able hand would give an account of the sufferings of our poor men, PRISONERS in New-York: but my expectation being hitherto disappointed, if you have nothing better offered upon the subject, you may, if you please, publish what I herewith send you, being the account which the prisoners themselves give.

As soon as they were taken, they were robbed of all their baggage, of whatever money they had, though it were paper, and could be of no advantage to the enemy, of their silver shoe-buckles, knee-buckles, &c. and many were stripped almost naked of cloaths; especially those who had good cloaths were stripped at once, being told, *that such cloaths were too good for rebels.* Thus, deprived of their cloaths and baggage, they were unable to shift even their linen, and were obliged to wear the same shirts for three or four months together, whereby they became extremely nasty and lousy; and this itself had been sufficient to bring on them many mortal diseases.

After they were taken, they were in the first place put on board the ships, and thrust down into the hold, where not a breath of fresh air could be obtained, and they were nearly suffocated for want of air; particularly some who were taken at Fort Washington, were first in this manner thrust down into the holds of vessels, in such numbers, that even at the cold season of November, they could scarcely bear any cloaths on them, being kept in a constant sweat. Yet these same persons, after lying in this situation for a while, till the pores of their bodies were as perfectly open as possible, were of a sudden taken out, and put into some of the churches in New-York, without covering or a spark of fire, where they suffered as much by the cold as they did by the sweating stagnation of the air in the other situa-

tion; and the consequence was, that they took such colds as brought on the most fatal diseases, and swept them off almost beyond conception.

Besides these things, they suffered extremely for the want of provisions, and even water. The Commissary pretended to allow them half a pound of bread, and four ounces of pork, per day; but of this pittance they were much cut short. What was given them for three days, was not enough for one day, and in some instances they went for three days without a single mouthful of food of any kind. They were pinched to that degree, that some on board the ships would pick up and eat the salt which happened to be scattered there; others gathered up the bran which the light horse wasted, and eat that mixed with dirt and filth as it was. Nor was this all, both the bread and pork which they did allow them, was extremely bad; for the bread, some of it was made out of the bran which they brought over to feed their light horse, and the rest of it was so mouldy, and the pork was so damnified, being soaked in bilge water, in the transportation from Europe, that they were not fit to be eaten by human creatures; and when they were eaten were very unwholesome. Such bread and pork as they would not pretend to give to their own men, they gave to our poor, sick, dying prisoners.

Nor were they in this doleful situation allowed a sufficiency of water. One would have thought that water is so plenty and cheap an element, that they would not have grudged them that. But there are, it seems, no bounds to their cruelty. The water allowed them was so brackish, and withal nasty, that they could not drink it until reduced to extremity. Nor did they let them have a sufficiency even of such water as this.

When winter came on, our poor people suffered extremely for want of fire and cloaths to keep them warm.

They

'They were confined in churches, where there were no fire-places, that could make no fires even if they had had wood. But wood was allowed them only for cooking their pittance of victuals; and for that purpose very sparingly. They had none to keep them warm even in the extremest of the weather, although they were almost naked, and the few cloaths they had left them were thin summer cloaths. Nor had they a single blanket, nor any bedding, not even straw, allowed them, till a little before Christmas; but during all the summer, and the cold weather in the fall, &c. they were wholly destitute of these necessary articles.

At the time that these were taken on Long-Island, a considerable part of them were sick of the dysentery, and with this distemper on them were crouded first on board of the ships, afterwards into the churches in New-York, three, four, or five hundred together, without any blankets, or any thing for even the sick to lie upon, but the bare floors or pavements. In this situation, that contagious distemper soon communicated from the sick to the well, who probably would have remained so, had they not been in this manner thrust in together, without regard to sick or well, or to the sultry, unwholesome season, it being then the heat of summer. Of this distemper numbers died daily, and many others, by their confinement and the sultry season, contracted fevers and died of them.— During their sickness with these and other diseases, they had no medicine, nothing soothing or comfortable for sick people, and were not so much as once visited by any physician by the month together.

Nor ought we to omit the insults which the *humane* Britons offered to our people, nor the artifices which they used to induce them to inlist into their service, and fight against their country. It seems that one *end*

of their starving our people, was to bring them by dint of necessity, to turn rebels to their own country, their consciences, and their God; for while thus famishing, they would come and say to them, " This is the just punishment of your rebellion,— nay, you are treated too well for rebels,—you have not received half you deserve, nor half you shall receive; but if you will *inlist* into his Majesty's service, you shall have victuals and cloaths enough."

As to insults, the British officers, besides continually cursing and swearing at them as rebels, often threatened to hang them all; and at a particular time ordered a number to choose each man his halter, out of a parcel offered, wherewith to be hanged; and even went so far as to cause a gallows to be erected before the prison, as if they were immediately to be executed. They further threatened to send them all to the East-Indies, and sell them there for slaves. In these and numberless other ways, did the British officers seem to rack their inventions to insult, terrify, and vex the poor prisoners. The meanest upstart officers among them would insult and abuse our Colonels and chief officers.

In this situation, without cloaths, without victuals or drink, and even water, or with those which were so bare and unwholesome; without fire; a number of them sick at first with a nauseous and contagious distemper: these with others, crowded by hundreds into close confinement, at the most unwholesome season of the year, and continued there for four months; without blankets, bedding or straw; without linen to shift, or cloaths to cover their bodies,—no wonder that they all became sickly, and having at the same time no medicine, no help of physicians, nothing to refresh or support nature; no wonder they died by scores in a night. And those who were so far gone, as to be unable to help themselves, the workings of their distemper passing through them, as they lay, could not be cleansed for want of cloaths; so that many lay for six, seven or eight days in all the filth of nature and of the dysentery, till death, more kind than Britons, put an end to their misery.

By these means, and in this way, above fifteen hundred brave Americans, who had nobly gone forth in the defence of their injured oppressed country, but whom the chance of war had cast into the hands of our enemies, died in New-York: many of whom were very amiable promising youths, of good families, the flower of our land. And of those who lived to come out of prison, the greatest part, so far as I can learn, are either dead or dying: their constitutions are broken, their stamina of nature worn out, they cannot recover, they die. Even the few that might have survived, are dying of the small pox; for it seems that our enemies, determined that even those, whom a good constitution and a kind Providence had carried through unexampled sufferings, should not at last escape death, just before their release from imprisonment, infected them with that fatal distemper.

To these circumstances, I shall subjoin the manner in which they buried those of our people who died :—They dragged them out of their prisons by one leg or one arm; piled them up without doors; there let them lie, till a sufficient number were dead, to make a cart load; then loaded them up in a cart; drove the cart thus loaded out to the ditches made by our people when fortifying New-York, there they would tip the cart, tumble the corpses together into the ditch, and afterwards slightly cover them with dirt.

By these things, we learn the temper of our enemies. As Britons, they boast of their politeness, humanity and compassion; and now we see what reason they have to boast of those virtues : their politeness leads them to insult and vex the distressed, the disarmed, who have not the means of liberty to redress; yea, even the sick and dying: their humanity and compassion led them, in cold blood to slaughter by hundreds and thousands, their fellowmen, who had submitted to their power: and not barely to kill them, but to kill them by inches, to starve them to death, to treat them ten times more cruelly, than if they had hung them all, the day they took them. Where were savages ever found in the wilds of America, more cruel, more inhuman, more blood thirsty, more brutal, more destitute of every human virtue ? Where, in all history, can we find an instance of more horrid treatment of prisoners ? Even the famous instance of Calcutta is not to be compared with this: that respected a few, only 140; this, more than 3000; that was finished in one night; this was continued for four or five months : in that was expressed cruelty in one way only; in this it is expressed many ways: that appears to have been the fault of either inconsideration, or sudden heat of passion; this must have been the effect of cool reflection, and a preconcerted system : and which of the two is the worst, which is the most diabolical admits of no dispute.

While our poor prisoners have been thus treated by our foes, the prisoners we have taken from them, have enjoyed liberty to walk and ride about within large limits, at their pleasure; have been fully supplied with every necessary, and have ever lived on the fat of the land; so that some have been so healthy, so merry, so plump and well fed as they. And this generous treatment, it is said, they could not but remember; for when they were returned in the exchange of prisoners, and saw the miserable, famished, dying state of our prisoners, conscious of the treatment they had received,

ceived, they could not refrain from tears.

This doleful tale needs no comment or painting; the bare narration " makes both the ears to tingle," and is more affecting than all the figures of rhetoric. I shall not therefore enlarge further; but only add, that this teaches us what spirit our enemies are of, and what we are to expect from them, if we either submit to be taken, or to be pardoned by them: for cruelty runs through a man's whole conduct, and he that is so cruel in one part of his conduct will be cruel throughout; and I am persuaded, that the indignation of that merciful Being, who " hath no pleasure in the death even of the wicked," is raised against the authors of this barbarity;—fo the indignation of every friend to right, to mercy and to mankind, ought to be roused hereby, together with a determinate resolution to resist to the last, such barbarous —— who delight in torture and blood; and not to let the blood of so many of our famished, tortured fellow citizens, cry for vengeance in vain.

Philadelphia, June 25.
Extract of a letter from GENERAL WASHINGTON *to Congress, dated Middle-Brook, June 20, 1777.*

" When I had the honour of addressing you last, I informed you that the main body of the enemy had marched from Brunswick, and extended their van as far as Somerset Court-house. I am now to acquaint you, that after encamping between these two posts, and beginning a line of redoubts, they changed their ground yesterday morning and in the course of the preceding night, and returned to Brunswick again, burning as they went several valuable dwelling-houses.

" I must observe, and with peculiar satisfaction I do it, that on the first notice of the enemy's movements, the militia assembled in the most spirited manner, firmly determined to give them every annoyance in their power, and to afford us every possible aid. This I thought it my duty to mention, in justice to their conduct; and I am inclined to believe, that Gen. Howe's return, thus suddenly made, must have been in consequence of the information he received, that the people were in, and flying to, arms in every quarter to oppose him."

Extract of another letter from GEN. WASHINGTON *to Congress, dated Head Quarters, Middle-Brook, June 22, 11 o'clock, P. M.*

" I have the honour and pleasure to inform you, that the enemy evacuated Brunswick this morning, and retired to Amboy, burning many houses as they went along; some of them, from the appearance of the flames, were considerable buildings.

" From several pieces of information, and from a variety of circumstances, it was evident that a move was in agitation, and it was the general opinion that it was intended this morning. I therefore detached three brigades, under the command of Major-general Green, to fall upon their rear, and kept the main body of the army paraded upon the heights, to support them if there should be occasion. A party of Col. Morgan's regiment of light infantry attacked and drove the Hessian picquet about sunrise, and upon the appearance of Gen. Wayne's brigade, and Morgan's regiment (who got first to the ground) opposite Brunswick, the enemy immediately crossed the bridge to the east side of the river, and threw themselves into redoubts which they had before constructed. Our troops advanced briskly upon them, upon which they quitted the redoubts, without making an opposition, and retired by the Amboy road. As all our troops, from the difference of their stations in camp, had not come up, when the enemy began to move off,

K k

off, it was impoffible to check them, as their numbers were far greater than we had reafon to expect, being, as we were informed afterwards, between four and five thoufand men. Our people purfued them as far as Pif-cataqua, but finding it impoffible to overtake them, and fearing they might be led on too far from the main body, they returned to Brunfwick. By information of the inhabitants, Gen. Howe, Lord Cornwallis, and Gen. Grant, were in the town when the alarm was firft given, but they quitted it very foon after.

" In the purfuit, Col. Morgan's riflemen exchanged feveral fharp fires with the enemy, which, it is ima-gined, did confiderable execution. I am in hopes that they afterwards fell in with Gen. Maxwell, who was de-tached laft night with a ftrong party to lie between Brunfwick and Am-boy, in order to interrupt any con-voys or parties that might be paffing; but I have yet heard nothing from him.

" Gen. Green defires me to make mention of the conduct and bravery of Gen. Wayne and Col. Morgan, and of their officers and men upon this occafion, as they conftantly ad-vanced upon an enemy far fuperior to them in numbers, and well fecured behind ftrong redoubts.

" Gen. Sullivan advanced from Rocky-Hill to Brunfwick with his divifion; but as he did not receive his order of march till very late at night, he did not arrive till the enemy had been gone fome time.

Publifhed by order of Congrefs,
CHARLES THOMSON, Sec.
Extract of a letter from the Camp at Middle-Brook, dated June 23.

" I wrote two letters yefterday by different expreffes, giving an account of our being in poffeffion of Brunf-wick, and the enemy retreating to Amboy, where we now hear their main body have reached; their ad-vance guard about four miles between Woodbridge and Bonum-town; Ge-

neral Maxwell was near them, alfo General Parfons, with his brigade, and Lord Stirling, with his divifion, is between them and our camp here; near 6000 remain (of our troops) in Brunfwick.

" The enemy have thrown their bridge (defigned for the Delaware) acrofs the Sound from Amboy to Staten Ifland, by which it is clear they defign to retreat, if clofely pufh-ed: the weather laft night and this morning has been fo wet that nothing could be done, otherwife I believe, we fhould have moved nearer to them; their retreat has been attended with fuch a deftruction of property, that marks their defpair of poffeffing this country; and Sir William Howe's reputation as a General, muft be greatly leffened in their own eyes. A want of confidence in a Commander in Chief, and the troops difpirited as their's muft be, can leave them no great profpect of ending the campaign with much advantage, which has opened fo ingloriously."

Extract of a letter from a General Officer in GENERAL WASHING-TON'*s camp at Middle-Brook, dated the 23d of June,* 1777.

" The enemy a few days ago form-ed a defign of going to Philadelphia by land, and on the 13th inft. marched with one divifion of the army to So-merfet Court-houfe, in hopes of making Gen. Wafhington quit his place, and proceed on in their front to the Delaware; but finding themfelves overpowered, the militia of this and the neighbouring States daily coming in and furrounding them, and our light troops harraffing them every night and day, killing and taking numbers, obliged them to quit their advanced poft about *one in the morn-ing of the* 19th (with more precipita-tion than you can imagine) and re-treat to Brunfwick, burning and de-ftroying all farm houfes on the road. Their cruelty fhewn the inhabitants is beyond the powers of human utterance to exprefs; not content with plundering, they ruined and defaced every public edifice, particularly thofe which were erected and dedicated to Almighty God.

"A Council of War was held on the night of the 21ft, and refolved to march a part of our army to their lines near Brunfwick, and give them battle, if their numbers were equal. For this purpofe three brigades were ordered to parade and move after dufk, under the command of Major Gen. Green and Brigadiers Wayne, Varnum and Debore. At fun rife Wayne's arrived at their advanced picquet; our light troops on the left flank began to fkirmifh; the guards gave way after a faint refiftance, and the brigade advanced in good order, took poffeffion of the heights above Brunfwick, on the eaft and weft fides of the Rariton. We foon perceived the whole of the enemy in motion; a column advanced with a fhew of attack, while their main body began to retreat: upon this difcovery our artillery began a warm cannonade on them, which occafioned them to abandon the town and their feveral encampments, leaving feveral tents, a vaft deal of blankets, camp-kettles, waggons, carts, horfes, &c. Such a running I never faw. We took poffeffion of the town in lefs than fifteen minutes.

The enemy's lofs of killed, wounded, and taken, amounts to between two or three hundred. They have gone to Amboy, and to-day we fhall oblige them to take poft on Staten Ifland, the place they left this time twelvemonth. Thus, Sir, have we drove the proud Britifh troops: they were to have deftroyed Brunfwick, but we advanced too foon for them. Not a houfe have they left on the road, except where the owners were Tories. The fpear General Howe leaned on in this State has at length pierced his hand; in the hour of his diftrefs fell from him like the autum-

nal leaves. What Gen. Howe will attempt next is uncertain; every fcheme is defeated, and we have, like the

"*Tyrannous breathings of the North,
Check'd all his buds from blowing.*"

N. B. Gen. Sullivan's divifion is encamped at Brunfwick. Our lofs are killed two, wounded feven.

Extract of a letter, dated Camp, Middle-Brook, June 22d, 1777.

"I have juft feen the examination of a perfon of veracity who is come out of New-York.—The defcription he gives of the treatment of our prifoners is fhocking, beyond defcription. They are allowed but three ounces of falt pork per day, which they are frequently obliged to eat raw, and three pounds of bread per week. The humane and compaffionate (for fuch it feems there are even among Tories) are debarred from affording them the leaft affiftance; and they are infulted and abufed in the groffeft and moft illiberal terms; for the flighteft offences they are confined in dungeons, and loaded with irons.—How long will the patience and humanity of the much injured Americans be proof againft fuch reiterated abufe and infult? One of our poor fellows in the prifon, in a fit of agony and defpair, threw himfelf on the floor and exclaimed,—"Good God! Am I then reduced to the fatal neceffity, either of taking up arms againft my country, or perifhing with hunger? No. I will die ten thoufand deaths firft." This is no exaggerated picture; they are fubftantial facts.

"The militia have turned out with amazing fpirit, and behaved (as Burgoyne faid on another occafion) "*to a charm.*" All party difputes have totally fubfided at Philadelphia; and they are now firmly united in fupport of the common caufe. Never fince the commencement of our prefent difputes have I felt my mind more at eafe about the iffue of it; and I doubt, we fhall put a glorious

end

end to the prefent campaign, and a final period to all pretence (in Great-Br'tain) of domination over America."

———————

Whitehall, Auguſt 22, 1777.
Copy of a letter from the Honourable General Sir WILLIAM HOWE *to Lord* GEORGE GERMAIN.
New-York, July 5, 1777.
My Lord,

Having eſtabliſhed a corps ſufficient for the defence of Amboy, the army aſſembled at Brunſwick on the 12th of June.

The enemy's principal force being encamped upon the mountain above Quibble-town, with a corps of two thouſand men at Prince-town, it was thought adviſeable to make a movement in two columns from Brunſwick on the 14th in the morning, leaving Brigadier-general Matthew with 2000 men to guard that poſt. The firſt diviſion, under the command of Lord Cornwallis, advanced to Hillſborough, and the ſecond to Middle Buſh, under the command of Lieutenant-general De Heiſter, with a view of drawing on an action, if the enemy ſhould remove from the mountain towards the Delaware ; but on finding their intention to keep a poſition which it would not have been prudent to attack, I determined, without loſs of time, to purſue the principal objects of the campaign by withdrawing the army from Jerſey ; and in conſequence of this determination returned to the camp at Brunſwick on the 19th, and marched from thence to Amboy on the 22d, intending to croſs to Staten Iſland, from whence the embarkation was to take place.

Upon quitting the camp at Brunſwick, the enemy brought a few troops forward with two or three pieces of cannon, which they fired at the utmoſt range without the leaſt execution or any return from us ; they alſo puſhed ſome battalions into the woods to harraſs the rear where Lord Cornwallis commanded, who ſoon diſperſed them with the loſs of only two men killed and thirteen wounded ; the enemy having nine killed, and about thirty wounded.

The neceſſary preparations being finiſhed for croſſing the troops to Staten Iſland, intelligence was received that the enemy had moved down from the mountain, and taken poſt at Quibble-town, intending, as it was given out, to attack the rear of the army removing from Amboy ; that two corps had alſo advanced to their left,—one of 3000 men and 8 pieces of cannon, under the command of Lord Stirling, Generals Maxwell and Conway ; the laſt ſaid to be a Captain in the French ſervice,—the other corps conſiſted of about 700 men, with only one piece of cannon.

In this ſituation of the enemy, it was judged adviſeable to make a movement that might lead on to an attack, which was done the 26th in the morning in two columns ; the right, under the command of Lord Cornwallis, with Major-general Grant, Brigadiers Matthew and Leſlie, and Colonel Donop, took the rout by Woodbridge towards Scotch Plains ; the left column where I was, with Major-generals Sterne, Vaughan and Grey, Brigadiers Cleaveland and Agnew, marched by Metuchin Meeting-houſe to join the rear of the right column in the road from thence to Scotch Plains, intending to have taken ſeparate routs about two miles after the junction, in order to have attacked the enemy's left flank at Quibble-town. Four battalions were detached in the morning, with ſix pieces of cannon, to take poſt at Bonham-town.

The right column, having fallen in with the aforementioned corps of 700 men ſoon after paſſing Woodbridge, gave the alarm, by the firing that enſued, to their main army at Quibble-town, which retired to the mountain with the utmoſt precipitation. The ſmall corps was cloſely puſhed

puſhed by the light troops, and with difficulty got off their pieces of cannon.

Lord Cornwallis, ſoon after he was upon the road leading to Scotch Plains from Metuchin Meeting-houſe, came up with the corps commanded by Lord Stirling, who he found advantageouſly poſted in a country much covered with wood, and his artillery well diſpoſed. The King's troops, vying with each other upon this occaſion, preſſed forward to ſuch cloſe action, that the enemy, though inclined to reſiſt, could not long maintain their ground againſt ſo great impetuoſity, but were diſperſed on all ſides, leaving behind three pieces of braſs ordnance, three Captains and ſixty men killed, and upwards of two hundred officers and men wounded and taken.

His Lordſhip had five men killed, and thirty wounded. Captain Finch of the light company of the guards was the only officer who ſuffered, and to my great concern the wound he received proving mortal, he died the 29th of June at Amboy.

The troops engaged in this action were the 1ſt light infantry, 1ſt Britiſh grenadiers, 1ſt, 2d, and 3d Heſſian grenadiers; 1ſt battalion of guards, Heſſian chaſſeurs, and the Queen's rangers. I take the liberty of particulariſing theſe corps, as Lord Cornwallis, in his report to me ſo highly extols their merit and ardour upon this attack. One piece of cannon was taken by the guards, the other two by Colonel Mingerode's battalion of Heſſian grenadiers.

The enemy were purſued as far as Weſtfield with little effect, the day proving ſo intenſely hot, that the ſoldiers could with difficulty continue their march thither; in the mean time it gave opportunity for thoſe flying to eſcape by ſculking in the thick woods, until night favoured their retreat to the mountain.

The army lay that night at Weſt-field, returned the next day to Raway, and the day following to Amboy. On the 30th, at ten o'clock in the forenoon, the troops began to croſs over to Staten Iſland, and the rear guard, under the command of Lord Cornwallis, paſſed at two in the afternoon, without the leaſt appearance of an enemy.

The embarkation of the troops is proceeding with the utmoſt diſpatch, and I ſhall have the honour of ſending your Lordſhip further information as ſoon as the troops are landed at the place of their deſtination.

With the moſt perfect reſpect I have the honour to be your Lordſhip's moſt faithful and moſt obedient ſervant,
W. HOWE.

Extract of another letter from the Honourable General Sir WILLIAM HOWE *to Lord* GEORGE GERMAIN *dated New-York,* July 15, 1777.

Various accounts have been lately brought from the northern part of this province, in regard to the army from Canada; and I have this day had the ſatisfaction to receive a letter from Lieutenant-general Burgoyne, with a confirmation of his being before Ticonderoga; a copy of which your Lordſhip has incloſed; intelligence otherwiſe received leaves no room to doubt his being in poſſeſſion, but it does not come from authority ſo certain as to juſtify me in a poſitive declaration of the fact.

I am extremely concerned, my Lord, to cloſe this letter with a circumſtance as diſtreſſing as it was unexpected. An expreſs is juſt arrived from Rhode-Iſland with intelligence, that a ſmall party of the rebels made a deſcent there on the night of the 10th inſtant, ſurprized Major-general Preſcot in his quarters, carried him off, and Lieutenant Barrington of the 7th regiment, with ſuch diſpatch and ſecrecy as to fruſtrate every attempt to reſcue them.

Extract

Extract of a letter from Lieutenant-general BURGOYNE *to the Honourable Sir* WILLIAM HOWE, *dated Camp before Ticonderoga, July 2, 1777.*

I wait only fome neceffaries of the heavy artillery, which have been retarded by contrary winds upon Lake Champlain, to open batteries upon Ticonderoga.

The army is in the fulleft powers of health and fpirit. I have a large body of favages, and fhall be joined by a larger in a few days. Ticonderoga reduced, I fhall leave behind me proper engineers to put it in an impregnable ftate; and it will be garrifoned from Canada, where all the deftined fupplies are fafely arrived. My force therefore will be left complete for future operations.

Admiralty-Office, Auguft 23, 1777.
Extract of a letter from Sir GEORGE COLLIER, *Commander of his Majefty's fhip the Rainbow, to Mr.* STEPHENS, *dated at Halifax, July 12, 1777.*

I failed from this port in the morning of Sunday the 6th inftant, and in the afternoon difcovered three fail, to which we immediately gave chace; but from the diftance I could form no judgment of their force, or what they were; the Victor brig was at this time in company three or four miles aftern, and as her rate of failing was inferior to that of the Rainbow, I made the fignal for her making more fail, to avoid feparating from her: at fun-fet we had gained fo much on the chace as to difcover they were large fhips, ftanding as we were on the ftarboard tack, with the wind at W. N. W. I judged from thence, that they were bound to fome of the ports of New-England.

I followed them with all the fail I could croud, and at dawn of day next morning we faw them again about three points on the weather bow, with a floop in company; the preft fail I carried all night had increafed the diftance from the Victor

brig fo much, that fhe was no longer difcernable from the maft-head.

The fhips we were in chace of were about 5 or 6 miles diftant, and from many circumftances I had no doubt were part of the rebel fleet, which had failed fome time before from Bofton, under the command of Manley; continuing the chace, and gaining upon them, they quitted the floop, and fet her on fire, going off in a regular line of battle ahead, and fetting top gallant royals, and every fail that could be ufeful to them.

A little after fix we difcovered another fail ftanding towards the rebel fhips; fhe croffed us on the contrary tack at about four miles diftance, and put about when fhe could fetch their wakes; from her not making the private fignal to me, I concluded that fhe was another of the rebel frigates, and therefore paid no regard to an Englifh red enfign fhe hoifted, and two guns fhe fired to leeward.

About ten in the morning the enemy's fhip went away lafking, and three quarters of an hour afterwards I was furprized to fee feveral fhot exchanged between the fternmoft of them and the ftranger who had laft joined, and whom I had hitherto looked upon as another of their fleet. I then hoifted my colours; fhortly after which the two fternmoft of the rebel frigates hawled their wind, whilft the headmoft kept away about two points from it. This brought the Englifh fhip (which I afterwards found was the Flora) more abreaft of them, who paffed to windward, exchanging a broadfide with each, and purfuing the fugitive, who, from the alteration two or three times of her courfe, feemed uncertain which way to fteer. The Flora gaining faft upon her, which fhe perceiving, hawled her wind again, and foon afterwards tacked and ftood after her comrades, exchanging a broadfide with the Flora as they paffed each other.

I was juft putting about after the

two

two ships, when I observed this unexpected manœuvre of the rebel frigates, which made me stand on something longer before I tacked, hoping to get her within reach of my guns as she passed me: I accordingly did so, but had not the good fortune to bring down either a mast or sail by my fire.

I tacked immediately after her, and soon afterwards saw the headmost rebel frigate put about; she passed me just out of gunshot to windward, and appeared a very fine ship of 34 guns, with rebel colours flying. One of the gentlemen of my quarter-deck had been a prisoner lately at Boston, and knew her to be the Hancock, on board of whom Manley commanded; the sea-officer in whom the Congress place great confidence, and who is the second in rank in their navy.

The ship I had fired upon I found outsailed me, and soon after my tacking went away lasking, whilst the other frigate kept her wind. I then saw with concern, that one of the three must unavoidably escape, if they thus steered different courses; I therefore judged it best to put about and follow the Hancock, which appeared the largest ship. Whilst I was in stays, the Flora passed me very near in pursuit of the ship I had fired upon.

It was about two o'clock in the afternoon of Monday the 7th of July, that I tacked after Manley, who seemed at first rather to outsail the Rainbow; but I understood afterwards, that to endeavour making his ship sail better, he started all his water forward, and by that means put her out of trim. An hour before the close of day, he altered his course, and kept away large; however, we got so near to him before dark, as enabled us, by means of a night-glass, to keep sight of him all night. At dawn of day he was not much more than a mile a-head of me; soon after which we saw a small sail to

leeward, which we found to be the Victor brig, who, as we passed, fired at the rebel frigate, and killed one of the men at the wheel, but was not able, from bad sailing, to keep up, or come near any more. About four in the morning I began firing the bow-chace upon her, with occasional broadsides loaded with round and grape, as I could bring them to bear, some of which struck her masts and sails. At half an hour past eight I was so near as to hail her, and let them know, that if they expected quarter, they must strike immediately. Manley took a few minutes to consider; and a fresher breeze just then springing up, he availed himself of it, by attempting to set some of the steering sails on the other side, I therefore fired into him; upon which he struck the rebel colours to his Majesty's ship, after a chace of upwards of 39 hours.

I sent my first Lieutenant, Mr. Haynes, to take possession. She proved to be a rebel frigate, fitted out by the Congress, called the Hancock, of 32 guns, mostly 12 pounders, and had about 229 men on board: her complement is 290 men; the remainder were in the Fox. She is a very large frigate, quite new off the stocks; and I am informed that, though from her foulness and their mismanagement we came up with her, yet that she is one of the fastest sailing ships ever built.

Mr. Manley informed me, that the ship the Flora was in chace off was his Majesty's ship the Fox of 28 guns, which he had lately taken on the Banks of Newfoundland; and that the other frigate was the Boston of 30 guns, commanded by M'Neal. I found Captain Fotheringham, late commander of the Fox, and forty of his people, on board the Hancock; but his officers and some of his men were put on board the Boston frigate, and the remainder sent in a fishing vessel to Newfoundland.

After

After taking out the prisoners, I found it necessary, from their numbers being very near as many as my own ship's company, to return to Halifax, where I arrived with my prize on the 11th instant.

I had the great satisfaction on my arrival to find the Flora and the Fox both here: she had retaken the latter shortly after I passed her.

Sir George Collier, in the above letter, gives an account,

That, advice being received on the 16th of June, of a party of the rebels, supposed to consist of about 200 men, having landed in the river St. John's, he ordered Captain Hawker of the Mermaid, with the Gage armed sloop and Nova Scotia armed schooner, to proceed with the utmost expedition into that river; that Major-general Massey ordered some of the Highland regiment to embark on board the Mermaid; that he also ordered the Vulture sloop and Hope schooner from the bason of Minas and Annapolis, to join Captain Hawker; and that a detachment was likewise sent from Fort Cumberland, under Brigadier-major Stedholm, who was to command all the troops on this service. That Captain Hawker arriving off St. John's-Road on the 27th, found the Vulture in that river, and was informed by Captain Feattus, that the rebels had taken possession of the town, and had fired on his boats, and wounded six of his men on their attempting to land. That when the Mermaid anchored in the road, the rebels quitted the town, and posted themselves in the woods, round the harbour; that neither the Hope, nor any of the armed vessels with the troops from Fort Cumberland were arrived; but that Captain Hawker, nevertheless thinking he had a sufficient force to attack the rebels, made a disposition accordingly; that Major Stedholm critically arriving, took the command of the detachment upon their landing, and marched them into the woods,

dividing his party so well, and giving so brisk a fire, that the rebels were soon put to flight; and being better acquainted with the country than the King's troops, made their escape by gaining the whale-boats, and pushed up the river above the falls. The loss on either side was very inconsiderable.

———————

Distribution of the British Forces under the command of Sir WILLIAM HOWE, *K. B.*

Head Quarters, Amboy, June 23, 1777.

The army to be brigaded, and to embark in the following manner:

British,—General Sir William Howe, Lieutenant - general Earl Cornwallis.

2 Battalions of Light Infantry.—— Lieut. Colonel Abercrombie and Major Craig; Major Maitland and Major Straubenzie.

2 Battalions of Grenadiers,——Lieut. Col. Medows and Major Mitchell; Lieut. Colonel Monckton and Major Gardiner.

Brigade of Guards, 1st and 2d Battalion,——Brigadier-general Matthew.

1st Brigade,—No Officer appointed, 4th, 23d, 28th, and 49th regiments.

2d Ditto,——Major-general Grant, 5th, 10th, 27th, 40th, and 55th reg.

3d Ditto,——Major-general Gray, 15th, 42d, 2 battalions, 44th, and 17th regiments.

4th Ditto,—Brigadier-general Agnew, 33d, 37th, 46th, and 64th regiments.

5th Ditto,—Brigadier-general Leslie, 71st, 3 battalions.

16th Light Dragoons.

Hessians.——Lieut. General Kniphausen.

Hessian and Anspach Chasseurs,—— Colonel Donop.

Mungerode,——Lengerkin and Linsign's Battalions of Grenadiers.— Major-general Scirn.

Du

Du Corps,—Merbach, Donop, and Loofe's Battalions.
1ft Battalion of Anfpach.
On York-Ifland and King's-Bridge.
Lieut. General Sir Henry Clinton.
At King's-Bridge.
Major-general Vaughan.
7th, 26th, 35th, and 63d regiments of foot, 17th light dragoons.
Heffians.—Major-general Schmidt.
Prince Carl, Srein, Trimbach, Weffenback, and Kolher's grenadiers.
Major-general Tryon, three battalions of Provincials.
At New-York. Major-general Jones.
38th and 45th regiments, and a Heffian regiment, Prince Hereditaire.
Staten-Ifland.
Brigadier-general Campbell.
52d regiment, Waldeck's regiment, and two battalions of Anfpach.
Paulus Hook. 57th regiment.
Long-Ifland.
A battalion of Provincials,
At Rhode-Ifland.
Major-general Pigot and Brigadier-general Smith.
22d, 43d, and 54th regiments.
Heffians.—Colonel Loiberg,
Ditforth, Huzze, Bunaw, and Wittginaw.

New-York, July 21.
Copy of a letter fent by a Flag of Truce, from J. VERNUM, *Brigadier-general in the rebel army, to Colonel* LOSSBERG, *Commanding Officer of the Heffian troops at Rhode-Ifland, dated Head Quarters, Tiverton.*

" Sir,

" The afcendancy of vice, the controul of paffions alone, have rendered war neceffary and lawful. It cannot precede an actual tyranny and a refufal of reparation which fuppofed a demand. Reprifals are frequently attended with declarations and confequential hoftilities. The caufe of humanity, the importance of civil focieties, make thefe pre-requifites fo much efteemed by the law of Na-

ture. Religion, in its matchlefs evangelick difplay, excites us to an univerfal philanthropy, and confequently not to levy war but from neceffity. Have thefe or fimilar meafures been adopted by the Prince of Heffe Caffel, in fending his troops to America? What compaction, what tie, what breach of faith, what injury, what national caufe relative to Heffe Caffel and America, anteceded your ravages in the country? Two countries, two territories, kingdoms or ftates, not united by political ftipulations, are like two individuals in a ftate of nature, equally independent. The firft violation amounts to murder, robbery, or plunder. By every reafon, by every law, you are entitled to vindictive juftice, but the plenitude of American pity, tendernefs, and mercy, has caufed your deluded troops, captives in our poffeffion, to tafte thofe fweets of freedom to which before they were perfect ftrangers. The man who nobly fights in the caufe of his country, in defence of his violated laws and liberties, while he feels the approbation of an honeft man, while he enjoys the praifes of all the virtuous and brave; he anticipates the joys of Heaven, preluded by the rectitude of his mind. But the man who fights for gain (a fordid mercenary) what is he? Why do Heffians contend with Americans? By Nature they are brethren, the offspring of one univerfal Parent, bound by the univerfal laws of God to mutual benevolence. The glittering coin of Britain, or her dark intrigues, has interpofed. The confequence you know. You are ftrangers to your brethren here, except a daftard few, they love you, and wifh you well. Thefe few may join with Britain. You call us rebels. Did ever America rebel againft the laws of Heffe Caffel? A general breach of laws conftitutes rebellion. Think again, and change ye the epithet. Could you know the caufe, the man-

L l   ners,

ners, the religion, and the injuries of America, you would add your numbers to her virtuous sons, and live in peace and plenty. I am, Sir, your most obedient and humble servant,

J. VARNUM.

To the Heffian Officer first in Rank, Rhode-Island.

By his Excellency Sir WILLIAM HOWE, *Knight of the Most Honourable Order of the Bath, General and Commander in Chief, &c. &c. &c.*

PROCLAMATION.

Whereas many veffels have arrived, and are daily arriving in this port, with cargoes of different kinds for the ufe of his Majefty's forces, under my command, and for the ufe of the inhabitants of fuch parts of the province of New-York as are or may be under the protection of his Majefty's forces; in order that the importers may not fuffer by the detention of fuch cargoes on board fhips, as well as to prevent any part thereof from being clandeftinely conveyed to the rebels: I have thought fit to iffue this Proclamation, appointing Andrew Elliot, Efq. to be Superintendant of all imports and exports to and from the Ifland of New-York, Long-Ifland, and Staten-Ifland, (tranfports, victuallers, and prizes excepted): hereby ordering and commanding all mafters of merchant fhips, immediately on their arrival, to make entry of the veffels, and deliver in proper manifefts of their cargoes, on oath, at the Superintendant's office; and any goods found on board, not inferted in the faid manifefts, fhall be feized and forfeited; and if any mafter of a veffel, arriving in this port or its dependencies, as aforefaid, fhall break bulk, or fuffer the fame to be done, before he has obtained a permiffion in writing from the Superintendant or his deputy, any part of the cargo fo landed fnall be feized and forfeited, and the mafter liable to imprifon-

ment; and all rum, fpirits, fugar, molaffes, and falt imported, are to be ftored at the expence of the owners or importers, in warehoufes by them to be provided, under the infpection of the faid Superintendant or his officers, with whom the keys are to be lodged, who will grant permiffions when the fame or any part thereof is fold for the ufe of the army, navy, or inhabitants, fuch permiffion always fpecifying the quantity, and to whom the fame is difpofed.

And I do further order and direct, that no goods or merchandize whatever fhall be laden on board any fhip or veffel (fuch as are in his Majefty's fervice excepted) until permiffion in writing is firft obtained from the Superintendant's office, fpecifying the quantity and quality of the goods fo intended to be laden, with the veffel and mafter's name, and where bound; and all goods and merchandize found on board any fhip or veffel for which permiffion has not been obtained, fhall be feized and forfeited, together with the veffel, and the mafter liable to imprifonment.

And I do further order, that no fhip or veffel (fuch as are in his Majefty's fervice excepted) fhall leave this port or its dependencies, until the mafter fhall deliver in at the Superintendant's office a manifeft on oath, fpecifying the quantity and quality of the goods, and by whom fhipped, together with the permiffions granted for the loading of the veffels, as above directed; and if it fhall appear to the Superintendant or his deputies, that no fraud has been committed, and the intention of this Proclamation is fully complied with, he is hereby directed to grant a certificate of the fame, annexed to a certified copy of fuch manifeft, with permiffion to leave the port; and any veffel leaving this port (except as above excepted) without having firft complied with the directions herein before contained, fhall be forfeited, together with

with the cargo on board, and the master liable to imprisonment; neither are vessels in ballast to depart the port without permission from the Superintendant, as aforesaid.

And in order that the inhabitants of Long-Island and Staten-Island may be furnished with necessaries, and at the same time to prevent supplies being conveyed to the rebels through those channels, I do further direct that no vessel or small craft whatever shall carry from the Island of New-York to Long-Island or Staten-Island, at one time, without permission from the Superintendant's office, any larger quantities of rum, spirits, sugar, or molasses, than one barrel of each, and of salt four bushels, nor of any other kind of merchandize more than may be judged sufficient for the use of one family, under forfeiture of such vessel or small craft, together with the goods found on board, and the master or person having the direction thereof shall be liable to imprisonment.

And as a further security for obedience to the orders herein contained, and as an encouragement for others to detect those who shall presume to act contrary thereto, any person or persons who shall give information to to the Superintendant or his deputies, of any goods or merchandize shipped or imported contrary to the tenor of this Proclamation, so that the person or persons offending can be detected, such informer or informers shall be entitled to one moiety of the value arising from the sale of the goods or merchandize so forfeited.

All merchants, traders, masters of vessels and others, are hereby strictly commanded to pay due obedience to the Superintendant and his officers, in the execution of their duty, as they shall answer the contrary at their peril: and all officers civil and military, are required to aid and assist them in all cases where the same shall be found necessary.

The Superintendant, his deputy, and all persons acting under them, having their salaries appointed as a full compensation for the services required of them, no fees are to be offered on any account whatever.

Given under my hand at Head Quarters, in New-York, the 17th July, 1777. W. HOWE.
By his Excellency's command,
ROBERT MACKENZIE, Secretary.

Philadelphia, June 12.
We hear that upwards of three hundred Tories, belonging to General Delancey's brigade at Fort Independence, have deserted, and joined General Putnam's army, near Peek's-kill. Their leader was the Rev. Mr. Sayre, an Episcopal Minister, well known formerly for his attachment to the English Government; but severity of duty, scarcity of provisions, and ill treatment in other respects, were the reasons of their deserting; and from their miserable appearance, being greatly emaciated, and almost destitute of cloathing, there is no room to doubt of the veracity of what the poor devils now assert, and that they have, in some measure, done penance for their misconduct and credulity.

Philadelphia, June 16, 1777.
Letter from General ARNOLD to General MIFFLIN.
Corell's Ferry, June 15, 1777; Eleven o'clock at night.
" Dear General,
" I have received no intelligence from General Washington since four o'clock last evening, at which time the enemy were encamped at Somerset Court-house, supposed to be seven thousand in number, under command of General Howe and Cornwallis. This is doubtless their main body. Their first design seems to have been to cut off General Sullivan's retreat, and possess themselves of this place. Finding General Sullivan had frustrated their intentions by a forced

march,

march, they appeared to have given over their first defign, and now wifh to draw Gen. Wafhington from his ftrong hold; which, if they effect, probably a body from Brunfwick will take poffeffion of it. General Wafhington will doubtlefs difappoint them, as he remains quiet in his encampment. The militia turns out in great numbers in the Jerfeys. Gen. Sullivan is gone to Fleming-town, twelve miles from this. The troops that arrive here are immediately fent after him. I am very fearful the enemy will retire to Brunfwick before you arrive with your reinforcements, and oblige us to attack them at a difadvantage; for fight them we muft, when all our reinforcements are in, we cannot avoid it with honour. Our men are in high fpirits, and in four days we fhall have upwards of twenty thoufand. General Putnam has eight thoufand with him. General Wafhington has wrote three days fince for four thoufand to be fent immediately to him. I expect every minute to hear from our army and the enemy. Every intelligence of confequence fhall be forwarded to you directly. I am, &c.

B. Arnold.

Major General Mifflin.

Laft night arrived an exprefs from the Jerfeys, by which we learn, that the enemy were in motion at one o'clock, on yefterday morning, but which way was not known. That General Sullivan was hourly receiving reinforcements from the Jerfeys militia, and was within fix miles of the enemy, where he determined to make a ftand if they came that way; and that he had taken one of the enemy's light horfe, who was with a fmall party reconnoitring.

Philadelphia.

Extract of a letter from General Washington *to* Congrefs, *dated Camp at Quibble-town, June 25,* 1777.

" Sir,

" When I had the honour to ad-

drefs you laft, it was on the fubject of the enemy's retreat from Brunfwick to Amboy, and of the meafures purfued to annoy them. At the time of writing, the information I had received refpecting their lofs was rather vague and uncertain; but we have reafon to believe, from intelligence through various channels fince, that it was pretty confiderable, and fell chiefly on the grenadiers and light infantry, who formed their covering party. The inclofed copy of a letter correfponds with other accounts on this head, and with the declarations of fome deferters. Some of the accounts are, that officers were heard to fay, they had not fuffered fo feverely fince the affair at Prince-town.

" After the evacuation of Brunfwick, I determined, with the advice of my general officers, to move the whole army next morning to this poft, where they would be nearer the enemy, and might act according to circumftances. In this I was prevented by rain, and they only moved yefterday morning.

" It is much to be regretted, that an exprefs fent off to Gen. Maxwell on Saturday night, to inform him of Gen. Green's movements towards Brunfwick, that he might conduct himfelf accordingly, did not reach him. Whether the exprefs went defignedly to the enemy, or was taken, is not known, but there is reafon to believe he fell into their hands. If Gen. Maxwell had received the order, there is no doubt but their whole rear guard would have been cut off. This the enemy confeffed themfelves, as we are well informed by perfons in Bonham-town.

" By a reconnoitring party juft returned, it is reported as a matter of doubt whether any of the enemy have removed from Amboy; though it is almoft certain they have tranfported a great deal of their baggage.

I have the honour to be, &c.

G. Washington."

" May

"May it pleafe your Excellency,

"I have thought proper to trouble your Excellency with the following intelligence, received by three different ways, that the greatest part of the fleet, from New-York harbour, has removed to the Watering Place and Princes Bay, where the baggage and troops, paffing from the Jerfeys, are conftantly embarking—that the tranfport at New-York, cut down for a floating battery, has twentyfix 24 and 18 pounders, and lies off the grand battery in the river; another, which they have been fitting for the fame purpofe, is neglected and unfinifhed. Gen. Howe arrived at New-York on Sunday afternoon, the whole of which day they were employed in removing the wounded foldiers from the docks to the hofpitals there, faid to amount to five hundred men. Col. Campbell, of the 57th regiment of Britifh troops, garrifons New-York, with the affiftance of the inhabitants, fifty of whom are obliged to do duty every day,

I am, &c."

Publifhed by order of Congrefs,
CHARLES THOMSON, Secretary.
Philadelphia, July 3.

Copy of a letter from Gen. WASHINGTON *to Congrefs, dated Camp at Middle-Brook, June 28, 1777.*

"Sir,

"On Thurfday morning Gen. Howe advanced with his whole army, in feveral columns, from Amboy, as far as Weftfield. We are certainly informed, that the troops fent to Staten-Ifland returned the preceding evening, and, it is faid, with an augmentation of marines—fo that carrying them there was a feint; with intention to deceive us. His defign, in this fudden movement, was either to bring on a general engagement upon difadvantageous terms, confidering matters in any point of view, or to cut off our parties, and Lord Stirling's divifion, which was fent down to them, or to poffefs himfelf of the heights and paffes in the mountains on our left. The two laft feemed to be the firft objects of his attention, as his march was rapid againft thefe parties, and indicated a ftrong difpofition to gain thofe paffes. In this fituation of affairs, it was thought abfolutely neceffary that we fhould move our force from the low ground to occupy the heights before them, which was effected. As they advanced they fell in with fome of our light parties, and part of Lord Stirling's divifion, with which they had fome pretty fmart fkirmifhing, with but very little lofs, I believe, on our fide, except in three field pieces, which unfortunately fell into the enemy's hands; but not having obtained returns yet, I cannot determine with certainty, nor can we afcertain what the enemy's lofs was. As foon as we had gained the paffes, I detached a body of light troops, under Brigadier-general Scott, to hang on their flank, and to watch their motions, and ordered Morgan's corps of riflemen to join him fince. The enemy remained at Weftfield till yefterday afternoon; when about three o'clock they moved towards Spank-town, with our light troops in their rear and purfuing. The enemy have plundered all before them, and, it is faid, burnt fome houfes. I have the honour to be, &c.

G. WASHINGTON."

Extract of a letter from the fame to Congrefs, dated Head Quarters, Middle-Brook, June 29, 1777, nine o'clock, P. M.

"Sir,

"I have not been able to afcertain yet, with any degree of precifion, the lofs fuftained by the enemy in the feveral fkirmifhes on Thurfday, though we have many reafons to believe was much more confiderable than what it was apprehended to be when I had the honour of addreffing you on the fubject.

"As to our lofs, I am affured by Lord Stirling, that it was trifling; and

and by such deserters as have come in, that they saw but very few prisoners taken. It would have been certainly known before this—(that is the number not yet returned) had not some of the parties, and I believe the most which were then out joined the corps since detached.

I have the honour to be, &c.

G. Washington."

June 30. P. S. The prisoners taken by us were thirteen, two of which are light dragoons, the rest infantry.

G. Washington.

Published by order of Congress,

Charles Thomson, Secretary.

Williamsburgh, July 18.

His Excellency the Governor received the following dispatches yesterday afternoon from Congress, which arrived in Philadelphia just as the post was setting out.

Copy of a letter from General Washington *to Congress.*

Head Quarters, Morristown, July 7.

"Sir,

"I was this morning honoured with your's. No change has taken place in the situation of the enemy upon Staten-Island, since I wrote to you on the 5th, but I have this morning received an account from Elizabeth-town, which mentions, that a person just come from the island, who informs, that small craft are constantly plying between New-York and the fleet, laden with officers baggage, and stores put up in packages, and marked with their names and regiments, and that transports are fitted up with stalls over their main decks, for their reception. *This looks as if a longer voyage was intended than up the North River. I have given notice to all the Eastern States to be upon their guard, should the fleet put to sea and steer that way; and I think the works upon Delaware should be carried on with spirit, and be completed as fast as possible, lest they should visit that quarter.* I think the Southern States should be also advised of the uncertainty of the next operation of the enemy, that they may also be making such preparations as they judge necessary.

G. Washington."

P. S. The inclosed piece of intelligence is just sent to me by General Forman, which is confirmed in several particulars by two deserters from the fleet, who left it yesterday morning. Bernard Ditchway, a deserter from the hospital ship Dutton, left her on Saturday night, 12 o'clock, 5th July, 1777. The examinant informs, that the ships that went from Prince's Bay on Tuesday and Wednesday last, had Hessian troops on board; that they now lie within the Narrows, and, as it is reported among the shipmen, they are to wait there till the remainder of the troops are embarked. That the light and draught horses were all embarked yesterday (Saturday 5th instant) on board of about 50 brigs, schooners, and sloops. That on Thursday the troops began to embark at the Watering Place, and were going on board every day; the British light infantry embarked on Saturday, That a great number of baggage-waggons, cannons, &c. &c. are put on board. The examinant farther says, that the hospital ships are filled with sick; that the present reigning disease among them is the bloody flux. That the troops appear much dejected. That he assisted to row one boat to New-York, with 52 wounded men, on Thursday the 3d of July, and that several other boats were then employed in the same way. That all the transports are come from New-York, and now lie from the point of the Narrows towards the Kills, to the amount of 300 ships, snows, &c. That no ships have, to his knowledge, gone up the North River with troops; that the common report among the sailors and soldiers is, that the fleet is going to Delaware.

Sworn to before me,

David Forman, Brig. Gen.

Freehold, July 9, 1777.

Philadelphia,

Philadelphia, July 22.

Extract of a letter from General WASHINGTON *to Congress, dated Camp at the Clove, July 16, 1777.*

" Sir,

" I beg leave to congratulate Congress on the captivity of Major-general Prescott, and one of his Aids-de-Camp. The particulars of this fortunate event you will find in the inclosed extract of a letter this minute received from General Spencer, which I presume are at large in the packet Mr. Greenleaf will deliver. Lieut. Col. Barton, with the small handful under his command, who conducted the enterprize, have great merit."

Extract of a letter from Major-general SPENCER, *dated Providence, July 11, 1777.*

" Sir,

" I have the pleasure to congratulate your Honour, and the Hon. Continental Congress, on the late success of Lieut. Col. Barton, who, with the number of forty, including Captains Adams and Philips, and a number of brave officers, last night went on Rhode-Island, and brought off Major-general Prescott, and Major William Barrington, one of his Aid-de-Camps, and the sentry at the General's door, all that were at the General's quarters. This was done with such prudence, that no alarm was given unto the enemy until our party had got near the main, on their return. They are now in this town.

" Col. Barton went with his party in four whale-boats from Warwick Neck, about ten miles by water, to the west side of the island, landed about half way from Newport to Bristol Ferry, then marched one mile to the General's quarters, returned again to Warwick, and had the good fortune to escape the discovery of the enemy's guard boats, although several ships of war lay round in those parts. Several attempts of this nature have been made without any loss on our side, and with some small success. The above named Capt. Philips, some time since, with a party of about 200, brought off one Ensign Clark of the 43d regiment, now a prisoner. Another party attacked one of the enemy's guards, dispersed them, killed three, and wounded one. We have had several deserters from the British regiments."

Published by order of Congress,

CHARLES THOMSON, Secretary.

General Lee, we have the pleasure to inform the public, is in good health and spirits, although a close prisoner on board the Centurion man of war; but the exploit of Col. Barton, in seizing and bringing off, *with so much address and gallantry,* the British Major-general Prescott, will no doubt secure his enlargement in a very short time, and restore our brave old General to the bosom of his friends.

———————

In Congress, Feb. 25th, 1777.

To the end that the most speedy stop may be put to the pernicious and unsoldierly practice of deserting, and that such offenders who receive the public money for services that they design not to perform, may be certainly and speedily carried back to the corps they have deserted from, it is earnestly recommended to the Committees of Observation or Inspection in these United States, that they cause diligent enquiries to be made in their respective counties or districts, for all deserters that may be lurking and harboured therein, and cause such whenever found to be immediately secured and conveyed to the nearest Continental Officer, and all such Officers are hereby directed to receive and secure such deserters, that they may be safely delivered to their respective regiments, and brought to a speedy trial and exemplary punishment; and farther to pay to the persons delivering such deserters, ferters, eight dollars for each deferter fo brought and delivered, and twelve ninetieths of a dollar, in lieu of expences for every mile from the place where the deferter was taken up, to the place where he is delivered to the Officer.

ARTICLES of WAR. Section VI.

ART. 1. All officers and foldiers, who having received pay, or having been duly inlifted in the fervice of the United States, fhall be convicted of having deferted the fame, fhall fuffer death, or fuch other punifhment as by a Court Martial fhall be inflicted.

ART. 2. Any non-commiffioned officer or foldier, who fhall, without leave from his Commanding Officer, abfent himfelf from his troop or company, or from any detachment with which he fhall be commanded, fhall, upon being convicted thereof, be punifhed according to the nature of his offence, at the difcretion of a Court-Martial.

ART. 3. No non-commiffioned officer or foldier fhall inlift himfelf in any other regiment, troop or company, without a regular difcharge from the regiment, troop or company, in which he laft ferved, on the penalty of being reputed a deferter, and fuffering accordingly: and in cafe any officer fhall knowingly receive and entertain fuch non-commiffioned officer or foldier, or fhall not, after his being difcovered to be a deferter, immediately confine him, and give notice thereof to the corps in which he laft ferved, he, the faid officer fo offending, fhall by a Court-Martial be cafhiered.

Ordered, That the foregoing refolve, and the three Articles of War, be publifhed in the feveral news-papers for fix months, and the feveral printers are hereby requefted to publifh them accordingly.

JOHN HANCOCK, Prefident.

Philadelphia, April 22.

The Supreme Executive Council has appointed John Armftrong, John Cadwallader, James Potter, and Samuel Meredith, Efquires, Brigadier-Generals of the Militia of this State.

In Congrefs, April 9, 1777.

Refolved, That the Pay-mafter, and the Deputy Pay-mafters-general, be directed forthwith to confult the Commander in Chief of their refpective diftricts, and appoint deputies to repair to fuch pofts and places of rendezvous, and anfwer the draughts of fuch officers ftationed thereat, as the faid Commanders in Chief fhall refpectively direct; that the deputies be fupplied with money by the refpective Pay-mafters and Deputy Pay-mafters-general, and account with them therefore; and that all other Pay-mafters of the army ceafe to act at the pofts and places provided with deputies as aforefaid.

April 10. Refolved, That the Commanders in Chief of the feveral departments, previous to the difcharge of any regiment or corps of militia reinforcing the army, be refpectively directed to iffue their warrants on the Pay-mafter and Deputy Pay-mafter-general, for the amount of the pay due to the fame; and, when the military cheft is unfupplied, the Pay-mafter or Deputy Pay-mafter-general is authorized to draw on the Prefident for the amount of fuch warrants.

Extract from the Minutes.

Publifhed by Order of Congrefs,

CHARLES THOMSON, Sec.

In Congrefs, April 14, 1777.

Whereas the State of Pennfylvania is threatened with an immediate invafion; and, from the adjournment of the Legiflative and Executive Authorities of the Commonwealth, it is impracticable to carry into immediate execution many meafures of the utmoft importance, not only to the fafety of this Commonwealth, but likewife

wife to the general welfare of the United States.

Refolved, That it is the indifpenf able duty of Congrefs to watch over all matters, (the neglect of which may, in its confequences, deeply af-fect the welfare of the United States) till fuch time as the Legiflative and Executive Authorities of the Com-monwealth of Pennfylvania, can re-fume the regular exercife of their dif-ferent functions.

Refolved, That his Excellency the Prefident of the Supreme Executive Council of the Commonwealth of Pennfylvania, be requefted forthwith to convene the Legiflative and Exe-cutive Authorities of this State, in order that proper meafures may be purfued for the defence of the fame.

Refolved, That a Committee of three be appointed to confer with the Prefident of the Supreme Executive Council, with fuch other Members of the faid Council as can be con-vened with the Board of War for the State of Pennfylvania, and with the Delegates of the faid State in Con-grefs, concerning the mode of autho-rity which they fhall conceive moft eligible to be exercifed during the re-cefs of the Houfe of Affembly, and the Council, in order, that if the fame be approved by Congrefs, may be immediately adopted.

The Members chofen, Mr. S. A-dams, Mr. Duer, and Mr. R. H. Lee.

Extract from the Minutes,
CHARLES THOMSON, Sec.

In Congrefs, April 15, 1777.

The Committee appointed by Con-grefs on the 14th day of April, to confer with the Prefident and Mem-bers of the Supreme Executive Coun-cil of the Commonwealth of Pennfyl-vania, the Board of War of faid State, and the Delegates reprefenting the fame in Congrefs, concerning the authority which fhould be deemed eligible to be exercifed during the re-

cefs of the Council and Affembly, re-port,

That a conference, agreeable to the order of Congrefs, has been held, when the following Gentlemen were prefent:

His Excellency Thomas Wharton, jun. Efquire, Prefident of the Su-preme Executive Council.

Board of War. Owen Biddle, Efq. Chairman, Jofeph Dean, Richard Bache, John Shee.

Delegates for the State of Pennfyl-vania in Congrefs. Robert Morris, James Wilfon, Daniel Roberdeau, George Clymer, Efquires.

Committee of Congrefs. Mr. Sa-muel Adams, Mr. Richard H. Lee, Mr. Duer.

That it appears clearly to the Members in conference, that the Exe-cutive Authority of the Common-wealth of Pennfylvania is incapable of any exertion, adequate to the pre-fent crifis, and that it is of the greateft importance, that every power fhould be called forth into action, which may conduce to the fafety of this State, with which the liberties and profpe-rity of the whole are fo intimately connected. From this confideration, and at the particular inftance and re-queft of the Prefident of the Supreme Executive Council and Board of War of the State of Pennfylvania, they beg leave to recommend the following refolutions to be adopted by Con-grefs:

Refolved, That the Prefident of the Supreme Executive Council of the Commonwealth of Pennfylvania, to-gether with as many Members of faid Council as can be convened, the Board of War, and (in fuch cafes as relate to the marine) the Navy Board of faid State, fhould, in the prefent critical exigency of affairs, exercife every authority to promote the fafety of the State, till fuch time as the Le-giflative and Executive Authorities of the Commonwealth of Pennfylvania can be convened.

M m

Refolved,

Resolved, That it be, and it is hereby earnestly recommended by Congress, to the good people of Pennsylvania, chearfully to submit to the exertion of an authority which is indispensably essential to the preservation of the lives, liberties, and property of themselves, their families, and posterity.

Resolved, That the Commanding Officer of the Continental Forces in this city, afford every possible assistance in carrying into execution all such measures as may be recommended to him by the authority above-mentioned.

Resolved, That Congress will chearfully co-operate with the authority above-mentioned, in facilitating every measure which may be deemed conducive to the safety of the State

Congress taking into consideration the foregoing report,

Resolved, That the same be concurred in, and that the resolutions proposed be agreed to.

Extract from the Minutes,
CHARLES THOMSON, Sec.

In Congress, April 14, 1777.

Resolved, That from and after the publication hereof, the second article of the 8th section, the first article of the 11th section, the eight article of the 14th section, and the second article of the 18th section, of the Rules and Articles for the better Government of the Troops raised, or to be raised, and kept in pay by, and at the expence of the United States of America, passed in Congress, the 20th day of September, One thousand seven hundred and seventy-six, shall be, and they are hereby repealed, and that the four following articles be substituted in the place and stead thereof:

ART. I. All officers and soldiers shall have full liberty to bring into any of the forts or garrisons of the United American States, any quantity of eatable provisions, except where any contracts are, or shall be entered into by Congress, or by their order, for furnishing such provisions, and with respect only to the species of provisions so contracted for.

ART. II. If any Officer shall think himself to be wronged by his Colonel or the Commanding Officer of the regiment, and shall, upon due application made to him, be refused to be redressed, he may complain to the Continental General, commanding in the State where such regiment shall be stationed, in order to obtain justice, who is hereby required to examine into the said complaint, and take proper measures for redressing the wrong complained of, and transmit as soon as possible to Congress, a true state of such complaint, with the proceedings had thereon.

ART. III. No sentence of a General Court-martial shall be put in execution, till after a report shall be made of the whole proceedings to Congress, the Commander in Chief, or the Continental General commanding in the State where such a General Court-martial shall be held, and their, or his orders, be issued for carrying such sentence into execution.

ART. IV. The Continental General commanding in either of the American States for the time being, shall have full power of appointing General Courts-martial to be held, and of pardoning or mitigating any of the punishments ordered to be inflicted for any of the offences mentioned in the afore-mentioned Rules and Articles for the better Government of the Troops, except the punishment of offenders under sentence of death by a General Court-martial, which he may order to be suspended, until the pleasure of Congress can be known; which suspension, with the proceedings of the Court-martial, the said General shall immediately transmit to Congress for their determination. And every offender convicted by any regimental Court-martial may be pardoned, or have his punishment mitigated by the
Colonel

Colonel or Officer commanding the regiment.

By Order of Congress,

JOHN HANCOCK, President.

In Congress, April 14, 1777.

Refolved, That it be recommended to the Executive Powers of each of the United States, to enquire into the conduct of all officers on the recruiting fervice, within them refpectively, to remove all fuch as belong to the battalions of their refpective quotas, who have neglected their duty, or abufed the truft repofed in them, and fhall be found within their refpective jurifdiction, and to fill up all vacancies which may happen by fuch removals; to tranfmit to Congrefs all fuch teftimony as fhall be taken againft any officer or officers who may have marched or removed from the State to whofe battalions he or they belong, and againft any officer or officers belonging to the quota of another State, who may have been guilty of neglect or mifbehaviour in the State where the enquiry fhall be made.

That it be recommended to the faid Executive Powers to procure exact returns of the Continental troops in each, and tranfmit the fame to Congrefs without delay. And all officers and foldiers of the Continental army are hereby required to pay the ftricteft regard to the orders of the Executive Powers of the feveral States, touching the aforefaid premifes.

Refolved, That it be recommended to the Legiflatures of each of the United States to enact laws exempting from actual fervice any two of the militia, who fhall, within the time limited by fuch laws, furnifh one able-bodied recruit, to ferve in any battalion of the Continental army, for the term of three years, or during the prefent war. — Such exemption to continue during the term for which the recruit fhall inlift, and every fuch recruit to be entitled to the Continental bounty, and other allowances.

That it be recommended to the Legiflatures aforefaid refpectively, to enact laws compelling all fuch perfons as are by laws exempted from bearing arms or performing militia duties, other than fuch as are fpecified in the foregoing refolve, to furnifh fuch number of able-bodied foldiers as the faid Legiflatures refpectively fhall deem a proper equivalent for fuch exemptions, fuch foldiers to be entitled to the Continental bounty and other allowances, over and above fuch gratuities as they may receive from thofe who procure them to inlift.

Alfo to permit the inlifting of fervants and apprentices, and to prohibit the imprifoning or otherwife reftraining the perfons of foldiers in the Continental fervice for any debt not exceeding fifty dollars.

And whereas it is of the greateft moment to the caufe of American Freedom, that an army of confiderable ftrength take the field early the enfuing campaign;

Refolved, That if the feveral quotas of the States cannot be furnifhed by any of the means recommended in the foregoing refolutions, or any other means by the faid Legiflatures devifed, before the fifteenth day of May next, it is recommended to each State to caufe indifcriminate draughts to be made from their refpective militia.

That it be recommended to the faid Legiflatures to apply all the means by thefe refolutions recommended in the manner which they fhall judge moft effectual for fpeedily compleating the army, and in cafe they fhall prove unfuccefsful that they caufe the draughts aforefaid to be made.

Refolved, That the Executive Power of each State to be authorized and impowered to order fuch officers as they fhall judge proper from the refpective battalions and companies of their refpective quotas, to remain within the State, for the purpofe of aiding in inlifting and collecting the recruits which may be furnifhed under

the

the above recommended regulations, and to convey the fame to the battalions and companies to which they shall belong, such officers to be under the direction of such Executive Powers respectively.

By Order of Congress,

JOHN HANCOCK, President.

PENNSYLVANIA WAR-OFFICE.
Philadelphia, April 17, 1777.
Resolved,

1. That a Committee of fifty be appointed to have the direction and superintendance of the removal of all the provisions and other stores, now in this city, or near the river Delaware in this State, below the Falls of Trenton, that will be useful to our enemies, should they get possession of them, or that may be necessary to the army of the United States.

2. That the inhabitants of this city or liberties, be allowed to retain as much provisions of all kinds as is usual and customary for families to be possessed of at this season, it being the intention of this Board to remove the extraordinary stores only, of those who have been returned, as having greater quantities than is usually laid up by families of similar circumstances in common times.

3. That all provisions, the property of private persons, so returned to this Board, over and above what is customary as aforesaid, be removed into the country, to such place or places as this Board may direct.

4. That the said Committee be empowered to appoint one or more Commissary or Commissaries, to take charge of such provisions or stores as the said Committee are empowered to remove, who are to be paid a reasonable allowance for their services.

5. That the said Committee of fifty be fully authorized and empowered to take all the said provisions, over and above the customary quantities at this season, and deliver it into the hands of their Commissaries, for which

the said Commissaries are to give receipts, specifying the kinds and quantity to the respective owners, and for which the said Commissaries shall be accountable.

6. That the said Committee of Fifty be authorized to take possession of all tanned and dressed leather, bar-iron, &c. &c. the Commissaries giving receipts to the owners for the same as aforesaid, which they shall have removed to such place or places as aforesaid.

7. That the said Committee may on application, if they think proper, deliver any quantity of the said provisions, &c. to the respective owners, they giving receipts for the same, provided it be not intended to expose them to the enemy, or will eventually put them in their power.

8. That if the Committee of Fifty have just reasons to suspect that any provision or stores as aforesaid shall be concealed, they are hereby authorized and impowered to take every necessary means for discovering and taking possession of the same.

9. That the necessary waggons be supplied by the Quarter-master General, to whom the Committee are directed to apply.

10. That the Commanding Officer be applied to for a party of men, when necessary, to assist the said Committee, or such discreet person or persons as they may appoint to search the houses and stores of such of the inhabitants as have, or may refuse to submit to the resolves of the Honourable Congress, and this Board, in not making report of their stock of provisions when called upon, or have made, or may make a false report thereof: and that the said Committee be requested immediately to order diligent search to be made accordingly.

11. That Messieurs William Tharp, Alexander Fullerton, John Galloway, John M'Calla, Robert Knox, George Goodwin, William M'Mullin, William Drewry, Thomas Irwin, Charles Massey,

Maffey, Joseph Grafeberry, Ephraim Bonham, Charles W. Peale, Lawrence Birnie, John Young, Jacob Schriener, Andrew Guyer, Jacob Godfhall, Ifaac Roufh, Samuel Griff, William Heyfham, Mofes Bartram, Robert Smith, Samuel Simpfon, John Pollard, William Olephant, Jacob Bright, Samuel Taylor, John Hall, Benjamin Armitage, Samuel M'Clane, Richard Sewell, George Claypoole, Edward Evans, John Snowden, Nathaniel Donnell, John M'Culloch, James Montgomery, John Donaldfon, Thomas Leech, Charles Rifk, Thomas Bradford, Jehu Eyres, James Longhead, Jofeph Copperthwaite, John Williams, John Barnhill, John Lifle, Lambert Wilmer, and Adam Foulk, be the faid Committee, who are to divide themfelves for particular diftricts, or to act altogether in conjunction, as they may think proper.

12. That if any perfon or perfons think themfelves aggrieved by the faid Committee in the premifes, fhall have a right of an appeal to this Board in writing.

By order of the Board,

OWEN BIDDLE, Chairman.

PENNSYLVANIA WAR-OFFICE.

Philadelphia, April 19, 1777.

Whereas this Board have thought it neceffary to give orders for the removal of fuch provifions and other ftores out of this city as may not be immediately neceffary for the fubfiftence of the inhabitants; and this Board being informed that quantities of flour are daily brought into this city for fale, which greatly defeats the purpofes of the above meafure.

Refolved, That no flour in barrels fhall be fuffered to be brought into this city until further orders from this Board, and fhould any be brought in, the owners thereof fhall be immediately required and directed to carry it out again at their own expence, unlefs it fully appears to the Com-

mittee of Fifty, that they knew nothing of the orders of this Board for the removal of ftores and provifions.

By order of the Board,

OWEN BIDDLE, Chairman.

CONTINENTAL NAVY-BOARD.

Philadelphia, April 21, 1777.

All furgeons and warrant officers in or near this city, belonging to the navy of the United States, and not in actual fervice, are hereby directed to give perfonal attendance at the Continental Navy-Board, every Monday and Thurfday, between the hours of ten and one in the forenoon, to receive the orders of the faid Board.

JOHN NIXON,

FRANCIS HOPKINSON,

JOHN WHARTON.

Notice is hereby given, That the Lieutenant of Philadelphia has divided the city into the four following diftricts:

1. Mulberry Ward.

2. Upper Delaware, Lower Delaware, High ftreet, and North Wards.

3. Cheftnut, Walnut, Middle, and South Wards.

4. Dock Ward.

In purfuance of an Act of the General Affembly of the Commonwealth of Pennfylvania, entituled "An Act to regulate the Militia, &c." I hereby require all the male white inhabitants between the ages of eighteen and fifty-three years, capable of bearing arms, refiding in the diftrict of Mulberry Ward, to meet at Leonard Melchard's tavern, in Second-ftreet, on Wednefday next.

And all male white inhabitants, between the ages aforefaid, refiding in the diftrict of Upper Delaware, Lower Delaware, High-ftreet, and North Wards, to meet on the fame day, at Ifrael Jacobs's, at the fign of the Bunch of Grapes, in Third-ftreet.

And all the male white inhabitants, between the ages aforefaid, refiding in the diftrict of Cheftnut, Walnut,

and

and South Wards, to meet on Thursday next, at the sign of the Indian Queen, in Fourth-street.

And all the male white inhabitants, between the ages aforesaid, residing in Dock Ward, to meet also on Thursday, at James Alexander's tavern, near the draw-bridge.—Respectively to elect by ballot, between the hours of ten in the morning and six in the afternoon, on the days above-mentioned, three Field Officers, (that is to say, one Colonel, one Lieutenant-colonel, and one Major) each of whom shall be a freeholder.—It is expected that the citizens will be punctual in their attendance, as the choice of Field Officers is of the greatest importance at this critical juncture.

GEORGE HENRY, Lieutenant of the city of Philadelphia.
Philadelphia, April 18, 1777.

PENNSYLVANIA WAR-OFFICE.
Philadelphia, May 1, 1777.

I Abraham Chovet do pledge my faith and sacred honour, that I will not say, do, or cause to be said or done, any thing that may injure the welfare of the United Independent States of America, by holding any correspondence with the enemies thereof, or those in any way opposing the measures entered into by them in defence of their liberty, or that may in any wise be construed so to be. In testimony whereof I have hereunto set my hand, the day and year above written.   ABRA. CHOVET.

I do solemnly swear, that I will bear true allegiance to the United Independent States of America. That I will not directly nor indirectly hold any treasonable correspondence with the enemies thereof, nor with any person acting under the authority of the King of Great-Britain, and that I will not promote or be concerned in any plot or conspiracy against the Independency of the said United States, nor be privy to any plot or conspiracy without giving notice thereof immediately to proper authority now established in this State, but in all things behave myself as a peaceable and dutiful subject of these States.

WILLIAM D. SMITH.
Sworn the 26th April, 1777, before me, JAMES YOUNG, one of the Justices, &c.

I do solemnly swear, that I will bear true allegiance to the United Independent States of America, that I will not directly nor indirectly hold any treasonable correspondence with the enemies thereof, nor with any person whatever, acting under the authority of the King of Great-Britain, and that I will not promote or be concerned in any plot or conspiracy against the Independency of the said United States, nor be privy to any plot or conspiracy, without giving notice thereof immediately to proper authority, now established in this State, but in all things behave myself as a peaceable and dutiful subject of these States.   CHARLES STEDMAN, jun.
Sworn the 26th April, 1777, before me JAMES YOUNG, one of the Justices, &c.

We do solemnly swear, that we will bear true allegiance to the United Independent States of America. That we will not directly nor indirectly hold any treasonable correspondence with the enemies thereof, nor with any person whatever acting under the authority of the King of Great-Britain, and that we will not promote, or be concerned in any plot or conspiracy against the Independency of the said States, nor be privy to any plot or conspiracy without giving notice thereof immediately to proper authority now established in this State, but in all things behave ourselves as peaceable and dutiful subjects of these States.

Signed   ROBERT DOVE,
        GEORGE HARRISON.
Sworn the 2d May, 1777, before me, JAMES YOUNG.
Philadelphia,

Philadelphia, May 6, 1777.

The whole reinforcement expected this summer to join the British army in America, amounts only to 10,000 Germans, and 3000 British troops, the whole of whom are raw and undisciplined. From this trifling addition, the whole force of Great-Britain in America, will not be greater this year than it was last. We have certain information, that there *are now* 40,000 *men enlisted in the American* army in the different States on the Continent, and that the recruiting service goes on more rapidly than ever. If a mixed body of men, composed of militia and regular troops, seldom exceeding in number 20,000 men fit for duty, kept Gen. Howe at bay last year, and prevented his conquering more of our country than he could defend with his ships, and occupy with his camps, what may we not expect this year with more than double that number of only regular troops, a majority of whom are well disciplined, and have seen service? O! ye of little faith! Ye timid Whigs and Tories, if ye will not trust like honest men in the goodness of our cause, nor in the many pledges which Divine Providence has given us of our future success, you may venture to put your trust in the present strength and resources of your country, which far exceed the strength and resources of our enemies in the field. Come and contribute your labours, your advice, and your wealth, towards the support of the common cause, and be assured, that you will find security for your property, liberty, and lives, in no part of the Thirteen United States, but in the power of the Congress.

The Government of New-York has imposed an oath of allegiance upon every idle, neutral, and suspected person in their State. They have obliged such persons as refuse to take it to join Gen. Howe *and have condemned several of their estates as forfeited property.* Nothing can be more just and reasonable than this. Suppose a number of people should be confined in a leaky vessel together, at a great distance from a harbour; and suppose part of them should refuse to pump, or while others were pumping, should refuse to steer, or to unfold a sail, would not they be looked upon as highly criminal, and accessary to the ruin of those who were active in saving the ship? It is exactly the same with idle, neutral, and suspected people in the present controversy. They should be compelled to do something for the States, or to join the enemy. " He that is not for us (says the Author of all truth) is against us."

Much has been said of a war between France and Great-Britain this summer. I am one of those politicians that wish it may not take place till the present campaign is over. After the experience we have acquired in the art o war; after the manufactory and importation of every thing necessary to support a war; after raising an army sufficient, if properly employed, to crush the army of Great-Britain in a month or two, and thereby to deter all the powers of Europe from making war upon us; I say after these things, shall we wish to see France step in, and by drawing off the force of Britain from this country, rob us of that glory, that prerogative of free and independent States, the power of *self-defence* which Divine Providence intends for us? Besides, should France declare war at this time in our favour, she would render us such *apparent,* essential services, that she might hereafter lay some exclusive claims upon our commerce or our liberties. A peace, or a cessation of hostilities *just now* in America, would leave us for ever in the puny condition of a seven months child. One campaign more, or two at most, will compleat our national and military character. France will not declare war against Britain till her *own* interest, reft, and not *curs*, require it. This, according to the prefent ftate of injuries and refentment, and the natural progrefs of both, between rival nations, muft inevitaly happen in a year or two.

It appears from an orderly book found with the Heffians who were taken at Trenton laft December, that the following letter was given out in the general orders of the 29th of Auguft laft, figned Van Heifter, who fays it was fent to him by General Howe.

Copy of a letter from a Gentleman of Long-Ifland to General HOWE.

" I was this morning an unwilling fpeftator of fuch outrages as I never believed could be committed in a Chriftian country. The Heffian troops have plundered this unfortunate place entirely, and without diftinction of perfons. They have driven every poor family out of their houfes, and robbed them of their property, which I believe will have the moft unhappy confequences.

" I am fure the commanding General will not permit fuch dreadful havock, and I entreat you to acquaint him with it, that we may be freed from our mifery as quickly as poffible." *Written Auguft 28, 1776.*

In confequence of the above letter, the General iffued his orders, forbidding fuch conduct in the troops under his command; but it appears from the book above-mentioned, that fimilar complaints were repeatedly made, and no effectual means taken to prevent them.

The following anecdote being a lively reprefentation of the *bleffings of Britifh Government, is* recommended to the ferious perufal of all timid, cool-hearted Americans.—On Monday the 19th of May laft, one Mr. Anderfon, a houfe carpenter, living in Chapel-ftreet, New-York, had a difference with a Tory, who infulted Mr. Anderfon as he was going home from his work, with his tools on his fhoulder, by tauntingly faying to him, " Times are changed with you— So! you are obliged to carry your axe—Where is your gun now, that you ufed to carry !" This brought on a further altercation, and at length blows enfued : upon which the Tory lodged a complaint with Gen. Pigot ; Mr. Anderfon could not be heard in his defence, but was ordered to receive 500 lafhes ; and, notwithftanding the interceffions of his wife and children, and a number of his friends, this inhuman fentence was carried into execution with the greateft rigour, againft a reputable freeholder and citizen, he fainting away twice during the execution ; after which he was put into confinement on board a man of war.

Extracts from the Journals of the Affembly of Pennfylvania.

Friday, June 13. On motion, refolved, that Mr. Parker, Col. Coats, and Mr. Whitehill, be a Committee to purchafe a coach, and prefent the fame to the Honourable Mrs. Wafhington, the worthy Lady of his Excellency General Wafhington, as a fmall teftimonial of the fenfe this Affembly have of his great and important fervices to the American States.

On motion, refolved, That it be recommended to his Excellency the Prefident and Council to iffue a Proclamation, ftrictly forbidding all recruiting officers within this State to enlift fervants or apprentices, on pain of being profecuted with the utmoft rigour of the law.

Refolved, That no perfon within this State, who is, by the militia law of this Commonwealth, obliged to do or perform any military duties, fhall be excufed or exempted from fuch duties, under pretence of his having procured a perfon to enlift in the Continental army, either for three years, or during the war.

Refolved, That this Houfe will, at their next fitting, confider the cafe
of

of those whose servants and apprentices have been already enlisted.

Saturday, June 14. The Committee appointed to purchase a coach to be presented to the Hon. Mrs. Washington, reported that they had bought a very elegant one, and, in the name of the House, had presented it to that Lady, by whom it had been politely accepted.

On motion, resolved, That the President and Council be authorized and impowered to remove, as they may think proper, all the bells belonging to the several churches, and other public buildings, as also the copper and brass, in the city, to some place of safety.

Philadelphia, May 6.
In Congress, May 3, 1777.

The Committee upon the Treasury report,

That the Commissioners for settling the accounts of the army in the Northern department have produced to the Treasury Board, among other accounts adjusted by them, a general account of the receipts and disbursements of Major-general Schuyler; and a separate account of the disposal of specie remitted to him by Congress and otherwise, for carrying on the military operations in Canada. That the last mentioned account has, at Gen. Schuyler's immediate request, been examined by the Board of Treasury, with the several vouchers: that it appears to this Board, That before Gen. Schuyler was supplied by Congress with any specie at all, he sent into Canada, for the public service, more than 3250 dollars in specie. That he sent such further sums in specie into Canada, raised on his private credit, that when the army retreated from thence, he was in advance upwards of the value of 10,000 dollars in specie above what he had been supplied with by Congress.——That to reimburse his friends, who

had lent him the said specie, he, after his retreat from Canada, drew out of the Military Chest several sums in specie, with which it was supplied after such retreat; but that he remains, upon the final settlement of the said account, in advance for the public in specie, upwards of the value of 3250 dollars more than he ever received in specie, having taken Continental money in payment thereof. That it further appears from the said account and vouchers, that none of the specie supplied to him by Congress before the retreat from Canada, remained in his hands more than two days, the same being delivered over to the Deputy Pay-master General.

Resolved, That the said report be accepted, and that the same be published. Extract from the Minutes,

CHARLES THOMSON, Secretary.

We hear from New-Jersey, that the Governor and Council of Safety of that State have recommended it to the Speaker to call their General Assembly (which stood adjourned to the 21st of May inst.) to meet at Haddenfield, on the 7th, on the urgent necessity of convening before the time appointed.

The Honourable the Congress have promoted Brigadier-general Arnold to the rank of Major-general.

In Congress, May 14, 1777.
Resolved,

I. That the Quarter-master General of the army may be authorized and impowered to appoint one Commissary of forage for the army, and one for each of the military departments thereof, with such and so many Forage-masters as he shall judge necessary.

II. That the duty of the Commissary of forage shall be to purchase such quantities of forage, and store the same in such magazines as the Quarter-master General or the Deputy Quarter-master General of any department shall, from time to time, order and direct: That the Commiffaries fhall conform themfelves in making purchafes to fuch rules and regulations as fhall be prefcribed to them by the Quarter-mafter General or Deputy Quarter-mafter General of the department to which they fhall feverally belong.

III. That all forage purchafed by any Commiffary of forage, and delivered into any magazine, fhall be received by the Forage-mafter thereunto appointed, who fhall give his receipt therefore, fpecifying the fort, quantity and quality, as a voucher for the Commiffary of forage, to be by him produced to the Quarter-mafter General, or Deputy Quartermafter General, of the department, in fupport of his account.

IV. That the Commiffaries of forage fhall make a monthly return to the Quarter-mafter General or Deputy Quarter-mafter General of the department, of all forage by them purchafed, fpecifying to what Foragemafter and in which magazine the fame was delivered, that the Foragemafter may ftand charged therewith.

V. That no Forage-mafter to whofe care any magazine of forage fhall be committed fhall iffue any part thereof, unlefs by a written order from the Commander in Chief, the Commander in Chief of the department, the Commanding Officer of the poft where fuch magazine may be eftablifhed, the Quarter-mafter General or Deputy Quarter-mafter General of the department, or one of his affiftants, the Waggon-mafter General or any other Waggon-mafter; fuch orders to fpecify for whofe ufe the forage is intended, and every fuch order to be filed by the Forage-mafter, and a regular entry thereof made in a book to be by him kept for that purpofe, as a voucher for the expenditure of the forage by him received.

VI. That the forage-mafters fhall make monthly returns to the Quarter-

mafter General and Deputy Quartermafter General of the departments they belong to, of the ftate of their magazines, fpecifying the quantity left in ftore at the firft and every fucceeding return, the quantity received fince the laft return, the expenditure fince fuch return, and what remains on hand.

VII. And whereas it frequently happens that there is a neceffity to detain hired carriages (the owners whereof were to find their own forage) far beyond the time for which the owners thereof agreed to ferve, and who, if their own forage is expended, muft have recourfe to the public magazine—It is refolved, That fuch perfons fo detained and become deftitute of forage, fhall, upon the written order of any of the officers mentioned in the fifth refolution, be fupplied out of the public magazines, and that the Waggon-mafter, before he figns the difcharge for any fuch hired carriage, fhall direct the Foragemafter to indorfe thereon the quantity, fort and quality of the forage furnifhed fuch perfon, that the fame may be deducted out of the wages due to the owner of fuch hired carriage, all of which deduction fhall, by the Quarter-mafter General or Deputy Quarter-mafter General of the department, be carried to the credit of the Forage-mafter's account, who fhall have furnifhed the forage.

VIII. That if the Commiffary of forage in any department fhould be ordered to procure fuch large quantities of forage as to render it impoffible for him to do it without affiftance, the Quarter-mafter General or Deputy Quarter-mafter General of the department, fhall direct one or more of his affiftants to aid the Commiffary of forage, pointing out the diftricts in which they are feverally to purchafe, that one may not enhance the price by bidding above another.

IX. Whereas, notwithftanding the orders

orders that have been, from time to time, iſſued by General Officers of our army to prevent the loſs and embezzlement of intrenching tools and other military ſtores, great waſte has been made; to prevent which for the future, it is reſolved, That every Commiſſary of ſtores, Store-keeper, or perſon to whoſe charge and care any military ſtores, of what kind ſoever, ſhall be committed, ſhall paſs his receipt for and ſtand charged to be accountable for the ſame, and ſhall not iſſue any of them without taking a receipt therefor, the receiver promiſing to be accountable: and if any perſon having received any ſuch ſtores ſhall loſe or embezzle the ſame, the Commiſſary, Store-keeper, or perſon by whom they were delivered, ſhall charge him with the value thereof, and tranſmit a copy of ſuch charge to the Pay-maſter General or Deputy Pay-maſter General of the department, who is to charge the ſame to the Pay-maſter of the corps ſuch perſon may belong to, unleſs it ſhall appear that ſuch loſs happened without any blameable negligence or omiſſion. And if any perſon in the Continental ſervice ſhall ſell or otherwiſe diſpoſe of any ſtores committed to his care, without a written order for ſo doing, iſſued by the Commander in Chief, or Commander in Chief of the department, or General Officer commanding at a ſeparate poſt, he ſhall be puniſhed for theft.

X. That the Waggon-maſter General of the army, or Waggon-maſter in any of the departments thereof, ſhall receive from the Quarter-maſter General or Deputy Quarter-maſter of any department, all ſuch horſes, cattle, and carriages, as the ſervice may require; and that neither the Waggon-maſter General, or any other Waggon-maſter, ſhall, on any account, preſume to purchaſe any horſes, cattle, or carriages, for the public ſervice, without the expreſs order of the Commander in Chief, the Commander in Chief of the department, the Quarter-maſter General, or Deputy Quarter-maſter General of a department; nor ſhall the Waggon-maſter General, or any other Waggon-maſter, hire any horſes, cattle, or carriages, unleſs by the authority aforeſaid, or by that of an Aſſiſtant Deputy Quarter-maſter General.

XI. That the Quarter-maſter General appoint ſuch Aſſiſtants, and make ſuch arrangements for conducting the buſineſs of his department, as to him and to the Commander in Chief, or Commander of a department, ſhall ſeem moſt conducive to the public weal; that a copy of ſuch arrangement, ſpecifying the names of the Aſſiſtants, Commiſſaries of Forage, Waggon-maſters, Forage-maſters, and Clerks of the ſeveral departments, be tranſmitted to the Board of War. That every Aſſiſtant of the Quarter-maſter General of the Army, and every Aſſiſtant of the Deputy Quarter-maſter General of the ſeveral departments thereof, ſhall make monthly returns of every article of what kind ſoever that may be in or at any of the forts, encampments, magazines, or places in the diſtrict, committed to his care, to the Deputy Quarter-maſter General of the department, noting what is good, what is reparable, and what is unfit for further ſervice, in ſeparate columns, from which returns the Deputy Quarter-maſter General ſhall make one general return, in which ſhall be ſpecified the total of all the articles in every diſtrict within his department; one copy whereof ſhall be monthly tranſmitted to the Board of War, one to the Commander in Chief of the department, and one to the Quarter-maſter General, from which return the Quarter-maſter General ſhall make a general return, ſpecifying what is in each department, and every diſtrict thereof; one copy whereof ſhall be monthly tranſmitted to the Board of War, one to the Commander in Chief, and one to the Commander of each department.

XII. That every Affistant Quartermafter, Commiffary of Forage, Waggon-mafter General, Forage-mafter, and every other perfon employed in the Quarter-mafter General's branch, who fhall negleçt or refufe to make fuch monthly returns, fhall be difmiffed the fervice by the Quarter-mafter General, or the Deputy Quartermafter General, of the department to which fuch delinquent belongs.

XIII. And, in order that all Deputy Quarter-mafters General and Affiftants may make their returns in fuch a manner as to avoid that great confufion which has heretofore arifen from a want of method, the Quarter-mafter General is to furnifh his Deputies with a form, copies whereof they are to deliver to the Affiftants, and to every perfon in the Quartermafter General's branch, who may be called upon for a return.

XIV. That the Quarter-mafter General, and the Deputy Quartermafters General in the feveral departments, have full power, and be authorized, with the confent of the Commander in Chief, or the Commander of the department, to difmifs any perfon by them employed, who fhall refufe or negleçt any duty enjoined by the foregoing Refolutions, or any other duty he may be charged with, and appoint others in the ftead of fuch as may be difmiffed.

XV. That the General and Commander in Chief of our armies, and the Commander of any department thereof, be allowed as much forage for their horfes, and thofe of their fuite, as the fervice may require.

XVI. That a Major General and Brigadier General, not having the command of a feparate department, fhall each be allowed forage for fix horfes for themfelves, their Aids de Camp or Brigade Majors, and fervants.

XVII. That the Commander in Chief, and the Commander in any feparate department, be authorized to allow fuch forage, and for and during fuch times as they fhall think proper, to the Quarter-mafter General and his Deputies, to the Mufter-mafter General and his Deputies, the Chief Engineer and his Affiftants, the Commiffary General and his Deputies, the Direçtor General of the Hofpital, his Subs and Surgeons General, to the Adjutant General and his Deputies, to the Colonels, Lieutenant Colonels, Majors, Adjutants, Quarter-mafters, and Surgeons of regiments, and to Provoft Martials, or to fuch and fo many of the beforementioned Officers and their Deputies, as the fervice fhall neceffarily require: provided always, That, if any of the Officers above-mentioned, their Deputies or Affiftants, fhould be allowed forage, in confequence of any General Orders hereafter given, and fhould neverthelefs not keep any or fo many horfes as they would be permitted to draw forage for, in fuch cafe no forage fhall be iffued for more horfes than they really have, nor fhall they, at any time thereafter, be allowed any forage as back allowance, or any money in lieu thereof.

XVIII. That a Deputy Quartermafter General be appointed to each department, and one to each grand divifion of the army: the rank of the former to be that of a Colonel, and of the latter that of a Lieutenant Colonel.

XIX. That the Quarter-mafter General, with the approbation of the Commander in Chief, or Commander of any feparate department, appoint a competent number of Deputy Quarter-mafters General, a Waggon-mafter General, and fo many Waggon-mafters as the fervice, from time to time, may require, and make a return to the Board of War of the names of the perfons fo appointed.

XX. That Major General Mifflin be

be allowed, for his services as Quarter-master General, one hundred and sixty-six dollars per month, in addition to his pay as Major General.—That the pay of a Deputy Quarter-master General of a grand division of the army be seventy-five dollars per month.—That the pay of an Assistant Deputy Quarter-master General be forty dollars per month, and that he have the rank of Captain.—That the pay of a Waggon-master General be seventy-five dollars per month.—That the pay of a Deputy Waggon-master General be fifty dollars per month.—That the pay of a Barrack-master General be seventy-five dollars per month.—That the pay of a Waggon-master, or Conductor of Waggons, be forty dollars per month.—That the pay of a Forage-master be forty dollars per month.

XXI. That every Officer, non-commissioned Officer, or Soldier, in the army of the United States, who shall, on any pretence whatever, presume to take out of any stable, pasture, park, or carriage, any horse or horses belonging to the public, or any belonging to private persons actually employed in the public service, without having authority so to do, by written order of the Commander in Chief, the Commander of any department, the Commanding Officer of any post where such horses may be, the Quarter-master General, or any of his Deputies or Assistants, or by the Commanding Officer of Artillery, or any detachment thereof, who may give order for the taking of horses assigned to that corps only, such orders to specify the particular service for which such horse or horses are taken, shall be for such offence, as soon as may be, brought to a General Court-martial; and if the fact is proved to the satisfaction of the Court, the Commander in Chief, or other General Officer, having given orders for such Court to convene, shall, upon con-

viction, immediately dismiss from the service such offender, if an officer, unless from some circumstances the Commander in Chief or such General Officer shall see cause to pardon the offence: and if a non-commissioned Officer or private, he shall order such corporal punishment to be inflicted as he may think proper, not exceeding one hundred lashes, unless from some circumstances the Commander in Chief or such General Officer shall see cause to pardon the offence.

Extracts from the Minutes,
Charles Thomson, Secretary.

————————

In Congress, June 10, 1777.

Resolved, That for supplying the army of the United States with provisions, one Commissary-general and four Deputy Commissaries-general of purchases, and one Commissary-general and three Deputy Commissaries-general of issues, be appointed by Congress.

2. That each of the said Commissaries and Deputy Commissaries be authorized to appoint for himself one Clerk.

3. That the Deputy Commissaries-general have authority to appoint as many Assistant Commissaries to act under them as may, from time to time, be necessary, and the same to displace at pleasure, making returns thereof to the Commissaries-general respectively, who shall have full power to limit their numbers, to displace such as they shall think disqualified for the trust, and direct their respective Deputy Commissaries-general to appoint others in their stead: that special care be taken by the officers empowered as aforesaid, to appoint none but persons of probity, capacity, vigilance, and attachment to the United States, and the cause they are engaged in, and to make returns to the Board of War, the Commander in Chief, and the Commander of the respective department of the Assistant Commissaries by them respectively appointed,

appointed, their several places of abode, the time of their appointment and dismission, and the post, place, magazine or district, to which they are severally assigned; and that the Deputy Commissaries-general of purchases and issues in the same district make similar returns to each other.

4. That the Commissary-general of purchases shall superintend the Deputy Commissaries-general of purchases, and assign to each a separate district, who shall constantly reside therein, and not make any purchases beyond the limits thereof; and every purchaser employed therein shall also have a certain district assigned him by the respective Deputy Commissary-general, in which he shall reside, and beyond the limits of which he shall not be permitted to make any purchases, unless by special order of his superior, directing the quantity and quality of provisions so to be purchased beyond his limits, and informing such purchaser of the prices given by the stationed purchaser in the district to which he may be sent

5. That the Commissary-general of purchases shall direct the Deputy Commissary-general in their respective districts to inform themselves and assistants, as nearly as may be, of the prices for which the articles, which they are to procure, may be purchased, and that neither they nor any of the said assistants, employed under their direction, exceed such prices; and if any Deputy Commissary-general of purchases shall neglect his duty, or be guilty of any fraud or misconduct in his office, the Commissary-general may suspend him, and shall immediately certify the same to Congress, with the reasons for such suspension, and appoint a person to act in his stead with all the powers of a Deputy Commissary-general, until the sense of Congress shall be known thereon.

6. That the present Commissary-general, by himself or his deputies,

deliver unto the Commissary-general of issues, or his deputies or assistants, all and every kind of provisions and other public stores in the Commissary-general's department, that now are, or at the time when such delivery shall be made, may be, in any of the posts, places, magazines and store-houses, belonging to the United States, taking duplicate receipts for the same, one set whereof, together with a general return of all stores so delivered, to be sent to the Board of Treasury, that the Commissary-general of issues may be charged therewith.

7. That it shall be the duty of the Commissary-general of purchases, with the assistance of the Deputy Commissaries-general and Assistant Commissaries of purchases, to purchase all provisions and other necessaries allowed, or which may hereafter be allowed by Congress to the troops of the United States, and deliver the Commissary-general of issues, or his deputies or assistants, in such quantities and at such places or magazines, as the Commander in Chief, or the Commander in the respective department, shall direct.

8. That the Commissary-general of issues shall direct the respective Deputy Commissaries-general to station one of their assistants at every fort, post, place or magazine, where provisions are or may be stored.

9. That the Commissary-general of purchases shall furnish each of the Deputy Commissaries-general and assistants with a book, in which is to be entered every purchase by them respectively made: and, that all the accounts may be kept in the same form, he shall cause the pages of such books to be divided into ten columns: in the first of which shall be entered the year, month and day in which any purchase is made; in the second, the names of the persons from whom; in the third, in what place; in the fourth, the species and quantity of provisions,

provifions, and, if live-ftock, the number, colour and natural marks; in the fifth, the artificial marks and number; in the fixth, the prices; in the feventh, the amount of the purchafe-money; in the eighth, ninth and tenth, the weight of the meat, hides and tallow of the live-ftock, as hereafter directed: and the Commiffary-general of iffues fhall furnifh each of the iffuing Deputy Commiffaries-general and Affiftants with a fimilar book, in which fhall be entered all provifions received by them from the purchafers refpectively: the firft column to contain the time of receiving fuch provifion; the fecond, the name of the purchafer; and in each of the other columns, the entries before directed.

10. That each purchafer fhall enter, in different pages of the faid book, each fpecies of provifions by him purchafed, and, at the end of every month, fhall foot and transfer the faid entries to a general account, fpecifying the quantity, amount and average coft of each article, and fhall alfo, in the courfe of the next fucceeding month, fend a copy of fuch account to the refpective Deputy Commiffary-generals, who fhall thereupon make out a monthly return of all the provifions purchafed in his diftrict, fpecifying the quantity, amount and average coft of each fpecies, as before directed, together with a copy of each purchafer's accounts, to the Board of War and Commiffary-general of purchafes within the time limited as aforefaid.

11. That the purchafing Commiffaries deliver live-ftock and other provifions required by the Commiffary, or feveral Deputy Commiffaries-general of iffues, at fuch places as they fhall refpectively direct.

12. That the Deputy Commiffary-general of purchafes, in each diftrict, fhall fpecially appoint one or more affiftants to purchafe live-ftock, who fhall caufe to be branded on the horns of all cattle by them purchafed, the number and initial letters of their names refpectively, and fhall alfo have power to employ drovers, and a perfon at each place, to which they may refpectively be directed to fend cattle, to receive, kill and deliver, the fame as hereafter directed.

13. That each drove of live-ftock, or quantity of provifions or other ftores, that may be fent to any poft, place or magazine, by any purchafer, fhall be accompanied with duplicate invoices, taken from the entries directed to be made in the books of the purchafing Commiffaries, one of which, together with the live-ftock or other ftores, fhall be delivered at fuch poft, place or magazine, to the perfon appointed to receive live-ftock, or to the iffuing Commiffaries refpectively, who, on the other, fhall give his receipt for the articles received, to be tranfmitted to the purchafer by the perfon delivering the faid articles; provided that if any live-ftock, under the care of the drover, fhall be wanted at any other poft than that to which they were ordered, the purchafer's Deputy at fuch poft may detain them, taking a copy of the invoice, as far as it refpects the live-ftock detained, and giving his receipt for the fame on the back of the faid invoice, fpecifying their marks and numbers, and the perfon to whom the refidue may be delivered, fhall give his receipt therefor on the fame invoice, and detain the other for his ufe as aforefaid

14. That each drove of live-ftock fhall be killed under the direction of the Purchafer's Deputy receiving the fame, who fhall weigh and deliver the meat to the Commiffary of iffues of the refpective poft, together with duplicates of the invoice left by the drover, entering in the eighth column the weight of the quarters of the feveral creatures; in the ninth, the weight of the hide; in the tenth, the weight of the tallow; and at the foot of each invoice, the number of heads

and

and tongues : and the Commiffary of iffues fhall indorfe his receipt on one of the invoices, and deliver it to the Deputy aforefaid, who fhall return it to the purchafer as his voucher, and to enable him to fill up the eighth, ninth and tenth columns of the entries in his book ; and the other fhall be kept by the iffuing Commiffary for his own ufe.

15. That the Commiffary-general of purchafes fhall contract by himfelf, or the refpective Deputy Commiffaries-general, with one or more perfons in each diftrict, to make or fupply a fufficient quantity of vinegar for the ufe of the army.

16. That the Deputy Commiffaries-general of purchafes take fpecial care to procure full fupplies of vegetables, as being effentially neceffary to the health of the army ; and they are refpectively empowered and directed, with the advice of the Commander in Chief, or Commander of the refpective Diftrict, to hire land therein, and raife fuch quantities of vegetables as are wanted and cannot be otherwife procured for the army ; and for this purpofe, to employ fuitable perfons to conduct, and labourers to affift in carrying on the faid bufinefs.

17. That the Commiffary-general of purchafes fhall, from time to time, apply to Congrefs for all the money wanted in his department, and fhall make the neceffary advances to the refpective Deputy Commiffaries-general, calling them to account as often as he fhall judge it neceffary ; and the Deputy Commiffaries-general fhall, in like manner, make advances of the money received of the faid Commiffary-general, to their refpective affiftants, and call them to account as aforefaid.

18. That the Commiffary or Deputy Commiffaries-general of purchafes and Iffues fhall refpectively be accountable for the conduct of the officers of their own appointment ; and

all the accounts of purchafes, and iffues, fhall, once in fix months, be fettled by the refpective Commiffaries-general with the proper Commiffioners of Accounts ; each account of purchafes to be vouched by the feveral bills and receipts of the venders, fpecifying the coft, and the receipts of the iffuing Commiffaries fhewing the delivery of all articles therein charged ; and each account of iffues by the victualling returns hereafter directed to be made ; and receipts for all provifions charged therein as rations, or fent by the refpective iffuing Commiffary to any other. And the Commiffaries-general fhall produce the monthly returns of the feveral purchafing and iffuing Commiffaries, to be ufed by the Commiffioners in adjufting their refpective accounts.

19. That the Commiffaries-general of purchafes and iffues, and their refpective Deputies, for the neglect of duty, or other offences in their refpective offices, fhall be fubject to military arreft and trial by order of the Commander in Chief, or any General Officer commanding a divifion in the army, poft or department, where fuch neglect of duty or offence may happen ; and the refpective Affiftants of the Deputy Commiffaries-general of purchafes and iffues fhall, for the fame caufes, be liable to military arreft as commiffioned officers in the army, by any General Officer, or any Officer commanding at a detached poft to which fuch Affiftants may be affigned.

20. That the Commiffary-general of iffues fhall fuperintend the refpective Deputy Commiffaries-general, and affign to each a feparate diftrict ; and have full powers to fufpend them, and appoint others for a time, as already appointed for the Commiffary-general of purchafes.

21. That every iffuing Commiffary fhall enter in diftinct pages of the book mentioned in the ninth article, each fpecies of provifions or other ftores received by him, including the provifions

fions delivered by other iffuing Commiffaries or the prefent Commiffary-general, and the fame entries fhall be made with refpect to thefe, as therein are directed, when provifions are received from the purchafers ; excepting that the prices and coft of articles delivered by the faid Commiffaries may be omitted.

22. That every iffuing Commiffary fhall be furnifhed with a book of iffues in which he fhall open a feparate account with each regiment, corps or detachment to which he may iffue, or Commiffary to which he may fend or deliver provifions ; and each page thereof fhall be divided into columns, in the firft of which fhall be entered the time of delivery ; in the fecond, the name of the officer, upon whofe return provifions are iffued, or by whom fent to any other iffuing Commiffary ; in the third, the number of rations, and in other feparate columns the feveral quantities of each fpecies of provifions delivered as rations, or fent to the Commiffaries as aforefaid: And on the laft day of every month, he fhall foot the faid accounts, and alfo all the accounts of provifions received and entered in the book mentioned in the preceding article.

23. That every iffuing Commiffary fhall take duplicate receipts for each quantity of provifions and ftores by him fent to any poft, place or magazine, agreeably to the form of the entries directed to be made in the book of iffues, one of which he fhall deliver to the officer, or perfon employed to deliver the faid provifions or ftores ; and the iffuing Commiffary at fuch poft, place or magazine, or at any intermediate poft, who may receive fuch provifions or ftores, or any part thereof, fhall certify the quantity on the back of the faid receipt, which the officer or perfon, who delivered the provifions, fhall return to the Commiffary that fent them as his voucher. And in cafes of deficiency, the Commiffary who fent the provifions fhall

credit the Commiffary to whom they were directed for the quantity loft, if the fame has been placed to his debit, and fhall charge twice the amount thereof to the account of the officer or perfon employed to deliver it, and fhall alfo tranfmit a copy of the faid account to the Pay-mafter or Deputy Pay-mafter General in the diftrict, who fhall fend to the iffuing Commiffary a receipt for fuch account, to be produced by him on fettlement, and fhall alfo deduct the amount thereof from the pay of the delinquent, and credit the United States therefor: provided that if any provifions or ftores fhall be loft by unavoidable accident, and the fame is proved by fworn evidences before the commanding officer of the poft from or to which fuch provifions or ftores were fent, his certificate, with the proof annexed, fhall authorize the Commiffary to cancel fuch charge.

24. That no provifions be iffued to any perfons but by the written order of the Commander in Chief, the Commander of any department, the Quarter-mafter General, any of his Deputies or Affiftants, the Commanding Officer of a poft, defcribing the perfon in whofe favour fuch order fhall be given ; or upon a return figned by the Commanding Officer of a corps or detachment thereof, whether commiffioned or non-commiffioned, or by the regimental Quarter-mafter.

25. That when any troops are ordered to quit a poft, and the iffuing Commiffary remains at fuch poft, the refpective Commanding Officers of the feveral regiments or corps fhall call on the iffuing Commiffary for a certificate, fpecifying the day to which they were victualled inclufively ; and in cafe detachments of different regiments or corps are made, the Commanding Officer of fuch detachments fhall procure a certificate from the Commiffary, in which fhall be inferted the days to which the different troops, of which his detachment may be com-

pofed

pofed, were victualled, and the next and fubfequent provifion return for fuch detachment fhall diftinguifh the corps out of which it is formed, and the number of each corps, to the end that the Commiffary may charge each corps with the provifion iffued to it; and if any Commiffary, at any other poft, fhall victual any other corps or detachment comprehended in the foregoing defcription before fuch certificates are produced, he fhall charge the officer commanding the fame with twenty days provifion for the whole number of men under his care, and make return thereof to the Pay-mafter General, or Deputy Pay-mafter General in the Diftrict, who fhall make the proper ftoppages, and alfo to the Board of Treafury, who fhall charge him therefor. Provided, That if fuch certificates be procured and delivered within thirty days after the firft drawing of fuch certificate, the Commiffary-general fhall cancel the charge, keeping the certificate as a voucher for fo doing: provided alfo, That not-withftanding fuch certificate may be produced, if it fhall appear that the officer commanding any corps or detachment has drawn more provifion than the corps or detachment was entitled to, he fhall ftand charged the double quantity fo over-drawn.

26. That every iffuing Commiffary fhall take receipts for the number of rations, and for fo much of every fpecies of provifions as he may iffue therefor.

27. That every iffuing Commiffary on the laft drawing day, preceding the laft drawing day of every month, fhall victual the troops up to the laft day of the month inclufive; and if provifions fhould be ordered for troops going on detachments for fuch time as would run beyond that day, two returns fhall be made out, one to the laft day of the month inclufive, and one from the firft day of the month inclufive to the time ordered.

28. That every iffuing Commiffary fhall number the provifion returns, and indorfe the fame with the date thereof, and the number of men victualled, and put the returns of each detachment or corps on feparate files, each to contain the returns of a month for fuch corps or detachment.

29. That wherever any capital magazine fhall be eftablifhed, the Commander in Chief, or Commanding Officer of the department, fhall order ftore-houfes to be built, and barracks for fifty men, and the fame to be inclofed with a ftockade.

30. That whenever any of the provifions or ftores in any of the magazines become fo damaged as to threaten a total lofs of all fuch damaged provifions, the Commiffary of iffues, to whofe care fuch provifions may be committed, fhall make return thereof immediately to the Deputy Commiffary-general of iffues, who is to apply to the Commander in Chief, or fome General Officer, to order a Court of Enquiry, who fhall thereupon grant one, and fuch provifions as may by the Court be condemned, fhall be fold at public vendue, under the direction of the Deputy Commiffary-general of iffues, public notice being given of fuch fale by advertifements, at leaft ten days before the day of fale, unlefs the Court fhould determine that the fame ought to be fold at an earlier day.

31. That every Affiftant Commiffary of iffues fhall, within fix days after the laft day of every month, make a return to the Deputy Commiffary-general of the diftrict, of all provifions and ftores in his magazine or ftore at the laft preceding return; of all provifions by him received in the preceding month; from whom and whence; of what he has iffued, fpecifying the regiment and corps, and the number of rations and quantity of each fpecies of provifions drawn by the fame; and of what remains in ftore.

32. That each Deputy Commiffary-

sary-general of issues shall, from the monthly returns of the Assistant Commissaries, make out a general return for the district, specifying what remained in the magazines or stores at the last return; what has been received since; the number of rations and quantity of provisions issued, and what remains in store, distinguishing the several posts, places, magazines and regiments or corps as aforesaid; one to be sent to the Board of War, one to the Commander in Chief, one to the Commander of the department, one to the Commissary-general of purchases, and one to the Commissary-general of issues.

33. That the Commissary-general of purchases and Commissary-general of issues, each in his own department, make a general monthly return to the Board of War, the Commander in Chief, and the Commanding Officer of the respective districts, and take special care constantly to provide and furnish each of the officers under him with printed forms of the books, invoices, receipts and returns to be used by them respectively, agreeable to these resolves.

34. That no returns of rations drawn or returned by the several regiments, be hereafter made by the issuing Commissaries to the Commissary-general of musters, or by him to the Adjutant-general, or by the Adjutant-general to the Board of War, as directed in the regulations of the Muster-master General's department, passed by Congress, the fourth day of April last.

35. That the Commissaries-general, and the respective officers under them, apply to the Quarter-master General or his respective officers for waggons, teams and horses, wanted in the several districts; and if at any time it shall be necessary to hire the same, they are not to exceed the rates stipulated by Congress, or the Quarter-master General aforesaid.

36. That all persons employed to purchase for the United States any articles in the several departments of the Commissary-general of purchases, Quarter-master, Director, or Clothier-general, or the Commissary-general of military stores, shall previously apply to them, or the principal officers under them respectively, for certificates of the several prices by them allowed for such articles, and shall not, on any pretence whatsoever, exceed such prices. And it is recommended to the several States to give to their purchasers respectively similar directions.

37. That the Commissary-general of purchases, from time to time, provide sufficient quantities of salt, and deliver it to the Commissary-general of issues, or the respective officers under him, who are directed to issue to the troops only such quantities and in such manner as the Commander in Chief, or Commander of the respective district, shall direct. And the Commissary-general of issues shall direct the respective Deputy Commissaries General to employ a suitable number of coopers and packers, who shall salt and pack provisions at the several magazines and stores, and take the proper precautions with respect to all provisions therein deposited.

38. And whereas great confusion hath arisen from the manner in which officers and soldiers have been paid for rations and parts of rations allowed to, but not drawn by them respectively;

Resolved, That the parts of a ration be estimated as follows, viz. for the daily allowance of beef, pork or fish, four ninetieths of a dollar; of bread or flour, two ninetieths; of pease or beans, one ninetieth; of milk, one ninetieth; of beer, one ninetieth; of rice, one half of a ninetieth; and of soap one half of a ninetieth; making in the whole ten ninetieths of a dollar for each ration: and that for the future the

Quarter-

Quarter-mafter, or other perfon, drawing provifion for any regiment, corps or detachment, fhall, on the laft day of every month, make out an abftract of the number of retained rations due to each officer refpectively, and alfo the number of each part of a ration due to fuch regiment, corps or detachment, and deliver the fame to the refpective iffuing Commiffary, who fhall compare it with his books, and finding it right, fhall certify thereon that the feveral charges in the abftract are juft, and that fuch a fum as he fhall find to be due, fhould be paid to the refpective Pay-mafter of the regiment, corps or detachment, who fhall annex the faid abftract to the pay-roll, that the Pay-mafter, or Deputy Pay-mafter General, of the diftrict may pay, and he is hereby required to pay fuch ration-abftract to the regimental Pay-mafter, who is directed to pay the refpective officers and foldiers, and take their receipts. And when any regiment, corps or detachment, or iffuing Commiffary, is ordered to leave a poft before the end of the month, the ration-abftracts fhall be made up to the day of his or their leaving the poft, and certified by the Commiffion as aforefaid.

29. That the Commiffary of iffues at every poft where cattle are killed for the ufe of the army, appoint a careful perfon to take charge of the hides and tallow, to fee that the former are properly dried, and that the latter is properly rendered, and that both are difpofed of as the Commiffary-general of iffues, by order of Congrefs, fhall direct.

PENNSYLVANIA WAR-OFFICE,

Philadelphia, May 2, 1777.

Application having been made to the Board by the Honourable Major-general Schuyler for affiftance in procuring blankets for the ufe of the Continental troops; and the Honour-

able Congrefs having recommended to the Legiflative Bodies of the feveral States, to make an affefment of blankets on the inhabitants, agreeable to their circumftances: and whereas the Prefident of the Supreme Executive Council, with the Vice Prefident, and fuch members of the faid Council, in conjunction with the Board of War for this State, and (in fuch cafes as relate to the marine) the Navy-Board, are, in the prefent critical exigency of affairs, by refolve of the Honourable Congrefs, vefted with the exercife of every authority to promote the fafety of the State, till fuch time as the Legiflative and Executive Authorities of the Commonwealth of Pennfylvania can be convened: and as the want of blankets for the troops may occafion ficknefs, and the death of many valuable men, and reduce the ftrength of our army, and it appearing to this Board that an immediate fupply is neceffary; therefore

Refolved, That four thoufand blankets be collected in this State from the inhabitants, in fuch quantities as is proportionate to the number they have in family, and the ftock of blankets they may be poffeffed of; for which blankets they fhall be paid the full value, according to an appraifement to be made of them, as will be hereafter directed.

Refolved, That the city and counties fhall fupply of the faid four thoufand blankets in the proportion as follows:

The city of Philadelphia -	667
County of Philadelphia - -	667
Bucks - - - -	333
Chefter - -	500
Lancafter - -	500
Berks - -	333
Northampton -	167
York - - -	500
Cumberland - -	333
	4000

Refolved, That twelve Gentlemen be appointed in the city, and the fame number

number in each of the said counties, to be Commissioners, to aid and assist this Board in carrying into execution, in their respective districts, every measure that may be recommended for the safety of this Commonwealth. And that they employ proper and discreet men, in such numbers as they may think necessary, to collect immediately from every family their proportion of blankets for the purposes aforesaid, and that they direct the proportion to be supplied by every family or families within their respective districts; for which purpose, they are to take every necessary measure to do equal justice to the people, and to facilitate the collecting of the same.

Resolved, That the said Commissioners direct an appraisement to be made of such blankets, and order immediate payment to be made for the same, and that a sufficient sum of money be sent to the said Commissioners to pay for the blankets so collected.

Resolved, That George Henry, Richard Humphreys, Charles Wilson Peale, John Dunlap, Thomas Irwin, Casper Guyer, Robert Smith, Jacob Graff, Alexander Boyd, Ephraim Benham, Jacob Bright, and Jacob Schriener, be appointed Commissioners for the aforesaid purpose, in the city of Philadelphia; and that William Coats, Jacob Eagle, Samuel Dewees, George Smith, Archibald Thomas, William Antis, Daniel Heester, John Moore, Benjamin M'Veaugh, William Dean, Robert Curry, and Isaac Warner, be appointed Commissioners for the aforesaid purpose, in the county of Philadelphia. That Joseph Kirkbride, John Gill, Samuel Smith, William Crawford, John Lacey, Andrew Kachlien, Joseph Hart, James Benezet, Henry Wynknop, Major M'Irvaine, John Kidd, and Richard Gibbs, be appointed Commissioners for the aforesaid purpose in the county

of Bucks. That Robert Smith, Benjamin Brannon, Thomas Strawbridge, Thomas Cheney, Lewis Gronow, Andrew Boyd, Richard Thomas, Caleb Davis, Nicholas Fairlamb, William Evans, and William Clinghan, be appointed Commissioners for the aforesaid purpose in the county of Chester. That Bartram Galbraith, James Crawford, Adam Ordt, Robert Thomson, Joshua Elder, Christopher Crawford, William Atlee, John Hubley, Alexander Lowry, Curtis Grub, Philip Marsteller, Matthias Slough, and Adam Keigart, be appointed Commissioners for the aforesaid purpose in the county of Lancaster. That Richard M'Allister, Hans Morrison, John Hays, James M'Caulis, John Carson, Joseph Donnaldson, James Smith, Martin Eichelberger, James Edgar, Francis Crazer, and John Hay, be appointed Commissioners for the aforesaid purpose in the county of York. That Jacob Morgan, John Old, Abraham Lincoln, Henry Shoemaker, Christian Lower, jun. Valentine Eckart, James Read, Henry Haller, Adam Whitman, Benjamin Spiker, Mark Bird, Daniel Hunter, and Gabriel Heister, be appointed Commissioners for the aforesaid purpose in the county of Berks. That James Galbraith, James Gregory, Benjamin Blythe, Robert M'Coy, George Sharp, John Harris, William Lyon, George Stephenson, William Clark, John Harris, William Duffield, and Hugh Alexander, be appointed Commissioners for the aforesaid purpose in the county of Cumberland. That John Weizel, Jacob Shoemaker, David Deshler, Arthur Lartimer, John Chambers, Colonel Laber, Abraham Berlin, Simon Drisbach, Peter Rhodes, Robert Lettis Hooper, and Jacob Stroud, be appointed Commissioners for the aforesaid purpose in the county of Northampton.

Resolved, That the said Commissioners

fioners be allowed per diem, for each day they are employed in the bufinefs aforefaid.

Refolved,. That no blankets be collected but fuch as are fit for field ufe, and that the Lieutenants, or Sub-lieutenants, of the refpective counties, fupply the faid Commiffioners with a fufficient body of the militia to carry thefe Refolves into execution, whenever they find it neceffary to apply to them for that purpofe. By order,

THOMAS WHARTON, jun. Prefident.

PENNSYLVANIA WAR-OFFICE,
May 5, 1777.

Whereas by a Refolve of the Honourable Congrefs of the 14th of April, it is recommended to the different Legiflatures to authorize the enlifting of apprentices and fervants to compleat the regiments raifing in their refpective States. And whereas by the recefs of the Legiflature of this State, no law, however neceffary, can at this time be enacted: therefore

Refolved, That his Excellency the Prefident of the Supreme Executive Council, together with this Board, entirely concurring with that Honourable Body in the propriety and neceffity of the meafure recommended, are fully of opinion, that the enlifting of apprentices and fervants, of the age of fixteen years and upwards, to compleat the troops of this State at the prefent critical juncture, ought to be allowed of, declaring at the fame time, that they fhall efteem it their duty to ufe their influence (if neceffary) with the Legiflature of this State, as foon as convened, to pafs a law to make full compenfation to fuch mafters of apprentices and fervants as have or may fuffer by this neceffary meafure being carried into execution, and that for the future none are to be enlifted under the age of fixteen years.

By order of the Board,

JACOB S. HOWELL, Secretary.

Philadelphia, June 10, 1777.

The following is an extract from the inftructions given by the town of Bofton, on the 26th ult. to their Reprefentatives in Affembly, viz.

" You are to move, that immediate application be made to Congrefs, that all the States money might be redeemed with Continental currency, and each State charged by the Continent for what they receive. If this could be accomplifhed, and the money redeemed by loan certificates, it would operate doubly in favour of the States, for as they carry intereft, they would be fpeedily hoarded; and being taken out of circulation, would give the remaining currency a proportionably greater value, and in that cafe would be nearly equal to a tax; befides, the currency being all of the fame fpecies, a counterfeit would be more eafily difcovered, than when a great variety of money is paffing, and then it would be the joint intereft of all the States to keep the credit good, and might be a farther means of ftrengthening the union."

It is reported, and believed, that ammunition and cloathing are depofited, by order of a certain European Court, at New Orleans and the Havannah, with directions to lend them to fuch American veffels as may call for them.

In Congrefs, June 7, 1777.

Whereas complaint has been made that many of the regimental Paymafters abfent themfelves from the army, by which the public fervice greatly fuffers.

Refolved therefore, That the Commander in Chief, and the Commander in each feparate department, be directed to take the moft effectual means for compelling all regimental Pay-mafters to attend punctually to the duties of their office, and that fuch as are negligent be punifhed and difplaced, and that they be refpectively impowered to appoint others of ability, diligence and integrity, in the room of such as are displaced. Extract from the Minutes,

CHARLES THOMSON, Sec.

The liberal provision made by Congress in the new medical arrangement, joined with a humane desire to prevent the repetition of the distresses which afflicted the brave American soldiers the last campaign, have drawn men of the first abilities into the field, to watch over the health, and preserve the lives of the soldiers, many of them from very extensive and profitable practice, and every species of domestic happiness. Dr. William Brown of Virginia, Dr. James Craik of Maryland, and Dr. Thomas Bond, jun. of Philadelphia, are appointed Assistant Director-generals. Dr. Walter Jones of Virginia, and Dr. Benjamin Rush of Philadelphia, Physician and Surgeon-generals of the hospitals of the middle department. Under these none but gentlemen of the best education, and well qualified, are employed as senior Physicians, Surgeons, &c. The Eastern and Northern departments are filled with gentlemen of the first characters in those countries; and the public may depend on it, that the greatest exertions of skill and industry shall be constantly made, and no cost spared, to make the sick and wounded soldiery comfortable and happy. As a consequence of the above liberal arrangement of the Honourable Congress, we do, with great pleasure, and equal truth, assure the public (notwithstanding the many false and wicked reports propagated by the enemies of American liberty, and only calculated to retard the recruiting service) that all the military hospitals of the United States are in excellent order, *and that the army enjoy a degree of health seldom to be be seen or read of.*

W. SHIPPEN, jun. Director-general of the American hospitals.

JOHN COCHRAN, Physician and Surgeon-general of the army in the middle department.

Head Quarters, Middle-brook, June 4.

Philadelphia.

A SUPPLEMENT *to the Act intituled, "An Act for making the Continental Bills of Credit, and the Bills of Credit emitted by Resolves of the late Assemblies legal tender," and for other purposes therein mentioned.* (See page 126.)

Whereas in the Act of General Assembly of the Commonwealth of Pennsylvania, passed the twenty-ninth day of January last past, intituled, "An Act for making the Continental bills of credit, and the bills of credit emitted by the Resolves of the late Assemblies legal tender, and for other purposes therein mentioned," no mention is made in express words of bodies politic and corporate; for which reason it has been construed, by some persons, that such bodies are not comprehended within the meaning of the said Act: in order, therefore, that the said bills of credit, and also the bills of credit emitted, and to be emitted by virtue of an Act intituled, "An Act for emitting the sum of two hundred thousand pounds in bills of credit for the defence of this State, and providing a fund for sinking the same by a tax on all estates, real and personal, and on all taxables within the same," shall be alike taken and made current in all payments by all persons, as well in their private as in their politic or corporate capacity.

Be it enacted, by the representatives of the freemen of the Commonwealth of Pennsylvania in General Assembly met, and by the authority of the same, That all the bills of credit declared to be legal tender by the said first recited Act, and also the bills of credit emitted, and to be emitted by virtue of the said last recited Act, shall be legal tender, not only to those persons and creditors therein mentioned, but also to all bodies politic and corporate, which said bodies shall be deemed and taken to be subject in all respects to all the fines and forfeitures in the said Acts mentioned, which the persons or creditors therein named

named are or ought to be subject to for any offence committed against the above recited Acts, as fully and effectually to all intents and purposes as if the said bodies politic or corporate had been expressly named in the said Act.

JOHN BAYARD, Speaker.

Enacted into a law the thirteenth day of June, in the year one thousand seven hundred and seventy-seven.

JOHN MORRIS, junior, Clerk of General Assembly.

STATE of NEW JERSEY.
In Council of Safety.

Whereas in and by a certain Act of the Legislature of this State, passed at Haddenfield, the fourth day of this present month of June, intitled, " An Act for rendering more effectual two certain Acts therein mentioned," it is among other things enacted, that the Governor or Commander in Chief for the time being, and Council of Safety, be authorized and impowered to grant passports or permissions to pass through any parts of this State, and also to authorize such and so many persons in every county within the same, to grant such passports and permissions, and under such regulations as they shall think necessary; and to detain under guard all persons suspected of dangerous designs against this State, travelling without such passports or permissions, until they shall satisfy the Governor and Council aforesaid, or the persons so by them authorized, of their being well affected to the State, or of their travelling without any designs injurious to it; and that every person who shall be convicted of counterfeiting such passports or permissions, shall suffer six months imprisonment; as by the said Act, reference being thereunto had may appear.

We do thereby, by these presents, authorize and appoint to grant such passports and permissions as aforesaid, the officers following, to wit, all the Members of the Council and of the General Assembly of this State, the Justices of the Supreme Court, the Judges of the Inferior Court of Common Pleas, the Justices of the Peace, and the Field Officers of the Militia of this State, that is to say, such of the said Justices of the Peace and Field Officers as have been duly qualified, and taken the oaths of abjuration and allegiance prescribed by law; which passports and permissions are hereby directed to be to the following effect, viz.

County of —— ss. *The Bearer hereof, —— aged about — years, of a — complexion, rather — of stature, with — eyes, a traveller from — to — has permission to pass to said — behaving h self civilly. Dated at — the — day of — 1777.*

Which passport or permission the said officer is to subscribe with his name and title of office; and all ferrymen and inn-keepers within this State are hereby prohibited to convey over any creek or river, or to entertain any traveller (excepting the said officers hereby authorized to grant such passports or permission, and all persons belonging to the army of the United States) who shall refuse to produce such passport or permission upon being thereto requested, which every ferry-man and inn-keeper is hereby enjoined to do.

Dated at Haddenfield, the ninth day of June, in the year of our Lord one thousand seven hundred and seventy-seven.

WILLIAM LIVINGSTON, President.

STATE of NEW JERSEY.

An Act for rendering more effectual two certain Acts therein mentioned.

Whereas two certain Acts of the Council and Assembly of this State, the one intitled, " An Act to punish traitors and disaffected persons," passed the fourth day of October last, and the other intitled, " An Act for investing the Governor and a Council consisting of twelve, with certain
powers

powers therein mentioned for a limited time," passed the fifteenth day of March last, have been found insufficient to answer all the salutary purposes thereby intended: wherefore, for the greater security of the State, the more vigorous suppression of its internal enemies, and to render the said Acts more operative and effectual.

1. Be it enacted, by the Council and General Assembly of this State, and it is hereby enacted by the authority of the same, That if any person being a member of, or owing allegiance to this Government as described in the first section of the Act herein first mentioned, shall be apprehended on his way to the enemy with intent to go into their lines or encampments, or into any places in their possession, without the licence, permission or passport of the Commander in Chief of the army of the United States of America, or of the Governor or Commander in Chief of this State for the time being, or of some General Officer of the army of the said United States, or of one of the Brigadiers-general of the militia of this State, such person is hereby declared to be guilty of a capital felony, and being thereof legally convicted, shall suffer death, accordingly. Provided nevertheless, That if any person so offending as aforesaid, shall, at the time of his examination before the Governor and Council of Safety aforesaid, or within six days thereafter, declare his willingness to enlist, and shall actually enlist with the leave of the Governor and Council aforesaid, to serve on board any of the vessels of war belonging to the United States, it shall be lawful for them to suffer him so to enlist, and thereupon to discharge him from his confinement, and such his enlistment shall be deemed a full pardon of his offence aforesaid, any thing herein before contained to the contrary thereof notwithstanding.

2. And be it further enacted, by the authority aforesaid, That if any person being a member of, or owing allegiance to this Government, as in the said first mentioned Act is described, who hath since the fourth day of October last voluntarily gone into any of the enemy's lines or encampments, or into any places in their possession, shall return to any parts of this State in a secret or clandestine manner, or without any leave, licence or passport previously obtained from the Governor or Commander in Chief of this State for the time being, or from a General Officer of the army of the United States, or of one of the Brigadiers-general of the militia of this State, such person is hereby declared to be guilty of a capital felony, and being thereof convicted, shall suffer death accordingly. Provided nevertheless, that he may enlist as aforesaid, and that such enlistment shall be considered and operate in like manner as the enlistment of a person committing the offence specified in the last preceding section of this Act.

3. And be it further enacted, by the authority aforesaid, That the Governor or Commander in Chief for the time being, and Council aforesaid, are hereby authorized and impowered to grant passports or permissions to pass through any parts of this State, and also to authorize such and so many persons in every county within the same to grant such passports and permissions, and under such regulations as they shall think necessary, and to detain under guard all persons suspected of dangerous designs against this State, travelling without such passports or permissions, until they shall satisfy the Governor and Council aforesaid, or the persons by them so authorized, of their being well affected to the State, or of their travelling without any designs injurious to it; and every person who shall be convicted of counterfeiting any such passports or permissions,

P p   shall

shall suffer six months imprisonment.

4. And be it further enacted, by the authority aforesaid, That it shall and may be lawful to and for the Governor, or Commander in Chief for the time being, and Council aforesaid, to send into the enemy's lines such of the wives and children of persons lately residing within this State, who have gone over to the enemy, as they shall think necessary.

5. And whereas by reason of the irruption of the enemy into several parts of this State, and the arts and influence of disaffected persons residing in the same, either no trials at all, or no fair and impartial trial of traitors and disaffected persons can be had in several counties of this State:

Be it therefore further enacted, by the authority aforesaid, That every person who shall be charged with, or committed for, any of the crimes or offences specified in the first, second or third sections of the said Act, intitled, " An Act to punish traitors and disaffected persons," may be tried for the same in any county of this State by a jury of that county, at the discretion of the Governor and Council aforesaid, though the offence he is charged with, and was committed for, was done and perpetrated in any other county, any law, usage or custom to the contrary thereof in any wise notwithstanding. Provided nevertheless, that the Governor and Council aforesaid may permit any person suspected of, or charged with any of the said crimes or offences, to enlist on board any of the vessels of war belonging to the United States instead of confining them for trial, and such inlistment shall be deemed a full pardon of the said crime or offence, any law to the contrary thereof notwithstanding.

6. And be it further enacted, by the authority aforesaid, That, if any person, who shall be convened before the Governor and Council aforesaid, by warrant, summons, or otherwise, on suspicion of being dangerous or disaffected to the present Government, shall neglect or refuse to take the oaths of abjuration and allegiance set forth in an Act intitled, " An Act for the security of the Government of New-Jersey," passed the nineteenth day of September, one thousand seven hundred and seventy-six, upon the same being tendered to him by them, and and such person as shall appear to the Government and Council too dangerous to the State to be suffered to go at large, upon giving security to appear at the next Court of General Quarter Sessions of the Peace, and to be in the mean time of good behaviour, the Governor and Council aforesaid are hereby authorized and impowered to commit such person to close gaol, and certify the same, with the cause of commitment, under the hand and seal of the Governor, to the next Court of General Quarter Sessions of the Peace, where, if such person shall refuse to take the oaths, he shall be bound to his good behaviour, or be fined or imprisoned as the said Court shall deem necessary, any thing in the said Act, intitled, " An Act to punish traitors and disaffected persons," to the contrary notwithstanding.

7. And be it enacted, by the authority aforesaid, That whenever the Governor, or Commander in Chief for the time being, and any four of the said Council of Safety, are met upon business, and a fifth member is not immediately expected to complete the quorum required by the said Act, entitled, " An Act for vesting the Governor and Council, consisting of twelve, with certain powers therein mentioned for a limited time," it shall and may be lawful for the said Governor or Commander in Chief for the time being, and the members of the said Council so met, to send for any Judge of the Court of Common Pleas, or any Justice of the Peace in the

the county in which they are fo affembled, to fupply the place of the fifth abfent member, and fuch Judge or Juftice fhall, during his fitting with them, be deemed and efteemed to all intents and purpofes a member of the faid Council.

8. And be it further enacted, by the authority aforefaid, That the Governor, or Commander in Chief for the time being, by and with the advice and confent of the Council aforefaid, is hereby authorized and impowered to carry all their lawful orders and directions into execution by any fuch detachment of the troops in the fervice of the United States as he may be able to procure for that purpofe, at the expence of the faid States, in the fame manner as he is by the faid laft mentioned act authorized and impowered to do, by any of the militia of this State.

9. And be it further enacted, by the authority aforefaid, That any dwelling-houfe, out-houfe, or guard room, in which the Governor or Commander in Chief for the time being, and Council aforefaid, fhall confine any perfon for any offence committed againft the faid Act, entitled, " An Act to punifh traitors and difaffected perfons," fhall be deemed and adjudged a legal gaol to that purpofe.

10. And be it further enacted, by the authority aforefaid, That, after the condemnation of any offender for any crime committed againft the faid laft mentioned Act, for which fuch offender is fentenced to fuffer death, the Judge, who fhall pafs fentence on fuch offender, fhall refpite his execution, until the directions of the Governor or Commander in Chief for the time being, and the Council aforefaid, can be held thereon, who may, and are hereby authorifed, at their difcretion, either to fuffer fuch offender to be executed purfuant to his fentence, or to fend him on board any of the veffels of war belonging to the

United States. Provided neverthelefs, that nothing herein contained fhall extend in anywife to diminifh the power and authority invefted by the Conftitution of this State in the Governor and Council of this State, of granting pardons to criminals, after condemnation, in all cafes of treafon, felony, and other offences.

11. And be it further enacted, by the authority aforefaid, That the Governor or Commander in Chief for the time being, and the Council of Safety aforefaid, fhall be, and they are hereby authorized to caufe to be cleanfed fuch of the towns of this State in which any troops have been quartered, as they fhall think neceffary, to prevent infectious diftempers, and the expence thereof fhall be defrayed by warrants drawn by the Governor or Commander in Chief for the time being, in the faid Council of Safety, on the Treafurer of this State, not exceeding three hundred pounds.

12. And whereas the enemy has lately adopted the mean and unmanly practice of encouraging our difaffected fubjects fecretly, to apprehend and convey into their lines fuch of the loyal fubjects of this State as have rendered themfelves more peculiarly obnoxious to their refentment, on account of their fingular patriotifm, and more eminent fervices to their country.

Be it therefore enacted, by the authority aforefaid, That it fhall and may be lawful for the Governor or Commander in Chief for the time being, and Council of Safety aforefaid, forthwith and from time to time hereafter to apprehend and imprifon fuch and fo many perfons difaffected to this State, as they fhall think fufficient to induce the enemy to releafe fuch of the fubjects of this State as have already been, or hereafter may be fo fecretly apprehended and conveyed away as aforefaid and detained by the enemy, and them to caufe to be treated in like

manner

manner as the enemy treat such prisoners of this State, until they shall be released and set at liberty to return to their respective places of abode.

13. And be it further enacted, by the authority aforesaid, That whenever the Governor or Commander in Chief for the time being, by reason of his absence out of this State, or of sickness though within it, or by any other reasonable impediment, is prevented from attending the Council of Safety, the Vice-President of the Council of this State shall be, and he is hereby invested with same power and authority as the Governor or Commander in Chief for the time being is invested with by this present act, or the said act, intitled, " An Act for investing the Governor and a Council consisting of twelve, with certain powers therein-mentioned, for a limited time."

14 And be it further enacted by the same authority, That this act shall continue in force during the continuance of the said last mentioned act, and no longer.

Passed at Haddenfield,
4th June, 1777.

In Council, Philadelphia, July 5,
1777.

Whereas the Constitution of the Commonwealth of Pennsylvania, in section 30th, ordains, " That Justices of the Peace shall be elected by the freeholders of each ward, district or township, as the law shall direct; and that their names shall be returned to the President in Council, who shall commissionate one, or more of them, for each ward, district or township, so returning, for seven years."

And whereas an act of Assembly, intitled, " An Act directing the mode and times of electing Justices of the Peace for the city of Philadelphia, and and the several and respective counties of this Commonwealth, and for other purposes therein mentioned,"

was passed on the 11th of February last.

And whereas by inattention, misapprehension, absence of great numbers of the freeholders in the defence of their country, (the militia of several of the counties being then in actual service) shortness of the times that had been appointed, neglect, and other causes, some districts, and also some townships, (in counties in which a township has been made a district for this purpose) did not hold the election of Justices on the days by said act appointed ; and it was likely, that like omissions would happen in other places, of which the times for such elections had not then elapsed.

And whereas on the fifteenth day of March last past, a supplement to to the said recited act of Assembly was passed to remedy all mistakes and lapses thereby given to the freeholders in cases to make such their election ; which time is now also passed. And whereas in and by the said supplement, further provision was made in the premises, in the words following:

" And whereas the freeholders of the several wards in the city of Philadelphia have neglected to elect Justices of the Peace, as by the said act was directed, and it may happen that some other parts of the State may also neglect to elect Justices, at the time in the said act and by this act directed : Be it enacted, by the authority aforesaid, That where any such neglect has been, or may be, at the time by the above recited act, or by this act directed for the election of Justices, for any district in any or either of the said counties, the Commissioners and Assessors of such county or counties, or any five of them (in such county or counties where they are directed so to do by the said act) are hereby enjoined and required to appoint a time and place for election of Justices of Peace for such district, and give notice thereof to the freeholders, who shall hold the

the said election, and in all things relating thereto, act and do agreeable to the directions of the act, to which this act is a supplement; and when they shall have elected Justices, they shall be deemed and taken to be Justices of the Peace, as is in and by the said act declared."

And whereas, notwithstanding the last recited section of said supplementary act, the freeholders of some districts may yet neglect to elect Justices of the Peace, in manner aforesaid, provision by said supplement is further made, that upon application in writing, by twenty or more of the freeholders of any such district, to the President of this State, it shall be lawful for the President in Council to appoint and commissionate one, or more Justice, or Justices of the Peace, as the case may require for any such district, which may still neglect to elect Justices of the Peace. Wherefore, notice is hereby given to the freeholders of any district as aforesaid, wherein no election of Justices of the Peace hath been hitherto holden, of the remedy provided by law, and of the mode in which they ought to proceed, in order to have justice duly administered. And it is recommended, because of these words in the third section of said supplement, above transcribed, "in such county and counties, where they are so directed to do by the said act," words which seem to confine the appointment of the time and place of the election to the Commissioners and Assessors of the counties of Philadelphia, Bucks, Chester, Lancaster, Berks, York, and Northampton; that in case of the return of any choice yet to be made, of Justices in Cumberland, Bedford, Northumberland, and Westmoreland, that said return be accompanied with an application in writing, from twenty or more of the freeholders of the district, to the President, to appoint, as aforesaid, in order to make the commission valid; whatever said recited words

may purport—at the same time, the freeholder may be assured, that their election, and the return thereof, shall be regarded as in other cases.

N. B. Some districts have perhaps made elections regularly, but their officers may not have made returns of the persons elected, or having made their returns, their returns may have miscarried, or fallen into the hands of ill-disposed persons, and may have been suppressed. In such cases new returns are wanted, and it would be safe to send duplicates. These lapses and defects prevent a second Commission of the Peace for each county from being issued, while they should include all the vacant districts for single commissions, being a great expence on the counties.

Extract from the Minutes,

T. MALTACK, Secretary.

Annapolis, July 10.
An Act for the better security of the Government.

Whereas, in every free state, allegiance and protection are reciprocal, and no man is entitled to have the benefit of the one, who chuses to yield to the other; and as every inhabitant of this state enjoys the protection and benefit of the Government, and laws thereof; and it is reasonable that every person, if required, should give testimony of his attachment and fidelity to this State, and the present Government thereof as now established.

Be it enacted, by the General Assembly of Maryland, That every free male person within this State, above eighteen years of age, unless a Quaker, Menonist, or Dunker, if required, shall take, repeat, and subscribe the oath of fidelity and support to this State, contained in the act, intitled, " An Act to punish certain crimes and misdemeanors, and to prevent the growth of Toryism;" and every free male Quaker, Menonist, or Dunker, within this State, above eighteen years of age, if required, shall solemnly, sincerely,

sincerely, and truly declare and affirm, in the words of the said oath, and thereto subscribe his name.

And be it enacted, That if any Judge or Justice, of his own knowledge, or from the information of some credible and reputable person, shall have good cause to suspect any person to be disaffected or dangerous to this State, or the present Government thereof, it shall and may be lawful for such Judge or Justice; and he is hereby authorized and required, to issue his warrant to bring such person before any Judge or Justice; and if the Judge or Justice shall adjudge such person dangerous or disaffected to this State, or the present Government thereof, he shall require such person to take, repeat, and subscribe the said oath; or make, repeat, and subscribe the said declaration; and on his refusal, shall require such person to enter into a recognizance of bail, with sufficient security for his appearance at the next court to be held for his county; and on his refusal to give such bail, shall commit such person to the public gaol, there to remain till discharged by due course of law; and the Judge or Justice shall certify the name of every person so refusing, to his next county court; and, if the court shall adjudge such person disaffected to this State, or the present Government thereof, they shall require such person to take, repeat, and subscribe the said oath; or to make, repeat, and subscribe the said declaration; and if such person so required shall refuse to take the said oath, or make the said declaration, the said court shall record such refusal, and thereupon such person shall be so far considered as an outlaw, as to be incapable of commencing or prosecuting any suit in any court of this State, for the recovery of any debt or damages, for any money or tobacco, due or owing to him in his own right, unless, previous to suit, he shall take, repeat, and subscribe the said

oath, or make, repeat, and subscribe the said declaration, before some Judge or Justice; and in case of neglect thereof, the Court, before whom such suit shall be brought, shall, *ex officio*, enter judgment of nonsuit, and such person shall also be disabled to use or practise the science of physic or surgery, or the art of an apothecary, or the trade of merchandize, or buying and selling, or any liberal science, for his gain, within this State, until such time as he shall take and subscribe the said oath, or make and subscribe the said declaration, before some Judge or Justice, and shall also be for ever incapable to hold or exercise any office, civil or military, within this State, and obliged by such Court, to enter into recognizance, with sufficient security for his good behaviour, for so long time as the Court shall adjudge, not exceeding the present war with Great-Britain; and if such person shall be adjudged by the Court a dangerous person to reside in this State, the Court shall require such person to enter into recognizance, with sufficient security for his appearance before the Governor and the Council, or the next General Court, and on his refusal to enter into such recognizance, shall commit such person to the public gaol, there to remain till discharged by due course of law; and if the Governor and the Council, or the General Court, shall adjudge such person's residence in this State dangerous to the State or Government thereof, they shall adjudge such person to be banished this State for ever, and in case of return, to be close imprisoned for life in such gaol as the Governor shall direct; and the Governor and the Council, or the General Court, may allow such person a reasonable time, not exceeding two months, to dispose, sell, or carry away his property, provided such person shall enter into recognizance, or give a bond, with sufficient security for his

his good and peaceable behaviour in the mean time, and provided such person shall also enter into bond, with sufficient security to the Chancellor for the payment of all debts which he may owe to any of the subjects of this or any other of the United States, and in case of refusal to enter into such recognizance, or to give such bond, such person shall be immediately banished, and his property invested in such Commissioners as the Governor and Council, or the Court by their order, may appoint, who shall thereout, and by public sale thereof, pay the debts of such person, and the balance, if any, shall be by them paid to the order of such person; and the said Commissioners shall have, and may retain in their hands a commission of five per cent. for their trouble; and the said Commissioner may enter into and possess the estate of such person, or recover in law or equity, in their names, any debts or other property belonging to such person, in the same manner as such person would or might have done, by the laws of this State, for the purposes aforesaid.

And be it enacted, That if any constable shall refuse or neglect to execute such warrant from any Judge or Justice, he shall forfeit and pay the sum of 5l. current money, and shall be entitled to receive seven shillings and sixpence from the person on whom he shall serve such warrant.

And be it enacted, That the Clerk at the General and every County Court shall, without fee or reward, keep a fair transcript in his office of the said oath and declaration to be subscribed by any person taking or making the same in open Court, and shall make an entry in his minutes, and in the records of the proceedings of his Court, of the time when any person shall take or make the said oath or declaration; and if such person shall hold or exercise any office of profit or trust in this State, he shall

also note what office such person shall hold or exercise. And every Judge or Justice shall keep in his house a fair transcript of the said oath and declaration for every person to subscribe, who shall take or make the same before him, and shall also certify to his next General or County Court the name of every person who shall take or make the said oath or declaration before him, and the time when, and the office of profit or trust such person shall hold, or enjoy, and the Clerk of the Court to which such certificate shall be entered, shall enter the same among the records of the proceedings of his Court; but no Judge or Justice shall be obliged to administer such oath, or take such declaration, out of Court, unless at the house where he shall usually live or reside.

Whereas several Officers under the late Government, and other persons, late inhabitants of this State, have fled from and deserted the defence of this country in the present just and necessary war, leaving considerable estates to be defended by the blood and treasure of the good people of this State, and it appearing very unreasonable that such persons should return, unless within a limited time, to this State, which they have deserted in the hour of distress and danger, to enjoy, without any risque, every benefit from the war, if our arms should be blessed with success:

Be it enacted, That no person who fled from this State since the fourteenth day of August, seventeen hundred seventy-five, and did not subscribe the association, unless he shall return to this State within twelve months from the end of this present session, shall ever return to this State. And if such person shall return to this State within or after the twelve months aforesaid, and shall not take, repeat, and subscribe the said oath, or make, repeat, and subscribe the said declaration of fidelity and support to this State, within ten days after his return,

he

he shall be close imprisoned for life in such gaol as the Governor shall direct, and shall also forfeit all his property within this State; and such property shall, on conviction in the General Court of his flight as aforesaid, and return and neglect as aforesaid, be invested in such Commissioners as the Court shall appoint, who shall thereout, and by public sale thereof, first pay the debts of such person, to any of the subjects of this or any of the United States, and afterwards, the balance, if any, to the Treasurer of their shore, for the use of this State; and the said Commissioners shall have, and may retain in their hands, five per cent. commission for their trouble.

Whereas it appears to be reasonable, that the property within this State of such persons who may have fled as aforesaid, and also of all such who shall refuse, when required, to take the said oath, or make the said declaration, as required by this Act, should pay a sum of money in lieu of the danger and risque of pains and forfeitures which they might incur, if engaged in the service and defence of this State;

Be it enacted, that the Justices of the several County Courts shall annually, at their respective august Courts, make diligent enquiry after every person who has fled from their country as aforesaid, and shall enter his name, together with the name of every person who shall refuse as aforesaid to take the said oath, or make the said declaration. on the Minutes of the proceedings of their Court at their then sitting, and shall annually, during the lives of such persons who shall refuse to comply as aforesaid with the directions of this Act, assess and rate the estate of such person in any sum not exceeding five pounds current money for every hundred pounds of property belonging to such person within this State, in lieu of the risque and danger of pains and

forfeitures such persons might incur if engaged in the service and defence of this State; and the Clerk of the Court shall annually, before the fifth day of September, deliver a copy of such assessment to the Collector of his county, who shall collect the same in the same manner as the rate and assessment by the Act intitled, " An Act to assess and impose an equal tax on all property within this State," is to be collected and levied; and if the property of such person shall lie in any other county, such Clerk shall send a certificate of such person's flight, refusal or neglect, to the Court of the county or counties in which the property of such person may lie, and such Court shall assess and rate the property of such person as aforesaid, and the Collector of such county or counties shall collect and levy such rate as aforesaid.

By the House of Delegates, June 19, 1777. Read the first time, and ordered to lie on the table.

By order,
    G. Duvall, Cl. H. D.

By the House of Delegates, June 21, 1777. Read the second time, and will pass. By order,
    G. Duvall, Cl. H. D.

By the Senate, June 23, 1777. Read the first time, and ordered to lie on the table. By order,
    A. C. Hanson, Cl. Sen.

By the Senate, June 26, 1777. Read the second time, and will not pass. By order,
    A. C. Hanson, Cl. Sen.

An Act to reinforce the American Army.

Be it enacted by the General Assembly of Maryland, That if any person within this State, between sixteen and fifty years of age, shall, on or before the fifteenth day of August next, furnish and deliver to any recruiting Serjeant appointed by the Governor and the Council, or any officer in any of the battalions raised

by

by this State, an healthy, able bodied recruit, being a freeman, or an Irifh or American indented fervant, or apprentice, not employed in the trade of a fhip-carpenter, gunfmith, blackfmith, tavlor, fhoemaker, or weaver, in any linen, woollen, iron, or wire manufactory, to ferve in any one of the battalions raifed by this State for the term of three years, fuch perfon fhall be exempt from any militia or military duty for the faid term of three years; and fuch perfon is hereby required not to give more than thirty dollars reward to fuch recruit.

And be it enacted, That in cafe any two perfons, in confequence of the recommendation of Congrefs, have, before the paffing of this Act, furnifhed one able bodied recruit as aforefaid, to ferve for the aforefaid term of three years, fuch two perfons, by furnifhing one other able bodied recruit as aforefaid, to ferve for the term of three years aforefaid, fhall be entitled to the above exemption.

And be it enacted, That fuch recruit fhall be entitled to receive the Continental bounty and other allow. ances: and the officer to whom he fhall be delivered, fhall give a certificate, expreffing the name of the recruit, the time when he enlifted, and the name of the perfon who fhall furnifh and deliver the recruit.

And be it enacted, That every healthy, able bodied man as aforefaid (not furnifhed by or receiving any reward from perfons exempted as aforefaid) who fhall hereafter enter into any of the battalions raifed by this State for three years, fhall be entitled to receive, from this State, a bounty of thirty dollars above the Continental allowance, and that the Governor and the Council be empowered to draw on the Treafurers for money fufficient for this purpofe, and to appoint recruiting Serjeants in each county, who fhall be paid the Continental allowance for their trouble.

And be it enacted, That the Governor and Council be empowered to order any part of the artillery companies raifed for the immediate defence of this State, not exceeding fifty-fix privates, under officers proper for fuch a number of artillerifts, to march with all expedition to the city of Philadelphia, there to obey the orders of Congrefs, or of his Excellency General Wafhington, and to remain in the Continental fervice during this campaign, or fo long as the Commander in Chief fhall require their fervice, unlefs the exigencies of this State fhould require their recall by the Governor and the Council.

And be it enacted, That no officer of the United States fhall enlift any of the inhabitants of this State in the fervice of the United States, unlefs in fome one of the battalions from this State, under the penalty of one hundred pounds for each perfon enlifted contrary hereto.

An Act to punifh Forestalling and Engroffing, and for other purpofes.

Whereas all endeavours to enhance the common price of merchandize, or the neceffaries of life, and all practices for that purpofe ought to be reftrained as far as poffible, and the art and avarice of foreftallers and engroffers in this State having been grievous and oppreffive to the inhabitants thereof, therefore

Be it enacted, by the General Affembly of Maryland, That if any perfon fhall buy, or caufe to be bought, any goods, wares, or merchandize, except the articles of grain and lumber, coming to any market or fair within this State to be fold in fuch market or fair, or coming to any city, or town, port, harbour, haven, or creek, within this State, to be fold, or fhall make any bargain, contract or promife for the having or buying of any goods, wares or merchandize, except as before excepted, or any part thereof, fo coming

Q q   as

as aforesaid, before the same shall be in the market, fair, city, town, port, harbour, haven, or creek, ready there to be sold, or shall dissuade any person coming to this State, or to any market or fair therein, to abstain or forbear to bring any goods, wares, or merchandize to this State, or any part thereof, shall be adjudged a forestaller, and on conviction thereof in the general or any county court, shall be fined by the court, not exceeding five hundred pounds, or imprisoned not exceeding one year, or both, in the discretion of the court. Provided, that buying by any person any goods, wares, or merchandize, coming to market, for the use and consumption of himself and family for a year, shall not be deemed forestalling.

And be it enacted, That if any person within this State shall buy, to sell again within this State, or in any of the adjoining States, any butter, beef, pork, cotton, wool, flax, woollens, hemp, tallow, raw hides, tanned leather, shoes, or salt, of the produce or growth of, or raised or manufactured in this State; or if any person within this State shall obtain or get into his hands, by buying, contracting or promise taking, (other than by demise, grant, or lease of land, or in payment for debt) any goods, wares or merchandize, within this State, except from the original importer, with intent to sell the same again within this State, or in any of the adjoining States, such person shall be adjudged an engrosser, and, on conviction thereof, in the general or any county court, shall forfeit any of the articles aforesaid so bought or got into his possession, one half to the State, and the other half to the informer, and may be fined not exceeding five hundred pounds, or imprisoned not exceeding one year, or both, in the discretion of the court. Provided always, and it is hereby declared, that the buying of any goods,

wares, or merchandize, by any agent of this or the United States, or the purchasing materials for the carrying on manufactories, and so converted in the house of the purchaser, or the buying of provisions by any licenced ordinary keepers, for the use of his ordinary, shall not be deemed engrossing within this Act.

And be it enacted, That the importer or manufacturer of all goods, wares and merchandizes, shall be allowed to sell the same by wholesale or retail.

And be it enacted, That no person shall purchase any goods imported into, or manufactured within this State, to sell, barter, or exchange again, unless he shall purchase the same from the original importer or manufacturer, under the forfeiture of the goods so purchased, one half to the State, and the other half to the informer, and under the penalty of five hundred pounds for each offence. But this restraint shall not extend to licenced ordinary keepers, so as to prohibit them from purchasing liquors, and other necessaries, for the common use of their ordinaries.

And be it enacted, That any person who shall purchase goods, wares, or merchandize in any of the United States, and bring them into this State for sale, shall be considered as a purchaser within this State, (unless such goods were imported by him through the Capes of Chesapeake-Bay, or through some one of the inlets of some neighbouring State) and shall sell them for ready money, if required, at not more than the rate of thirty *per centum* profit on the purchase-money, and the charges of transportation or carriage to the place where they shall be exposed to sale; except the articles of salt and brown sugar, which shall be sold at not more than thirty-five *per centum* upon the purchase-money and the charges aforesaid.

And be it enacted, That every retailer shall sell goods, purchased of the

the importer or manufacturer, for ready money, if required, at not more than at the rate of thirty *per centum* profit on the purchase-money paid to the importer or manufacturer, and the charges of transportation or carriage to the place where exposed to sale, except the articles of salt and brown sugar, which shall be sold at not more than thirty-five *per centum* profit on the purchase-money, with the charges aforesaid. And the importer, if a resident of this State, shall deliver into his county court-office, on or before the first day of each county court, a list on oath, signed by him and the purchaser, of the names of all persons to whom he shall sell at wholesale, and the price; and if a foreigner shall be the importer, he shall deliver such list as aforesaid into the naval office of the district; in which the vessel bringing the goods shall be entered; and such list, or an attested copy thereof, by the clerk of the county or naval officer, shall be evidence on a prosecution or suit against the retailer.

And if any such retailer shall refuse to sell any goods, wares, or merchandize, at the price above limited, for ready money, if required, he shall forfeit and pay five pounds for each refusal; and if any importer shall neglect to lodge the list as above required, he shall forfeit and pay five hundred pounds for each neglect.

And be it enacted, That no person shall purchase any goods, wares, or merchandize, condemned in the Courts of Admiralty, from the original purchaser thereof, to sell, barter, or exchange again, and the original purchaser shall sell the same, reserving sufficient for the use of himself and his family for one year, for ready money, if required, at not more than the rate of thirty *per centum* profit on the purchase-money, and the charges of transportation or carriage to the place where exposed to sale, except the articles of salt and

brown sugar, which shall be sold at not more than thirty-five *per centum* profit on the purchase money, with the charges aforesaid. Provided, that if the owners of any prize become purchasers, they shall be considered as importers, and at liberty to sell by wholesale or retail.

And be it enacted, That if such purchaser of condemned goods shall refuse to sell, at the price above limited, for ready money, if required, he shall forfeit and pay five hundred pounds for each refusal.

Whereas it is represented to this General Assembly, that several persons from some of the neighbouring States have engrossed very large quantities of iron, rum, sugar, cotton, salt, and molasses:

Be it enacted, That none of the said articles shall be carried out of this State; and that the purchasers thereof shall sell the same by retail within this State, to the inhabitants thereof, if required, at not more than the rate of ten *per centum* profit on the purchase-money; and if any of the said purchasers, their agents, factors, storekeepers, or trustees, in whose possession any of the said articles may be, shall refuse to sell the said articles, or any of them, at the rate aforesaid, to any of the inhabitants of this State, as aforesaid, he or they so refusing, shall, for every offence, forfeit the sum of five pounds current money, one half thereof to the informer, and the other half to the use of this State; and shall also forfeit, to the uses aforesaid, the goods so as aforesaid refused to be sold.

And be it enacted, That no goods, wares, or merchandize, shall be exposed to sale by public vendue (except household furniture, goods condemned in the Court of Admiralty, or sold under contract for that purpose, heretofore made, or by distress for rent, or by process out of the courts of law or equity, or by the executor or administrator for any deceased person) under

penalty

penalty of one hundred pounds on the perfon felling or buying at fuch vendue.

And whereas it is reprefented to this General Affembly, that divers perfons, inhabitants of this State, have engroffed large quantities of falt, rum, fugar, molaffes, coffee, and iron, with intent to fell the fame again at high and exorbitant prices, by means whereof the inhabitants are greatly oppreffed ; and whereas alfo feveral perfons of this State may have purchafed and laid up for the ufe of their families, more falt than is fufficient for to ferve their families for one year, from this time :

Be it enacted, That all and every of the perfons who have fo engroffed the faid articles as aforefaid, fhall fell the fame by retail to the inhabitants of this State, at not more than the rate of ten *per centum* profit on the purchafe-money, referving fo much of the faid articles as may be neceffary for himfelf and family for one year, and not felling more of the overplus of the article of falt to any perfon than fhall be fufficient for the ufe of his family for one year, allowing one peck to each individual of fuch family : and if any of the faid perfons who have engroffed any of the faid articles as aforefaid, fhall refufe to fell the fame at the rate aforefaid, and in the manner aforefaid, he fhall, for every offence, forfeit the fum of five pounds current money, and the goods fo refufed to be fold, one half thereof to the ufe of the informer, and the other half to the ufe of this State.

And be it further enacted, That if any perfon or perfons, in this State, hath, or have purchafed, or laid up for the ufe of his or their family or families, more falt than fhall be fufficient for his or their family or families for one year from this time, fuch perfon or perfons fhall fell the overplus to the inhabitants of this State by retail, at the fame rate, and in the fame manner and proportion, as the perfons who have engroffed falt as above-metioned, are directed to fell the fame ; and if any perfon fhall refufe to fell the overplus of his falt, at the rate and manner aforefaid, he fhall forfeit, for every offence, the fum of five pounds current money, and the overplus of his falt fo refufed to be fold, one half to the informer, and the other half to the ufe of this State.

And be it enacted, That if the owner or poffeffor of any of the articles above-mentioned, fhall attempt to remove any of them out of this State, it fhall and may be lawful for any perfon to feize the fame, and every fuch article, fo attempted to be carried out of this State, fhall be forfeited, one half to the perfon feizing the fame, and the other half to the ufe of this State.

And be it enacted, That the Governor and the Council be empowered to draw on the Treafurer of the Weftern fhore, for a fum not exceeding two thoufand pounds, and to apply the fame, or fo much as they may think neceffary, in erecting falt works in fuch part or parts of this State as they may think moft proper, and to employ a manager, and to direct any quantity made to be fold and diftributed in the feveral counties, in proportion to the number of inhabitants in each county, allowing a peck to each perfon for the year.

And be it enacted, That the following bounties be allowed to private adventurers (to whom no money has been or fhall be advanced by the public) who fhall, before the firft day of February next, make falt within this State, to wit : for fifty bufhels, the fum of five pounds ; for one hundred bufhels, ten pounds ; for two hundred bufhels, twenty pounds ; and for five hundred bufhels, fifty pounds ; and the Treafurer of either fhore fhall pay the faid bounties to any perfons bringing a certificate, expreffing the quantity, and the place and time

when

when and where made, from the Court of the county wherein the falt fhall be made.

And be it enacted, That a premium of two hundred pounds fhall be paid by either of the treafurers to the firft perfon to whom no money has been or fhall be advanced by the public, who fhall produce a certificate from any county Court of this State, of his having made one thoufand bufhels of falt within this State, before the firft day of February next.

And be it enacted, That the Governor and the Council be empowered to draw on the Treafurer of the Weftern fhore for any fum not exceeding one thoufand pounds, to be advanced by them in any fum not exceeding two hundred and fifty pounds, to any one adventurer, who they fhall think fit and trufty, and who will enter into bond with fecurity, faithfully and without delay to apply the fame in erecting falt works within this State, and to repay the fame without intereft, after one year from the advance.

This Act to continue and be in force for and during the term of one year, and to the end of the next feffion of Affembly, which fhall happen after the expiration of the faid one year.

Annapolis, July 3.

On Sunday laft the General Affembly of this State adjourned to Monday the 8th of September next, after having paffed the following laws:

1. An Act to continue an Act for the fufpending the power of the Commiffioners for building a Court-houfe and prifon in Hartford county.

2. An Act directing the Juftices of Frederick county to afcertain the number of taxables in Wafhington and Montgomery counties, and to enable the Sheriffs of thofe counties to collect their proportion of the public levy, as fettled by the Juftices of Frederick county.

3. An Act to enable the corpora-

tion of the city of Annapolis to fell or leafe certain lands, and to enlarge and afcertain the jurifdiction of the Mayor's Court of the faid city.

4. An Act to revive and aid the proceedings of Cæcil County Court.

5. An Act for the recovery of fines on non-enrollers.

6. An Act to revive the proceedings of Saint Mary's County Court.

7. An Act to continue an Act for enlarging the powers of the Governor and the Council.

8. An Act to reinforce the American army.

9. An Act to remove the records of the Prerogative Office.

10. An Act to repeal part of an Act to promote the recruiting fervice.

11. An Act to punifh foreftalling and engroffing, and for the other purpofes.

12. An Act for the fpeedy recovery of fmall debts out of Court.

13. An Act for the fpecial appointment of Infpectors.

14. A fupplement to the Acts for affeffment of property,

15. An Act for the relief of Jean Collineau, of Marfeilles, in the kingdom of France, (a private Act.)

16. An Act relating to the Treafurers.

17. An Act to regulate the militia.

18. An Act for the payment of the journals of accounts.

19. An Act to direct the recording of a deed to William Smith, (a private Act.)

By his Excellency THOMAS JOHNSON, Efq. Governor of Maryland.

A PROCLAMATION.

Whereas many of the foldiers who inlifted in the late Col. Smallwood's battalion, and the independent companies, have not yet joined any of the regiments of Continental troops raifing in this State, I have therefore thought fit, at the requeft of the General Affembly, to publifh this my Proclamation, hereby requiring fuch
of

of them as are on the Eastern shore to appear on or before the last day of July next, at farthest, at any place where Col. Richardson's regiment shall be ; and such of them as shall be on the Western shore, to appear on or before the last day of July next, at the city of Annapolis, or Baltimore, or Frederick-town, under the penalty of being treated as deserters ; and do promise to such who shall so appear, that they shall be indulged to enter for three years in any of the battalions raised by this State, and shall thereupon receive the Continental bounty, and other allowances. And that all persons concerned may have due notice of this my Proclamation, the several Sheriffs within this State are hereby commanded to make the same public in their respective counties.

Given at Annapolis, this thirtieth day of June, in the year of our Lord one thousand seven hundred and seventy-seven.

THO. JOHNSON.

By his Excellency's command,

T. JOHNSON, jun. Sec.

God save the State.

By His Excellency JOHN M'KINLY, Esquire, *President, Captain-general and Commander in Chief, of the Delaware State.*

A PROCLAMATION.

Whereas I have received information, that sundry base and sordid persons, inhabitants of the county of Sussex, in this State, do carry on a criminal intercourse and traffic with the crews of the enemy's ships of war, which are stationed on that coast, and supply them with provisions, to the great damage of the public, and in direct violation of an Act of Assembly of the said State. In order therefore that such traitors to their country should be brought to condign and exemplary punishment, I have thought fit, with the advice of the Privy Council, to issue this my Proclamation, hereby strictly enjoining and requiring all Judges, Justices, Sheriffs, Constables, and other officers, as well as all other the inhabitants of this State, to make diligent inquiry after every person carrying on such criminal intercourse and traffic with our enemies, and to use all possible means for apprehending and securing all such persons, that they may be dealt with as their crimes deserve, and the law directs. And I do hereby promise and engage, that the public reward of two hundred dollars shall be paid to any person or persons, who shall apprehend, and secure, in one of the goals in this State, any person trafficking as aforesaid, who shall be legally convicted thereof : and I do promise, moreover, a full pardon for every such offence to any person who shall give due information, whereby any such trafficker shall be apprehended and convicted according to law.

Given under my hand, and the Great Seal of the State, the second day of July, in the year of our Lord one thousand seven hundred and seventy-seven.

JOHN M'KINLY.

By his Excellency's Command,

JAMES BOOTH, Sec.

By his Excellency JOHN M'KINLY, Esquire, President, Captain-general and Commander in Chief of the Delaware State.

A PROCLAMATION.

Whereas I have received information, That divers counterfeit bills, of the likeness of paper bills of credit of the denomination of thirty dollars, issued by the Honourable the Continental Congress, May 10, 1775, have been passed and uttered in the county of Sussex, in this State : and whereas Dorman Loffland, late Sheriff of the said county, stands charged, on oath, with the uttering of divers of the said counterfeit bills, and that he hath fled for the same : and as it is necessary, as well for the security of the interest of individuals

as

as for the profperity of the United States of America, that the counterfeiting of the paper money, emitted by Congrefs, and uttering the fame, fhould be prevented, and the actors therein be brought to condign and exemplary punifhment, I have thought fit, with the advice and confent of the Privy Council, to iffue this my Proclamation, hereby ftrictly enjoining and requiring all Judges, Juftices, Sheriffs, Conftables and other officers, as well as all other the inhabitants within this State, to make diligent fearch and enquiry after the faid Dorman Loffland, and to ufe all poffible means for apprehending and fecuring him, that he may be proceeded againft according to law. And I do hereby promife and engage, that the public reward of three hundred dollars fhall be paid to any perfon or perfons who fhall apprehend and fecure the faid Dorman Loffland in one of the gaols of this State, fo that he may be profecuted on the charge aforefaid.

Given under my hand and the Great Seal of the State, the third day of July, in the year of our Lord one thoufand feven hundred and feventy-feven. JOHN M'KINLY.

By his Excellency's command,
JAMES BOOTH, Sec.

Virginia.

Abftract of an Act for eftablifhing an Office for the purpofe of borrowing money for the ufe of the Commonwealth.

Whereas it is expedient that one million of dollars, or the value thereof in other money, fhould be immediately borrowed, to prevent, as far as may be, the farther emiffion of large fums of paper money: be it therefore enacted by the General Affembly, That George Webb, Efq. or the Treafurer for the time being, fhall open an office for that purpofe in the city of Williamfburgh, previous to which, as well for the faithful difcharge of the duties thereof as what may be farther required of him by this Act, he fhall give bond, with good fecurity, in the fum of two hundred thoufand pounds, payable to the Governor and his fucceffors, for the ufe of the Commonwealth. And the faid George Webb, or the Treafurer for the time being, is empowered and directed to receive from any perfon whatever fum of fpecie, Continental paper dollars, or bills of credit iffued by authority of this Commonwealth, he or fhe fhall be willing to lend, for any term not exceeding three years, fo as fuch fum be not lefs than three hundred dollars, or the value thereof in other money, lent by any one perfon, and to give the lender a receipt for the money lent in the form following, that is to fay: *The Treafurer of the Commonwealth of Virginia acknowledgeth the receipt of   dollars from   which he promifes to pay to the faid   or bearer, on the   day of   with intereft, at the rate of fix per centum per annum, agreeable to an Act paffed at a General Affembly, begun and held at the Capitol, in the city of Williamfburg, on Monday the fifth day of May, in the year of our Lord one thoufand feven hundred and feventy-feven. Witnefs the hand of the Treafurer, this   day of   . Which* receipt fhall be figned by the Treafurer, who fhall keep a book containing a counterpart thereof, of which, fo often as he receives money lent, he fhall cut a certificate indent ways, fill up and deliver the fame to the lender, keeping the book as a check in his office. He fhall, moreover, keep regular books, in which due entries fhall be made of the fums borrowed, of the time when, and of the names of the perfons by whom, the faid fums were lent, for which fervices he fhall be allowed to retain one eighth *per centum* on all monies received into his office, in lieu of all claims he may

may have for transacting the business thereof.

Provided always, That when the said sum of one million of dollars, or the value thereof in other money, is borrowed, the said George Webb, Esq. or the Treasurer for the time being, shall forbear receiving any more money upon such loans.

And be it further enacted, That the Treasurer shall pay the interest of the money due upon such certificates annually, and take in and discharge the principal thereof at the time or times therein limited for that purpose; or should the lender or bearer of such certificates desire to have the same paid and discharged before the time limited for that purpose, the Treasurer is hereby authorized to comply therewith, provided the state of the Treasury will admit of the same, without prejudice to the Public.

And be it further enacted, That if any person within this Commonwealth shall forge or counterfeit, alter or erase, any certificate of money lent as aforesaid, or transfer any certificate to another, or demand payment at the office of principal or interest thereupon, knowing the same to be forged or counterfeited, altered or erased, every person so offending, and being lawfully convicted, shall forfeit his whole estate, real and personal, receive on his bare back, at the public whipping-post, thirty-nine lashes, and shall be obliged to serve on board some armed vessel in the service of this State, without wages, not exceeding seven years.

Williamsburg, (Virginia) June 27.

Last Tuesday Richard Henry Lee, Esq. was chosen one of the Delegates to represent this State in General Congress, in the room of George Mason, Esq. who has declined his appointment.

In the HOUSE of DELEGATES,
Friday, June 20, 1777.

Resolved, That the thanks of this House be given by the Speaker to Richard Henry Lee, Esq. for the faithful services he has rendered his country in the discharge of his duty as one of the Delegates from this State in General Congress.

And thereupon Mr. Speaker gave Mr. Lee, he standing up in his place, the thanks of the House as follows:

Sir,

It is with a particular pleasure that I obey this command of the House; because it gives me an opportunity, whilst I am performing an act of duty to them, to perform an act of justice to you. Serving with you in Congress, and attentively observing your conduct there, I thought that you manifested in the American cause a zeal truly patriotic; and, as far as I could judge, exerted the abilities you are confessedly distinguished for, to promote the good and prosperity of your own country in particular, and of the United States in general. That the tribute of praise deserved may reward those who do well, and encourage others to follow your example, the House has come to this resolution:

Resolved, That the thanks of this House be given by the Speaker to Richard Henry Lee, Esq. for the faithful services he has rendered his country in the discharge of his duty as one of the Delegates from this State in Congress.

To which Mr. Lee answered:

Mr. Speaker,

I thank the House for this instance of candour and justice, which I accept the more willingly, as my conscience informs me, it is not undeserved. I consider the approbation of my country, Sir, as the highest reward for faithful services; and it shall be my constant care to merit that approbation by a diligent attention to public duties.

My thanks are particularly due to you, Sir, for the obliging manner in which you have been pleased to signify the vote of this House; and I pray you, Sir, to receive my grateful acknowledgments.

In

In SENATE, *June* 21, 1777.

On a motion made, Resolved, as a just tribute to Richard Henry Lee, Esq. our worthy Delegate in General Congress, that the Speaker be desired to present him the warmest thanks of this House for his unwearied diligence and fidelity in discharge of that important trust.

The above Resolve was enclosed in a letter from the Speaker to Richard Henry Lee, Esq. in answer to which the Senate received the following letter, directed to the Speaker:

Sir, *June* 23, 1777.

As nothing can be more valuable to a citizen than the approbation of his countrymen, so I have received, with singular pleasure, the honourable testimony that the House of Senators has been pleased to give of my conduct in Congress as a Delegate from this Commonwealth.

That community which is willing to acknowledge the fidelity of its servants, can never want such as are zealous to promote its best interest, honest and diligent in discharge of their duty.

It shall be my care, Sir, to deserve, on all occasions of public trust, the reward that the Honourable Senate have now conferred upon me. I am, with sentiments of duty and respect for the Honourable House, Sir, your most humble servant,

RICHARD HENRY LEE.

Williamsburg, July 18, 1777.

By his Excellency PATRICK HENRY, *Esq. Governor or Chief Magistrate of the Commonwealth of Virginia*;

A PROCLAMATION.

Whereas I have been credibly informed, that several persons are going about in the different parts of this State, some of them in the guise of officers, engrossing the commodities of the country at the most extravagant prices, with a view, as is supposed, of depreciating our currency, and discouraging people, moreover, by their false and injurious reports of the condition of our army under his Excellency General Washington, and of the general posture of our affairs, from engaging in the American service: to the end, therefore, that all such persons may be vigilantly inspected, and particularly that they may be obliged to give that security for their friendship which the Act of the last session of Assembly requires of all persons coming within this State from any other of the United States, and that such of them as may appear to violate another Act of a former session, by discouraging people from enlisting as soldiers, may be brought to condign punishment, I have thought proper, by and with the advice of the Council, to issue this my Proclamation, hereby requiring all officers, both civil and military, within this Commonwealth, and all other subjects thereof, to be aiding and assisting in this business as they tender the welfare of their country, and as they shall answer the contrary at their peril.

Given under my hand, this 8th day of July in the 2d year of the Commonwealth, *annoque Domini,* 1777. PATRICK HENRY.

The AMERICAN CRISIS, No. III.

By the Author of COMMON-SENSE.

(*Published at Philadelphia, the* 19*th of April last.*)

IN the progress of politics, as in the common occurrences of life, we are not only apt to forget the ground we have travelled over, but frequently neglect to gather up experience as we go. We expend, if I may so say, the knowledge of every day on the circumstances that produce it, and journey on in search of new matter and new refinements: but as it is pleasant, and sometimes useful, to look back, even to the first periods

R r of

of infancy, and trace the turns and windings through which we have paſſed, ſo we may likewiſe derive many advantages by halting a while in our political career, and taking a review of the wondrous complicated labyrinth of little more than yeſterday.

Truly, may we ſay, that never did man grow old in ſo ſhort a time! We have crowded the buſineſs of an age into the compaſs of a few months, and have been driven through ſuch a rapid ſucceſſion of things, that, for the want of leiſure to think, we unavoidably waſted knowledge as we came, and have left nearly as much behind us as we brought with us: but the road is yet rich with fragments, and, before we fully loſe ſight of them, will repay us for the trouble of ſtopping to pick them up.

Were a man to be totally deprived of memory, he would be incapable of forming any juſt opinion; every thing about him would ſeem a chaos; he would even have his own hiſtory to aſk from every one; and by not knowing how the world went on in his abſence, he would be at a loſs to know how it ought to go on when he recovered, or rather, returned to it again. In like manner, though in a leſs degree, a too great inattention to paſt occurrences retards and bewilders our judgment in every thing; while, on the contrary, by comparing what is paſt with what is preſent, we frequently hit on the true character of both, and become wiſe with very little trouble. It is a kind of countermarch, by which we get into the rear of Time, and mark the movements and meaning of things as we make our return. There are certain circumſtances, which, at the time of their happening, are kind of riddles; and as every riddle is to be followed by its anſwer, ſo thoſe kind of circumſtances will be followed by their events, and thoſe events are always the true ſolution. A conſiderable ſpace of time may lapſe between,

and unleſs we continue our obſervations from the one to the other, the harmony of them will paſs away unnoticed: but the misfortune is, that partly from the preſſing neceſſity of ſome inſtant things, and partly from the impatience of our tempers, we are frequently in ſuch a hurry to make out the meaning of every thing as faſt as it happens, that we thereby never truly underſtand it; and not only ſtart new difficulties to ourſelves by ſo doing, but, as it were, embarraſs Providence in her good deſigns.

I have been civil in ſtating this fault on a large ſcale; for, as it now ſtands, it does not appear to be levelled againſt any particular ſet of men; but were it to be refined a little further, it might afterwards be applied to the Tories with a degree of ſtriking propriety: thoſe men have been remarkable for drawing ſudden concluſions from ſingle facts. The leaſt apparent miſhap on our ſide, or the leaſt ſeeming advantage on the part of the enemy, have determined the fate of a whole campaign. By this haſty judgment they have converted a retreat into a defeat; miſtook generalſhip for error; while every little advantage purpoſely given the enemy, either to weaken their ſtrength by dividing it, embarraſs their councils by multiplying their objects, or to ſecure a greater poſt by the ſurrender of a leſs, has been inſtantly magnified into a conqueſt. Thus, by quartering ill policy upon ill principles, they have frequently promoted the cauſe they deſigned to injure, and injured that which they intended to promote.

It is probable the campaign may open before this number comes from the preſs. The enemy have long lain idle, and amuſed themſelves with carrying on the war by Proclamations only. While they continue their delay, our ſtrength increaſes; and were they to move to action now, it is a circumſtantial proof they have no reinforcement

inforcement coming; wherefore, in either cafe, the comparative advantage will be ours. Like a wounded difabled whale, they want only time and room to die in: and though in the agony of their exit, it may be unfafe to live within the flapping of their tail, yet every hour fhortens their date, and leffens their power of mifchief. If any thing happens while this Number is in the prefs, it will afford me a fubject for the laft pages of it. At prefent I am tired of waiting; and as neither the enemy, nor the ftate of politics, have yet produced any thing new, I am thereby left in the field of general matter undirected by any ftriking or particular object. This Crifis, therefore, will be made up rather of variety than novelty, and confift more of things ufeful than things wonderful.

The fuccefs of the caufe, the union of the people, and the means of fupporting and fecuring both, are points which cannot be too much attended to. He who doubts of the former is a defponding coward, and he who wilfully difturbs the latter is a traitor. Their characters are eafily fixed, and under thefe fhort defcriptions I leave them for the prefent.

One of the greateft degrees of fentimental union which America ever knew, was in denying the right of the Britifh Parliament " TO BIND THE COLONIES IN ALL CASES WHATSOEVER." The declaration is in its form an almighty one, and is the loftieft ftretch of arbitrary power that ever one fet of men, or one country claimed over another. Taxation was nothing more than putting the declared right into practice; and this failing, recourfe was had to arms, as a means to eftablifh both the right and the practice, or to anfwer a worfe purpofe, which will be mentioned in the courfe of this Number. And in order to repay themfelves the expence of an army, and to profit by their own injuftice, the

Colonies were, by another law, declared to be in a ftate of actual rebellion, and of confequence all property therein would fall to the conquerors.

The Colonies, on their part, firft, denied the right; fecondly, they fufpended the ufe of taxable articles, and petitioned againft the practice of taxation: and thefe failing, they, thirdly, defended their property by force, as foon as it was forcibly invaded; and in anfwer to the declaration of rebellion and non-protection, publifhed their declaration of Independence, and right to felf-protection.

Thefe, in a few words, are the different ftages of the quarrel; and the parts are fo intimately and neceffarily connected with each other, as to admit of no feparation. A perfon, to ufe a trite phrafe, muft be a Whig or a Tory in the lump. His feelings, as a man, may be wounded; his charity, as a Chriftian, may be moved; but his political principles muft go through all the cafes on one fide or the other. He cannot be a Whig in *this* ftage, and a Tory in *that*. If he fays he is againft the United Independence of the Continent, he is to all intents and purpofes againft her in all the reft; becaufe THIS LAST comprehends the whole. And he may juft as well fay, that Britain was right in declaring us rebels; right in taxing us: and right in declaring her " RIGHT TO BIND THE COLONIES IN ALL CASES WHATSOEVER." It fignifies nothing what neutral ground, of his own creation, he may fkulk upon for fhelter; for the quarrel in no ftage of it hath afforded any fuch ground; and either we or Britain are abfolutely right or abfolutely wrong through the whole.

Britain, like a gamefter nearly ruined, hath now put all her loffes into one bet, and is playing a defperate game for the total. If fhe win it, fhe wins from ME my life; fhe wins the Continent as the forfeited

property

property of rebels; the right of taxing those that are left as reduced subjects; and the power of binding them as slaves: and the single die which determines this unparalleled event is, Whether we support our Independence, or she overturn it. This is coming to the point at once. Here is the touch-stone to try men by. *He that is not a supporter of the Independent States of America, in the same degree that his religious and political principles would suffer him to support the government of any other country of which he called himself 'a subject, is, in the American sense of the word.* A TORY; *and the instant that he endeavours to bring his Toryism into practice, he becomes* A TRAITOR. The first can only be detected by a general test, and the law hath already provided for the latter.

It is unnatural and impolitic to admit men who would root up our Independence to have any share in our legislation, either as electors or representatives; because the support of our Independence rests, in a great measure, on the vigour and purity of our public bodies. Would Britain, even in time of peace, much less in time of war, suffer an election to be carried by men who professed themselves not to be her subjects, or allow such to sit in Parliament? Certainly not.

But there a certain species of Tories with whom conscience or principle hath nothing to do, and who are so from avarice only. Some of the first fortunes in the Continent, on the part of the Whigs, are staked on the issue of our present measures. And shall disaffection only be rewarded with security? Can any thing be a greater inducement to a miserly man, than the hope of making his mammon safe? And though the scheme be fraught with every character of folly, yet, so long as he supposes, that by doing materially criminal against America on one part, and by expressing his private disapprobation against Independence, as a palliative with the enemy on the other part, he stands thereby in a safe line between both, while, I say, this ground be suffered to remain, craft and the spirit of avarice will point it out, and men will not be wanting to fill up this most contemptible of all characters.

These men, ashamed to own the sordid cause from whence their disaffection springs, and thereby add meanness to meanness, by endeavouring to shelter themselves under the mask of hypocrisy; that is, they had rather be thought to be Tories from *some kind of principle*, than Tories by having *no principle at all*. But till such time as they can show some real reason, natural, political or conscientious, on which their objections to Independence are founded, we are not obliged to give them credit for being Tories of the first stamp, but must set them down as Tories of the last.

In the second number of the Crisis I endeavoured to shew the impossibility of the enemy making any conquest of America; that nothing was wanting on our part but patience and perseverance, and that, with these virtues, our success, as far as human speculation could discern, seemed as certain as fate. But as there are many among us, who, influenced by others, have regularly gone back from the principles they once held, in proportion as we have gone forward; and as it is the unfortunate lot of many a good man to live within the neighbourhood of disaffected ones, I shall therefore, for the sake of confirming the one and recovering the other, endeavour, in the space of a page or two, to go over some of the leading principles, in support of Independence. It is a much pleasanter task to prevent vice than to punish it; and however our tempers may

may be gratified by refentment, or our national expences eafed by forfeited eftates, harmony and frienfhip is, neverthelefs, the happieft condition a country can be bleft with.

Firft,—The natural right of the Continent to Independence.

Secondly,—Her intereft in being independent.

Thirdly,—The neceffity.—And

Fourthly,—The moral advantages arifing therefrom.

1. The NATURAL RIGHT of the Continent to Independence, is a point which never yet was called in queftion. It will not even admit of a debate. To deny fuch a right, would be a kind of atheifm againft Nature: and the beft anfwer to fuch an objection would be, *The fool hath faid in his heart, There is no God.*"

2. The INTEREST of the Continent in being independent is a point as clearly right as the former. America, by her own internal induftry, and unknown to all the powers of Europe, was at the beginning of the difpute, arrived at a pitch of greatnefs, trade and population, beyond which it was the intereft of Britain not to fuffer her to pafs, left fhe fhould grow too powerful to be kept fubordinate. She began to view this country with the fame uneafy malicious eye, with which a covetous guardian would view his ward, whofe eftate he had been enriching himfelf by for twenty years, and faw him juft arriving at manhood. And America owes no more to Britain for her prefent maturity, than the ward would to his guardian for being twenty-one years of age. That America hath flourifhed *at the time* fhe was under the government of Britain, is true; but there is every natural reafon to believe, that had fhe been an independent country from the firft fettlement thereof, uncontrouled by any foreign power, free to make her own laws, regulate and encourage her own commerce, fhe had by this time been of much greater worth than now. The cafe is fimply this: the firft fettlers in the different colonies were left to fhift for themfelves, unnoticed and unfupported by any European government; but as the tyranny and perfecution of the old world daily drove numbers to the new, and, as by the favour of Heaven on their induftry and perfeverance, they grew into impoitance, fo, in a like degree, they became an object of profit to the greedy eyes of Europe. It was impoffible in this ftate of infancy, however thriving and promifing, that they could refift the power of any armed invader that fhould feek to bring them under his authority. In this fituation, Britain thought it worth her while to claim them, and the Continent received and acknowledged the claimer. It was, in reality, of no very great importance who was her mafter, feeing, that from the force and ambition of the different powers of Europe, fhe muft, till fhe acquired ftrength enough to affert her own right, acknowledge fome one. As well, perhaps, Britain as another; and it might have been as well to have been under the States of Holland as any. The fame hopes of engroffing and profiting by her trade, by not oppreffing it too much, would have operated alike with any mafter, and produced to the Colonies the fame effects. The clamour of protection, likewife, was all a farce; becaufe, in order to make THAT protection neceffary, fhe muft firft, by her own quarrels create us enemies. Hard terms, indeed!

To know whether it be the intereft of the Continent to be independent, we need only afk this eafy, fimple queftion: is it the intereft of a man to be a boy all his life? The anfwer to one will be the anfwer to both. America hath been one continued fcene of legiflative contention from the firft King's reprefentative to the laft; and this was unavoidably founded in the natural oppofition of

intereft

interest between the old country and the new. A Governor sent from England, or receiving his authority therefrom ought never to have been considered in any other light than that of a genteel commissioned spy, whose private business was information, and his public business a kind of civilized oppression. In the first of these characters he was to watch the tempers, sentiments and disposition of the people, the growth of trade, and the increase of private fortunes; and in the latter, to suppress all such Acts of the Assemblies, however beneficial to the people, which did not directly or indirectly throw some increase of power or profit into the hands of those who sent him.

America, till now, could never be called a *free country*; because her legislation depended on the will of a man three thousand miles distant, whose interest was in opposition to ours, and who, by a single " NO," could forbid what law he pleased.

The freedom of trade, likewise, is, to a trading country, an article of such vast importance, that the principal source of wealth depends upon it; and it is impossible that any country can flourish, as it otherwise might do, where commerce is engrossed, cramped and fettered by the laws and mandates of another---yet these evils, and more than I can here enumerate, the Continent has suffered by being under the government of Great-Britain. By an Independence we clear the whole at once—put an end to the business of unanswered petitions and fruitless remonstrances——exchange Britain for Europe—shake hands with the world—live at peace with mankind—and trade to any market where we best can buy and sell.

3. The NECESSITY, likewise, of being independent, even before it was declared, became so evident and important, that the Continent ran the risk of being ruined every day she delayed it. There were reasons to believe, that Britain would endeavour to make a European matter of it, and rather than lose the whole, would dismember it like Poland, and dispose of her several claims to the highest bidder. Genoa, failing in her attempts to reduce Corsica, made a sale of it to the French, and such traffics have been common in the old world. We had at that time no Ambassador in any part of Europe, to counteract her negociations, and by that means she had the range of every foreign Court uncontradicted on our part. We even knew nothing of the treaty for the Hessians till it was concluded, and the troops ready to embark. Had we been independent before, we probably had prevented her obtaining them. We had no credit abroad, because of our rebellious dependency. Our ships could claim no protection in foreign ports, because we afforded them no justifiable reason for granting it to us. The calling ourselves subjects, and at the same time fighting against the power we acknowledged, was a dangerous precedent to all Europe. If the grievances justified our taking up arms, they justified our separation; if they did not justify our separation, neither could they justify our taking up arms. All Europe was interested in reducing us as rebels, and all Europe (or the greatest part at least) is interested in supporting us as Independent States. At home our condition was still worse: our currency had no foundation, and the fall of it would have ruined Whig and Tory alike. We had no other law than a kind of moderated passion; no other civil power than an honest mob; and no other protection than the temporary attachment of one man to another. Had Independence been delayed a few months longer, this Continent would have been plunged into irrecoverable confusion: some violent for it, some against it, till in the general cabal the rich would have been ruined,

ed, and the poor deſtroyed. It is to Independence that every Tory owes the preſent ſafety he lives in; for by THAT, and THAT ONLY, we emerged from a ſtate of dangerous ſuſpence, and became a regular people.

The neceſſity likewiſe of being independent, had there been no rupture between Britain and America, would in a little time have brought one on. The encreaſing importance of commerce, the weight and perplexity of legiſlation, and the entangled ſtate of European politics, would daily have ſhewn to the Continent the impoſſibility of continuing ſubordinate; for, after the cooleſt reflections on the matter, THIS MUST be allowed, that Britain was too jealous of America, to govern it juſtly; too ignorant of it, to govern it well; and too diſtant, to govern it at all.

4. But, what weigh moſt with all men of ſerious reflection, are the MORAL ADVANTAGES ariſing from Independence: war and deſolation are become the trades of the old world; and America neither could, nor can be under the government of Britain without becoming a ſharer of her guilt, and a partner in all the diſmal commerce of death. The ſpirit of duelling, extended on a national ſcale, is a proper character for European wars. They have ſeldom any other motive than pride, or any other object than fame. The conqueror and the conquered are generally ruined alike, and the chief difference at laſt is, that the one marches home with honours, and the other without them. 'Tis the natural temper of the Engliſh to fight for a feather, if they ſuppoſe *that feather* to be an affront; and America, without the right of aſking why, muſt have abetted in every quarrel, and abided by its fate. It is a ſhocking ſituation to live in, that one country muſt be brought into all the wars of another, whether the meaſure be right or wrong, or whether

ſhe will or not; yet this, in the fulleſt extent, was, and ever would be, the unavoidable conſequence of the connection. Surely! the Quakers forgot their own principles, when in their late teſtimony they called *this connection*, with theſe military and miſerable appendages hanging to it, *The happy conſtitution.*

The free ſpirit on which the American cauſe is founded, diſdains to mix with ſuch an impurity, and leave it a rubbiſh fit only for narrow and ſuſpicious minds to grovel in: ſuſpicion and perſecution are weeds of the ſame dunghill, and flouriſh beſt together. Had the Quakers minded their religion and buſineſs, they might have lived through this diſpute in enviable eaſe, and none would have moleſted them. The common phraſe with theſe people is, *Our principles are peace.* To which may be replied, *And your practices are the reverſe;* for never did the conduct of men oppoſe their own doctrine more notoriouſly than the preſent race of the Quakers. They have artfully changed themſelves into a different ſort of people to what they uſed to be, and yet have the addreſs to perſuade each other they are not altered; like antiquated virgins, they ſee not the havock deformity hath made upon them; but pleaſantly miſtaking wrinkles for dimples, conceit themſelves yet lovely, and wonder at the ſtupid world for not admiring them.

Did no injury ariſe to the public by this apoſtacy of the Quakers from themſelves, the public would have nothing to do with it; but as both the deſign and conſequences are pointed againſt a cauſe in which the whole community are intereſted, it is, therefore, no longer a ſubject confined to the cognizance of the meeting only, but comes as a matter of criminality before either the authority of the particular State *in which* it is acted, or of the Continent *againſt which* it operates. Every attempt

now

now to support the authority of the King or Parliament of Great-Britain over America, is treason against *every* State; therefore it is impossible that any *one* can pardon or skreen from punishment an offender against *all*.

But to proceed: while the infatuated Tories of this and other States were last spring talking of Commissioners, accommodation, making the matter up, and the Lord knows what stuff and nonsense, their *good* and Ministry were glutting themselves with the revenge of reducing America to an *unconditional submission*, and solacing each other with the certainty of conquering it in *one campaign*. The following quotations are from the Parliamentary Register of the Debates of the House of Lords, March 5th, 1776:

"The Americans, says Lord Talbot *, have been obstinate, undutiful and ungovernable from the very beginning, from their first early and infant settlements; and I am every day more and more convinced that this people will never be brought back to their duty, and the subordinate relation they stand in to this country, till *reduced to an unconditional effectual submission; no concession on our part, no lenity, no endurance,* will have any other effect but that of encreasing their insolence."

"The struggle, says Lord Townshend †, is now a struggle for power; the die is cast, and the ONLY POINT which now remains to be determined, is, in what manner the war can be most effectually prosecuted and speedily finished, in order to procure that *unconditional submission*, which has been so ably stated by the noble Earl with the white staff (meaning Lord Talbot); and I have no reason to doubt that the measures now pursuing will put an end to the war in the course of a SINGLE CAMPAIGN. Should it linger longer, we shall

then have reason to expect that some foreign power will interfere, and take advantage of our domestic troubles and civil distractions."

Lord Lyttelton. "My sentiments are pretty well known. I shall only observe now, that lenient measures have had no other effect than to produce insult after insult; that the more we conceded, the higher America rose in her demands, and the more insolent she has grown. It is for this reason that I am now for the most effective and decisive measures; and am of opinion, that no alternative is left us, but to relinquish America for ever, or finally determine to compel her to acknowledge the legislative authority of this country; and it is the principle of an *unconditional submission* I would be for maintaing."

Can words be more expressive than these? Surely the Tories will believe the Tory Lords! The truth is, *they do believe them*, and know as fully as any Whig on the Continent knows, that the and Ministry never had the least design of an accommodation with America, but an absolute unconditional conquest. And the part which the Tories were to act, was, by downright lying, to endeavour to put the Continent off its guard, and to divide and sow discontent in the minds of such Whigs as they might gain an influence over. In short, to keep up a distraction here, that the force sent from England might be able to conquer in "*one campaign*." They and the Ministry were, by a different game, playing into each other's hands. The cry of the Tories in England was, *No reconciliation, no accommodation*, in order to obtain the greater military force; while those in America were crying nothing but *Reconciliation and accommodation*, that the force sent might conquer with less assistance.

But *this* "*single campaign*," is over,

---

* Steward of the King's Houshold.
† Formerly General Townshend at Quebeck, and late Lord Lieutenant of Ireland.

over, and America not conquered. The whole work is yet to do, and the force much less to do it with. Their condition is both despicable and deplorable : out of cash—out of heart—and out of hope. A country furnished with arms and ammunition, as America now is, with three millions of inhabitants, and three thousand miles distant from the nearest enemy that can approach her, is able to look and laugh them in the face.

Howe appears to have two objects in view, either to go up the North river, or come to Philadelphia.

By going up the North river, he secures a retreat for his army through Canada ; but the ships must return, if they return at all, the same way they went ; and as our army would be in the rear, the safety of their passage down is a doubtful matter. By such a motion he shuts himself from all supplies from Europe but through Canada, and exposes his army and navy to the danger of perishing. The idea of his cutting off the communication, between the eastern and southern States, by means of the North river, is merely visionary. He cannot do it by his shipping ; because no ship can lay long at anchor in any river within reach of the shore ; a single gun would drive a first rate from such a station : this was fully proved last October at Forts Washington and Lee, where one gun only, on each side the river, obliged two frigates to cut and be towed off in an hour's time. Neither can he cut it off by his army ; because the several posts they must occupy, would divide them almost to nothing, and expose them to be picked up by ours like pebbles on a river's bank ; but admitting he could, where is the injury ? Because while his whole force is cantoned out, as centries over the water, they will be very innocently employed, and the moment they march into the country, the communication opens.

The most probable object is Philadelphia, and the reasons are many. Howe's business in America is to conquer it, and in proportion as he finds himself unable to the task, he will employ his strength to distress women and weak minds, in order to accomplish, through *their* fears, what he cannot effect by his *own* force. His coming or attempting to come to Philadelphia is a circumstance that proves his weakness : for no General, that felt himself able to take the field and attack his antagonist, would think of bringing his army into a city in the summer time ; and this mere shifting the scene from place to place, without effecting any thing, has feeblencss and cowardice on the face of it, and holds him up in a contemptible light to any one who can reason justly and firmly. By several informations from New-York, it appears, that their army in general, both officers and men, have given up the expectation of conquering America ; their eye, now, is fixed upon the spoil. They suppose Philadelphia to be rich with stores, and as they think to get more by robbing a town than by attacking an army, their movement towards this city is probable. We are not now contending against an army of soldiers, but against a band of thieves, who had rather plunder than fight, and have no other hope of conquest than by cruelty.

They expect to get a mighty booty, and strike another general panic by making a sudden movement, and getting possession of this city ; but unless they can march *out* as well as *in*, or get the entire command of the river, to remove off their plunder, they may probably be stopped with the stolen goods upon them. They have never yet succeeded wherever they have been opposed, but at Fort Washington. At Charlestown their defeat was effectual. At Ticonderoga they ran away. In every skirmish at Kingsbridge and the White Plains,

S s

they

they were obliged to retreat ; and the inftant our arms were turned upon them in the Jerfeys, they turned likewife, and thofe that turned not were taken.

The neceffity of always fitting our internal police to the circumftances of the times we live in, is fomething fo ftrikingly obvious, that no fufficient objection can be made againft it. The fafety of all focieties depends upon it ; and where this point is not attended to, the confequence will either be a general languor or a tumult. The encouragement and protection of the good fubjects of any State, and the fuppreffion and punifhment of bad ones, are the principal object for which all authority is inftituted, and the line in which it ought to operate. We have in this city a ftrange variety of men and characters, and the circumftances of the times require they fhould be publicly known ; it is not the number of Tories that hurt us, fo much as the not finding out who they are ; men muft take one fide or the other, and abide by the confequences : the Quakers, trufting to their fhort-fighted fagacity, have, moft unluckily for them, made their declaration in their laft teftimony, and we ought now to take them at their word. They have voluntarily read themfelves out of the Continental meeting, and cannot hope to be reftored to it again, but by payment and penitence. Men whofe political principles are founded on avarice, are beyond the reach of reafon ; and the only cure for Toryifm of this caft, is to tax it. A fubftantial good drawn from a real evil, is of the fame benefit to fociety, as if drawn from a virtue ; and where men have not public fpirit to render themfelves ferviceable, it ought to be the ftudy of Government to draw the beft ufe poffible from their vices. When the governing paffion of any man or fet of men is once known, the method of managing them is eafy ; for even mifers,

whom no public virtue can imprefs, would become generous, could a heavy tax be laid upon covetoufnefs.

The Tories have endeavoured to injure their property with the enemy, by forfeiting their reputation with us ; from which may be juftly inferred, that their governing paffion is avarice. Make them as much afraid of lofing on one fide as the other, and you ftagger their Toryifm ; make them more fo, and you reclaim them ; for their principle is to worfhip any power they are moft afraid of.

This method of confidering men and things together, opens into a large field for fpeculation, and affords me opportunity of offering fome obfervations on the ftate of our currency, fo as to make the fupport of it go hand in hand, with the fuppreffion of difaffection and the encouragement of public fpirit.

The thing which firft prefents itfelf in infpecting the ftate of the currency, is, that we have too much of it, and that there is a neceffity of reducing the quantity, in order to encreafe the value. Men are daily growing poor by the very means they take to get rich ; for in the fame proportion that the prices of all goods on hand are raifed, the value of all money laid by is reduced. A fimple cafe will make this clear : let a man have one hundred pounds cafh, and as many goods on hand as will to-day fell for 20l. but not content with the prefent market-price, he raifes them to 40, and by fo doing, obliges others in their own defence to raife *cent. per cent.* likewife ; in this cafe, it is evident that his hundred pounds laid by is reduced fifty pounds in value ; whereas, had the markets dropped *cent. per cent.* his goods would have fold but for ten, but his hundred pounds would have rifen in value to two hundred ; becaufe it would then purchafe as many goods again, or fupport his family as long again as before. And ftrange as it may feem, he is one hundred and fifty pounds the

the poorer for raising his goods, to what he would have been had he lowered them; because the forty pounds his goods sold for, is by the general rise of the markets, cent. per cent. rendered of no more value than the ten pounds would be, had the market fallen in the same proportion; and, consequently, the whole difference of gain or loss is on the different values of the hundred pounds laid by, viz. from fifty to two hundred. This rage for raising goods is for several reasons much more the fault of the Tories than the Whigs; and yet the Tories (to their shame and confusion ought they to be told of it) are by far the most noisy and discontented. The greatest part of the Whigs, by being now either in the army or employed in some public service, are *buyers* only, and not *sellers*; and as this evil has its origin in trade, it cannot be charged on those who are out of it.

But the grievance is now become too general to be relieved by partial methods, and the only effectual cure is to reduce the quantity of money; with half the quantity we should be richer than we are now, because the value of it would be double, and consequently our attachment to it increased; for it is not the number of dollars a man has, but how far they will go, that makes him either rich or poor.

These two points being admitted, viz. that the quantity of money is too great, and that the prices of goods can be only effectually reduced by reducing the quantity of the money, the next point to be considered is, the method how to reduce it?

The circumstances of the times, as before observed, require that the public characters of all men should *now* be fully understood; and the only general method of ascertaining it, is by an oath or affirmation, renouncing all allegiance to the King of Great-Britain, and to support the Indepen-

dency of the United States as declared by Congress. Let, at the same time, a tax of ten, fifteen or twenty *per cent. per annum*, to be collected quarterly, be levied on all property. These alternatives, by being perfectly voluntary, will take in all sorts of people. Here is the test; here is the tax. He who takes the former, conscientiously proves his affection to the cause, and binds himself to pay his quota by the best *services* in his power, and is thereby justly exempt from the latter; and those who choose the latter, pay their quota in money, to be excused from taking the former, or rather it is the price paid to us for their supposed, though mistaken, insurance with the enemy.

But this is only a part of the advantage which would arise by knowing the different characters of men. The Whigs stake every thing on the issue of their arms, while the Tories, by their disaffection, are sapping and undermining their strength, and, of consequence, the property of the Whigs is the more exposed thereby; and whatever injury their estates may sustain by the movements of the enemy, must either be borne by themselves, who have done every thing which has *yet* been done, or by the Tories, who have not only done nothing, but have, by their disaffection, invited the enemy on.

In the present crisis we ought to know square by square, and house by house, who are in real allegiance with the United Independent States, and who are not. Let but the line be made clear and distinct, and all men will then know what they are to trust to. It would not only be good policy, but strict justice, to raise fifty or an hundred thousand pounds, or more, if it is necessary, out of the estates and property of the King of England's votaries, resident in Philadelphia, to be distributed, as a reward to those inhabitants of the City and State, who should turn out

and

and repulse the enemy, should they attempt their march this way; and likewise, to bind the property of all such persons to make good the damage which that of the Whigs might sustain. In the undistinguishable mode of conducting a war, we frequently make reprisals at sea on the vessels of persons in England, who are friends to our cause, compared with the residentiary Tories among us.

In every former publication of mine, from Common Sense down to the last Crisis, I have generally gone on the charitable supposition, that the Tories were rather a mistaken than a criminal people, and have applied argument after argument with all the candour and temper I was capable of, in order to set every part of the case clearly and fairly before them, and, if possible, to reclaim them from ruin to reason. I have done my duty by them, and have now done with that doctrine, taking it for granted, that those who yet hold their disaffection, are, either a set of avaricious miscreants, who would sacrifice the Continent to save themselves, or a banditti of hungry traitors, who are hoping for a division of the spoil. To which may be added, a list of Crown or Proprietary dependents, who, rather than go without a portion of power, would be content to share it with the Devil. Of such men there is no hope; and their obedience will only be according to the danger that is set before them, and the power that is exercised over them.

A time will shortly arrive, in which, by ascertaining the characters of persons now, we shall be guarded against their mischiefs then; for in proportion as the enemy despair of conquest, they will be trying the arts of seduction, and the force of fear by all the mischiefs they can inflict. But in war we may be certain of these two things, viz. that cruelty in an enemy, and motions made with more than usual parade, are always signs of weakness. He that can conquer, finds his mind too free and pleasant to be brutish; and he that intends to conquer, never makes too much show of his strength.

We now know the enemy we have to do with. While drunk with the certainty of victory, they disdained to be civil; and in proportion as disappointment makes them sober, and their apprehensions of an European war alarm them, they will become cringing and artful; honest they cannot be. But our answer to them, in either condition they may be in, is short and full, " As Free and Independent States, we are willing to make peace with you to-morrow; but we can neither hear or reply in any other character."

If Britain cannot conquer us, it proves, that she is neither able to govern or protect us, and our particular situation now is such, that any connection with her would be unwisely exchanging a half defeated enemy for two powerful ones. Europe, by every appearance and information, is now on the eve, nay, on the morning twilight of a war, and any alliance with   brings France and Spain upon our backs; a separation from him attach them to our side; therefore, the only road to *Peace*, *Honour*, and *Commerce*, is INDEPENDENCE.

COMMON-SENSE.
Philadelphia, April 19, 1777.
And in the fourth year of the UNION, *which* GOD *preserve!*

Philadelphia, June 28, 1777.
An Act obliging the male white inhabitants of this State to give assurances of allegiance to the same, and for other purposes therein mentioned.

Whereas the separation of the Thirteen United States form the Government of the Crown and Parliament of Great-Britain (who by their Acts of oppression and cruelty, as set forth

forth in the Declaration of Independence by Congrefs, bearing date the tenth of July, 1776, had rendered fuch feparation, on the part of the faid States, abfolutely neceffary for their own happinefs and the happinefs of fucceeding generations) the good people of this State of Pennfylvania are become free and independent of the faid Crown and Parliament.

And whereas from fordid, mercenary motives, or other caufes inconfiftent with the happinefs of a free and independent people, fundry perfons have, or may yet be induced to withhold their fervice and allegiance from the Commonwealth of Pennfylvania, as a free independent State, as declared by Congrefs: And whereas fundry other perfons, in their feveral capacities, have, at the rifk of their lives, or the hazard of their fortunes, or both, rendered great and eminent fervices in defence and fupport of the faid Independence, and may yet continue to do the fame ; and as both thofe forts of perfons remain at this time mixed, and in fome meafure undiftinguifhed from each other, the difaffected deriving undeferved fervice from the faithful and well affected : And whereas allegiance and protection are reciprocal ; and thofe who will not bear the former, are not (nor ought not) to be entitled to the benefit of the latter : Therefore be it enacted, by the Reprefentatives of the Freemen of the Commonwealth of Pennfylvania, in General Affembly met, and by the authority of the fame, That all male white inhabitants of this State, except of the counties of Bedford, Northumberland and Weftmoreland, above the age of eighteen years, fhall, on or before the firft day of July next, take and fubfcribe the following oath or affirmation before fome one of the Juftices of the Peace of the city or county where they fhall refpectively inhabit ; and the inhabitants of the faid counties of Bedford, Northumberland and Weftmoreland, above the faid age, fhall, on or before the firft day of Auguft next, take and fubfcribe the faid oath or affirmation, before fome one of the Juftices of the faid three counties laft mentioned, in which they fhall refpectively inhabit ; and the faid Juftices fhall give a certificate thereof to every fuch perfon ; and the faid oath or affirmation fhall be as followeth, viz.

I [——— ———] do fwear or affirm, that I renounce and refufe all allegiance to George the Third, King of Great-Britain, his heirs, and fucceffors ; and that I will be faithful and bear true allegiance to the Commonwealth of Pennfylvania, as a free and independent State, and that I will not at any time do, or caufe to be done, any matter, or thing that will be prejudicial or injurious to the freedom and independence thereof, as declared by Congrefs. And alfo, that I will difcover and make known to fome one Juftice of the Peace of the faid State, all treafons or treacherous confpiracies, which I now know, or hereafter fhall know, to be formed againft this, or any of the United States of America.

And the form of the certificate fhall be as followeth, viz.

I do hereby certify that [——— ———] hath voluntarily taken and fubfcribed the oath or affirmation of allegiance and fidelity, as directed by an Act of General Affembly of Pennfylvania, paffed the 13th of June, 1777. Witnefs my hand and feal, the day of   A. D.
                              (L. S.)

And be it further enacted, by the authority aforefaid, That the Juftice or Juftices of the Peace before whom fuch oath or affirmation fhall be fubfcribed, fhall keep fair regifter of the names and firnames fo fworn or affirmed, and the time when, and fhall, on or before the firft day of October in every year, tranfmit in writing, under his or their hands and feals,

feals, to the office of Recorder of Deeds for the said city or county, a true list of the names and surnames of those, who, within the same year, have so sworn or affirmed before them respectively; and the said Justice or Justices shall have and receive therefor, and for the said certificate, the sum of one shilling and no more, for every person so sworn or affirmed; and the said Justice or Justices shall lay their accounts before the county Commissioners, or any two of them, from time to time, to be examined and allowed; and the said Commissioners shall draw orders on the county Treasurers for such sums as shall be so allowed, which orders the said Treasurers are hereby authorized and required to pay out of the State taxes; and the Recorders of Deeds in the city and several counties of this State, are hereby enjoined to record the said lists in books to be prepared for that purpose, and shall be paid for the same in the same manner as the Justices, at the rate of five pounds for every hundred names.

And be it further enacted, by the authority aforesaid, That every person above the age aforesaid, refusing or neglecting to take and subscribe the said oath or affirmation, shall, during the time of such neglect or refusal, be incapable of holding any office or place of trust in this State, serving on juries, suing for any debts, electing or being elected, buying, selling, or transferring any lands, tenements or hereditaments, and shall be disarmed by the Lieutenant or Sub-lieutenants of the city or counties respectively.

And whereas there is a danger of having the seeds of discord and disaffection greatly spread by persons, whose political principles are not known, removing or travelling from one part of the State to another; and it is well known that this State is already become (and likely to be more so) an asylum for refugees flying from the just resentment of their fellow citizens in other States: for remedy whereof, be it enacted, by the authority aforesaid, That every person above the age aforesaid, who shall travel out of the county or city in which he usually resides, without the certificate aforesaid, may be suspected to be a spy, and to hold principles inimical to the United States, and shall be taken before one of the Justices nearest to the place where he shall be apprehended, who shall tender to him the said oath or affirmation, and upon his refusal to take and subscribe the said oath or affirmation, the said Justice shall commit him to the common gaol of the city or county, there to remain without bail or mainprize, until he shall take and subscribe the said oath or affirmation, or produce a certificate that he had already done so.

And be it further enacted, by the authority aforesaid, That all persons coming from any of the other United States into this State, are hereby required to apply to one of the nearest Justices after he enters this State, and take and subscribe the said oath or affirmation, upon the penalty of being dealt with as in the case of persons travelling or removing out of the city or county in which they usually reside, unless he can produce a certificate that he hath taken the oath or affirmation, in the like nature, in the State from whence he came.

Provided always nevertheless, That Delegates in Congress, prisoners of war, officers and soldiers in the Continental army, merchants and mariners trading in the ports of this State from foreign powers in amity with the United States, and not becoming resident, are declared not to be within the intent and meaning of this Act.

And be it further enacted, That if any person shall forge such certificate, as by this Act is to be made out, and given by any of the Justices of the Peace of this State; or shall

cause

cause or procure others to forge or counterfeit the name and seal of the Justice of the Peace to such certificate, or shall by erasing or otherwise taking out, or covering or passing over, a man's name that was wrote in a true and genuine certificate, alter the same as to serve his own, or any other man's purposes; or shall produce and make use of any such certificate, knowing it to be forged or altered, every such person and persons so offending, and being thereof legally convicted before any Court of General Quarter Sessions of the Peace of the city or county where such offence shall be committed, shall be fined the sum of fifty pounds, and be committed to gaol until he pays the fine, and cost of prosecution. And if he shall not within the space of thirty days satisfy the judgment of the Court, he shall be whipped with any number of lashes not exceeding thirty-nine, on his bare back, well laid on.

JOHN BAYARD, Speaker. Enacted into a law June the 13th, 1777. JOHN MORRIS, jun. Clerk of the General Assembly.

[*The same Act has been passed by the Assemblies of the other twelve Colonies.*]

A CHARGE, *on the Rise of the American Empire, delivered by the Hon.* WILLIAM-HENRY DRAYTON, *Esq. Chief Justice of South-Carolina, to the Grand Jury for the district of Charles-town.*

South-Carolina, Charles-town District,

At a Court of General Sessions of the Peace, Over and Terminer, Assize and General Gaol Delivery, begun and holden at Charlestown, for the district of Charlestown, on Tuesday, October 15th, in the year of our Lord, 1776— before the Honourable WILLIAM-HENRY DRAYTON, Esq. Chief Justice, and his associates, Justices of the said Court,

Ordered, That the Charge delivered by his Honour the Chief Justice to the Grand Jury, and their Presentments at this Sessions, be forthwith published.

By order of the Court, JOHN COLCOCK, C. C. S.

The CHARGE to the GRAND JURY.

Gentlemen of the Grand Jury,

The last time I had the honour to address a Grand Jury in this Court, (*See vol. iii. page* 321.) I expounded to them the Constitution of their country, as established by Congress on the 26th day of March last, independent of Royal authority. I laid before them the causes of that important change of our Government—a comparison of these, with those that occasioned the English Revolution of 1688—and, the law resulting from the injuries in each case. I spoke to that Grand Jury of the late Revolution of South-Carolina. I mean to speak to you on a more important subject—the Rise of the American Empire.

The great Act in March last upon the matter, constituted our country totally independent of Great-Britain. For, it was calculated to place in our hands, the whole legislative, executive and judicial powers of Government; and to enable us in the most effectual manner, by force of arms to oppose, resist and war against the British Crown. The Act naturally looked forward to an accommodation of the unhappy difference between that power and America: in like manner, every declaration of war between independent States, implies a future accommodation of their disputes. But, although by that Act, we were upon the matter made independent; yet, there were no words in it, specially declarative of that Independency. Such a declaration was of right to be made only by the General Congress; because the united voice and strength of America, were necessary to give a desireable credit and prospect of stability, to a declared state of total separation from Great-Britain: and the

the General Congrefs, as the only means left by which they had a chance to avert the ruin of America, have iffued a declaration, by which all political connection between you and the State of Great-Britain, is totally diffolved.

Carolinians! heretofore you were bound—by the American Revolution you are now free. The change is moft important—moft honourable—moft beneficial. It is your birth right by the law of Nature—it is even valid by the fundamental laws of your country—you were placed in poffeffion of it by the hand of God!—— Particulars evidencing a fubject of the higheft import—Gentlemen of the Grand Jury, it is my duty to mark to you, the great lines of your conduct; and fo to endeavour to explain the nature of each, that you may clearly fee your way, and thereby be animated in your progrefs to difcharge thofe fervices which are required at at your hands. And hence, it is neceffary for me to lay before you fome obfervations upon the nature of the American Revolution, which, by every tie, divine and human, you are bound to fupport. I fhall, therefore, endeavour to draw your attention to this great fubject, neceffarily including the lines of your particular conduct.

It is but to glance an eye over the hiftoric page, to be affured that the duration of empire is limited by the Almighty decree. Empires have their rife to a zenith—and their declenfion to a diffolution. The years of a man, nay, the hours of an infect on the bank of the Hypanis, that lives but a day, epitomize the advance and decay of the ftrength and duration of dominion! One common fate awaits all things upon earth—a thoufand caufes accelerate or delay their perfection or ruin. To look a little into remote times, we fee, that from the moft contemptible origin upon record, Rome became the moft powerful

State the fun ever faw: the world bowed before her imperial fafces!— yet, having run through all the viciffitudes of dominion, her courfe was finifhed. Her empire was diffolved, that the feparated members of it might arife to run through fimilar revolutions.

Great-Britain was a part of this mighty empire. But, being diffolved from it, in her turn fhe alfo extended her dominion:—arrived at, and paffed her zenith. Three and thirty years numbered the illuftrious days of the Roman greatnefs—Eight years meafure the duration of the Britifh grandeur in meridian luftre! How few are the days of true glory! The extent of the Roman period is from their complete conqueft of Italy, which gave them a place whereon to ftand, that they might fhake the world, to the original caufe of their declenfion, their introduction of Afiatic luxury. The Britifh period is from the year 1758, when they victorioufly purfued their enemies into every quarter of the globe; to the immediate caufe of their decline—their injuftice difplayed by the Stamp Act.——In fhort, like the Roman Empire, Great-Britain, in her Conftitution of Government, contained a poifon to bring on her decay; and in each cafe, this poifon was drawn into a ruinous operation, by the riches and luxuries of the Eaft. Thus, by natural caufes and common effects, the American States are become diffolved from the Britifh dominion.—And is it to be wondered at, that Britain has experienced the invariable fate of empire! We are not furprized when we fee youth or age yield to the common lot of humanity.—Nay, to repine, that in our day, America is diffolved from the Britifh State, is impioufly to queftion the unerring wifdom of Providence. The Almighty fetteth up; and he cafteth down: he breaks the fceptre, and transfers the dominion: he has made choice of the prefent generation

neration to erect the American Empire. Thankful as we are, and ought to be, for an appointment, of the kind, the moſt illuſtrious that ever was; let each individual exert himſelf in this important operation, directed by Jehovah himſelf. From a ſhort retroſpect, it is evident, the work was not the preſent deſign of man.

Never were a people more wrapped up in a King, than the Americans were in George the Third, in the year 1763. They revered and obeyed the Britiſh Government, *becauſe it protected them*—they fondly called Great-Britain—Home! But, from that time, the Britiſh Counſels took a ruinous turn; ceaſing to protect—they ſought to ruin America. The Stamp Act, Declaratory Law, and the duties upon tea and other articles, at once proclaimed their injuſtice, and announced to the Americans, that they had but little room for hope; infinite ſpace for fear. IN VAIN THEY PETITIONED FOR REDRESS! Authorized by the law of Nature, they exerted the inherent powers of ſociety, and reſiſted the edicts which told them, that they had no property; and that againſt their conſent, and by men over whom they had no controul, they were to be bound in all caſes whatſoever. Dreadful information!—Patience could not but reſent them. However, regardleſs of ſuch feelings, and reſolved to endeavour to ſupport thoſe all graſping claims, early in the year 1774, the Britiſh tyranny made other edicts—to overturn American charters—to ſuſpend or deſtroy, at the pleaſure of the , the value of private property—to block up the port of Boſton, *in terrorem*, to other American ports—to give murder the ſanction of law—to eſtabliſh the Roman Catholic religion, and to make the a deſpot in Canada; and as much ſo as he then choſe to be in Maſſachuſetts-Bay. And General

Gage was ſent to Boſton with a conſiderable force, to uſher theſe edicts into action, and the Americans into ſlavery.

Their petition thus anſwered——even with the ſword of the at their breaſt, the Americans thought only of new petitions. It is well known, there was not then even an idea that the Independence of America would be the work of this generation: for people *yet* had a confidence in the integrity of the Britiſh Monarch. At length ſubſequent edicts being alſo paſſed, to reſtrain the Americans from enjoying the bounty of Providence on their own coaſts; and to cut off their trade with each other and with foreign States—*the ſword yet* REEKING *with American blood*, and the ſtill deaf to the prayers of the people for " peace, liberty, and ſafety:" it was even ſo late as the latter end of the laſt year, before that confidence viſibly declined; and it was generally ſeen, that the quarrel was likely to force America into an immediate State of Independence. But, ſuch an event was not expected, becauſe it was thought, the from motives of policy, if not from inclination, would heal our wounds, and thereby prevent the ſeparation; and it was not wiſhed for, becauſe men were unwilling to break off old connections, and change the uſual form of government.

Such were the ſentiments of America, until the arrival of the Britiſh Act of Parliament declaring the Americans out of the Royal protection, and denouncing a general war againſt them. But, Counſels too refined, generally produce contrary and unexpected events. So the whole ſyſtem of Britiſh policy reſpecting America ſince the year 1763, calculated to ſurprize, deceive, or drive the people into ſlavery—urged them into Independence: and, this Act of Parliament, in particular, finally re-leaſed

T t

leafed America from Great-Britain. Antecedent to this, the by   hoftilities, had, as far as he perfonally could, abfolved America from the faith, allegiance, and fubjeſtion ſhe owed   ; becauſe the law of our land exprefsly declares, theſe are due only in return for   protection, allegiance being *founded* on the benefit of protection. But God knowing that we are in peril by falſe bre thren, as well as by real enemies, out of his abundant mercy has cauſed us to be releaſed from fubjection, by yet a better title than the mere oppreffions of a man in the   office. This title is ſingular in its kind.· It is the voluntary and joint act of the whole Britiſh Legiſlature, on the twenty-firſt day of December, 1775, releafing the faith, allegiance and fubjection of America to the

     , by folemnly declaring the former out of the protection of the latter; and thereby, agreeable to every principle of law, actually *diffolving* the original contract between   and people.

Hence, an American cannot, legally, at the fuit of

     , be indicted of high treaſon; becauſe the indictment cannot charge him with an Act *contra ligeantiæ ſuæ debitum*; for not being protected by that   the law holds that he does not owe   any faith and allegiance. So, an alien enemy, even invading the kingdom of England, and taken in arms, cannot be dealt with as a traitor, becauſe *he violates no truſt or allegiance*. In ſhort, this doctrine laid down in the beſt law authorities, is a criterion whereby we may ſafely judge, whether or not a particular people are fubject to a particular government. And, thus upon the matter, that deciſive Act of Parliament, *ipſo facto*, created the United Colonies, Free and Independent States.

These particulars evidence againſt the   calumniator in the ſtrongeſt manner. Let him not with unparalleled   from a continue to declare, that the Americans meant only to amuſe, by vague expreffions of attachment, and the ſtrongeſt profeffions of loyalty, whilſt they were preparing for a general revolt, for the purpoſe of eſtabliſhing an independent empire. On the firſt of September, 1775, Richard Penn and Arthur Lee, Eſquires, delivered to Lord Dartmouth, he being Secretary of State, a petition from the Congreſs to the King, when Lord Dartmouth told them, " No ANSWER WOULD BE GIVEN." The petition contained this remarkable paſſage, that the King would " *be pleaſed to direct ſome mode, by which the united applications of his faithful Coloniſts to the Throne, in preſence of their Common Councils, might be improved into a* PERMANENT AND HAPPY RECONCILIATION; *and that, in the mean time, meaſures might be taken for preventing the further deſtruction of the lives of his Majeſty's ſubjects.*" YET, NOTWITHSTANDING THIS, on the 26th of October following, from the   , the   charged the Americans with aiming at Independence! The facts I have ſtated, are known to the world; they are yet more *ſtubborn* than the   But let other facts be alſo ſtated againſt.

     .——There was a time, when the American army before Boſton had not a thouſand weight of gunpowder —the forces were unable to advance into Canada, until they received a ſmall ſupply of powder from this country, and for which the General Congreſs expreſsly ſent—and when we took up arms a few months before, we begun with a ſtock of five hundred weight!—Theſe *grand* magazines of ammunition, demonſtrate to be ſure, that America, or even Maſſachuſetts-Bay was preparing to enter the military road to Independence!—On the contrary, if we conſider the manner in which Great-Brtiain

Britain has conducted her irritating and hostile measures, we cannot but clearly see, that God has darkened her Counsels; and that with a stretched out arm, he himself has delivered us out of the house of bondage, and has led us on to empire.

In the year 1774, General Gage arrived at Boston, to awe the people into a submission to the edicts against America. The force he brought, was, by the oppressors, thought not only sufficient to compel obedience; but that this would be effected even at the appearance of the sword. But, the Continent being roused by the edicts, General Gage to his surprize found, that he had not strength sufficient to carry them into execution. In this situation things continued several months, while on the one hand, the General received reinforcements; and on the other, the people acquired a contempt for the troops, and found time to form their militia into some order to oppose the force they saw accumulating for their destruction. Hence, in the succeeding April, when the General commenced hostilities, he was defeated. The victory produced the most important effects.—The people were animated to besiege Boston, where it soon appeared, that the British troops were too weak to make any impression upon them, thus acquiring military knowledge by the actual operations of war.—The United Colonies were roused to arms.—They new-modelled their militia—raised regular troops—fortified their harbours—and crushed the Tory parties among them.—Success fired the Americans with a spirit of enterprize.

In the mean time, the _____ passed such other edicts, as, adding to the calendar of injuries, widened the civil breach; and narrowed the band of the American Union. And, such supplies were, from time to time, sent for the relief of Boston, as not in any degree sufficient to enable General Gage to raise the siege; answered no other ends, but to increase the number, heighten the spirit, advance the discipline of the American army; and to cause every Member of the Union to exert their ability to procure arms and ammunition from abroad. Thus *trained* on evidently by the Almighty, these troops, reproached by General Gage when they first sat down before Boston, that " with a preposterous parade of military arrangements, they affected to hold the army besieged;" in less than eleven months compelled that British army, although considerably reinforced, to abandon Boston by stealth, and to trust their safety, not to their arms, but to the winds. The British Ministry have attempted to put a gloss upon this remove of their army: however, the cannon, stores, and provisions they left in Boston, are in our hands substantial marks of their flight.

Thus there appears to have been a fatality in their Counsels, respecting Boston, the then grand seat of contention; their forces being inadequate to the enterprize on which they were sent: and under the same influence have their attacks been directed against Virginia and North-Carolina, Savannah, and this capital. Such a *series* of events is striking! It surely displays an over-ruling Providence that has confounded the British Counsels, to the end that America should not have been at first shackled, and thereby prevented from acquiring a knowledge of, and confidence in her strength, to be attained only by an experimental trial and successful exertion of it, previous to the British Rulers doing acts driving her, either into Slavery or Independence.—The same trace of an over-ruling Providence, is evident throughout the whole transaction of the English Revolution of 1688. King James received early information of the Prince of Orange's intention to invade England; and Lewis the XIV.

offered

offered the King a powerful affiftance: but his Counfels were confounded from on high: he paid little attention to the firft—he neglected the laft. The winds blew, and how opportunely have they aided us; the winds detained James's fleet at anchor; while they, *directing* the courfe of the Prince, enabled him without any lofs to land in England, at a time when no perfon thought of a Revolution, which was deftined to take place, within but a few weeks. Unexpected, wonderful, and rapid movements, characterize the Britifh and American Revolutions:—They do not appear to have been premeditated by man. And from fo clofe a fimilitude, in fo many points, between the two Revolutions, we have great reafon to hope, that the American, like the Britifh, will be ftable againft the   .

As I faid before, in my laft charge, I drew a parrallel between the caufes which occafioned the Englifh Revolution, and thofe which occafioned our local Revolution in March laft; and I examined the famous Refolution of the Lords and Commons of England, at Weftminfter, declaring the law upon James's conduct. The two firft points of it applied to our own cafe in the clofeft manner; and in applying the third, treating of James's withdrawing, I pointed out, that the abdication of the regal government among us, was immediately effected, not only by the withdrawing of the Regal Subftitute, with the Enfigns of Government; but that   had withdrawn himfelf, " by withdrawing the conftitutional benefits of the   office, and his protection out of this country." Thus couching my thoughts upon the article of the withdrawing, in order that the parallel fhould be continued throughout as clofe as the fubject would admit, without attempting to extract the effence from the fubftance of the refolution, to demonftrate that fuch a parallel was not

neceffary: a mode which, the fubject being new, might not then perhaps have been fo generally fatisfactory. But, as the American Revolution leads me again to mention that refolution, which in the ftrongeft manner juftifies it; I make no fcruple now to fay, that the Refolution, though appearing to point out feveral kinds of criminality, yet has only one idea thus varioufly reprefented.

" RESOLVED, That King James the Second *having endeavoured to fubvert* the Conftitution of the kingdom, by breaking the original contract between King and people; and by the advice of Jefuits, and other wicked perfons, *having violated* the fundamental laws; and *having withdrawn himfelf* out of the kingdom, has abdicated the government, and that the throne is thereby vacant."

But, before I make any further obfervation upon this Refolution, allow me to fhew you the fenfe of Scotland in the laft, and of America in the prefent century, touching an abdication of government; and you will find, that the voice of Nature is the fame in either extremity of the globe, and in different ages.

The eftates of Scotland having enumerated King James's mal-adminiftration, and in which there was no article of withdrawing, they declared, that " thereby he had forefaulted the Rights of the Crown, and the Throne was become vacant."—And the Reprefentatives of the United States of America, ftating their grievances under   , decreed, that " he has abdicated Government here, by declaring us out of his protection, and waging war againft us."—And, that " a   , whofe character is thus marked by every act which may define a   , is unfit to be the   of a free people."

Thus, in each cafe it is apparent, the abdication or forefaulting took place from but one and the fame caufe cause—*the failure of protection:*— And this is the single idea, that I apprehend is in the Resolution of Westminster. Search to understand, what is a breach of the original contract— what a violation of the fundamental laws—wherein consisted the criminality of James's withdrawing? Your enquiry must terminate thus—*a failure of protection.*— Independent of the nature of the subject, the history of that time, warrants this construction upon the withdrawing in particular. For upon James's first flying from Whitehall, quitting the administration without providing a power to protect the people, he was considered by the Prince of Orange, and the heads of the English nation, as having then absolutely abdicated the government, and terminated his reign; and they treated him accordingly upon his sudden return to Whitehall; from whence he was *immediately* ejected. In short, a failure of protection being once established, it necessarily includes, and implies a charge of a breach of original contract—a violation of fundamental laws—and a withdrawing of the King: I do not mean the individual person, but the officer so called. For, the officer being constituted to dispense protection, and there being a failure of it, it is evident *prima facie,* that the officer is withdrawn; and in reality, because the law will not admit, that the officer can be present and not dispense protection, as the law ascribes to the King in his political capacity absolute perfection; and therefore it will *intend* a withdrawing and abdication, in exclusion of any idea of his being present and doing wrong. Protection was the great end for which mankind formed societies. On this hang all the duties of a King. It is the one thing needful in royalty.

Upon the whole, what is Civil Liberty, or, by what conduct it may be oppressed; by what means the oppression ought to be removed, or an abdication or forefaulting of the government may be induced; cannot precisely be ascertained, and laid down as rules to the world. Humanity is interested in these subjects. Nature alone will judge; and she will decide upon the occasion, without regard to precedent. In America, Nature has borne British oppression, so long as it was tolerable; but, there is a load of injury which cannot be endured. Nature felt it. And, the people of America, acting upon natural principles, by the mouths of their representatives in Congress assembled, at Philadelphia, on the fourth day of July last, awfully declared—and revere the sentence!— " That these United Colonies are, and of right ought to be, Free and Independent States; that they are absolved from all allegiance to the   ; and that all political connection between them and the State of Great-Britain, is, and ought to be totally dissolved."

A DECREE is now gone forth, NOT to be recalled! And, thus has suddenly arisen in the world, a new empire, stiled, The United States of America. An empire, that as soon as started into existence, attracts the attention of the rest of the universe; and bids fair, by the blessing of God, to be the most glorious of any upon record. America hails Europe, Asia and Africa!—She proffers peace and plenty!

This Revolution, forming one of of the most important epocha's in the history, not of a nation, but, of the world, is, as it were, an eminence from which we may observe the things around us. And, I am naturally led to explain the value of that grand object now in our possession and view— to state the American ability by arms to maintain the acquisition—and to shew the conduct, by which a patriotic Grand Jury may aid the establishment of our infant empire.

To

To make men fenfible of the value of the object now in our poffeffion, we need no ingenuity of thought, or difplay of eloquence. To him who doubts of the meridian fun, it is fufficient to point to it. So in the prefent cafe, as well to demonftrate the value of the object, as the juftice of our claim to it, we need only hold it up to view. IT IS, TO MAINTAIN AMONG THE POWERS OF THE EARTH, THE SEPARATE AND EQUAL STATION TO WHICH THE LAWS OF NATURE AND OF NATURE's GOD ENTITLE US. A few months ago, we fought only to preferve to the labourer the fruits of his toil, free from the all-covering grafp of the Britifh , *alieni appetens*, *fui profufus*; and to defend a people from being like brute beafts bound in all cafes whatfoever. But, thefe two laft ingredients to make life agreeable, are now melted into, infeparably blended with, and wholly included in the firft, which is now become the OBJECT, for which America, *ex neceffitate*, wars againft Britain—And I fhall now point out to you the Continental ability, by arms to maintain this invaluable ftation.

When in modern times, Philip of Spain became the tyrant of the Low Countries in Europe; of feventeen provinces which compofed thofe territories, feven only effectually confederated to preferve their liberties, or to perifh in the attempt. They faw Philip, the moft powerful Prince in the Old World, and mafter of Mexico and Peru in the New—Nations, inceffantly pouring into his territories, floods of gold and filver. They faw him poffeffed of the beft troops, and the moft formidable navy in the univerfe; and aiming at no lefs than univerfal monarchy!——But, thefe feven provinces, making but a fpeck upon the globe, faw themfelves without armies, fleets, or funds of money: yet feeing themfelves on the point of being, by a tyrant, bound

in all cafes whatfoever, *nobly relying upon Providence and the juftice of their caufe*, they refolved to oppofe the tyrant's whole force, and at leaft *deferve* to be free. They fought, they bled; and were often brought to the door of deftruction. THEY REDOUBLED THEIR EFFORTS IN PROPORTION TO THEIR DANGER. And, the inhabitants of that *fpeck* of earth, compelled the mafter of dominions fo extenfive, that it was boafted the fun was never abfent, to treat with them as a free and independent people !

For a moment, and with the aid of a fearful imagination, let us fuppofe, that the American States are now as defencelefs as the Hollanders then were; and that the   is now as powerful as Philip then was. Yet even fuch a ftate of things, could not be a plea for any degree of fubmiffion on our part. Did not the Hollanders oppofe their weaknefs to the ftrength of Spain? Are not the Americans engaged in as good a caufe as the Hollanders fought in? Are the Americans lefs in love with liberty than the Hollanders were? Shall we not in this, a fimilar caufe, dare thofe perils that they fuccefsfully combated? Shall we not *deferve* freedom !—Our paft actions prefage our future achievements; and animate us in our military efforts for " peace, liberty and fafety."——But, fee the real powers of Great-Britain.

Staggering beneath the load of an enormous debt, the very annual intereft of which, in the year 1775, amounted to upwards of four millions eight hundred and eighty thoufand pounds fterling; Great-Britain fcarcely fupports the weight, which is yet rapidly increafing. During the prefent year, fhe profecutes the war at a charge of more than nineteen millions fterling, incurred by actual expences, and by lofs of revenue in confequence of the war. Her trade, her only refource for money, is now in a manner deftroyed;

destroyed; for her principal trade, which was to this Continent, is now at an end; and she sustains heavy, very heavy losses by the American captures of her West-India ships. Her manufactures are almost at their last morsel. Her public credit is certain to fail even by a short continuance of the war. Her fleets are not half manned. And she is so destitute of an army, that she is reduced to supplicate even the petty German Princes for assistance; and thinks it worth her while to make a separate treaty to procure only 668 men!—— *a last effort to form an army in America.* But, after all this humiliating exertion, she has, *even upon paper,* raised a German army of only 16,868 men, who, with about 14,000 national troops, and a few Hanoverian regiments, compose the whole military force that she can collect for the American service. Nay, so arduous a task was even this, that her grand army of about 26,000 men, could not open the present campaign before the end of August last. Add to these particulars, the troops are unaccustomed to the sudden vicissitudes of the American climate, and the extremes of cold, heat, and rain. They cannot proceed without camp equipage, because they are used to such luxuries. The very scene of their operations is a matter of discouragement to them, because they know not the country; and for their supplies of men, stores, and the greatest part of their provisions, they must look to Great-Britain—and there is a vast abyss between. Hence, their supplies must be precarious at best; and failing, they may be involved in ruin. A check may affect them as a defeat—a defeat in battle may annihilate their very army. Such seems to be the situation of Great-Britain, while *only* the American war is on her hands. But, do we not see France and Spain, her *inveterate* enemies, now watching for the critical

moment when they shall swallow up her West-India Islands! When this crisis appears, which from the now quick arrivals of French vessels in America; and from the forces already collected, and others now daily poured into the islands by those powers, cannot be far distant, what will be the situation of Great-Britain!

On the other hand, America is possessed of resources for the war, which appear as soon as enquired after; are found only by being sought for; and are but scarce imagined even when found. Strong in her union, on each coast and frontier, she meets the invaders, whether British or Indian savages, repelling their allied attacks. The Americans now live without luxury. They are habituated to despise their yearly profits by agriculture and trade. THEY ENGAGE IN THE WAR FROM PRINCIPLE. They follow their leaders to battle with personal affection. Natives of the climate, they bear the vicissitudes and extremities of the weather—hardy and robust, they need no camp equipage, and they march with celerity. The common people have acute understandings; and there are those in the higher stations, who are acquainted with the arts and sciences; and have a comprehensive view of things equally with those who act against them. In short, the American armies meet the war where they may be constantly recruited and subsisted; comforted by the aid of their neighbours, and by reflections upon the justice of their cause; and animated by seeing, that they are arrayed in the defence of all that is, or can be dear to them.

From such a people every thing is to be hoped for, nothing is to be doubted of. Such a people, though young in the practice of war, ever were superior to veteran troops. To prove this, shall I direct your attention to Europe, Asia, and Africa, in their histories to point out to you numberless

numberless inflances of this fort? No, Gentlemen, America now attracts the eyes of the world: fhe deferves our whole attention—let us not fearch abroad and in remote or modern times, for inflances of fuch a kind as we can find at home and in our own day. Need I mention, that fuch a people, young in the art of war, beat veteran troops at Lexington; flaughtered them at Bunker's-hill; and drove them out of Bofton! or remind you of Sullivan's Ifland, where, in an unfinifhed wooden fort, on a flat coaft, fuch men, during 11 hours, and at the diftance of 500 yards, flood the whole and uninter-mitted fire of a Britifh fquadron of 2 fhips of the line, 5 frigates and a bomb; and with 15 pieces of cannon, caufed the enemy to burn one of their largeft frigates, and to fly with the reft of the fquadron in a fhattered condition, from before our capital!

Such a contrafted flate of the powers of America and of Britain, is, I apprehend, a juft reprefentation of their abilities with regard to the prefent war; and if America behaves worthy of herfelf, I fee no caufe to fear the enemy. However, in fuch a con-flict, we ought to expect difficulties, dangers and defeats "What, fhall we receive good at the hand of God, and fhall we not receive evil?" Job's perfeverance in his duty under every calamity, at length raifed him to the height of human felicity; and, if we are firm, even our defeats will operate to our benefit. Let us remember, that it was to the danger in which the Roman State was reared, that fhe owed her illuftrious men and imperial fortune. The Roman dignity was never fo majeftic; her glory never fo refplendent; her fortitude and exertions never fo confpicuous and ner-vous, as when Hannibal, in the fuc-ceffive battles of Trabia, Thrafymenus, and Cannae, having almoft ex-tirpated their whole military force, *the very State was on the brink of*

diffolution. The Romans *deferved—* and they *acquired* victory!

And now, Gentlemen of the Grand Jury, having in this manner confidered the nature of the American Revolution upon circumftances of fact, and principles of law, I am to mark the conduct which you ought to purfue, and which will enable you to aid the eftablifhment of our infant empire. But, that I may naturally introduce this fubject, I fhall firft ftate and explain to you, the principal articles of the enquiry which you are fworn to make on the part of the State, and for the body of this diftrict; and thefe articles I fhall arrange under two heads. The one relating to crimes and mifdemeanours immediately injurious to individuals—the other relating to fuch as are injurious to the State.

Thofe criminal injuries that affect individuals, refpect either their perfons, habitations, or property. Of thefe injuries, the moft important are fuch as affect the perfon; and of fuch, the act depriving the perfon of life is the moft enormous.

In the contemplation of law, every taking of life is a homicide; and according to the particular circumftances of each cafe, this homicide is purely voluntary, including the cafes of felony, as felf-murder, murder refpecting another, and manflaughter: or, the homicide is purely involuntary, as *per infortunium*, mifadventure: or, of a mixed kind, *ex neceffitate*; as *fe defendendo* inducing a forfeiture; or being under the requifition or permiffion of law and not inducing any: and thus, homicide is either juftifiable, excufable or felonious.

It is juftifiable in all cafes *ex neceffitate*; as when the life is taken by the legal execution of a criminal; or for the advancement of juftice; or for the prevention of fome atrocious crime.

It is excufable in cafes *per infortunium*, mifadventure; as when life is taken

taken by the doing a lawful act without any evil intention : so in cases *se defendendo*, as a man being attacked without any provocation on his part, and having *bona fide* retreated as far as he safely could, when for self-preservation he kills the aggressor. And although this last arises *ex necessitate*, and it would therefore seem to be rather justifiable than excuseable, yet the law intitles it *necessitas culpabilis*, and thereby distinguishes it from the other. For, the law so highly respects the life of a man, that it always intends some misbehaviour in the person who takes it away without an express legal command or permission.

But, homicide is felonious in all cases of manslaughter, murder, and self-murder. In cases of manslaughter, as killing another without any degree of malice ; and this killing may be either voluntary, by a sudden act of revenge on a sudden provocation and heat ; or it may be; *yet not strictly so*, involuntary, being in the commission of some unlawful act under the degree of felony ; for this killing being the consequence of the unlawful act *voluntarily* entered upon, the law, because of the *previous intent*, will transfer *this*, from the original to the *consequential* object.

In cases of murder, as killing another person *ex malitia præcogitata :* and here it is necessary that I particularly explain what the law considers as malice prepense.—Malice prepense then, is an inclination of the mind, not so properly bearing ill-will to the person killed, the commonly received notion, as containing *any evil design*, the dictate of a wicked and malignant heart. The discovery of this secret inclination of the mind must arise, because it cannot any otherwise, only from the external effects of it ; and by such evidence, the malignity of the mind is held either express in fact, or implied in law. Thus, malice prepense is held to be express in fact, when there is evidence of a laying in wait, or of menacings antecedent, grudges, or deliberate compassings to do some bodily harm; Even upon a sudden provocation, the one beating or treating another in an excessive and cruel manner, so that he dies, though he did not intend his death, the slayer displays an express *evil design*, the genuine sense of malice. This is evidence of a bad heart, and the act is equivalent to a deliberate act of slaughter. So any wilful action; likely in its nature to kill, without its being aimed at any person in particular : for this shews an enmity to all mankind. So if two or more come to do any felony, or any unlawful act, the *probable* consequence of which *might* be bloodshed, and one of them kills a man, it is murder in them all, because of the unlawful act, the *malitia præcogitata*, or *evil intended*. But, malice prepense is held to be implied in law, when one kills an officer of justice in the execution of his office, or any person assisting him, though not specially called. Or when without sufficient provocation, and no affront by words or gestures only, is a sufficient provocation, a man suddenly kills another. Or, when upon a chiding between husband and wife, the husband strikes the wife with a pestle, or other dangerous weapon, and she presently dies. These and similar instances are evidences of a malice prepense on the part of the slayer; and he shall be held guilty of murder.——In cases of self-murder, there must be a voluntary and deliberate putting an end to one's existence ; or doing some unlawful malicious act, the consequence of which is his own death. In a word, all homicide is *presumed* to be malicious, until the contrary is made to appear in evidence.

There is a regular gradation of importance in the component parts of

U u

the

the univerſal ſyſtem ; and therefore, there muſt be a ſcale marking the degrees of injury. We have examined the higheſt injury that can be committed or perpetrated upon the perſon of an individual——let us now turn our attention to ſuch injuries againſt the perſon, as are of an inferior nature.

Of theſe, the firſt in degree is mayham, which is the cutting out, with malice prepenſe, or diſabling the tongue, putting out an eye, ſlitting the noſe, cutting off a noſe or lip, or depriving another of the uſe of ſuch of his members as may render him the leſs able to defend himſelf, or annoy his adverſary. The next is rape. Then the infamous crime againſt nature. Theſe are felonies. But, there are yet other injuries againſt the perſon, which being of a leſs flagrant degree, are, by the tenderneſs of the law, deſcribed under the gentler term of miſdemeanors. Such are aſſaults, batteries, wounding, falſe impriſonment, and kidnapping. Here, in a manner, terminates the ſcale of injuries againſt the perſon : we will now ſtate ſuch as may be perpetrated againſt his manſion, or habitation.

By the univerſal conſent of all ages, the dwelling-houſe of man was, and is endowed with peculiar immunities and valuable privileges. Among the ancients, if even an enemy reached the fire-place of the houſe, he was ſure of protection. Thus we find Coriolanus at the fire-place of Tullus Aufidius, chief of the Volſcian nation, diſcovering himſelf to Aufidius, his public and private enemy, and ſupplicating and receiving his protection againſt Rome, from whence he was baniſhed. And, on this ſubject of a dwelling, Cicero, the great Roman lawyer, orator, and ſtateſman, thus pathetically expreſſes himſelf. "What is more inviolable, what better defended by religion, than the houſe of a citizen ? Here are his altars, here his fire-hearths are contained——this

place of refuge is ſo ſacred to all men, that to be dragged from thence is unlawful." In like manner we find, that at Athens the habitation was particularly protected by the law : burglary was there puniſhed with death, although theft was not. And our law hath ſo ſpecial a regard to a man's dwelling-houſe, that it terms it his caſtle, and will not ſuffer it to be violated with impunity. The law ranges the injuries againſt it under two heads—Arſon, and hameſecken or houſebreaking : and, this laſt it divides into legal or proper burgulary, which is nocturnal houſebreaking, and houſebreaking by day.

Arſon is an injury that tends by fire to annihilate the habitation of another perſon ; or other houſe, that, being within the curtilage or homeſtall, may be reaſonably eſteemed a parcel of it, though not contiguous. So a barn in the field with hay or corn in it. But, this injury by fire, muſt be done with a malicious intent; otherwiſe it is only treſpaſs.

Burglary, is a breaking and entering in the night time, the manſion-houſe of another, with intent to commit ſome felony therein, whether the felonious intent be executed or not : and all ſuch houſes are the objects of burglary, and of houſebreaking, as are deſcribed in the caſe of Arſon

But, to violate this place of protection in the day, by robbing therein, and putting any dweller in fear, although there be no actual breach of the houſe : or by breaking and robbing in the houſe, a dweller being therein and not put in fear : or by robbing and breaking the houſe actually taking ſomething, none being in the houſe : or by feloniouſly taking away ſomething to the value of 35s. currency, or upwards, no perſon being in the houſe : or by breaking the houſe with intent to commit a felony, any perſon being in the houſe and put in fear, though nothing be actually taken :

taken: any fuch violation is called houfebreaking—a crime not of fo atrocious a nature as burglary. For, in the contemplation of our law, as well as of all others, violences perpetrated in the night, are of a more malignant tendency than fimilar ones by day: becaufe, attacks in the night occafion a greater degree of terror; and becaufe, they are in a feafon by Nature appropriated to the neceffary reft and refrefhment of the human body, which is then, by fleep, difarmed of all attention to its defence.

With refpect to injuries againft a man's perfonal property, they are to be confidered under three heads.—Larceny, malicious Mifchief, Forgery. And Larceny, the firft of thefe, is either fimple or mixt.

Simple larceny, or common theft, is a felonious and fraudulent taking and carrying away, the mere perfonal goods of another—here, no violence or fear is implied. If goods fo taken are above the value of *feven fhillings* currency, the offence is termed *grand larceny:* but if they are not exceeding that value, the act is *petit larceny.*—Mixt larceny, has in it all the ingredients of fimple larceny; but it is aggravated by a taking from the houfe or perfon; and this taking, is yet aggravated if it is under the impreffion of violence or fear. Such a taking in the houfe with or without violence or fear, may or may not fall within the crimes of burglary or houfebreaking, according to the circumftances. And, fuch a taking from the perfon, without, or with violence or fear, will be put fimple larceny in the firft cafe; in the other, it is a robbery, and the value is of no confideration.

Malicious mifchief, is a fpecies of injury that bears a near relation to the crime of arfon. A dwelling is the object of arfon; but, other property is the fubject for malicious mifchief to operate upon; and indeed this fpirit of wanton cruelty has a wide field of action. This horrible fpirit difplays itfelf by burning or deftroying the property of another, as a ftack of rice, corn or other grain; or any tar-kiln, barrels of pitch, turpentine, rofin, or other growth, product, or manufacture of this State: or killing or deftroying any horfes, fheep, or other cattle.

At length, the crime of forgery concludes the calendar of public offences againft the property of an individual: I need only define the crime: it is a fraudulent making or alteration of a writing to the prejudice of another perfon.

Having in this manner marked out to you, the diftinguifhing features of the principal crimes and injuries againft the perfon, habitation and property of an individual, I now defire your attention, and I fhall not long detain it, while I delineate thofe againft the State; objects which ought moft carefully to be obferved wherever they appear. I have purpofely thus referved this fubject, as well, becaufe it is of the moft important nature, and virtually includes the other; as that by being the *laft* defcribed, you may be the *more likely to* retain the impreffion of it. Every outrage and violence againft the perfon, habitation or property of an individual, is a crime, a mifdemeanor, or a contempt, and therefore an injury againft the State, bound by original compact to protect the individual in his rights. For, no man conceiving himfelf injured, has any authority or fhadow of it, to redrefs himfelf; becaufe the State has eftablifhed courts which are *vindices injuriarum.* Hence, every criminal injury againft the individual, muft ultimately *wound* the State; and be included in the offences againft the body politic, which muft be more important in their nature than thofe relating to the individual, becaufe they are the more extenfive, and of a higher degree of criminality. It behoves you,

therefore,

therefore, to watch for the public safety ; for this is to be attentive to your private security.

It is not by any means necessary that that I trace these crimes, as they are branched by the law. The present public service requires your immediate particular attention to offences done against only four acts of Assembly---the patrol and Negro laws----the law against counterfeiting the certificates issued by the late Houses of Assembly, or the currency issued by the Congress of the Continent of this country,---and, the law to prevent sedition, and to punish insurgents and disturbers of the public peace.

The two first laws are calculated to keep our domestics in a proper behaviour. The two last were expresly formed, as two pillars to support our new Constitution ; and, therefore, these last are your most important objects.—I shall fully explain them.

The Act against counterfeiting extends to all persons who counterfeit, raze or alter, or utter, or offer in payment, knowing the same to be counterfeited, razed or altered, any certificate or bill of credit under the authority of the late Common House of Assembly, or the Congresses of this country, or of the Continent.

The law to prevent sedition, guards against those actions as, in such a crisis as this, might reasonably be expected to operate against our present honourable and happy establishment. And the variety and importance of those actions, make it necessary for me to particularize them to you.

This salutary act touches all persons taking up arms against the authority of the present Government ; or who, by violence, words, deeds or writing, cause, or attempt to cause, induce, or persuade any other person to do so. In like manner, all persons who give intelligence to, or hold correspondence with, or aid or abet any land or naval force sent by Great-Britain, or any other force or body of men within this State, with hostile intent against it. So those who compel, induce, persuade or attempt to do so, any white person, Indian, free Negro, or slave, to join any force under authority derived from Great-Britain. And so, all persons who collect or assemble with any others, or procure them to be assembled with intent, in a riotous and seditious manner, to disturb the public peace and tranquility ; and by words, or otherwise, create and raise traiterous seditions or discontents, in the minds of the people against the public authority.

Thus having stated to you such criminal injuries against an individual, or the State, as may be most likely to come within your notice : it is a natural consequence, that I describe the person by law held capable of committing such injuries.

In the first place, the party must be of sound memory at the time of committing the offence ; and it is the leading principle in every case. If the party is under seven years of age, no evidence can possibly be admitted to criminate ; because the law holds, that the party cannot discern between good and evil. But if the accused is above seven and under fourteen, he is liable to be criminated, if at the time of his committing the injury, his understanding was so ripe as to occasion him to shew a consciousness of guilt, the rule being, *malitiâ supplet ætatem*. And if the party is of the age of fourteen, which is the age of discretion ; the law *prima facie* considers him capable of committing offences, as a person of full age. Also, a lunatic for crimes perpetrated in a lucid interval. Also, a man for crimes done in a state of drunkenness voluntarily contracted ; and so far is this artificial insanity from excusing, that it tends to aggravate the offence.

All those particulars relating to the person,

perfon, habitation and property of an individual; thofe refpecting the fafety, peace and tranquility of the State; and thefe defcribing the perpetrator of criminal injuries, are fo many proper heads for your diligent enquiry: and fuch offenders and offences being within your knowledge, you muft make due prefentment of them. You are to hear evidence only on the part of an information to you of an offence; for an indictment by you is only in the nature of a folemn and public accufation, which is afterwards to be tried and determined by others: you are only to examine, whether there be fufficient caufe to call upon the party to anfwer. Twelve of you at leaft muft agree in opinion, that the accufed ought to undergo a public trial—fo twelve other jurors are to declare him innocent or guilty. Happy inftitution, whereby no man can be declared a criminal, but by the concurring voices of at leaft four and twenty men, collected in the vicinage by blind chance, upon their oaths to do juftice, and againft whom even the party himfelf has no exception!

Thus, Gentlemen of the Grand Jury, with the beft intentions for the public fervice, however executed; having declared to you, that you are not *bound* under, but *freed* from the dominion of the   ; I thought myfelf neceffarily obliged, and I have endeavoured to demonftrate to you, that the rife and fall of empires are natural events—that the Independence of America *was* not, at the commencement of the late civil war, or even at the conclufion of the laft year, *the aim of the Americans*—that their fubjection to the

being releafed by the action of *Britifh oppreffion*, the ftroke of *the Britifh fword*, and the tenor of *a Britifh Act of Parliament*; their natural rife to empire was conducted by the hand of God!—that the fame ftrong hand, by proceedings equally

unexpected, wonderful and rapid, **as** in our cafe, conducted the Englifh Revolution of 1688---that the Revolutions in England and Scotland at that period, and in America now giving a new epocha to the hiftory of the world, were founded in the *fame* immediate caufe, a failure of protection ---that thofe Revolutions concurred, *in one grand evidence* of the feelings of Nature on fuch a fubject---that every fpecies of mal-adminiftration in   is to be traced to a failure of protection, which is the only inftrument working his abdication---that the object for which we contend, is *juft* in its nature, and of *ineftimable* value---that the American Revolution may be fupported with the faireft profpect of fuccefs by arms---and that it may be powerfully aided by a Grand Jury.

Gentlemen! I do moft cordially congratulate you, placed as you are in a ftation, honourable to yourfelves, and beneficial to your country. Guardians of the innocent, you are appointed to fend the robber, the murderer, the incendiary and the traitor to trial. Your diligence in enquiring for fuch offenders, is the fource of your honour, and a means of your country's fafety; and although no fuch offenders be found, your laudable fearch will yet tend to curb a propenfity to robbery, murder, fedition and treafon. See, Gentlemen, what great advantages may refult from your vigilant and patriotic conduct! Your ears ought to be *fhut* to the petitions of friendfhip, and to the calls of confanguinity---but, they ought to be *expanded* to receive the *complaints of your injured country*, and the *demands of impartial juftice*. Brutus inflicted upon his fons the *ultimum fupplicium*, for confpiring to re-eftablifh the Regal Government in Rome. And, if a fimilar occafion fhould arife in America, which God forbid, I truft, a Brutus will not be wanting. Let thofe, if there are any
such,

such, who treacherously or pusilanimously hanker after a return of Government, remember such things and tremble. Let us ever remember, rejoice and teach our children, that the American Empire is composed of States that are, and of right ought to be, free and independent; " that they are absolved from

and that all political connection between them and the State of Great-Britain, IS, AND OUGHT TO BE, TOTALLY DISSOLVED."

South-Carolina.

At a Court of General Sessions of the Peace, Oyer and Terminer, Assize and General Gaol Delivery, begun to be held at Charles-town, for the district of Charles-town, on Tuesday, October 15th, in the year of our Lord one thousand seven hundred and seventy-six.

The Presentments of the Grand Jury for the said district.

1. It is with most cordial satisfaction we embrace this opportunity of offering our congratulations on the late Declaration of the Continental Congress, constituting the United Colonies of North-America Independent States; an event, however once dreaded as repugnant to those hopes of peace and friendship with the British State, which was then ardently entertained, yet which every American must now most joyfully embrace, as the only happy means of salvation and security, and the surest prevention to the treacherous and cruel designs of a wicked and detestable enemy.

2. As the kind and beneficent hand of a wise and bounteous Providence has so ordered and disposed of human events, that from calamities which were dreaded as the most miserable and destructive to America, benefits the most advantageous, honourable and desirable have arisen to her, which now give a very joyful

prospect of liberty and happiness. We think our grateful sense of such peculiar care and protection cannot be manifested in a way more acceptable and proper than in a strict regard to the duties which mankind owe to their God.

3. We present the growing evil of many churches established by law, falling to decay, and some remaining without ministers to perform divine service, in divers parishes in this district, by which means the spirit of religion will decline, and become prejudicial to the manners of the people.

4. We present and recommend a proper militia law to be made, in such manner as to compel impartially and equally all degrees of persons liable to do the duty therein required, so as to enable the good people of this State (who are now become principally the guardians thereof) to repel any domestic or foreign enemy as far as possible.

5. We present and recommend, that care may always be had, that none but gentlemen of weight and influence, and good example, be prevailed on to qualify and act in the Commission of Peace, by whose influence, licentiousness, sedition and profligacy, may be suppressed, and good order maintained.

6. We present and recommend, that some office may be created in this district, whereby executions and sales by the Sheriff may be recorded, so that on the death or removal of the Sheriff recourse may be had to such records by those concerned.

7. We present and recommend, that Jews and others may be restrained from allowing their Negroes to sell goods in shops, as such practice may induce other Negroes to steal and barter with them.

8. We present the ill practice of Jews opening their shops and selling of goods on Sunday, to the profanation of the Lord's-Day.

9. We

9. We present the Barrack-master, Philip Will, for seizing of fire-wood on the wharfs, under pretence of the public, when he applies the same to his own use, to the distressing of the inhabitants. By information of Mr. Patrick Hinds, one of the Grand Jurors.

10. We present the want of more constables in this district, we being informed that there are only four in this town.

11. We return our thanks to his Honour the Chief Justice for his excellent charge delivered at the opening of the sessions, and desire that the charge and these presentments be forthwith printed and published.

JOSEPH GLOVER, Foreman, (L. S.)
BENJAMIN BAKER, (L. S.)
BENJAMIN DART, (L. S.)
JOHN FULLERTON, (L. S.)
CHRIST. FITZSIMONS, (L. S.)
WILLIAM HOPTON, (L. S.)
WILLIAM HALE, (L. S.)
PATRICK HINDS, (L. S.)
CHARLES JOHNSTON, (L. S.)
ANDREW LORD, (L. S.)
JOHN MILES, (L. S.)
WILLIAM RUSSEL, (L. S.)
STEPHEN TOWNSEND. (L. S.)

Charles-Town, South-Carolina, July 4, 1777.

June 26. ARTICLES *of the Definitive Treaty of Peace, concluded on, and signed at Dewit's Corner the 20th day of May, 1777, between the States of South-Carolina and Georgia and the Cherokee Indians.*

ARTICLE 1. The Cherokee Nations acknowledge, that the troops during last summer repeatedly defeated their forces, victoriously penetrated through their Lower Towns, middle settlements and vallies, and quietly and unopposed built, held, and continue to occupy, the Fort at Seneca, thereby did effect and maintain the conquest of all the Cherokee lands, eastward of the Unacaye Mountain; and to, and for their people, did acquire, possess, and yet continue to hold, in and over the said lands, all and singular the rights incidental to conquest; and the Cherokee Nation, in consequence thereof, do cede the said lands to the said people, the people of South-Carolina.

ARTICLE 2. South-Carolina will immediately send a supply of goods into the Cherokee Nation and settlements for sale, and permit the Cherokees, during their good behaviour, to inhabit the middle settlements and vallies westward of the highest part of the Occonnee Mountain; but they shall not, beyond a line extended south-west and north-east across the highest part of the Occonnee Mountain, proceed or advance, without permission from the Commanding Officer at Fort Rutledge; to apply for which, one runner may at any time be sent by the Cherokees: Provided nevertheless, that during this present year the Cherokees may raise, gather and remove the corn they have planted on the east side of the Occonnee Mountain.

ARTICLE 3. The Government of South-Carolina will endeavour that the Cherokees be furnished with supplies of goods as usual; and that the trade shall be put under the best regulations. Every person who, without a proper pass or licence, shall arrive in the Cherokee nation or settlements, the Cherokees shall immediately apprehend, and deliver to the Commanding Officer at Fort Rutledge, and seize to their own use, all the cattle, horses, goods and effects conducted into their settlements by every such person.

ARTICLE 4. Every white person who instigated, or endeavoured to instigate, the Cherokees to the late war, or encouraged or aided them, or endeavoured to do so in the prosecution of it, and who now is, or hereafter may be, in their power, shall, without delay, by the Cherokees,

kers, be apprehended and delivered to the Commanding Officer at Fort Rutledge; and the Cherokees shall take to their own use all the effects, which in their nation or settlements they may find in the possession of, or belonging to, every such white person, and for every such white person so delivered, shall be paid five hundred pounds weight of dressed leather, or the value therof.

ARTICLE 5. Any Indian who, in the Cherokee Nation or settlements, shall murder a white person, shall be immediately apprehended and conveyed to Fort Rutledge by the Cherokees, who, in presence of the Commanding Officer at that post, shall put the murderer to death; and if any white or other person belonging to South-Carolina or Georgia, shall in the Cherokee Nation, or any white or other person shall, in South Carolina or Georgia, murder a Cherokee Indian, every such person, duly convicted thereof, shall suffer death in presence of the Cherokee Indians, if any shall attend at the time and place of execution; and that they may have an opportunity of attending, due notice of the time and place of such intended execution shall be sent to the Cherokees.

ARTICLE 6. All white and Indian persons shall be set at liberty as soon as possible; all Negroes taken during the late war, and who now are, or hereafter may be, in the power of the Cherokees, shall, as soon as possible be delivered to the Commanding Officer at Fort Rutledge, together with the horses, by any of their people before the late war, stolen from South-Carolina, Georgia, North Carolina, or Virginia, and which now are, or hereafter may be, in the power of the Cherokees, to the end that restitution may be made to their true owners.

ARTICLE 7. For every run-away Negro that shall be apprehended and delivered by the Cherokees to the Commanding Officer at Fort Rutledge, shall be paid one hundred pounds weight of leather, or the value thereof.

ARTICLE 8. The hatchet shall be for ever buried, and there shall be an universal peace and friendship re-established between South-Carolina, including the Catawba and Georgia on the one part, and the Cherokee Nation on the other; there shall be a general oblivion of injuries; the contracting parties shall use their utmost endeavours to maintain the peace and friendship now re-established, and the Cherokees shall, at all times, apprehend and deliver to the Commanding Officer at Fort Rutledge, every person, white or red, who in their nation or settlements, shall by any means endeavour to instigate a war by the Cherokee Nation, or hostility, or robbery, by any of their people, against or upon any of the American States, or subjects thereof.

In witness of all and every thing herein determined between South-Carolina, Georgia, and the Cherokee Nation, we their underwritten Commissioners and Deputies, by virtue of our full powers, severally, and not one for the other, have signed this present definitive treaty, in their respective names, and have caused our seals to be hereunto affixed.

Done at Dewit's Corner, this twentieth day of May, in the year of our Lord one thousand seven hundred and seventy-seven.

An Ordinance for regulating the militia of the province of Quebec, and rendering it of more general utility, towards the preservation and security thereof.

Whereas his Excellency the Captain-general and Governor in Chief of this province is, by virtue of his Majesty's commission under the Great Seal of Great-Britain, empowered to levy,

levy, arm, muster, command, and employ all persons within the province, and, as occasion shall serve, them to march or transport from one place to another, for the purpose of resisting and withstanding of all enemies, pirates, and rebels, both by land and by water; which commission, in the absence of the Captain-general, the Lieutenant-governor, or Commander in Chief, for the time being, is authorized to execute :—— and whereas the well ordering and training of the said militia, may hereafter be of great use towards preserving and securing the province from all hostile invaders thereof, be it enacted by the Captain-general and Governor in Chief of the province, by and with the advice and consent of the Legislative Council of the same, That

ART. 1. All persons, as well in the towns as in the country, from the age of sixteen years to sixty, are bound to serve in the militia of that parish wherein they reside; and from and after the publication of the present ordinance, every person (excepting such as are herein after excepted) refusing to serve, or neglecting to get himself inrolled under the officers appointed by his Excellency the Captain-general or Governor in Chief, in the different parishes, shall forfeit five pounds; and upon a second refusal, he shall, over and above a like forfeiture of five pounds for such second refusal, be rendered incapable of keeping by him, or bearing any fire-arm whatsoever, under the like penalty of five pounds, and one month's imprisonment, for every time he shall be convicted of having used or kept such fire-arm.

ART. 2. Every militia-man, whose conduct or behaviour proves unworthy of, or dishonourable to the corps, shall be expelled therefrom, and in like manner rendered incapable of keeping by him, or using any fire-arm, under the penalties mentioned

in the foregoing Article; and as well those who have refused or neglected to enroll themselves, as those who are expelled therefrom, shall furnish sleighs, and other carriages for the King's service, when called upon, in a double proportion to their neighbours of the same parish, doing duty as militia-men readily and chearfully, and for half the price; provided always that, after the expiration of one year, any person, who has committed any of the above recited offences, and suffered the penalties directed by this and the foregoing Articles, upon making his submission to the Captain of militia, in the presence of the most reputable inhabitants of the parish, at the church door, on a Sunday, or some other feast day, shall, after a report has been made thereof to the Colonel of militia of the district, and being approved by the Captain-general, or in his absence, the Lieutenant-governor, or Commander in Chief, for the time being, be restored to the corps, intitled to the priviliges thereof; and act therein, as if no such offence had been committed.

ART. 3. The Captain or Captains of militia in every parish, shall, twenty days after the publication of the present ordinance, or sooner, if it can be done, transmit to the Colonels of militia, or Inspectors, when such shall be appointed, for the respective districts, an account of the number of officers and militia-men fit for service in their respective companies; as also a list of such as may have refused to inroll themselves, or disobeyed the orders of their superior officers; and hereafter such lists, as well as of any alterations that may have happened within the last twelve-month, are to be transmitted by the Captains to the Colonels of militia, or Inspectors when such shall be appointed, by the tenth or fifteenth of March in every year at farthest.

ART. 4. No person belonging to
a particular

X x

a particular company of militia, shall leave his usual residence, whereby he became subject thereto, without giving due notice to his Captain or Commanding Officer, and of the place where he intends to settle; and every person, so settling in another parish, shall give notice thereof to the Captain or Commanding Officer of the parish wherein he settles, under a penalty of forty shillings for the first offence, and for the second, the like sum, and one month's imprisonment.

ART. 5. Upon the two last Sundays in the month of June, and the two first in July, the Captains or Commanding Officers of the militia, shall draw out their companies in the most convenient place of their respective parishes, in order to inspect their arms, fire at marks, and instruct them in their duties; and such as disobey, and do not appear on such training days, or at such other times as the Colonels of militia, Inspectors, or other persons authorized to review or exercise them by special orders from the Captain-general, or, in his absence, the Lieutenant-governor, or Commander in Chief, for the time being, shall direct, are to forfeit ten shillings for every offence, except they shall have first asked and obtained leave of absence, on shewing reasonable cause for the same.

ART. 6. In time of war, rebellion, or when any other pressing exigency of the State requires it, such number of officers, serjeants, and militia-men, as the Governor, Lieutenant-governor, or Commander in Chief, for the time being, thinks fit to direct, shall be drawn out of the different companies, marched from their respective parishes, to such place as they shall be ordered to, and serve, though still as militia, in conjunction with his Majesty's forces, under the guidance and superintendance of the officers whom the Commander in Chief shall be pleased to appoint for that purpose: and at the end of the campaign, or of the service they were ordered upon, shall return to their own homes, but not before they have been regularly dismissed from the same; any person refusing to obey such order, absconding, or not repairing to the place he is ordered to, shall incur double the penalties inflicted by the first Article of this ordinance; and any one quitting the service when so embodied, before he is discharged therefrom, shall moreover be expelled the corps, and never allowed to re-enter the same: and any person buying or purchasing arms, ammunition, or equipments, delivered out of his Majesty's stores to the militia, when embodied, or any ammunition, furnished out of the said stores, for training and exercising the said militia, shall incur a penalty of 5l. for every such offence, to be recovered upon the oath of one credible witness before any one Commissioner of the Peace in the district where such offence has been committed.

ART. 7. All inhabitants above the age of 60, and having one servant, as well as all others holding lands *en roture*, and not exempted therefrom by this ordinance, shall, when ordered by Government, and called upon by the Captains of the militia, in rotation, furnish carts, sleighs, or order carriages for the King's service, at such price per day, as shall be fixed upon by the Commander in Chief; and any who shall neglect or refuse to furnish the same, or shall desert or quit that service, without being duly discharged therefrom, shall likewise incur the penalties directed by the first Article.

ART. 8. The Captains and other officers of militia not paying due obedience to their superiors, or who shall be convicted of having acted with partiality, of exempting some, without being properly authorized so to
do

do, or ordering others out of their turn, out of pique or refentment, fhall be deprived of their commiffions, and obliged to ferve as private militia-men.

ART. 9. The Captains, and other officers of militia, fhall take up all deferters, whether foldiers or failors, all ftragglers and other perfons, travelling through their refpective parifhes, fufpected of being emiffaries from conveying intelligence to, or corresponding with the rebellious colonies, all perfons fpreading falfe reports to the detriment of Government, and perfons leaving the province without a pafs from the Captain-general, or, in his abfence, the Lieutenant-governor or Commander in Chief, for the time being; and any perfon, either in town or country, lodging or concealing fuch deferters, ftragglers, or fufpected perfons as above, or aiding and affifting any perfon leaving the province without a pafs, without giving immediate notice thereof to the Captains of their refpective companies in the country, and if in the towns of Quebec, Montreal, and Trois Rivieres, to the Colonels or Commanding Officers, or other officers appointed for that purpofe, fhall, for the firft offence, if inhabitants of the towns, forfeit ten pounds, and be imprifoned one month; refiding in the country, fhall forfeit five pounds, and be imprifoned for the fame time; and double the fame and double the time of imprifonment, for the fecond, and every other fubfequent offence of the like nature.

ART. 10. In all cafes where the manner of profecuting for the penalties inflicted by this ordinance has not been directed, where the fine impofed does not exceed the fum of forty fhillings, any one Field Officer of the militia, or Infpector, when fuch officer fhall be appointed, of the diftrict wherein the offence fhall have committed, being a Commiffioner of the peace; and where the penalty

exceeds the fum of forty fhillings, or directs the imprifonment of the offender, any two Field Officers, or one Field Officer and Infpector, as before, belonging to the diftrict in which the offence fhall have been committed, being Commiffioners of of the Peace, or any other two Commiffioners of the Peace for that diftrict, is and are hereby authorized, upon information laid before them, to take cognizance of, and hear in a fummary manner, all offences committed againft the intent and meaning of this ordinance, to inflict the penalties, and levy the fines by warrant under his or their hands and feals, and all monies arifing therefrom, to be by him or them tranfmitted to the Receiver-general of the province, and applied, as other public monies to his Majefty's ufe; fubject, neverthelefs, in cafes where the penalty is of or exceeds ten pounds, and where the party offending is to be imprifoned for more than one month, or to be expelled the militia, to an appeal before the Governor, or, in his abfence, the Lieutenant-governor, or Commander in Chief for the time being, and any five members of his Majefty's Council (the Commiffioners of the Peace who fhall have heard the fame and given judgment therein only excepted) who are hereby appointed a Court of Appeals for that purpofe, and authorized to hear and finally to detrmine the fame.

ART. 11. The members of his Majefty's Council, Judges, and others officers of civil government, the Seigniors, ftiled here, *Seigneurs primitifs*, the nobleffe, fo acknowledged under the ancient Government of the country, half pay or reduced officers, clergy, ftudents of the feminaries of Quebec and Montreal, and perfons employed in offices of public utility, are exempted from ferving in the militia or furnifhing carriages: provided always, that nothing in this ordinance contained be conftrued to exempt the

Seigniors,

Seigniors, or nobleſſe, from rendering ſuch perſonal ſervices as are agreeable to the ancient uſage, and to which they are bound by the tenure of their lands, whenever the Governor, or in his abſence, the Lieutenant-governor, or Commander in Chief, for the time being, ſhall judge it neceſſary to call upon them for the ſame.

This ordinance to be in force for two years, and to the ſeſſion of the Legiſlative Council of this province, which will be held in the year one thouſand ſeven hundred and ſeventy-nine. GUY CARLETON.

Enacted by the authority aforeſaid, and paſſed in Council under the Great Seal of the province, at the Council Chamber in the Caſtle of St. Lewis, in the city of Quebec, the twenty-ninth day of March, in the ſeventeenth year of the reign of our Sovereign Lord George the Third, by the grace of God, of Great-Britain, France, and Ireland, King, Defender of the Faith, and ſo forth, and in the year of our Lord, one thouſand ſeven hundred and ſeventy ſeven.

By his Excellency's command,
J. WILLIAMS, C. L. C.

Whitehall, Auguſt 25, 1777.
The following letter from Lieutenant-General Burgoyne to Lord George Germain was received the 23d inſtant, by Captain Gardiner, firſt Aid de Camp to Lieutenant-General Burgoyne, who arrived in the Royal George armed tranſport from Quebec.
Head Quarters, Skeneſborough-Houſe,
July 11, 1777.

My Lord,

I have the honour to acquaint your Lordſhip, that the enemy diſlodged from Ticonderoga and Mount Independence on the 6th inſtant, and were driven on the ſame day beyond Skeneſborough on the right, and to Huberton on the left, with the loſs of 128 pieces of cannon, all their armed veſſels and batteaux, the greateſt part of their baggage and ammunition, proviſion and military ſtores to a very large amount.

This ſucceſs has been followed by events equally fortunate and rapid. I ſubjoin ſuch a detail of circumſtances as the time will permit; and, for his Majeſty's further information, I beg leave to refer your Lordſhip to Captain Gardiner, my Aid de Camp, whom I have thought it neceſſary to diſpatch with news ſo important to the King's ſervice, and ſo honourable to the troops under my command.

Journal of the late principal proceedings of the army.

Having remained at Crown Point three days, to bring up the rear of the army, to eſtabliſh the magazines and the hoſpital, and to obtain intelligence of the enemy, on

June 30, I ordered the advanced corps, conſiſting of the Britiſh light infantry and grenadiers, the 24th regiment, ſome Canadians and ſavages, and ten pieces of light artillery, under the command of Brigadier-General Frazer, to move from Putnam Creek, where they had been encamped ſome days, up the weſt ſhore of the lake to Four Mile Point, ſo called from being within that diſtance of the fort of Ticonderoga. The German reſerve, conſiſting of the Brunſwick chaſſeurs, light infantry and grenadiers, under Lieutenant-Colonel Breymen, were advanced at the ſame time upon the eaſt ſhore.

July 1. The whole army made a movement forward. Brigadier Frazer's corps occupied the ſtrong poſt called Three Mile Point on the weſt ſhore; the German reſerve the eaſt ſhore oppoſite; the right wing of the line encamped at Four Mile Point; the left wing nearly oppoſite on the eaſt ſhore. The Royal George and Inflexible frigates, with the gun boats, were anchored juſt without the reach of the enemy's batteries. The reſt of the fleet had been ſome time without guns,

guns, in order to affist in carrying provisions over Lake Champlain.

The enemy appeared to be posted as follows: a brigade occupied the old French lines upon the height north-ward of the fort of Ticonderoga. These lines were in good repair, and had several intrenchments behind them, chiefly calculated to guard the north-west flank, and they were further sustained by a blockhouse. To the left of these works about a mile, the enemy had saw-mills, and a post sustained by a blockhouse, and an-other blockhouse, and an hospital at the entrance of Lake George. Upon the right of the French lines, and be-tween them and the old fort, there were two new blockhouses, and a con-siderable battery close to the water-edge.

It seemed that the enemy had em-ployed their chief industry, and were in greatest force, upon Mount Inde-pendence, which is high and circular; and upon the summit, which is table-land, were a star fort made with pickets and well supplied with artil-lery, and a large square of barracks within it.

The foot of the Mount, which pro-jects into the Lake, was intrenched and covered with a strong abattis close to the water. This intrenchment was lined with heavy artillery pointing down the Lake, flanking the water-battery above described, and sustained by another battery about half-way up the Mount. On the west-side the Mount runs the main river, and in its passage round is joined by the water which comes down from Lake George. On the east-side of the Mount the water forms a small bay, into which falls a rivulet, after having encircled in its course part of the Mount to the south-west. The side to the south could not be seen, but was described as inaccessible. There was a bridge between the Mount and Ticonderoga, which also was unseen.

July 2. About nine in the morning a smoke was observed towards Lake George, and the Indians brought in a report that the enemy had set fire to their further blockhouse, and had abandoned the saw-mills; and that a considerable body were advancing from the lines towards a bridge upon the road which led to the right of the British camp. A detachment of the advanced corps was immediately put in march under Brigadier Frazer, sup-ported by a brigade of the line and some artillery, under the command of Major-General Phillips, with orders to proceed towards Mount Hope, which is to the north of the lines, to reconnoitre the enemy's position, and to take advantage of any post they might abandon, or be driven from.

The Indians under Captain Frazer, supported by his company of marks-men, were directed to make a circuit to the left of Brigadier Frazer's line of march, and endeavour to cut off the retreat of the enemy to their lines; but this design miscarried, through the impetuosity of the Indians, who attacked too soon, and in front, and the enemy were thereby able to retire with the loss of one officer and a few men killed, and one officer wounded. Major-General Phillips took possession of the very advantageous post of Mount Hope this night, and the enemy were thereby entirely cut off from a com-munication with Lake George.

July 3. Mount Hope was occu-pied in force by Brigadier Frazer's whole brigade, the first brigade Bri-tish, and two entire brigades of artil-lery. The second brigade British en-camped upon the left of the first, and the brigade of Gall having been drawn from the east there to occupy the ground where Frazer's corps had been on Three Mile Point, the line became compleat, extending from the shore to the westernmost part of Mount Hope. On the same day Major-General Rei-defel encamped on the east shore in a parallel line with Three Mile Point, having pushed the reserve forward
near

near the rivulet which is on the east of Mount Independence. The enemy cannonaded the camps of Mount Hope and of the German reserve most part of the day, but without effect.

July 4. The army worked hard at their communications, and got up the artillery, tents, baggage and provisions. The enemy at intervals continued the cannonade upon the camps, which was not in any instance returned.

The Thunderer Radeau carrying the battering train and stores, having been warped up from Crown Point, arrived this day, and immediately began to land the artillery.

July 5. Lieutenant Twiss, the commanding engineer, was ordered to reconnoitre Sugar Hill on the south-west side of the communication from Lake George into Lake Champlain. It had appeared from the first to be a very advantageous post; and it is now known that the enemy had a council some time ago upon the expediency of possessing it; but the idea was rejected upon the supposition that it was impossible for a corps to be established there in force. Lieutenant Twiss reported this hill to have the entire command of the works and buildings both of Ticonderoga and Mount Independence; that the ground might be levelled so as to receive cannon; and that a road to convey them, though difficult, might be made practicable in twenty-four hours. This hill also entirely commanded in reverse the bridge of communication, saw the exact situation of the vessels, nor could the enemy during the day make any material movement or preparation without being discovered, and even having their numbers counted.

It was immediately determined that a battery should be raised upon Sugar-hill for light twenty-four pounders, medium twelves, and eight-inch howitzers. This very arduous work was carried on so rapidly, that the battery would have been ready the next day.

It is a duty in this place to do some justice to the zeal and activity of Major-general Phillips, who had the direction of the operation; and having mentioned that most valuable officer, I trust it cannot be thought a digression to add, that it is to his judicious arrangements and indefatigable pains, during the general superintendency of preparations which Sir Guy Carleton entrusted to him in the winter and spring, that the service is indebted for its present forwardness; the prevalence of contrary winds and other accidents having rendered it impossible for any necessaries prepared in England for the opening of the campaign yet to reach the army.

July 6. Soon after day-light an officer arrived express on board the *Royal George*, where in the night I took my quarters as the most central situation, with information from Brigadier Frazer that the enemy were retiring, and that he was advancing with his piquets, leaving orders for the brigade to follow as soon as they could accoutre, with intention to pursue by land. This movement was very soon discernable, as were the British colours which the Brigadier had fixed upon the fort of Ticonderoga. Knowing how safely I could trust to that officer's conduct, I turned my chief attention to the pursuit by water, by which route I had intelligence one column were retiring in two hundred and twenty batteaux, covered by five armed gallies.

The great bridge of communication, through which a way was to be opened, was supported by twenty-two sunken piers of large timber at nearly equal distances: the spaces between were filled by separate floats, each about fifty feet long and twelve feet wide, strongly fastened together by chains and rivets, and also fastened to the sunken piers. Before this bridge was

was a boom made of very large pieces of round timber, faftened together by rivetted bolts and double chains made of iron an inch and half fquare.

The gun boats were immediately moved forward, and the boom and one of the intermediate floats were cut with great dexterity and difpatch : and Commodore Lutwidge, with the officers and feamen in his department, partaking the general animation, a paffage was found in half an hour for the frigates alfo, through impediments, which the enemy had been labouring ten months together to make impenetrable. During thefe operations Major-general Reidefel had paffed to Mount Independence, with the corps of Breymen and part of the left wing. He was directed to proceed by land to fuftain Brigadier Frazer, or to act more to the left, if he faw it expedient fo to do. The 62d regiment Britifh, and the Brunfwick regiment of Prince Frederic, were left at Ticonderoga and Mount Independence, in the place of the parties of Frazer's brigade, which had remained in poffeffion of the ftores, and the reft of the army were ordered to follow up the river, as they could be collected, without regard to the place of corps in the line. About three in the afternoon I arrived with the Royal George and Inflexible, and the beft failing gun boats and batteaux at South Bay, within three miles of Skenefborough, at which latter place I learned the enemy were pofted in a ftockaded fort, and their armed gallies at the falls below.

The foremoft regiments, viz. the 9th, 20th, and 21ft, were inftantly difembarked and afcended the mountain, with intention of burning the fort and cutting off the retreat of the enemy, but their precipitate flight rendered this manœuvre ineffectual. The gun boats and frigates continued their courfe to Skenefborough falls. Captain Carter, with part of his brigade of gun boats, immediately attacked the gallies, and with fo much fpirit that two of them very foon ftruck, the other three were blown up ; and the enemy having previoufly prepared combuftible materials, fet fire to the fort, mills, ftorehoufes, batteaux, &c. and retired with the detachment left for that purpofe, the main body having gone off, when the troops were afcending the mountain. A great quantity of provifion and fome arms were here confumed, and moft part of their officers baggage was burned, funk or taken. Their lofs in the attack is not known ; about thirty prifoners were made, among which were two wounded officers. During thefe operations upon the right, Brigadier Frazer had continued his purfuit on the road to Caftletown 'till one o'clock, having marched in a very hot day from four in the morning. Some ftragglers of the enemy had been picked up, from whom the Brigadier learnt, that their rear guard was compofed of chofen men, and commanded by Colonel Francis, one of their beft officers. While the men were refrefhing, Major-general Reidefel came up, and arrangements having been concerted for continuing the purfuit, Brigadier Frazer moved forward again, and during the night lay upon his arms in an advantageous fituation.

July 7. At three in the morning he renewed his march, and about five his advanced fcouts difcovered the enemy's centries, who fired their pieces, and joined their main body. The Brigadier obferving a commanding ground on the left of his light infantry, immediately ordered it to be poffeffed by that corps ; and a confiderable body of the enemy attempting the fame, they met. The enemy were driven back to their original poft. The advanced guard under Major Grant were by this time engaged, and the grenadiers were advanced to fuftain them, and to prevent the right flank from being turned. The Brigadier remained on the left, where the

the enemy, aided by logs and trees, defended themselves long. After being dislodged and prevented getting to the Castletown road by the grenadiers, they rallied and renewed the action. They were again driven, and attempted to retreat by Pittsford Mountain : but the grenadiers scrambled up what had appeared an inaccessible part of the ascent, and gained the summit before them. This threw them into confusion. They were still, nevertheless, greatly superior in number, and consequently in extent, and the Brigadier, in momentary expectation of the arrival of the Germans, had latterly weakened his left to support his right. At this critical moment Major-general Reidesel arrived with the foremost of his column, viz. the chasseur company and eighty grenadiers and light infantry. His judgment instantly pointed to him the course to take. He extended upon Brigadier Frazer's left flank. Major Berner led the chasseurs into action with great gallantry, and they were equally well sustained. The enemy fled on all sides, leaving dead upon the field Colonel Francis and many other officers, and upwards of two hundred private men. Above six hundred were wounded, many of whom perished in the woods attempting to get off; and one Colonel, seven Captains, ten subalterns, and two hundred and ten men, were made prisoners. The number of the enemy before the action amounted, by the report of the prisoners, to two thousand men, and they were strongly posted. The British detachment under Brigadier Frazer, (the parties left at Ticonderoga the day before not having been able to rejoin) consisted only of eight hundred and fifty fighting men. The bare relation of so signal an action is sufficient for its praise. Should the attack against such inequality of numbers before the Germans came up seem to require explanation, it is to be considered that the enemy might

have escaped by delay; that the advanced guard found themselves on a sudden too near the enemy to avoid action without retreating; and that the Brigadier had supposed the German troops to be very near. The difference of time in their arrival was merely accidental. Major-general Reidesel and those he commanded pressed for a share of glory, and they arrived in time to obtain it. I have only to add upon this event, that the exertions of Brigadier Frazer were but a continuance of that uniform intelligence, activity, and bravery, which distinguish his character upon all occasions, and entitle him to be recommended in the most particular manner to his Majesty's notice. The other officers and soldiers of this corps have prevented any distinctions of individuals by a general and equal display of spirit.

On the same day, July 7, the country people about Skenesborough having reported that part of the enemy were still retreating upon Wood Creek, the 9th regiment was detached to take post near Fort Anne, to observe their motions. This was effected, though with much difficulty, the roads being extremely bad, and the bridges broken. The other troops were employed all that day and night in dragging fifty batteaux over the falls to facilitate the movement of the rest of the first brigade to Fort Anne, to dislodge the enemy there.

July 8. A report was received from Lieutenant-colonel Hill, commanding the 9th regiment, that the enemy had been reinforced in the night by a considerable body of fresh troops; that he could not retire before them with his regiment, but would maintain his ground. The two remaining regiments of the first brigade under Brigadier Powell were ordered to quicken their march; and, upon second intelligence of the force of the enemy, and firing being heard, the 20th regiment were ordered forward, and

EXPLANATION.

A. Cheonderoga.
B. Intrenchment & front of the Attack in 1758.
C. Lake Champlain.
D. Wood Creek.
E. A Mountain over looking the Fort.
F. Our Rafts with 3 Cannon & 1 Howhits.
G. Where the Army lay the 7th.
H. Saw Mill & Fall. ⎫ The Carrying Place is from
I. Ovens. ⎭ H. to I. is about 2 Miles.
K. Where the Army lay the 6th.
L. Where the Army fell in with 450 of the Enemy, and Lord Howe was Kill'd.
M. The Army marching in four Columns.
N. Landing Place.
O. Mutton Island.
P. Bare Mountain Entrance of the Narrows.
Q. Saw Mill Creek.

LAKE GEORGE

Jnᵒ Lodge Sculp

London. Printed according to Act of Parliament, for J. Almon, in Piccadilly, Augᵗ 25, 1777.

and Major-general Phillips, with some pieces of artillery, was sent to take the command. A violent storm of rain, which lasted the whole day, prevented these troops from getting to Fort Anne so soon as was intended; but the delay gave the 9th regiment an opportunity of distinguishing themselves by standing and repulsing an attack of six times their numbers. The enemy finding the position not to be forced in front, endeavoured to surround it; and, from the superiority of their numbers, that inconvenience was to be apprehended, and Lieutenant-colonel Hill therefore found it necessary to change his ground in the heat of action. So critical an order was executed by the regiment with the greatest steadiness and bravery. The enemy, after an attack of three hours, were totally repulsed with great loss. They fled towards Fort Edward, setting fire to Fort Anne, but leaving a saw mill and blockhouse in good repair, which latter was afterwards possessed by the King's troops. The 9th regiment acquired, during their expedition, about thirty prisoners, some stores and baggage, and the colours of the second Hampshire regiment. The accidents to counterballance these several successes are few. The service has lost an officer of great gallantry and experience in Major Grant. The other officers killed are also to be much regretted Captain Montgommery of the 9th regiment, an officer of much merit, was wounded in the leg early in the action, and was in the act of being dressed by the surgeon, when the regiment changed ground; being unable to help himself, he and the surgeon were taken prisoners. I hear he has been well treated, and is in a fair way of recovering at Albany. The wounded officers and men in general here are also likely to do well.

July 9 *and* 10. The army much fatigued, many parts of it having wanted their provisions for two days,

almost the whole of their tents and baggage, assembled in their present position. The right wing occupies the height of Skenesborough in two lines, covered on the right flank by Reidesel's dragoons, *en potence*; the left flank to Wood Creek. The Brunswic troops, under General Reidesel, are upon Castleton river with Breymen's corps, upon the communication of roads towards Pulteney and Rutland. The regiment of Hesse Hanau are at the head of East Creek, to preserve the communication with the camp at Castleton, and secure the batteaux. Brigadier Frazer's corps is in the centre to move on either wing of the army.

The remains of Tieonderoga army are at Fort Edward, where they have been joined by considerable corps of fresh troops.

Roads are opening to march to them by Fort Anne, and the Wood Creek is clearing of fallen trees and sunken stones, and other obstacles, to give passage to batteaux carrying artillery, stores, provisions and camp equipage. These are laborious works: but the spirit and zeal of the troops are sufficient to surmount them. In the mean time all possible diligence is using at Ticonderoga to get gunboats, batteaux and provision vessels, into Lake George. A corps of the army will be ordered to penetrate by that route, which will be afterwards the route of the magazines; and a junction of the whole is intended at Fort Edward.

I transmit to your Lordship herewith, returns of the killed and wounded, and lists of such parts of the artillery, provisions and stores taken from the enemy as could be collected in so short a time. By a written account found in the Commissary's house at Ticonderoga, six thousand odd hundred persons were fed from the magazines the day before the evacuation. I have the honour to be, &c.

J. BURGOYNE.

List

Lift of the killed and wounded of the troops under the command of Lieutenant-general Burgoyne, from the 2d of July to the 8th, 1777.

July 2. *Captain Frafer's Rangers.* 1 Indian *killed.* 1 Lieutenant, 3 Indians, *wounded.* 1 Rank and File *prifoners.*

July 6. *Royal Artillery.* 1 Lieutenant, 1 Rank and File, *killed.* 1 Rank and File *wounded.*

Britifh Brigadier-General Frazer's Corps.

Light Infantry. 1 Lieutenant, 1 Serjeant, 10 Rank and File, *killed.* 1 Major, 2 Captains, 2 Lieutenants, 4 Serjeants, 74 Rank and File, *wounded.*

Grenadiers. 11 Rank and File *killed.* 1 Major, 3 Captains, 3 Lieutenants, 4 Serjeants, 35 Rank and File, *wounded.*

2 *Companies of the 24th Regiment prefent.* 1 Major, 3 Rank and File, *killed.* 2 Serjeants *wounded.*

Total. 1 Major, 1 Lieutenant, 1 Serjeant, 24 Rank and File, *killed.* 2 Majors, 5 Captains, 5 Lieutenants, 10 Serjeants, 109 Rank and File, *wounded.*

Germans, Lieutenant-Colonel Breyman's Corps.

July 7. *De la Compagnie des Chaffeurs.* 4 Rank and File, *killed.* 1 Lieutenant, 6 Rank and File, *wounded.*

Du Battaillon de L'Infanterie legere. 3 Rank and File, *killed.* 4 Rank and File, *wounded.*

Des Grenediers. 2 Rank and File, *killed.* 1 Serjeant, 1 Rank and File, *wounded.*

Total. 9 Rank and File, *killed.* 1 Lieutenant, 1 Serjeant, 11 Rank and File, *wounded.*

July 8. *9th Regiment.* 1 Lieutenant, 1 Serjeant, 11 Rank and File, *killed.* 1 Captain, 2 Lieutenants, 19 Rank and File, *wounded.* 1 Captain, 1 Surgeon, *prifoners.*

Total of the Killed and Wounded in the above Actions.

1 Major, 3 Lieutenants, 2 Serjeants, 45 Rank and File, 1 Indian, *killed.* 2 Majors, 6 Captains, 9 Lieutenants, 11 Serjeants, 140 Rank and File, 3 Indians, *wounded.* 1 Captain, 1 Surgeon, 1 Rank and File, *prifoners.*

Britifh Officers Killed and Wounded.

July 2. *53d Regiment.* Lieutenant Haughton, *wounded.*

July 6. *Royal Artillery.* Second Lieutenant Cleland, *killed.* Volunteer Sutton, *wounded.*

KILLED.

July 7. Major Grant, *24th Regiment.* Lieutenant Douglas, *29th Reg.* Lieut. Hoggart, of the *Marines.*

WOUNDED.

Light Infantry. Captain Harris, *54th Regiment.*
Captain Craig, *43d Ditto.*
Major Earl of Balcarras, *53d Ditto.*
Lieutenant Jones, *62d Ditto.*
Grenadiers. Captain Stapylton, *9th Ditto.*
Lieutenant Row, *9th Ditto.*
Major Ackland, *20th Ditto.*
Lieutenant Steele, *29th Ditto.*
Captain Rofs, *34th Ditto.*
Lieutenant Richardfon, *34th Ditto.*
Captain Shrimpton, *62d Ditto.*
Volunteer Lindfay.

KILLED.

July 8. Lieutenant Weftrop, *9th Regiment.*

WOUNDED.

July 8. Captain Montgomery, *9th Regiment,* and prifoner with the Enemy.
Lieutenant Stavely, *9th Regiment.*
Lieutenant Murray, *Ditto.*
Adjutant Fielding, *Ditto.*

July 7. The Germans had one officer wounded of the Chaffeur Company, Lieutenant Crufe.

(Signed)

R. Kingfton, *Dep. Adj. Gen.*

Return

Return of the different Provisions taken at Ticonderoga and Fort Independence, on July 6, 1777.

Ticonderoga. 57 Barrels of flour, 19 barrels of pork, 31 bushels of salt, 50 barrels of biscuit.

Fort Independence. 1711 barrels of flour, 630 barrels of pork, 5 barrels of beef, 60 barrels of pease, 120 gallons of rum.

Total. 1748 barrels of flour, 649 barrels of pork, 5 barrels of beef, 60 barrels of pease, 31 bushels of salt, 120 gallons of rum, 50 barrels of biscuit.

1768 barrels of flour, at 195lb. each, is	344,760
50 ditto of biscuit, at 100lb. each, is —	5,000
	349,760

649 Barrels of pork, at 220lb. each,	142,780
5 Ditto of beef, at 210lb. each, —	1,050
	143,830

N. B. 87 Barrels more of beef and pork, supposed to be damaged.

Return of the Ordnance, Shot, and Shells, &c. taken at Ticonderoga and Mount Independence, July 6, 1777.

IRON ORDNANCE.

Thirty-two pounders 2, 1 spiked. Twenty-four pounders 2, 1 spiked. Eighteen pounders 10, 6 spiked. Twelve-pounders 10, 8 spiked. Nine-pounders 18, 6 spiked. Six-pounders 34, 15 spiked. Four-pounders 9, 1 spiked. Two-pounder 1, not spiked. One-pounder 2, not spiked. 8 Inch howitzers 2. Petards 2. Brass mortars 5 $\frac{1}{2}$ inch 1. Total 93.

SHOT.

Round Shot. Thirty-two Pounders 30. Twenty-four-pounders 54. Eighteen-pounders 268. Twelve-pounders 359. Nine-pounders 280. Six-pounders 886. Four Pounders 12. Three-pounders 70.

Grape Shot. Thirty-two pounders 19. Twenty-four-pounders 40. Eighteen-pounders 66. Twelve-pounders 15. Nine-pounders 8. Six-pounders 84. 8 Inch howitzers 10.

Double-headed Shot. 32 Pounders 20. Eighteen-pounders 68. Twelve-pounders 46. Nine-pounders 90. Six-pounders 52.

SHELLS,

Thirteen-inch 30. Ten-inch 40. Eight-inch 187. Five and $\frac{1}{2}$ inch 219. Four and $\frac{1}{4}$ inch 170.

Iron Round Shot of $\left\{\begin{matrix} 2 \text{ oz.} \\ 1\frac{1}{2} \end{matrix}\right\}$ Boxes 39.

Corned Powder in Barrels. Whole Barrels 29. Broken ditto 9.

Besides the above ordnance there is also taken great quantities of military stores of every denomination, intrenching tools, &c. &c. &c.

Return of Ordnance taken and destroyed in the five armed vessels at Skenesborough, July 6, 1777.

Iron Ordnance taken. Eighteen-pounders 2. Six-pounders 2. Four-pounders 6. Two-pounders 4. Total 14.

Iron Ordnance destroyed. Twelve-pounders 2. Six-pounders 2. Four-pounders 13. Two-pounders 4. Total 35 taken and destroyed.

One vessel loaded with powder, taken—Quantity not known.

One vessel loaded with powder, blown up—Quantity not known.

Total of Artillery taken 107
Total of Artillery destroyed 21

General Total 128 Pieces.

Exclusive of shot and shells, &c. described in the above return, there were also great numbers of batteaux loaded with military stores and powder, which were all burnt or blown up by the rebels at Skenesborough, July 6, 1777.

Admiralty-

Admiralty-office, August 23, 1777.

Lieutenant Sayer, of his Majesty's ship Garland, arrived here this morning, with a letter from Captain Pearson, commander of that ship, and senior sea officer in the river St. Laurence, to Mr. Stephens; of which the following is an extract:

Garland, Quebec, July 22, 1777.

You will be pleased to inform my Lords Commissioners of the Admiralty, that the rebels having abandoned Ticonderoga on the 6th of this month, without making any other defence than from two or three of their armed vessels, which some of our gun-boats soon silenced; I herewith inclose, for their Lordships further information, a copy of a letter of the 7th instant, from Capt. Lutwedge of his Majesty's ship Triton, commanding in the naval department on the lakes; who also informs me, by letter of the 18th, which arrived here this day, that many of our gun-boats were got over land into Lake-George; that every thing was going on as well as could be wished; and that there was every appearance of a successful campaign.

Copy of a letter from Captain Lutwedge to Captain Pearson, dated on board the Royal George, off Skenesborough, July 7, 1777.

I have the pleasure to acquaint you, that, very early this morning the rebels abandoned Ticonderoga and Mount Independent, leaving behind all their artillery, stores, and a quantity of provisions. A part of them moved off by land (by No. 4) towards New England, and the remainder in batteaux, with their armed vessels, up to Skenesborough.

Three British regiments, with the Hesse Hanau regiment, and some gun batteaux, moved up the river in pursuit of them. At nine A. M. the Royal George and Inflexible sailed up, through the bridge at Ticonderoga, and, with a favourable wind, got up within half a mile of Skenesborough, where I found the gun batteaux engaged with the enemy's vessels.

The ships were not able to get near enough to be of any use, except from their appearance; and soon after the firing from the enemy's vessels ceased. The crews of two of their vessels were obliged to quit them, from the fire of the gun-boats people, who acted with great spirit on the occasion; and the other three were burnt and blown up. General Burgoyne, who was on board the Royal George, went round and landed, with a part of the army, in South Bay, and came to Skenesborough in the evening.

A great quantity of arms, stores, officers baggage, &c. were destroyed in the batteaux of the rebels, which were burnt with the vessels. From the best intelligence we have, the rebel army is entirely dispersed, and no probability of their joining again to interrupt the progress of our army southward.

Annexed is a list of the rebel fleet taken and destroyed; and they have now no armed vessels of any kind left.

I am, &c.

SKEFF. LUTWEDGE.

A list of vessels taken and destroyed at Skenesborough, July 6, 1777.

Trumbull Galley. 2 Eighteen-pounders. 2 Six-pounders. 6 Four-pounders. 4 Two-pounders, and 12 Swivels.----taken.

Liberty schooner, laden with powder, taken.

Revenge sloop, burnt and blown up.

Gates Galley. 2 Twelve-pounders, 2 Six-pounders, 3 Four-pounders, 4 Two-pounders, and 8 Swivels----burnt and blown up.

Enterprize Schooner, a provision vessel, burnt.   [*London Gazette.*
                                         Extract

Extract of a letter from General SCHUYLER *to General* WASHINGTON.

Saratoga, *July* 7, 1777.

Dear Sir,

Soon after I had difpatched the letter, which I did myfelf the honour to addrefs to your Excellency from Stillwater, I met with Lieut. Colonel Hay, Deputy Quarter-mafter General, who was at Ticonderoga: he informs me, that on Saturday, it had been agreed upon to retreat from Ticonderoga and Mount Independence; that between two and three o'clock on Sunday morning, General St. Clair, with the reft of the General Officers and the army, marched out of the lines at Mount Independence; that Col. Long, with about 600 men, embarked on board our few veffels, and in batteaux; that juft before they arrived at Skenefborough, they were overtaken by the enemy's veffels, in which we loft all our ammunition.

The troops under Col. Long are arrived at Fort Ann; where Gen. St. Clair is with the main body, I have not yet learned. Col. Hay imagined he would come by the way of Skenefborough; if fo, he will fall in with the enemy, who have taken poffeffion there. Capt. Duntignore, who is juft arrived here, confirms Col. Hay's account, except as to Gen. St. Clair, who, he underftood, was to march to No. 4; this is not likely. I have difpatched an officer to meet General St. Clair, and requefted that he fhould march by the fhorteft rout to Fort Edward. As I have related the above from memory, I may have omitted fome, and mifapprehended other circumftances. It is impoffible to fay what poft we fhall take; it depends on the rout the enemy mean to purfue.

Publifhed by order of the Congrefs,

CHARLES THOMSON, Sec.

Philadelphia, *July* 22.

Copy of a letter from General ST. CLAIR *to Congrefs, dated Fort Edward, July* 14, 1777.

Sir,

Congrefs may proably think it extraordinary that fo much time fhould have elapfed before they heard from me, after a ftep of fuch confequence, as the evacuation of the pofts that had been intrufted to my care; but it was not in my power to write whilft on the march to this place. I am forry to find that my letter to General Schuyler, the night the evacuation took place, has not come to his hands, as for want of that, though he has doubtlefs informed Congrefs of the matter, he could not give them the reafons that induced it. They were thefe:

Seeing that the pofts of Ticonderoga and Mount Independence were nearly invefted, and having intelligence by my fpies that they would be completely fo in 24 hours, when we fhould be cut off from all poffibility of fuccour, that the batteries of the enemy were ready to open, and the whole of our encampment on the Ticonderoga fide expofed to their fire; confidering at the fame time the weaknefs of the garrifon, that the effective numbers were not fufficient to man one half of the works, and that confequently the whole muft be upon conftant duty, which they could not poffibly long fuftain, and that of courfe, the places, with the garrifon, muft inevitably, in a very few days, fall into the enemy's hands, I faw no alternative but endeavouring to evacuate them, and bring off the army; whereupon I called the General Officers together, to take their fentiments: they were unanimoufly of opinion, that the places fhould be evacuated, without the leaft lofs of time, and it was accordingly fet about that night, the 5th inftant. After embarking in boats as much of our cannon, provifions, and ftores, as

was

was poffible, with the boats which were ordered to Skeenfborough, I fent Col. Long, an active, diligent, and good officer, to take the command there, with his regiment and the invalids, until I fhould join him with the army, which was to march to that place by Caftleton. The body of the army reached Caftleton the next evening, 30 miles from Ticonderoga, and 12 from Skeenfborough; but the *rear guard*, under the command of Col. Warner, which, with the ftragglers and infirm, amounted to *near* 1200, ftopped fhort at that place fix miles, and were next morning attacked by a ftrong detachment the enemy had fent to hang upon our rear, and retard our march. Two regiments of militia, who had left us the evening before, and had halted about two miles from Col. Warner, were immediately ordered to his affiftance, but to my great furprize they marched directly down to me; at the fame time I received information that the enemy were in poffeffion of Skeenfborough, and had cut off all our boats and armed veffels. This obliged me to change my route, that I might not be put betwixt two fires, and at the fame time be able to bring off Col. Warner, to whom I fent orders, if he found the enemy too ftrong, to retreat to Rutland, where he would find me to cover him, that place lying nearly at an equal diftance from both. Before my orders reached him, his party was difperfed, after having for a confiderable time fuftained a very warm engagement, *in which the enemy fuffered fo much, that they purfued but a fmall diftance.* Our lofs I cannot afcertain, *but believe it does not exceed* 40 *killed and wounded.* About 200 of the party have joined me at Rutland and fince, but great numbers of them are ftill miffing, and I fufpect have got down to New-England by the way of Number Four. After a very fatiguing march of feven days, in which the army fuffered much from

bad weather and want of provifions, I joined General Schuyler the 12th inftant.

It was my original plan to retreat to this place, that I might be betwixt General Burgoyne and the inhabitants, and that the militia might have fomething in this quarter to collect to. It is now effected, and the militia are coming in, fo that I have the moft fanguine hopes that the progrefs of the enemy will *be checked*, and I may yet have the fatisfaction to experience, that although I have loft *a poft, I have eventually faved a State.* Perhaps I may be cenfured, by thofe who are unacquainted with the fituation I was in, for not calling the militia fooner to my affiftance. I think I informed Congrefs that I could not do that for want of provifions; and as foon as I got a fupply I did call for them, and was joined by near 900 the day before the evacuation, but they came from home fo ill provided, that they could not, nor did not, propofe to ftay with me but a few days. The two Maffachufetts regiments of militia likewife, which compofed part of the garrifon, gave me notice that their time expired in two days, and they intended then to go home. In vain did I beg of their officers to exert every influence they had over them; and from their fubfequent behaviour, I am fully perfuaded the officers are moft to blame. They kept with me, however, for two days on the march; but their conduct was fo licentious and diforderly, and their example beginning to affect the Continental troops, I was conftrained to fend them off.

Enclofed is a copy of the Council of war, in which you will find the principles upon which the retreat was undertaken. As I found all the General Officers fo fully of opinion, that it fhould be done immediately, I forbore to mention to them many circumftances which might have influenced them, and which I fhould have laid before them had they been

of

of different fentiments; for I was, and ftill am, fo firmly convinced of the neceffity, as well as the propriety of it, that I believe I fhould have ventured upon it, had they been every one againft it.

I have the utmoft confidence in the candour of Congrefs; and perfuade myfelf, notwithftanding the lofs they have fuftained, when they have impartially confidered that I was pofted with little more than ooo men in a place that required 10,000 to defend it, that thefe 2000 were ill equipped, and worfe armed, not above one bayonet in ten, an arm effential in the defence of lines: that with thefe 2000 I have made good a retreat from under the nofe of an army at leaft four times their number, and have them now betwixt the enemy and the country, ready to act againft them, that my conduct will appear at leaft not deferving cenfure.

I have the honour to be, &c.
AR. ST. CLAIR.

P. S. The enemy's force, from the beft accounts, is 3500 Britifh, 4000 Brunfwick and Heffe Hanau, 200 Indians, and 200 Canadians.

The Hon. John Hancock, Efq.

At a Council of General Officers held at Ticonderoga, July 5, 1777; prefent Major-general St. Clair, Brigadier-general De Roche Fermoy, Brigadier-general Poor, Brigadier-general Patterfon, and Colonel Commandant Long.

General St. Clair reprefented to the Council, that as there is reafon to believe that the batteries of the enemy are ready to open upon the Ticonderoga fide, and that the camp is very much expofed to their fire, and to be enfiladed on all quarters, and as there is alfo reafon to expect an attack upon Ticonderoga and Mount Independence at the fame time, in which cafe neither could draw any fupport from the other, he defires their opinion, whether it would be moft proper to remove the tents to the low ground, where they would be lefs expofed, and wait the attack at the Ticonderoga lines; or whether the whole of the troops fhould be drawn over to Mount Independence, the more effectually to provide for the defence of that poft?

At the fame time the General begged leave to inform them, that the whole of our force confifted of 2089 effective rank and file, including 124 artificers unarmed, befides the corps of artillery, and about 900 militia that have joined us, and cannot ftay but a few days.

The Council were unanimoufly of opinion, that it is impoffible with our force to defend Ticonderoga and Mount Independence, and that the troops, cannon, and ftores, fhould be removed this night, if poffible, to Mount Independence.

2d. Whether, after the divifion of the army at Ticonderoga have retreated to Mount Independence, we fhall be in a fituation to defend that poft; or, in cafe it cannot be defended, if a retreat into the country will be practicable?

The Council are unanimoufly of opinion, that as the enemy have already nearly furrounded us, and there remains nothing more to inveft us completely, but their occupying the neck of land betwixt the lakes and the eaft creek, which is not more than three quarters of a mile over, and poffeffing themfelves of the Narrows betwixt us and Skeenfborough, and thereby cutting off all communication with the country, a retreat ought to be undertaken as foon as poffible, and that we fhall be very fortunate to effect it.

A. ST. CLAIR, Maj. Gen.
DE ROCHE FERMOY, B. G.
Signed, ENOCH POOR, B. G.
JOHN PATTERSON, B. G.
Col. Commandant LONG.

A true copy taken from the original.
ISAAC BUDD DUNN, A. D. C.

Publifhed by order of Congrefs,
CHARLES THOMSON, Sec.

The

The New-York Gazette contains the following apology, written by a General Officer in the Northern army, for the evacuation of Ticonderoga.

Our force confifted of about 4000 men, including the corps of artillery and artificers, who were not armed; a confiderable part of which were militia; we could not bring above 3000 fit for duty into the field; General Burgoyne came againft us with 8000 healthy, fpirited troops, with a lake force confifting of three 50 gun fhips, or under, mounting fourteen brafs 24 pounders; two thirteen inch mortars, a number of howitzers, feveral floops, gun-boats, &c. &c.

Their ftrength being fo very fuperior to ours, obliged us to tamely fit ftill, and fee them erect batteries all around us, without hazarding a fally; two batteries were erected in front of our lines, on higher ground than ours, within half a mile; on our left, they had taken poft on a very high hill overlooking all our works; our right would have been commanded by their fhipping and batteries they had erected on the other fide the lake, that our lines at Ticonderoga would have been of no fervice, and we muft have inevitably abandoned them in a few days after their batteries opened, which would have been the next morning. We then fhould have been neceffitated to retire to Fort Independence; the confequence of which, I conceive, would have been much worfe than the mode adopted; for the moment we had left Ticonderoga Fort, they could fend their fhipping by us, and prevent our communication with Skeenfborough; then the only avenue to Fort Independence would have been by a narrow neck of land leading from the Mount to the Grants; to this neck they had almoft cut a road, a day more would have compleated it. A few troops ftationed at Ticonderoga would have prevented our communication with Lake George, as our own works would have been againft us. Their fhipping would have deftroyed our connection with Skeenfborough, and their main body might have been placed on this neck of land, who, by a few works, might have prevented all fupplies and reinforcements; we might have ftaid at the Mount as long as our provifions would have fupported us; we had flour for thirty days, and meat fufficient only for a week. Under thefe circumftances General St. Clair, on the 16th inftant, called a Council of War, and an evacuation was accordingly agreed upon, as the only means of faving the army from captivity. It was neceffary alfo that our retreat fhould be precipitate, as the communication was almoft cut off, and they would foon be apprized of our defigns.

Philadelphia, Aug. 6. On the 29th ult. the Congrefs met, and came to the following refolutions:

Refolved, That an enquiry be made into the reafons of the evacuation of Ticonderoga and Mount Independence, and into the conduct of the General Officers who were in the Northern department at the time of the evacuation.

That a Committee be appointed to digeft and report the mode of conducting the enquiry.

July 30. Refolved, That Majorgeneral St. Clair, who commanded at Ticonderoga and Mount Independence, forthwith do repair to Head Quarters.

Auguft 1. Refolved, That Majorgeneral Schuyler be directed to repair to Head Quarters.

That General Wafhington be directed to order fuch General Officer as he fhall think proper, immediately to repair to the Northern department, to relieve General Schuyler in his command there.

That Brigadier Poor, Brigadier Patterfon, and Brigadier Roche de Fermoy,

Fermoy, be directed to repair to Head Quarters.

August 3. Refolved, That General Wafhington be directed to order the General whom he fhall judge proper, to relieve Gen. Schuyler in his command, to repair with all poffible expedition to the Northern department, giving him directions what number of the militia to call in from the States of New-Hampfhire, Maffachufetts - Bay, Connecticut, New-York, New-Jerfey, and Pennfylvania.

That notice be immediately fent to the executive powers of the faid States, and that they be earneftly requefted to get the militia in thofe parts of their refpective States moft contiguous to the Northern department, ready to march at a moment's warning, and to fend with all poffible expedition fuch parts of them as the General commanding in the Northern department fhall require, to ferve till the 15th of November, if not fooner relieved by Continental troops, or difmiffed by the Commanding Officer of the department, and be entitled to Continental pay and rations.

That the Commanding Officer in the Northern department have difcretionary power to make requifitions in the States aforefaid, from time to time, for fuch additional numbers of the milita to ferve in that department as he fhall judge neceffary for the public fervice.

Whereas it is reprefented to Congrefs, that Gen. Wafhington is of opinion, that the immediate recall of all the Brigadiers from the Northern department may be productive of inconvenience to the public fervice ;

Refolved, That the order of Congrefs of the firft day of this month, refpecting the Brigadiers, be fufpended until General Wafhington fhall judge it may be carried into effect with fafety.

Refolved, That Congrefs have a juft fenfe of the merit of Lieutenant Col. Meigs, and the officers and men under his command, who diftinguifhed their prudence, activity, enterprize, and valour in the late expedition to Long-Ifland ; and that an elegant fword be provided by the Commiffary-general of military ftores, and prefented to Lieutenant-colonel Meigs.

Refolved, That Congrefs have a juft fenfe of the gallant behaviour of Lieutenant-colonel Barton of a militia regiment of the State of Rhode-Ifland and Providence Plantation, and the brave officers and men of his party, who diftinguifhed their valour and addrefs in making prifoners of Major-general Prefcott of the Britifh army, and Major William Barrington, his Aid de Camp : and that an elegant fword be provided by the Commiffary-general of military ftores, and prefented to Lieutenant-colonel Barton. Extract from the minutes.

CHARLES THOMSON, Sec.

Whitehall Sept. 24, 1777.
Copy of a letter from Lieutenant-general Burgoyne to Lord George Germaine, dated Head Quarters upon Hudfon's River, near Fort Edward, July 30, 1777, received this day by the Silver Eel ordnance tranfport from Quebec.

My Lord,

By my difpatch of the 11th inftant, committed to the care of Capt. Gardner, my Aid de Camp, I had the honour to inform your Lordfhip of the fuccefsful progrefs which had then been made by the army under my command.

Although the continued retreat of the enemy from one poft to another fince that period has prevented any material action, I think the bare date of a letter from Hudfon's River matter of intelligence not to be deferred : and I take this occafion to give your Lordfhip the further fatisfaction of

knowing

knowing, that the march hither, though scarce a day passed without firing, was effected without any loss of the regulars. A few wounds only were received by the Indians and Provincials. The losses of the enemy, including killed and prisoners in the several skirmishes, amount to about 300 men.

The toil of the march was great, but supported with the utmost alacrity. The country being a wilderness in almost every part of the passage, the enemy took the means of cutting large timber trees on both sides the road, so as to fall across and lengthways, with the branches interwoven. The troops had not only layers of these to remove, in places where it was impossible to take any other direction, but also they had above forty bridges to construct, and others to repair, one of which was of log work over a morass two miles in extent.

I was not unapprized that great part of these difficulties might have been avoided by falling back from Skeensborough to Ticonderoga by water, in order to take the more commodious route by Lake George. But besides wishing to prevent the effect which a retrograde motion often has, to abate the pannic of an enemy, I considered that the natural consequence would be a resistance, of delay at least, at Fort George; where, as the retreat was open, the enemy could wait securely, the preparation of batteries, or at least a landing in force for the purpose of investment.

The issue has justified my perseverance. The garrison of Fort George, in manifest danger of being cut off by the direct movement from Skeensborough to Hudson's River, took the measure I expected of abandoning the fort, and burning the vessels, thereby leaving the lake entirely free. A detachment of the King's troops, which I had ordered to be ready for that event, with a great embarkation

of provision, passed the lake on the same day that I took possession of this communication by land: and I have the happiness upon the whole to find, that the necessaries for continuing the progress of the army are more forward in point of time than they could have been by any other means.

The enemy is at present in force near Saratoga, where they profess an intention of standing a battle, and they have drawn a supply of artillery from New-England for that purpose. The King's troops are employed in bringing forward from Fort George, provisions, batteaux, artillery, and other materials necessary for proceeding. I have the honour to be, &c.
J. BURGOYNE.

Admiralty-Office, Sept. 24, 1777.
Extract of a letter from Capt. Pearson, of his Majesty's ship the Garland, to Mr. Stephens, dated off Quebec the 13th of August, 1777, received this day by the Silver Eel ordnance transport.

By the last accounts from Gen. Burgoyne's army, dated the 2d instant, they were encamped at and near Fort Edward; which place the rebel army a few days before abandoned, and were then retiring towards Saratoga. General Arnold has lately joined and now commands their Northern army: he brought with him twelve pieces of brass cannon, with which it is expected he means to make a stand at Saratoga. Gen. Burgoyne, with his army, all well, and in great spirits, purposed marching on the 5th, to attack them.

Admiralty-Office, Sept. 27, 1777.
The following letter from Lieut. Bazely, Commander of his Majesty's cutter the Alert, to Mr. Stephens, was this day received:

Sir, *Plymouth, Sept. 24, 1777.*
I have the pleasure to acquaint you of my arrival here, having met with the Lexington brig, armed by the American Congress, with 16 four pounders, 12 swivels, and 84 men,

men, commanded by Henry Johnstone, (late master of the Yankee privateer, who made his escape from the Mars at Blackstakes in September, 1776) which I took the 19th instant, W. b. S. 14 leagues from Ushant, two days from Morlaix, bound to Boston with dispatches for Congress, which were thrown overboard.

I gave chace at five in the morning, and came up with him at half past seven, had a close engagement till ten, when he bore up and made sail: as soon as I got my rigging to rights, again gave chace, and came up with him at half past one, renewed the action till half past two, when he struck. I have been so fortunate as to have had only 2 men killed and 3 wounded, one of which is since dead, with my mast, rigging, and sails much cut and damaged.

The loss on the rebels side is 7 men killed and 11 wounded: in the former are the Master and Lieutenant of Marines; in the latter, the first Lieutenant and gunner; with her rigging, mast and sails, much damaged.

It blowing strong easterly the night of the 20th, with a large swell and thick weather, I parted company; but am in expectation of her arrival in this port every hour.

I am to beg you will acquaint their Lordships with the very gallant behaviour of my officers and people on this occasion. I am, Sir, your very humble servant, JOHN BAZELY.

N. B. The Lexington arrived in the Downs the 25th instant, and is put into Dover to repair her damages.

The Alert had 10 carriage guns, four pounders, 10 swivels, and 60 men. [London Gazette.

London, August 27.
Monday night arrived from New-York, the Lord Shuldham armed vessel, with Lieut. General Heister, and two or three other officers in the

Hessian corps. This vessel left New-York on the 29th of July, and brings advice, that Lord and General Howe, with the fleet and army, sailed from Sandy Hook on the 24th of July, and steered away to the southward. It is not certainly known where they are gone; but it is generally supposed at New-York, that General Howe intends going up Chesapeak-Bay, and to march towards Lancaster, in order to get between Gen. Washington and his principal magazines; and that General Howe's design in this measure, is, to bring Gen. Washington out of Jersey, and oblige him to risk a battle to protect his magazines. This ship brings further advice, that General Washington upon hearing of Ticonderoga being taken, had detached three thousand men to support the Northern army; the King's troops while in Jersey, were exceedingly fatigued with severe duty, and in their retreat were exceedingly harrassed. In the two last skirmishes they had the advantage at first, but were finally repulsed. It is the prevailing opinion in General Howe's army, that the engineers in the American army, are all French and Germans. General Howe is greatly chagrined at being obliged to leave Jersey: it was the darling wish of his heart to march through Jersey to Philadelphia: his mortification is greater than can be expressed. Though no one can tell where General Howe intends to go, it is certain he does not take more than thirteen thousand men, effective, with him. Wherever he intends to land, it is not probable he will meet with any opposition from General Washington, and therefore that he may ravage, and desolate the country, for a little while, with impunity; plunder farms, burn villages, &c. but all this is no permanent advantage. The country force will be collected, and he will be again driven to his ships. There is not a sensible

man

man in the army in America, who does not now reprobate all the *notions* and *nonsense* of *conquering* that *immense country.*

London, Aug. 29. General Heister is so much offended with our Ministry, or military, or both, that he has requested to go home, and to be excused coming to London; which was granted.

London, September 9. The real truth brought by transports and other private vessels from America, from time to time, never leaks out till some days after their arrival. The ministerial runners are so eager to circulate *their part* of the story, that the rest is not attended to, till the false glare of the first tale is pretty well over; and then a few of the thinking part of mankind begin to enquire a little further. In this situation exactly, stand the last accounts from New-York and Canada. The ministerial runners have had their day: and they have made the most of every particular, that could be twisted in favour of their party. The Americans have very few friends in England. The very extensive influence of corruption, and the very general prevalence of the fashionable vices of the age, have almost extinguished that love of truth, which was, till lately, the warmest passion in an Englishman's breast. However, though the charge is just, and pretty generally acknowledged to be so, there is yet a very respectable body of men in this country, who are an exception to it. To these therefore, the following *truths* are addressed :—

General Howe left New-York full of anxiety, grief, and vexation. The Scotch, in the army, had formed themselves into a faction; and were full of complaints against him, pretendedly for not fighting Mr. Washington, but really because they expected great plunder in marching through Jersey. Their example has infected the English soldiery: the army in general is become a banditti of robbers. General Howe has repeatedly attempted to check this disorder: and to this is to be ascribed the illiberal abuse daily poured out against him, in the several prints under ministerial direction by the different Court writers, who are kept in constant pay, for this and other dirty purposes. Every body remembers the daily abuse here, upon General Gage while he was at Boston. The Scotch in America, and the Scotch in England perfectly understand each other. General Howe wished to have waited at New-York till the arrival of General Robertson from England; by whom he expected *orders,* or at least very *interesting advices.* But the Scotch were clamorous. He was afraid to disoblige them. He knew their influence at home. He embarked on the 23d of July, at the moment he wished to have waited for the arrival of General Robertson. General Howe kept the object of his expedition as secret as possible, and in order to deceive the American General, he, on the 22d of July, sent a floating battery, and some transports up the North River; but they came down again time enough to sail at the tail of the fleet. However this feint had its intended effect; for on the 24th Gen. Washington detached a large body of his army over the North River.

General Howe intended to have left at New-York only 3000 men, and had actually embarked all the rest of the army, to go on the expedition to Chesapeak-Bay, when a representation was made by General Clinton, that 3000 men were not sufficient for the defence of New-York, that if the Provincial officers knew what they *ought* to do, they would attack New-York, &c. upon which General Howe ordered 6000 men to be disembarked and sent to New-York for the certain security of that place.

Copy

Copy of a letter from New-York, dated July 1, 1777.

" You charge me, and other well-wishers to a reconciliation, with want of activity in that desireable object. The stake I hold in this country, has not left me an idle spectator. I have contributed my small powers in several ways to this restoration, and would to God I could see it effected. Peace we may have; that is, armies may cease to desolate the country. But simply not being at war, falls short of the terms we ought to be upon: for where all amity is dead, all intercourse, but on compulsion, I fear, is at an end. How far it will be either to the interest, or in the power of Great-Britain, to hold this Continent on such terms, is at present beyond my foresight. You have long been possessed of my sentiments, with respect to the opposition made, the provocation, &c. and the conditions I have recommended, at some risque to myself. The unconditional submission you require, if made, is the least likely to be binding. Where want of power, and not of will, to resist, are the terms, the tenor of your security will be very frail. You are no stranger to the divided opinions that reigned, when that important subject of independence was agitated. The tempting circumstance of an enlarged commerce, to a country whose existence is trade, has staggered many, whose inclinations then opposed it. I can aver these ideas have been created by the effects of the war, and never before existed. However, to justify the measures taken, you assert, was the original design of the Colonies; many, therefore, wish the establishment of this independence, who affect publicly to oppose it. This unconditional submission is the fatal rock that our hopes are split upon. Could your honour, or dignity, or personal resentment, have condescended to have been explicit, and proposed terms less severe, much

might have been done. No concessions, no terms to the dishonour of England, were wished for; we must have degraded ourselves in the very act. A large field was open, on which the important subject of peace might have been discussed, without the smallest sacrifice to your pride of power or dignity, that feather so many millions have been spent to keep up. A few ages hence will read the history of this war with as little faith, as we do that of Titans. History may relate, without credit, the disgraceful story, that Britons, who pride themselves for humanity in their wars, have, against people united to them by so many ties, employed wretches who disgrace their Creator. You will, I know, retort, that you only imitated our endeavours. If the charge is just, there is no similitude in the consequences. But a strict neutrality has been recommended here. Had they been employed in the American armies, their rage, and dreadful manner of making war, could only have been opposed to men, to men in arms, for only such could have appeared as enemies; but where they are, the large scene they have to act in, will present numberless objects to their infernal rage, as being connected with those in opposition. Age, infancy, and sickness, women, children at the breast, and in the womb, are all, all alike, subject to their merciless fury. The distinguished honour of admitting these creatures, has been given to *Burgoyne.* The generous *Carleton* forbid and refused it, clearly convinced he could subdue armies without courage, discipline, cloathing, &c. &c. in short, destitute of things necessary to make them in any degree formidable to veteran troops, in the full enjoyment of every thing the others wanted. Figure to yourself an English General, surrounded by his suite, receiving from the hands of an Indian Chief, besmeared with blood, the

scalps

scalps of an hundred defenceless women and innocent children, torn half dead from them; for to kill outright, is a mercy they (always) have neither time nor inclination to give. Blood thus spilt, is to cement our future union. These are the acts by which confidence is to be regained. I am sick of the subject. Reflect—Great-Britain is not the only power in the world, and be wise in time."

New-York, Aug. 8. For some time past the demand for goods of all sorts, and the high prices given for them has made the fortunes of those who brought out cargoes with them This lucrative traffic has been confined to a few favourites, chiefly Scotchmen. It was thought the British Prohibitory Act would have prevented the arrival, in America, of all British goods; but so far from it, that Act has thrown the *whole* trade into the hands of a few, who make a monopoly of it. But the departure of the fleet and army, which has carried off 24,000 people, soldiers, sailors, and attendants, together with a proclamation issued out, prohibiting all intercourse with the Jerseys, has made trade very dull of late; however, many of those who came out lately, and have not got their cargoes sold, are reshipping their goods, to be ready to sail whenever intelligence arrives of Sir William Howe having made good his landing, where they intend to dispose of their goods to great advantage. Fresh provisions are exceedingly scarce and dear, beef 1s. 9d. sterling a pound, and other articles in proportion.

A letter from Paris, August 4, 1777.

" As I find by the last letters from England, that all apprehensions respecting the ill designs of France, were removed by the late order of this Court respecting American privateers, I beg leave to inform you of a few facts, which you will probably think worth publication.—By the treaties subsisting with England, France has obliged herself to afford no aid or succour to the privateers of of any nation at war with England; and the established laws and marine regulations of France forbid the privateers of all nations whatever from continuing in the ports of this kingdom more than 24 hours; these laws and regulations have been repeatedly dispensed with in favour of the American rebels, but the doing it is so contrary to the treaties and to the neutrality professed by the French Ministers, that it is impossible they should, at any time, upon proper application, refuse to order the American privateers out of their harbours, unless they would have thrown off the mask, and provoked immediate hostilities. When Capt. Wickes first arrived here with Dr. Franklin, no notice was taken of him by Lord Stormont, and he was suffered quietly to dispose of his two prizes, and refit for a cruize; but when he afterwards brought five other prizes, and among them the Lisbon packet-boat, into Port L'Orient, the Ambassador complained, and Wickes was in consequence ordered out; though, it is true, the order, like all orders given here against the Americans, was never executed: Wickes therefore leisurely sold his prizes, refitted his vessel, and went out upon another cruize, after having been joined by the Lexington and Dolphin privateers; the last of which, contrary to treaties, was armed and fitted out by the American Agents at Nantz. When Wickes with his little squadron again returned into the ports of France, after having captured eighteen British vessels, the insult and the injury offered us by France, were thought insupportable, and Lord Stormont having received instructions for that purpose, went about the 9th of July to Versailles, and delivered strong complaints, with threats of returning immediately to England, unless satisfaction

tisfaction was given, at leaft in re-fpect of the American privateers. The French Court not being yet prepared for war, (though Spain apparently is) and being defirous at leaft of putting off hoftilities until their feamen fhould have returned from the fifheries, promifed to inforce an obfervance of the eftablifhed regulation, which allows privateers to ftay but 24 hours in the harbours of France, and orders were given accordingly; but when thefe orders reached St. Maloes and Morlaix, it was found that Wickes and Johnfon could not, without great inconvenience, comply with them; the former, whilft chaced by the Burford fhip of war, had, to efcape, thrown over all his guns, and fawed three of the beams of his fhip afunder; and the veffels of both were in want of careening. To give them time for this, and yet fave appearances with England, was difficult; but a rare expedient was foon contrived to effect it, which was, to arreft the three privateers;‘ and accordingly Wickes, Johnfon and Nicholfon, were made to fign parole engagements not to go to fea without the leave of this Government; fo that they now refit at leifure, and as foon as they fhall be ready for putting to fea, leave for their doing it will doubtlefs be likewife ready. In this pretty manner it is that we are duped, whilft we even fuppofe ourfelves to have obtained mighty conceffions from France. But in other places the French Miniftry have taken no kind of pains even to fave appearances. The order obtained by Lord Stormont required not only all privateers, but their prizes, to leave the ports of this kingdom; but not one of them has obeyed it: on the contrary, all thofe fent into Nantz, &c. by Wickes's fquadron have been unladen and fold; and the fame has been done to the Guernfey brig at Cherbourg; nor has any privateer quitted the French

ports in confequence of the order about which you in England are exulting. Cunningham had been long ready, and waiting for an opportunity to efcape the Britifh cruizers, who were watching for him; and the Admiralty at Dunkirk even affifted in enabling to deceive and efcape them. The General Mifflin privateer too is ftill at Breft: fhe arrived there foon after the order in queftion had been received; but, pretending to be leaky, fhe was not only permitted to ftay and repair, but has been actually fupplied with materials out of the royal yard there. This privateer on her arrival at Breft, faluted the Admiral du Chaffault commanding there, who, after confulting all his officers, returned the falute to the flag of the rebel Colonies, thereby acknowledging their Independency, and infulting Great-Britain in the moft public manner. After this the officers of the French fleet dined on board the rebel privateer, and in their excefs of zeal and mirth, as I am told, drank fuccefs to the united arms of France and America, confufion to Great-Britain, and other laudable toafts; for which the Britifh tars, it is hoped, will one day remember them. Thefe facts have been obtained from an authentic and more than common fource. They may enable your readers to judge whether England has indeed reafon to be fatisfied with the proceedings and fecret defigns of France, efpecially when it is known and confidered that uncommon exertions are now making here to increafe the naval force of this nation; that feveral more frigates, and an additional body of troops, are about to be fent to the Weft-Indies; and that the French fifhermen, from fome caufe or other, were (if we may believe the accounts lately arrived from thofe places) preparing to return home a month fooner than ufual.

Extract

Extract of a letter from Paris, dated Aug. 5.

The Court of London have sent one Ambaffador to this capital. The Congrefs of America have fent two to France. All have been officially received by the Court of Verfailles. All are equally protected by that Court. The difference only amounts to this; that Franklin hath his fecret, Stormont his open interviews. In other refpects the advantage is on the fide of the Americans. Stormont hath fecured Maurepas, the Americans are favoured by the Queen. Hence the Emperor had a very long, although private interview with Doctor Franklin, whilft he only deigned to notice Stormont in the circle. This is a fact. Let authority deny it, and it fhall be proved to the eternal infamy of your Minifters.

Extract of a letter from Paris, Aug. 20.

" I congratulate you on the pleafing change of affairs, in regard to your nation. By the fpirited refolution of Lord Stormont, orders have been iffued at all the fea-ports of France not to permit the American privateers to difpofe of their prizes in this kingdom, nor permit them to remain in any of the ports longer than 24 hours. Orders have likewife been iffued to inform the merchants, that if they directly or indirectly affift the Americans with ftores, &c. they are to take the rifk of their ladings, as no protection will be given them by the Crown of France; and Lord Stormont has declared, that every French fhip which fhall be taken by the Englifh cruizers, bound to any of the American ports with any kind of merchandize, to affift the Americans, will be deemed lawful prizes by the Court of Great-Britain."

Extract of a letter from a Gentleman at Paris to his friend, an American merchant at Nantz.

——'Tis with the greateft pleafure in the world that I can affure you,

notwithftanding the public profeffions extorted from our Minifters by Lord Stormont's remonftrances, that the real intentions of our Court are in favour of the Americans. The great benefit which France enjoys from the commerce of the Colonies, who pour all their treafures into its lap, ought not nor cannot be rejected or flighted.

This kingdom flourifhes by exchanging its commodities for thofe of America; and the fale of fhips and cargoes continually brought into our harbours, gives fuch a life and fpirit to our merchants and traders, that our Governors are too wife not to cherifh this traffick for their own fakes. Be not then alarmed at the orders iffued againft the American privateers, who are commanded to leave our fea-ports in 24 hours. Time, under various pretences, will always be allowed to difpofe of prizes, &c.

[It is a certain, and notorious FACT, that not one of the American privateers failed out of any of the French ports, in confequence of thefe orders; and that not one prize, or veffel taken by the American privateers, has been refufed admittance into any of the French ports, in confequence of thefe orders.]

London, Sept. 10. Several French veffels having been taken by the Britifh cruizers lately, upon a fuppofition that thofe veffels were carrying arms, and other ftores and goods, to the affiftance of the Americans, the French Court have complained of thefe proceedings, and claimed their veffels; our Court have refolved " To *reftore* the French veffels;" and orders are given accordingly.

London, Sept. 11. Authentic information from France has been received, that the Clarendon, and Hanover Packet, two rich fhips from Jamaica for London, have been taken by two American privateers, who have carried them into Nantz.

A

As soon as this information arrived, Beelton Long, Esq. waited upon Lord North on the subject, the cargoes or principal part being consigned to him and Co. Lord North could do nothing in the affair; but referred him to Lord Weymouth. This noble Lord seemed to rejoice at the information; and told Mr. Long he was glad to have his intelligence, for he wanted something of this kind, to push at this moment; and ordered Mr. Long to put his information into writing, with every particular he could recollect. Mr. Long did so. Lord Weymouth sent Mr. Long's paper to Lord Stormont. Upon the affair being thus stated, and complained of, to the French Ministry, they pretended ignorance of the whole transaction; made strong professions of the sincerity of the King, their master, of his intentions of living in perfect friendship with the King of Great-Britain; but required authentic documents, or testimonies of the facts stated; in order, as they said, to make the necessary enquiries. Lord Stormont, upon receiving these flattering assurances, was overjoyed. But instead of writing to Lord Weymouth, he fell, some how or other, into the *little*, underhand way of corresponding with the *agent* (for Mr. Long is but an agent in the whole affair) and not with the Minister. He wrote to Mr. Long, to impower him to demand the ships and cargoes; to send him over to Paris a *Letter, or Power of Attorney*, to act for him, (Mr. Long) to demand the goods, therein marked and specified; and he would endeavour to get the owners indemnified. Mr. Long, proud of his correspondence with the Peer, and nephew of the Earl of Mansfield, makes the matter publicly known at Lloyd's, upon the Exchange, &c. He prepared the Letter of Attorney for Lord Stormont, and sent it to his Excellency; but the Marquis de Noailles, at the Court of London,

did not authenticate it; he would not affront Lord Stormont so grossly. Thus the matter was taken out of the hands of the national Ministers: it became a *private* affair, between Mr. Long, and his attorney, Lord Stormont. The attorney takes it up, and proceeds, *in his own way*, appearing as Mr. Long's advocate, claiming Mr. Long's goods, through the tedious process of the French Courts of Law.

On the 7th of October, Mr. Long's Agent at Nantz waited (as he had done many times before on this business) on the Judge of Admiralty there, who told him he had at last received *directions* to try the cause of the two ships and cargoes in question; that the Minister (the French Minister) *had never given a promise to Lord Stormont, to restore these ships and cargoes*, but that the matter *should be tried* in the Court of Admiralty at Nantz. The Judge also acquainted Mr. Long's Agent, that the question to be tried, was, *to whom did they belong?* That the affair would be *a work of time*; and desired the Agent to prepare, and make a regular application. He added, that one of the ships would not be fit to go to sea again.—[The ships were unrigged, and lying upon mud at a place called Pombay, in Nantz river. Mr. Long's Agent allows the crews one livre per diem each man.]

From these facts, it was obvious to all impartial men, that the refusal of the French Ministry, to deliver the vessels and cargoes, until a *formal trial* was had, in the Court of Admiralty at Nantz, for the purpose of ascertaining, as well the claim of the captors, as that of Mr. Long, fully proved that the French Court conceive the COMMISSION, under which the captors found the validity of their caption, *to have been granted by a power competent to the issuing it.*

London, Nov. 8. The French Government have at last declared, " The

A a a

two

two ships, the *Clarendon* and *Hanover Packet*, belonging to Mr. Long, which were taken and carried into Nantz, *to be forfeited to the French King*." This pretence under which the said prizes are confiscated in France, is the highest indignity to Great Britain, and a full acknowledgment of the *Independency* of the Colonies; for unless the Congress commission was allowed *a valid one, no capture under it could alter the property* of those ships; *nor could any improper entry of them* by the Americans (which is the sole ground for declaring them forfeited to the King) after they were unjustly taken by force, affect or alter the rights of the real owners.

Extract of a genuine letter from Paris, dated November 4.

" All is cabal and intrigue at Fontainbleau. Dr. Franklin went there a few days ago. Great changes are said to be making in our Ministry. The greatest preparations are making in the marine department. Several frigates are building, upon a new construction, to carry 32 twenty-four pounders upon one deck, designed to be a match for the English frigates. The troops are all sailed for the West-Indies; when they arrive there, the French will have in their islands an army of upwards of 21,000 men; besides what Spain has at the Havannah. Many single ships have since sailed, at different times, to the West-Indies. Should another campaign take place in America, it will be impossible to avoid a war; nothing prevented it last summer but our Ministry permitting their seamen and vessels to be sent out to the fisheries, after they had resolved and actually issued orders to stop them. Being once gone, it was in the power of Great-Britain, to intercept their return, and therefore they were obliged to remain quiet during the summer, and content themselves with giving the Colonies secret assistance. They have,

however, seen and repented of their mistake in that proceeding, and will not again tie up their hands in the same manner. One of the American Agents said a few days ago, That nation would be the *wisest* that first acknowledged the Independency of America."

London, October 22. On Sunday last a noble Earl arrived in town from France. The intelligence this Nobleman brings of the state of public affairs in France, ought to awaken this country. The French Court have ordered 50,000 of their troops to march down to the sea-coast *immediately.* The troops are drawn from the garrisoned towns, in the frontiers, of Flanders, and Germany. Lisle, in particular, is, in a manner, dismantled; and very few troops are left in any of the towns. Part are arrived at Montreuil (near Bologne) and places adjacent upon the coast. The encouragement given to the American privateers at Dunkirk is *perfectly notorious.* Every thing in France wears the face of war.

Our Ministers have, for some days, been a good deal alarmed by the conduct of France. A few weeks since, they ordered several more ships into commission. France laughed at the menace; she knew (all the world knows it) we cannot get hands for half of those that were in commission before. France in return now menaces us with her army. Thus the two nations are bullying each other. They are both like tinder; and the smallest spark will kindle a war. Nothing but the good sense and prudence of Capt. Jarvis prevented it, when the Robuste bore down upon him. Was he not obliged to snatch the matches out of the hands of his people, to prevent their firing? Nobody doubts Capt. Jarvis's bravery; but will not every man say, that if he had fired, the two nations would, at this moment, have been at open war. A war between England and France is much dreaded.

dreaded. It is fuspended by a thread. It is in the power of any Captain of a fhip to begin it to-morrow.

Lord Mulgrave in his late cruize fell in with, at fea, a Dutch fhip, which he brought to and fearched, but could not difcover to what place fhe was bound. She had fome arms on board, and twenty-feven French officers, moft of them gentlemen of of diftinction and rank. Some of the people on board having a difference among themfelves, gave information that fhe was bound to North-America, upon which Lord Mulgrave brought her into Portfmouth. In the firft tranfports of rage and vexation, it was refolved to fend the French gentlemen to the common gaol; but before the order was executed; the Minifters altered their minds, and releafed them.

A letter from Benjamin Franklin and Silas Deane, Efqrs. to Lord Stormont, at Paris.

Paris, Feb. 23, 1777.

" My Lord,

" Captain Weeks, of the Reprifal frigate, belonging to the United States of America, has now in his hands near one hundred Britifh feamen, prifoners. He defires to know, whether an exchange may be made with him for an equal number of American feamen now prifoners in England? We take the liberty of propofing this matter to your Lordfhip, and of requefting your opinion (if there be no impropriety in your giving it) whether fuch an exchange will probably be agreed to by your Court?

If your people cannot be foon exchanged here, they will be fent to America. We have the honour to be,

With great refpect,

Your Lordfhip's moft obedient,
Humble fervants,

B. FRANKLIN.
S. DEANE."

Right Hon. Lord Vifcount Stormont.

Another.

Paris, April 2, 1777.

" My Lord,

" We did ourfelves the honour of writing fome time ago to your Lordfhip, on the fubject of exchanging prifoners. You did not condefcend to give us any anfwer, and therefore we expect none to this. We however take the liberty of fending you copies of certain depofitions, which we fhall tranfmit to Congrefs, whereby it will be known to your Court, that the United States are not acquainted with the barbarous treatment their people receive, when they have the misfortune of being your prifoners here in Europe: and that if your conduct towards us is not altered, it is not unlikely that fevere reprifals may be thought juftifiable, from the neceffity of putting fome check to fuch abominable practices.

" For the fake of humanity, it is to be wifhed that men would endeavour to alleviate, as much as poffible, the unavoidable miferies attending a ftate of war. It has been faid, that among the civilized nations of Europe, the ancient horrors of that ftate are much diminifhed; but the compelling men by chains, ftripes, and famine, to fight againft their friends and relations, is a new mode of barbarity which your nation alone had the honour of inventing; and the fending American prifoners of war to Africa and Afia, remote from all probability of exchange, and where they can fcarce hope ever to hear from their families, even if the unwholefomenefs of the climate does not put a fpeedy end to their lives, is a manner of treating captives that you can juftify by no other precedent of cuftom, except that of the black favages of Guinea. We are,

Your Lordfhip's moft obedient
Humble fervants,

B. FRANKLIN,
S. DEANE."

Lord Vifcount Stormont.

Another

Another.

Paris, 3d of April, 1777.

" My Lord,

" In anſwer to a letter which concerns ſome of the moſt material intereſts of humanity, and of the two nations, Great-Britain and the United States of America, now at war, we received the incloſed *indecent* paper, as coming from your Lordſhip, which we return, for your Lordſhip's more mature conſideration.

(Signed)   B. FRANKLIN.

SILAS DEANE.'

N. B. The words of the paper ſent by Lord Stormont, and referred to in the above letter were, " The King's Ambaſſador receives no applications from rebels, unleſs they come to implore his Majeſty's mercy."

London, Nov. 10. Advice has been received from Paris, that Mr. Hodge, who had been committed to the Baſtile ſome time ago, at the requeſt of Lord Stormont, *was releaſed.* He was noticed by the Scotch Lord, for having acted very publicly at Dunkirk, in fitting out Captain Cunningham, acting there as his agent, in the moſt notorious manner, &c. Lord Stormont made a moſt heavy complaint of this conduct, and threatened, that if he was not apprehended and committed, a fleet of Britiſh men of war would intercept and ſeize the French Newfoundland fleet, &c. Upon this Mr. Hodge was committed to the Baſtile. The Newfoundland fleet having part arrived, and the reſt hourly expected, Dr. Franklin, Mr. Deane, and the other American Commiſſioners, applied for his releaſe. The King of France anſwered, " That as he wiſhed to live upon good terms with America, and the preſent harmony between them not to be interrupted, he granted their requeſt." Mr. Hodge was immediately ſet at liberty. While in the Baſtile, Mr. Hodge ſays, he was treated conſtantly with the utmoſt politeneſs and civility; and entertained, every day, in the moſt elegant 'manner, at the King of France's expence.

In the Legiſlative Council,

The 3d day of February, 1777.

Ordered, That the Bill, intitled, " A Bill for eſtabliſhing the Conſtitution of the State of South-Carolina," as it came up to this Houſe from the General Aſſembly, be printed and made public.

By order of the Houſe,

THOMAS FARR, Clerk.

A Bill for eſtabliſhing the Conſtitution of the State of South-Carolina.

That, inaſmuch as the Conſtitution, or form of government, agreed to, and reſolved upon, by the freemen of this country, met in Congreſs the 26th day of March laſt, was temporary only, calculated for, and ſuited to, the then ſituation of their public affairs, looking forward to an accommodation with Great-Britain, an event then deſired : and whereas the American States have been ſince conſtituted Independent States, and the political connection heretofore ſubſiſting between them and Great-Britain entirely diſſolved, by the Declaration of the honourable the Continental Congreſs, dated the 4th day of July laſt, for the many great and weighty reaſons, therein particularly ſet forth : it therefore becomes abſolutely neceſſary, to frame a laſting Conſtitution ſuitable to that great event : Be it therefore conſtituted and enacted, by his Excellency John Rutledge, Eſquire, Preſident and Commander in Chief, in and over the State of South-Carolina, by the Honourable the Legiſlative Council, and General Aſſembly, and by the authority of the ſame, That the following articles, agreed upon by the freemen of this State, now met in General Aſſembly, be henceforth and for ever (unleſs altered by the Legiſlative Authority of this State) looked upon as the Conſtitution and form of government thereof.

1. That

1. That the stile of this country be, hereafter, the State of South-Carolina.

2. That the Legislative authority be vested in a Legislative Council and General Assembly.

3. That as soon as may be, after the first meeting of the Legislative Council and General Assembly, they shall jointly, in the General Assembly, choose by ballot, from among themselves, or from the people at large, a President and Commander in Chief, and a Vice-president of the State, and Privy Council, to continue for two years: and till such choice shall be made, the former President and Commander in Chief, Vice-president, and Privy Council, shall continue to act as such.

4. That a member of the Legislative Council, or General Assembly, being chosen, and acting as President and Commander in Chief, or Vice-president, shall vacate his seat, and another person shall be elected in his room.

5. That every person who shall be elected President and Commander in Chief of the State, or Vice-president, or a member of the Privy Council, shall be qualified as followeth, that is to say, the President and Vice-president, shall have been residents in this State for ten years, and the members of the Privy Council five years, preceding their said election, and shall have in this State, a settled plantation or freehold, in their and each of their own right, of the value of at least ten thousand pounds currency, clear of debt; and, on being elected, they shall take an oath of qualification, in the General Assembly.

6. That no future President or Commander in Chief, who shall serve for two years, shall be eligible to serve in the said office, after the expiration of the said term, until the full end and term of four years.

7. That no person in this State shall hold the office of President thereof, or Vice-president, and any other office or commission, civil or military, except in the militia, either in this State, or under the authority of the Continental Congress, at one and the same time.

8. That in case of the death of the President and Commander in Chief, or his absence from the State, the Vice-president of the State shall succeed to his office, and the Privy Council shall choose, out of their own body, a Vice-president of the State. And in case of the death of the Vice-president of the State, or in his absence from the State, one of the Privy Council, to be chosen by themselves, shall succeed to his office, until a nomination to those offices respectively, by the General Assembly and Legislative Council, for the remainder of the time for which the officer so dying or being absent was appointed.

9. That the Privy Council, whereof the Vice-president of the State shall of course be a member, and President of the Privy Council, shall consist (including the Vice-president) of nine members; five of whom shall be a Quorum. Provided always, That no officer of the army or navy, in the service of the Continent or this State, nor Judge of any of the courts of law, shall be eligible,—nor shall the father, son, or brother to the President for the time being, be elected in the Privy Council during his administration. A member of the Legislative Council or General Assembly, being chosen of the Privy Council, shall not thereby lose his seat in the Legislative Council or General Assembly, unless he be elected Vice-president of the State, in which case he shall, and another person shall be chosen in his stead. The Privy Council is to advise the President and Commander in Chief when required; but he shall not be bound to consult them, unless directed by law. If a member of the Privy Council shall die, or depart this State, another shall

shall be chosen in his room, in manner above-mentioned.

10. That in case of the absence from Charles-Town, or sickness of the President, the Vice-president, or in case of his absence, any one of the Privy Council, may be impowered by the President, under his hand and seal, to act in his room.

11. That the executive authority be vested in the President and Commander in Chief, limited and restrained in manner herein after mentioned.

12. That each parish and district throughout this State, shall, on the last Monday in November and the day following, which will be in the year of our Lord one thousand seven hundred and seventy-eight, and on the same days of every second year thereafter, elect by ballot, one member of the Legislative Council (except the district of St. Philip and St. Michael's parishes, Charles-town, which shall elect two members; and except also the district between Broad and Saludy Rivers, in three divisions, viz. the lower district, Little River district, and upper or Spartan district, each of which said divisions, shall elect one member) to meet on the second Monday in January, at the the usual place in Charles-town, unless the casualties of war, or contagious disorders, should render it unsafe to meet there, in which case the President and Commander in Chief for the time being, may, by Proclamation, with the advice and consent of the Privy Council, appoint a more secure and convenient place of meeting, and to continue for two years, from the said last Monday in November. And that no person shall be eligible to a seat in the said Council until he hath attained the age of thirty years. Not less than thirteen members shall be a Quorum to do business; but, the Speaker, or any three members, may adjourn from day to day. No person who resides in the parish or district for which he

is elected, shall take his seat in the Legislative Council, unless he possesses a settled estate and freehold, in his own right, in the said parish or district, of the value of two thousand pounds currency at least, clear of debt. And no non-resident shall be eligible to a seat in the said Council, unless he is owner of a settled estate and freehold in his own right, in the parish or district where he is elected, of the value of seven thousand pounds currency at least, also clear of debt.

13. That on the last Monday in November and the day following, which shall be in the year of our Lord one thousand seven hundred and seventy-eight, and on the same days of every second year thereafter, members of the General Assembly shall be chosen, to meet on the second Monday in January then next, at the usual place in Charles-town, unless the casualties of war, or contagious disorders, should render it unsafe to meet there, in which case the President and Commander in Chief for the time being, may, by Proclamation, with the advice and consent of the Privy Council, appoint a more secure and convenient place of meeting, and to continue for two years from the said last Monday in November. Each parish and district within this State shall send members to the General Assembly in the following proportions, that is to say,

The parishes of St. Philip and St. Michael, Charles-town, thirty members.

The parish of Christ-church, six members.

The parish of St. John, in Berkley county, six members.

The parish of St. Andrew, six members.

The parish of St. George, Dorchester, six members.

The parish of St. James, Goosecreek, six members.

The parish of St. Thomas and St. Dennis, six members.

The parish of St. Paul, six members.
The

The parish of St. Bartholomew, six members.

The parish of St. Helena, six members.

The parish of St. James, Sanfee, six members.

The parish of Prince George, Winyah, six members.

The parish of Prince Frederick, six members.

The parish of St. John, in Colleton county, six members.

The parish of St Peter, six members.

The parish of Prince Williams, six members.

The parish of St. Stephen, six members

The district to the eastward of the Wateree River, ten members.

The district of Ninety-six, ten members.

The district of Saxe-Gotha, six members.

The district between Broad and Saludy Rivers, in three divisions, viz.

The Lower District, four members.

The Little River District, four members.

The Upper or Spartan District, four members.

The district between Broad and Catawba Rivers, ten members.

The district called the New Acquisition, ten members

The parish of St. Matthew, six members.

The parish of St. David, six members.

The district between Savannah River and the North Fork of Edisto, six members.

And the election of the said members shall be conducted, as near as may be, agreeable to the direction of the Election Act. And where there are no Churches or Churchwardens in a district or parish, the General Assembly, at some convenient time before their expiration, shall appoint places of election, and persons to receive votes and make returns. The qualification of the electors shall be, that every free white man, and no other person, who acknowledges the Being of a God, and believes in a future state of rewards and punishments, and who has attained to the age of one and twenty years, and hath been a resident and an inhabitant in this State for the space of one whole year, before the date of the writs for the election he offers to give his vote at, and hath a freehold at least of fifty acres of land, or a town lot, and hath been legally seized and possessed of the same, at least six months, previous to such election, or hath paid a tax the preceding year, or was taxable the present year, at least six months previous to the said election, in a sum equal to the tax on fifty acres of land, to the support of this government, shall be deemed a person qualified to vote for, and may be capable of electing, a representative or representatives, to serve as a member or members, in the Legislative Council and General Assembly, for the parish or district where he actually is a resident, or in any other parish or district in this State where he hath the like freehold. Electors shall take an oath, or affirmation of qualification, if required by the returning officer. The qualification of the elected, if residents in the parish or district for which they shall be returned, shall be the same as mentioned in the Election Act, and construed to mean clear of debt. But no non-resident shall be eligible to a seat in the General Assembly, unless he is owner of a settled estate and freehold, in his own right, of the value of three thousand and five hundred pounds currency at least, clear of debt, in the parish or district for which he is elected.

14. That if any parish or district neglects or refuses to elect members; or, if the members chosen do not meet in General Assembly; those who do meet shall have the powers of the General Assembly. Not less than

than forty-nine members shall make an House, to do business; but the Speaker, or any seven members, may adjourn from day to day.

15. That when proper information can be had of the particular and comparative strength and taxable property of the different parts of the State, that then the present representation be proportioned in the most equal and just manner, regard being always had to the number of white inhabitants and taxable property of the people.

16. That all money bills for the support of government, shall originate in the General Assembly, and shall not be altered or mended by the Legislative Council, but may be rejected by them: but that no money be drawn out of the public treasury, but by the Legislative authority of the State. All other bills and ordinances may take rise in the General Assembly or Legislative Council, and be altered, amended, or rejected by either. Bills having passed the General Assembly and Legislative Council, shall be signed by the President and Commander in Chief for the time being, the Speaker of the Legislative Council, and the Speaker of the General Assembly, in the Council Chamber, and shall then have all the force and validity of an Act of General Assembly of this State. And the General Assembly and Legislative Council respectively, shall enjoy all other privileges which have, at any time, been claimed or exercised by the Commons House of Assembly.

17. That the General Assembly and Legislative Council may adjourn themselves respectively; and the President and Commander in Chief shall have no power to adjourn, prorogue, or dissolve them: but may, if necessary, by and with the advice and consent of the Privy Council, call them, before the time to which they shall stand adjourned. And where a bill hath been rejected, it may, on a meeting after an adjournment for not less than three days, of General Assembly and Legislative Council, be brought in again.

18. That the General Assembly and the Legislative Council shall each choose their respective Speakers, and their own officers, by ballot, without controul. And that, during a recess, the Speakers, of either House, shall issue writs for filling up vacancies, occasioned by death, in their respective Houses, giving at least three weeks, and not more than thirty-five days previous notice, of the time appointed for the election.

19. That if any parish or district shall neglect to elect a member or members, on the day of election; or, in case any person chosen a member of the Legislative Council or General Assembly, shall refuse to qualify and take his seat as such, or die, or depart the State; the said Legislative Council or General Assembly, as the case may be, shall appoint proper days, for electing a member or members of the said Legislative Council or General Assembly, in such cases respectively.

20. That if any member of the General Assembly, or of the Legislative Council, shall accept any place of emolument, or any commission (except in the militia) he shall vacate his seat, and there shall thereupon be a new election; but he shall not be disqualified from serving, upon being re-elected, without he is appointed Secretary of the State, a Commissioner of the Treasury, an Officer of the Customs, Register of Mesne Conveyances, a Clerk of one of the Courts of Justice, Powder-receiver, Clerk of the Legislative or Privy Council, Clerk of the General Assembly, Surveyor-general, or Commissary of Military Stores; which officers are hereby declared disqualified, from being members either of the Legislative Council or General Assembly.

21. That

21. That no Minister of the Gospel, or public preacher, of any religious persuasion, be eligible, for the future, either as a member of the Legislative Council, or of the General Assembly.

22. That the Delegates of this State in the Continental Congress, be chosen, annually, by the General Assembly and Legislative Council jointly, by ballot, in the General Assembly; and nothing contained in this Constitution shall be construed to extend to vacate the seat of any member, who is, or may be, a Delegate from this State to the Continental Congress, as such.

23. That the Vice-president of the State and the Privy Council, or the Vice-president and a majority of the Privy Council for the time being, shall exercise the powers of a Court of Chancery. And there shall be an Ordinary, who shall exercise the powers heretofore exercised by that officer in this State.

24. That the jurisdiction of the Court of Admiralty be confined to maritime causes.

25. That Justices of the Peace shall be nominated by the General Assembly, and commissioned by the President and Commander in Chief, during pleasure. They will not be intitled to fees, except on prosecutions for felony; and, not acting in the magistracy, they shall not be entitled to the privileges allowed them by law.

26. That all other judicial officers shall be chosen, by ballot, jointly by the General Assembly and Legislative Council, in the General Assembly, and, except the Judges of the Court of Chancery, commissioned by the President and Commander in Chief, during good behaviour: but shall be removed, on address of the General Assembly and Legislative Council.

27. That the Sheriffs, qualified as by law directed, shall be chosen by the freeholders in each district throughout the State, and commissioned by the President and Commander in Chief, for two years only.

28. That the Commissioners of the Treasury, the Secretary of the State, the Register of Mesne Conveyances, Attorney-general, Powder-receiver, Collectors, Comptrollers, Waiters, and Surveyor-general, be chosen by the General Assembly and Legislative Council jointly, by ballot, in the General Assembly, and commissioned by the President and Commander in Chief, during good behaviour; but shall be removed on address of the General Assembly and Legislative Council.

29, That all Field Officers in the army, and all Captains in the navy, shall be, by the General Assembly and Legislative Council, chosen jointly, by ballot, in the General Assembly, and commissioned by the President and Commander in Chief, except in cases where they are to receive their commissions from Congress. And that all other officers, in the army and navy, shall be commissioned by the President and Commander in Chief.

30. That in case of vacancy in any of the offices above directed to be filled by the General Assembly and Legislative Council, the President and Commander in Chief, with the advice and consent of the Privy Council, may appoint others in their stead, until there shall be an election by the General Assembly and Legislative Council to fill those vacancies respectively.

31. That the President and Commander in Chief, with the advice and consent of the Privy Council, may appoint, during pleasure, until otherwise directed by the resolution of the General Assembly and Legislative Council, all other necessary officers, except such as are by law directed to be otherwise chosen.

32. That the President and Commander

B b b

mander in Chief shall have no power to commence war, or conclude peace, or enter into any final treaty, without the consent of the General Assembly and Legislative Council.

33. That the resolutions of the late Congresses of this State, and all laws now of force here (and not hereby altered) shall so continue, until altered or repealed by the Legislature of this State, unless where they are temporary, in which case they shall expire at the times respectively limited for their duration.

34. That the President and Commander in Chief, Vice-president of this State, and Privy Council respectively, shall have the same personal privileges, as are allowed by Act of Assembly to the Governor, Lieutenant-governor, and Privy Council. That the President and Commander in Chief for the time being, by and with the advice and consent of the Privy Council, may lay embargoes, or prohibit the exportation of any commodity, for any time not exceeding thirty days, in the recess of the General Assembly.

35. That all persons who shall be chosen and appointed to any office, or to any place of trust, civil or military, before entering upon the execution of office, shall take the following oath:

" I A. B. do acknowledge the State of South Carolina, to be a Free, Independent, and Sovereign State, and that the people thereof owe no allegiance or obedience to   of Great-Britain: and I do renounce, refuse, and abjure, any allegiance or obedience to him. And I do swear, or affirm [as the case may be] that I will, to the utmost of my power, support, maintain and defend the said State, against the said   and his heirs and successors, and his or their abettors, assistant, and adherents, and will serve the said State in the Office of

which I now hold, and in any other office which I may hereafter hold, by the appointment, or under the authority, of the said State, with fidelity and honour, and according to the best of my skill and understanding.

36. That the following yearly salaries be allowed to the public officers under-mentioned: the President and Commander in Chief, five thousand five hundred and thirty-eight dollars and one half: the Chief Justice, two thousand one hundred and twenty-one dollars: the Assistant Judges, one thousand seven hundred and twenty-four dollars each: the Attorney-general, one thousand two hundred and ninety-three dollars, in lieu of all charges against the public for fees on criminal prosecutions: the three Commissioners of the Treasury, one thousand two hundred and thirty-one dollars each.

37. That all persons and religious societies, who acknowledge, that there is one God, and a future state of rewards and punishments, and that God is publicly to be worshipped, shall be freely tolerated. The Christian religion shall be deemed, and is hereby constituted, and declared to be, the established religion of this State. That all denominations of Christians in this State, demeaning themselves peaceably and faithfully, shall enjoy equal religious privileges To accomplish this desireable purpose, without injury to the religious property of those societies of Christians which are by law already incorporated, for the purposes of religious worship; and to put it fully into the power of every other society of Christians, either already formed, or hereafter to be formed, to obtain the like incorporation; It is hereby constituted, appointed, and declared, That the respective societies of the Church of England, That are already formed in this State, for the purposes of religious worship, shall still continue incorporate,

corporate, and hold the religious property now in their possession : and that, whenever fifteen or more male persons, not under twenty-one years of age, professing the Christian religion, and agreeing to unite themselves in a society for the purposes of religious worship, they shall (on complying with the terms herein after mentioned) be, and be constituted, a Church, and be esteemed and regarded in law as of the established religion of the State, and on petition to the Legislature, shall be intitled to be incorporated, and to enjoy equal privileges : that every society of Christians, so formed, shall give themselves a name or denomination, by which they shall be called and known in law ; and all that associate with them for the purposes of worship, shall be esteemed as belonging to the society so called ; but that, previous to the establishment and incorporation of the respective societies of every denomination as aforesaid ; and in order to intitle them thereto, each society so petitioning, shall have agreed to, and subscribed, in a book, the following five articles, without which, no agreement or union of men, upon pretence of religion, shall intitle them to be incorporated, and esteemed as a church of the established religion of this State. First, That there is one eternal God, and a future state of rewards and punishments. Second, That God is to be publicly worshipped. Third, The Christian religion is the true religion. Fourth, That the Holy Scriptures of the Old and New Testament, are divinely inspired, and are the rule of faith and practice. Fifth, That it is lawful, and the duty of every man being thereunto called by those that govern, to bear witness to truth, That every inhabitant of this State, when called to make an appeal to God, as a witness to truth, shall be permitted to do it in that way which is most agreeable to the dictates of his own conscience. And,

that the people of this State may for ever enjoy the right of electing their own pastors or clergy ; and, at the same time, that the State may have sufficient security, for the due discharge of the pastoral office, by those who shall be admitted to be a clergyman on the establishment, no person shall officiate as minister of any established church, who shall not have been chosen by a majority of the society to which he shall minister, or by persons appointed by the said majority to choose and procure a minister for them, nor until the minister so chosen and appointed, shall have made and subscribed to the following declaration, over and above the aforesaid five articles, viz. That he is determined, by God's grace, out of the Holy Scriptures, to instruct the people committed to his charge, and to teach nothing (as required of necessity to eternal salvation) but that which he shall be persuaded may be concluded and proved from the Scripture ; that he will use both public and private admonitions, as well to the sick as to the whole, within his cure, as need shall require and occasion shall be given ; and that he will be diligent in prayers, and in reading of the Holy Scriptures, and in such studies as help to the knowledge of the same ; that he will be diligent to frame and fashion his own self, and his family, according to the doctrine of Christ, and to make both himself and them, as much as in him lieth, wholesome examples and patterns to the flock of Christ ; that he will maintain and set forwards, as much as he can, quietness, peace, and love, among all Christian people ; and especially among those that are or shall be committed to his charge. No person shall disturb or molest any religious assembly, nor shall use any reproachful, reviling or abusive language, against any church ; that being the certain way of disturbing the peace, and of hindering the conversion of any to the truth by engaging them in quarrels and animosities,

B b b 2

sities, to the hatred of the professors, and that profession which otherwise they might be brought to assent to. Any person consenting to associate with, and subscribing to, the writing or instrument by which any denomination of Christians shall form themselves into a society, before any five members, shall thereby be made a member thereof. Any person striking out his name from such writing or instrument as aforesaid, or having his name struck out, by any person thereto authorized by the society to which he belongs, shall cease to be a member. No person whatsoever shall speak any thing, in their religious assembly, irreverently, or seditiously of the government of this State. No person shall, by law, be obliged to pay towards the maintenance and support of a religious worship that he does not freely join in, or has not voluntarily engaged to support: but, the churches, chapels, parsonages, glebes, and all other property, now belonging to any societies of the Church of England, or any other religious societies, shall remain, and be secured, to them for ever. No person shall be capable of any place of honour, trust or profit, under the authority of this State, who is not a member of some church of the established religion thereof. Marriages shall be solemnized, after publication three several Sundays preceding such marriage, in some public place of worship, in the parish or district where the woman resides, or by licence, which shall be directed to any Minister of the Gospel, without specifying the denomination, or prescribing the mode of solemnization. The poor shall be supported, and elections managed in the accustomed manner, until laws shall be provided, to adjust those matters in the most equitable way.

38. That no Clergyman, Preacher, or Minister of the Gospel, shall be intitled to any greater exemption from punishments inflicted by law, by reason of any benefit of clergy, than if such Clergyman, Preacher, or Minister, was a layman; but that every such Clergyman, Preacher, or Minister, being found guilty of any offence which is clergyable or not clergyable by the law, shall suffer as a layman.

39. That no part of this Constitution shall be altered without a notice of ninety days being previously given: nor shall any part of the same be changed, without the consent of a majority of the members of the General Assembly and Legislative Council.

40. That the General Assembly and Legislative Council shall not proceed to the election of a President or Vice-president, until there be a majority of both Houses present.

———————

The following Paper is supposed to have been written by a *celebrated* American Philosopher, at Paris; for the purpose of borrowing money for the use of the United States of America; and it has had a wonderful effect; large sums having been lent, in consequence of the sound and irrefutable facts and arguments contained in it. It has been translated into the French and Dutch languages, and printed; and it is now circulating in Holland, Flanders, &c.

In borrowing money a man's credit depends on some or all of the following particulars:

First, His known conduct respecting former loans, and his punctuality in discharging them.

Secondly, His industry.

Thirdly, His frugality.

Fourthly, The amount and the certainty of his income, and the freedom of his estate from the incumbrances of prior debts.

Fifthly, His well founded prospects of greater future ability, by the improvement of his estate in value, and by aids from others.

Sixthly,

Sixthly, His known prudence in managing his general affairs, and the advantage they will probably receive from the loan which he defires.

Seventhly, His known probity and honeft character, manifefted by his voluntary difcharge of his debts, which he could not have been legally compelled to pay.——The circum-ftances which give credit to an indi-vidual, ought to, and will have their weight upon the lenders of money, to public bodies or nations. If then we confider and compare' Britain and America, in thefe feveral particulars, upon queftion, " *To which is the fafeft to lend money ?*" We fhall find, 1. Refpecting *former loans*, that America, which borrowing ten mil-lions during the laft war for the main-tainance of her army of 25,000 men, and other charges, had faithfully dif-charged and paid that debt, and all her other debts in 1772. Whereas Britain, during thofe ten years of peace and profitable commerce, had made little or no reduction of her debt, but on the contrary, from time to time, diminifhed the hopes of her creditors by a wanton diverfion and mifapplication of the finking fund de-ftined for difcharging it.

2. Refpecting *induftry*, Every man is employed; the greater part in cul-tivating their own lands; the reft in handicrafts, navigation, and com-merce. An idle man is a rarity; idlenefs and inutility are difgraceful. In England, the number of that cha-racter is immenfe; fafhion has fpread it far and wide; hence the embarraf-ments of private fortunes, and the daily bankruptcies arifing from an univerfal fondnefs for appearance and expenfive pleafures; and hence, in fome degree, the mifmanagements of public bufinefs; for habits of bufinefs and ability in it are acquired only by practice, and where univerfal diffipa-tion, and the perpetual purfuit of amufement are the mode, the youth, educated in it, can rarely afterwards acquire that patient attention and clofe application to affairs, which are fo neceffary to a Statefman charged with the care of national welfare. Hence the frequent errors in policy; and hence the wearinefs at public councils, and backwardnefs in going to them; the conftant unwillingnefs to engage in any meafure that requires thought and confideration, and the readinefs for poftponing every new propofition, which ' poftponing is therefore the only part of bufinefs that they come to be expert in, an expert-nefs produced neceffarily by fo much daily practice. Whereas in America, men bred to clofe employments in their private affairs, attend with eafe to thofe of the public, when engaged in them, and nothing fails through negligence.

3. Refpecting *frugality*; the man-ner of living in America is more fimple and lefs expenfive than that in Eng-land; plain tables, plain cloathing, and plain furniture in houfes prevail, with few carriages of pleafure; there, an expenfive appearance hurts credit, and is avoided: in England it is often *affumed* to gain credit, and *continued* to ruin. Refpecting public affairs, the difference is ftill greater. In England, the falaries of officers, and emoluments of office, are enormous. The King has a million fterling per annum, and yet cannot maintain his family free of debt. Secretaries of State, Lords of Treafury, Admiralty, &c. have vaft appointments. An Auditor of the Exchequer has fixpence in the pound, or a fortieth part of all the public money expended by the nation; fo that, when a war cofts forty millions, one million is paid to him. An Infpector of the Mint, in the laft new coinage, received as his fee 65,000l. fterling per annum; to all which rewards, no fervice thefe Gentlemen can render the public is by any means equivalent. All this is paid by the people, who are op-preffed by taxes fo occafioned, and thereby

thereby rendered less able to contribute to the payment of necessary, national debts. In America, salaries, where indispensible, are extremely low, but much of the public business is done gratis. The honour of serving the public ably and faithfully, is deemed sufficient. Public spirit really exists there, and has great effects. In England, it is universally deemed a non-entity, and whoever pretends to it, is laughed at as a fool, or suspected as a knave. The Committees of Congress, which form the Board of War, the Board of Treasury, the Board of Foreign Affairs, the Naval Board, that for Accounts, &c. all attend the business of their respective functions, without any salary or emolument whatever, though they spend in it much more of their time than any Lord of Treasury or Admiralty in England can spare from his amusements. A British Minister lately computed, that the whole expence of the Americans, in their civil government, over three millions of people, amounted to but 70,000l. sterling, and drew from thence a conclusion, that they ought to be taxed, until their expence was equal in proportion to that which it costs Britain to govern eight millions. He had no idea of a contrary conclusion, that if three millions may be well governed for 70,000l. eight millions may be as well governed for three times that sum, and that therefore the expence of his own government should be diminished. In that corrupted nation, no man is ashamed of being concerned in lucrative Government jobbs, in which the public money is egregiously misapplied and squandered, the Treasury pillaged, and more numerous and heavy taxes accumulated, to the great oppression of the people. But the prospect of a greater number of such jobbs by a war, is an inducement with many to cry out for war upon all occasions, and to oppose every proposition of peace. Hence the con-

stant increase of the national debt, and the absolute improbability of its ever being discharged.

4. Respecting the amount and certainty of income, and solidity of security, the whole Thirteen States of America are engaged for the payment of every debt contracted by the Congress, and the debt to be contracted by the present war, is the only debt they will have to pay; all, or nearly all the former debts of particular colonies being already discharged. Whereas England will have to pay, not only the enormous debt this war must occasion, but all their vast preceding debt, or the interest of it; and while America is enriching itself by prizes made upon the British commerce, more than it ever did by any commerce of its own under the restraints of a British monoply, Britain is growing poorer by the loss of that monopoly, and the diminution of its revenues, and of course less able to discharge the present indiscreet increase of its expences.

5. Respecting *prospects of greater future ability*, Britain has none such. Her islands are circumscribed by the ocean; and excepting a few parks or forests, she has no new land to cultivate, and cannot therefore extend her improvements. Her numbers too, instead of increasing from increased subsistence, are continually diminishing from growing luxury, and the increasing difficulties of maintaining families, which of course discourages early marriages. Thus she will have fewer people to assist in paying her debts, and that diminished number will be poorer. America, on the contrary, has besides her lands already cultivated, a vast territory yet to be cultivated, continually increase in value with the increase of people; and the people, who double themselves by a natural propagation every twenty-five years, will double yet faster by the accession of strangers, as long as lands are to be had for new families;

families; fo that every twenty years, there will be a double number of inhabitants obliged to difcharge the public debts; and thofe inhabitants being more opulent, may pay their fhares with greater eafe.

6. Refpecting *prudence* in general affairs, and the advantages to be expected from the loan defired. The Americans are cultivators of land, thofe engaged in fifhery and commerce are few, compared with the others. They have ever conducted their feveral governments with wifdom, avoiding wars, and vain expenfive projects, delighting only in their peaceable occupations, which muft, confidering the extent of their uncultivated territory, find them employment ftill for ages. Whereas England, even unquiet, ambitious, avaricious, imprudent, and quarrelfome, is half of the time engaged in war, always at an expence infinitely, greater than the advantage to be obtained by it, if fuccefsful. Thus they made war againft Spain in 1739, for a claim of about 95,000l. (fcarce a groat for each individual of the nation) and fpent forty millions fterling in the war, and the lives of fifty thoufand men; and finally made peace without obtaining fatisfaction for the fum claimed. Indeed, there is fcarce a nation in Europe, againft which fhe has not made war on fome frivolous pretext or other, and thereby imprudently accumulated a debt that has brought her on the verge of bankruptcy. But the moft indifcreet of all her wars is the prefent againft America; with which fhe might, for ages, have preferved her profitable connection, only by a juft and equitable conduct. She is now acting like a mad fhop-keeper, who, by beating thofe that pafs his doors, attempts to make them come in, and be his cuftomers. America cannot fubmit to fuch treatment, without being firft ruined; and being ruined, her cuftom will be worth nothing. England,

to effect this, is increafing her debt, and irretrievably ruining herfelf. America, on the other hand, aims only to eftablifh her Liberty, and that freedom of commerce which will be advantageous to all Europe; and by abolifhing that monopoly which fhe laboured under, fhe will profit infinitely more than enough, to repay any debt which fhe may contract to accomplifh it.

7. Refpecting *character in the honeft payment of debts.* The punctuality with which America has difcharged her public debts, was fhewn under the firft head; and the general good difpofition of the people to fuch punctuality, has been manifefted in their faithful payment of private debts to England, fince the commencement of this war. There were not wanting fome politicians, who propofed ftopping that payment, until peace fhould be reftored, alledging that in the ufual courfe of commerce, and of the credit given, there was always a debt exifting equal to the trade of 18 months. That the trade amounting to five millions fterling per annum, the debt muft be feven millions and an half; that this fum paid to the Britifh merchants, would operate to prevent that diftrefs, intended to be brought upon Britain, by our ftoppage of commerce with her. For the merchants receiving this money, and no orders with it for farther fupplies, would either lay it out in the public funds, or in employing manufacturers to accumulate goods, for a future hungry market in America, upon an expected accommodation; by which means the funds would be kept up, and the manufacturers prevented from murmuring. But againft this it was alledged, that injuries from Minifters fhould not be revenged on merchants; that the credit was in confequence of, private contracts, made in confidence of good faith; that thefe ought to be held facred, and faithfully complied with; for that whatever public utility might

might be supposed to arise from a breach of private faith, it was unjust, and would in the end be found unwise; honesty, being in truth, the best policy. On this principle, the proposition was universally rejected; and, though the English prosecuted the war, with unexampled barbarity, burning our defenceless towns in the midst of winter, and arming savages against us, the debt was punctually paid; and the merchants of London have testified to the Parliament, and will testify to all the world, that from their experience in dealing with us, they had, before the war, no apprehension of our unfairness, and that since the war, they have been convinced, that their good opinion of us was well founded. England, on the contrary, an old, corrupt, extravagant, and profligate nation, sees herself deep in debt, which she is in no condition to pay; and yet is madly, and dishonestly, running deeper, without any possibility of discharging her debt, but by a public bankruptcy.

It appears, therefore, from the general industry, frugality, ability, prudence, and virtue of America, that she is a much safer debtor than Britain; to say nothing of the satisfaction generous minds must have in reflecting, that by loans to America, they are opposing tyranny, and aiding the cause of liberty, which is the cause of all mankind.

———————

The following is a translation of an ADDRESS *circulating among the* HOLDERS *of* BRITISH STOCK *in* HOLLAND, *viz.*

" To you, the people of Holland, and of the other United Provinces, I address myself. You are all my countrymen, and many of you are my friends. You have lent the enormous sum of thirty millions sterling to Great-Britain; and the nation that owes you this, owes near four times as much to others, and is now on the verge of bankruptcy and ruin. Six months ago you appeared sensible of the insufficiency of her security, and you wisely determined not only to desist from farther loans to her, but to sell out your several interests in the British funds, as fast as possible, without sinking them too rapidly. I approved this determination, and was silent. But I now find that some of you, wanting other ways to employ your money, have began to risk it again on British national security, and for the sake of a temporary interest, are about to lose the principal. I must therefore seriously call your attention to the real situation of Great-Britain. At the beginning of the year 1762, the British three per cent. consolidated annuities were worth only 60 per cent. (near 20 per cent. less than their present extravagant price) and yet Great-Britain was then at the summit of her glory; her commerce and her victories were extended to every quarter of the globe; her public debt was small in comparison to its present enormous amount; and she had neither lost, nor was likely to lose, any of her possessions in India or America, but on the contrary, she had made important conquests from her enemies, and could at any time have secured peace, by restoring but a part of those conquests.

" What now is the situation of Great-Britain? What increase of national prosperity does she enjoy to occasion the present advanced price of her stocks? By a continuance in the most infatuated conduct; she has brought upon herself calamities infinitely greater than what any former war could have involved her in. She has *irrecoverably lost* almost the whole of her vast possessions on the continent of America. More than three millions of people, who had been affectionately united under her government, and had fought hand in hand with her, have revolted, and are fighting against her: instead of their affection, she has provoked their utmost hatred;
and

and inftead of monopolizing their whole commerce, (that commerce which yielded her a clear profit of two millions *per ann.* and which carried her triumphantly through the laft war) fhe no longer retains the fmalleft fhare of it; nor can fhe even proteƈt the trade of her own ifland. Both the arms and the commerce of America, which were the principal fupports of Britain, are now employed againft her. For three years fhe has endeavoured to reduce the revolted Colonies, but has only wafted her own blood and treafure, and confirmed their hatred and their independency. At the commencement of each year, we have been told that the next campaign would be the laft; and yet the end of each year has left her fituation worfe than the beginning. Still, however, fhe obftinately purfues the fame deftruƈtive courfe. Every man knows, that without the dominion and trade of the United Colonies, Great-Britain cannot pay either the intereft or principal of her enormous debt; and every *wife* man knows, that fhe has already *loft* the Colonies, and the *poffibility of ever recovering them.* Her national debt is now increafed to almoft the immenfe fum of *one hundred and fifty millions fterling*, and yet we fhall very foon fee her coming in the face of all Europe, to borrow other millions for another hopelefs campaign in America. Like a ruined gamefter, having loft or mortgaged her eftate above its value, fhe defperately hazards the money of every one who will lend her, vainly hoping to recover fome part of her former loffes. But will you, my countrymen, famed as you are for cautious prudence, will you furnifh the ftake which is to continue this defperate game? Will you, in this fallen ftate of Britain, purchafe her ftocks at 20 *per cent.* more than their value, when fhe was in her moft triumphant and profperous condition? Will you not rather feize the prefent

favourable moment, and fell out, as faft as poffible, the interefts which you have too long retained in her precarious funds? If ever national calamities could give a caufe for finking the price of the Britifh ftocks, they ought now to be at the loweft ftate of depreciation. Her misfortunes are now infinitely greater than at any former period. Thofe annuities, which in 1762 were worth but fixty *per cent.* cannot, in the prefent diftreffed fituation of Britifh affairs, be worth half as much. It is time, my countrymen, that you fhould open your eyes, and ceafe to be any longer deluded by the artful falfhoods, the infidious mifreprefentations, and fruitlefs promifes, which the adherents, and hireling fcribblers of the Britifh Government have propagated, in regular fucceffion, year after year. Experience has proved the dangerous fallacy of thefe their praƈtices. Great-Britain now totters towards her fall: the only folid foundation of her wealth and power is taken away, and fhe muft neceffarily fink under the enormous weight of her public debt. Take care then, my countrymen, that you are not involved in her ruin.

I am, &c.

PENSACOLA.
18th November, 1775.

Sir,

The Earl of Dartmouth having been pleafed to fignify to me in a letter of the 5th of July laft, his Majefty's royal wifhes that I fhould afford every poffible proteƈtion to fuch of his fubjeƈts in the Colonies in rebellion as fhall be too weak to refift the violence of the times, and too loyal to concur in the meafures of thofe who have avowed and fupported that rebellion, and are defirous of feeking an afylum in this Province; and that I fhould countenance and proteƈt all fuch as may be induced under the circumftances above ftated to retreat hither, and give them grants

C c c · of

of land, by way of bounty and encouragement, exempt from quit-rent for ten years; and that I should also give every possible encouragement in my power to the exportation of lumber from hence to the West-India Islands: I therefore thought proper to direct a Proclamation to issue, notifying and declaring this royal bounty and encouragement, but I am afraid, from the circumstances of the times, that it will not be in my power to have it so generally dispersed and published as I could wish, we having no printing-press in the Colony; and therefore I have taken liberty to inclose a copy of this proclamation to your Excellency, and to request that you·will be pleased to direct that a number of copies of the same may be printed and published in your government.

I have further to request, that your Excellency will be pleased to afford every assistance in your power to have these his Majesty's most gracious intentions carried into execution.

I am,
With great regard and esteem,
Sir,
Your most obedient humble servant,
PETER CHESTER.
His Excellency William Tryon, Esq.

WEST-FLORIDA.
By his Excellency PETER CHESTER,
Esq.

Captain General, Governor and Commander in Chief, in and over his Majesty's said Povinces of West Florida, and the territories depending thereon in America, Chancellor, Vice-admiral, and Ordinary of the same, &c.

A PROCLAMATION.

Whereas his Majesty by his royal instructions, dated at St. James's the the third day of February, in the year of our Lord one thousand seven hundred and seventy-four, and in the fourteenth year of his reign, did think fit, with the advice of his Privy Council, to revoke and annul all the powers and authorities which before that time had been given by his Majesty to the Governors of this Province, for the laying out and passing grants of land within the same, and to direct and appoint certain rules and regulations to be thenceforth strictly and punctually observed for the future disposal, by public sale, of such lands, tenements, and hereditaments, as then were or hereafter should be in his Majesty's power to dispose of within this province, in the manner by the said instructions particularly mentioned and directed. And whereas his Majesty has been graciously pleased to signify his royal wishes that the Governor of this province should afford every possible protection to such of his subjects in the colonies in rebellion, as shall be too weak to resist the violences of the times, and too loyal to concur in the measures of those who have avowed and supported that rebellion, and are desirous of seeking an asylum in West-Florida; and to that end his Majesty has been pleased to direct that the execution of the instructions of the third day of February, in the year of our Lord one thousand seven hundred and seventy-four herein before mentioned, should be suspended for the present within this colony. And whereas his Majesty has also been pleased to signify his further pleasure to the Governor of this province, to give every possible encouragement to the exportation of lumber from this colony to his islands in the West-Indies, it is therefore hereby notified to all his Majesty's good and faithful subjects, who may be induced under the circumstances above stated, to seek a retreat in this province, that the Governor of the said province, will afford them every possible protection and countenance in his power; and that they upon their arrival in this province, and applying to the Governor thereof in Council, for grants of
land,

land, fhall obtain the fame, exempt from quit-rents for ten years, under the following regulations; to wit, That one hundred acres of land will be granted to every fuch perfon being mafter or miftrefs of a family, for himfelf and herfelf; and fifty acres for every white or black man, woman, or child, of which fuch perfon's family fhall confift at the actual time of making the grant. And in cafe any fuch perfon, well affected to the conftitution, applying to the faid Governor in Council for grants of land, fhall be defirous of taking up a larger quantity than the actual number of perfons in his or her family would intitle fuch perfon to take up, that the faid Governor in Council, will grant to every fuch perfon or perfons fuch further quantity of land as they may defire, not exceeding one thoufand acres over and above what they are intitled to by the number of perfons in their refpective families. Provided, it fhall appear to the faid Governor, that they are in a condition and intention to cultivate the fame. And provided alfo, that they, at the time of fuch application, do give good evidence to the Governor of the faid province, of their real attachment to the conftitution, and of their non-concurrence in the rebellious proceedings in the other colonies. And it is hereby further notified, that the Governor of this province will afford every poffible encouragement to all his Majefty's good fubjects, who may think proper to be concerned in the exportation of lumber, and all other produce from this province to the Weft-Indies, and that he will grant his licence to any fuch perfon or perfons to cut wood and convert it into lumber, upon any part of his Majefty's lands within this province. Provided always, that proper fecurity be given upon the exportation of any lumber, that the fame fhall be landed in fome of the Weft-India Iflands belonging to the King.

Given under my hand, and the Great Seal of his Majefty's faid province, in the Council Chamber at Penfacola, the eleventh day of November, in the year of our Lord one thoufand feven hundred feventy-five, and in the fixteenth year of his Majefty's reign.

PETER CHESTER.

By his Excellency's command,

ALEX. MACULLOUGH, D. Sec.

GOD SAVE THE KING.

Whitehall, November 1, 1777.

The following letter from General Sir William Howe to Lord George Germain was received the 28th of laft month, by the Swallow Packet from Maryland.

Camp at the Head of Elk, Auguft 30, 1777.

My Lord,

The duplicates of your Lordfhip's difpatches, No. 10, 11, and 12, with an original, No. 13, I had the honour to receive on the 16th inftant, by the Eagle Packet.

My laft difpatches advifed your Lordfhip of the embarkation of the army at Staten Ifland, from whence the fleet failed on the 23d of July, and arrived off the Capes of Delaware on the 30th following; when, from information, I judged it moft advifeable to proceed to Chefapeak Bay: but meeting with conftant unfavourable winds, we did not enter the Bay until the 16th inftant; from which time the winds proving fair, the fleet arrived at the mouth of the Elk River on the 22d, through a very difficult navigation; and the army landed on the 5th at Elk ferry, the enemy's army being then in the neighbourhood of Philadelphia.

On the 28th a corps of the army marched from the ferry to this place, by the weft fide of the river, leaving Lieutenant-general Knyphaufen with three brigades in that camp, and one brigade on the communication.

The corps commanded by General Knyphaufen

C c c 2

Knyphaufen will crofs the ferry to Cecil Court-houfe to-morrow, and is to form a junction with this on the 3d next enfuing, about eight miles on this fide of Chriftian-bridge.

The enemy's army is at this time encamped behind Brandy's-wine Creek, with an advanced corps on White-clay Creek: their force confifts of about fifteen thoufand men, including militia; neverthelefs, I am of opinion, it will be a difficult matter to bring them to a general action, even though it fhould be in the defence of Philadelphia.

The inclofed Declaration I have publithed, to endeavour to quiet the minds of the people at large in Pennfylvania, and the counties to which it has relation, led aftray by the leaders in rebellion.

By his Excellency Sir William Howe, K. B. General and Commander in Chief, &c. &c. &c.
DECLARATION.
Sir William Howe, regretting the calamities to which many of his Majefty's faithful fubjects are ftill expofed by the continuance of the rebellion, and no lefs defirous of protecting the innocent, than determined to purfue with the rigours of war all thofe whom his Majefty's forces, in the courfe of their progrefs, may find in arms againft the King, doth hereby affure the peaceable inhabitants of the province of Pennfylvania, the lower counties on Delaware, and the counties of Maryland on the eaftern fhore of Chefapeak Bay. That in order to remove any groundlefs apprehenfions which may have been raifed of their fuffering by depredations of the army under his command, he hath iffued the ftricteft orders to the troops for the prefervation of regularity and good difcipline, and has fignified, that the moft exemplary punifhment fhall be inflicted upon thofe who fhall dare to plunder the property, or moleft the perfons, of any of his Majefty's well difpofed fubjects.

Security and protection are likewife extended to all perfons inhabitants of the province and counties aforefaid, who, not guilty of having affumed legiflative or judicial authority, may have acted illegally in fubordinate ftations, and, confcious of their mifconduct, been induced to leave their dwellings; provided fuch perfons do forthwith return, and remain peaceably at their ufual places of abode.

Confidering moreover, that many officers and private men, now actually in arms againft his Majefty, may be willing to relinquifh the part they have taken in this rebellion, and return to their due allegiance, Sir William Howe doth therefore promife a free and general pardon to all fuch officers and private men, as fhall voluntarily come and furrender themfelves to any detachment of his Majefty's forces, before the day on which it fhall be notified that the faid indulgence is to be difcontinued.

Given under my hand, at Head Quarters of the army, the 27th day of Auguft, 1777.
W. Howe.
By his Excellency's command,
Robert Mackenzie, Sec.

Admiralty-Office, November 1, 1777.
The following is an extract of a letter from Lord Vifcount Howe, Commander in Chief of his Majefty's fhips and veffels in North-America, to Mr. Stephens, received the 28th of laft month, by the Swallow Packet, from Maryland:
Eagle, Elk River, Auguft 28, 1777.
Sir,
I informed you in my laft letter, of the 9th of July, that the part of the army intended by the General for a particular fervice was embarked.
I put to fea from Sandy-Hook with the fleet, confifting in the whole of 267 fail, the 23d of the fame month, being

being the earliest opportunity the weather would admit; but having frequent calms, and constant south-west and southerly winds in the mean time, the progress of the armament was so much retarded, that we were not advanced along the coast so far as the Delaware before the 29th, nor off the capes of Virginia, the destination of the fleet, until the 14th instant.

The wind then changing to the eastward, the fleet proceeded on, and anchored the next day within the entrance of Chesapeak Bay. By the attention of Capt. Griffith, commanding in the rear, and the general good disposition of the masters of the transports, the passage was effected without separation.

Captain Hammond, who had acquired a very correct knowledge of the navigation, was withdrawn from the Delaware, the Roebuck being replaced by the Liverpool, and charged with the care of stationing proper pilot vessels to mark out the channel up the Chesapeak Bay. The fleet, with that, and the further assistance of good pilots, being safely conducted up to the head of the Bay, anchored between the Safafras and Elk Rivers the 22d.

Having attended the General to reconnoitre the adjacent shores next day, the descent was fixed to be made on the 25th in the Elk.

The debarkation of the army was to be made on this occasion in five divisions, correspondent to the number of men which could be regularly landed from the flat-boats at the same time.

The covering ships, consisting of the Roebuck, with the Apollo, Sphynx, Vigilant, Senegal, and Swift, moving up the river in the morning of the 25th, the flat-boats under the chief command of Captain Duncan, with the infantry of the first division, advanced, and were followed in succession by the transports of the second and third divisions.

No preparation being made to oppose the descent, the transports of the other divisions were also ordered forward; and the whole army, with the necessary proportion of artillery and stores, were landed on the same day on the northern shore, opposite to Cecil Court-house, about six miles from Turkey Point.

Whitehall, Nov. 1, 1777.

The following letter from Lieutenant-General Burgoyne to Lord George Germain was yesterday received by an armed transport that sailed from Quebec the 7th of October:

Camp, nearly opposite to Saratogha, August 20, 1777.

My Lord,

In my last dispatch (a duplicate of which will be inclosed herewith) I had the honour to inform your Lordship of the proceedings of the army under my command to the 30th of July.

From that period to the 15th of August, every possible measure was employed to bring forward batteaux, provision and ammunition from Fort George to the first navigable part of Hudson's River; a distance of 18 miles; the roads in some parts steep, and in others wanting great repair. Of the horses furnished by contract in Canada, not more than a third part was yet arrived. The delay was not imputable to neglect, but to the natural accidents attending so long and intricate a combination of land and water carriage. Fifty teams of oxen, which had been collected in the country through which I had marched, were added to assist the transport; but these resources together were found far inadequate to the purposes of feeding the army and forming a magazine at the same time. Exceeding heavy rains augmented the impediments. It was often necessary

ceſſary to employ ten or twelve oxen upon a ſingle batteaux : and after the utmoſt exertions for the fifteen days above ſtated, there were not above four days proviſions beforehand, nor above ten batteaux in the Hudſon's River.

Intelligence had reached me, that Lieutenant-colonel St. Leger was before Fort Stanwix, which was defended. The main army of the enemy oppoſed to me was at Still Water, a place between Saratogha and the mouth of the Mohawk.

A rapid movement forward appeared to be of the utmoſt conſequence at this period. The enemy could not have proceeded up the Mohawk without putting themſelves between two fires, in caſe Lieutenant-colonel St. Leger ſhould have ſucceeded, and at beſt being cut off by my army from Albany ; they muſt either therefore have ſtood an action, have fallen back towards Albany, or have paſſed the Hudſon's River, in order to ſecure a retreat to New-England higher up. Whichever of theſe meaſures they had taken, ſo that the King's army had been enabled to advance, Colonel St. Leger's operations would have been aſſiſted, a junction with him probably ſecured, and the whole country of the Mohawk opened.

To maintain the communication with Fort George during ſuch a movement, ſo as to be ſupplied by daily degrees at a diſtance continually increaſing, was an obvious impoſſibility. The army was much too weak to have afforded a chain of poſts : eſcorts for every ſeparate tranſport would have been ſtill a greater drain ; nor could any have been made ſo ſtrong as to force their way through ſuch poſitions as the enemy might take in one night's march from the White Creek, where they had a numerous militia. Had the enemy remained ſupine through fear, or want of comprehending ſo palpable an advantage, the phyſical impoſſibility of being

ſupplied by degrees from Fort George was ſtill in force, becauſe a new neceſſity of land carriage for nine miles ariſes at Still Water ; and in proportion that carriages had been brought forward to that place, the tranſport muſt have ceaſed behind.

The alternative therefore was ſhort ; either to relinquiſh the favourable opportunity of advancing upon the enemy, or to attempt other reſources of ſupply.

It is well known that the enemy's ſupplies in live cattle from a large tract of country, paſſed by the route of Mancheſter, Arlington, and other parts of the Hampſhire grants to Bennington, in order to be occaſionally conveyed from thence to the main army. A large depôt of corn and of wheel carriages was alſo formed at the ſame place, and the uſual guard was militia, though it varied in number from day to day. A ſcheme was formed to ſurprize Bennington. The poſſeſſion of the cattle and carriages would certainly have enabled the army to leave their diſtant magazines, and to have acted with energy and diſpatch. Succeſs would alſo have anſwered many ſecondary purpoſes.

Lieutenant-colonel Baum, an officer well qualified for the undertaking, was fixed upon to command. He had under him two hundred diſmounted dragoons of the regiment of Reiſdeſel, Captain Frazer's markſmen, which were the only Britiſh, all the Canadian volunteers, a party of the provincials who perfectly knew the country, an hundred Indians, and two light pieces of cannon. The whole detachment amounted to about five hundred men. The inſtructions were poſitive to keep the regular corps poſted while the light troops felt their way, and not to incur the danger of being ſurrounded, or having a retreat cut off.

In order to facilitate this operation, and to be ready to take the advantage of its ſucceſs, the army moved up the

eaſt

eaft fhore of Hudfon's River on the 14th, a bridge was formed of rafts, over which the advanced corps paffed, and encamped at Saratogha ; Lieutenant-colonel Breyman's corps were pofted near Batten-kiln, and upon intelligence from Lieutenant-colonel Baum, that the enemy was ftronger at Bennington than expected, and were aware of his attack, that corps, confifting of the Brunfwick grenadiers, light infantry, and chaffeurs, were fent forward to fuftain him.

It fince appears that Lieutenant-colonel Baum, not having been able to complete his march undifcovered, was joined at a place called Stantcoick Mills, about four miles fhort of Bennington, by many people profeffing themfelves to be loyalifts. A provincial gentleman of confidence, who had been fent with the detachment, as knowing the country, and the characters of the inhabitants, was fo incautious as to leave at liberty fuch as took the oath of allegiance. His credulity and their profligacy caufed the firft misfortune : Colonel Baum was induced to proceed without fufficient knowledge of the ground ; his defign was betrayed ; the men who had taken the oaths were the firft to fire upon him ; he was attacked on all fides ; he fhewed great perfonal courage, but was overpowered by numbers.

During this time Lieutenant-colonel Breyman was upon the march through a heavy rain. And fuch were the other impediments ftated in that officer's report, of bad roads, tired horfes, difficulties in paffing artillery carriages, &c. that he was from eight in the morning of the 15th to four in the afternoon the following day making about twenty-four miles. He engaged, fought gallantly, and drove the enemy from three feveral heights, but was too late to fuccour Colonel Baum, who was made prifoner, and a confiderable part of his dragoons were killed or taken. The failure of ammunition, from the accidental breaking to pieces of a tumbril, unfortunately obliged Lieutenant-colonel Breyman to retire conquering troops, and to leave behind two pieces of cannon, befides two which had been loft by Lieutenant-colonel Baum. The Indians made good their retreat from the firft affair, as did Captain Frazer, with part of his company, and many of the Provincials and Canadians.

The lofs, as at prefent appears, amounts to about four hundred men killed and taken in both actions, and twenty-fix officers, moftly prifoners ; but men who were difperfed in the woods drop in daily. A correct return fhall be tranfmitted to your Lordfhip the firft opportunity.

This, my Lord, is the true ftate of the event. I have not dwelt upon errors, becaufe in many inftances they were counterbalanced by fpirit. The enemy will of courfe find matter of parade in the acquifition of four pieces of cannon, but that apart they have fmall caufe for exultation : their lofs in killed and wounded being more than double to ours, by the confeffion of their prifoners and deferters, and of many inhabitants who were witneffes to the burial of the dead.

The chief fubject of regret on our fide, after that which any lofs of gallant men naturally occafions, is the difappointment of not obtaining live cattle, and the lapfe of time in bringing forward the magazines.

The heavy work is now nearly compleated, and a new bridge of boats is thrown over the Hudfon's River oppofite to Saratogha, the former one of rafts having been carried away by the fwell of water after the late continual rains. When enabled to move, nothing within my fcale of talent fhall be left unattempted, to fulfil his Majefty's orders ; and I hope circumftances will be fuch, that my endeavours may

be

be in some degree assisted by a co-operation of the army under Sir William Howe.

I have the honour to be, &c.
J. BURGOYNE.

Extract of a letter from Lieutenant-colonel St. Leger to Lieutenant-general Burgoyne, brought through the woods by an Indian, dated before Fort Stanwix, August 11, 1777.

After combating the natural difficulties of the river St. Lawrence, and the artificial ones the enemy threw in my way at Wood Creek, I invested Fort Stanwix the 3d instant. On the 5th I learnt from discovering parties on the Mohawk River, that a body of one thousand militia were on their march to raise the siege. On the confirmation of this news, I moved a large body of Indians, with some troops the same night, to lay in ambuscade for them on their march. They fell into it. The compleatest victory was obtained: above 400 lay dead on the field, amongst the number of whom were almost all the principal movers of rebellion in that country. There are six or seven hundred men in the fort. The militia will never rally; all that I am to apprehend therefore that will retard my progress in joining you, is a reinforcement of what they call their regular troops, by the way of Half-moon, up the Mohawk River. A diversion therefore from your army by that quarter, will greatly expedite my junction with either of the grand armies.

Letters have been also received from General Sir Guy Carleton, giving an account of an attempt made by a large body of the rebels on Ticonderoga and Fort Independence, on the 16th of September. That they surprised and made prisoners part of four companies of the 53d regiment that were stationed at the Carrying-place and Sugar Loaf Hill, and had destroyed some waggons, boats, &c. but had beaten off from the forts by the garrisons, and upon the approach of a reinforcement from Crown Point had withdrawn intirely. That Colonel St. Leger, finding Fort Stanwix too strongly fortified, and the garrison too numerous to be taken by assault, and the Indians being alarmed by a false report of the approach of a large body of the rebel continental troops, he had given over the attempt of forcing a passage down the Mohawk River, and returned to Montreal, from whence he had proceeded to Ticonderoga, intending to join Lieutenant-general Burgoyne by that route.

That the 31st regiment had been ordered there with Brigadier-general Maclean by Sir Guy Carleton, who had gone up to St. John's, where he had received a letter from the Brigadier, of which the following is an extract:

Extract of a letter from Brigadier-general Maclean to Governor Sir Guy Carleton, dated at Ticonderoga, September 30, 1777.

This morning an express arrived from General Burgoyne with a verbal account of a very smart and long action that happened on the 19th. There is no list of killed and wounded, but what Mr. Philips relates verbally. The action lasted from 12 o'clock till dark; the ground was so very disadvantageous, that only three British regiments were fairly engaged. Our loss is about 150 killed on the spot, and 350 wounded. Nine officers killed, and a great many wounded. It is said we buried 600 of the enemy, and that vast numbers are wounded. We did not gain the field till after dark. Arnold commanded. The rebels retired to their camp, half a league from the field of battle.
[*London Gazette.*

General BURGOYNE's *Instructions to Lieutenant-colonel BAUM.*

The object of your expedition is, to try the affection of the country;

to difconcert the Councils of the enemy; to mount the Rudeffells dragoons; to compleat Petre's corps; and to obtain large fupplies of cattle, horfes, and carriages.

The feveral corps, of which the inclofed is a lift, are to be under your command.

The troops muft take no tents, and what little baggage is carried by the officers, muft be on their own battalion horfes.

You are to proceed from Batten Kill to Arlington, and take poft there till the detachment of the Provincials, under the command of Captain Sherwood fhall join you from the fouthward.

You are then to proceed to Manchefter, where you will again take poft, fo as to fecure the pafs of the mountains, on the road from Manchefter to Rockingham; from thence you will detach the Indians and light troops to the Northward, towards Otter Creek. On their return, and receiving intelligence that no enemy is upon the Connecticut River, you will proceed by the road over the mountains to Rockingham, where you will take poft. This will be the moft diftant part of the expedition, and muft be proceeded upon with caution, as you will have the defiles of the mountains behind you, which might make a retreat difficult. You muft therefore endeavour to be well informed of the force of the enemy's militia in the neighbouring country: fhould you find it may with prudence be effected, you are to remain there while the Indians and light troops are detached up the river; and you are afterwards to defcend the river to Brattleborough, and from that place, by the quickeft march, you are to return by the great road to Albany.

During your whole progrefs, your detachments are to have orders to bring into you all horfes fit to mount the dragoons under your command, or to ferve as battalion horfes for the troops; together with as many faddles and bridles as can be found: the number of horfes requifite, befides thofe neceffary for mounting the regiment of dragoons, ought to be thirteen hundred; if you can bring more for the ufe of the army, it will be fo much the better. Your parties are likewife to bring in waggons and other convenient carriages, with as many draught oxen as will be neceffary to draw them; and all cattle fit for flaughter (milch cows excepted, which are to be left for the ufe of the inhabitants); regular receipts, in the form hereto fubjoined, are to be given in all places, where any of the above articles are taken, to fuch perfons as have remained in their habitations, and otherwife complied with the terms of General Burgoyne's Manifefto; but no receipt to be given to fuch as are known to be acting in the fervice of the rebels. As you will have with you perfons perfectly acquainted with the country, it may perhaps be advifeable to tax the feveral diftricts with the portions of the feveral articles, and limit the hours for the delivery; and fhould you find it neceffary to move before fuch delivery can be made, hoftages of the moft refpectable people fhould be taken to fecure their following you the next day. All poffible means are to be ufed to prevent plundering. As it is probable that Capt. Sherwood, who is already detached to the fouthward, and will join you at Arlington, will drive a confiderable quantity of cattle and horfes to you, you will therefore fend in thefe cattle to the army, with a proper detachment from Petre's corps to cover them, in order to difincumber yourfelf; but you muft always keep the regiment of dragoons compact. The dragoons themfelves muft ride and take care of the horfes of the regiment. Thofe horfes that are deftined for the ufe of the army, muft be tied in ftrings of ten each, in order that one man may lead ten horfes.

D d d   You

You will give the unarmed men of Petre's corps to conduct them, and inhabitants whom ye can trust.

You must always keep your camps in good position, but at the same time where there is pasture; and you must have a chain of centinels around your cattle when grazing.

Colonel Skene will be with you as much as possible, in order to distinguish the good subjects from the bad; to procure the best intelligence of the enemy, and choose those people who are to bring me the accounts of your progress and success.

When you find it necessary to halt a day or two, you must always intrench the camp of the regiment of dragoons, in order never to risque an attack or affront from the enemy.

As you will return with the regiment of dragoons mounted, you must always have a detachment of Captain Frazer's, or Petre's corps, in front of the column, and the same in the rear, in order to prevent your falling into an ambuscade when you march through the woods.

You will use all possible means to make the country believe, that the troops under your command are the advanced corps of the army; and that it is intended to pass to Connecticut, on the road to Boston: you will likewise insinuate, that the main army from Albany is to be joined at Springfield, by a corps of troops from Rhode Island.

It is highly probable, that the corps under Mr. Warner, now supposed to be at Manchester, will retreat before you; but should they, contrary to expectation, be able to collect in great force, and post themselves advantageously, it is left to your discretion to attack them or not; always bearing in mind, that your corps is too valuable to let any considerable loss be hazarded on this occasion.

Should any corps be moved from Mr. Arnold's main army, in order to interrupt your retreat, you are to take as strong a post as the country will afford, and send the quickest intelligence to me; and you may depend upon my making such movements as shall put the enemy between two fires, or otherwise effectually sustain you.

It is imagined the progress of the whole of this expedition may be effected in about a fortnight; but every movement of it must depend on your success in obtaining such supplies of provisions as will enable you to subsist for your return in this army, in case you can get no more. And should not the army be able to reach Albany before your expedition should be compleated, I will find means to send you notice of it, and give your route another direction.

All persons acting in Committees, or any officers under the direction of the Congress, either civil or military, to be made prisoners.

I heartily wish you success, and have the honour to be, Sir,

Your humble servant,

J. BURGOYNE, Lieut. General.

Head Quarters, Aug. 9, 1777.

Fish-kill, Aug. 21.

Extract of a letter from Albany, Aug. 18.

" Since my last I have had the pleasure of seeing Col. Wallers; he nearly agrees with the account I gave you in my last of the engagement he had with the enemy. He however adds, that from all the accounts he could collect from the Indians and inhabitants near the fort, Sir John Johnston fell in the engagement. The killed and wounded of the enemy in both engagements, from all that can be collected, exceeds three hundred. Those that were with General Harkemen all agree, that they killed and wounded that number; for they say, that the Indians were more than half drunk, and shewed themselves more openly than has ever been known, and the regulars marched on very boldly three deep, and our people,

known

known to Indian wars, placed themselves immediately behind trees, and made great havock among them; their cartridges being made up of three buck shot and a bullet. Some say they have seen three fall by a shot; however, the most moderate computation exceeds three hundred. The Indians got a severe drubbing, that the greater part have left them, and are gone home.

" The day before yesterday we received an account that Walter Butler, with fourteen white men, and fourteen Indians, had come to the German Flats, with a manifesto from Barry St. Leger (the General commanding the enemy's army in that quarter) being on a truce to the inhabitants of Tryon Country, signed Daniel Clans and John Butler, exhorting the people to lay down their arms; and a letter from two persons, supposed to be taken prisoners among them, giving an account of the humanity that was shewn to them, and also exhorting the inhabitants tamely to submit. The letter is a forgery, and the former clearly indicates, that they are unable to subdue us by arms, and that their only way to obtain their wishes is, to deceive and mislead the credulous. Mr. Butler paid for his pains, for himself and party were immediately made prisoners.

" An Hessian officer and four privates, deserted from Fort Edward, inform, that about 6000 of the enemy's troops were at Fort Edward. Gen. Arnold is gone to the westward. Gen. Gates is arrived at Albany; his coming is very animating to our army. Great numbers of the back inhabitants are flocking down with their families, having left most part of their substance behind them.—Their case is truly deplorable."

Extract of a letter from a gentlemen in Quebec to his friend at Cork, dated Sept. 6, 1777.

" I shall now give you some little account of the manœuvres, since the opening of the campaign in this province. Some time before Gen. Burgoyne set out, he dispatched Col. St. Leger and Sir John Johnston, the former having about 600 regulars, and the latter 900 savages, of the Upper Nations, both to act in conjunction: their route was by Number 4, to go down the Mohawk River, and to surprize the rebels at Fort Stanwix. Here they were disappointed, as the former were well advised of their coming, and were as well prepared, as you will find hereafter. When they came within 12 miles of that fort, they had advice of a party of 8 or 900 of the rebels coming to reinforce the garrison. The King's troops posted themselves in a very advantageous spot, between them and the fort, and lay in ambush till they came up, when the savages sallied out together with the troops, which so surprised the rebels, that there were more than half of them cut off or taken prisoners.

" Soon after that skirmish, they marched against the fort, and opened some batteries on it, which had little or no effect, they having no more artillery than 2 six pounders, 2 threes, and 2 or three small mortars. The rebels made a sally out, in which time there was a smart fire; they retired with the loss of some men into the fort. There were about 30 savages killed, among who were some of their Chiefs, which struck the others with such terror, that they immediately proposed to Col. St. Leger to raise the siege. A scouting party of the savages that were out, brought advice that a large body of rebels were within two miles of them, and that they should be surrounded. A little after they saw four men go into the fort, through a swamp they before thought impassable.

" This alarmed the troops, and got in order for an immediate retreat, which they effected in the night, leaving every thing behind them. The savages being disappointed of the spoil they expected in the fort,

now

now began to plunder the camp: they began with the officers cafes of liquor, and every thing that came in their way after, nor dare any officer to prevent them, they being more than double their number, and it was with the greateſt precaution they kept them from falling on the remainder of the troops and officers, to put them all to death. Their route was the ſame road as when they advanced. The ſavages finding their proviſion ſhort, took the beſt part of it, and left them, taking to the woods. Col. St. Leger and his men ſuffered much for the neceſſaries of life, as they were four days without any thing to eat or drink. General Burgoyne's foraging party, 30 miles from Saratoga, were defeated with great loſs, and every man would have been cut off but for the ſhelter of the night. Here thirty ſavages were killed, among them two or three of their Chiefs. In a day or two after this, ſome ſavages went to an houſe, where they found a woman and her daughter, a girl of about 18, whom they butchered in a moſt inhuman manner, which coming to the knowledge of General Burgoyne, had the aſſaſſins tried at a Court-Martial, and condemned to be hanged; but remonſtrances from their Chiefs, and promiſes for their future good behaviour, they were pardoned. In a day or two after, moſt of them left the camp, and went to their families, fifty excepted, who came here two days ago, and told General Carleton they were reſtrained by General Burgoyne, and that they would not have gone ſo near this campaign, if they knew they were to have a new father; that they heard from their lands, that many men of their nation were diſaffected, and were ready to take the oppoſite ſide: but they doubted not to be able to bring them over to the King's intereſt.

"All this was nothing but flattery; as they were diſappointed in plunder, they came to get preſents, &c. A good number of the Albany people

joined General Burgoyne's foraging party, and many of them were taken by the enemy, and every priſoner put to death. Nine tenths of the Canadians are ſtrong rebels. There were upwards of 900 on the foraging party, and one half of them did not get back. Since this loſs, Gen. Burgoyne has been obliged to make a ſtand at Saratoga, but advice has been received that they were to be in motion on the 4th inſt. to go towards Albany, be the conſequence what it may.

"Private letters ſay, that the ſkirmiſh with the foraging party happened on the 16th ult. at Van Skoiks Mills, near Bennington. Lieutenant Baume commanded the party, which conſiſted of part of the regiment of Ridſal's dragoons, Capt. Frazer's company, 150 Provincials, and 1000 ſavages. The dragoons were all cut off, the Commander, with moſt of his officers, taken priſoners, 33 ſavages killed, and near 50 wounded, and had not a reinforcement came up, the whole party would have been killed or taken priſoners. On this loſs, ſavages went expreſs acroſs to Col. St. Leger's, which occaſioned them to abandon him, and the few men he brought back had nothing with them but the cloaths on their backs and their firelocks; every article of their camp equipage was left behind, even to their napſacks."

By the Hon. BENEDICT ARNOLD, *Eſq. Major-general and Commander in Chief of the army of the United States of America on the Mohawk River.*

Whereas a certain Barry St. Leger, a Brigadier-general in the ſervice of the ———— George of Great-Britain, at the head of a banditti of robbers, murderers, and traitors, compoſed of ſavages of America, and more ſavage Britons, (among whom is a noted Sir John Johnſton, John Butler, and Daniel Claus) have lately appeared in the frontiers of this State, and have threatened ruin and deſtruction to all

the

the inhabitants of the United States. They have also, by artifice and misrepresentation, induced many of the ignorant and unwary subjects of these States, to forfeit their allegiance to the same, and join with them in their atrocious crimes, and parties of treachery and parricide.

Humanity to those poor deluded wretches, who are hastening blindfold to destruction, induces me to offer them, and all others concerned whether savages, Germans, Americans, or Britons) PARDON, provided they do, within ten days from the date hereof, come in and lay down their arms, sue for protection, and swear allegiance to the United States of America.

But if still blind to their own interest and safety, they obstinately persist in their wicked courses, determined to draw on themselves the first vengeance of Heaven, and of this exasperated country, they must expect no mercy from either.

B. ARNOLD, M. G.

Given under my hand, Head-Quarters, German Flats, 20th August, 1777.

———

Philadelphia, Sept. 3. Congress took into consideration the report of the Committee on the mode of conducting the inquiry into the causes of the evacuation of Ticonderoga and Mount Independence; and into the conduct of the General officers in the Northern department at the time of the evacuation, whereupon,

Resolved, That a Committee of three members of the Congress be appointed and authorized to correspond with public bodies, or private persons, by letter or otherwise, in this and the neighbouring States, in order to collect the clearest and fullest evidence of the state of the army in the Northern department, and also of the state of the troops, military stores and provision at the said post, before and at the time when the evacuation was determined upon.

To call for and examine the Minutes of the Council of war; and to enenquire what orders were given, from time to time, by the Commander in Chief of that department.

To inquire particularly if the barracks and stores, were destroyed, or left standing.

To inquire of the Quarter-master General, and Commissary General, what quantity of provision had been laid up at Ticonderoga, or near it, for the use of the garrison, and what measures were taken or taking for throwing in further supplies.

To inform themselves, as fully as possible, of the number, appointments of the enemy from the time of their landing to the time of evacuating the fort; and also of the number, quality and condition of the garrison, and if any, and what measures were taken to gain intelligence of the strength of the enemy, by the Commander in Chief, or the Commanding Officer at Ticonderoga.

To inquire of the Clothier General what cloathing, from time to time, had been issued for the use of the Northern department; and from other public officers, into the expenditure of such general issues.

To inquire into the number, equipment, and behaviour of the militia, and the term of service for which they were engaged, at and before the time of the evacuation; into the situation and condition of the lines at Ticonderoga, and the fortifications upon Mount Independence. What works had been thrown up by the enemy, what posts they had taken, and the distance of their works; what orders had been given by the Commanding Officer for directing and regulating a retreat, and the manner in which the retreat was conducted; what orders were given relative to the sick, and what care taken of them. Whether any Continental troops, and what number were at Albany, or in the neighbourhood, how long they had been there, and why they were not ordered to Ticonderoga.

To

To inquire into the number and size of cannon, and whether any were removed before the evacuation; the quantity and species of military stores; the state of the arms, both of the Continental soldiers and militia, whether the troops were furnished with bayonets, and whether there were any, and what number of pikes or spears proper for defending lines.

That upon such inquiry and collection of facts, a copy of the whole be transmitted, by the said Committee, to General Washington, and that thereupon he appoint a Court Martial for the trial of General Officers who were in the Northern department when Ticonderoga and Mount Independence were evacuated, agreeable to the rules and articles of war.

August 28. Congress proceeded to the election of the Committee to collect evidence and facts relative to the evacuation of Ticonderoga, &c. and the ballots being taken,

Mr. Laurens, Mr. Richard Henry Lee, and Mr. John Adams, were elected.

Published by order of Congress,

CHARLES THOMSON, Sec.

In Congress, Sept. 1, 1777.

Resolved, That General Washington be directed to appoint a Court of Enquiry relative to the late expedition by General Sullivan against the British forces on Staten-Island.

Copy from the Journals.

WILLIAM CH. HOUSTON, D. Sec.

The public now beholds the fate of that army, on which they were taught to believe, two months ago, that the event of the American war principally depended. What stories did we not hear of a junction to be formed with General Howe, of the New-England provinces to be subdued, of Washington to be got between two fires, and the communication to be cut off between the Northern and Southern parts of America. Let us now mark the event. If Gen. Burgoyne should

winter in Albany, his situation for eight months to come, will be as deplorable as even his enemies could desire. Every load of fuel, and every pound of provision he has in his army, must be obtained by detachments sent into the country; these detachments will be attacked; his quarters will be for ever beat up; his men will be worn down with fatigue, till, by the end of the winter, of a gallant army of 7000 men, with which he marched out of Canada, hardly so many hundreds, probably, will remain. Such will be the case, supposing him to accomplish his intention of getting to Albany. But it is next to a certainty, that he has before this began his retreat into Canada; and his situation, on that supposition, is dreadful to think of. With a victorious army pursuing him in the rear with bodies interposed before him, with the militia of all the New-England provinces, flocking down upon him on all sides; he has a march to perform of a hundred miles, through a country, in which, according to his own account, he was sometimes unable to proceed more than 18 miles in 15 days. The difficulties of moving large bodies in such countries, people, it is to be hoped, will begin at last to understand, and not suppose that an army in a wilderness, is to proceed at the same rate as an ordinary foot-traveller on a turnpike-road. By the time his army gets back into Canada, their losses and distresses may be such as humanity shudders to think of: but if the accounts received be true, of the Provincials having destroyed all the batteaux on Lake George, no man can say whether ever five hundred of them will get back to Canada at all. Such is the fate of the second expedition, which has now been attempted from Canada to Albany; by means of which, as the Ministry have always told us, the reduction of America was principally to be accomplished. The silly account of Burgoyne's goyne's having obtained a victory over Arnold, and killed so many thousand of his men, are fit only to be circulated in the Drawing-room at St. James's. People, at all acquainted with affairs, know the falsehood of such intelligence by the mere consideration of the dates and distances. Thus much we know for certain from General Burgoyne's own accounts, published in the Gazette, that he had lost in actions with the enemy upwards of 1000 men, and at the time of his writing had only four days provisions in advance. The nation will now determine, whether, under the assurances of men who have thus deceived them, they will persist in prosecuting a war, intended originally to subvert the liberties of the Empire, and ending, on every supposition, in the ruin of this country.

———————

The misfortunes and disgraces of our arms, in this unhappy, and insane American war, are not owing to our Generals, Admirals, or other officers, but to the want of ability in our Ministers; or rather, to speak properly, to the misconduct of Lord George Germain. This noblemen went into his present office, where, by his situation, and department, he must have the conducting of the war; and for this express and particular purpose he went into that office. He accepted the seals on the 4th of November, 1775. On the 20th of March, 1776 (near *five* months after, he became the War Minister), General Howe was driven out of Boston. He was necessitated, in the most hazardous season, to go to Halifax, there being no other place open to him. However, he left Commodore Bankes (since dead of a broken heart) at the mouth of Boston harbour, in case any advices should come from England, to send them to Halifax. On the 12th of May he sent an account of the measures he had been obliged to take. This letter he directed to the Earl of Dartmouth. He did not know that Lord Dartmouth was removed from the American office. Lord George Germain had not sent him even a common official notice of his own appointment. General Howe was left to act *as he could*. Lord George sent him no orders; he had prepared no plan of operations for the campaign, although he had now been so many months in office. Foreign troops were hired; an immense expence was incurred; all was hurry and bustle at the Secretary's office; fine speeches, and great promises, were made in Parliament. Still there was no *plan of operations* framed. Every thing was *left to chance*. When the Minister heard of the evacuation of Boston, he did not send any instructions to Gen. Howe; although the General had taken the precaution to station Commodore Bankes, to forward any to him, in case any should come. On the 10th of June, General Howe left Halifax; and on the 29th he arrived at Staten-Island. On the 6th of May the foreign troops, and on the 12th of May Lord Howe, sailed from Portsmouth for America. General Howe was totally ignorant of the designs of the Ministry; and the Ministry were totally ignorant of the designs of General Howe. Here the ill effects began to appear, of there being *no plan of operations* laid down. The foreign troops were obliged to go to Halifax, to know where General Howe was; and Lord Howe, though he sailed after them, was obliged to do the same. When they arrived at Halifax, they were told General Howe was gone to the neighbourhood of New-York. The army and Admiral proceeded like the first adventurers, along the coast of America, looking out for a place to land at, in a great, populous, and hospitable country, that but yesterday (as it were) was all our own; but which, the mad policy of an ignorant and infamous Ministry, had

had made defperate. On the 12th of August, the fleets and armies all joined at Staten-Ifland. The feafon being fo far advanced, nothing was done this campaign, but taking New-York. It was not General Howe's fault, that more was not done, but the fault of the Minifter, who acted upon no fyftem, who laid down no plan; who left every thing to chance. Great promifes were again made in Parliament; America was to be conquered in 1777; and the army being there, and on the fpot, the conqueft would go on moft rapidly. Lord George Germain, it may be prefumed, by this time, faw his error in not having laid down *fome plan of operations.* He conceived a defign of marching through the country, from Canada to New-York. This was his *firft,* and the *only plan* he has formed fince he came into office. Of the *folly* of this plan, the fact is recent, and undeniable. It has been rendered abortive. But fuppofe it to have been fuccefsful, of what *ufe* was it? General Burgoyne might be faid to have marched acrofs the country; but it could not be faid, that he had *conquered* an inch of it. But the plan was imperfect; which fhews the *want of wifdom* in the framer. To have enfured the fuccefs of it, General Howe fhould have had orders to go up the Hudfon's River. In that cafe the two armies might, and in all probability would, have met. But General Howe had no fuch orders: he was left to himfelf, to act as he pleafed. And now, the imperfection of the plan being obvious, and it having mifcarried through want of wifdom in the framer, the *blame* is thrown upon General Howe. Every runner, from Mr. Hans Stanley downward, are violent againft the Howes. Even Lord Mansfield abufes the Howes. This is the *old trick,* of throwing the blame, that juftly belongs to the Miniftry, upon the unfortunate officers. As to the expedition againft Carolina,

under Sir Peter Parker and General Clinton, and the expedition on the Mohawk River, under Colonel St. Leger, the man deferves to be fet down as a lunatic, who contrived them. And as to the operations of General Howe, the feafon is too far advanced for them to be attended with any material confequences, except giving further inftructions to the Americans in the art of war.

———————

It is curious to recollect the fucceffion of minifterial falfhoods, with which England, and all Europe has, from year to year, been deluded. At the paffing of the Bofton Port Bill, we were told that Bofton would be immediately at the Minifter's feet; that the other towns of Maffachufetts Bay would defert their capital, and rejoice at the profpect of increafing their own trade, at the expence of Bofton. When the contrary of this happened, when not only the whole province of Maffachufetts Bay, but all New England, efpoufed the caufe of Bofton, we were then told that the New Englanders *were hated* by the *Southern* Colonies, and would be deferted by them. When this too proved falfe, and when it was refolved to affemble a Congrefs, we were for feveral months affured, that the members would never meet; when they had met, we were promifed that they would quarrel and feparate; and when they had formed their non-importation and non-exportation agreement, we were told that thofe agreements would never be obferved. When it was found that they were moft ftrictly obferved, and that hoftilities were likely to commence, we were told that the cowardly Americans would never dare to affemble in arms, and that two Britifh regiments would, in two months, march through and fubdue all the rebellious colonies, when at *Lexington, Concord, and Bunker's Hill,* we had woeful experience to the contrary; when

twenty

twenty British regiments were buried near twelve months in Boston, and finally driven out of it, we were gravely told, that General Howe had *only changed his position*, and gone to *Halifax in his way to New-York*; that New-York was the place from whence all America would be speedily subdued; when New-York was obtained, and when General Howe's operations from thence were frustrated, viz. those against New England at the *White Plains*, and those against Philadelphia at *Trenton, Prince-town, &c.* we were then told, that the fleet, the army, the German and British reinforcements, &c. had arrived at New-York too late in the season; but that being now all on the spot, ready for early action, Philadelphia at least would be taken in the ensuing April, and all America subdued before August. April and May however passed, and Philadelphia was unmolested. In June the reinforcements and supplies from Europe being arrived, an attempt was made to advance to Philadelphia; it was frustrated, and the British army driven entirely out of Jersey, where they had suffered so much to maintain a footing during the winter. It having been thus discovered that New-York was not the proper place from which to conquer America, we were told that another *change of position* would be useful; that the Quakers of Philadelphia had changed their religion, and taken up arms; and that the British army must go up the Delaware by sea and join the Quakers, and put an end to the Congress and the rebellion at once. When General and Lord Howe had sailed up the Delaware, and found it necessary to sail *down* again, because there were not quite 5000 Quakers in arms, it was then discovered that the best way to preserve the health of an army, was to croud the soldiers into the holds and transports, feed them on salted provisions, and send them on a sea voyage for four or five weeks, in

the hot months of July and August; and that the direct way to Philadelphia was to sail from the Delaware southwards to Virginia, and then northwards up Chesapeak Bay through Maryland. When this shall be done, and when the British army annoyed by Washington's forces, and by autumnal agues, &c. finds another *charge of position* expedient, we shall then be told that *Georgia* is the place, from which, above all others, America can be best over-run and subdued. I say Georgia, because every other place between that and Halifax has been already tried, either by General Howe, or by General Clinton and Sir Peter Parker. In reflecting upon this regular succession of Court tales and promises, one is at a loss whether he should most admire the impudence of those who propagate, or the folly of those who believe them; and who are still ready to believe, that the Colonies will yet be subdued, after having three years baffled all our efforts, having formed and firmly established their respective constitutions of government, trained and disciplined their inhabitants, inlisted and collected a large regular army to serve during the war, procured immense supplies of artillery, arms, ammunition, cloathing, &c. and become strong enough in that country, and at that distance, *to resist all Europe*.

Admiralty-Office, Oct. 6, 1777.
Copy of a letter from Lieutenant BOURCHIER, *commanding his Majesty's ship Druid, to Mr.* STEPHENS, *Secretary of the Admiralty.*
Druid, at Spithead, Oct. 3, 1777.

" Sir,

" I beg you will please to acquaint the Right Hon. the Lords Commissioners of the Admiralty, I arrived at this place at nine o'clock this morning, with his Majesty's sloop Druid under my command, under the directions of the Hon. Capt. William Finch,

E e e

Finch, of his Majesty's ship Camel; and to inform their Lordships, that on the 4th of September, in the latitude 40. 33. N. longitude 50. 17. W. at half past four in the evening, we discovered a strange sail on our larboard quarter, bearing West, and steering for us: we were then (from the irregularity of the fleet) about five miles distant from the Camel, to windward, repeating the signal for the convoy to go under the Camel's stern, and obliging those ships to bear down; the Weazle at a great distance to leeward, and out of our sight.

" We cleared ship for action, and turned all hands to quarters. At five o'clock she came within pistol shot, when I could plainly perceive her to be a rebel privateer, mounting 38 or 40 guns, her decks and tops full of men; she hailed, and desired us to strike to the honour of the Congress's colours, hoisted her ensign, and began to engage. The first broadside sent a shot through Captain Carteret's thigh bone, and killed the master.

" I then took the command on the quarter deck, and continued the action. At half past five she came close alongside, and kept an irregular, but very hot firing. At six she made sail a-head. I attempted to do the same, and keep her broadside on, but the shattered condition of the rigging rendered the sails almost useless to the ship. As the had-sails only were of service, we edged away, and kept her nearly on our bow till twenty minutes past six. She then had the wind abaft, sheered off, hauled down her colours, and made sail. I attempted to wear ship, and rake her; but the rigging being entirely shot to pieces, could not bring her round. I then tried to make what sail I could, and pursue the enemy, but found most of the masts and yards wounded, and the rigging, &c. as in the inclosed defect of the ship, with four feet ten inches water in the hold.

" At half past seven we brought to, with our foresail and mizen on our larboard tack, to plug the shot holes between wind and water, clear the wreck, and pump the ship out.

" I then perceived another rebel privateer laying to, bearing S. S. W. six or seven miles off, and by her appearance I suppose she mounted about 20 guns. The Camel was then in chace about two or three miles distant; soon after the Weazle spoke to us, and gave chace also.

" I am sorry to inform their Lordships, that the first broadside which was fired killed the Master and wounded Capt. Carteret in the left thigh, of which he died the next morning, after undergoing an amputation. I should do the greatest injustice was I to omit acquainting their Lordships, that although Capt. Carteret was so dangerously wounded, it was with great difficulty he could be persuaded to quit the deck: his fortitude and intrepidity was such, that he wished to have remained on deck to see the service performed; but the loss of blood was so great, it was absolutely necessary to carry him to the surgeon. And I should be wanting in gratitude and justice, if I omitted to mention the remarkable bravery of the officers, seamen, and marines, during the action, and the alertness they shewed, with the fatigue they went through to put the ship in a state of service, when action was hourly expected; for three days and nights the rebels were in sight.

" Inclosed you have a list of the killed and wounded.

I have the honour to be, Sir, Your most obedient humble servant,
JOHN BOURCHIER."

A list of men killed on board his Majesty's sloop Druid the 4th of September, 1777, in action with a rebel privateer, viz.

Mr. John Wilson, Master; John Crambron, seaman; George Baker, Simon Salisbury, Lawrence Macely, marines; and Henry Hallcott, a boy.

Died

Died of their wounds since action.

Peter Carteret, Esq. Commander; George Smith, invalid; George White, marine, on the 5th of September; Patrick Lowry, seaman, on the 19th of September; and John Fennigan, seamen, on the 21st.

Wounded.

Mr. John Wiggan, Master Mate; Mr. James Nicholson, Lieutenant of marines; John Plumbley, James Connel, James Stanton, Daniel Butler, Peter Chapman, John Scully, Richard Austin, William Wallbrook, Charles Robertson, James Thomas, Thomas Connolly, and John Wood, seamen; Mr. Nicholas Poulson, Surgeon's Mate; Thomas Dunn, James Miller, Thomas Allbut, James Murray, Robert Osborn, marines; and Samuel Ketson, a boy.

JOHN BOURCHIER.

Extract of a letter from Commodore THOMPSON, *to the* MARINE COMMITTEE *of* CONGRESS, *dated on board the Raleigh, at sea, Sept. 28, 1777, in latitude 49. 35. North, long. 13. 13. West, from London, viz.*

" Honourable Gentlemen,

" I have the honour to acquaint you, that we had a fine passage off of the coast of America. The third day after sailing I fell in with and took a small schooner from New-York, bound to Halifax, in ballast, excepting 20 barrels of flour, 275 Spanish milled dollars, 137 counterfeited bills, of 30 dollars each, in imitation of the bills emitted by Congress, May the 10th, 1775; and 40 *counterfeited* bills, of seven dollars each, imitating the Massachusetts sword-in-hand money; the whole making 4390 dollars, which I shall commit to the flames, after preserving samples. The schooner being of little value we burnt her. Next day we fell in with a Bermudas vessel from Halifax, which I released after supplying the Captain with provisions, which they had refused to sell him, or permit him to carry out of Nova Scotia."

" At day-light, Sept. 2, we took a snow called the Nancy, Capt. Hooper, from St. Vincent's, being part of the Windward Island fleet, which had out sailed her the day before. Having by this capture discovered the situation of the fleet, and found that they were convoyed by the Camel, Druid, Weazel, and Grasshopper ships of war (the former a very large lofty ship, carrying twenty-two 12 pounders)." The Commodore continues, " After dispatching the snow for the first safe port in the United States, we made sail in quest of the fleet, and next morning discovered them from the mast head; at sun-set we were near enough to distinguish the leading ship, as well as their number, which was sixty sail, bearing East by North; the wind being then West, I made a signal, as being one of the fleet left astern (for I had possessed myself of the signal from the prize). I hailed Capt. Hinman, and told him my intention was to run into the fleet in the morning, and attack the convoy, which I thought we were able to destroy; I therefore ordered him to keep close under the Raleigh's stern, until we come alongside the Commodore, which ship we would both attack. Unluckily in the night, the wind shifted to North; the fleet then hauled up close to the wind, which brought us to leeward; in the morning it came to blow fresh; at day-light we saw the body of the fleet bearing about N. E. at two or three leagues distance, steering East North East: we made sail, and the Raleigh soon fetched up to the fleet, under double reefed topsails; but the Alfred being tender-sided, could not carry sail, and therefore fell a great way to leeward, and astern. I could not take in any sail, for fear of being discovered to be a strange ship; we there-

fore

fore kept our sails shaking in the wind, thinking the Alfred might come up; but Capt. Hinman made signal that his ship was overpressed with sail; seeing no chance of his coming up, and being fearful of being discovered, I determined to make sail, and stand into the fleet, and take my chance alone. While we were laying to, most of the merchant ships had got a-head into the fleet; however, I hauled in and passed a few of them, and desired them to go under the Commodore's stern. By this they took us to be some British frigate which had joined the fleet. I stood on close to the wind, making for one of the ships of war which was to the windward of all the fleet, repeating the Commodore's signals. Our ports were down, and our guns housed, and we shot up alongside, within pistol shot; then we up sails, out guns, hoisted Continental colours, and bid them strike to the Thirteen United States: sudden surprize threw them into confusion, and their sails flew all aback; upon which we complimented them with a gun for each State (a whole broadside into their hull); there was a great swell, which made our shots uncertain; however, they seemed to tell pretty well; the enemy then returned the fire, and the action commenced. Our second broadside was aimed at their rigging, which had its desired effect: our shot cut away their topsail sheets, topsail yards, part of the main yard, braces, bowlines, and at once disabled and rendered them incapable of steering the ship, or making sail, towards the Commodore, who lay to the leeward. In about a quarter of an hour *all hands quitted quarters on board the British man of war; we cleared her decks totally; not a man was seen, nor a gun fired on board her, for twenty minutes before we left her. She lay like a log alongside of us, entirely at the mercy of our shot, which flew very thick; we fired twelve broad-*

sides, besides a constant fire from our musquetry; we were alongside of her forty-five minutes; when we left her, she seemed to be water logged, and in a most shattered condition. During this little engagement, my officers and men behaved with the greatest fortitude and resolution, particularly the green hands. I was very glad of this little opportunity to try the men and guns, both of which exceeded my expectations. We received but little damage; one of the enemy's shot went through our side, and several stuck in it; they fired high, and shot away some of our running rigging; their grape shot and musquetry made several holes through our sails. If it could be supposed that they had any fixed intention after such a surprize, it was to disable us, that the other ship might come up to their assistance. My intention was to sink the enemy's ship, if I could not bring her off, and I should have effectually sunk her in a few minutes more, could we have staid. Our firing had thrown the fleet into confusion; a squall prevented them from seeing us at first; when it cleared up, one was running one way, and one another: some upon the wind, and some before it: their Commodore, and the other ships of force, tacked and stood right for us; but had not the wind favoured him, and we drifted to leeward, he could not have fetched us, and I should certainly have sunk the ship: however I staid by her, until he came pretty near, and we being in danger of being surrounded, I made sail and ran down to the Alfred, who was lying about four miles to the leeward. Capt. Hinman, on seeing me engaged, had hauled up his courses, and hoisted Continental colours; when we had got pretty near the Alfred, I took in top gallant sails, and shortened sail to wait for the British Commodore, but he soon tacked and stood again into the fleet; it was then about sun-set;

we

we have since challenged him for three days succeſſively to come out of his fleet, and engage us, but he declines the challenge : himſelf and the other armed ſhips keep cloſe together, a little aſtern of the fleet, and fine weather favours them ; we wait for a ſtorm, and then if any advantage of-fers, intend to make the beſt uſe of it ; but we muſt not venture among them as they are now prepared, nei-ther can we truſt to the Alfred's ſailing. Had ſhe been a ſtiff ſhip, and ſailed equally well with the Raleigh, we ſhould in all probability have deſtroy-ed the convoy, and diſperſed the whole fleet, badly manned as we are, having only 180 men, chiefly green hands : I cannot truſt to working the ſhip were I to go into the fleet ; but if the enemy will attack where we have room, we are able to defend ourſelves, or deſtroy them. I could at firſt have cut off ſeveral of the mer-chantmen, but muſt by that means have been diſcovered, and thereby have loſt our chance at the King's ſhips ; *and I am determined never to war againſt the merchants, where I have an opportunity of waring againſt the King.* I ſhould have preferred ſinking that ſhip to the richeſt capture in the fleet. My officers are invariably of the ſame ſentiments. Our loſs in the action was only one boy killed and another wounded, excepting that the firſt Lieutenant received a ſlight wound in the thigh. Our rigging and ſails were damaged, but are now in good repair.

I am, Hon. Gentlemen,
Your moſt obedient humble ſervant,
(Signed)   THOMAS THOMPSON."

Liſt of Ships and Veſſels taken by American Privateers, continued from page 108.

Ships Names and Maſters.	From and to	
Active, Clarke,	Quebec to England,	retaken.
Active, Fairbone,	Ireland to New-York.	
Adventure, Noinſkley,	Leeward Iſlands to Halifax.	
Adventure,	Newfoundland to Bilboa.	
Ann Suſanna, Johnſon,	Jamaica to London.	
Anna, Skilton,	Briſtol to Dominica.	
Annabella, Ladd,	Corke to Jamaica.	
Apalachicola, Ogilvie,	London to St. Auguſtine.	
Apollo, Collins,	Corke to the Weſt-Indies.	
Argo, Smith,	London to New York.	
Argus, Donaldſon,	Barbadoes to Quebec,	retaken.
Ariadne, Cox,	Antigua to Londonderry.	
Arthur and Betty, Prittijohn,	on the Banks of Newfoundland.	
Athol, Wadie,	Halifax to Dominica.	
Bedford, De Goris,	Cowes for Quebec.	
Belliſle, Ribble, M'Gomery,	From Whitehaven.	
Betſey, Toleman,	Leeward Iſlands to New-York, retaken.	
Betſey, Waring,	Barbadoes to Quebec,	retaken.
Betſey,	Oporto to Briſtol.	
Betſey, Horrick,	on the Banks of Newfoundland.	
Betſey, Keyhoe,	Dublin to Jamaica.	
Betty, Darcy,	Dublin to Antigua.	
Betſey, Muir,	belonging to Antigua.	
Bloſſom,	cut out of Kingſton Harbour.	
Bonetta, Fox,	on the Banks of Newfoundland.	
Bonne Intelligence, Bienvenu,	Rotterdam to Guernſey.	

Brig,

Ships Names and Masters.	From and to	
Brig,	London to Limerick,	worth 15,000l.
Britannia, Crockatt,	London to Tobago.	
Brothers, Herbert,	Liverpool to Jamaica.	
Brothers, Atkinson,	Newry to Antigua,	ransomed.
Brothers, Murphy,	London to Chepstow,	burnt.
Brothers, Kelly,	Dublin to Oporto.	
Brunswick, Service,	Glasgow to Newfoundland.	
Catherine, Truman,	Jamaica to London,	retaken.
Catherine, Scallion,	Dublin to Antigua.	
Cæsar, Tolias,	West-Indies to New-York.	
Cæsar, O'Brien,	London to Barbadoes.	
Cæsar, Sedgley,	Newfoundland to New-York.	
Charlotte, Paxton,	Jamaica to Bristol.	
Charming Jenny, Walker,	Memel to Workington.	
Charming Polly,	Jamaica to London.	
Charming Sally, Hill,	Malaga to London.	
Christian, Dourich,	belonging to St. Vincent's.	
Christian, Danett,	West Indies to Ireland.	
Christie, Hall.		
Clarendon, Crowley,	Jamaica to London.	
Cleveland, Norman,	London to Halifax.	
Clifton, Obryan,	Jamaica to Quebec.	
Conde Arande, Wakeham,	St. John's to West-Indies.	
Cornwall, Hardcastle,	Antigua to London.	
Crawfurd, Alexander,	Greenock to St. Ubes.	
Devonshire, Fisher,	Tortola to England.	
Diana,	Halifax to Newfoundland.	
Dorothy, M'Donough,	Bristol to Jamaica.	
Dover, Walsby,	Oporto to London,	retaken.
Dublin, Durham,	Halifax to the West-Indies.	
Eastley, Austin,	Newfoundland to Oporto.	
Edward and Ann, Brown,	Koningsberg to Liverpool.	
Eleanor, Bailey,	on the Banks of Newfoundland.	
Elizabeth, Byrne,	Liverpool to West-Indies.	
Elizabeth, Douting,	belonging to Corke.	
Emperor of Germany,	Bristol to West-Indies,	retaken.
Endeavour, Mellish,	London to Spain.	
Esther, a victualler,	Corke to New-York.	
Expedition, Braithwaite,	Whitehaven to Norway.	sunk.
	———— ————,	retaken.
Fanny, Berwick,	Christiana to London,	burnt.
Favourite, Grave,	Morpeth to Dublin,	sunk.
Flora, Heberdine,	West-Indies to New-York.	
Flora, a schooner,	belonging to Jamaica.	
Fly, Charter,	Corke to New-York.	
Fly, Hawry,	Alicant to Newfoundland,	retaken.
Fowey, Channel,	Waterford to Halifax.	
Fox, an English frigate,	in America,	retaken.
Friends, Crediton,	West-Indies to New-York.	
Friendship, Taylor,	Bay of Roses to London.	

Friendship,

Ships Names and Masters.	*From and to*	
Friendship, Esthill,	New-York to London.	
Fox, Forley,	London to Africa.	
Free Mason, Stevens,	West-Indies to New-York.	
Fortune, Kinguen,	London to Cadiz,	a rich French ship.
Gascoyne, Thoburn,	Africa to West-Indies.	
General Payne, Adams,	St. Kitt's to London.	
Grace, Woodley,	Jamaica to Liverpool,	retaken.
Greystock, Clerk,	Workington to Dublin,	funk.
Grog, Cocken,	Corke to Antigua,	with provisions.
Hanover Planter, Luncy,	Jamaica to London.	
Harmony, Friendship,	Corke to New-York.	
Harriott, Wilson,	Antigua to London,	ship restored.
Hermit, M'Dowland,	Jamaica to London.	
Honour, Casey,	Corke to Newfoundland.	
Jamaica, Watts,	Jamaica to London.	
James, Russel,	from Glasgow,	funk.
Jane,	belonging to Jersey.	
Jane, Wallace,	London to Tortola.	
Janet,	belonging to Irvine.	
Jason, Hitchinson,	Whitehaven to Petersburgh.	
Jasper, Cuthbut,	London to New-York,	with stores.
Jenny and Peggy, Howe,	Whitehaven to Ireland,	funk.
Jenny and Sally, Drummond,	Glasgow to Norway.	
Jenny, Russel,	on the Banks of Newfoundland.	
Jenny, Wood,	Falmouth to Quebec,	retaken.
Industry, Bodmin,	belonging to Jersey,	retaken.
John, Wilkie,	Glasgow to St. Ubes,	restored.
John and Thomas, Yowart,	Norway to Dublin,	retaken.
Judith, Lesthouse,	London to St. Augustine.	
Juno, Barnes,	Newfoundland to Poole.	
Kinnoul, Ramsay,	Barcelona to Stettin.	
Lark, Whalley,	Corke to Barbadoes.	
Larke, Kentisbeer,	belonging to Poole.	
La Ville de Bayonne, Regnier,	Topsham to Naples,	a French ship.
Le Lorging,	Yarmouth to Genoa.	
Leonara,	from Mountsbay,	plundered.
Little Betsey, Freeman,	London to Venice.	
Littleton, Johnson,	London to New-York,	
Lively Martindale,	———— ————	retaken.
Lively, Morris,	Antigua to New-York,	dismissed.
Lovely Peggy, Fitzgerald,	Waterford to Newfoundland.	
Lucy, Nichols,	Liverpool to Jamaica.	
Lucy, Watson,	Corke to Quebec.	retaken.
Lydia, Evans,	Liverpool to Jamaica.	
Manning, Brewer,	Jamaica to London.	
Margaret and Mary, Izat,	Halifax to London.	
Maria,	Lynn to Bristol,	burnt.
Maria, Wames,	———— ————,	burnt.
Mary, Meudall,	Cadiz to Newfoundland.	
Mary and Betty, Thornton,	Liverpool to Banishannon.	
Mary, Price,	Newfoundland to a market.	

Mercury.

Ships Names and Masters.	From and to	
Mercury, Rowland,	Leith to Gibraltar.	
Merlin, Taylor,	Greenock to the West-Indies.	
Mercury, Pearce,	Newfoundland to a market.	
Molly, Bouschel,	Greenock to Milthorp.	
Nancy, Gibbs,	Pensacola to Jamaica,	retaken
Nancy, Hooper,	St. Vincent's to London.	
Nancy, Laury,	Jamaica to London,	retaken.
Nancy, Payne,	Malaga to Dublin,	retaken.
Nautillus, Coney,	Greenland to England.	
New Exeter, Manning,	Malaga to London.	
Norman,	London to Halifax.	
Northampton, Gray,	belonging to Lynn.	
Patty, Green,	—————— ——————	ransomed.
Pegginwall,	belonging to Belfast.	
Peggy, Attride,	Corke to Liverpool.	
Peter, Salmon,	Newfoundland to Bilboa,	plundered.
Polly, Thompson,	Leeward Islands to New-York,	with rum.
Prince Masserano, Warren,	Bergen to Venice.	
Prince George,	Whitehaven to Jamaica,	retaken.
Prince George, White,	Bristol to Madeira.	
Priscilla, Cassida,	Sligo to Liverpool,	retaken.
Property, Hill,	South-Carolina to Nantz,	retaken.
Patsey, Handy,	on the Banks of Newfoundland.	
Queen of Portugal, Tibby,	Corke to Lisbon.	
Rebecca, Witherington,	Corke to the West-Indies.	
Rebecca, Bell,	Liverpool to Limerick.	
Rebecca, Calton,	St. Kitt's to London.	
Restoration, Robbins,	Quebec to Oporto,	retaken.
Rhoda, Butcher,	London to Venice.	
Richard, Ledger,	Workington to Dublin,	sunk.
Rising Sun, Salter,	Liverpool to Halifax.	
Rose, Lewis,	Africa to Jamaica,	with slaves.
Royal Bounty,	Greenland to Leith.	
Sally, Mole,	New-York to Barbadoes.	
Sally, Simpson,	—————— ——————	retaken.
Sally, Cleland,	Lancaster to Antigua,	retaken.
Sally, M'Croskie,	Halifax to Waterford.	
Sally, Rose,	Philadelphia to Nantz,	retaken.
Sally, Marshall,	Dartmouth to St. John's.	
Samuel, Roberts,	West-Indies to New-York,	rum and sugar.
Schooner, a, Atkins,	from New-York,	with money.
Sir William Erskine,	Clyde to New-York,	retaken.
Sisters, Graham,	Africa to the West-Indies.	
Seberio,	Honduras to London,	plundred.
Sophia, Ayres,	Leeward Islands to London,	retaken.
St. George, Moore,	Africa to Grenada,	450 slaves, ivory, gold dust, &c.
Success, Crook,	London to West-Indies,	retaken.
Swift, Edwards,	Dublin to Jamaica.	
Thames, Hill,	Oporto to Hull,	retaken.
Thomas, Hall,	Jamaica to New-York.	

Thomas

Ships Names and Masters.	From and to	
Thomas and Elizabeth, Watson,	Peterburgh to Leith,	burnt.
Thomas and Mary. Dorrefter,	belonging to Waterford,	retaken.
Three Brothers, Johnson,	Newfoundland for Barbadoes,	retaken.
Three Sifters, Malone,	Corke to Lifbon.	
Tranfport fhip,	London to New-York,	with 80 Heffians.
Triton, Bertram,	Jerfey to Honduras,	
Triumph, Cole,	Ireland to the Mediterranean.	
True Briton, Venture,	belonging to London.	
Two Friends, Birch,	Halifax to Louifburgh.	
Two Friends, M'Gregor,	Cadiz to New-York.	
Venus, Wilkes,	Greenland to Liverpool.	
Unicorn, Mafters,	Honduras to London.	
Union, Bell,	Miffifippi to Dublin.	
Unity, Worth,	Lifbon to Corke.	
Weymouth Packet Boat,	Weft-Indies to Falmouth.	
William, Callaghan,	Corke to Bourdeaux.	
William and Mary, Platt.		
William, Wadden,	belonging to Wexford.	
William and Polly, Simmonds,	Newfoundland to London.	
Wolfe, Marfhal,	Jamaica to Glafgow.	
Young Jacob, Cook,	Newfoundland to a market.	

The LONDON GAZETTE *Extraordinary.*

Whitehall, December 2, 1777.

Yesterday morning Major Cuyler, first Aid de Camp to Gen. Sir William Howe, arrived from Philadelphia, with difpatches to Lord George Germain, of which the following are copies and extracts:

Copy of a letter from General Sir WILLIAM HOWE *to Lord* GEORGE GERMAIN, *dated Head-quarters, German-town, Oct.* 10, 1777.

My Lord,

In my laft difpatch of the 30th of Auguft I had the honour to advife your Lordfhip of the army having landed on the weft fide of Elk River, and of its being afterwards divided into two columns; one under the command of Lord Cornwallis at the head of Elk; and the other commanded by Lieutenant-general Knyphaufen at Cecil Court-houfe: I am therefore to give your Lordfhip an account of the operations from that period, wherein will be included two general actions, in both of which I have the fatisfaction to premife, that

fuccefs has attended his Majefty's arms.

On the 3d of September, Major-general Grant with fix battalions remaining at the head of Elk to preferve the communication with the fleet, the two columns joined at Pencadder, lying four miles to the eaftward of Elk on the road to Chriftien-bridge. In this day's march the Heffian and Anfpach chaffeurs, and the 2d battalion of light infantry, who were at the head of Lord Cornwallis's column, fell in with a chofen corps of 1000 men from the enemy's army, advantageoufly pofted in the woods, which they defeated with the lofs of only two officers wounded, three men killed, and 19 wounded, when that of the enemy was not lefs than 50 killed, and many more wounded.

On the 6th, Major-general Grant, after Capt. Duncan, who fuperintended the naval department, had deftroyed fuch veffels and ftores as could not be removed from the head of Elk, joined the army.

The whole marched on the 8th by Newark,

F f f

Newark, and encamped that evening in the township of Hokessen, upon the road leading from Newport to Lancaster, at which first place General Washington had taken post, having his left to Christien-creek, and his front covered by Red Clay-creek.

The two armies in this situation being only four miles apart, the enemy moved early in the night of the 8th, by the Lancaster road, from Wilmington, and about ten o'clock next morning crossed Brandywine-creek at Chad's-ford, taking post on the heights on the eastern side of it.

On the 9th in the afternoon, Lieutenant-general Knyphausen marched with the left of the army to New-garden and Kennet's-square, while Lord Cornwallis with the right moved to Hokessen's Meeting-house, and both joined the next morning at Kennet's-square.

On the 11th, at day-break, the army advanced in two columns, the right commanded by Lieutenant-general Knyphausen, consisting of four Hessian battalions under Major-general Stern, the first and second brigades of British, three battalions of the 71st regiment, the Queen's American rangers, and one squadron of the 16th dragoons under Major-general Grant, having with them six medium twelve pounders, four howitzers, and the light artillery belonging to the brigades. This column took the direct road to Chad's-ford, seven miles distant from Kennet's-square, and arrived in front of the enemy about ten o'clock, skirmishing most part of the march with their advanced troops, in which the Queen's rangers, commanded by Capt. Wemyss of the 40th regiment, distinguished themselves in a particular manner.

The other column under the command of Lord Cornwallis, Major-general Grey, Brigadier-generals Matthew and Agnew, consisting of the mounted and dismounted chasseurs, two squadrons of the 16th dragoons, two battalions of light infantry, two battalions of British, and three of Hessian grenadiers, two battalions of guards, the 3d and 4th brigades, with four light 12 pounders, and the artillery of the brigades, marched about twelve miles to the forks of the Brandywine, crossed the first branch at Trimbles-ford, and the second at Jeffery's-ford, about two o'clock in the afternoon, taking from thence the road to Dilworth, in order to turn the enemy's right at Chad's-ford.

General Washington having intelligence of this movement about noon, detached Gen. Sullivan to his right with near 10,000 men, who took a strong position on the commanding ground above Birmingham church, with his left near to the Brandywine, both flanks being covered by very thick woods, and his artillery advantageously disposed.

As soon as this was observed, which was about four o'clock, the King's troops advanced in three columns, and upon approaching the enemy, formed the line with the right towards the Brandywine; the guards being upon the right, and the British grenadiers upon their left, supported by the Hessian grenadiers in a second line: to the left of the centre were the two battalions of light infantry, with the Hessian and Anspach chasseurs, supported by the 4th brigade. The 3d brigade formed the reserve.

Lord Cornwallis having formed the line, the light infantry and chasseurs began the attack; the guards and grenadiers instantly advanced from the right, the whole under a heavy train of artillery and musquetry; but they pushed on with an impetuosity not to be sustained by the enemy, who falling back into the woods in their rear, the King's troops entered with them, and pursued closely for near two miles.

After this success a part of the enemy's

my's right took a second position in a wood about half a mile from Dilworth, from whence the 2d light infantry and chasseurs soon dislodged them, and from this time they did not rally again in force.

The 1st British grenadiers, the Hessian grenadiers, and guards, having in the pursuit got entangled in very thick woods, were no further engaged during the day.

The 2d light infantry, 2d grenadiers, and 4th brigade, moved forward a mile beyond Dilworth, where they attacked a corps of the enemy that had not been before engaged, and were strongly posted to cover the retreat of their army by the roads from Chad's-ford to Chester and Wilmington; which corps not being forced until after it was dark, when the troops had undergone much fatigue, in a march of 17 miles, besides what they supported since the commencement of the attack, the enemy's army escaped a total overthrow, that must have been the consequence of an hour's more day-light.

The 3d brigade was not brought into action, but kept in reserve in the rear of the 4th brigade, it not being known before it was dark how far Lieutenant-general Knyphausen's attack had succeeded; nor was there an opportunity of employing the cavalry.

Lieutenant-general Knyphausen, as had been previously concerted, kept the enemy amused in the course of the day with cannon, and the appearance of forcing the ford, without intending to pass it until the attack upon the enemy's right should take place: accordingly when it began, Major-general Grant crossed the ford with the 4th and 5th regiments; and the 4th regiment passing first forced the enemy from an intrenchment and battery, where three brass field-pieces and a five and half inch howitzer were taken, that had been placed there to command the ford. The enemy made little stand on that side

after the work was carried, when the guards appearing on their right flank, the retreat became general, but darkness coming on before Lieutenant-general Knyphausen's corps could reach the heights, there was no farther action on that side.

From the most correct accounts, I conclude the strength of the enemy's army opposed to Lieutenant-general Knyphausen and Lord Cornwallis was not less than 15,000 men, a part of which retired to Chester, and remained there that night, but the greater body did not stop until they reached Philadelphia. Their loss was considerable in officers killed and wounded, and they had about 300 men killed, 600 wounded, and near 400 made prisoners.

The loss on the side of his Majesty's troops, and the ordnance, ammunition, and stores, taken from the enemy, will appear in the inclosed returns.

The army laid this night on the field of battle, and on the 12th Major-general Grant, with the 1st and 2d brigades, marched to Concord. Lord Cornwallis, with the light infantry and British grenadiers, joined him next day, and proceeded to Ashtown, within five miles of Chester.

On the same day (the 13th) the 71st regiment was detached to Wilmington, where the enemy had thrown up works, both to the land and to the river, with seven pieces of cannon in the latter; but these works being evacuated, Major M'Donell took possession of the place without opposition, and made Mr. M'Kinley, the new appointed President of the lower counties on Delaware, his prisoner.

On the 14th, Lieutenant-colonel Loos, with the combined battalion of Khal's brigade, escorted the wounded and sick to Wilmington, whither the battalion of Mirbach was sent two days afterwards to join them.

The army moved in two columns towards Goshen on the 16th; and

intelligence

intelligence being received upon the march that the enemy was advancing upon the Lancaster road, and were within five miles of Goshen, it was immediately determined to push forward the two columns and attack them; Lord Cornwallis to take his route by Goshen Meeting-house, and Lieutenant-general Knyphausen by the road to Downing-town.

The two divisions proceeded on their march, but a most violent fall of rain setting in, and continuing the whole day and night without intermission, made the intended attack impracticable.

The 1st light infantry, at the head of Lord Cornwallis's column, meeting with a part of the enemy's advanced guard, about a mile beyond Goshen, defeated them, killing 12, and wounding more, without the loss of a man.

Nearly at the same time the chasseurs in front of Lieutenant-general Knyphausen's column fell in with another party, of which they killed an officer and five men, and took four officers prisoners, with the loss of three men wounded.

The enemy being thus apprized of the approach of the army, marched with the utmost precipitation the whole night of the 16th, and got in the morning to the Yellow Springs, having, as is since known, all their small ammunition damaged by the excessive rain.

In the evening of the 17th Lord Cornwallis advanced to the Lancaster road, and took post about two miles distant from Lieutenant-general Knyphausen.

The army joined in the Lancaster road at the White Horse on the 18th, and marched to Truduffrin, from whence a detachment of light infantry was immediately sent to the Valley Forge upon Schuylkill, where the enemy had a variety of stores, and a considerable magazine of flour. The 1st battalion of light infantry and the British grenadiers took post there next day, and were joined on the 20th by the guards.

The enemy crossed the Schuylkill on the 18th, above French-creek, and encamped upon the river, on each side of Perkyomy-creek, having detached troops to all the fords of Schuylkill, with cannon at Swedesford and the fords below it.

Upon intelligence that General Wayne was lying in the woods with a corps of 1500 men, and four pieces of cannon, about three miles distant, and in the rear of the left wing of the army, Major-general Grey was detached on the 20th, late at night, with the 2d light infantry, the 42d and 44th regiments, to surprize this corps. The most effectual precaution being taken by the General to prevent his detachment from firing, he gained the enemy's left about one o'clock, and having, by the bayonet only, forced their out-centries and pickets, he rushed in upon their encampment, directed by the light of their fires, killed and wounded not less than 300 on the spot, taking between 70 and and 80 prisoners, including several officers, the greater part of their arms, and eight waggons loaded with baggage and stores. Upon the first alarm, the cannon were carried off, and the darkness of the night only saved the remainder of the corps. One Captain of light infantry and three men were killed in the attack, and four men wounded. Gallantry in the troops, and good conduct in the General, were fully manifested upon this critical service.

On the 21st the army moved by Valley Forge, and encamped upon the banks of Schuylkill, extending from Fat Land-ford to French-creek. The enemy upon this movement quitted their position, and marched towards Potsgrove in the evening of this day.

On the 22d the grenadiers and light infantry of the guards crossed

over

over in the afternoon at Fat Land-ford, to take poft, and the chaffeurs crofting foon after at Gordon's-ford, oppofite to the left of the line, took poft there alfo. The army was put in movement at midnight, the van-guard being led by Lord Cornwallis, and the whole crofted the river at Fat Land-ford without oppofition. Major-general Grant, who com-manded the rear-guard with the bag-gage, pafled the river before two o'clock in the afternoon, and the ar-my encamped on the 23d, with its left to the Schuylkill, and the right upon the Monatomy road, having Stony Run in front. The 2d batta-lion of light infantry was detached to Swede's-ford, which a fmall part of the enemy quitted immediately, leav-ing fix pieces of iron cannon behind them.

On the 25th the army marched in two columns to German-town; and Lord Cornwallis, with the Britifh grenadiers, and two battalions of Heffian grenadiers, took poffeffion of Philadelphia the next morning.

In the evening of the 26th, three batteries for fix medium 12 pounders and four howitzers were begun at Philadelphia, to act againft the ene-my's fhipping and craft that might approach the town. Thefe batteries were unfinifhed on the 27th, when two frigates, a number of gallies, gondolas, and other armed veffels, came up from Mud Ifland, and at-tacked the lower battery of two guns and two howitzers. The largeft fri-gate, called the Delaware, mounting 30 guns, anchored within 500 yards of the battery, and the other frigate fomewhat more diftant; the gallies, gondolas, and other veffels, taking their refpective ftations as they could bring their guns to bear. About ten in the morning they began a heavy cannonade upon the town as well as the battery, but the tide falling the Delaware grounded; upon which the four battalion guns of the grenadiers

being brought to bear upon her to the greateft advantage, they did fuch execution in a fhort time, that fhe ftruck her colours, and was taken poffeffion of by the marine company of grenadiers commanded by Captain Averne.

Brigadier-general Cleveland, who attended the batteries in perfon, fee-ing the effect of the battalion guns upon the Delaware, turned the di-rection of his fire to the fmaller fri-gate and armed veffels, which forced all of them, excepting a fchooner that was difabled and driven on fhore, to return to their former fituation, under the protection of the fort, where there were two floating batteries in the manner of hulks, of confiderable ftrength, with three ranges of funken machines, which they term chevaux de frize, to obftruct the paffage of the river, the loweft row being three miles below the fort.

The enemy had a redoubt upon the Jerfey fhore, at a place called Billing's-point, with heavy guns in it, to prevent thefe machines from being weighed up.

Upon the reprefentation of Capt. Hammond, commanding his Majefty's fhip Roebuck, who was lying off Chefter with fome other fhips of war, that the poffeffion of Billing's-point would give him the lower chevaux de frize, the 10th and 42d regiments were detached on the 29th, under the command of Lieutenant-colonel Stir-ling. This detachment croffing the river next day from Chefter, took poffeffion on the 1ft of October of the enemy's works at the point, which 300 men pofted there evacuated, af-ter fpiking the guns and burning the barracks. Lieutenant-colonel Stir-ling purfued them about two miles, but to little purpofe, as they retired with the utmoft precipitation. Capt. Hammond immediately opened the navigation at that place, by removing a part of the chevaux de frize.

On the 3d the regiment of royal

Welch

Welch fuzileers was detached to Philadelphia, with orders to proceed next day to Chester, where they were to be joined by the 10th and 42d regiments on their return from Jersey, and to form an escort for a convoy of provisions to the army.

The enemy having received a reinforcement of 1500 men from Peek's-kill, 1000 from Virginia, and presuming upon the army being much weakened by the detachments to Philadelphia and Jersey, thought it a favourable time for them to risque an action. They accordingly marched at six o'clock in the evening of the 3d, from their camp near Shippach-creek, about 16 miles from German-town.

This village forms one continued street for two miles, which the line of encampment, in the position the army then occupied, crossed at Right Angles near a mile from the head of it, where the 2d battalion of light infantry and the 40th regiment were posted.

In this line of encampment, Lieutenant-general Knyphausen, Major-generals Stirn and Grey, Brigadier-general Agnew, with seven British and three Hessian battalions, the mounted and dismounted chasseurs, were upon the left of the village, extending to the Schuylkill, the chasseurs being in front.

Major-general Grant and Brigadier-general Matthew, with the corps of guards, six battalions of British, and two squadrons of dragoons, were upon the right; the 1st battalion of light infantry, and the Queen's American rangers, were advanced in the front of this wing.

At three o'clock in the morning of the 4th, the patrols discovered the enemy's approach, and upon the communication of this intelligence the army was immediately ordered under arms.

Soon after the break of day, the enemy began their attack upon the 2d light infantry, which they sustained for a considerable time, supported by the 40th regiment; but at length being overpowered by increasing numbers, the light infantry and a part of the 40th retired into the village, when Lieutenant-colonel Mulgrave, with six companies of the latter corps, threw himself into a large stone house in the face of the enemy, which, though surrounded by a brigade, and attacked by four pieces of cannon, he most gallantly defended, until Major-general Grey, at the head of three battalions of the 3d brigade, turning his front to the village, and Brigadier-general Agnew, who covered Major-general Grey's left with the 4th brigade, by a vigorous attack repulsed the enemy that had penetrated into the upper part of the village, which was done with great slaughter: the 5th and 55th regiments, from the right, engaging them at the same time on the other side of the village, compleated the defeat of the enemy in this quarter.

The regiments of Du Corps and Donop being formed to support the left of the 4th brigade, and one battalion of the Hessian grenadiers in the rear of the chasseurs, were not engaged; the precipitate flight of the enemy preventing the two first corps from entering into action, and the success of the chasseurs, in repelling all efforts against them on that side, did not call for the support of the latter.

The 1st light infantry, and pickets of the line in front of the right wing, were engaged soon after the attack began upon the head of the village; the pickets were obliged to fall back, but the light infantry, being well supported by the 4th regiment, sustained the enemy's attack with such determined bravery, that they could not make the least impression on them.

Two columns of the enemy were opposite to the guards, 27th and 28th regiments, who formed the right of the line.

Major-

Major-general Grant, who was upon the right, moved up the 49th regiment, with four pieces of cannon, to the left of the 4th regiment, about the time Major-general Grey had forced the enemy in the village, and then advancing with the right wing, the enemy's left gave way, and was pursued through a strong country between four and five miles.

Lord Cornwallis, being early apprized at Philadelphia of the enemy's approach, put in motion the two battalions of British and one of the Hessian grenadiers, with a squadron of dragoons; and his Lordship getting to German-town just as the enemy had been forced out of the village, he joined Major-general Grey, when placing himself at the head of the troops, he followed the enemy eight miles on the Skippach road, but such was the expedition with which they fled, he was not able to overtake them.

The grenadiers from Philadelphia, who, full of ardour, had run most of the way to German-town, could not arrive in time to join in the action.

The country in general was so strongly inclosed and covered with wood, that the dragoons had not any opening to charge, excepting a small party on the right, which behaved most gallantly.

The enemy retired near 20 miles by several roads to Perkyomy-creek, and are now encamped near Skippach-creek, about 18 miles distant from hence.

They saved all their cannon by withdrawing them early in the day.

By the best accounts their loss was between 200 and 300 killed, about 600 wounded, and upwards of 400 taken. Among the killed was General Nash, with many other officers of all ranks, and 54 officers among the prisoners.

Since the battle of Brandywine 72 of their officers have been taken, exclusive of ten belonging to the Delaware frigate.

Your Lordship will see the loss on the part of the King's army in return No. 3. and among the killed will be found the names of Brigadier-general Agnew and Lieutenant-colonel Bird of the 15th regiment, both of whom are much to be lamented as officers of experience and approved merit.

Lieutenant-colonel Walcot of the 5th regiment is among the wounded, but I have the satisfaction to report that he is now in a fair way of recovery, though at first his wound was thought mortal. His behaviour on this occasion reflects upon him infinite honour.

In these several engagements, the successes attending them are far better vouchers than any words can convey of the good conduct of the General Officers, and of the bravery of the other officers and soldiers. The fatigues of a march exceeding 100 miles, supported with the utmost chearfulness by all ranks, without tents, and with very little baggage, will, I hope, be esteemed as convincing proofs of the noble spirit and emulation prevailing in the army to promote his Majesty's service.

Major Cuyler, my first Aid de Camp, will have the honour to deliver my dispatches, and I flatter myself is well informed to answer your Lordship's further enquiries.

With most perfect respect,

I have the honour to be, &c.

W. HOWE.

Return of the killed, wounded, and missing, of the army under the command of his Excellency Sir WILLIAM HOWE, in the general engagement with the rebel army, on the heights of the Brandywine, Sept. 11, 1777.

Royal artillery. 5 Rank and file, killed; 1 Lieutenant, 2 Serjeants, 9 rank and file, wounded.

1st Battalion of light infantry. 1 Lieutenant,

Lieutenant, 9 rank and file, *killed*; 3 Captains, 3 Lieutenants, 8 Serjeants, 1 drummer, 36 rank and file, *wounded*.

2d Battalion of ditto. 6 Rank and file, *killed*; 3 Captains, 4 Lieutenants, 2 Serjeants, 2 drummers, 41 rank and file, *wounded*.

1st Battalion of grenadiers. 3 Lieutenants, 1 Serjeant, 8 rank and file, *killed*; 1 Lieutenant-colonel, 2 Captains, 4 Lieutenants, 3 Serjeants, 46 rank and file, *wounded*; 2 rank and file, *missing*.

2d Battalion of ditto. 1 Captain, 1 Lieutenant, 1 Serjeant, 9 rank and file, *killed*; 1 Captain, 1 Lieutenant, 7 Serjeants, 61 rank and file, *wounded*; 1 rank and file, *missing*.

Brigade of foot guards. 1 Rank and file, *killed*; 5 rank and file, *wounded*; 1 rank and file, *missing*.

1st Brigade, 4th regiment. 2 Rank and file, *killed*; 1 Captain, 20 rank and file, *wounded*.

1st Brigade, 23d regiment. 1 Serjeant, 1 rank and file, *killed*; 4 rank and file, *wounded*.

1st Brigade, 28th regiment. 2 Rank and file, *killed*; 1 Lieutenant, 8 rank and file, *wounded*.

1st Brigade, 49th regiment. 1 Serjeant, 2 rank and file, *killed*; 1 Captain, 1 drummer, 9 rank and file, *wounded*.

2d Brigade, 5th regiment. 1 Ensign, 1 Serjeant, 12 rank file, *wounded*.

2d Brigade, 10th regiment. 2 Rank and file, *killed*; 6 rank and file, *wounded*.

2d Brigade, 27th regiment. 1 Rank and file, *killed*; 2 rank and file, *wounded*.

2d Brigade, 40th regiment. 1 Rank and file, *wounded*.

2d Brigade, 55th regiment. 1 Rank and file, *wounded*.

4th Brigade, 33d regiment. 1 Rank and file, *killed*; 1 Serjeant, 11 rank and file, *wounded*; 1 rank and file, *missing*.

4th Brigade, 37th regiment. 1 Serjeant, 6 rank and file, *wounded*.

4th Brigade, 46th regiment. 1 Rank and file, *killed*; 1 Ensign, 1 Serjeant, 12 rank and file, *wounded*.

4th Brigade, 64th regiment. 1 Captain, 4 rank and file, *killed*; 1 Major, 3 Lieutenants, 2 Ensigns, 5 Serjeants, 31 rank and file, *wounded*.

Two Battalions of the 71st regiment. 3 Rank and file, *wounded*.

Queen's American rangers. 1 Captain, 1 Serjeant, 12 rank and file, *killed*; 4 Captains, 5 Lieutenants, 1 Ensign, 4 Serjeants, 43 rank and file, *wounded*; 1 rank and file, *missing*.

Ferguson's corps of riflemen. 2 Rank and file, *killed*; 1 Captain, 5 rank and file, *wounded*.

Total British. 3 Captains, 5 Lieutenants, 5 Serjeants, 68 rank and file, *killed*; 1 Lieutenant-colonel, 1 Major, 16 Captains, 22 Lieutenants, 5 Ensigns, 35 Serjeants, 4 drummers, 372 rank and file, *wounded*; 6 rank and file, *missing*.

Hessian yagers. 1 Serjeant, 3 rank and file, *killed*; 1 Captain, 3 Serjeants, 12 rank and file, *wounded*.

Battalion Linsing. 2 Lieutenants, 1 Serjeant, 2 rank and file, *wounded*.

Ditto Lengerke. 1 Rank and file, *killed*.

Regiment du Corps. 1 Rank and file, *killed*; 2 rank and file, *wounded*.

Ditto Mirbach. 2 Rank and file, *wounded*.

Anspach yagers. 1 Serjeant, 1 rank and file, *killed*; 1 Lieutenant, 1 Serjeant, 5 rank and file, *wounded*.

Total Foreign. 2 Serjeants, 6 rank and file, *killed*; 1 Captain, 3 Lieutenants, 5 Serjeants, 23 rank and file, *wounded*.

Total British and Foreign. 3 Captains, 5 Lieutenants, 7 Serjeants, 74 rank and file, *killed*; 1 Lieutenant-colonel, 1 Major, 17 Captains, 25 Lieutenants, 5 Ensigns, 40 Serjeants, 4 drummers, 395 rank and file, *wounded*; rank and file, 6 *missing*.

Names

Names and rank of officers killed and wounded in the general engagement of the 11th of September, 1777.

Royal artillery. Lieutenant Shand, *wounded.*

1st Battalion of light infantry. 38th company, Lieutenant Johnston, *killed*; 23d Capt. Meccan, 33d Capt. Dancey, 15th Capt. Douglas, 27th Lieut. Birch, 33d Lieut. Nicholl, 15th Lieut. Leigh, *wounded.*

2d Battalion of light infantry, 49th company, Capt. Wade, 55th Capt. Downing, 57th Captain Sir James Murray, 40th Capt. De Courcy, 45th Lieut. Ruxton, 49th Lieut. Armstrong, 63d Lieut. Ball, *wounded.*

1st Battalion of grenadiers, 15th company, Lieut. Faulkener, 27th Lieut. Minchin, 40th Lieut. Barber, *killed*; 55th Lieut. Col. Medowes, 15th Captain Cathcart, 40th Capt. Simcoe, 33d Lieuts. Harris and Drummond, 37th Lieuts. Chapman and Cooke, *wounded.*

2d Battalion of grenadiers, 63d company, Capt. Drury, 52d Lieut. D'Oyly, *killed*; 44th Capt. Fish, 64th Lieut. Peters, *wounded.*

4th regiment, Captain Rawdon, *wounded.*

28th reg. Lieut. Edwards, *wounded.*

49th reg. Capt. Stewart, *wounded.*

5th reg. Ensign Andrew, *wounded.*

46th reg. Ensign Bristow, *wounded.*

64th reg. Capt. Nairne, *killed*; Major Macleroth, Lieuts. Jacob, Torianno, and Wynyar, Ensigns Freeman and Grant, *wounded.*

Queen's American rangers. Capt. Murden, *killed*; Capt. Williams, Saunders, M'Kay, M'Crea, Lieuts. Ker, Agne, Smith, Jeel, and Close, Ensign M'Kay, *wounded.*

Ferguson's corps. Capt. Ferguson, *wounded.*

Hessian yagers. Capt. Trantvitter, *wounded.*

Battalion of Linsing. Lieuts. De Buy and De Brumbak, *wounded.*

Anspach yagers. Lieut. De Forstner, *wounded.*

Volunteers serving with the Queen's rangers. Capt. Burns, *wounded.*

Ditto with first battalion of light infantry. Captains Cummings, Currey, M'Intosh, and M'Kenzie, *wounded.*

Ditto with 2d battalion of light infantry. Capt. Moultrie, Evans, Fone, *wounded.*

Return of ordnance, ammunition, and stores, taken from the rebels by his Majesty's troops, in the action near Brandywine-creek, Sept. 11, 1777.

Ordnance mounted on travelling carriages.

Brass six-pounders, 1 Rebel States, 1 Hessian, 1 English; four-pounders, 4 French; three-pounders, 1 Hessian, 1 French; five and half inch howitzer, 1 Rebel States.

Iron four-pounders, 1 Rebel States. Total 11.

Shot fixed, with powder. Grape quilted, six-pounders, 188; three-pounders, 20; ditto round, six-pounders, 76; three-pounders, 23; ditto case, six-pounders, 130; three-pounders, 225.

Shot fixed to wood bottoms. Round, six-pounders, 6; case, six-pounders, 4; eight inch howitzers, 38; five and half ditto, 39.

Shot, round loose. Twelve-pounders, 6; six-pounders, 29; four-pounders, 12; three-pounders, 20.

Cartridges. Paper filled with powder, six-pounders, 24; three-pounders, 46; flannel ditto, for five and half inch howitzer, 28; musquet filled with ball, 6000.

Powder. Whole barrels, 3.

Budge barrels, 4.

Waggons covered for ammunition, 9; open ditto, 1.

A quantity of damaged tubes, port fires, and intrenching tools.

The two Hessian guns were taken by the rebels at Trentown, and one of them since bored to a six-pounder.

The English gun was left at Princetown, the carriage being broke.

Return

Return of the killed, wounded, and missing, of the army under the command of his Excellency General Sir WILLIAM HOWE, *in the engagement with the rebel army at Germantown, in Pennsylvania, on the 4th of October,* 1777.

Royal artillery. 1 Lieutenant, 1 Serjeant, 13 rank and file, *wounded.*

1st Battalion of light infantry. 1 Serjeant, 5 rank and file, *killed*; 2 Lieutenants, 1 Serjeant, 36 rank and file, *wounded*; 2 rank and file, *missing.*

2d Battalion of light infantry. 2 Serjeants, 7 rank and file, *killed*; 1 Captain, 3 Lieutenants, 3 Serjeants, 1 drummer, 51 rank and file, *wounded*; 1 Captain, 4 rank and file, *missing.*

Brigade of foot guards. 3 rank and file, *wounded.*

4th regiment. 1 Serjeant, 8 rank and file, *killed*; 1 Captain, 3 Lieutenants, 4 Ensigns, 2 Serjeants, 46 rank and file, *wounded*; 3 rank and file, *missing.*

5th. 1 Drummer, 9 rank and file, *killed*; 1 Lieutenant-colonel, 1 Captain, 2 Ensigns, 5 Serjeants, 37 rank and file, *wounded.*

15th. 1 Lieutenant-colonel, 1 Ensign, 5 rank and file, *killed*; 2 Captains, 1 Lieutenant, 1 Ensign, 2 Serjeants, 42 rank file, *wounded.*

17th. 1 Ensign, 1 Serjeant, 4 rank and file, *killed*; 3 Serjeants, 21 rank and file, *wounded.*

33d. 2 Serjeants, 2 rank and file, *killed*; 13 rank and file, *wounded.*

37th. 3 rank and file, *killed*; 1 Lieutenant, 20 rank and file, *wounded.*

40th. 4 Rank and file, *killed*; 2 Lieutenants, 1 Ensign, 3 Serjeants, 23 rank and file, *wounded*; 3 rank and file, *missing.*

44th. 1 Lieutenant-colonel, 5 rank and file, *killed*; 1 Ensign, 1 Serjeant, 31 rank and file, *wounded*; 1 rank and file, *missing.*

46th. 2 Rank and file, *killed*; 1 Serjeant, 5 rank and file, *wounded.*

49th. 1 Serjeant, 11 rank and file, *wounded.*

55th. 3 Rank and file, *killed*; 1 Captain, 1 Ensign, 13 rank and file, *wounded.*

64th. 1 Rank and file, *killed*; 6 rank and file, *wounded.*

Queen's American rangers. 1 Rank and file, *wounded.*

Total British. 2 Lieutenant-colonels, 2 Ensigns, 7 Serjeants, 1 drummer, 58 rank and file, *killed*; 1 Lieutenant-colonel, 6 Captains, 13 Lieutenants, 10 Ensigns, 23 Serjeants, 1 drummer, 372 rank and file, *wounded*; 1 Captain, 13 rank and file, *missing.*

Hessian chasseurs. 10 rank and file, *wounded.*

Hessian reg. du corps. 1 Serjeant, 13 rank and file, *wounded.*

Total Hessians. 1 Serjeant, 23 rank and file, *wounded.*

Total British and Hessians. 2 Lieutenant-colonels, 2 Ensigns, 7 Serjeants, 1 drummer, 58 rank and file, *killed*; 1 Lieutenant-colonel, 6 Captains, 13 Lieutenants, 10 Ensigns, 24 Serjeants, 1 drummer, 395 rank and file, *wounded*; 1 Captain, 13 rank and file, *missing.*

N. B. *16th light dragoons.* 1 Man, *killed*; 3 horses, *killed*; and 4 *wounded.*

Names and rank of the officers killed and wounded in the engagement at German-town, on the 4th of October, 1777.

Royal artillery. Lieutenant James Froit, *wounded.*

1st Light infantry. Lieutenant Morgan, 17th, *dead of his wounds.* Lieut. Champaigne, 4th *wounded.*

2d Light infantry. Captain Sir James Baird, 71st, Captain Weir, 43d, Lieutenant St. George, 52d, Lieutenant Campbell, sen. 71st, *wounded*; Capt. Speke, 37th, *prisoner.*

4th Regiment. Captain Thorne, Lieutenants Arbuthnot and Kemble, Ensigns Dickson, Schoen, Hadden, and

and Blenman, Adjutant Hunt, *wounded.*

5th Regiment. Lieutenant colonel Walcot, Captain Charleton, Enfigns Thomas and Stuart, *wounded.*

15th Regiment. Lieutenant-colonel Bird, Enfign Anthony Frederick, *killed*; Captains T. G. Goldfrapp, Henry Ditmas, Lieutenant G. Thomas, Enfign William Ball, *wounded.*

17th Regiment. Enfign Nathaniel Philips, *killed.*

37th Regiment. Lieutenant Buckeridge, *wounded.*

40th Regiment. Lieutenants Doyle and Forbes, Enfign Campbell, *wounded.*

44th Regiment. Lieutenant-colonel Agnew (Brigadier general) *killed*; Enfign David Stack, *wounded.*

55th Regiment. Captain Fifher, Enfign Shuldham, *wounded.*

Volunteers ferving with 1ft light infantry. James Forreft, William M'Intofh, *wounded.*

Ditto ferving with 2d light infantry. Smithf. Waller, half-pay Enfign Gordon, *wounded.*

N. B. Captain Wolfe, of the 40th light infantry, killed, and Lieutenant Hunter, of the 52d ditto, *wounded*; one Serjeant and one rank and file, *killed*, and eight rank and file *wounded*, 20th September, on a detachment under the command of Major-general Grey, in Pennfylvania.

Extract of a letter from General Sir WILLIAM HOWE *to Lord* GEORGE GERMAIN, *dated Philadelphia, October* 21, 1777.

Since the march of the army from the head of the Elk, I have been honoured with your Lordfhip's feveral difpatches, No. 10, 11, 12, and feparate letter of the 20th of May, the duplicates of which were before received, alfo the original and duplicate of the 12th of June, enclofing the ftates of Heffian chaffeurs and recruits brought out by Major-general Robertfon, a circular letter of the fame date, and the original and duplicate of your Lordfhip's difpatch, No. 14. Thefe reached my hands at German-town on the 17th inftant, and on the 19th I had the further honour of your Lordfhip's difpatches of the 6th of Auguft, which came to New-York by the Le Defpencer packet.

The inclofed copies of reports from Lieutenant-general Sir Henry Clinton and Brigadier-general Campbell, will give your Lordfhip a particular information of the moft material tranfactions that have paffed on the fide of New-York. The very important and brilliant fuccefs fet forth in No. 3, does infinite honour to the General and his troops, and muft be attended with the beft confequences to his Majefty's fervice.

The lofs on the part of the King's troops on this laft occafion is contained in return No. 4.

One hundred of the enemy were killed in the different attacks, eight Field Officers, two Captains, twelve Subalterns, and about three hundred men made prifoners, by the beft accounts that could be obtained before Sir Henry Clinton's advices were difpatched.

On the 19th the army removed from German-town to this place, as a more convenient fituation for the reduction of Fort Ifland, which at prefent is an obftruction to the paffage of the river, as the upper chevaux de frize cannot be removed until we have poffeffion of that poft. The difficulty of accefs has rendered the reduction of it a much more tedious operation, than was conceived upon our arrival here.

I am to requeft that additional cloathing may be fent over for 5000 Provincials, which, by including the new levies expected to be raifed in this and the neighbouring countries, will certainly be wanting.

Extract

Extract of a letter from Lieutenant-general Sir HENRY CLINTON, *to General Sir* WILLIAM HOWE, *dated Kingsbridge, 23d Sept.* 1777.

In the laſt letter which I had the honour of writing to your Excellency of the 6th of this month, I mentioned my intention of making an incurſion into Jerſey; the object of which was to make a ſmall diverſion in favour of both armies, at what, I ſuppoſed, a critical time; having learnt by rebel accounts that you had landed on Elk River.

My principal motive was, if poſſible, to attempt a ſtroke againſt any detached corps of the enemy, if one offered, or, if not, to collect a conſiderable number of cattle, which would at the ſame time prove a ſeaſonable refreſhment to the troops, and deprive the enemy of reſources which I underſtood they much depended upon; and finally to retire, with our body, by the only road practicable with thoſe embarraſſments, to re-embark, return to our camp, or proceed to ſome other expedition if any thing preſented itſelf.

All arrangements being ſettled, the landing was made at the four following places, viz. at Elizabethtown Point by Brigadier-general Campbell, with the 7th, 26th, and 52d regiments, Anſpach and Waldeck grenadiers, and 300 Provincials,

At Schuyler's-ferry by Capt. Drummond, with two pieces of cannon, 250 recruits of the 71ſt regiment, and ſome convaleſcents.

At Fort Lee by Major-general Vaughan, with Capt. Emmerick's chaſſeurs, five companies of grenadiers and light infantry, the 57th, 63d, and Prince Charles's regiment, and 5 pieces of very light artillery.

And at Tapan by Lieutenant-colonel Campbell, with 200 Provincials, and 40 marines.

The corps which landed at Elizabeth-town Point to proceed towards Newark, driving cattle, and diſarming the inhabitants, and if it met with the enemy in any force, ſo as to prevent its proceeding to Aquakinack, its retreat over the Paſaick River was ſecured by a ſmall corps with cannon on the heights of Schuyler, who had landed at Schuyler's-ferry, and were aportée to take poſſeſſion of the high grounds which command the environs of Newark, &c. If the Elizabeth-town corps continued its march to Aquakinack, it was there received by the corps which had landed at Fort Lee, and marched by Newbridge, Hackinſack and Slatterdam, where it was in a ſituation to fulfil that object. A poſt was left at Hackinſack, and I ordered General Vaughan to leave one battalion and two pieces of cannon at Newbridge to cover that very important paſs. Lieutenant-colonel Campbell, who had landed at Tapan, to remain there, and if preſſed to fall back on Newbridge; this however ſubject to any alterations that General Vaughan ſhould think neceſſary to make. Finding that Brigadier-general Campbell had landed on Friday the 12th, about four o'clock in the morning, without oppoſition, I then went by Newark Bay to Schuyler's Landing on Hackinſack River. The cannon were that inſtant landed, and I ordered them to proceed through the Cedar Swamp, to the high grounds near Schuyler's houſe, where Capt. Sutherland with 250 men had been for ſome time. Finding it neceſſary to amuſe the enemy, who being informed of the landing at Elizabeth-town Point, were retiring with their cattle, the troops were ordered to ſhew themſelves, and about noon the enemy were much encreaſed in number, and had got one piece of cannon. They had all the boats on their ſide of the river.

Firing of muſquetry and cannon continued the whole day with little or no loſs on either ſide. Much looſe
firing

firing was heard beyond Newark, and at night we had a private report that Gen Campbell had taken poſſeſſion of that town. I ſent immediately to tell him our ſituation, but ſoon afterwards, by the noiſe of cattle driving and march of troops, found he had continued his route, was oppoſite to us, and on his way to Aquakinack. I judged it beſt to order him to halt till morning. At daybreak the rebels appeared in ſome force, and about noon they had three pieces of cannon in battery on their ſide of the ravine. I went over to obſerve them, and had every reaſon to ſuppoſe, from their cloathing and artillery, that they were reinforced by what is called continental troops. To try their countenance, and give an opportunity to the Provincials, I ordered Burkick's battalion to march through a corn-field, with an intention of taking in flank a body of the rebels poſted behind a ſtone wall, and which it would have been difficult to have removed by a front attack. The regiment marched with great ſpirit, and their march, with ſome little movement to favour it, obliged the rebels to quit without a ſhot. I then repaſſed the river, deſiring General Campbell to loſe no opportunity of giving them a bruſh, and, if poſſible, of taking their cannon.

In the evening the rebels retired, as we ſuppoſed, to the neighbouring woods, and I waited only to hear of the arrival of a ſquadron of cavalry, which I had ordered to join General Vaughan from Paulus Hook, to ſettle a plan in which part of General Vaughan's corps might co-operate with General Campbell's, in endeavouring to ſurround them. In the mean time I received a letter from General Vaughan, acquainting me, that, by information from his patrols, the rebels were aſſembling in great force at the Clove. This intelligence, and their leaving us ſo ſuddenly, gave me ſome ſuſpicion of

their intention, and made it neceſſary for me to aſſemble our little army as ſoon as poſſible, occupy Newbridge in ſome force, and ſend Lieutenant-colonel Campbell from Newbridge towards Tapan, to obſerve their motions in that quarter.

General Campbell began his march at day-break, and was not followed. I ordered the ſmall corps on the heights of Schuyler, reinforced with two companies of grenadiers, to fall back and cover the entry of the defile; and when the cattle we had got on that ſide had paſſed the river, they were to paſs alſo, and remain with their cannon on the other ſide.

I then went to General Vaughan at Slatterdam, and having aſſembled the little army and the cattle, I ordered him to march to Newbridge, and General Campbell towards Hackinſack.

The whole aſſembled at Newbridge on the 15th, and then hearing nothing of the enemy, having collected our cattle, the ſoldiers without tents or blankets, and the weather threatening, I thought it adviſeable to fall back. I accordingly ordered General Campbell to continue his march to Engliſh Neighbourhood, taking with him the cattle, amounting to 400 head, including 20 milch cows, for the uſe of the hoſpital, (which was all I would ſuffer to be taken from the inhabitants) 400 ſheep, and a few horſes.

On the 16th, General Campbell marched to Bergen-point, where he embarked for Staten Iſland, and General Vaughan to Fort Lee, not followed by a ſingle man, where he repaſſed the North River, and the whole returned to their former ſtations by two o'clock.

I wiſh upon this occaſion to expreſs the very great aſſiſtance I have received from the navy; indeed I have experienced it in every inſtance; but the excellent arrangement of the boats in this affair, and the ſecrecy with
which

which every thing was conducted, demand my particular acknowledgment.

Your Excellency will permit me to give the highest commendation to the regularity of the troops, both British, Foreign, and Provincials, during this excursion. Their strict attention to discipline did them and their officers great credit.

Return of the killed, wounded, prisoners, and missing, of the following corps during an excursion to Jersey, from the 12th to the 16th of September, 1777.

English Fuzileers. 1 Lieutenant, 1 rank and file, wounded.

26th Regiment. 2 Rank and file, killed; 2 rank and file, wounded.

2d Regiment. 6 Rank and file, wounded; 1 Serjeant, 5 drummers, 4 rank and file, missing; 5 rank and file, taken prisoners.

57th Regiment. 3 Rank and file, killed; 2 rank and file, wounded; 2 rank and file, missing.

71st Regiment. 1 rank and file, wounded.

Gen. Skinner's brigade. 3 Rank and file, killed; 5 rank and file, wounded; 3 rank and file, missing.

Total. 8 Rank and file, killed; 1 Lieutenant, 17 rank and file, wounded; 1 drummer, 9 rank file, missing; 5 rank and file, taken prisoners.

Lieutenant Haymer of 7th regiment, wounded.

(Signed)

H. CLINTON, Lieut. Gen.

Copy of a letter from Brigadier-general CAMPBELL to Sir HENRY CLINTON, dated Head Quarters, Staten Island, August 23, 1777.

Sir,

I had the honour of informing you yesterday morning of a descent made by the rebels on this island, and of my being on my march with the 52d regiment of British and 3d regiment of Waldeck, with two field pieces to each battalion, to reconnoitre, and if possible to attack them. I am sorry now to add, that the enemy effected

almost a total surprize of two battalions of the Jersey Provincials, which occasioned nearly the whole loss sustained by his Majesty's troops, as will appear by the inclosed return.

Soon after I wrote, I had intelligence that the enemy was moving towards Richmond, with an intention (as I conjectured) of occupying the adjacent heights, and thereby be enabled to cut off the retreat of three Provincial regiments stationed beyond that village, which determined me to move forward to prevent the sacrifice of that corps; but a messenger soon after arrived from Lieutenant-colonel Dongan, with information, that an attack had likewise been made on the west part of the island; that Lieutenant-colonel Lawrence and a good many of his corps had been made prisoners; but that he and Lieutenant-colonel Allan, and their battalions, with a few of Lawrence's that had joined them, had taken possession of some works formerly thrown up by the rebels near Princes Bay, where they should be able to defend themselves until supported, or that boats should arrive to carry them off. This strengthening me in my former resolution. I advanced on the footsteps of the enemy, and proceeded without the least interruption to the village of Richmond, where I was obliged to halt to bring up the rear, and to refresh the troops, who were even at this time very much fatigued from excessive heat. From this place Brigadier-general Skinner was directed to send repeated expresses to inform Colonel Dongan of my approach, and desiring him to endeavour a junction. I had proceeded but a short way beyond Richmond, when I was informed, that the rebels had reached the Old Blazing Star, and were using the greatest diligence in transporting their troops to the Jersey shore. At this very instant an officer arrived from Colonel Dongan, that he was a little more than at a mile's distance on his way to join me; whereupon I sent him

him orders to turn towards the enemy, and to attack whatever body he could come up with, and I was following with all expedition, and would immediately support him. He obeyed my orders with spirit, bravery, and resolution, and engaged their rear for near half an hour, when the 52d regiment coming up, exchanging some shots, and moving to take them in flank, and the cannon having by this time begun to play upon their boats, about 150 surrendered themselves prisoners to Lieutenant-colonel Campbell of the 52d regiment, and the remainder, of nearly the same number, retreated towards the extremity of the island opposite Amboy, of which last number I have since learned was Brigadier-general De Bore; and reports render it still doubtful whether he has as yet made his escape from off the island: however, the troops were by this time so much fatigued, that I found it altogether impossible to pursue them; and I fear the greater part, if not the whole, found means to cross over near Amboy.

The troops lay for that night under arms, and this morning I detached the greater part of General Skinner's brigade towards Amboy, and proceeded with the regular troops on my return. A party was this day also ordered to bring off the enemy's boats under the cover of a piece of cannon, which was effected without any loss.

I must not forget to mention, that Colonel Buskirk's battalion was early in the day ordered to attack a party left to cover the enemy's boats, which they did with charge of bayonet, and obliged them to retreat to the Jersey shore.

By prisoner's reports, and from an inclosed order found in Gen. Smallwood's, Major of Brigades, pocket, who was killed, it appears, that this attack was carried on by select and chosen troops, and formed from three brigades.—Sullivan's, Smallwood's, and De Bore's, and

headed by their respective Generals, besides Drayton's and Ogden's battalions. We have taken in all 259 prisoners, among whom are 1 Lieutenant-colonel, 3 Majors, 2 Captains, and 15 inferior officers. Their loss in killed cannot be ascertained, but must have been considerable.

I cannot do too much justice to the bravery and spirit of the troops. Both officers and men seemed only anxious to engage, and emulous who should be foremost in the race of glory. And I must add, that the several Commanding Officers did justice to the ardour of their troops, which they knew how to temper with judgment and conduct. For further particulars I refer you to Brigade Major Campbell, who was present at the whole affair, and charged with the delivery of this. I have, &c.

(Signed)

JOHN CAMPBELL, Brigadier-gen.

Copy of a letter from Lieutenant-general Sir HENRY CLINTON *to General Sir* WILLIAM HOWE, *dated Fort Montgomery, Oct. 9, 1777.*

Sir,

In the last letter which I had the honour to write to your Excellency, I mentioned my intention, with the small force that could be spared from the important post you had left under my command, to make an attack upon Forts Clinton, Montgomery, &c. Your Excellency recollects the situation of these forts, that they are separated by a creek which comes from the mountain, and communicate with each other by a bridge.

In my opinion, the only way of effecting it was by a coup de main in the unguarded state they then were. The Commodore and I having made our arrangements, and every proper jealousy having been given for every object but the real one, the little army, consisting of about 3000 men, arrived off Veerplanks point, preceded by the gallies under the command of Sir James Wallace. On
our

our appearance the enemy retired without firing a shot, leaving a twelve pounder behind them ; and Sir James moved up to Peek's-kill Neck to mask the only communication they had across the river on this side of the Highlands.

At day-break on the 6th, the * troops disembarked at Stoney-point. The avant guarde of 500 regulars and 400 Provincials, commanded by Lieutenant-colonel Campbell, with Colonel Robinson of the Provincials under him, began its march to occupy the pass of Thunder-hill. This avant guarde, after it had passed that mountain, was to proceed by a detour of seven miles round the hill, and debouchee in the rear of Fort Montgomery, while Gen. Vaughan with 1200 † men, was to continue his march towards Fort Clinton, covering the corps under Lieutenant-colonel Campbell, and àportée to co-operate, by attacking Fort Clinton, or in case of misfortune to favour the retreat. Major-general Tryon, with the remainder, being the rear ‡ guard, to leave a battalion at the pass of Thunder-hill, to open our communication with the fleet.

Your Excellency recollecting the many, and, I may say, extraordinary difficulties of this march over the mountains, every natural obstruction, and all that art could invent to add to them, will not be surprized, that the corps, intended to attack Fort Montgomery in the rear, could not get to its ground before five o'clock; about which time I ordered General Vaughan's corps, àportée, to begin the attack on Fort Clinton, to push, if possible, and dislodge the enemy from their advanced station behind a stone breast-work, having in front, for half a mile, a most impenetrable

abbatis. This the General, by his good disposition, obliged the enemy to quit, though supported by cannon, got possession of the wall, and there waited the motion of the co-operating troops, when I joined him, and soon afterwards heard Lieutenant-colonel Campbell begin his attack. I chose to wait a favourable moment before I ordered the attack on the side of Fort Clinton; which was a circular height, defended by a line for musquetry, with a barbet battery in the centre of three guns, and flanked by two redoubts. The approaches to it through a continued abbatis of 400 yards, defensive every inch, and exposed to the fire of ten pieces of cannon. As the night was approaching, I determined to seize the first favourable instant. A brisk attack on the Montgomery side ; the gallies with their oars approaching, firing, and even striking the fort ; the men of war that moment appearing, crouding all sail to support us ; the extreme ardour of the troops, in short, all determined me to order the attack ; General Vaughan's spirited behaviour and good conduct did the rest. Having no time to lose, I particularly ordered that not a shot should be fired ; in this I was strictly obeyed, and both redoubts, &c. were stormed. General Tryon advanced with one battalion to support Gen. Vaughan, in case it might be necessary, and he arrived in time to join in the cry of victory.

Trumbach's regiment was posted at the stone-wall to cover our retreat in case of misfortune. The night being dark, it was near eight o'clock before we could be certain of the success of the attack against Fort Montgomery, which we found afterwards had succeeded at the same instant that of

* 52d and 27th regiments, Loyal Americans, New-York volunteers, and Emerick's Provincial chasseurs.
† Grenadiers and light infantry, 26th and 63d regiments, one company of the 71st, one troop of dismounted dragoons, Hessian chasseurs.
‡ Royal fuzileers, and Hessian regiment of Trumbach.

Fort

Fort Clinton did, and that by the excellent difposition of Lieutenant Colonel Campbell, who was unfortunately killed on the firft attack, but feconded by Colonel Robinfon of the Loyal American regiment, by whofe knowledge of the country I was much aided in forming my plan, and to whofe fpirited conduct in the execution of it I impute in a great meafure the fuccefs of the enterprize.

Our lofs was not very confiderable excepting in fome refpectable officers, who were killed in the attack.

About ten o'clock at night the rebels fet fire to their two fhips, Montgomery and Congrefs, fome gallies and other armed veffels, with their cannon, ftores, &c. in them.

I have the honour to fend your Excellency a return of the cannon, ftores, &c. taken. That of ftores is very confiderable, this being, I believe, their principal magazine.

The Commodore has affifted me with his advice, and every effort. We fent a joint fummons to Fort Conftitution, but our flag meeting with an infolent reception, unknown in any war, we determined to chaftize, and therefore an embarkation under Major-general Tryon, and Sir James Wallace, with the gallies, was ordered. They found the Fort evacuated in the greateft confufion, their ftore-houfes burnt, but their cannon were left unfpiked. The Commodore immediately ordered Sir James Wallace up the river, and if it fhould be poffible to find a paffage through the chevaux de frize, between Polypus Ifland and the Main, he may probably do moft effential fervice.

In juftice to Captain Pownal, who commanded the flat boats, and the officers under him, I muft mention to your Excellency that that fervice could not have been more zealoufly or punctually attended to.

I have the honour to be, &c.
(Signed)   H. CLINTON, Lt. Gen.

October 9, 10 o'clock at night.

P. S. Major General Tryon, whom I detached this morning with Emerick's chaffeurs, 50 yagers, the Royal Fuzileers and regiment of Trumbach, with two three-pounders, to deftroy the rebel fettlement called the Continental Village, has juft returned, and reported to me that he has burned barracks for 1500 men, feveral ftorehoufes, and loaded waggons. The extreme badnefs of the weather making it neceffary to be as expeditious as poffible, no account could be taken of the ftores, but I believe them to have been confiderable. I need not point out to your Excellency the confequence of deftroying this poft, as it was the only eftablifhment of the rebels in that part of the Highlands, and the place from whence any neighbouring body of troops drew their fupplies. Fanning's and Bayard's corps marched from Verplanks Point to co-operate with General Tryon, but finding he met with no oppofition, they were ordered back to their poft.   Signed H. C.

Return of cannon, ftores, ammunition, &c. taken and deftroyed upon the expedition up the North River, Oct. 6, 1777.

Cannon. Thirty-two pounders 6; eighteen-pounders 3; twelve-pounders 7; nine-pounders 3; fix-pounders 41; four-pounders 3; three-pounders 2; two-pounders 2; *Total* 67.

Two frigates built for 30 and 36 guns were burnt by the rebels on the forts being taken. The guns aboard them, and two gallies which were likewife burnt, amounted to above 30. One floop with 10 guns fell into our hands. The whole lofs therefore is above 100 pieces.

Powder. 54 cafks; 11 ¼ barrels; 12,236lb. exclufive of what was aboard the veffels.

Cartridges fitted. 1852 cannon; 57,396 mufquet.

Cannon fhot. 9530 round; 886 double headed; 2483 grape and cafe:

H h h

cafe : 36 cwt. 1. qr. 15 lb. Land-gridge.

For mufquets. 1279 wt. of ball ; 116 wt. of buck fhot ; 5400 flints.

Every article belonging to the Laboratory in the greateft perfection. Other ftores, fuch as port-fires, match, harnefs, fpare gun carriages, tools, inftruments, &c. &c. in great plenty. A large quantity of provifions. The boom and chain which ran acrofs the river from Fort Montgomery to St. Anthony's Nofe is fuppofed to have coft the rebels 70,000l. Another boom which we deftroyed near Fort Conftitution muft likewife have coft the rebels much money and labour. Barracks for 1500 men were deftroyed by Major-general Tryon at Continental Village, befides feveral ftore-houfes and loaded waggons, of the articles contained in which no accounts could be taken.

Return of the killed, wounded, and miffing of the troops under the command of Lieutenant-general Sir HENRY CLINTON, *in the ftorm of Forts Clinton and Montgomery on the 6th of October, 1777.*

Light infantry and grenadiers. 1 Captain, 3 rank and file, *killed* ; 1 Captain, 1 Lieutenant, 1 Serjeant, 30 rank and file, *wounded* ; 3 rank and file, *miffing.*

26th regiment. 1 Rank and file, *killed* ; 1 Lieutenant, 1 rank and file, *wounded.*

52d. 1 Lieutenant-colonel, 2 rank and file, *killed* ; 2 Lieutenants, 1 Enfign, 13 rank and file, *wounded.*

57th. 2 Serjeants, 4 rank and file, *killed* ; 1 Captain, 1 drummer, 18 rank and file, *wounded.*

63d. 1 Major, 1 Lieutenant, 1 Serjeant, 6 rank and file, *killed* ; 2 Captains, 2 Serjeants, 27 rank and file, *wounded.*

One company in 71ft. 1 Lieutenant, 3 rank and file, *killed* ; 1 Lieutenant, 1 Serjeant, 7 rank and file, *wounded.*

Heffian chaffeurs. 3 rank and file, *killed* ; 11 rank and file, *wounded.*

Heffian regiment of Trumbach. 2 rank and file, *wounded.*

Capt. Emerick's Provincial corps. 1 rank and file, *killed* ; 5 rank and file, *wounded.*

Loyal Americans. 1 Enfign, 2 rank and file, *wounded.*

New-York volunteers. 1 Major, 7 rank and file, *killed* ; 10 rank and file, *wounded* ; 2 rank and file, *miffing.*

Total. 1 Lieutenant-colonel, 2 Majors, 1 Captain, 2 Lieutenants, 1 Enfign, 3 Serjeants, 30 rank and file, *killed* ; 4 Captains, 5 Lieutenants, 2 Enfigns, 4 Serjeants, 1 drummer, 126 rank and file, *wounded* ; 5 rank and file, *miffing.*

Names and ranks of the officers killed and wounded in the above return.

Light infantry and grenadiers. Capt. Stuart, 26th, killed. Captain D'Eeb, Anfpach grenadiers, Lieut. M'Donell, 26th, wounded.

26th regiment. Lieutenant Delhunty, wounded.

52d. Lieutenant-colonel Campbell, killed ; Lieutenants Grofe, Ruffel, Enfign Thomas, wounded.

57th. Capt. Brownlow, wounded.

63d. Major Sill, Lieutenant Wrixen, killed ; Captains Nefbitt, Jones, wounded.

71ft. Lieutenant M'Kenzie, killed ; Lieutenant Frazer, wounded.

Loyal Americans. Enfign Ward, wounded.

New-York volunteers. Major Grant, Enfign M'Donell, killed.

N. B. Count Graboufkie, a Polifh Nobleman acting as Aid du Camp to Lieutenant-general Clinton, killed, not included in the above return.

Copy of a letter from General Sir WILLIAM HOWE *to Lord* GEORGE GERMAIN, *dated Philadelphia,* 25th October, 1777.

My Lord,

The enemy having entrenched about eight hundred men at Red Bank, upon the Jerfey fhore, fome little diftance above Fort Ifland, Colonel Donop, with three battalions

of

of Heſſian grenadiers, the regiment of Mirbach, and the infantry, chaſſeurs, croſſed the Delaware on the 21ſt inſtant to Cooper's Ferry, oppoſite to this town, with directions to proceed to the attack of that poſt. The detachment marched a part of the way on the ſame day, and on the 22d in the afternoon was before Red Bank : Colonel Donop immediately made the beſt diſpoſition, and led on the troops in the moſt gallant manner to the aſſault. They carried an extenſive outwork, from whence the enemy were driven into an interior intrenchment, which could not be forced without ladders, being eight or nine feet high, with a parapet boarded and fraized. The detachment in moving up and returning from the attack was much galled by the enemy's gallies and floating batteries.

Colonel Donop and Lieutenant-colonel Minningerode being both wounded, the command devolved upon Lieutenant-colonel Linſing, who, after collecting all the wounded that could be brought off, marched that night about five miles towards Cooper's-ferry, and on the following morning returned with the detachment to camp.

Colonel Donop unfortunately had his thigh ſo much fractured by a muſquet ball, that he could not be removed, but I ſince underſtand there are ſome hopes of his recovery. There were ſeveral brave officers loſt upon this occaſion, in which the utmoſt ardour and courage were diſplayed by both officers and ſoldiers.

On the 23d the Auguſta in coming up the river, with ſome other ſhips of war, to engage the enemy's gallies near the fort, got aground, and by ſome accident taking fire in the action, was unavoidably conſumed ; but I do not hear there were any lives loſt. The Merlin ſloop alſo grounded, and the other ſhips being obliged to remove to a diſtance from the exploſion of the Auguſta, it became expedient to evacuate and burn her alſo.

Theſe diſappointments however will not prevent the moſt vigorous meaſures being purſued for the reduction of the fort, which will give us the paſſage up the river.

I have the honour to be, &c.
W. HOWE.

P. S. I have the ſatisfaction to incloſe to your Lordſhip a report juſt received of a very ſpirited piece of ſervice performed by Major-general Vaughan, and Sir James Wallace, up the Hudſon's River.

Copy of Major-general VAUGHAN's
Report.

On board the Friendſhip off Eſopus, Friday, October 17, 10 o clock, morning.

Sir,

I have the honour to inform you, that on the evening of the 15th inſtant I arrived off Eſopus; finding that the rebels had thrown up works, and had made every diſpoſition to annoy us, and cut off our communication, I judged it neceſſary to attack them, the wind being at that time ſo much againſt us that we could make no way. I accordingly landed the troops, attacked their batteries, drove them from their works, ſpiked and deſtroyed their guns. Eſopus being a nurſery for almoſt every villain in the country, I judged it neceſſary to proceed to that town. On our approach they were drawn up with cannon, which we took and drove them out of the place. On our entering the town they fired from their houſes, which induced me to reduce the place to aſhes, which I accordingly did, not leaving a houſe. We found a conſiderable quantity of ſtores of all kinds, which ſhared the ſame fate.

Sir James Wallace has deſtroyed all the ſhipping except an armed galley, which run up the Creek with every thing belonging to the veſſels in ſtore.

H h h 2   Our

Our lofs is fo inconfiderable that it is not at prefent worth while to mention. I am, &c.

(Signed) JOHN VAUGHAN.

Admiralty-Office, December 1, 1777. *Copy of a Letter from Vice Admiral Lord Vifcount* HOWE *to Mr.* STEPHENS. *Dated on board his Majefty's fhip* Eagle, *in the River Delaware, October* 25, 1777.

The Lords Commiffioners of the Admiralty will be informed by my laft letter of the 28th of Auguft of the arrival of the fleet at the head of Chefepeak Bay, and the debarkation of the army the 25th in the River Elk.

The provifions, military ftores, and baggage required having been landed under the direction of Captain Duncan, by the 7th of the next month the army advanced towards the rebel forces affembled near Wilmington on the fide of the Delaware.

The enemy confiding in the ftrength of their fituation, and waiting the approach of the army, were charged the 11th in the evening with fo much fpirit, that notwithftanding the advantages of their poft, they were quickly forced on every part, and retreated in great confufion towards the town of Philadelphia.

When this account was forwarded, the lofs in either army was not afcertained. But twelve pieces of cannon had been taken in the field; and the victory would have probably been compleat, but for the great fatigue of the King's forces in a long and difficult march round by the Forks of the Brandywine, to arrive in the deftined pofition for the commencement of the attack.

Upon intelligence of this event received the 13th, preparation was made for taking the firft favourable opportunity to move the fleet round to a proper anchorage for preferving a free communication with the army in this river.

The progrefs down the Bay was confiderably retarded by the ftate of the weather and intricacy of the navigation which did not admit of continuing under fail during the night, wherefore, though quitting the Elk the 14th, the fleet could not put to fea from the Capes of Virginia until the 23d of the fame month. I then proceeded forward in the Eagle with the Vigilant and Ifis, and a fmall divifion of the tranfports in which fome articles of provifions and military ftores, likely to be fooneft wanted for the army, had been for that purpofe embarked, and left the body of the fleet to be conducted by Captain Griffith with the reft of the fhips of war.

Having had very tempeftuous weather of fome duration to the Northward, in the paffage down Chefepeak Bay, the profpect was favourable for the fpeedy arrival of the fleet in the Delaware.

But when the two divifions (little feparated) were advanced within a few leagues of the entrance of the river, the wind changed in a fudden fquall from the Southward in the evening of the 25th; and having continued between the North-Weft and North-Eaft with a degree of force much too great for the tranfports to make any way againft it, I was unable to get into the river (followed a few days after by the firft convoy, which I had left in the care of Captain Cornwallis when the weather became more fettled) until the evening of the 4th inftant.

The larger convoy with Captain Griffith, though much more difperfed, arrived between the 6th and 8th of the month, with no other material accident except the lofs of the tranfport named the Father's Good Will, which having fprung a leak when no affiftance could be given during the bad weather, funk at fea, but the crew were faved.

The fhips of war and tranfports were anchored in the moft convenient fituations

fituations in the weſtern ſhore from Newcaſtle down towards Rudy Iſland.

On my arrival off Cheſter on the 6th inſtant, I learnt that the rebel army, ſince the 11th of laſt month, had always been retiring with precipitation to avoid a general action, ſometimes attempting advantages by ſurprize; but the King's forces maintaining their uſual aſcendancy on every occaſion.

The General was in poſſeſſion of Philadelphia, and a frigate of 32 guns named the Delaware, attempted to be paſſed above the town, had been taken by the troops which were firſt poſted there.

Captain Hammond (who was returned here in the Roebuck) had moved up the river with the Pearl, Camilla, and Liverpool, as the army advanced.

When I came to this ſtation, he was lying with thoſe frigates off Billingport, where the rebels had nearly compleated a very extenſive work for defending the approach to the firſt double line of ſunk frames or chevaux de frize, which croſſed the navigable channel in that part of the river.

The General having a few days before appointed a ſtrong corps of infantry to be landed on the Jerſey ſhore, to diſlodge the enemy from that poſt, they abandoned it at his approach. The front to the river had thereupon been deſtroyed, and the troops that evening withdrawn.

A trial had in the mean time been begun for opening a paſſage through that firſt obſtruction, which the enemy, with their fire rafts, gallies, and other armed craft, repeatedly endeavoured to prevent under cover of the night; but without any material injury to the frigates: and a ſufficient channel was at length (though not without much difficulty) made for the larger ſhips, by the advanced ſquadron; the conduct of which was on every occaſion to be much approved.

The remaining obſtructions to an uninterrupted communication with the town of Philadelphia, conſiſted of an incloſed work erected on a flat muddy iſland, named Fort Iſland, a little diſtance below the entrance of the Schuylkill, ſtrengthened by four block-houſes; with two floating batteries of nine guns each, and twelve or fourteen gallies mounting heavy cannon, beſides many other armed craft of leſſer force, and ſeveral fireſhips. Oppoſite thereto, on the eaſtern ſhore at Red Bank, above Manto Creek, a redoubt was conſtructed, under which their moveable water force could find protection occaſionally.

In the front of theſe defences, to the extent of half a mile or more below the iſland, (being the part of the channel where the navigation was contracted in the width to about 100 fathoms) ſeveral rows of the chevaux de frize were ſunk ſo as to render the nearer approach of the ſhips impracticable; and no attempt could be made for moving the ſunk frames, or otherwiſe clearing the channel, till the command of the ſhores on each ſide of the river could be obtained.

For theſe purpoſes the General ordered ſome batteries to be erected on the weſtern ſhore to diſlodge the enemy from the iſland; and a body of troops to be landed for forcing the redoubt on Red Bank.

It was intended that the Vigilant ſhould paſs through a ſhallow and very confined channel between Hog Iſland (next below Fort Iſland) and the Pennſylvania ſhore; to arrive and act upon the rear and leſs defenſible part of the work; and the circumſtances of the navigation not admitting of a more ſerious attack, for the reaſons before-mentioned, a diverſion was propoſed to be made at the ſame time by the advanced frigates, together with the Iſis and Auguſta, in the eaſtern or main channel of the river,

river, as well for engaging the attention of the enemy at Fort Island and the redoubt, as to reftrain the motions of the gallies and other armed craft which had retired under the works at Red Bank, when they difcovered the danger they would be expofed to in their former ftations near Fort Island from our batteries on the weftern fhore.

The wind continuing from the northward feveral fucceffive days, the Vigilant could not proceed according to her deftination at the time intended. The Augufta, Roebuck, Liverpool, and Pearl, were neverthelefs ordered above the firft line of chevaux de frize the 22d inftant, to be in readinefs for fuch fervice as they fhould be able to render when the redoubt fhould be attacked; and Captain Reynolds, being the fenior officer, fucceeded to the command of the advanced fquadron.

The detachment of the army, confifting of Heffian troops under Col. Donop, appointed to attack the redoubt, croffed the Delaware oppofite to Philadelphia the 21ft inftant, in a divifion of flat boats, which Captain Clayton conducted in the night by Fort Ifland along the weftern fhore for that purpofe.

The attack of the redoubt being obferved to take place the evening of the 22d, juft upon the clofe of day, Captain Reynolds immediately flipped, and advanced with the fquadron, (to which the Merlin had been joined) as faft as he was able with the flood, to fecond the attempt of the troops, which were feen to be very warmly engaged: but the change in the natural courfe of the river, caufed by the obftructions appearing to have altered the channel, the Augufta and Merlin unfortunately grounded fome diftance below the fecond line of the chevaux de frize; and the frefh northerly wind, which then prevailed, greatly checking the rifing of the

tide, they could not be got afloat on the fubfequent flood.

The diverfion was endeavoured to be continued by the frigates, at which the fire from the enemy's gallies was chiefly pointed for fome time. But as the night advanced, the Heffian detachment having been repulfed, the firing ceafed.

The rebels difcovering the ftate of the Augufta and Merlin in the morning of the 23d, renewed the fire from their gallies, works and floating batteries. But their moveable force approaching little nearer than a random fhot, the injury was inconfiderable to the fhips; and by the alertnefs and fpirit of the officers and feamen (of the tranfports as well as fhips of war) attending in the boats of the fleet on this occafion, four fire veffels, directed againft the Augufta, were fent without effect.

The Ifis was at this time warping through between the lower chevaux de frize. Empty tranfports had been ordered up from the fleet, and other preparations made for lightening the Augufta; when by fome accident, no otherwife connected with the circumftances of the action, but as it was probably caufed by the wads from her guns, the fhip took fire abaft, and it fpread with fuch rapidity, that all endeavours to extinguifh it were ufed in vain. The men were thereupon taken out, except a very fmall number not yet afcertained. The fecond Lieutenant Baldock, the Chaplain and Gunner appear to be of that number.

In this ftate of the proceeding it was neceffary to withdraw the frigates, for fecuring them from the effect of the blaft. And as the Merlin could not be protected from the fame injury, I judged it requifite to give orders for the floop to be evacuated and deftroyed. The other fhip dropped down nearer to Billingport.

Much

Much commendation is due to the several Captains, inferior officers and seamen concerned in this service; and particularly in their resolute exertions to assist in saving the crew of the Augusta.

Admiralty-Office, December 1, 1777.

Copy of a letter from Commodore HOTHAM to Vice-Admiral Lord Viscount HOWE, and by his Lordship transmitted to Mr. STEPHENS, dated on board His Majesty's ship the Preston, off Peek's-Kill Creek, the 9th of October, 1777.

Sir Henry Clinton having thought it adviseable to make a diversion up the North River, and the necessary arrangements being made in consequence, the flat boats and batteaux on the 3d instant proceeded to Spikendevil-creek in three divisions, under the Captains Pownall, Jordan, and Stanhope: Captain Pownall having the direction of the whole.

A body of about 1100 troops were embarked in them that evening, and the same night proceeded to Tarry Town, where they landed at daybreak, and occupied the heights adjoining. A second division, nearly of that number, marched out at the same time from Kingsbridge, and formed a junction by land with those who passed by water. The squadron under Captain Ommanney had moved up the day before to receive them, the smaller part of it, namely, the galleys and armed vessels, (as they might be to act separately) I thought it adviseable on this occasion to make a distinct command, and could not place them better than under the direction of Sir James Wallace, whose knowledge of the river, as well as Captain Ommanney's, we fully experienced the advantage of.

The third division of troops were embarked in transports, and on the 4th in the morning left New-York, under convoy of the Preston, and in the course of the same tide arrived off Tarry Town.

The general embarkation was that night made, and the wind being still favourable, the whole, preceded by the squadron under Sir James Wallace as an advanced guard, reached Vere Planks Point at noon the day following, and those in the flat boats landed with appearance only of an opposition. Sir James Wallace was immediately dispatched higher up the river to cut off the enemy's communication by Peak's-kill-ferry.

The 6th at day-break the general debarkation took place, and all the troops, except about four hundred, who were left to secure Vere Plank Neck, were soon landed at Stoney Point, upon the opposite shore, from whence they had about twelve miles to march through a mountainous and rugged road to Fort Clinton and Montgomery.

The ships and transports then moved higher up, and anchored opposite Peek's-kill landing.

In the afternoon the advanced squadron and the two frigates got under sail and opened Fort Montgomery, with a view only to make an appearance, and thereby to cause a diversion in favour of the attack, which we observed had now begun. Sir James by the help of his oars got near enough in with the gallies to throw some shot into the fort. The cannonading and fire of musquetry continued 'till night, when, by a most spirited exertion, a general and vigorous assault was made, and the two important Forts of Clinton and Montgomery fell by storm to his Majesty's arms. On which I have the honour to congratulate your Lordship most sincerely. The rebel frigates are both burnt, with a galley, and a sloop of ten guns is taken.

The loss on the enemy's side is not yet exactly known, but they are supposed to have had about 100 killed and 250 taken prisoners. The greatest loss on the side of the King's troops are about 40 killed, among whom

are

are some valuable officers, namely, Lieutenant Colonel Campbell, Major Sill, Major Grant, and Captain Stewart, and about 150 wounded.

A summons signed by Sir Henry Clinton and myself was the next day sent up to Fort Constitution, by a flag of truce, which being fired at, returned, and determined the General immediately to correct the insult by an attack. An embarkation was accordingly made on the morning on the 8th, and proceeded up the river for that purpose, under cover of the galleys.

We found upon our arrival the Fort had been abandoned in great confusion, their barracks burnt, but all their artillery left. The whole number of cannon taken in three forts amount to 67, with a large quantity of provisions, ammunition, and stores of all kinds to a very considerable amount. I have directed such part of the chain and bomb as cannot be saved to be destroyed: the construction of both give strong proofs of labour, industry, and skill.

Sir James Wallace, with his flying squadron, is gone still higher up the river, and if he passes the chevaux de frize at Pellipus Island, he may do essential service, as there can be nothing to give him any interruption.

When it is considered that this attack was made after a most fatiguing march over precipices, and through roads almost impenetrable, which made it impossible for the troops to avail themselves of the use of cannon so unnecessary for such a purpose, and the little assistance they could therein promise themselves from the ships; the access through the highlands to the forts, rendering the approach to them so precarious, it redounds the more to the credit of an enterprize, which was formed and executed with equal judgment, valour, and success.

The Captains, officers, and men under my command have been so strenuously zealous in their exertions upon this occasion, that every testimony is due from me in approbation of their conduct during this service of fatigue, of which Capt. Pownal has had his share, and is well able to inform your Lordships of every particular.

I have the farther pleasure to acquaint your Lordship, that General Tryon is just returned from Continental Village, where he has destroyed barracks for 1500 men, with stores to a considerable amount.

Copy of a letter from Sir James Wallace *to Commodore* Hotham, *dated, Gallies and Armed Vessels off Esopus Creek, October* 17, 1777.

Sir,

We proceeded up the river, destroying a number of vessels as we sailed along, without stopping till we arrived at Esopus-creek, where we found two batteries; one of two guns, the other of three guns erected, and an armed galley at the mouth of the creek, who endeavoured to prevent our passing by their cannonade. General Vaughan was of opinion such a force should not be left behind. It was determined to land and destroy them, and immediately executed, without retarding our proceeding up the river. The General marched for the town and fired it. The boats from the armed vessels went up the creek, burnt two brigs, several large sloops and other craft, with all their apparatus that was in store upon the shore. Lieutenant Clark of the Dependence, with two or three others, in firing the stores were blown up, but we flatter ourselves not dangerously.

The officers and men upon this occasion behaved with the greatest spirit.
[*London Gazette.*

———————

Philadelphia, September 12.
Letter from General Washington.
" Sir, *Chester, Sept.* 11, 1777.
" I am sorry to inform you, that in this day's engagement we have been obliged to leave the enemy mas-
ters

ters of the field. Unfortunately the intelligence received of the enemy's advancing up the Brandywine, and croffing the ford about fix miles above us, was uncertain and contradictory, notwithstanding all my pains to get the best. This prevented my making a difposition adequate to the force with which the enemy attacked us on our right. In confequence of which the troops first engaged were obliged to retire before they could be reinforced.

" In the midft of the attack on the right, that body of the enemy which remained on the fide of Chad's-ford, croffed it, and attacked the division there, under the command of General Mayne, and the light troops under General Maxwell, who, after a fevere conflict, alfo retired. The militia, under General Armftrong, being pofted at a ford, about two miles below Chad's-ford, had no opportunity of engaging; but we fought under many difadvantages, and were, from the caufes above-mentioned, obliged to retire; yet our lofs of men is, I am perfuaded, very confiderable. but I believe much lefs than the enemy; we have alfo loft eight pieces of cannon, according to the beft information I can obtain; the baggage having been previoufly moved off, is all faved, except the men's blankets, which being at their backs, many of them, doubtlefs, were loft. I have directed all the troops to affemble behind Chefter, where they are now arranging for this night. Notwithftanding the misfortune of the day, I am happy to find the troops in good fpirits, and I hope another time we fhall compenfate for the lofs we have fuftained. The Marquis la Fayette is wounded in the leg, and General Woodford in the hand. Divers other officers are wounded, and fome flain; but the number of either cannot now be afcertained.

.I have the honour to be, &c.
G. Washington."

" P. S. It is not in my power to fend you certain intelligence, the prefent being the firft leifure moment I have had fince the action."

Published by order of Congrefs,
Charles Thomson, Sec.

___

Bofton, October 2.
Extract of a letter from a gentleman of diftinction in Philadelphia to his friend in this town dated Sept. 15, 1777.

Dear Sir,

In my laft I wrote you, that we were every moment in expectation of engaging the enemy. They advanced by flow degrees up the river Brandywine, with an evident intention of croffing one of the fords. Our army of courfe moved on the other fide of the river to prevent it. But as there were three fords within the compafs of ten miles, we were obliged to divide our army, to guard each pafs; the greateft probability was, that they would crofs the middle one, called Chad's; accordingly our greateft force was pofted there, and General Maxwell, with about 1000 light troops, were fent acrofs to take poffeffion of the oppofite height. In the night of the 10th inftant, they threw up a flight breaft-work of limbs of trees. The next morning, about eight o'clock, the enemy appeared in fight, and moved on a party to difpoffefs Maxwell, and at a little diftance opened upon our people a heavy cannonade with 8 pieces of cannon, which was returned by our cannon, with good effect. General Maxwell drove back the party which was fent againft him with great lofs; they were reinforced a fecond time, and came on, but were again repulfed, and followed fome diftance by the General's party. But as they could not carry their fcheme into execution while our light troops remained on the other fide the river, they were determined, at all events, to oblige them to retire; accordingly they

I i i

they sent a very strong party round a piece of woods, in order to come upon his flank, while the other attacked him in front. The General perceived this movement, and retreated across, where he joined the main body, with the trifling loss of three killed, and eight or nine wounded. A very intelligent fellow, who was in the action, told me, that when they pursued the enemy, he was confident he saw near 500 lying on the field; but the General, who is very modest in his account of the matter, imagines there were at least 300 killed and wounded. I was with the main body on this side the river, and had the pleasure to see the British troops run. The distance from us was not much more than a quarter of a mile.

The enemy still kept up their cannonade, and some of their troops paraded on the heights, and appeared as if they intended to attempt Chad's-ford, but their main body filed off to the left, and crossing the upper ford, marched on to Birmingham Meeting-house, near which our right wing was posted. Unfortunately the accounts our General received of this movement were various and contradictory, which prevented a sufficient force being sent on to sustain the attack in that quarter. Lord Stirling's, and another officer's divisions, were there, and General Sullivan was sent on to reinforce, but unhappily his division took rather too large a circuit, and rising a hill, were attacked by the whole force of the enemy, before they had time to form. This sudden and unexpected attack threw them into confusion, and they retreated with the utmost precipitation.

The other divisions were also obliged to retreat, after maintaining a very warm conflict for some time, and were closely pursued by the enemy, who took advantage of their retreat, till they fell in with General Green's division, and the one that was Lin-

coln's, but now commanded by General Waine. Here a most terrible and bloody battle took place, which was maintained with the greatest bravery and intrepidity for upwards of half an hour, when our people were obliged to quit the field, and the day closing prevented any further pursuit. We lost in this action nine pieces of cannon, a number of officers and men, but none of higher rank than Major Bush, of Col. Hartley's regiment, who was killed.

The Marquis la Fayette was wounded in the leg, but is in a fair way. Gen. Woodford was shot through the hand.

In the evening the General retreated to Chester, in order to collect his troops, and to permit them to take some refreshment, having had no food the whole day, and little or no sleep for 48 hours before.

I forgot to mention, that at the time they attacked us on the right, the party which possessed the heights opposite Chad's-ford, attempted to pass it, but were attacked by Gen. Maxwell, who again obliged them to retreat, with the loss of 30 men, among whom was a Capt. Campbell, out of whose pocket was taken the orders of the 10th instant, and some other important papers.

By General Howe's orders, it appears, that very little reliance is to be placed upon his promises of protection; for he there commands his troops to bring in all the cattle and horses they can lay their hands on, and promises to pay the soldiers who bring them in, a guinea a head for horses, a dollar for horned cattle, and a crown for fat sheep; in consequence of which, they have plundered all the inhabitants without distinction.

The regiment of artillery, with their General, behaved with their usual coolness and intrepidity. Some of them could scarce be prevailed upon to quit their guns, even when
                                    surrounded

furrounded by the enemy, and forsaken by our infantry.

The Bofton boys did themfelves great honour. I rode up to Captain Allen, at the beginning of the action; young Cooper was with him at the fame gun, and a number of our Bofton lads; they feemed in high fpirits. I told them not to forget old times. Colonel Proctor, with his corps of artillery, alfo behaved to admiration. In the infantry, the brigade which compofed Green's and Waine's divifion, particularly Wenden's and Woodford's, behaved admirably. They fuftained a clofe and heavy fire from the enemy for a long time, without ftarting an inch. Spottwood's and Stewart's regiments diftinguifhed themfelves greatly. The former is a Virginia, and though not a large one, is the beft difciplined and moft orderly regiment in the fervice. The Commander is a fenfible, brave, and cool gentleman, and his whole foul feems to be engroffed in the care and difcipline of his regiment; of confequence they are always clean and healthy.

Many others (Virginia efpecially) which I have not time to defcribe, behaved in a manner that would do honour to veteran troops. The Marylanders got no great credit; but it is faid to be the fault of their principal Commander. How this is, time will difcover; their Brigadier-general (B——re) is fufpended. He has fince refigned his commiffion.

A great number of French officers were in the action. The Marquis de la Fayette, that moft accomplifhed youth, behaved with a bravery equal to his birth and amiable character. The Polifh Count Pulafki, with a party of light horfe, rode up to reconnoitre the enemy, within piftol fhot of their front. Chevalier du Pleffi, who is one of Gen. K's family, had three balls through his hat. Young Fleuri's horfe was killed under him. He fhewed fo much bravery,

and was fo ufeful in rallying the troops, that the Congrefs have made him a prefent of another. I fhould not do juftice if I did not add, that the foreign officers in general behaved exceeding well.

I fhall follow the ufual cuftom of the drama, by introducing the greateft hero at the laft. The character of our worthy General needs no eulogium. He is at all times great, but on that day he really outfhone himfelf.

In the beginning of the action he rode from one end to the other of the line, cheering and encouraging the men with fuch benignity and affability, as almoft feemed to be more than human. Defcription would fail me, were I to attempt to reprefent how much the men feemed animated by his prefence; they could give no other vent to their feelings but by fhouts of applaufe, which feemed to rend the air.

Never were men in better fpirits, and I am confident as I am of my own exiftence, that if the attack had been made where it was expected, Mr. Howe and his army would certainly have been entirely routed. As the enemy were in poffeffion of the field of battle, and our troops much fatigued, we could not very fuddenly form a judgment of the killed and wounded on either fide. It was, however, agreed on all hands, that the lofs of the enemy was infinitely greater than ours; and the accounts which have been received confirm the conjecture. They have loft upwards of 2000 men in killed and wounded, and confefs, that though they have gained the victory, they have paid very dear for it. In fhort, it is another Bunker's-hill action. From the beft accounts that can be gathered, our lofs does not exceed 1000. They have fent to us furgeons to affift in dreffing the wounded, and feveral have been fent by our General.

As it was not improbable the enemy
would

would purſue their advantage, and immediately puſh for this city, Gen. Waſhington thought it beſt to be before-hand with them and accordingly marched here, with his troops, but, from the accounts afterwards received, finding that they were greatly diſabled, and would probably wait for a further reinforcement before they came on, he yeſterday (Sunday) croſſed the Schuylkill, and has moved on the Lancaſter road, towards the enemy, who ſtill remain near the field of battle, and it is probable, you will ſoon hear of another engagement, which will doubtleſs decide the fate of the preſent campaign.

It is with the greateſt pleaſure I can aſſure you, that notwithſtanding the hardſhips they have endured, and the blood which has been ſpilt, our men are in high ſpirits, and ſeem more eager than ever to engage the enemy. It is not therefore improbable that the next battle will be a very bloody one.

We hear that there is a very conſiderable number of Virginia and Maryland militia on their way under General Smallwood. Four thouſand will be raiſed immediately in the Jerſeys, and three thouſand of General Putnam's diviſion are ordered, and, I ſuppoſe, are now on their march, ſo that I apprehend we ſhall ſtill be able to maintain a countenance.

I wait the arrival of the poſt, and ſhall leave this letter open till the laſt moment, that I may give you all the intelligence I poſſibly can.

Tell Henley the battle exceeded any thing he ever ſaw. I know he will be mortified that he was not a party concerned.

Fifteenth inſt. The poſt arrived yeſterday, and brought your's of the 4th inſt. The ſupply of blankets and ſtockings, brought in the veſſels from Spain, has arrived in a very lucky time, as our men began to want them exceedingly, and would have ſuffered ſoon.

Mr. Hancock, at whoſe houſe I write this, deſires me to acquaint his friends, that he is ſo much engaged in public matters, that he has not time to write by this poſt. Indeed he is very much engaged. The whole buſineſs part of the Congreſs lies upon his ſhoulders, and he is conſtantly employed both night and day. It is high time he ſhould have a little relaxation, but although his deſire to viſit his native town is exceedingly ſtrong, yet he is too much of the ſoldier to quit in time of danger; he is therefore determined to wait the iſſue of the preſent campaign; and when that is happily ended, as I doubt not it will, he will then, in all probability, pay you a viſit.

Sixteenth. How uncertain is human life! how ſoon are the brighteſt proſpects changed! Poor Gen. Coudray, who, this morning at eleven o'clock, I ſhook hands with in high ſpirits, in half an hour after was no more. He ſet out with a number of French gentlemen to join General Waſhington, as volunteers. The boats on the river Schuylkill are ſo conſtructed, that horſes and carriages drive immediately into them without unharneſſing. The General was on a young mare, full of ſpirits; he rode her into the boat, but not being able to ſtop her career, ſhe went out at the other end with the General on her back into the river. He diſengaged himſelf from her, and Major Rogers, his Aid de Camp, jumped immediately in after him, and being a good ſwimmer, ſuſtained him for a few minutes, but finding he could get no aſſiſtance, and the General ſtruggling, he was obliged (in order to ſave his own life) to quit him. The unfortunate General ſunk, and the tide being ſtrong, they have not yet been able to find the body, notwithſtanding the moſt diligent ſearch they could make. The General was greatly eſteemed by all who knew him, as well for his good ſenſe and courteous diſpoſition, difpofition, as for his knowledge of military affairs. His lofs is, of confequence, much lamented, particularly by his countrymen, to whom he feemed to be a father and protector.

Seventeenth. A letter was received laft night from Col. Biddle by Gen. Mifflin, who is fick in this city. Biddle fays, the enemy advanced yefterday about two o'clock, and attacked our picquet, which of courfe retired ; they then attacked the front of our army, and an engagement began, but rain coming on, both fides were forced to defift. The rain continues this day, but I fuppofe, as foons as it clears up, the action will be renewed. Our men are all in high fpirits, well pofted, and thofe of them who retreated in the laft action, have been collected, and are determined to make their ftand there. The action muft have been very bloody to the enemy ; feveral deferters who have come in fay, they had obliged the inhabitants to bury their dead ; that 1060 Britifh and foreign troops were buried in the neighbourhood This is exclufive of what was killed by Gen. Maxwell.

Their wounded men are fent to Wilmington, and as they are under apprehenfions from Gen. Smallwood and Col. Gift, who are in their rear, with 2000 men, they are obliged to leave a ftrong guard at Wilmington, to defend their fick and wounded.

Yefterday Congrefs was informed by exprefs, that 4000 Britifh forces were landed at Elizabeth-town Point. This was done, no doubt, with a view of making a diverfion in favour of Howe ; but as we have a fufficient force, which may foon be brought to oppofe them in that quarter, we are under no apprehenfions of their remaining long there.

The enemy are now within 10 miles of Swedes-ford, on the Schuylkill. This ford is about fixteen miles above Philadelphia. They mean to crofs it, no doubt, but the point will be very warmly difputed.

Gen. Wafhington and his army are at the Warren Tavern, on the Lancafter road, the other fide of Schuylkill.

The AMERICAN CRISIS.
Number IV.

Thofe who expect to reap the bleffings of freedom, muft, like men, undergo the fatigue of fupporting it. The event of yefterday is one of thofe kind of alarms which is juft fufficient to rouze us to duty, without being of confequence enough to deprefs our fortitude. It is not a field of a few acres of ground, but a caufe that we are defending ; and whether we defeat the enemy in one battle, or by degrees, the confequence will be the fame.

Look back at the events of laft winter, and the prefent year ; then you will find that the enemy's fuccefles have always contributed to reduce them. What they have gained in ground, they paid fo dearly for in numbers, that their victories have in the end amounted to defeats. We have always been mafters at the laft pufh, and always fhall, while we do our duty. Howe has been once on the banks of the Delaware, and from thence driven back with lofs and difgrace ; and why not be again driven from the Schuylkill ? His condition and ours are very different. He has every body to fight ; we have only his one army to cope with, and which waftes away at every engagement ; we cannot only reinforce, but can redouble our numbers ; he is cut off from all fupplies, and muft fooner or later inevitably fall into our hands. Shall a band of ten or twelve thoufand robbers, who are this day fifteen hundred or two thoufand men lefs in ftrength than they were yefterday, conquer America, or fubdue even a fingle State ? The thing cannot be, unlefs unless we sit down, and suffer them to do it. Another such a brush, notwithstanding we lost the ground, would, by still reducing the enemy, put them in a condition to be afterwards totally defeated.

Could our whole army have come up to the attack at one time, the consequence had probably been otherwise; but our having different parts of the Brandywine-creek to guard, and the uncertainty which road to Philadelphia the enemy would attempt to take, naturally afforded them an opportunity of passing with their main body at a place where only a part of ours could be posted: but it must strike every thinking man with conviction, that it requires a much greater force to oppose an enemy in several places, than is sufficient to defeat them in any one place.

Men who are sincere in defending their freedom, will always feel concern at every circumstance which seems to make against them; it is the natural and honest consequence of all affectionate attachments, and the want of it is a vice. But the dejection lasts only for a moment; they soon rise out of it with additional vigour, the glow of hope, courage, and fortitude, will in a little time supply the place of every inferior passion, and kindle the whole heart into heroism.

There is a mystery in the countenance of some causes, which we have not always present judgment enough to explain. It is distressing to see an enemy advancing into a country, but it is the only place in which we can beat them, and in which we have always beaten them, whenever they made the attempt. The nearer any disease approaches to a crisis, the nearer it is to a cure: danger and deliverance make their advances together; and it is only at the last push that one or the other takes the lead.

There are many men who will do their duty when it is not wanted: but a genuine public spirit always appears most when there is most occasion for it. Thank God! our army, though fatigued, is yet intire. The attack made by us yesterday, was under many disadvantages naturally arising from the uncertainty of knowing which route the enemy would take; and from that circumstance, the whole of our force could not be brought up together, time enough to engage all at once. Our strength is yet reserved; and it is evident that Howe does not think himself a gainer by the affair, otherwise he would this morning have moved down and attacked General Washington.

Gentlemen of the city and country, it is in your power, by a spirited improvement of the present circumstance, to turn it to a real advantage: Howe is now weaker than before, and every shot will contribute to reduce him. You are more immediately interested than any other part of the continent: your All is at stake; it is not so with the general cause; you are devoted by the enemy to plunder and destruction: it is the encouragement which Howe, the chief of the plunderers, has promised his army. Thus circumstanced, you may save yourselves by a manly resistance, but you can have no hope in any other conduct. I never yet knew our brave General or any part of the army, officers or men, out of heart, and I have seen them in circumstances a thousand times more trying than the present. It is only those that are not in action, that feel languor and heaviness, and the best way to rub it off, is to turn out, and make sure work of it.

Our army must undoubtedly feel fatigue, and want a reinforcement of rest, though not of valour. Our own interest and happiness call upon us to give them every support in our power, and make the burden of the day, on which the safety of this city depends,

depends, as light as poffible. Remember, gentlemen, that we have forces both to the northward and fouthward of Philadelphia, if the enemy be but ftopt till thofe can arrive, this city will be faved, and the enemy finally routed. You have too much at ftake to hefitate; you cught not to think an hour upon the matter, but fpring to action at once. Other ftates have been invaded, and have likewife driven off the invaders. Now our time and turn is come, and perhaps the finifhing ftroke is referved for us. When we look back on the dangers we have been faved from, and reflect on the fucceffes we have been bleffed with, it would be finful either to be idle or defpair.

I clofe this paper with a fhort addrefs to General Howe. You, Sir, are only lingering out the period that fhall bring with it your defeat. You have yet fcarce began upon the war, and the farther you enter, the fafter will your troubles thicken. What you now enjoy is only a refpite from ruin; an invitation to deftruction; a fomething that will lead on to our deliverance at your expence. We know the caufe we are engaged in, and though a paffionate fondnefs for it may make us grieve at every injury which threatens it, yet when the moment of concern is over, the determination to duty returns. We are not the hireling flaves of a beggarly ——; nor the cringing flattererers of an infamous Court. We are not moved by the gloomy fmile of a worthlefs ——, but by the ardent glow of generous patriotifm. We fight not to enflave but to fet a country free, and to make room upon earth for honeft men to live in. In fuch a caufe we are right; and we leave to you the defpairing reflection of being the tool of a miferable ——

COMMON SENSE.

Philadelphia,
Sept 12, at noon.

Philadelphia.
Extract of a letter from Head-Quarters, dated Sept. 9, three o'clock, A. M.

I embrace this opportunity to inform you, that the movements of the enemy yefterday gave the greateft reafon to apprehend they were endeavouring to force a march to Philadelphia, which they will profecute this day, or give us battle. Yefterday they advanced towards us, and our army prepared to give them battle, but whether from a diflike to our fituation, or a defire to fteal a march, I know not, they have and are ftill doing their utmoft to file to the right of us.

Philadelphia, Sept. 5. Within thefe few days feveral perfons of this city, have been apprehended as inimical to the United States. Many of thefe are Quakers. Yefterday a remonftrance from three of that body was prefented to the Prefident and Council of Pennfylvania, wherein they fay, that Lewis Nicola, Town-major, who commands here, having orders to confine them, they fay fuch confinement is againft law, and defire to be heard firft. Signed Ifrael Pemberton, John Hunt, Samuel Pleafants.

In a paper written by an advocate for the meafure, it is obferved, " People ought not to be furprized at Congrefs recommending this ftep. The right to bail has often been fufpended in England. In the year 1745, when the Scotch rebels invaded England. This is at prefent the cafe in America. Read General Burgoyne's general warrant to Lieut. Col. Baum, to feize *all pointed out* by Col. Skeene.

In Congrefs, Aug. 28, 1777.

The Committee to whom the papers, fent by General Sullivan, were referred, reported

That the feveral teftimonies fince the commencement of the prefent conteft contest between Great-Britain and America, and the uniform conduct of several persons who belong to the society of people called Quakers, render it certain that those persons are with much rancour and bitterness disaffected to the American cause.

Resolved, That it be recommended to the Supreme Executive Council of Pennsylvania, forthwith to apprehend and secure the persons of Joshua Fisher, Abel James, James Pemberton, Henry Drinker, Israel Pemberton, John Pemberton, John James, Samuel Pleasants, Thomas Wharton, sen. Thomas Fisher, and Samuel Fisher, sons of Joshua.

Sept. 3. A letter from G. Bryam, Esq. Vice-president of the Executive Council was read, setting forth that the above-named Persons were apprehended, and desiring the advice of Congress, whether Augusta and Winchester, in Virginia, would not be suitable places to secure them.

Resolved, That in the opinion of Congress, Stanton, in the county of Augusta, is the most proper place in the State of Virginia, for their residence and security.

The remonstrance from twenty-one Quakers, at present confined in the Mason's Lodge, was read.

The remonstrance of Israel Pemberton, &c. was read.

Ordered to lie on the table.

Resolved, That it be recommended to the Executive Council, to hear what the remonstrants can alledge against the charges of corresponding with the enemy, and to remove the suspicions of their being disaffected to the United States, and to act therein as they shall judge most conducive to the public safety.

Extract from the Journals.

Wm. Ch. Houston, Dep. Sec.

In Council, Philadelphia, Sept. 9, 1777.

Resolved, That James Pemberton, Henry Drinker, Israel Pemberton, John Pemberton, Samuel Pleasants, Thomas Wharton, sen. Thomas Fisher, son of Joshua, Samuel Fisher, son of Joshua, Myers Fisher, Elijah Brown, John Hunt, Phineas Bond, Rev. Thomas Coombe, Charles Jervis, William Drewet Smith, Charles Eddy, Thomas Pike, Owen Jones, jun. Edward Penington, William Smith, Thomas Gilpin, and Thomas Affleck, apprehended by Council as persons who have uniformly manifested, by their general conduct and conversation, a disposition highly inimical to the cause of America, and now imprisoned in the Free Masons Lodge in this city, they refusing to confine themselves to their several dwellings, and thereby making the restraint of their persons in another manner necessary, and having refused to promise to refrain from corresponding with the enemy, and also declined giving any assurance of allegiance to this State, as of right they ought, do thereby renounce all the privileges of citizenship; and that it appears they consider themselves as subjects of the King of Great-Britain, the enemy of this and the other United States of America; and that they ought to be proceeded with accordingly.

Resolved, That persons of like character, and in emergencies equal to the present, when the enemy is at our doors, have, in the other States, been arrested and secured upon suspicions arising from their general behaviour and refusal to acknowledge their allegiance to the States of which they were proper subjects; and that such proceedings may be abundantly justified by the conduct of the freest nations, and the authority of the most judicious civilians, therefore

Resolved, That the persons whose names are mentioned above, be, without farther delay, removed to Staunton in Virginia, there to be treated according to their characters, and stations, as far as may be consistent with the securing of their persons. Also

Resolved,

Resolved, That William Imlay, said to be a subject of the state of New-York, having behaved in like manner as the persons above-mentioned, and in particular declined to give assurance of allegiance to the state of New-York, be removed and secured with the rest.

Ordered, That Col. Nicola, the Town-major, secure the prisoners above-named, now in the Masons Lodge, and assist in removing them out of the city.

Extract from the Minutes,

T. MATLACK, Sec.

GENERAL ORDERS.

Wilmington, Sept. 5.

From every information of the enemy's design, and from their movements, it is manifest that their aim is, if possible, to possess themselves of Philadelphia. This is with them a capital object; it is what they last year strove to effect, but were happily disappointed. They made a second attempt at the opening of this campaign; but after vast preparation and expence for that purpose, they abandoned their design, and totally evacuated the Jerseys. They are now making their last effort. It seems they first intended to come up the Delaware, but from the measures taken against them in the river, judged the enterprize that way too hazardous. At length they have landed on the eastern shore in Maryland, and advanced some little way into the country; but the General thinks they will be again disappointed in their views, should they push their design against Philadelphia on this route. Their All is at stake. They will put the contest on the event of a single battle; if they are overthrown, they are utterly undone—the war is at an end. Now then is the time for our strenuous exertions; one bold stroke will free the land from rapine, devastation, and burnings, and female innocence from brutal lust and vio-

lence. In every other quarter the American arms have been of late rapidly successful; great numbers of the enemy have fallen in battle, and still greater numbers have been taken prisoners. The militia to the northward have fought with a resolution that would have done honour to the oldest soldiers; they bravely fought and conquered, and glory attends them. Who can forbear to emulate their noble spirits? Who is there without ambition to share with them the applause of their countrymen, and of all posterity, as the defenders of liberty, and preservers of peace and happiness to millions in the present and future generations?

Two years we have maintained the war, and struggled with difficulties innumerable; but the prospect has since brightened, and our affairs put on a better face. Now is the time to reap the fruits of all our toils and dangers; if we behave like men, this third campaign will be our last. Ours is the main army; to us our countrymen look for protection; the eyes of all America and Europe are turned upon us, as on those by whom the event of the war is to be determined; and the General assures his countrymen and fellow-soldiers, that he believes the critical, the important time is at hand, which demands their most spirited exertions in the field.

Here glory waits to crown the brave.—Peace, freedom, and happiness, will be the rewards of victory. Animated by motives like these, soldiers fighting in the cause of innocence, humanity, and justice, will never give way; but with undaunted resolution press on to conquest. And this the General assures himself is the part the American forces, now in arms, will act; and thus acting, he will ensure them success.

Williamsburg, Aug. 22. Upon notice of the British fleet being within our Capes, the Council met at the Capitol, and orders were issued to the

K k k   county

county Lieutenants, to march their several corps of militia to Williamsburg, York, Portsmouth, &c. to receive the enemy wherever they should make a descent. All the militia marched instantly with a chearfulness and alacrity not to be equalled. The Sussex militia, though they received their orders on Saturday, encamped on Sunday evening on the banks of James River, above forty miles from home. Thomas Nelson, jun. Esq. Brigadier-general, was appointed Commander in Chief.

Extract of a letter from Chester-town, dated August 30.

" The enemy have robbed our people of about one hundred negroes. Our people were told they might have what they wanted, and no violence should be committed: when they applied for their negroes, a day was formally appointed for a restoration, and when the day came, they were told they should be paid when the army returned.

" Our shores are crowded with dead bodies, both men and horses."

Philadelphia, Sept. 6. As Mr. W. Hughes, an old gentleman, of Chester county, was going a few days ago, into Newcastle county, to see what was become of his daughter, he was met by six Hessians, who took his horse from him, stripped him, and then with the most cruel barbarity, because he complained of his usage, they scourged the old gentleman in such a manner as would shock humanity. This account is from a lady who saw his back at the hospitable house, to which, with difficulty, he made shift to crawl.

Ordered by the subscriber commanding in Philadelphia, Sept. 23, 1777, That every decked vessel in the river Delaware between Market-street Wharf and Burlington, be next flood taken up to Burlington, and put under the care of the naval officer there. All such as are below

Market-street Wharf and Fort Mifflin, to be taken down the river, and put under the care of the naval officer commanding there. All such vessels, &c. as do not observe these orders, will be burned by boats and guards sent for that purpose. Every boat, batteau, &c. between Fort Mifflin and Burlington, must be immediately moved into Timber-creek, Anncocus, or Burlington-creeks. All merchandize and provisions brought into this city since the 19th instant, must be immediately removed, and none brought in, but what is *immediately* necessary for the use of the inhabitants. All others to be removed, if time will permit, or destroyed. The expence of removing to be charged to the owners.

Lewis Nicola, Col. of Invalids.

By Philip Schuyler, *Esq.*

Major-general in the army of the United States of America, and Commander in Chief of the Northern department.

To the inhabitants of Castleton, of Hubberton, Rutland, Tinmouth, Powlet, Wells, Granville, with the neighbouring districts; also the districts bordering on White-Creek, Cambden, Cambridge, &c. &c. &c.

Whereas Lieutenant-general John Burgoyne, commanding an army of the British troops, did, by a written paper, by him subscribed, bearing date at Skeensborough House, on the 10th day of July instant, require you to send from your several townships, deputations consisting of ten persons or more from each township, to meet Col. Skeens at Castle-town, on Wednesday, July 15th, at ten in the morning, for sundry purposes in said paper mentioned, and that you were not to fail in paying obedience thereto, under pain of military execution. Whatever, my countrymen, may be the ostensible reasons for such meeting, it is evident the enemy mean to
prevail!

prevail on you, by threats and promises, to forsake the cause of your injured country; to assist them in forcing slavery on the United States of America, and under the specious pretext of affording you protection, to bring on you that misery, which their promises of protection drew on such of the deluded inhabitants of New-Jersey, who were weak enough to confide in them; but who soon experienced their fallacy, by being treated indiscriminately with those virtuous citizens who came forth in the defence of their country, with the most wanton barbarity, and such as hitherto hath not even disgraced barbarians. They cruelly butchered, without distinction to age or sex; ravished children from ten to women of eighty years of age;—they burnt, pillaged and destroyed whatever came into their power; nor did those edifices dedicated to the worship of Almighty God escape their sacreligious fury. Such were the deeds; such they were incontestibly proved to be, which have marked the British arms with the most indelible stains. But they having, by the blessing of Divine Providence on our arms, been obliged totally to abandon that state; they left those who were weak or wicked enough to take protection under them to bemoan their credulity, and to cast themselves on the mercy of their injured countrymen. Such will be your fate, if you lend a willing ear to their promises, which I trust, none of you will do. But left any of you should so far forget the duty you owe to your country, as to join with, or in any manner of way assist, or give comfort to, or hold correspondence with, or take protection from the enemy—Be it known to each and every of you, the inhabitants of said townships, or any other the inhabitants of the United States, that you will be considered and dealt with as traitors to said States, and that the laws thereof will be put in execution against every person so offending, with the utmost rigour. And I do hereby strictly enjoin and command all officers, civil and military, to apprehend all such offenders. And I do further strictly enjoin and command such of the militia of said townships as have not yet marched, to do so without delay, to join the army under my command, or some detachment thereof.

Given under my hand at Head-Quarters, Fort Edward, July 13th, 1777.

PHILIP SCHUYLER.

By the General's command,

HENRY B. LEVINGSTON, A. D. C.

Head-Quarters, Aug. 25, 1777.

Sir,

A messenger is just arrived with the inclosed letters from General Arnold and Colonel Gansevoort; I am happy in communicating them to your Excellency. Great honour is due to Col. Gansevoort, Lieut. Col. Willett; and the offices and soldiers of the garrison under their command; I cannot too warmly recommend them to Congress. The gallant defence of Fort Stanwix must convince all the Western nations of Indians of the superiority of the Americans arms.

I am, Sir,

Your most obedient humble servant,

HORATIO GATES.

His Excellency JOHN HANCOCK, *Esq. President of Congress.*

Head-Quarters, Aug. 28, 1777.

Sir,

In the packet I have the honour to transmit to your Excellency a copy of a letter I received last night from Major-general Arnold. The defeat and disgrace with which the enemy have been obliged to retreat from Fort Schuyler, added to the compleat and brilliant victory gained by General Stark and Colonel Warner, at Bennington, gives the brightest lustre to the American arms, and covers the enemies of the United States with

K k k 2

infamy

infamy and fhame. The horrid murders and fcalpings, paid for and encouraged by Lieutenant-general Burgoyne, previous to his defeat at Bennington, will for ever ftain the honour of the Britifh arms. In one houfe, the parents, with fix children, were moft cruelly butchered; and this polite macaroni paid ten dollars for each of their fcalps. Heaven has, I hope, in ftore fome punifhment for fuch unheard-of crimes. I am, Sir,

Your moft obedient humble fervant,
HORATIO GATES.
The Hon. JOHN HANCOCK, *Efq.*

Fort Schuyler, Aug. 22.
Dear Sir,

This morning at eleven o'clock, I began a heavy cannonade upon our enemies works, which was immediately returned by a number of fhells and cannon. About three o'clock feveral deferters came in, who informed me that General St. Leger, with his army, was retreating with the utmoft precipitation; foon after which I fent out a party of about fixty men, to enter their camps, who foon returned, and confirmed the above account. About feven o'clock this evening Hanjort Schuyler arrived here, and informed me that General Arnold, with 2000 men, were on their march for this poft; in confequence of which I fend you this information. I am, dear Sir,

Your's, &c.
PETER GANSEVOORT, Col.
To the Hon. Gen. ARNOLD, or Officer commanding the army on their march to Fort Schuyler.

Mohawk River, ten miles above Fort Daton, Auguft 23, five o'clock, P. M.
Dear General,

I wrote you, the 21ft inftant, from German-flats, that from the beft intelligence I could procure of the enemy's ftrength, it was much fuperior to ours; at the fame time I inclofed you a copy of the refolutions of a

Council of War, and requefted you to fend me a reinforcement of one thoufand light troops. As the enemy had made their approaches within two hundred yards of the fort, I was determined, at all events, to hazard a battle, rather than fuffer the garrifon to fall a facrifice. This morning I marched from German-flats for this place. The exceffive bad roads, and the neceffary precautions in marching through a thick wood, retarded us fo much, that we have but this moment reached this place, where I have met an exprefs with the inclofed letter from Colonel Ganfevoort, acquainting me that the enemy had yefterday retired from Fort Schuyler with great precipitation. I am at a lofs to judge of their real intentions, whether they have returned home, or retired with a view of engaging us on the road; I am inclined to the former, from the account of their deferters, and from their leaving their tents and confiderable baggage, which our people fecured.

I fhall immediately detach about nine hundred men, and make a forced march to the fort, in hopes of coming up with the rear, and fecuring their cannon and heavy baggage.

I am, dear General,
Your affectionate obedient humble fervant,
B. ARNOLD.
Hon. Major-general GATES.

Fort Schuyler, Aug. 24, 1777, *ten o'clock at night.*
Dear General,

I wrote you yefterday, that the enemy had retreated from this place. At five o'clock in the evening, by a forced march of twenty-two miles, through a thick wood, I reached this place, in expectation of harraffing the enemy in their retreat; Col. Ganfevoort had anticipated my defign, by fending out a fmall party, who brought in four royals, and a confiderable quantity of baggage, with a number

number of prisoners and deserters. The enemy went off with the greatest precipitation, leaving their tents standing, their provisions, ammunition, &c. &c. which have fallen into our hands. I am, dear General,

Your affectionate,

B. ARNOLD.

Hon. Major-general GATES.

Published by order of Congress,

CHARLES THOMSON, Sec.

Kingston, September 8. On Friday last came to town from Fort Schuyler, Col. Peter Gansevoort, who lately so gallantly defended and drove the enemy from that fortress. From accounts brought by him we have collected the following further particulars relating to that important affair, viz.

Towards the close of the engagement, on the 6th of August, between about three or four hundred of the militia of Tryon county, under Gen. Harkemer, and about twelve hundred of the enemy, they, it seems, were ordered back to the fort, in consequence of the sally made or intended to be made, under Lieut. Col. Willet. This occasioned their sudden retreat, leaving our people in possession of the ground, and providentially saved them from being cut off. Among the prisoners they took of our people, were Col. Bellinger and Major Frey, two gentlemen who always had acted as hearty friends to America. On the 8th came to the fort, with a flag, Col. Butler, Capt. Gilbert Tice, of John's-town, and a Doctor. They brought from Gen. St. Leger, a Proclamation or Manifesto signed by him, but otherwise in the same words as Gen. Burgoyne's; also a letter from the two prisoners, which they were doubtless compelled to sign, and a verbal message to Col. Gansevoort from St. Leger, giving a pompous account of his forces and ability to take the fort. But that, to prevent the effusion of blood, through humanity and tenderness to

the besieged, he had deferred his attack upon the fort till he had previously disposed the Indians to forbear all manner of violence or injury to the prisoners: that he had succeeded in his design with the Indians, and could now assure Col. Gansevoort, and all the people under his command, that not the least injury should be offered them, provided they immediately delivered up the fort, with all its contents—And this he required and earnestly intreated Col. Gansevoort to do, for that if he did not, the Indians were determined to destroy all the men, women, and children, on the Mohawk River, and as soon as they got into the fort, to kill every man belonging to it, which Gen. St. Leger would be unable to prevent.—That it was vain for Col. Gansevoort to expect to defend the fort, for that the reinforcements coming to him were defeated and cut off—That Albany being in possession of the King's forces, it included the conquest of the Mohawk River, and therefore that an attempt to defend the fort would occasion the certain destruction of all the people in it, as well as many others. To the same purpose was the letter subscribed by Col. Bellinger and Major Frey.

Col. Gansevoort refusing to make any answer, or to listen to these or any proposals unless made in writing, the next day, August 9, Gen. St. Leger sent to the fort another flag, with the following letter, viz.

Camp before Fort-Stanwix, August 9. 1777.

Sir,

Agreeable to your wishes, I have the honour to give you on paper, the message of yesterday, though I cannot conceive, explicit and humane as it was, how it could admit of more than one construction. After the defeat of the reinforcement, and the fate of all your principal leaders, on which naturally, you built your hopes; and having the strongest reason from verbal

bal intelligence, and the matter contained in the letters that fell into my hands, and knowing thoroughly the situation of General Burgoyne's army, to be confident that you are without resource—in my fears and tenderness for your personal safety, from the hands of Indians, enraged for the loss of some of their principal and most favourite leaders—I called to council, the chiefs of all the nations, and after having used every method that humanity could suggest, to soften their minds, and lead them patiently to bear their own losses, by reflecting on the irretrievable misfortune of their enemies; I, at last, laboured the point my humanity wished for; which the chiefs assured me of, the next morning, after a consultation with each nation, that evening, at their fire places—Their answer in its fullest extent, they insisted should be carried by Colonel Butler, which he has given you in the most categorical manner; you are well acquainted that Indians never send messages without accompanying them with menaces on non-compliance, that a civilized enemy would never think of doing: you may rest assured therefore, that no insult was meant to be offered to your situation, by the King's servants, in the message they peremptorily demanded to be carried by Colonel Butler.

I am now to repeat what has been told you by my Adjutant-general. " That provided you will deliver up your garrison, with every thing as it stood, at the moment the first message was sent, your people shall be treated with every attention that a humane and generous enemy can give."

I have the honour to be,
Sir, Your most obedient,
humble servant,
BARRY ST. LEGER.

Brig. Gen. of his Majesty's forces.

P. S. I expect an immediate answer, as the Indians are extremely im-patient; and if this proposal is rejected, I am afraid it will be attended with very fatal consequences, not only to you and your garrison, but the whole country down the Mohawk River—such consequences as will be very repugnant to my sentiments of humanity, but after this, entirely out of my power to prevent.

BARRY ST. LEGER.
Colonel GANSEVOORT, *commanding Fort Stanwix.*

To this letter Col. Gansevoort returned a written answer, in substance as follows, viz. That being by the United States of America entrusted with the charge of the garrison, he was determined to defend it to the last extremity, against all enemies whatsoever, without any concern for the consequences of doing his duty.

On the receipt of this answer, the enemy renewed their firing at the fort, with cannon, bombs and small arms, which continued, and was returned from the fort (with some interval days of cessation on both sides) till the 22d of August, during which time the enemy had gradually made their approach to within one hundred and fifty paces of the fort, but were so much annoyed by our musquetry, that they came no nearer. A few of our people were killed and a few more wounded, six deserted to the enemy, and a few from them to the fort. On the 22d a deserter from the enemy informed Col. Gansevoort, that General St. Leger had been informed that Gen. Burgoyne's army had been entirely defeated, and that Gen. Arnold was near at hand with a re-inforcement for the garrison, of three thousand men with ten pieces of cannon---and that on this intelligence St. Leger, with all his troops, had precipitatly retreated, leaving their tents standing with considerable baggage, &c. This account was soon after confirmed by four more deserters. Col. Gansevoort then sent out two waggons with fifty men, who killed

killed two Indians, took four prisoners, and loaded the waggons. At night two more deserters came in, one of whom was called John Jost Cuyler, who was the person that gave Gen. St. Leger the intelligence that frightened him away.

On the 23d, parties were sent out, who brought in three prisoners, 4 four and two fifths inch royals, a three pound field-piece carriage, with all its apparatus, a quantity of baggage, ammunition, camp equipage, &c. the principal articles of which, and a great number of other articles left by the enemy, which fell into our hands, were as follow, viz.

Twenty-three batteaus; 19 waggons, the wheels cut; 2 travelling and lumber carriages; 155 three and six pound round shot; 87 ditto, fixed with flannel cartridges; 27 oil, and 2 hair cloths; 1 coil and 300 fathoms rope; 128 four and 2 fifths inch shells; 27 boxes cartridges, damaged; 30 copper hoops; 11 sets mens harness; one ditto, horse harness; 8 boxes musquet balls; 2160 musquet cartridges; 2 tanned hides; 5 deerskins; 5 camp stools; 6 matrosses; 1 pair curtains; 6 pair sheets; 18 bed cases; 10 knap-sacks; 1 case soap; 4 yards stroud; 4 brass candlesticks; 12 pewter plates; 250 weight iron; 128 weight steel; 106 spades; 100 picks; 80 falling axes; 1 set blacksmith's tools; 2 casks of nails; 2 whip saws; 3 cross cut ditto; 2 hand ditto; 2 barrels tar; 1 ditto pitch; 100 tent poles; 54 tents; 5 bell ditto, 1 brass, 24 camp kettles; 40 canteens; 4 frying pans; 56 blankets; 40 coats; 36 blanket ditto; 34 pair breeches; 2 pair of white ditto; 20 white, and 49 speckled shirts; 54 pair stockings; 20 handkerchiefs; and abundance of smaller articles; also a number of milch cows and horses, and 30 or 40 casks of flour, which had been staved, but not spoiled.

On the 24th, several scouts returned, with a German prisoner, who reported, that the enemy Indians, ten miles from the fort, fell upon the scattered regulars and Tories, took their arms, and stabbed them with their own bayonets. That for fear of them, he and nine more Germans, had fled to the woods, whence none but he had got in, not knowing what had become of the rest.

This afternoon arrived at the fort the Honourable Major-general Arnold, with 1000 men, who were saluted by a discharge of the cannon and mortars of the garrison, and with three cheers from the troops on the bastions.

The names of the deserters and prisoners then in the fort, were as follow, viz.

Edward Taylor of the 8th regiment.

Thomas Cook, Frederick Barkoff, William M'Intosh, Henry Innis, Patrick Karney, 34th regiment.

Charles Gray, 48th.

David Douglas, Benj. Harvey, artillery.

Joseph Cassier, German hunter.

David Sanguine, Ind. batteau man.

Donald Grant, Henry Whitmore, John Maddock, John Freeland, John Jost Cuyler *, John Lawrence, — Johnston.

AL-

* This Cuyler was one of Butler's Tories, sent out with a flag, to terrify and seduce the inhabitants on the Mohawk river; but being with his party, taken by our people, (as mentioned in the papers) and expecting to be punished with death, he was released on his parole, to be pardoned on condition of bringing good intelligence from the enemy, and his brother to be detained as a hostage for his return. On his passage from Gen. Arnold's camp to the fort, he fell in with a scout of the enemy, and pretended to have made his escape from our army, went with the scout to General St. Leger, to whom he related, that having been for some days a prisoner in our army, under General Arnold, and condemned to suffer death, he was going to execution, when finding himself not very closely guarded, he took an opportunity

ALBANY, 15th August, 1777.

SIR,

Inclosed I send you Lieut. Col. Marinus Willett's narration of occurrences at Fort Stanwix, since the approach of the enemy to invest that fortress. The narration must afford much pleasure to the public—at the same time, that it reflects great honour upon the gallant defenders of that important post.

I am, Sir,
Your humble servant.
JONATHAN TRUMBULL, jun.

Mr. John Holt.

On Saturday evening, August 2d, five batteaus arrived with stores for the garrison, about the same time we discovered a number of fires a little better than a mile from the N. West corner of the Fort. The stores were all got safe in, and the troops which were a guard to the batteaus, marched up. The Captain of the batteaux, and a few of his men, delaying their time about the boats, were fired on by a party of Indians, which killed one man and wounded two; the Captain himself was taken prisoner.

Next morning the enemy appeared in the edge of the woods, about a mile below the fort, where they took post, in order to invest it on that quarter, and to cut off the communication with the country; from whence they sent in a flag, who told us of their great power, strength, and determination, in such a manner as gave us reason to suppose they were not possessed of strength sufficient to take the fort. Our answer was, a determination to support it. All day on Monday we were much annoyed by a sharp fire of musketry from the Indians and German rifle-men, which, as our men were obliged to be exposed on the works, killed one and wounded seven. The day after, the firing was not so

heavy, and our men under better cover; all the damage was, one man killed by a rifle-ball.

This evening indicated something in contemplation by the enemy, the Indians were uncommonly noisy they made most horrid yelling great part of the evening in the woods, hardly a mile from the fort. A few cannon were fired among them.

Wednesday morning there was an unusual silence; we discovered some of the enemy marching along the edge of the woods downwards. About eleven o'clock, three men got into the fort, who brought a letter from Gen. Harkeman, of the Tryon county militia, advising us that he was at Eriska (eight miles from that fort) with part of his militia, and proposed to force his way to the fort, for our relief.—In order to render him what service we could in his march, it was agreed that I should make a sally from the fort with two hundred and fifty men; consisting one half of Gansevoort's, and one half of Massachusetts men, and one field piece, (an iron three pounder.) The men were instantly paraded, and I ordered the following dispositions to be made: Thirty men for the advanced guard to be commanded by Capt. Van Benscoten and Lieut. Stockwell; thirty for the rear guard under the command of Capt. Allen of the Massachusetts troops, and Lieut. Deuffendreff; thirty for flank guards, to be commanded by Capt. ——, from Massachusetts, and Ensign Chase. The main body formed into eight subdivisions, commanded by Capt. Bleeker, Lieutenants Conine, Bogardus, M'Clenner, and Ostraunder, Ensigns Bayley, Lewis, and Dennison, Lieut. Ball, the only supernumerary officer, to march with me, Capt. Johnson to bring up the rear of the main body —— Capt. Swart-

to run off, thinking, at worst, he might as well be shot as hanged---That though several shot we c fired at him, he got off quite unhurt. Being asked the force of General Arnold, he says his army consisted of 3000 w th ten field pieces, that he was on his march and must be very near at hand. On this intelligence, St. Leger decamped precipitately.--In the retreat Cuyler found means to conceal himself, and when the rest were gone, came into the fort.

Swartwourdt, with Enfigns Magee and Ament, and fifty men to guard the field piece, which was under the direction of Major Badlam. Nothing could be more fortunate than this enterprize. We totally routed two of the enemy's encampments, deftroyed all their provifion that was in them, brought off upwards of fifty brafs kettles, and more than a hundred blankets, (two articles which were much needed by us) with a number of mufkets, tomahawks, fpears, ammunition, cloathing, deer fkins, a variety of Indian affairs, and five colours, which on our return to the fort, were difplayed on our flag ftaff, under the Continental flag. The Indians took chiefly to the woods, the reft of their troops to the river. The number of men loft by the enemy is uncertain, fix lay dead in their encampment, two of which were Indians, feveral fcattered about in the woods, but their greateft lofs appeared to be in croffing the river, and no inconfiderable number on the oppofite fhore. I was happy in preventing the men from fcalping even the Indians, being defirous, if poffible, of teaching even the Savages humanity. But the men were much better employed, and kept in excellent order. We were out fo long, that a number of Britifh regulars, accompanied by what Indians, &c. could be rallied, had marched down to a thicket on the other fide of the river, about fifty yards from the road we were to pafs on our return ; near this place I had ordered the field piece. The ambufh was not quite formed when we difcovered them, and gave them a well directed fire.—Here efpecially, Major Badlam, with his field piece, did confiderable execution—here, alfo, the enemy were annoyed by the fire of feveral cannon from the fort, as they marched round to form the ambufcade. The enemy's fire was very wild, and though we were very much expofed, did no execution at all.

We brought in four prifoners, three of which were wounded. One of the prifoners is Mr. George Singleton of Montreal ; he is Lieutenant in a company of which Mr. Stephen Watts of New-York (brother-in law to Sir John Johnfon) was Captain, and who was himfelf killed in the battle with the militia, about two hours before. Mr. Singleton told me that Sir John was with him when we attacked their camp, and he thinks he ran to the river ; it is faid by fome of the Oneida Indians, that he is killed, which does not appear unlikely.

From thefe prifoners, we received the firft accounts of Gen. Harkeman's militia being ambufhed on their march and of a fevere battle they had with them about two hours before, which gave us reafon to think they had, for the prefent, given up their defign of marching to the fort.

I fhould not do juftice to the officers and foldiers who were with me on this enterprize, if I was not in the moft pofitive terms to affure their countrymen that they in general behaved with the greateft gallantry upon this occafion ; next to the very kind and fignal interpofition of Divine Providence, which was powerfully manifefted in their favour, it was undoubtedly owing to that noble intrepidity which difcovered itfelf in this attack, and ftruck the enemy with fuch a panick as difenabled them from taking pains to direct their fire, that we had not one man killed or wounded. The officers in general behaved fo well that it is hardly right to mention the names of any particular one for their fingular valour ; but fo remarkably intrepid was Capt. Van Benfcoten, and fo rapid was his attack, that it demands from me this particular teftimony of his extraordinary fpirit.

Among other things taken from the enemy, were feveral bundles of papers and a parcel of letters belonging to our garrifon, which they had taken from our militia, but not yet open-

opened. Here I found one letter for myself; there were likewise papers belonging to Sir John Johnson, and several others of the enemy's officers, with letters to and from Gen. St. Leger, their Commander; these papers have been of some service to us. On the evening of the next day, the enemy fired a few cannon at us from high ground, about half a mile north of the fort, where they have erected a small battery. Next day, being Friday the 8th, they threw a parcel of shells from the same battery, none of which did any execution. This evening they sent us a flag, with which came their Adjutant-general, Capt. Armstrong, Col. Butler, and a surgeon, the surgeon to examine Singleton's wounds; the principal business of the flag was to acquaint us, that Gen. St. Leger had, with much difficulty, prevailed on the Indians to agree, that if the Commanding Officer would deliver up the fort, the garrison should be secured from any kind of harm, that not a hair of their heads should be touched; but if not, the consequences to the garrison, should it afterwards fall into their hands, must be terrible; that the Indians were very much enraged, on account of their having a great number of their Chiefs killed in the late actions, and were determined, unless they got possession of the fort, to go down the Mohawk River, and fall upon its inhabitants. Our answer was, that should this be the case, the blood of these inhabitants would be upon the hands of Mr. Butler and his employers, not upon us, and that such proceedings would ever remain a stigma upon the name of Britain; but for our parts, we were determined to defend the fort.

That evening it was agreed by the Field Officers, that I should undertake, with Lieut. Stockwell, who is a good woods-man, to endeavour to get down into the country, and by making a proper representation of our affairs, endeavour to procure such force as may be sufficient, entirely to extirpate this miscreant band. After a most severe march, of about fifty miles through the wilderness, we have arrived at this place, and am in no doubt of beholding, in a few days, a few force sufficient to accomplish this important piece of business. By the best accounts, the loss of the Indians, in both actions, is very considerable, and they are quite sick of the expedition.

MARINUS WILLET.

German-flats, August 11, 1777.

A return of ammunition and artillery stores taken at the camp before Fort Schuyler, August 21*st,* 1777.

4 Royals, 42 5 inches diameter, 126 shells for ditto, 3 travelling carriages damaged, 2 damaged limbers for ditto, 135 three-pound round shot, 20 six-pound ditto, 72 three-pound shot flannel cartridges, 4 tin tube boxes, 60 tubes, 11 cannisters, 1 set horse-harness, 1 set of men's ditto, 4 sponges, 3 ladles, 3 wad-hooks, 28 boxes musket balls, 2 powder-horns, 2 lanthorns, 4 hand-spikes, 3 haversacks, 1 drudging-box, 2 linstocks, 2 port-fires, 1 apron, 1 pair of good limbers, 27 oil-cloths, 2 pair cloathes, 1 coil-rope, a large quantity of junk, a quantity of woollen yarn, 17 three-pound boxes of cartridges damaged, 5 six-pound ditto, 2160 good musquet cartridges, a large number of ditto damaged, 30 copper hoops.

———————

Boston, Sept. 20. The 10th of August, Barry St. Leger, Esq. Commander of the forces which besieged Fort Schuyler, sent by a flag to the fort, a proclamation almost verbatim with that of Burgoyne's, which proved a stimulus to that garrison's holding out.

The following is a copy of John Johnson and Company's address to the inhabitants of Tryon county, in order to dissuade them from taking

up

up arms to relieve Fort Schuyler, while besieged.

Camp before Fort Stanwix, Aug. 13.
To the Inhabitants of Tryon County.

Notwithstanding the many and great injuries we have received in person and property at your hands, and being at the head of victorious troops, we most ardently wish to have peace restored to this once happy country; to obtain which we are willing and desirous, upon a proper submission on your parts, to bury in oblivion all that is past, and hope that you are or will be convinced in the end, that we were your friends and good advisers, and not such wicked designing men as those who led you into error, and almost total ruin. You have, no doubt, great reason to dread the resentment of the Indians, on account of the loss they sustained in the late action, and the mulish obstinacy of your troops in this garrison, who have no resource but in themselves, for which reason the Indians declare, that if they do not surrender the garrison without further opposition, they will put every soul to death, not only the garrison, but the whole country, without any regard to age, sex, or friends—for which reason, it is become your indispensible duty, as you must answer the consequences, to send a deputation of your principal people, to oblige them immediately, to what in a very little time they must be forced, the surrender of the garrison—in which case we will engage on the faith of Christians to protect you from the violence of Indians.

Surrounded as you are by victorious armies, one half (if not the greater part) of the inhabitants friends to government, without any resource, surely you cannot hesitate a moment to accept the terms proposed to you, by friends and well-wishers to the country.

JOHN JOHNSON,
D. W. GLAUS, } Superintendants.
JOHN BUTLER,

In Congress, Sept. 6, 1777.

The Committee on the Treasury having taken into consideration the letter from Gen. Gates of the 28th of August, respecting cloathing for the army under his command, referred to them by Congress, report,

That it appears from the Clothier-general's report, that he has ordered considerable supplies of cloathing to be forwarded to the army in the Northern department from Boston, and that he has little doubt of being able to furnish, in the course of the year, the specific articles of cloathing directed to be given as a bounty to the troops; and as it will be equally disadvantageous to the soldiers, and to the service, should they receive money instead of such cloathing, the Board disapprove of the stoppages made by the Deputy Pay-master General in the Northern department out of the pay of troops in that department on account of cloathing, and direct the money to be returned, except in cases where a regiment shall have been furnished with more cloathing than the bounty.

That the greatest care ought to be taken to do justice to the soldiers as well as the public in this essential article. It is not sufficient, in the opinion of this Board, that the Clothier-general charges the regiment with the articles delivered, and takes the receipt of the Colonel or Commanding Officer; and that the Colonel or Commanding Officer, on delivering the cloathing to the Captain or Commanding Officer of each respective company, takes his receipt; every Commanding Officer of a company ought moreover strictly to be required to keep a cloathing account with his company, distinguishing the several articles delivered to each non-commissioned officer and private, and taking receipts for the same as his vouchers; and when each non-commissioned officer and private respectively shall have received his bounty of cloathing, the Command-

ing

ing Officer of the company to which he belongs shall deliver the account and receipts to the Commanding Officer of the regiment, to enable him to settle the cloathing account with the Clothier-general, as well as to discover whether equal justice has been done to the company.

That such troops as have not been supplied with cloathing ought to be furnished their full bounty without delay, which the Board have earnestly recommended to the attention of the Clothier-general, and he, on his part, has engaged to exert every means in his power to accomplish.

That such of the troops as, at their own expence, shall have provided themselves with any of the articles of cloathing allowed as a bounty, or shall not draw their cloathing in the course of the year, shall be entitled to receive the full value thereof at the average price which the cloathing of the army shall cost the public.

And whereas, when the bounty of cloathing was provided by Congress, it was conceived that it might be impracticable to obtain a sufficient quantity of cloth for regimental coats for the troops, and for that reason two hunting shirts were substituted; but in the event, so considerable a supply has been procured, that the Clothier-general has been enabled to furnish most of the troops with regimental coats instead of hunting shirts; and experience having shewn, that a further alteration of the articles of cloathing, allowed as a bounty, may be made to the advantage of the soldiers, and without loss to the public, therefore it is the opinion of the Committee that it be

Resolved, That the Clothier-general be directed, as far as he shall have it in his power to furnish all the non-commissioned officers and privates in the service of the United States, who have not yet received their bounty of cloathing, at their election, either with the several articles allowed by Congress in the resolution of the 8th of October, 1776, or in lieu thereof the following articles, viz.

One regimental coat, averaged at eight dollars and two thirds.

One jacket without sleeves, two dollars and two thirds.

One pair of buckskin and two pair of linen or woollen breeches, eight dollars.

One hat or leather cap, two dollars and two thirds.

Two shirts, eight dollars.

One hunting shirt, four ditto.

Two pair of overalls, six ditto.

Two pair of stockings, four ditto.

Two pair of shoes, six ditto.

One blanket, six ditto.

First cost estimated at fifty-six dollars.

But as the whole of the articles last specified exceeds that of the cloathing allowed as a bounty to the troops by eight dollars and one third of a dollar, so much shall be stopped out of the pay of every non-commissioned officer and private who shall be supplied in the manner last directed, as will make the amount of cloathing, he shall receive, equal to the value of the bounty of cloathing, which upon an average of the price of the several articles is estimated at forty-seven dollars and two thirds of a dollar.

The said report being twice read; on the question put,

Resolved, That Congress agree to the foregoing report and resolves.

By order of Congress,

JOHN HANCOCK, President.

Extract of a letter from a gentleman at Quebec, dated Sept. 7.

" In my last, I informed you of the success Gen. Burgoyne had met with by getting possession of Ticonderoga, &c. since which time however, he has received a check, by the defeat of a foraging party of about 600 whom he sent out to Bennington, distant from Saratoga, where his main body

body was, 30 miles. They were met and attacked by between 3 and 4000 of the rebels, and stood their ground for some time, till finding themselves surrounded and overpowered by numbers, they cut their way through them, and joined the main body. The loss upon this occasion is said to be 300, some say 500, killed, wounded and prisoners. Every attempt of this kind miscarrying, is productive of worse consequences to us than the loss of the men; it inspires them with courage. Our last accounts from Burgoyne's army say, that he was to leave Saratoga (where he has been for some time, waiting for stores coming up) the 4th inst. and proceed to Albany; so that in a few days, we may expect to hear something very capital. Col. St. Leger, who has a separate command of about 1000 Indians, 250 regulars, and as many of the faithful, went up by Niagara, and after clearing the country of the rebels, was to have gone down the Mohawk River and join Gen. Burgoyne at Albany. He was upon his way to attack Fort Stanwix, where the rebels had a garrison, when information was brought him, that a number of the enemy was coming by another route to reinforce it, he directly sent off a party consisting of Indians, and part of Sir John Johnson's corps, under the command of Sir John, to lie in ambush for them; they waited till the rebels came up, when they fired upon them, and throwing away their musquets, they ran in among them with their tomahawks and bayonets, and made a most dreadful slaughter, upwards of 600 rebels were left dead on the spot, and the few more that the party consisted of made their escape; our loss was very trifling. Col. St. Leger after this opened a battery upon the fort, but for want of heavy artillery could make no impression upon it. The Indians finding this, grew impatient, and wanted the Co-

lonel to return, threatening to leave him there if he did not. He endeavoured to pacify them, but all to no purpose, and an account coming in soon after, that a large body of the rebels were at hand in order to attack them, they lost all patience, and after breaking up the officers trunks, and carrying off what they could lay their hands on, they run away; upon which the Colonel thought it prudent to retreat, which he did to Oswego, leaving behind him two field-pieces that he could not carry off. Thus has this plan miscarried through the treachery of the Indians, who go to war only for the sake of plunder, which if they do not get from the enemy, they take from their friends. This retreat of Col. St. Leger from Fort Stanwix, has so alarmed many in this place, that they fancy themselves in greater danger than even in the winter of the siege, and it has raised the spirits of a few Yankey rascals here, who wish for nothing better than a visit from them. You know the gang of them, what pitiful miscreants they are."

Hartford, August 21. The following are the particulars of the action between the militia, &c. and part of the British army, on the 16th instant, near Bennington.

Saturday Aug. 16. Was a memorable day on account of a signal victory the militia, under the command of General Starke, obtained over a body of the King's troops, commanded by Governor Skeene. It seems that General Burgoyne had detached this corps, consisting of about 1500 men, chiefly Waldeckers and Brunswickers, intermixed with some British troops and Tories a motley compound, to penetrate as far as Bennington, and farther if it should be found practicable, with a view to encrease the number of his friends, to disperse his protections in the country to procure provisions for his army,
and

and to wreak his wrath and vengeance upon all thofe who had difregarded his calls of mercy. Governor Skeene had advantageoufly pofted this corps within five miles of Bennington meeting-houfe, where in different places they made breaft works for their own fecurity. This digreffion was of fuch ill tendency, and favoured fo much of prefumption, that Gen. Starke, who was at that time providentially at Bennington, with his brigade of militia from New Hampfhire ftate, determined to give them battle. Col. Simond's regiment of militia in Berks county was invited to his affiftance ; and 'a part of Col. Brown's arrived feafonably to attend on the action, and fome volunteers from different towns, and Col. Warner with a part of his own regiment joined them the fame day. The General wifely laid his plan of operations, and Divine Providence bleffing us with good weather, between three and four o'clock, P. M. he attacked them in front and flank in three or four different places with irrefiftible impetuofity.\ The action was extremely hot for between one and two hours; the flanking parties had carried their points with greater eafe, when the front preffed on to their breaft work with an ardour and patience beyond expectation. The blaze of the guns of the contending parties reached each other, the fire was fo extremely hot, and our men eafily furmounting their breaft works, amidft peals of thunder and flafhes of lightning from their guns, without regarding the roar of their field pieces, that the enemy at once deferted their cover and ran; and in about five minutes their whole camp was in the utmoft confufion and diforder; all their battalions were broken and fled moft precipitately ; at which inftant our whole army preffed after with redoubled ardour, purfued them a mile, made confiderable flaughter amongft them, and took many prifoners. One field piece had

already fallen into our hands. At this time our men ftopped to take breath, when the enemy being reinforced, our front fell back a few rods for conveniency of ground, and being collected and directed by Col. Roffelar, and reinforced by Major Stanten, renewed the fight with redoubled ardour, and fell in upon them with great impetuofity, put them to confufion and flight, and purfued them about a mile, making many prifoners, 2 or 3 more brafs field pieces falling into our hands, and are fuppofed to be the whole they brought with them. At this time darknefs came upon us, and prevented our fwallowing up the whole of this body. The enemy fled precipitately towards the North River. Governor Skeene in furprize and confternation, took horfe and fled. This action, which redounds fo much to the glory of the Great Lord of the Heavens and God of armies, affords the Americans a lafting monument of Divine power and goodnefs, and a moft powerful argument of love, and truft in God. Our lofs is about 40 or 50 killed, and more wounded. The enemy lofs is greater, and many more wounded. Their baggage fell into our hands. The number of prifoners taken, is about fix hundred. Two of their Colonels were amongft the prifoners, and mortally wounded. A number of inferior officers have alfo fallen into our hands, and in particular the General's Aid-de-Camp. A good number deferted and joined us. A large body of militia are now collecting to act in conjunction with the Northern army. General Starke will be endeared to us for ever.

v

Bofton, Sept. 18.
Head Quarters of the King's army upon Hudfon's River, Auguft 30, 1777.
Sir,
Major-general Reidefel has requefted me to tranfmit the inclofed to
Lieu-

Lieutenant colonel Baum, whom, the fortune of war, put into the hands of your troops at Bennington.

Having never failed in my attention towards prisoners, I cannot entertain a doubt of your taking this opportunity to shew me a return of civility ; and that you will permit the baggage and servants of such officers, your prisoners, as desired, to pass to them unmolested.

It is with great concern I find myself obliged to add to this application, a complaint of the bad treatment the provincial soldiers in the King's service received after the affair at Bennington. I have reports upon oath, that some were refused quarter after having asked it. I am willing to believe this was against the order and inclination of your officers ; but it is my part to require an explanation, and to warn you of the horrors of retaliation, if such a practice is not in the strongest terms discountenanced and reprehended.

Duty and principle, Sir, make me a public enemy to the Americans, who have taken up arms ; but I seek to be a generous one ; nor have I the shadow of resentment against any individual, who does not induce it by acts derogatory to those maxims, upon which all men of honour think alike.

Persuaded that a gentleman of the station to which this letter is addressed, will not be comprized in the exception I have made.

I am, personally, Sir,
your most humble servant,
J. BURGOYNE,
Lieut. General.
Major Gen. Gates.

Major-general GATES's answer.
Head Quarters of the army of the United States, Sep. 2, 1777.
Sir,

Last night I had the honour to receive your Excellency's letter of the first instant. I am astonished you should mention inhumanity, or threaten retaliation. Nothing happened in the action at Bennington, but what is common when works are carried by assault.

That the savages of America should, in their warfare, mangle and scalp the unhappy prisoners who fall into their hands, is neither new nor extraordinary ; but that the famous Lieutent-general Burgoyne, in whom the fine gentleman is united with the soldier and the scholar, should hire the savages of America to scalp Europeans, and the descendants of Europeans ; nay more, that he should pay a price for each scalp so barbarously taken, is more than will be believed in Europe, until authenticated facts shall, in every Gazette, confirm the truth of the horrid tale.

Miss Mc Rea, a young lady, lovely to the sight, of virtuous character, and amiable disposition, engaged to an officer of your army, was, with other women and children, taken out of a house near Fort Edward, carried into the woods, and there scalped and mangled in a most shocking manner. Two parents with their six children, were all treated with the same inhumanity, while quietly residing in their once happy and peaceful dwelling. The miserable fate of Miss Mc Rea was particularly aggravated, by her being dressed to receive her promised husband, but met her murderer employed by you. Upwards of one hundred men, women and children, have perished by the hands of the ruffians, to whom, it is asserted, you have paid the price of blood.

Inclosed are letters from your wounded officers, prisoners in my hands ; by them you will be informed of the generosity of their conquerors.

Such money, cloathing, attendants, and necessaries, which your Excellency pleases to send to the prisoners, shall be faithfully delivered. The late Colonel Baum's servant, who is

at

at Bennington, would have come to your Excellency's camp; but when I offered him a flag, he was affraid to run the risque of being scalped, and declined.

When I know what surgeon and attendants your Excellency is desirous of sending to Bennington, I shall dispatch an officer to your lines, to conduct them to my camp.

I am, Sir, your most
humble servant,
HORATIO GATES,
Major Gen.

Lieut. Gen. BURGOYNE.

Copy of a letter from Gen. BURGOYNE to Major General GATES.

Sir,   Sept. 6, 1777.

I received your letter of the 2d instant, and in consequence of your compliance with my proposal of sending a surgeon to visit the wounded officers in your hands, and some servants to carry money and necessaries to their masters, and remain with them, I have now to desire the favour of you to dispatch the officer you design with a drum and a flag of truce, so that he may arrive at Still Water about noon, on the 9th, and he shall be met there by the persons he is to conduct, accompanied also by a drum and a flag of truce. I trust, Sir, that it is understood between us that the surgeon shall have safe conduct to my outposts, when his visit shall be made, and he shall request it; and that you may be assured, on my part, that your officer shall meet with security and civility.

I have hesitated, Sir, upon answering the other paragraphs of your letter. I disdain to justify myself against the rhapsodies of fiction and calumny, which from the first of this contest, it has been an unvaried American policy to propagate, but which no longer imposes upon the world. I am induced to deviate from this general rule, in the present instance, lest my silence should be construed an acknowledgment of the truth of your allegations, and a pretence be thence taken for exercising future barbarities by the American troops.

By this motive, and upon this only, I condescend to inform you, that I would not be conscious of the acts you presume to impute to me, for the whole Continent of America, though the wealth of worlds were in its bowels, and a paradise upon its surface.

It has happened, that all my transactions with the Indian nations, last year and this, have been clearly heard, distinctly understood, accurately minuted, by very numerous, and in many parts, very unprejudiced persons. So immediately opposite to truth is your assertion, that I have paid a price for scalps, that one of the first regulations established by me at the great council in May, and repeated and enforced, and invariably adhered to since, was, that the Indians should receive compensation for prisoners, because it would prevent cruelty; and that not only such compensation should be withheld, but a strict account demanded for scalps. These pledges of conquest, for such you well know they will ever esteem them, were solemnly and peremptorily prohibited to be taken from the wounded, and even the dying, and the persons of aged men, women, children, and prisoners, were pronounced sacred, even in assaults.

In regard to Miss M'Rea, her fall wanted not the tragic display you have laboured to give it, to make it as sincerely abhorred and lamented by me, as it can be by the tenderest of her friends. The fact was no premeditated barbarity. On the contrary, two chiefs, who had brought her off for the purpose of security, not of violence to her person, disputed which should be her guard; and in a fit of savage passion in one, from whose hands she was snatched, the unhappy woman became the victim. Upon the first intelligence of
this

this event, I obliged the Indians to deliver the murderer into my hands ; and though to have punished him by our laws, or principles of justice, would have been perhaps unprecedented, he certainly should have suffered an ignominious death, had I not been convinced, from my circumstances and observation, beyond the possibility of a doubt, that a pardon under the terms which I presented and they accepted, would be more efficacious than an execution to prevent similar mischiefs.

The above instance excepted, your intelligence, respecting the cruelties of the Indians, is false.

You seem to threaten me with European publications, which affect me as little as any other threats you could make ; but in regard to American publications, whether your charge against me, which I acquit you of believing, was penned *from* a Gazette, or *for* a Gazette, I desire and demand of you, as a man of honour, that should it appear in print at all, this answer may follow it.

I am, Sir,
Your most humble servant,
J. BURGOYNE,
Lieutenant General.
Major General GATES.

Extract of a letter from Major General GATES *to the President of Congress.*

Sir,
Inclosed I have the honour to send you Lieutenant-general Burgoyne's answer to the letter I transmitted to Congress by the last express. All the reply I thought necessary to make to so extravigant a performance, is also in the packet. Having prepared every thing in concert with General Lincoln for the march of the army, I left Van Schaak's Island on Monday, and arrived here yesterday forenoon. The enemy gave no manner of interruption.

Head Quarters of the army of the United States, Sept. 8, 1777.

Sir,
Your Excellency may be satisfied that I will send an officer to Stillwater at the time you mention, to receive the surgeon, servants, and such comforts as your Excellency shall think proper to send to the prisoners in my hands.

I am, Sir,
Your most obedient,
humble servant.
HORATIO GATES. M. G.

Lieut. Gen. BURGOYNE.

Published by Order of CONGRESS,
CHARLES THOMSON, *Sec.*

———————

PORTSMOUTH, *Sept.* 27, 1777.
To the Hon. COMMITTEE *of* SAFETY *of this* STATE *at* EXETER.

Charles-town, Sept. 23, 1777.

Sir,
You will see by the inclosed, what we are doing here. General Lincoln is gone to join General Gates, and left us to act in this quarter with 1500 men, therefore request that all the militia, above Charles-town and eastward, may march to our assistance, with horses bringing flour and beef, to serve themselves one month ; by which time I hope the whole of General Burgoyne's army will be in our hands, I think now every man of spirit will turn out. Pasturing is good and plenty this way.

I am, your very humble servant,
JACOB BAYLEY, B. D. G.

I send about 100 prisoners to you, to dispose of as you think will be most safe ; some provisions must be sent to-morrow, to meet the prisoners, as far as one day's travel from hence, as we have none to spare ; the number to supply will be about 150 men. No time may be lost in sending along the militia. General Arnold has fought the right wing of

M m m   General

General Burgoyne's, won three field pieces, the field, and 250 prisoners. Great lofs on both fides.

(A true copy.)   B. BAYLEY.
Atteft. PETER LABEREE, Chairman.

Particulars of the movements of Gen. LINCLON, *from Sept.* 13th *to the* 21ft.

Thirteenth, marched in three divifions from Pawlet, commanded by Col. Brown, Johnfton, and Woodbury; Col. Brown to the South bay, to relieve our prifoners at the North Lake George; Colonel Johnfton, at the fame time to divert the enemy at Independence; Col. Woodbury at Skeenfborough, to cover Col. Brown's retreat, &c. On Wednefday morning, the 17th, at day break, Col. Brown began the attack, fet at liberty 100 of our men, who were prifoners; took prifoners 293 of the enemy, amongft which were two Captains, and feven Lieutenants, and two other officers; took Mount Defiance, Mount Hope, the French lines, and the Block Houfe, the Landing, 200 batteaux, one armed floop, and feveral gun boats. On Sunday took about 100 prifoners; the prifoners are marched for Connecticut, except 100; took a vaft quantity of plunder. His water craft are with a party fet out for the South end of Lake George, where are all their boats, baggage, and artillery. I have not the leaft doubt but they will fucceed; the divifion confifts of 500 men each; Col. Brown is reinforced now to 700; we mean to keep poffeffion of the ground at Ticonderoga. The field is now opened wide; the time is now come that we may entirely cut off General Burgoyne's whole army, if we exert ourfelves; our numbers are not fufficient to keep what we have, and can get. I think it the duty of every man to turn out, with his horfe, and one month's provifion, which will undoubtedly accomplifh our defign. I muft call on all our friends to America, to turn out, and come to our affiftance at Ticonderoga.

JACOB BAYLEY, B. D. G.

P. S. General Lincoln is gone to join General Gates.

(A true copy.)
Atteft. PETER LABEREE, Chairman.
Cafleton Sept. 21, 1777.
BOSTON, Oct. 2.
Copy of a letter from Col. BROWN *to the Hon. Major General* GATES, *dated North End of Lake George Landing, Thurfday, September* 18, 1777.

Sir,

With great fatigue, after marching all laft night, I arrived at this place at break of day, and after the beft difpofition of the men I could make, immediately began the attack, and in a few minutes carried the place. I then, without lofs of time, detached a confiderable part of my men to the mill where a great number of the enemy were pofted, who alfo were made prifoners; a fmall number of whom having taken poffeffion of a block houfe in that vicinity, were, with more difficulty, brought to fubmiffion; but at the fight of the cannon they furrendered.

During thefe feafons of fucceffes, Mount Defiance alfo fell into our hands. I have taken poffeffion of the old French lines at Ticonderoga. I have fent in a flag, demanding a furrender of Ticonderoga and Mount Independence, in the ftrongeft and moft peremptory terms. Have had as yet no information of the event of Col. Johnfton's attack on the Mount. My lofs of men in the feveral actions are not more than three or four killed, and five wounded. The enemy's lofs is lefs. I find myfelf in poffeffion of 293 prifoners, viz. two Captains, nine Subalterns, two Commiffaries, non-commiffioned officers and privates 143 Britifh, and 119 Canadians, 18 artificers, and retook more than 100 of our men; total 293, exclufive of the prifoners retaken. The water craft I have

Have taken are 150 batteaux above the Falls in Lake Champlain, 50 above the Falls, including several large gun boats, and an armed sloop; arms equal to the number of prisoners, some ammunition, and many other things, which I cannot as yet ascertain. I must not forget to mention a few cannon, which may be of so great service to us.

BOSTON, *September* 27.

General GATES's *General Orders, issued on the 6th instant, at Half Moon, previous to the army's marching to attack the enemy at Fort Edward.*

The Generals commanding divisions, and all the Generals and Colonels commanding brigades, to see that the commanding officers of regiments and companies have every thing in immediate readiness for a march; that when general orders are issued, the army may only have to strike their tents, load their baggage, and instantly at the word being given, march off the ground. A very large army of militia, with some Continental troops, under the command of Generals Lincoln and Starks, are now assembling in the Grants, and every necessary preparation for their acting in concert with this army upon the point of being compleated. This whole force must be prepared to march, upon the shortest notice, to drive the enemy with disgrace and defeat back to Canada, is the object of the present campaign. What has been successfully began, by General Starks and Colonel Warner, to the eastward, and General Harkeman and Colonel Gansevoort, at the westward, cannot, (with the blessing of Heaven) fail to be equally prosperous, in the hands of the generals and soldiers, appointed to face the enemy's main army, at the northward. If the murder of aged parents, with their innocent children, if mangling the blooming virgin, and inoffensive youth, are inducements to revenge—if the righteous cause of

freedom, and the happiness of posterity, are motives to stimulate the army to conquer their mercenary and merciless foes, the time is now come, when they are called upon, by their country, their general and every thing human and divine, to vanquish their enemy; each state in particular, and the Grand Convention of the United States, in general are, to this moment, industriously employed to provide their army with every comfort and necessary that can be procured; duty, gratitude and honour, must therefore inspire the heart of every officer and soldier, to do justice to their much injured country.

BOSTON, *October* 18, 1777.

Monday morning at three o'clock, an express arrived at General HEATH's, with the following letter, viz.

Camp three miles above Stillwater, October 9th, 1777.

Dear General,

" This will acknowledge the receipt of your's of the 29th ult. and will inform you, that on Tuesday last the enemy advanced from their right with a design to take post on our left. Our scouts were drove in—They continued advancing.

" Three regiments were ordered out, who met them a mile from our lines, a small eminence being between them, each pushed hard for it—Our troops gained it. The attack began at four o'clock, P. M. continued till dark without any intermission, during which we drove them two miles, and at last entered their works sword in hand. In the action, and in their works, were taken two brass 12 pounders and six 6 pounders, 3 ammunition waggons, about 300 tents, a great quantity of baggage, with upwards of 30 horses, waggons, &c. &c.

" It now became very dark, could not pursue them any further, nor was it safe or practicable, the woods being very thick.

M m m 2　　　　　　　　　We

" We halted half a mile in the rear of them, there remained the whole night with our arms in our hands, not a man slept.

" About four in the morning they began to move, we pushed on till they were drove into their strong works on the River Road—skirmishing parties were sent out the whole day; some prisoners taken, some killed and wounded on our side.

" Among the wounded is the good Major-general Lincoln shot through the leg. Wish he may save it, but it is much doubted.——The brave General Arnold was wounded in the action the day before.

" As we have not been able to get in returns, cannot give you a particular account of our loss; however, it is very inconsiderable—I believe I may venture to say not more than 30 killed, nor more than one hundred wounded.

" The enemy's loss on Tuesday must be great! Gen. Frazer wounded (since dead). Taken 3 field officers, 6 Captains, 10 Subalterns, 1 Quarter-master General, 190 private—taken in the hospital on Wednesday, about 300 sick and wounded, with some medicines, 200 barrels of flour, with many other articles. Besides these, upwards of 100 now lay dead on the ground, which we have not been able to bury.

" Much honour is due to our officers and men, who fought like heroes.

" The enemy began their retreat at about 11 o'clock at night, breaking up all the bridges and otherwise spoiling the roads in their rear.

" Thursday morning 300 men served with three days provision began their march to hang on their left flank (the river being on their right) and two brigades on the River Road in their rear, but could not proceed as it set in full of rain, and so continues. Shall push on immediately on its clearing up, when I hope to give

you a further account of them. Till then, I am your Honour's most obedient servant,

" JOHN GLOVER,
" Brigadier General.

" October 10, nine o'clock. Three thousand have already marched on their left flank; and our whole body is paraded, and will march immediately. J. G.

" P. S. 10th. A. M. This morning symptoms much in favour of General Lincoln, I am in hopes he will save his leg,

" The express heard a very heavy cannonade all the next day, while on his way hither."

Extract of another letter from a gentleman, dated Camp on Bemus's Heights, Oct. 9, 1777.

" With the greatest pleasure I can inform you of our having a most severe action on the 7th inst. Our army drove Britons and Germans, from the field into their works; but not being content with the honour of that, attacked their lines in the face of cannon and showers of musquetry, drove them from their works, took 9 pieces of brass artillery, 300 prisoners, among whom are 6 or 7 field officers, viz. 1 German Colonel, 2 Lieutenant-colonels, both since dead; Major Williams commandant of British artillery; 2 Brunswic Majors; Sir Francis Clark, Aid de Camp to General Burgoyne. The encampment of a German brigade, with all their equipage, fell into the hands of Col. Jackson's regiment, This is a short but as good an account as I can give of the matter at present. Thus ended the most capital affair the history of this war can produce. The enemy prepared yesterday for a retreat--this morning we find they are gone, leaving the sick and wounded, officers and men, in their camp. We shall march in half an hour in pursuit of them. They lost General Frazer in the last action, besides many others. You cannot conceive the bravery

bravery and spirit of our troops. Our loss was very trifling; we lost double the number of any other regiment, and had but 2 officers, and 8 or 10 men killed on the spot, and one officer, and 15 men wounded. We lost no field officer, nor that I can learn a Captain. Gen. Arnold entered the works, and immediately received a ball in his leg. Yesterday General Lincoln received an unfortunate wound in his leg from a random shot of the enemy ; his leg is to be taken off. I am in haste, being just going to mount for the pursuit."

The Honourable Continential Congrefs have removed from Philadelphia to York Town, in the Northern part of that State.

Boston, October 20, 1777.

Extract of a letter from a General Officer, dated Camp at Saratoga, Oct. 13, 1777.

" I received your esteemed favour of the 7th, and notice the contents, but cannot fully answer it at present. In my last I gave you an account of the action of the 7th, since which there has been skirmishing every day, in which we have taken great quantities of baggage, provisions, &c. prisoners about 120; deserters 160. The enemy have burnt every house but one, between their last encampment and the ground they now occupy, which is on the other side Saratoga-creek. We now lie within musket shot of them, *and are forming a circle round them*; and if the plan succeeds, shall have it complete in one night more. The Generals Lincoln and Arnold are both in a fine way, and keep their legs yet. The total destruction of General Burgoyne is very near, and, with the blessing of God, will soon be complete ; we have nothing to do but to act with prudence and firmness."

Extract of a letter from Albany, dated October 14, 1777.

" I have this moment received advice from the camp, that a party of our men have taken fifty batteaux of the enemy, loaded with provisions, stores, and medicines."

Extract of a letter from Saratoga, October 13, 1777.

" Yesterday Gen. Fellows, being on the other side of the river, took a number of boats from the enemy, confisting of near 1000 barrels of pork and beef ; together with three hogsheads of beaver hats, &c. &c."

Letter from Major-general GATES *to General* BURGOYNE.

Saratoga, Oct. 11, 1777.

Sir,

I had the honour to receive your Excellency's letter by Lady Acland. The respect due to her Ladyship's rank, the tendernefs due to her perfon and fex, were fufficient recommendations to entitle her to my protection. Confidering my preceding conduct with refpect to thofe of your army, whom the fortune of war had placed in my hands, I am furprized that your Excellency fhould think that I could confider the greateft attention to Lady Acland in the light of an *obligation*. The cruelties which mark the retreat of your army, in burning the gentlemens and farmers houfes as they went along, is almoft among civilized nations without a precedent ; they fhould not endeavour to ruin thofe they could not conquer ; this conduct betrays more the vindictive malice of a monk, than the generofity of a foldier. Your friend, Sir Francis Clark, by the information of Dr. Potts, the Director-general of my hofpital, languifhes under a very dangerous wound. Every fort of tendernefs and attention is paid to him, as well as to all the wounded who have fallen into my hands, and *the hofpital which you was neceffitated to leave to my mercy.*

At

At the folicitation of Major Williams, I am prevailed on to offer him and Major Meibom, in exchange for Col. Ethan Allen. Your Excellency's objections to my last proposals for the exchange of Col. Ethan Allen, I must consider as trifling, as I cannot but suppose that the Generals of the royal armies act in equal concert with those of the Generals of the armies of the United States.

The bearer delivers a number of letters from the officers of your army, taken prisoners in the action of the 7th instant.

I am, Sir,

Your most obedient servant,

HORATIO GATES,

Major General.

To Lieut. Gen. BURGOYNE

Whitehall, December 15, 1777.

This afternoon Captain Craig, of the 47th regiment, arrived from Quebec with the following duplicate of a letter from Lieutenant-general Burgoyne, to Lord George Germain, the original of which has not yet been received.

Albany, October 20, 1777

My Lord,

No possibility of communication with your Lordship having existed since the beginning of September, at which time my last dispatches were sent away, I have to report to your Lordship the proceedings of the army under my command from that period;—a feries of hard toil, incessant effort, stubborn action, till disabled in the collateral branches of the army by the total defection of the Indians; the desertion or the timidity of the Canadians and Provincials, some individuals excepted; disappointed in the last hope of any timely co-operation from other armies; the regular troops reduced by losses from the best parts to 3500 fighting men, not 2000 of which were British; only

three days provisions, upon short allowance, in store; invested by an army of sixteen thousand men, and no apparent means of retreat remaining, I called into Council all the Generals, Field Officers, and Captains, commanding corps, and by their unanimous concurrence and advice, I was induced to open a treaty with Major-general Gates.

Your Lordship will see by the papers transmitted herewith the disagreeable prospect which attended the first overtures, and when the terms concluded are compared, I trust that the spirit of the Councils I have mentioned, which, under such circumstances, dictated instead of submitting, will not be refused a share of credit.

Before I enter upon the detail of these events, I think it a duty of justice, my Lord, to take upon myself the measure of having passed the Hudson's River, in order to force a passage to Albany. I did not think myself authorized to call any men into Council, when the peremptory tenor of my orders, and the season of the year, admitting no alternative.

Provisions for about thirty days having been brought forward, the other necessary stores prepared, and the bridge of boats compleated, the army passed the Hudson's River on the 13th and 14th of September, and encamped on the heights and in the plain of Saratoga, the enemy being then in the neighbourhood of Stillwater.

15th. The whole army made a movement forward, and encamped in a good position in a place called Dovogot.

16th. It being found that there were several bridges to repair, that work was begun under cover of strong detachments, and the same opportunity was taken to reconnoitre the country.

17th.

17*th*. The army renewed their march, repaired other bridges, and encamped upon advantageous ground, about four miles from the enemy.

18*th*. The enemy appeared in considerable force to obstruct the further repair of bridges, and with a view as it was conceived to draw on an action where artillery could not be employed; a small loss was sustained in skirmishing, but the work of the bridges was effected.

19*th*. The passages of a great ravin, and other roads towards the enemy, having been reconnoitred, the army advanced in the following order:

Brigadier-general Frazer's corps, sustained by Lieutenant-colonel Breyman's corps, made a circuit in order to pass the ravin commodiously, without quitting the heights, and afterwards to cover the march of the line to the right: their corps moved in three columns, and had the Indians, Canadians, and Provincials upon their fronts and flanks. The British line, led by me in person, passed the ravin in a direct line south, and formed in order of battle as fast as they gained the summit, where they waited to give time to Frazer's corps to make the circuit, and to enable the left wing and artillery, which, under the command of Major-general Philips and Major-general Reidesel, kept the great road and meadows near the river, in two columns, and had bridges to repair, to be equally ready to proceed. The 47th regiment guarded the batteaux.

The signal guns, which had been previously settled to give notice of all the columns being ready to advance, having been fired between one and two o'clock, the march continued, the scouts and flankers of the column of the British line were soon fired upon from small parties, but with no effect; after about an hour's march, the picquets, which made the advanced guard of that column, were attacked in force, and obliged to give ground, but they soon rallied and were sustained.

On the first opening of the wood, I formed the troops; a few cannon shot dislodged the enemy at a house from whence the picquets had been attacked; and Brigadier-general Frazer's corps had arrived with such precision in point of time, as to be found in a very advantageous height on the right of the British.

In the mean time the enemy, not acquainted with the combination of the march, had moved in great force out of their intrenchments, with a view of turning the line upon the right; and being checked by the position of Brigadier-general Frazer, countermarched in order to direct their great effort to the left of the British.

From the nature of the country, movements of this nature, however near, may be effected without a possibility of their being discovered.

About three o'clock the action began by a very vigorous attack on the British line, and continued with great obstinacy till after sun-set. The enemy being continually supplied with fresh troops, the stress lay upon the 20th, 21st and 62d regiments, most parts of which were engaged near four hours without intermission: the 9th had been ordered early in the day to form in reserve. The grenadiers and 24th regiment were some part of the time brought into action, as were part of the light infantry; and all these corps charged with their usual spirit.

The riflemen, and other parts of Breyman's corps, were also of service; but it was not thought adviseable to evacuate the height where Brigadier-general Frazer was posted, otherwise than partially and occasionally.

Major-general Philips, upon first hearing the firing, found his way through a difficult part of the wood

to

to the scene of action, and brought up with him Major Williams and four pieces of artillery, and from that moment I stood indebted to that gallant and judicious second for incessant and most material services; particularly for restoring the action in a point which was critically pressed by a great superiority of fire, and to which he led up the 20th regiment at the utmost personal hazard.

Major-general Reidesel exerted himself to bring up a part of the left wing, and arrived in time to charge the enemy with regularity and bravery.

Just as the light closed, the enemy gave ground on all sides, and left us compleatly masters of the field of battle, with the loss of about 500 men on their side, and, as supposed, thrice that number wounded.

The darkness preventing a pursuit, the prisoners were few.

The behaviour of the officers and men in general was exemplary. Brigadier-general Frazer took his position in the beginning of the day with great judgment, and sustained the action with constant presence of mind and vigour. Brigadier-general Hamilton was the whole time engaged, and acquitted himself with great honour, activity, and good conduct. The artillery in general was distinguished, and the brigade under Captain Jones, who was killed in the action, was conspicuously so.

The army lay upon their arms the night of the 19th, and the next day took a position nearly within cannon shot of the enemy, fortifying their right, and extending their left so as to cover the meadows through which the great river runs, and where the batteaux and hospitals were placed. The 47th regiment, and the regiment of Hesse Hanau, with a corps of Provincials, encamped in the meadows as a further security.

It was soon found that no fruits, honour excepted, were attained by

the preceding victory; the enemy working with redoubled ardour to strengthen their left; their right was unattackable already.

On our side it became expedient to erect strong redoubts for the protection of the magazines and hospital, not only against a sudden attack, but also for their security in case of a march to turn the enemy's flank.

21st. A messenger arrived from Sir Harry Clinton, with a letter in cyphers, informing me of his intention to attack Fort Montgomery in about ten days from the date of his letter, which was the 10th of September. This was the only messenger of many that I apprehend were dispatched by Sir William Howe and him, that had reached my camp since the beginning of August. He was sent back the same night to inform Sir Harry of my situation, and of the necessity of a diversion to oblige General Gates to detach from his army; and my intention to wait favourable events in that position, if possible, to the 12th of October.

In the course of the two following days, two officers in disguise, and other confidential persons, were dispatched by different routes with verbal messages to the same effect; and I continued fortifying my camp, and watching the enemy, whose numbers encreased every day.

3d October. I thought it advisable to diminish the soldier's ration, in order to lengthen out the provisions, to which measure the army submitted with the utmost chearfulness. The difficulties of a retreat to Canada were clearly foreseen, as was the dilemma, should the retreat be effected, of leaving at liberty such an army as General Gates's to act against Sir William Howe.

This consideration operated forcibly to determine me to abide events as long as possible, and I reasoned thus: The expedition I commanded was

was evidently meant at firſt to be ha-zarded. Circumſtances might require it ſhould be devoted; a critical junction of Mr. Gates's force with Mr. Waſhington might poſſibly decide the fate of the war; the failure of my junction with Sir Harry Clinton, or the loſs of my retreat to Canada, could only be a partial misfortune.

7th. In this ſituation things continued 'till he 7th, when no intelligence having been received of the expected co-operation, and four or five days for our limited ſtay in the camp only remained, it was judged adviſeable to make a movement to the enemy's left, not only to diſcover whether there were any poſſible means of forcing a paſſage ſhould it be neceſſary to advance, or of diſlodging them for the convenience of retreat, but alſo to cover a forage of the army, which was in the greateſt diſtreſs on account of the ſcarcity.

A detachment of 1500 regular troops, with 2 twelve-pounders, 2 howitzers, and 6 ſix-pounders, were ordered to move, and was commanded by myſelf, having with me Major-general Phillips, Major-general Reideſel, and Brigadier-general Frazer. The guard of the camp upon the heights was left to Brigadiers-general Hamilton and Speicht; the redoubts and the plain to Brigadier-general Goll; and as the force of the enemy immediately in their front conſiſted of more than double their numbers, it was not poſſible to augment the corps that marched beyond the numbers above ſtated.

I formed the troops within three quarters of a mile of the enemy's left; and Captain Fraſer's rangers, with Indians and Provincials, had orders to go by ſecret paths in the woods to gain the enemy's rear, and by ſhewing themſelves there to keep them in check.

The further operations intended were prevented by a very ſudden and rapid attack of the enemy on our left, where the Britiſh grenadiers were poſted to ſupport the left wing of the line. Major Ackland at the head of them ſuſtained the attack with great reſolution; but the enemy's great numbers enabling them in a few minutes to extend the attack along the front of the Germans, which were immediately on the right of the grenadiers, no part of that body could be removed to make a ſecond line to the flank where the ſtreſs of the fire lay. The right was at that time unengaged; but it was ſoon obſerved that the enemy were marching a large corps round their flank to endeavour cutting off their retreat. The light infantry and part of the 24th regiment, which were at that poſt, were therefore ordered to form a ſecond line, and to ſecure the return of the troops into camp.

While this movement was proceeding, the enemy puſhed a freſh and ſtrong reinforcement to renew the action upon the left, which, overpowered by ſo great a ſuperiority, gave way, and the light infantry and 24th regiment were obliged to make a quick movement to ſave that point from being entirely carried, in doing which Brigadier-general Frazer was mortally wounded.

The danger to which the lines were expoſed becoming at this moment of the moſt ſerious nature, orders were given to Majors-general Phillips and Reideſel to cover the retreat, while ſuch troops as were moſt ready for the purpoſe returned for the defence of them. The troops retreated hard preſſed, but in good order. They were obliged to leave 6 pieces of cannon, all the horſes having been killed; and moſt of the artillery men, who had behaved as uſual with the utmoſt bravery, under the command of Major Williams, being either killed or wounded.

The troops had ſcarcely entered the camp, when it was ſtormed with

N n n   great

great fury, the enemy rushing to the lines under a severe fire of grape shot and small arms. The post of the light infantry under the command of Lord Belcarres, assisted by some of the line, who threw themselves by order into those entrenchments, was defended with great spirit; and the enemy, led on by General Arnold, was finally repulsed, and the General wounded; but unhappily the entrenchments of the German reserve, commanded by Lieutenant-colonel Breymen, who was killed, were carried, and although ordered to be recovered they never were so; and the enemy by that misfortune gained an opening on our right and rear. The night put an end to the action.

Under the disadvantages thus apparent in our situation, the army was ordered to quit the present position during the night, and take post upon the height above the hospital; thus, by an entire change of front, to reduce the enemy to form a new disposition. This movement was effected with great order and without loss, though all the artillery and camp were removed at the same time. The army continued offering battle to the enemy in their new position the whole day of the 8th.

8th. Intelligence was now received that the enemy were marching to turn the right, and no means could prevent this measure but retiring towards Saratoga. The army began to move at nine o'clock at night; Major-general Reidesel commanding the van guard, and Major-general Phillips the rear.

This retreat, though within musquet shot of the enemy, and encumbered with all the baggage of the army, was made without loss; but a very heavy rain, and the difficulties of guarding the batteaux which contained all the provisions, occasioned delays which prevented the army reaching Saratoga, till the night of the 9th; and the artillery could not

pass the fords of the Fish-kill till the morning of the 10th.

At our arrival near Saratoga, a corps of the enemy, of between five and six hundred, were discovered throwing up intrenchments on the heights, but retired over a ford of the Hudson's River at our approach, and joined a body posted to oppose our passage there.

It was judged proper to send a detachment of artificers, under a strong escort, to repair the bridges and open the road to Fort Edward. The 47th regiment, Capt. Fraser's marksmen, and Mackoy's provincials were ordered for that service; but the enemy appearing on the heights of Fish-kill in great force, and making a disposition to pass and give us battle, the 47th regiment and Fraser's marksmen were recalled: the provincials left to cover the workmen at the first bridge, ran away upon a very slight attack of a small party of the enemy, and left the artificers to escape as they could, without a possibility of their performing any work.

During these different movements, the batteaux with provisions were frequently fired upon from the opposite side of the river; some of them were lost, and several men were killed and wounded in those which remained.

11th. Attacks upon the batteaux were continued; several were taken and retaken; but their situation being much nearer to the main force of the enemy than to ours, it was found impossible to secure the provisions any otherwise than by landing them and carrying them upon the hill: this was effected under fire, and with great difficulty.

The possible means of further retreat were now considered in councils of war, composed of the general officers, minutes of which will be transmitted to your Lordship.

The only one that seemed at all practicable was by a night march to gain Fort Edward, with the troops carrying

carrying their provisions upon their backs; the impossibility of repairing bridges, putting a conveyance of artillery and carriages out of the question; and it was proposed to force the ford at Fort Edward, or the ford above it.

Before this attempt could be made, scouts returned with intelligence that the enemy were intrenched opposite those fords, and possessed a camp in force on the high ground between Fort Edward and Fort George, with cannon; they had also parties down the whole shore to watch our motions; and posts so near to us upon our own side of the water as must prevent the army moving a single mile undiscovered.

The bulk of the enemy's army was hourly joined by a new corps of militia and volunteers, and their number together amounted to 16,000 men.

Their position, which extended three parts in four of a circle round us, was from the nature of the ground, inattackable in all parts.

In this situation the army took the best position possible and fortified; waiting 'till the 13th at night in the anxious hope of succours from our friends, or the next desirable expectation, an attack from our enemy.

During this time the men lay continually upon their arms, and were cannonaded in every part; even rifle shot and grape shot came into all parts of the line, though without any considerable effect.

At this period an exact account of the provisions was taken, and the circumstances stated in the opening of this letter became compleat.

The Council of War was extended to all the Field Officers and Captains commanding corps of the army, and the Convention inclosed herewith, ensued; a transaction which I am sure was unavoidable, and which I trust in that situation will be esteemed honourable.

After the execution of the Treaty, General Gates drew together the force that had surrounded my position, and I had the consolation to have as many witnesses as I have men under my command, of its amounting to the numbers mentioned above.

During the events stated above, an attempt was made against Ticonderoga by an army assembled under Major-general Lincoln, who found means to march with a considerable corps from Hubberton undiscovered, while another column of his force passed the mountains between Skenesborough and Lake George; and on the morning of the 18th of September, a sudden and general attack was made upon the Carrying-place at Lake George, Sugar-hill, Ticonderoga, and Mount Independence. The sea-officer commanding the armed sloop stationed to defend the Carrying-place, as also some of the officers commanding at the posts at the Sugar-hill and at the Portage were surprized, and a considerable part of four companies of the 53d regiment were made prisoners; a block-house commanded by Lieutenant Lord of the 53d regiment was the only post on that side that had time to make use of their arms, and they made a brave defence, till cannon taken from the surprized vessel was brought against them.

After stating and lamenting so fatal a want of vigilance, I have to inform your Lordship of the satisfactory events which followed.

The enemy having twice summoned Brigadier-general Powell, and received such answers as became a gallant officer entrusted with so important a post; and having tried during the course of four days several attacks, and being repulsed in all, retreated without having done any considerable damage.

Brigadier-general Powell, from whose report to me I extract this relation, gives great commendations to

the

the regiment of Prince Frederick and the other troops stationed at Mount Independence. The Brigadier also mentions with great applause the behaviour of Captain Taylor of the 21st regiment, who was accidentally there on his road to the army from the hospital, and Lieutenant Beecroft of the 24th regiment, who, with the artificers in arms, defended an important battery.

On the 24th of September the enemy enabled by the capture of the gun boats and batteaux which they had made after the surprize of the sloop to embark upon Lake George, attacked Diamond Island in two divisions.

Captain Aubrey and two companies of the 47th regiment had been posted at that island from the time the army passed the Hudson's River, as a better situation for the security of the stores at the south end of Lake George, than Fort George, which is on the continent, and not tenable against artillery and numbers. The enemy were repulsed by Captain Aubrey with great loss, and pursued by the gun boats under his command to the east shore, where two of their principal vessels were retaken, together with all the cannon; they had just time to set fire to the other batteaux, and retreated over the mountains.

I beg leave to refer your Lordship for further particulars to my Aid-de-Camp Lord Petersham; and I humbly take occasion to recommend to His Majesty's notice that Nobleman, as one endued with qualities to do important services to his country in every station to which his birth may lead. In this late campaign, in particular, his behaviour has been such as to entitle him to the fullest applause, and I am confident his merit will be thought a sufficient ground for preferment, though deprived of the eclat and sort of claim which generally attends the delivery of fortunate dispatches.

I have only to add, my Lord, a general report of the killed and wounded. I do not give it as correct; the hurry of the time and the separation of the corps, having rendered it impossible to make it so. The British officers have bled profusely and most honourably; all who have fallen were valuable, but the extensive merits which marked the publick and private character of Brigadier-general Frazer will long remain upon the memory of this army, and make his loss a subject of particular regret. Those who remain unwounded have been equally forward; and the General Officers from the mode of fighting, have been more exposed than in other services. Among the rest I have had my escapes. It depends upon the sentence his Majesty shall pass upon my conduct; upon the judgment of my profession, and of the impartial and respectable parts of my country, whether I am to esteem them blessings or misfortunes.

I have the honour to be, &c.

J. BURGOYNE.

P. S. The above is an exact duplicate of the dispatch sent by Lord Petersham. Capt. Craig, of the 47th regiment, who has the charge of it, is an officer of great merit; and is particularly worthy of notice for having served with unabated zeal and activity through this laborious campaign, notwithstanding a wound through his arm, which he received at Hubberton.

No. I.

October 13, 1777.

Lieutenant-general Burgoyne is desirous of sending a field officer, with a message to Major-general Gates, upon a matter of high moment to both armies. He requests to be informed at what hour General Gates will receive him to-morrow morning.

Major-general GATES.

ANSWER.

ANSWER.

Major-general Gates will receive a Field Officer from Lieutenant-general Burgoyne at the advanced post of the army of the United States, at ten o'clock to-morrow morning, from whence he will be conducted to Head-quarters.

Camp at Saratoga, 9 o'clock,
P. M. October 13, 1777.
Lieutenant-general BURGOYNE.

No. II.

Major KINGSTON *delivered the following message to Major-general* GATES, *October 14, 1777.*

After having fought you twice, Lieutenant-general Burgoyne has waited some days, in his present position, determined to try a third conflict against any force you could bring to attack him.

He is apprized of the superiority of your numbers, and the disposition of your troops to impede his supplies, and render his retreat a scene of carnage on both sides. In this situation he is impelled by humanity, and thinks himself justified by established principles and precedents of state, and of war, to spare the lives of brave men upon honourable terms: should Major-general Gates be inclined to treat upon that idea, General Burgoyne would propose a cessation of arms during the time necessary to communicate the preliminary terms by which, in any extremity, he, and his army, mean to abide.

No. III.

Major-general GATES's *Proposals; together with Lieutenant-general* BURGOYNE's *Answers.*

I. General Burgoyne's army being exceedingly reduced by repeated defeats, by desertion, sickness, &c. their provisions exhausted, their military horses, tents and baggage, taken or destroyed, their retreat cut off, and their camp invested, they can only be allowed to surrender prisoners of war.

Answer. Lieutenant-general Burgoyne's army, however reduced, will never admit that their retreat is cut off, while they have arms in their hands.

II. The officers and soldiers may keep the baggage belonging to them. The Generals of the United States never permit Individuals to be pillaged.

III. The troops under his Excellency General Burgoyne will be conducted by the most convenient route to New-England, marching by easy marches, and sufficiently provided for by the way.

Answer. This Article is answered by General Burgoyne's first proposal, which is here annexed.

IV. The officers will be admitted on parole; may wear their side arms, and will be treated with the liberality customary in Europe, so long as they, by proper behaviour, continue to deserve it; but those who are apprehended having broke their parole, as some British officers have done, must expect to be close confined.

Answer. There being no officer in this army under, or capable of being under, the description of breaking parole, this article needs no answer.

V. All public stores, artillery, arms, ammunition, carriages, horses, &c. &c. must be delivered to Commissaries appointed to receive them.

Answer. All public stores may be delivered, arms excepted.

VI. These terms being agreed to and signed, the troops under his Excellency General Burgoyne's command may be drawn up in their encampment, where they will be ordered to ground their arms, and may thereupon be marched to the river side, to be passed over in their way towards Bennington.

Answer. This Article inadmissible in any extremity. Sooner than this army will consent to ground their arms in their encampment, they will rush on the enemy determined to take no quarter.

VII. A cessation of arms to continue

tinue till fun-fet, to receive General Burgoyne's anfwer.

(Signed) HORATIO GATES.
Camp at Saratoga, Oct. 14, 1777.

No. IV.

Major Kingfton met the Adjutant-general of Major-general Gates's army, October the 14th at fun-fet, and delivered the following meffage:

If General Gates does not mean to recede from the 6th Article, the treaty ends at once.

The army will to a man proceed to any act of defperation, rather than fubmit to that Article.

The ceffation of arms ends this evening.

No. V.

Lieutenant-general BURGOYNE's *Propofals, together with Major-general* GATES's *Anfwers.*

The annexed anfwers being given to Major-general Gates's propofals, it remains for Lieutenant-general Burgoyne, and the army under his command, to ftate the following preliminary Articles on their part:

I. The troops to march out of their camp with the honours of war, and the artillery of the entrenchments, which will be left as hereafter may be regulated.

I. The troops to march out of their camp with the honours of war, and the artillery of the intrenchments to the verge of the river where the old fort ftood, where their arms and artillery muft be left.

II. A free paffage to be granted to this army to Great-Britain, upon condition of not ferving again in North-America during the prefent conteft; and a proper port to be affigned for the entry of traufports to receive the troops whenever General Howe fhall fo order.

II. Agreed to for the port of Bofton.

III. Should any cartel take place, by which this army, or any part of it, may be exchanged, the foregoing article to be void as far as fuch exchange fhall be made.

III. Agreed.

IV. All officers to retain their carriages, bat-horfes, and other cattle; and no baggage to be molefted or fearched, the Lieutenant-general giving his honour, that there are no public ftores fecreted therein. Major-general Gates will of courfe take the neceffary meafures for the fecurity of this article.

IV. Agreed.

V. Upon the march the officers are not to be feparated from the men; and in quarters the officers fhall be lodged according to their rank; and are not to be hindered from affembling their men for roll-calling, and every other neceffary purpofes of regularity.

V. Agreed to, as far as circumftances will admit.

VI. There are various corps in this army, compofed of failors, batteaumen, artificers, drivers, independent companies, and followers of the army; and it is expected, that thofe perfons, of whatever country, fhall be included in the fulleft fenfe and utmoft extent of the above articles; and comprehended in every refpect as Britifh fubjects.

VI. Agreed to in the fulleft extent.

VII. All Canadians, and perfons belonging to the Eftablifhment in Canada, to be permitted to return there.

VII. Agreed.

VIII. Paffports to be immediately granted for three officers, not exceeding the rank of Captain, who fhall be appointed by General Burgoyne, to carry difpatches to Sir William Howe, Sir Guy Carleton, and to Great-Britain, by the way of New-York, and the public faith to be engaged, that thefe difpatches are not to be opened.

VIII. Agreed.

IX. The foregoing articles are to be confidered only as preliminaries for framing a treaty; in the courfe of which, others may arife to be confidered by both parties; for which

purpofe

purpose it is proposed, that two officers of each army shall meet and report their deliberations to their respective Generals.

IX. This capitulation to be finished by two o'clock this day, and the troops march from their encampment at five, and be in readiness to move towards Bolton to-morrow morning.

X. Lieutenant general Burgoyne will send his Deputy Adjutant-general to receive Major-general Gates's answer to-morrow morning at ten o'clock.

X. Complied with.

(Signed) HORATIO GATES.
Saratoga, Oct. 15, 1777,

No. VI.

The eight first preliminary articles of Lieutenant-general Burgoyne's proposals, and the 2d, 3d, and 4th of those of Major-general Gates of yesterday being agreed to, the foundation of the proposed treaty is out of dispute; but the several subordinate articles and regulations necessarily springing from these preliminaries, and requiring explanation and precision between the parties, before a definitive treaty can be safely executed, a longer time than that mentioned by General Gates in his answer to the 9th article, becomes indispensibly necessary. Lieutenant-general Burgoyne is willing to appoint two officers immediately to meet two others from Major-general Gates, to propound, discuss, and settle those subordinate articles, in order that the treaty in due form may be executed as soon as possible.

(Signed) JOHN BURGOYNE.
Camp at Saratoga, Oct. 15, 1777.

Major Kingston has authority to settle the place for a meeting of the officers proposed.

Settled by Major Kingston on the ground where Mr. Schuyler's house flood.

No. VII.

In the course of the night, Lieute-

nant-general Burgoyne has received intelligence, that a considerable force has been detached from the army under the command of Major-general Gates during the course of the negociation depending between them; Lieutenant-general Burgoyne conceives this, if true, to be not only a violation of the cessation of arms, but subversive of the principles on which the treaty originated, viz. a great superiority of numbers in General Gates's army; Lieutenant-general Burgoyne therefore requires, that two officers, on his part, be permitted to see that the strength of the forces now opposed to him is such as will convince him that no such detachments have been made; and that the same principles of superiority on which the treaty first began, still exist.

16th Oct.

No. VIII.

Articles of Convention between Lieutenant-general BURGOYNE, *and Major-general* GATES.

I. The troops under Lieutenant-general Burgoyne, to march out of their camp with the honours of war, and the artillery of the intrenchments, to the verge of the river, where the old fort flood, where the arms and artillery are to be left.—The arms to be piled by word of command from their own officers.

II. A free passage to be granted to the army under Lieutenant-general Burgoyne to Great-Britain, upon condition of not serving again in North-America, during the present contest; and the port of Bolton to be assigned for the entry of transports, to receive the troops, whenever General Howe shall so order.

III. Should any cartel take place, by which the army under Lieutenant-general Burgoyne, or any part of it, may be exchanged, the foregoing Article to be void, as far as such exchange shall be made.

IV. The army under Lieutenant-general Burgoyne is to march to Massachusetts fachufetts Bay, by the eafieft, and moft expeditious, and convenient route; and to be quartered in, near, or as convenient as poffible to Bofton, that the march of the troops may not be delayed when tranfports arrive to receive them.

V. The troops to be fupplied on the march, and during their being in quarters, with provifions, by Major-general Gates's orders, at the fame rate of rations as the troops of his own army; and, if poffible, the officers horfes and cattle are to be fupplied with forage at the ufual rates.

VI. All officers to retain their carriages, bat-horfes and other cattle, and no baggage to be molefted or fearched; Lieutenant-general Burgoyne giving his honour that there are no public ftores contained therein. Major-general Gates will of courfe take the neceffary meafures for the due performance of this Article: fhould any carriage be wanted during the march, for the tranfportation of officers baggage, they are, if poffible, to be fupplied by the country at the ufual rates.

VII. Upon the march, and during the time the army fhall remain in quarters, in the Maffachufetts Bay, the officers are not, as far as circumftances will admit, to be feparated from their men. The officers are to be quartered according to their rank, and are not to be hindered from affembling their men for roll-callings, and other neceffary purpofes of regularity.

VIII. All corps whatever of General Burgoyne's army, whether compofed of failors, batteau-men, artificers, drivers, independent companies, and followers of the army, of whatever country, fhall be included in the fulleft fenfe and utmoft extent of the above Articles, and comprehended in every refpect as Britifh fubjects.

IX. All Canadians and perfons belonging to the Canadian eftablifh-ment, confifting of failors, batteau-men, artificers, drivers, independent companies, and many other followers of the army, who come under no particular defcription, are to be permitted to return there; they are to be conducted immediately by the fhorteft route to the firft Britifh poft on Lake George, are to be fupplied with provifions in the fame manner as the other troops, and to be bound by the fame condition of not ferving during the prefent conteft in North-America.

X. Paffports to be immediately granted for three officers, not exceeding the rank of Captains, who fhall be appointed by Lieutenant-general Burgoyne, to carry difpatches to Sir William Howe, Sir Guy Carleton, and to Great-Britain, by the way of New-York; and Major-general Gates engages the public faith, that thefe difpatches fhall not be opened. Thefe officers are to fet out immediately after receiving their difpatches, and are to travel by the fhorteft route, and in the moft expeditious manner.

XI. During the ftay of the troops in the Maffachufets Bay, the officers are to be admitted on parole, and are to be permitted to wear their fide arms.

XII. Should the army under Lieutenant-general Burgoyne, find it neceffary to fend for their cloathing and other baggage from Canada, they are to be permitted to do it in the moft convenient manner, and neceffary paffports granted for that purpofe.

XIII. Thefe Articles are to be mutually figned and exchanged to-morrow morning at nine o'clock; and the troops under Lieutenant-general Burgoyne, are to march out of their intrenchments at three o'clock in the afternoon.

Camp at Saratoga, October 16, 1777.

HORATIO GATES, Major-general.

(True Copy.)

To prevent any doubts that might arife from Lieutenant-general Burgoyne's name not being mentioned in
the

the above treaty, Major-general Gates hereby declares, that he is understood to be comprehended in it, as fully as if his name had been specifically mentioned.

HORATIO GATES.

No. IX.

Minutes of a Council of War, held on the Heights of Saratoga, Oct. 19th, 1777.

PRESENT,

Lieutenant-general Burgoyne, Major-general Phillips, Major-general Reidefel, Brigadier-general Hamilton.

The Lieutenant-general states to the Council the present situation of affairs.

The enemy in force, according to the best intelligence he can obtain, to the amount of upwards of fourteen thousand men, and a considerable quantity of artillery, are on this side the Fish-kill, and threaten an attack. On the other side the Hudson's River, between this army and Fort Edward, is another of the enemy, the numbers unknown; but one corps, which there has been an opportunity of observing, is reported to be about fifteen hundred men. They have likewise cannon on the other side Hudson's River, and they have a brigade below Saratoga church, by which the two armies can communicate.

The batteaux of the army have been destroyed, and no means appear of making a bridge over the Hudson's River, were it even practicable from the position of the enemy.

The only means of retreat, therefore, are by the ford at Fort Edward, or taking the mountains, in order to pass the river higher up by rafts, or by another ford, which is *reported* to be practicable with difficulty, or by keeping the mountains, to pass the head of Hudson's River, and continue to the Westward of Lake George all the way to Ticonderoga; it is true, this last passage was never made but by Indians or very small bodies of men.

In order to pass cannon or any wheel carriages from hence to Fort Edward, some bridges must be repaired under fire of the enemy from the opposite side of the river; and the principal bridge will be a work of fourteen or fifteen hours; there is no good position for the army to take to sustain that work, and, if there were, the time stated as necessary would give the enemy on the other side Hudson's River an opportunity to take post on the strong ground above Fort Edward, or to dispute the ford while Gen. Gates's army followed in the rear.

The intelligence from the lower part of Hudson's River is founded upon the concurrent reports of prisoners and deserters, who say it was the news in the enemy's camp that Fort Montgomery was taken; and one man, a friend to Government, who arrived yesterday, mentions some particulars of the manner in which it was taken.

The provisions of the army may hold out to the 20th; there is neither rum nor spruce beer.

Having committed this state of facts to the consideration of the Council, the General requests their sentiments on the following propositions:

1st. To wait in the present position an attack from the enemy, or the chance of favourable events.

2d. To attack the enemy.

3d. To retreat, repairing the bridges as the army moves for the artillery, in order to force the passage of the ford.

4th. To retreat by night, leaving the artillery and the baggage; and should it be found impracticable to force the passage with musquetry, to attempt the upper ford, or the passage round Lake George.

5th. In case the enemy, by extending to their left, leave their rear open, to march rapidly for Albany.

Upon the first proposition resolved, That the situation would grow worse by by delay, that the provision now in store is not more than sufficient for the retreat, should impediments intervene, or a circuit of country become necessary; and as the enemy did not attack when the ground was unfortified, it is not probable they will do it now, as they have a better game to play.

The second unadviseable and desperate, there being no possibility of reconnoitring the enemy's position, and their great superiority of numbers known.

The third impracticable.

The fifth thought worthy of consideration by the Lieutenant-general, Major-general Phillips, and Brigadier-general Hamilton; but the position of the enemy yet gives no opening for it.

Resolved, That the fourth proposition is the only resource, and that, to effect it, the utmost secrecy and silence is to be observed; and the troops are to be put in motion from the right in the still part of the night, without any change in the disposition.

N. B. It depended upon the delivery of six days provision in due time, and upon the return of scouts, who had been sent forward, to examine by what route the army could probably move the first *four* miles undiscovered, whether the plan should take place on that day, or on the morrow.

The scouts on their return reported, that the enemy's position on our right was such, and they had so many small parties out, that it would be impossible to move without our march being immediately discovered.

Minutes and proceedings of a Council of War, consisting of all the General Officers and Field Officers, and Captains commanding Corps, on the Heights of Saratoga, October 13, 1777.

The Lieutenant-general having explained the situation of affairs, as in the preceding Council, with the ad-

ditional intelligence, that the enemy was intrenched at the fords of Fort Edward, and likewise occupied the strong position on the Pine Plains, between Fort George and Fort Edward, expressed his readiness to undertake at their head any enterprize of difficulty or hazard that should appear to them within the compass of their strength and spirit: he added, that he had reason to believe a capitulation had been in contemplation of some, perhaps of all, who knew the real situation of things; that upon a circumstance of such consequence to national and personal honour, he thought it a duty to his country, and to himself, to extend his Council beyond the usual limits; that the assembly present might justly be esteemed a full representation of the army; and that he should think himself unjustifiable in taking any step in so serious a matter, without such a concurrence of sentiments as should make a treaty the act of the army, as well as that of the General.

The first question therefore he desired them to decide was,

" Whether an army of 3500 fighting men, and well provided with artillery, were justifiable, upon the principles of national dignity, and military honour, in capitulating in any possible situation?"

Resolved nem. con. in the affirmative.

Question 2. " Is the present situation of that nature?"

Resolved, nem. con. that the present situation justifies a capitulation upon honourable terms.

The Lieutenant-general then drew up the message, marked No. 2, in the papers relative to the negociation; and laid it before the Council. It was unanimously approved, and upon that foundation the treaty opened.

October 14. Major Kingston having delivered the message marked No. 2, returned with the proposals marked

marked No. 3, and the Council of War being assembled again, the Lieutenant-general laid them before it, when it was resolved unanimously to reject the 6th Article, and not to admit of it in any extremity whatever.

The Lieutenant-general then laid before the Council the answers to Major-general Gates's proposals, as marked in the same paper, together with his own preliminary proposals, marked No. 4, which were unanimously approved of.

October 15. The Council being assembled again, Major-general Gates's answers to Lieutenant-general Burgoyne's proposals were laid before them, whereupon it was resolved, that they were satisfactory, and a sufficient ground for proceeding to a definitive treaty.

Reports of the killed, wounded, and prisoners of the British troops, (till exact returns can be collected) under the command of Lieutenant-general BURGOYNE, *to October* 12, 1777.

1 Brigadier-general, 1 Major, 2 Captains, 15 Lieutenants, 4 Ensigns, 12 Serjeants, 4 drummers, 313 rank rank and file, *killed*.

2 Lieutenant-colonels, 5 Majors, 17 Captains, 18 Lieutenants, 4 Ensigns, 1 Adjutant, 38 Serjeants, 4 drummers, 715 rank and file, *wounded*.

2 Majors, 2 Captains, 3 Lieutenants, 2 Ensigns, 1 Surgeon, 4 Serjeants, 2 drummers, 43 rank and file, *prisoners*.

Names of the Staff Officers, killed, wounded, and prisoners.

Brigadier-general Frazer, Sir James Clarke, Aid-de-Camp to Lieutenant-general Burgoyne, *killed*.

Captain Green of the 31st regiment, Aid-de-Camp to Major-general Phillips, Captain Bloomfield of the Royal Artillery, Major of Brigade to Major-general Phillips, *wounded*.

Captain Money of the 9th regiment, Deputy Quarter-master General, *prisoner*.

Names of Officers, killed, wounded, and missing.

Major Grant of the 24th regiment, *killed*.

Captains Wight of the 53d, Jones, Royal Artillery, *wounded*.

Lieutenants Weltrop and Wright, 9th regiment, Lucas, Cooke, Obins, 20th ditto, Currie, Mackenzie, Robertson, Turnbull, 21st ditto, Douglas, 29th ditto, Reynal, Harvey, Stuart, 62d ditto, Haggart, of the Marines, Cleyland, Second Lieutenant Royal Artillery, *killed*.

Ensigns Taylor, Phillips, Young, 62d ditto, *killed*.

Adjutant Fitzgerald, 62d ditto, *killed*.

Lieutenant-colonels Lynd, of 20th regiment, Anstruther, 62d ditto, *wounded*, in two different actions.

Major Forbes, 9th ditto, Acland, 20th ditto, Agnew, 24th ditto, Earl of Belcarres, 53d ditto, Harnage, 62d ditto, *wounded*, in two different actions.

Captains Montgomery, Sweetenham, Stapylton (since dead of his wounds) 9th ditto, Weyms, Dowling, Stanley, Farquire, 20th ditto, Strangeways, 24th ditto, Ramsey, 21st ditto, Blake, 24th ditto, Harris, Rofs, 34th ditto, Craig, 47th ditto, Shrimpton, Bunbury, 62d ditto, *wounded*.

Lieutenants, Battersby, light infantry, 29th ditto, Fisherton, grenadiers 21st ditto, Richardson, grenadiers 34th ditto (wounded in two different actions) Rowe, Stavely, Murray, Prince, 9th ditto, Dowling, 29th, doing duty with the 20th ditto, Doyle, 24th ditto, Rutherford, 21st ditto, Williams, Steel, 29th ditto, Richardson, 34th ditto, Haughton, Cullan, 53d ditto, Jones, 60th ditto, Smith, Howarth, Royal Artillery, *wounded*.

Ensigns Connel, 20th ditto, Blake, Hervey, 62d ditto, Baron d'Salons, 9th ditto, *wounded*.

O o o 2   Adjutant

‘Adjutant Fielding, 9th ditto, *wounded*.

Majors Acland, commanding the grenadiers, Williams, Royal Artillery, *prisoners*.

Captains Montgomery, Money, 9th ditto, *prisoners*.

Lieutenants Johnson, York, 29th ditto, Howarth, Royal Artillery, *prisoners*.

Ensigns D'Antroch, Naylor, 62d ditto, *prisoners*.

Surgeon Shelley, 9th ditto, *prisoner*.

J. Burgoyne, Lieutenant-general.

N. B. From the 12th, the loss by killed, prisoners, and desertion, was very confiderable. [*London Gazette*.

———

[*Obfervations on the preceding Gazette.*—Gen. Burgoyne says, at the beginning of his letter, *that the Indians, Canadians, &c. left him*; but it is not said, *where*, nor *when*, this happened. A little lower, he says, *I take upon myself the measure of having passed the Hudson's River*. Ministers say, he ought not to have passed the river, till he knew that General Howe, or Sir H. Clinton, or fomebody, were ready to co-operate with him. Further still, he says, *a critical junction of Mr. Gates's force with Mr. Washington, might possibly decide the fate of the war*. This is a pretty strong opinion of General Howe's situation; for if General Gates has joined General Washington (and there is no reason to doubt it) it is more than probable, the fate of the war is decided, before this time. General Burgoyne's next expression is, *the failure of my junction with Sir Harry Clinton, or the loss of my retreat to Canada, could only be a partial misfortune*. The misfortune is decisive, to all intents and purposes. In the paper, Number VII. General Burgoyne says, *he is informed General Gates has made a confiderable detachment from his army*. No answer is given to this paper. The firft, and fecond questions propofed to the Council of War, on the thirteenth of October, were fit to be debated only at Coach-makers Hall, or fome fuch place, not in a Council of War. Not a word is mentioned of the *King of Great-Britain*, or of *his army*, nor is the word *rebel* once made ufe of, throughout this Gazette. For thefe terms are fubftituted, *the army under Lieutenant-general Burgoyne, and the enemy*. It is alfo worthy of obfervation, that the *return* of the killed and wounded, is *only to the 12th of October*; and that at the *bottom* of the return, it is faid, " That *from the 12th, the lofs by killed, &c. is very confiderable.*" And why is it not faid, that *many*, if not all, the Brunfwickers have joined the Americans? The *fact is fo*.]

———

Albany, 19th of October, 1777.

Sir,

I have the pleafure to fend your Honourable Council the inclofed copy of a convention, by which Lieutenant-general Burgoyne furrendered himfelf and his whole army on the 17th inftant into my hands. They are now upon their march towards Bofton. General Glover and General Whipple, with a proper guard of militia, efcort them, and are to provide all fuch neceffary articles as may be wanted upon the march. I am fo extremely bufy in pufhing the army forward to ftop the cruel career of General Vaughan up Hudfon's River, that I have only time to acquaint you, that my friend General Lincoln's leg is in a fair way of doing well, and to teftify with what refpect I am,

Your much obliged,

and moft obedient,

humble fervant,

Horatio Gates.

To the Hon. the Prefident of the Council of the State of Maffachuffets Bay [The

[The American copy of the Convention is the same with that published in the London Gazette.]

In consequence of the foregoing convention at Saratoga the 17th of October, 1777,

The following numbers laid down their arms, and surrendered to General Gates, viz.

British troops - - -	2442
Brunswick and other German troops - - -	2198
Canadians, Volunteers, &c.	1100
Staff - - - - -	12
	5752

Sick and wounded left in the British camp when Gen. Burgoyne began his retreat, - - - 528

Besides the above there were killed, wounded, taken, and deserted, of British, German, and Canadian troops under General Burgoyne, between the 6th of July, and 16th of October, - - - 2933

In all 9213

Account of Brass Ordnance, &c. delivered up to General Gates on the 17th of October.

Viz.		
2	-	24 pounders
4	-	12 ditto
18	-	6 ditto
4	-	3 ditto
Royal Howitz. 5	-	5½ inch
Brass Mortars 2	=	8 inch
35		

All of brass, besides those taken at Bennington.

Stands of arms complete, 7000

Besides the military chest, large quantities of ordnance stores, cloathing for 7000 Provincials, tents, &c. &c.

BOSTON, October 30.

The following resolves passed the General Assembly of this State, previous to their adjournment, viz.

" Resolved, that the troops under General Burgoyne, be quartered in the barracks on Prospect and Winter Hills, and such others as a Committee of both Houses hereafter to be appointed shall judge most safe, retired, and easy guarded; and that they obtain suitable houses for the general officers, and proper rooms for the other officers of rank; the foreign troops to be kept separate from the British as far as practicable; both officers and soldiers to be prevented from coming into the town of Boston, or on this side Charles-town neck: and the Committee aforesaid are directed to fix such limits for the restraint of officers and soldiers, as may secure the public from any ill consequences, so far as may be consistent with a strict fulfilment of the Convention. That the representatives of the town of Boston be a Committee empowered to afford all such assistance to General Heath, in the procurement of fuel, by insurance or otherwise, as they shall judge will best favour the public interest. That every vessel coming from the eastward for this purpose, be furnished with a pass signed by Gen. Heath, certifying that the wood in those vessels is for the sole use of the army with Gen. Burgoyne, now prisoners of war in the state of the Massachusetts Bay: and that if she is taken, that army must be the sufferers.

And it is further resolved, That no inhabitant of the United States, or any other person whatever, shall at any time enter the limits assigned for preventing their communication with the prisoners, without a written licence obtained for that purpose, from the Council to General Heath, under the pain of military discipline, which Gen. Heath is hereby empowered and requested to inflict. That the Committee aforesaid be directed to appoint a proper number of of perfons of capacity and approved fidelity to buy and deliver out to the prifoners the various forts of provifions brought to Bofton market, the produce of this ftate, that they fhall need, over and above the rations to be fupplied by General Heath, in fuch quantities as will be needed for their confumption while here ; which fhall be purchafed with the currency of the United States, of fome of them; to be drawn out of the treafury by order of Council, and fold at the prices given for them; and if the fame is paid for in any part in gold or filver, the fame fhall be depofited in the public treafury, to be drawn thence as the court fhall order ; and the perfons appointed as above, fhall be under ftrict bond, of fuch tenor as the Council fhall order, for a faithful difcharge of their duty

Provided neverthelefs, That in cafe the Committee directed to appoint a number of perfons to buy and deliver out to the prifoners provifions, fhould find that mode of procedure does not anfwer the purpofe defigned, or fhould think it for the intereft of the government to difcontinue it; that upon their reprefenting the matter to Council, they, the Council, are hereby empowered to order the fame to be difcontinued, and to make fuch other regulations as they think necefffary. That the Honourable Council be requefted to order one thoufand men, including officers, and as many more as they find neceffary, from fuch part of the militia of this ftate as they fhall judge equitable, to ferve as guards, and to be under the command of Gen. Heath.

And that John Taylor and Nathan Cufhing, Efqrs. be a Committee, with fuch as the Honourable Houfe fhall join, to carry this refolve into execution ; and that they advife with General Heath, touching the feveral matters mentioned in the foregoing refolve.

Extract of a letter from the War-Office of the State of the Maffachufets Bay, to the American Deputies in France.

Bofton, Oct. 25, 1777.

" Gentlemen,

" You will doubtlefs be furprifed to find a veffel in ballaft addreffed to you, from this board, until we inform you, fhe is taken up by Government, to go exprefs upon the moft important occafion that this country ever experienced. But before we enter upon a detail of this happy event, it will not, we prefume, be unacceptable to give you a general view of our public affairs, fince the fortunate actions of Trenton and Princeton in the Jerfies. At the clofe of the laft campaign, Gen. Howe feeing his cantonements broke up, found it neceffary to collect his army at and about Brunfwick, on the river Rariton, where being intrenched, and covered on all fides, he was for a time inacceffible to General Wafhington, who contented himfelf, whilft his army was recruiting to beat back Gen. Howe's foragers, and harrafs his out-pofts. It is the prevalent opinion here, that the Britifh General originally defigned to penetrate to Philadelphia through the Jerfies, and actually made an effort, but whether he knew it to be impracticable from the beginning, or found it fo upon trial, we cannot determine, the fact is, that he retreated to Staten-Ifland. About Midfummer he embarked his troops, ftores, &c. from thence, and after a tedious paffage arrived in Chefapeak Bay, where he landed at the head of the river Elk, and marching through a dreary country, thinly inhabited, came to the river Brandy-wine, about 30 miles from Philadelphia. Although Gen. Howe made ufe of every poffible ftratagem to miflead Gen. Wafhington, he neverthelefs traverfed his defigns, and with a penetration, peculiar to himfelf, self, predicted, that the banks of the Delaware would be the scene of future contest. In that vicinity Gen. Washington met, and fought the enemy. But though neither courage was wanting in our troops, or conduct in our officers, a certain steadiness in charging, and quickness in forming, (which nothing but real action can give any troops) were wanting and we lost the ground, though it was dearly bought with British blood. By the fairest computation the enemy had 2000 killed and wounded, whilst ours by the most exact returns does not exceed half the number. However, matters were now brought to this crisis, that Gen. Howe should have the open country, and Gen. Washington the city, or the reverse; Gen. Washington chose the country, and the command of a fort on the Delaware, where the pass is so well defended by chevaux de frize, that the Roebuck; a British 40 gun ship, is already sunk, and two others have been repulsed, and which have hitherto prevented any vessels from getting up to the city.

" The second important action, was at or near German town, about 7 miles from Philadelphia, where the enemy were attacked, broken, and repulsed; their train of artillery was actually in our possession, and the wreath of victory just ready to crown the American hero, when an unfortunate circumstance snatched it from his brow. A division of the army, who acted as a corps de reserve, was ordered to advance nearer to their victorious brethren, who (owing to a thick fog, the smoke of the artillery, and from some fields of stubble fired by Gen. Howe's orders to cover the retreat) was mistaken for the enemy, which put our troops into disorder, and occasioned a retreat on our side, upon which the enemy rallied, soon recovered their artillery, and retook their own lines. Some General and

field officers were killed and wounded on both sides. We lost in the action, which continued upwards of two hours, including killed, wounded, and missing, officers and privates, only 700 men. With respect to the enemy, it is the opinion of the most judicious, that two more such actions (though on our side unsuccessful) would ruin Gen Howe's projects; what with killed, wounded, sickness, and desertion, an army which has no recruits flowing to it, exhausts beyond computation. Some advantages indeed the enemy derive from their fleet, and Generals Vaughan and Tryon have lately gone up Hudson's River with about 4000 men, and attacked Fort Montgomery, which was garrisoned with about 500; before we could relive it, they took it, but not without the expence of much blood; it commanded a strong pass in that river, and having fallen into their hands, we were obliged to burn the hulls of two Continental frigates. It is also said they have proceeded farther up, and have stolen some cattle, and destroyed several houses. However Gen. Putnam, with an equal number, is now in their rear, and Gen. Gates having disincumbered himself of his prisoners, and detatched 4000 men to repossess Ticonderoga, is advanced to Albany, and we hope will not long suffer them to remain unpunished. Gen. Parsons in the mean time has orders, if possible, to invest New-York; and 8000 men under Gen. Spencer are at their rendezvous upon an expedition against Newport and Rhode Island.

" Permit us now to point your attention to the North, where a blaze of glory reflects new lustre upon American arms ——An army, which Britain was a considerable time collecting, assisted by her allies, marched, well appointed from Canada early this spring, had before we suspected, that the enemy were so numerous in

that

that part of America, invested our fortress of Ticonderoga, the grand avenue to the New-England states. Time, and a strict scrutiny, will discover upon what grounds (but true it is) this important fortress, garrisoned by near 5000 troops, well armed and appointed under the command of Gen. St. Clair, was scarcely attacked before it was evacuated, and to our astonishment, in an instant was our country laid open to the triumphant entry of Lieutenant-general Burgoyne, and his cruel abettors, whilst our brave soldiers retreated before them, with sullen resentment, alternately against their own, and the enemy's General. But the militia composed of the main body of the people were by no means dismayed, and finding all the blessings of life at hazard, rushed to the field with ardour and emulation.

"Congress immediately superseded St. Clair, and appointed Gen. Gates, to conduct a band of hardy warriors, who only wanted good officers to lead them to victory. He rallied our broken army, and such was the deserved confidence in this great man, that when he gave the word to stand, each animated band, both of army and militia, were immoveable. Burgoyne, in the mean time, in all the wantonness of victory, suffered, if not encouraged his savages, and Canadians, to murder the distressed inhabitants, and advanced into the country as he too vainly thought, in the character of a conqueror.

"The first presage of his fate was a severe check at Fort Schuyler, (formerly Stanwix) an important post upon the Mohawk river; where a Colonel St. Leger, with a motley mixture of Britons, Waldeckers, and savages was sallied upon and dispersed by a brave little garrison, commanded by Colonel Gonsevelt. Had Gen. Burgoyne been wise, he would have taken this as a hint, that he was on

dangerous ground. Soon after this event a detachment of 2500 were sent to take post at Bennington, with orders in a *truly laughable stile*, " as opportunity offered to penetrate the country." These well armed and disciplened troops halted several miles short of their destination, and intrenched; and by a party of militia, under the command of the brave General Stacks; assisted by 300 Continental troops, of Colonel Warner's battalion, were twice attacked, *their lines carried by assault*, and one half of them were killed and made prisoners. This was followed by an action more important at Bemus's Heights, about 40 miles from Albany; and where night only prevented the Americans from another victory. The last effort of this baffled army was an attack upon the left and centre of General Gates's army, under the command of Generals Lincoln and Arnold. An action, which though marked with the unfortunate wounds of these brave Generals, terminated to the honour of American arms. General Frazer fell, with a great number of Britons, and the flower of the British army retreated in disorder, with great loss; they were pursued into their lines, their hospital, consisting of 300 sick and wounded, fell into our hands, and the baggage of a German batalion. During these transactions our light troops hung continually upon the flanks, and rear of the enemy; intercepted their convoys, destroyed their magazines, (daily beating in their guards and making prisoners. They, harrassed and exhausted by incessant duty, the sword, famine, or captivity became the wretched alternatives of this vaunting invader of America; *and he who, a few weeks before, in a pompous manifesto, proscribed the best blood of the country as traiterous*, was now at their mercy; his threats, that by the blessing of God, he would extend the influence of his arms far and near,

denouncing

denouncing fire and fword againft a much injured people, recoiled upon his own head; and of 10,000 men, who came out of Canada with him, full 4000 were killed, taken, and deferted, before the capitulation, and by which, he obliged the remainder to deliver their arms *as he did his own fword*, into the hands of his conqueror. For the articles of capitulation, and many important particulars, we refer you to the papers inclofed. We have the faireft profpect of playing the fame game with General Howe, as we have done with his coadjutor. Our Northern army have nothing now to obftruct their junction with General Wafhington.

" Having thus given you fome detail of our public affairs, you and your connections may form a judgment of the ridiculous infinuations of our treating with Britain, upon the terms that proud and cruel people prefcribe. No, Sirs! Was America harraffed, and beaten from the fea coaft to the Weftern world, and thence repulfed to the midland region, where our armies difpirited, broken, and imprifoned, our militia would replace them, and in fucceffion meet the tyrants in the field, fall there, a free, or, by driving them, live an independent people. We fhall be much more ftrenuous in thefe fentiments, when in one quarter our arms, are impreffive, and in another triumphant."

Extract of a Letter from Paris, dated Dec. 17, 1777,

" General Burgoyne was beaten in a fair battle, by our *militia*, his camp ftormed, and taken with cannon, baggage &c. The army fled to another fortified poft, where they were furrounded; the provifions coming to them from Canada taken, and General Gates on the point of attacking them again, when General Burgoyne agreed to capitulate. It is said, they had no bread for eight days; that they had only beef remaining for feven days, – which General Burgoyne propofed to his troops to divide among them, deftroy every thing cumberfome, and endeavour to fight their way through. This the *Englifh* agreed to, but the *Germans* and *Canadians* refufed, alledging it was a mad, hopelefs propofition, and would end in their total deftruction. So the capitulation took place. Burgoyne's further retreat had been cut off by the lofs of his batteaux. To fecure them, without leaving a guard, he had buried them; and filled the place with little erected boards, on every one of which was marked, HERE LIES THE BODY OF SUCH A ONE, &c. as if it had been a burying place of his foldiers. When our people came to the fpot, and examined it, they difcovered the ftratagem, *and the batteaux had a general and joyful refurrection.*

" General Burgoyne was to give his final anfwer at nine in the morning, October 17. He delayed it to the laft minute, when General Gates ordered the drums to beat for the affault. *He then came out on horfeback, rode up to General Gates, and prefented his fword.* The troops followed, and rank by rank as they paffed, laid down their arms. Our troops at the fame time marched into their lines, to the tune of *Yankee Doodle.* General Burgoyne was received with refpect, and dined with General Gates, who faid nothing unkind to him, except afking, how he could find in his heart to burn the poor country people's houfes wherever he paffed;—he anfwered,—that it was the ——'s orders. He was for moft part of the time very filent, and feemed much dejected. Some few of the New England men defired to have him in their hands for half an hour:—Being afked for what purpofe?—they faid, they would do him no manner of harm;—they would

only

only tar and feather him, and make him stand on the head of one of his empty beef barrels, *and read his own Proclamation.* Our militia is so greatly improved, as to attack British regular troops in their works, and carry them, though defended by equal numbers. We have had three instances of this in this campaign. The Indians all deserted General Burgoyne early;— the Tories, he complained, had deceived and betrayed him; and the Canadians, in his extremity, refused to fight for him.—Methink the *English* are unlucky in their *allies.* St. Leger's Indians plundered his camp, and left him—Just Heaven!——."

Copy of a letter from his Excellency Lieutenant-general BURGOYNE, *to his Excellency Sir* WILLIAM HOWE, *K. B. brought by Lieut.* VALANCY, *of the* 62d *Regiment.*

Albany, October 20, 1777.

" Sir,

" In conformity to my orders, to proceed by the most vigorous exertions to Albany, I passed the Hudson's River at Saratoga on the 13th of September. No exertions have been left untried. The army under my command has fought twice against great superiority of numbers. The first action was on the 19th of September, when, after four hours sharp conflict, we remained masters of the field of battle; the second action (on the 7th of October) was not so successful, and ended with a storm upon two parts of our entrenchments, the one defended by Lieutenant-colonel Breymen, who was killed on the spot, and the post was lost; the other defended by Lord Balcarres, at the head of the British light infantry, who repulsed the enemy with great loss. The army afterwards made good their retreat to the heights of Saratoga, unable to proceed further, the enemy having possession of all the fords, and the passes on the east side of Hudson's River.

" The army there waited the chance of events, and offered themselves to the attack of the enemy till the 13th instant, when only three days provision, at short allowance, remained. At that time the last hope of timely assistance being exhausted, my numbers reduced by past actions to three thousand five hundred fighting men, of which about nineteen hundred alone were British; invested by the enemy's troops to the amount of about sixteen thousand men, I was induced by the general concurrence and advice of the Generals, Field Officers, and Captains commanding corps, to open a treaty with Major-general Gates. Your Excellency will observe by the papers transmitted herewith, the disagreeable prospect that attended the first overtures. The army determined to die to a man, rather than submit to terms repugnant to national and personal honour. I trust you will think the treaty enclosed consistent with both. I am, with greatest respect and attachment, Sir,

" Your most obedient, and

" most humble servant,

" J. BURGOYNE."

All the private letters from General Burgoyne's army, speak in the highest terms, of the generosity and humanity of the Americans; particularly General Burgoyne's own letter to the Earl of Derby, which was yesterday shewn by his Lordship to several gentlemen, wherein the General particularly mentions one circumstance, that exceeds all that he had ever seen or read of —— This was, when the British soldiers had marched out of their camp, according to the Articles of Capitulation, to a fixed place, where they were to pile their arms, *not one of the American troops were to be seen.* General Gates had ordered his whole army out of sight, that not one of them should be spectators of the shame of the British troops, nor offer

offer the smallest insult to the vanquished. This refined delicacy, and most soldier-like politeness, reflects the greatest honour upon America; and is spoken of, by all our Officers, in the highest terms of admiration.

General Burgoyne and his troops were on the 27th of October at Northampton, which is 115 miles from Bolton. It was expected they would reach Cambridge on the 5th of November.

PHILADELPHIA, September 10.
Philadelphia, August 31, 1777.
" Much respected Sir,

" As I find that Congress have had no particular account of the expedition against Staten-Island, on the 22d instant, I take the liberty to lay before Congress, the whole of the transaction, with the motives that induced me to make it. I found that the troops stationed there, were frequently making incursions into the Jerseys, carrying off inhabitants, cattle, &c. and concluded, that reprisals ought to be made: upon enquiry I found that Col. Buskirk, with a regiment of two hundred and fifty, was encamped near Decker's ferry: Col. Barton, with his regiment, of equal number, near the New Blazing-Star ferry; Col. Lawrence, with a hundred and fifty, near the Old Blazing-Star ferry; Col. Dungan and Col. Allen, with about a hundred each, towards Amboy, about two miles asunder; the 55th and part of the 27th British, with two regiments of Anspachers and one of Waldeckers, were encamped near the Watering-place, by their fortifications. The strength of those I could not exactly learn, but have since learned that the 55th was 200 strong, the Anspachers 450 each, the regiment of Waldeckers about 400, detachment of the 57th about 100: I was also informed, that there were two small detachments of new recruits, the one lying at Rich-

mond, and the other at Cuckoldstown. My intention was to land so as to entrap the new recruits in their different encampments; the others, I apprehended, I could not force from their fortifications without cannon, and indeed I should in that case have to fight all the troops in New-York, as in a few hours they might reinforce with what number they pleased. I therefore concluded, that the attack must be as sudden as possible.

" As my troops lay twenty miles distant from the Island, I knew it would fatigue them much to march that distance, and then go through the necessary marchings on the Island; but this I could by no means avoid, as any movements of my troops nearer the Island would have given the alarm to the disaffected in the neighbourhood of Spanick-town, who would instantly communicate it to the island; I therefore determined to make my march as sudden and as secret as possible. I therefore selected from General Smallwood, and General De Borre's brigade, such men, as were best able to endure a march, amounting to near a thousand in the whole. These I ordered to march at two o'clock, P. M. from Hanover to Elizabeth-town, where they arrived at ten in the evening, Colonel Ogden, with his own, and Colonel Dayton's regiment, joined by a hundred militia, under Colonel Freelinghusen, were to march from Elizabeth-town in the evening, and cross the river against a creek called the Fresh-kill, and pass up the creek, and come in the rear of Lawrence's regiment before day, and attack him by day-light. The other troops were to cross from Halsey's-point. General Smallwood's brigade was to attack Buskirk's, and General De Borre's brigade was to attack Barton's regiment, each leaving one regiment on the main road, to cover their rear, and pick up such per-

sons

fons as might efcape Col. Ogden, or our attacking parties. Col. Ogden had orders, in cafe he compleated the reduction of Lawrence's regiment, to move on and attack Dungan and Allen; but in cafe he found too great a force collected againft him, he was to take an advantageous poft, and wait my coming up. We were able to collect only fix boats, of which I ordered three to Colonel Ogden, and kept three myfelf, but with thefe we croffed over before day-light, undifcovered to the enemy; and while on our march, heard a fevere firing in the quarter where Colonel Ogden was, which ceafed in about two minutes. General Smallwood proceeded on to Decker's ferry; but being deceived by his guide, fell in upon the wrong fide of the enemy, which gave them an opportunity of efcaping to their forts. The regiment turned out to be a Britifh regiment, they ran off and left their colours, which he took; they left their tents ftanding, which he deftroyed, with their ftores, magazine of hay, &c. He alfo burnt feven of their veffels, laden with dry goods. He killed fome few, and wounded others as they ran off, and took two prifoners. I went myfelf with the other brigade, and after having placed a regiment on the main road, and detached Colonel Price off to the right, to prevent efcapes, we marched brifkly up to Barton's quarters, where we found him drawn up to receive us. I ordered the main body to halt and form, and fent Lieutenant-colonel Smith round in their rear to prevent efcapes; but upon our main body moving up to charge, the enemy threw down their arms and ran off. Colonel Smith did every thing that man could do, to prevent their efcaping, and indeed fo did every officer and foldier; but they were fo well acquainted with the creeks and marfhes, that our men could not catch them, though

they killed many: feveral of them got into the boats which lay at the ferry, and came over to the Jerfey fhore. We took a confiderable number of arms, blankets, hats, cloathes, &c. Col. Barton, and above 40 privates, were made prifoners. We then came back, and formed a junction with General Smallwood, and proceeded up toward Colonel Ogden, from whom we could hear nothing. I concluded, as I heard firing from that quarter but once, that he had routed Lawrence; but had found the others too ftrong for him, and was waiting my coming up, I therefore found it neceffary to haften my march as much as poffible, and fent off a boat, to order the boats at Halfey's-point, to meet me at the Old Blazing-Star ferry, where we arrived at twelve o'clock, and found that Colonel Ogden had routed Lawrence, taken him and feveral officers, with eighty privates, prifoners, but that Dungan and Allen had efcaped. Colonel Ogden repaffed the river. The boats from Halfey's-point had not arrived with the provifions for the men; they had then been fafting near fourteen hours: I knew, that the longer they tarried, the more unfit for action they would be, and the longer time would be given the enemy to collect the force of the Ifland, and that of New-York and Powles-hook, to attack my rear, and that in cafe the enemy collected a force fuperior to mine, all poffibility of retreat would be cut off. I therefore began croffing the river as faft as poffible, with what boats I had; the others at Halfey's-point, had, upon feeing a veffel under fail, which Colonel Ogden had taken, been carried off by the boatmen, who miftook this veffel for a tender, and my meffenger could neither find boats nor boatmen. We had however got almoft the whole of our troops over, when the enemy having collected in force, appeared in fight to attack

our

our rear, the boats were then pushing off to bring over our rear guard, of a hundred men, who were posted on an eminence, about 20 rods from the ferry, and commanded by Major Steward and Major Tillard. The enemy being so superior in number, pressed on boldly, expecting to receive no opposition from so small a party; but in this they were much deceived; their officers drew them up, and gave the enemy so warm a reception, that they were various times driven back in the greatest confusion. They finding the enemy were about to surround them, retired to an eminence about thirty rods in the rear, and after some time to another, about ten rods more, where they maintained their ground with great valour, till their ammunition was all spent, and then finding that the boats kept in the river without coming over, and that there was no prospect of getting off, Major Steward, with about forty more surrendered prisoners of war, the rest went, some to Amboy, where I sent persons to bring them over, others swam the river, and landed safe on the opposite shore. Had the boatmen done their duty, not a man of them would have been lost; but the enemy bringing a field piece and a howitzer to play upon the water, they were so much frightened, that I could not prevail on them to come to one side or the other of the water. I ordered my men to fire upon them to drive them over, but it only caused them to row up toward Amboy. We should have suffered nothing more, had not some of the men evaded the vigilance of their officers, and were taken or killed by the enemy. In the morning of our landing, Major Powel, Captain Heron, and Lieutenant Hall, three brave officers, were taken or killed by the enemy, as they tarried in rear, to bring up the men. We had in the course of the day ten killed and fifteen wounded. Mr. Skinner sent me an account

of the prisoners taken by them, viz. nine officers, and a hundred and twenty-seven privates; among the officers were three Majors, viz. Steward, Tillard, and Woodson. From them we took eleven officers, among which were two Colonels; we took a hundred and thirty privates, and twenty-eight Tories. We must have killed and wounded for them at least four hundred, besides the injury we did them, in destroying their stores and vessels, and bringing off their arms and baggage, with a great number of cattle. My officers and men, through the whole, behaved with great spirit. Colonel Ogden and his party behaved with equal bravery. The Colonel gives them a very high, and I dare say a deserved, good character: he desires me particularly to mention Lieutenant-colonel Barber, who distinguished himself as an officer and soldier. Mr. Williams (a volunteer) and Mr. Brown, Cornet of Captain Barnell's company of horse, distinguished themselves by their spirit and activity. I should do injustice to Mr. Brown, if I did not mention the zeal and activity he discovered in procuring boats, and making preparations for the troops to cross. After having given Congress an account of the brave and spirited opposition made by Majors Tillard and Steward, with their small party against such superior number, it would be needless for me to say any thing more in their favour.

"I have the honour to be, dear Sir, with much esteem, your most obedient servant,

"JOHN SULLIVAN."

To the Hon. JOHN HANCOCK, *Esq.*

Published by order of Congress,

CHARLES THOMPSON,
Secretary.

In

In Congress, Oct. 14, 1777.

Whereas the British nation have received into their ports, and condemned as lawful prizes, several vessels, and their cargoes, belonging to these States, which the masters and mariners, in breach of the trust and confidence reposed in them, have betrayed, and delivered to the officers of the British Crown.

Resolved, therefore, that any vessel or cargo, the property of any British subject, not an inhabitant of Bermuda, or any of the Bahama islands, brought into any of the ports or harbours of any of these United States, by the master or mariners, shall be judged lawful prize, and divided among the captors, in the same proportion as if taken by any Continental vessel of war.

Extract from the Minutes,
CHARLES THOMSON, Sec.

Monday, October 27, 1777.
In Congress, September 10, 1777.

Resolved, That the interest which shall arise, after the date of this resolution, on Loan Office Certificates, already issued, or which shall be issued before the first day of March next, be annually paid at the respective Loan Offices *in Bills of Exchange on the Commissioners of the United States in Paris, at the rate of five livres of France for every Spanish milled dollar due for interest* as aforesaid, or in Continental Bills of Credit, at the option of the respective lenders. By order of Congress,

JOHN HANCOCK, President.

[It has been long notorious, that the Courts France and Spain have supplied the Colonies, with *arms, ammunition, artillery, cloathing, &c.* The above extraordinary resolution of Congress, demonstrates, that the Colonies are *subsidized* by these Courts; and that being thus secure of having the interest of their public debt discharged in Europe, they can want no other assistance for the establishment of their *Independence,* and the solidity of their national credit.]

The following extract from Governor POWNALL'*s Journal, was furnished by a friend, who obtained the Governor's permission to have it inserted in this work.*

[It must be observed, this Journal was made three and twenty years ago—Most likely there are many alterations in the state of the settlement of the country since that time; but the locality remains as it then was.]

Road from Philadelphia to Wright's Ferry, on the River Susquahanna, 1754.

From Philadelphia to Coaltusferry, over the Schuylkill, one mile three quarters, and fifty-two perches.

All the plans of Philadelphia represent it as extending from the River Delaware to the Schuylkill. This was, indeed, the original plan laid down on paper, and held out to the first settlers; and it is said, that Mr. Penn sold many of the lots on the banks of the Schuylkill almost as dear as those on the Banks of the River Delaware. That this town should ever have such extent is almost impossible; it does not extend one third of the way: those, therefore, who bought these lots on speculation were much deceived.

Another idea in the plan of this town was, that Front-street, next the Delaware, should have no houses immediately on the bank, but a parapet: the banks are pretty high, and had a large beach at the foot of them. After the first settlers had bought these lots in Front-street, it was found more convenient for the merchants and traders to build their warehouses, and even dwelling-houses, on the beach below, which they wharfed out. This part of the soil was not sold; several took long leases; and this became a street of the dwelling-houses, &c. of all the princi al

cipal merchants and rich men of bufinefs, and was called Water-ftreet.
A prodigious advantage arofe to Mr.
Penn's eftate upon the old long leafes
falling in. The ftreet on the top of
the bank, however, keeps its original name, and is called Front-ftreet.
The ftreet behind it, running parallel to it, is called Second-ftreet; the
next, Third-ftreet, and fo on. The
ftreets which run acrofs thefe, at
right angles, take their names from
different trees, as Pine-ftreet, Chef-
nut-ftreet, and fo on. At this day
there are remaining in fome of the
ftreets, the ftumps or roots of fome of
the original Pine-trees. Front-ftreet
ftretches further along the banks of
the Delaware than as defigned by the
original plan; the other ftreets are
more and more defalcated of their
length, fo that the fhape of the town
at prefent is that of a femi-oval. It
is built upon a point of land formed
by the confluence of the Delaware
and Schuylkill Rivers, and ftands a
few miles above that confluence, and
the fcite of it is that of a dead flat.
The two rivers have formed, by the
foil which they bring down mixing
with the filt which the tide brings
up, a low fwampy ifland, called
Mud Ifland, at their confluence.
The number * of inhabitants in Philadelphia now, 1755, about 20,000.
The houfes are all of brick; the
fronts of them precifely fuch as thofe
in Cheapfide, London; a pent over
the bafe ftory, and fhops, and a little
flip of a window to light a clofet by
the fide of the chimnies. On each
fide the ftreets there is a trottoir paved with brick: the ftreets are † not
yet paved, but formed with gravel,
as were the great ftreets of London
about 200 years ago.
The ferry-boats at Schuylkill,
(about a mile and three quarters from
Philadelphia) are the moft convenient

I ever faw; and the oars with which
they are rowed over, rigged out in a
manner the moft handy that can be
devifed; they are fixed in an iron
fork, fo as to have a perpendicular
motion, and they are loaded towards
the hand, fo as to be nearly bal-
lanced, leaving, however, the feather of the oar rather the more heavy;
this fork is fixed on a pivot, in the
gunwale of the boat, by which the
oar has free horizontal motion. By
this fimple contrivance of mecha-
nifm, a very flight boy can manage
a pair of large heavy oars, and row
over a large ferry-boat.
From Coultus-ferry.
Shadling, to the Black Horfe, four
miles and a quarter, and twenty-
one perches.
Meeting-houfe, a mile and a quarter, and twenty-nine perches.
Richard Hughs, the Three Tuns,
two miles and a half, and fifty-three
perches.
Ann Millar's, the Buck, one mile
and fixty-two perches.
Richard Berry's, the Plough, two
miles and three quarters, and fix
perches.
The Bull, —— Byer's, five miles
and a half, and twenty-nine perches.
‡ The Vernon, G. Afhton's, three
miles and a quarter, and fixty perches.
At the Plough is a new tavern juft
fet up, the Unicorn. A mile weft
of this, the road runs up the fouth
mountain of the valley, and goes
along the ridge of it until it defcends
into the valley at the Vernon's Head.
The road from the ferry to the Vernon runs inceffantly up hill and
down, and through woods (Oak,
Hickory, Chefnut) all the way, except here and there a plantation, and
the beginnings of others. The whole
land here is poffeffed by fettlers, but
not fully cultivated, becaufe the fettlers have all bought large tracts on

* In 1770 near 30,000.   † They have been paved fince this Journal was written.
‡ This fign was originally that of Admiral Vernon, but hath been regenerated, and is
now the Admiral Warren.

fpeculation;

speculation; the soil light, and rather stony; the face of the country like a large rolling sea.

To the White Horse, Hambright's, two miles and three quarters, and seventy-two perches.

To the Ship, Thomas Parks, eight miles and a quarter, and twelve perches.

At the Vernon's, or Warren's, Head, the road descends the south mountain into the valley, and then runs along the valley W, a little southerly, twelve miles. This is a narrow valley, but a most pleasing landscape; a little brook runs through it, which falls into the Schuylkill at Swede's-ford. The valley, fully settled and cultivated, every farmer has a lime-kiln for manure, or dressing, to his land; they raise chiefly wheat. The farm-houses all with sash-windows, and bulked up on each side with peach and apple orchards, and surrounded on all sides with every thing that looks like a man's own business being done there. The farms are such as yeomanry, not tenants, dwell in. The lands sell in the farm at about £.5 per acre for the freehold: lands on the west side of the North Mountain of this valley, sell at about £.3 per acre in the farm. Except round the houses in the bosom of the vale, the settlements not well cleared; the cause is, broken land, and large tracts. The sides of the two mountains, which enclose this vale, are covered with woods. The species as before.

To the Waggon, James Way's, six miles and a half, and twelve perches.

From the Ship to the Tun, by the Waggon Tavern, the road passes over the North Mountain of the valley, N. W. it rises by three ridges, between each of which there is a valley, each having a run of water through it. [To the Tun, John Millar's, six miles and sixty-four perches.] The first ridge is the least; the second and third, each bigger

than the former: broken land, oak, chesnut, and hickory. The road does not get quite clear of the mountain till it comes to the Sun. [To the Hat, Widow Caldwell's, six miles and a quarter, and twelve perches.] I could not ride this last thirteen miles with ease under three hours. I experienced the same on my return as in going. The road runs thence westerly over very hilly land to the Widow Caldwell's, at the Hat; yet all this hilly country is but a vale enclosed by the valley mountain on the left, and the Welch mountains on the right, but widens to the west. From hence to Conestoga-creek, pretty level, and so to Lancaster.

To the Red Lion, Joseph Steers, six miles and a half, and fifty-four perches.

To Conestoga-creek, four miles.

To Lancaster, one mile and three quarters, and thirty perches.

Lancaster, a pretty considerable town, encreasing fast, and growing rich; a manufactory here of saddles and pack-saddles, also of guns; a very considerable stage-town, in the way, by two roads, to the back-road and Indian country; about 500 houses.

To Mr. Wright's Ferry, at the Susquahanna River, ten miles.

The river wide, one mile and twelve perches.

Between Lancaster and Mr. Wright's, I saw one of the finest farms one can conceive, and in the highest culture, particularly one that was the estate of a Switzer. Here it was that I first saw the method of watering a whole range of pastures and meadows, on a hill side, by little troughs cut in the side of the hill, along which the water, from springs, was conducted, so as that when the out-let of those troughs were stopped at the end, the water ran over the sides, and watered all the ground between that and the trough next below it.

it. I dare fay this method may be in ufe in England, I never faw it there, but faw it here firft.

At Lancafter the road divides. There is another road which goes by Harris's Ferry over the fame river, but much higher to the northward.

To Scott's, nine miles.

At about three miles, the road croffes Little Coneftoga-creek; and at about four more, goes over a fteep fharp ridge. Hence, between Hughes and Sample's, the road paffes over a fharp high ridge, on the N. W. fide of which, at the foot, runs S. W. the Conewago-creek. Between thefe ridges, the land very hilly.

To Bayley's, three miles.

To Hughes's, four miles.

To Sample's, four miles.

To the Swatara-creek, three miles.

To Taylor's, three miles.

To Harris's Ferry, eight miles.

There is another great road, which goes from Philadelphia to the fame ferry, but keeps on the N. E. fide of the Schuylkill, and runs through German-town, &c. to Reading; but in this road I have not yet gone upon further than Norrington. There is a crofs road on the N. W. fide of the Welch Mountains, the Flying and Oley Hills, which going from Lancafter to Reading, chiefly through the vale of Coneftoga-creek, opens a communication between thofe two great roads. The ftages of which are,

From Reading to Sinking-fpring, four miles.

To Cocoefing-creek, a fmall branch, three miles.

To the main branch, one mile.

To Kiffinger's, three miles.

Here the road goes over high ridges.

To Cocôlico-creek, one mile.

To Donker's-town, Ephrata, at the mill, feven miles.

This is a branch of the great Coneftoga-creek.

Thefe people, called Donkers Doo-

pers, or Dimplers, are a ftrange fet of Proteftant regulars.

To Biar's mill, five miles.

To Lardis's, three miles.

To the Three Tuns, three miles.

This ftands on a branch of the Coneftoga, called Middle-creek.

Here the road coming from Lancafter divides into three.

To Lancafter, two miles.

Road from Philadelphia through the Lower Counties, and Maryland to Alexandria, on the Potômack River, in Virginia.

To the Lower Ferry, over the Schuylkill, four miles.

To Derby, three miles

Derby looks very pretty, feen from off any of the hills round about it, for it ftands in a bottom, furrounded with hills. The houfes, built in one ftreet, all ftand in this bottom, and the fides of the hills are covered with houfes and farms.

To Chefter, nine miles.

Some very good farms betwixt this and Chefter. Chefter ftands clofe upon the Delaware; employs nothing but fome fhalloops, and a fchooner or two.

To Chichefter and Marcus-hook, three miles.

A good pretty village; a place famous for cyder, as the country people fay.

To Wilmington, eleven miles

Wilmington is built on the fide of a hill on Chriftina-creek, and was, when firft fettled by the Swedes, called Chriftina. It is a regular well built town; but not trade enough here to draw together a fufficient number of people to compleat it to its plan. It forms a very delightful profpeft, feen from the oppofite fide of the river; the ftreets lying in parallel lines, one below another, on the defcent of the hill. Ships and large veffels come up to the town; fhalloops, &c. as high as Chriftinbridge; a ferry here.

Q q q The

The lands lying near the Delaware River, and on the banks of the rivers and creeks, are very fine meadow lands. The lands between these, hilly, gullied all the way, and in some places very stony.

To Newcastle, six miles.

From hence to Newcastle more level.

To Weatherspools, 20 miles.

In Maryland, level land all the way.

To Frederick's-town, twelve miles.

On Saffafras River, level.

To New-town or Chester, eighteen miles.

The country well settled, and excellent farms all the way.

To Docking Tavern, eighteen or twenty miles.

This lies on the east side of Chesapeak-bay.

To the Bay-side or ferry, 14 miles. This called the Narrows.—Here begin the plantations of Tobacco.

Across Kent Island, seven miles.

This all a flat, chiefly pine-lands.

Across the Bay, a ferry to Annapolis, twelve miles.

From Annapolis to Queen Ann's-town, on the river Patuxent, thirteen miles.

To Mr. Rosier's, on the banks of the River Potomack, between twenty and thirty miles.

Annapolis is the metropolis of Maryland; it is situated on the side of a sandy hill, in a little bay, within the main bay. It is said, that the original plan of the town was laid in circular streets, with cross streets running from the centre like radii. The State House, Governor's House, Assembly, Courts, &c. were to have formed the centre, at the top of the hill, with concentral streets going round the hill; but the town is far from being compleat, nor do the traces of such a plan appear in what is built; it makes a very irregular appearance, and is in size and form but a very poor town. In short, both Maryland and Virginia are so cut

by creeks and rivers, that almost every farm lies on some creek, or on the bay, with water carriage even for ships up its yard. In consequence of this, there is not, nor ever will be, in those parts, any one considerable port or town, but numbers of little ones, unless Alexandria, which has been settled about two years, and is situated at the feet of the great falls of Potmack River, at the head of Marine Navigation, up to which a twenty gun ship of war may come, (there are now two there) should upon the settling the back countries, become a barcadore and port to them. Alexandria has at present one exceeding good house of Lord Fairfax's, and about sixty or seventy others; it has also a Court House.

General WASHINGTON *to General* HOWE.

New-Jersey, July 16, 1777.

" Sir,

" The fortune of war having thrown Major-general Prescot into our hands, I beg leave to propose his exchange for Major-general Lee. This proposition being agreeable to the letter and spirit of agreement subsisting between us, will, I hope, have your approbation. I am the more induced to expect it, as it will not only remove the ground of controversy between us, but in its consequences effect the exchange of Lieutenant-colonel Campbell, and the Hessian Field Officers, for a like number of men of equal rank in your possession.

" I shall be obliged by your answer upon the subject, assuring you, that Major-general Prescot shall be sent in, if the proposed exchange shall be acceded to, either on the previous raleasement of General Lee, on your promise that the same shall immediately take place on General Prescot's return.

" I have the honour to be, &c.

" G. WASHINGTON."

Fis-

Fiſh-kill, Sept. 4.
Extract of a letter from Wilmington,
Aug. 26.

" The enemy have landed about two thouſand men, and are within four miles of the head of the Elk; they act with caution, even to timidity.

" His Excellency is gone out to reconnoitre the country near them, with three regiments of horſe; tomorrow we ſhall take our ſtations, ſo as to act againſt them; their horſes are dying faſt, nine have floated on ſhore within the ſpace of a mile.

" On the enemy's fleet appearing off Baltimore, the diſaffected inhabitants were all ſeized and ſent under a ſtrong guard to Frederick-town."

By his Excellency THOMAS JOHNSON, *Eſq. Governor of the State of Maryland.*

PROCLAMATION.

This State being now actually invaded by a formidable land and ſeaforce, and the enemy, in all probability, deſigning to land ſomewhere near the head of this bay, I have, in order to collect a body of militia, to be ready to act with the Continental army, which may ſoon be expected to meet the enemy, thought proper to iſſue this my Proclamation, hereby requiring and commanding the county Lieutenants, the Field and other proper officers of the militia of the Weſtern ſhore of this State, immediately to march at leaſt two full companies of each battalion of the militia to the neighbourhood of the Suſquahanna River, in Cecil and Hartford counties, where they ſhall receive orders. To defend our liberties, requires our exertions; our wives, our children, and our country implore our aſſiſtance; motives amply ſufficient to arm every one who can be called a man

Given at Annapolis this 22d day of Auguſt, in the year of our Lord, 1777.

T. JOHNSON.

Head-Quarters, September 26, 1777.

GENERAL ORDERS.

The public buſineſs having ſo entirely engaged the attention of the General, that he has not been properly at leiſure to return his grateful thanks to General Poor's and General Learned's brigades.—To the regiment of riflemen, to the corps of light infantry, and to Col. Marſhall's regiment, for their valiant behaviour in the action of the 19th inſtant, which will for ever eſtabliſh and confirm the reputation of the arms of the United States. Notwithſtanding the General has been ſo late in giving this public mark of honour and applauſe to the brave men, whoſe valour has ſo eminently ſerved their country, he aſſures them the juſt praiſe he immediately gave to the Honourable the Continental Congreſs, will remain a laſting record of their honour and renown.

By the account of the enemy, by their embarraſſed circumſtances, by the deſperate ſituation of their affairs, it is evident they muſt endeavour, by one raſh ſtroke, to regain all they have loſt.—*That failing*, their utter ruin is inevitable.—The General therefore intreats his valiant army, that they will, by the exactneſs of their diſcipline, by the alertneſs to fly to their arms on all occaſions, and particularly by their caution not to be ſurprized, ſecure that victory which Almighty Providence (if they deſerve it) will bleſs their labours with.

Copy of a letter from General WASHINGTON *to Congreſs.*

Camp near Penibacker's Mill, Oct. 5, 1777.

Sir,

Having received intelligence thro' two intercepted letters, that General Howe had detached a part of his force for the purpoſe of reducing Billings Fort, and the forts on Delaware, I communicated the accounts to my General Officers, who were

unanimouſly

unanimously of opinion, that a favourable opportunity offered to make an attack on the troops, which were at and near German-town. It was accordingly agreed, that it should take place yesterday morning, and the following dispositions were made: the divisions of Sullivan and Wayne, flanked by Conway's brigade, were to enter the town by the way of Chesneth-hill, while General Armstrong, with the Pennsylvania militia, should fall down the Manatawney road by Vandeoringa-mills, and get upon the enemy's left and rear. The divisions of Green and Stephens, flanked by M'Dougal's brigade, were to enter by taking a circuit by way of the Lime-kiln-road, at the Market-houses, and to attack their right wing, and the militia of Maryland and Jersey, under Generals Smallwood and Freeman, were to march by the Old York-road, and fall upon the rear of the right. Lord Stirling, with Nash and Maxwell's brigades, were to form a corps de reserve. We marched about seven o'clock the preceding evening, and General Sullivan's advanced party, drawn from Conway's brigade, attacked their picquet at Mount Ring, at Mr. Allan's house, about sun-rise the next morning, which presently gave way, and his main body, consisting of the right wing, following soon, engaged the light infantry and other troops encamped near the picquet, which they forced from the ground, leaving their baggage. They retreated a considerable distance, having previously thrown a party into Mr. Chew's house, who were in a situation not to be easily forced, and had it in their power, from the windows, to give us no small annoyance, and in a great measure to obstruct our advance. The attack from our left column under General Green began about three quarters of an hour after that from the right, and was for some time equally successful. But I cannot enter upon the particulars of what happened in that quarter, as I am not yet informed of them with sufficient certainty and precision.

The morning was extremely foggy, which prevented our improving the advantages we gained so well as we otherwise should have done. This circumstance, by concealing from us the true situation of the enemy, obliged us to act with more caution and less expedition than we could have wished; and gave the enemy time to recover from the effects of our first impression; and what was still more unfortunate, it served to keep our different parties in ignorance of each other's movements, and hindered their acting in concert. It also occasioned them to mistake one another for the enemy, which I believe more than any thing else contributed to the misfortune which ensued. In the midst of the most promising appearances, when every thing gave the most flattering hopes of a victory, the troops began suddenly to retreat, and entirely left the field, in spite of every effort that could be made to rally them.

Upon the whole, it may be said, the day was rather unfortunate than injurious. We sustained no material loss of men, and brought off all our artillery, except one piece, which was dismounted. The enemy are nothing the better by the event; and our troops, who are not the least dispirited by it, have gained what all young troops gain by being in action. We have had, however, several valuable officers killed and wounded, particularly the latter—General Nash is among the wounded, and his life is despaired of. As soon as it is possible to obtain a return of our loss, I will transmit it.

In justice to General Sullivan, and the whole right wing of the army, whose conduct I had an opportunity of observing, as they acted immedi-

ately

ately under my eye, I have the pleasure to inform you, both officers and men behaved with a degree of gallantry that did them the highest honour. I have the honour to be,

With great respect,

Sir, your most obedient servant,

GEORGE WASHINGTON.

P. S. The cannon mentioned above, has since been brought in a waggon to camp.

———

New-Windsor, October 11, 1777.

Dear General,

In consequence of a severe dose of tartar emetic, which I ordered to be given the spy, I have in my possession a small silver bullet, from which I have taken a letter from Clinton to Burgoyne, of which the inclosed is an exact copy.

With esteem, I am, dear General,

Your most obedient servant,

GEO. CLINTON.

To General PUTNAM.

———

Copy sent with the foregoing, viz.

Fort Montgomery, October 8, 1777.

Nous voici—and nothing now between us but *Gates.* I sincerely hope this *little* success of ours may facilitate your operations. In answer to your letter of the 28th of September, by C. C. I shall only say, I cannot presume to order, or even advise, for reasons obvious. I heartily wish you success. Faithfully your's,

H. CLINTON.

To General BURGOYNE.

———

Hill-town, October 8, 1777.

Dear Sir,

To-morrow we join General Washington at Montgomery township, Pennsylvania. Our troops last Saturday, although they came short of gaining a complete victory, did certainly give the enemy a sore basting, and if they are not able soon to raise the chevaux de frise, they will be obliged to make the best of their way from Philadelphia. The two Rhode Island regiments are ordered to Red Bank on Delaware, near the chevaux de frise, and leave us this evening. The express waits. I am with compliments to the General, &c.

Your's, &c.

JED. HUNTINGTON,

Brigadier-general.

To Col. Root.

———

PROCLAMATION,

By WILLIAM LIVINGSTON, *Esq.*

Governor of New-Jersey.

Whereas by a certain Act of the Council and General Assembly of this State, entitled, "An Act for rendering more effectual two certain acts therein mentioned," passed the 4th day of June last, it is among other things, enacted, that if any person being a member of, or owing allegiance to this government, as described in the first section of the act therein first mentioned, entitled "An Act to punish traitors and disaffected persons," passed the fourth day of October last, shall be apprehended on his way to the enemy with intent to go into their lines or encampments, or into any place in their possession, without the licence, permission, or passport of the Commander in Chief of the United States of America, or of the Governor or Commander in Chief of this State for the time being, or of some General Officer of the army of the said United States, or of one of the Brigadiers General of the militia of this State, such person is thereby declared to be guilty of a capital felony, and being thereof legally convicted, shall suffer death accordingly. Provided nevertheless, that if any person in so offending as aforesaid, shall, at the time of his examination before the Governor and Council of Safety, or within six days thereafter, declare his willingness to enlist, and shall actually enlist with the leave of the Governor and Council aforesaid, to serve on board any of the

the veffels of war belonging to the United States, it fhall be lawful for them to fuffer him fo to enlift. and fuch his enliftment fhall be deemed a full pardon of his offence aforefaid. any thing therein before contained to the contrary thereof notwithftanding.

And whereas it was by the faid act further enacted, that if any perfon, being a member of, or owing allegiance to this Government, as in the firft mentioned act is defcribed, who hath fince the fourth day of October laft, voluntarily gone into any of the enemy's lines or encampments, or into any places in their poffeffion, fhall return into any part of this State in a fecret or clandeftine manner, or without any leave, licence, or paffport previofly obtained from the Governor or Commander in Chief of this State for the time being, or from a General Officer of the army of the United States, or of one of the Brigadiers General of the Militia of the State, fuch perfon is thereby delared to be guilty of a capital felony, and being thereof convicted, fhall fuffer death accordingly. Provided neverthelefs, that he may enlift as aforefaid, and that fuch enliftment fhall be confidered and operate in like manner as the enliftment of a perfon committing the offence fpecified in the laft preceding fection of the faid act.

And whereas it has been reprefented to me, that notwithftanding this act (and I would prefume from a knowledge of the exiftence thereof) feveral officers of the Militia of this State, and others while ftationed in the fame, of inferior rank to thofe mentioned in the faid act, unauthorized thereby, and in violation thereof, have granted fuch licences, permiffions, and paffports, and frequently upon very frivolous occafions, and to perfons of fufpicious characters of both fexes; by means whereof a conftant communication and intercourfe has for fome time paft been fupported between the malignants of this State and the Britifh troops on Staten-Ifland and New-York; and many have been furnifhed with opportunities to carry on or tranfmit intelligence to the enemy, and to circulate difpatches from them among their fecret abettors in the interior parts of the country, and thereby facilitate their infamous attempts to difperfe their counterfeit bills and reprobated wares and merchandizes, as well as to feduce the loyal, and enlift into their fervice the difaffected inhabitants of our territories: for preventing of which unwarrantable, illegal, and pernicious practice, I have thought proper, by and with the advice of the Council of this State, to iffue this proclamation, hereby ftrictly prohibiting all the officers of the Militia of this State, and other perfons whatfoever (thofe fo as aforefaid authorized only excepted) to grant for the future any fuch licences, permiffions, or paffports, under any colour or pretence whatfoever, as they fhall anfwer to the contrary at their peril; and requiring all officers, both civil and military, within this State, to exert their utmoft endeavours in apprehending every perfon belonging to the fame, on his or her way to the enemy with intent to go into their lines or entrenchments, or any places in their poffeffion, without fuch licence, permiffion, or paffport, as for that purpofe is by the faid act required; or returning from thence without fuch leave, or paffport, as for that purpofe is thereby directed, have voluntarily gone into the fame fince the fourth day of October laft; and fuch offender to commit to fafe cuftody, tranfmitting the caufe of his or her caption, detention, and place of confinement, to the Governor or Commander in Chief for the time being of this State, with all

all convenient speed, in order that such offender may be brought to condign punishment: and all other subjects of this State are hereby required to be aiding and assisting in the apprehension of such offenders, as they tender the welfare of their country, and are ambitious in signalizing themselves in the glorious cause of liberty and virtue.

Given under my hand and seal, at Morris Town, the 4th day of August, in the year of our Lord 1777.

WILLIAM LIVINGSTON.

By his Excellency's Command,

WILLIAM LIVINGSTON,
Gun. D. Sec.

Speech of his Excellency WILLIAM LIVINGSTON, *Esq. Governor, Captain General, and Commander in Chief, in and over the State of New-Jersey, and the territories thereunto belonging, Chancellor, and Ordinary in the same.*

To the Honourable the Council and the General Assembly of the said State, in General Assembly convened.

Gentlemen,

I heartily congratulate you on the important success of the American arms at Bennington and Fort Schuyler, which at the same time that it reflects the brightest lustre on the bravery of our officers and men, may serve to teach Great Britain, that we are not to be subdued by proclamations; nor under any apprehensions from a menacing meteor, that, after the most portentous glare, so soon evaporates into smoke, or vanishes into nothing.

The same spirit which at first animated us to oppose the attempts of arbitrary power ; and, after all reasoning and expostulation had been found fruitless, compelled us, by force of arms to assert the unalienable rights of freemen, will ever enable us, in a reliance upon the Divine blessing to baffle the tyrannic and bloody purposes of an enemy divested of humanity, at open war with reason and justice, and out barbarizing all the barbarities in history. How conspicuous the finger of Heaven in their expulsion from this state, the most unobservant may recollect with wonder ; and every serious man will remember with devout gratitude. Let us only persevere with the same ardour, in repelling their unprovided hostilities, and they must, ere long, relinquish their desperate purpose, and return to the place from whence they came, with indelible infamy. Let us not therefore be discouraged by a few transient inconveniencies, the enduring of which may be productive of the most permanent blessings. In proportion of the value of the prize contended for, ought to be the vigour of our struggle ; and the blood and treasure we should be willing to expend in securing it. And what can be too valuable a sacrifice for securing that, without which, nothing else is of any value ? For, with the loss of liberty, every remaining possession, being held at the arbitrary will of another, becomes, beyond question, utterly worthless. To deter us into submission, the horrors of war may, by artful men, be drawn in strong and glowing colours ; and war is indeed a calamity most devoutly to be deprecated. But whence doth war derive its horrors, but from the temporary loss of some of those blessings of which the meditated despotism would totally deprive us, and that in perpetuity ? The establishment of tyranny will surely leave us nothing of which the effects of war can divest us. But a resolute opposition may prevent the establishment of tyranny, and secure freedom to our remotest posterity. Appeal to reason, and she cries aloud, resist, resist.

Gentle-

Gentlemen,

I shall now lay before you such matters as have occurred to me, as worthy your deliberation, during the present session.

The scarcity of salt is a matter of serious consideration, and has been industriously perverted by our internal enemies, to the most pestilent purposes. Nor can there be any reason for perpetuating this grievance, and the pernicious political consequences thence resulting, while a quantity sufficient for the consumption of all our inhabitants, may easily be manufactured in this state. It seems therefore worthy your attention, whether it would not be expedient for the legislature to erect such works at the public expence, and appoint proper persons to distribute the commodity in due proportions to the several counties, at nearly the prime cost. Thus might all the people be cheaply supplied, and the state be fully reimbursed.

The loss of a very considerable sum of money, together with a number of specialties, and other valuable papers belonging to the state, which had been committed to the custody of a late member of convention, appears a matter of too much importance to acquiesce in, without legal determination of his culpability or innocence. I find, indeed, by your Journals, that the House has made some enquiry into the matter. But the Assembly being no competent judicature, finally to determine whether the trustee is responsible for the loss of the deposite, the question still remains to be decided by a constitutional tribunal, which is either a court of law, or in a course of equity, according to the nature and circumstances of the case. I would therefore recommend it to you, in justice to the good people of this state, who are intimately concerned in the event of the trial to direct a prosecution for the purpose.

As our proportion of the heavy debt which will ienevitably be occasioned by the unnatural war, in which the avarice and ambition of Great Britain hath involved us, will be severely felt, unless seasonably discharged. I would most earnestly importune you, not to suffer this session to pass without sinking part of it by tax. Those who are for postponing this interesting affair, to a distant period, are not aware of the extensive mischief that will attend so fatal a measure.

I think it my indispensible duty, Gentlemen, to assure you of my repeated experience of the insufficiency of our militia law. In time of open war, and especially in case of an invasion, the military force of a state ought to be compellable to turn out. Any commutations, or pecuniary mulcts in lieu of actual service, render the act at such a critical juncture altogether ineffectual, and may finally terminate in our utter destruction. Experience, constant reiterated experience has shewn its insufficiency; and not to frame one more efficacious after such irresistible conviction, what will it be deemed but a kind of desertion of the cause; and leaving the state a victim to the enemy, at the most perilous crisis of the contest? It must, however, be acknowledged, to the honour of our militia (and it is with peculiar pleasure I embrace this opportunity to do it) that numbers of them have appeared in defence of their country with the greatest alacrity; and behaved in battle with such bravery, as would have encreased the renown of the most experienced veterans. But those gallant men were actuated by the spirit of patriotism, and scorned to measure their exertions for their country by the requisitions of its laws. Others by commuting for actual service by fines and forfeitures (and those not duly collected) throw a disproportional

onal burden upon the willing, who, by that means, are extremely harrassed, and have abundant reason for complaint and murmuring.

The necessity of a large supply of fire arms, and of public magazines of ammunition and warlike stores, is so obvious, that I doubt not your zeal for the public safety, will not suffer you to delay the necessary provision.

It is also worthy your deliberation, whether the workmen employed by such owners of furnaces, forges, and rolling mills, as are under contract to furnish the United States of America with cannon, cannon shot, camp kettles, or other implements of war for the use of their army, ought not to be exempted from the duties and services enjoined by the militia law, under such regulations for preventing any abuse of the indulgence as may be thought proper.

As a number of emissaries are employed by the enemy to circulate counterfeit bills made in imitation of the Continential currency, who frequently pass them in such of the counties of this State, in which either no trial at all, or no fair and impartial trial of such offenders can without difficulty, be had ; I would recommend the passing a law, for trying in any county of this state by a jury of that county, all such offenders already apprehended, and who may hereafter be apprehended, though the offence be committed in any other county.

Being fully convinced that the act, intitled, " An act of free and general pardon, and for other purposes therein mentioned," will in great measure be defeated by the fraudulent practices of the friends and agents of the offenders, whose personal estates are thereby declared forfeited ; it may deserve your consideration, whether it will not be necessary to pass another act for the more effectual securing the valuable ends thereby intended. What more particularly furnishes great opportunity for eluding the true intent of the law, is a want of authority in the commissioners to compel the appearance of persons suspected of concealing the property of the delinquent, or to be indebted to him, and to examine them, as well as other necessary witnesses, upon oath ; and also the want of proper penalties upon those who may be guilty of such concealment, which the superaddition of adequate rewards for encouraging a discovery.

As the present judgment in high treason cannot be awarded consistent with our constitution, and the courts having no authority to alter the sentence prescribed by law, I would recommend it to you to ascertain the punishment for that crime, by act of Assembly. For besides the style of the sentence, and the disposition of the head and quarters of the criminal, which the judges might perhaps think themselves at liberty to accommodate to our circumstances, the execution itself is so shocking and sanguinary, as the humanity of an American legislature cannot be presumed to have intended, and which indeed none but a savage, or a British subject can think of without horror.

Several persons to avoid receiving the money due to them by bond, bill or promissary note, bearing interest, frequently pretend, on tender of the money, that they are not possessed of such notes or specialities, having sent them to places of greater security ; and many obligees and creditors are themselves removed into other states, and places unknown to their debtors, who, though ready to discharge their debts, are thereby prevented from doing it ; the principal sum the mean while carrying interest, and the debtor obliged to keep the money at his own risque. To frustrate such iniquitous subterfuges

R r r

fuges, (the malignant defign of which is fufficiently evident) I would recommend an act to enable every obligor or debtor, whofe creditor is removed out of the ftate or cannot be found in it, or who refufes to receive the debt when tendered, to pay the fame into the Treafury for his ufe, and to be thereupon difcharged from the fum fo paid, and all the intereft thereafter accruing.

The act, intitled, " An act for rendering more effectual two certain acts therein mentioned," being nearly expired by its own imitation, it is of the laft moment to the common weal, to have it continued to fuch farther period as may be deemed neceffary to carry it fully into execution.

Gentlemen,

You are now approaching the clofe of the year, which has been chiefly fpent in ferving the public. That you have ferved it with fidelity, and with no inconfiderable degree of fuccefs, muft be a very pleafing reflection, and juftly entitles you to the applaufe of your country. May you ftill continue, in whatever ftation it fhall pleafe Providence to place you, to exert your endeavours for the profperity of a free and independent people; and during the whole courfe of the conflict, may our creed be, *Victory*; and our motto, *Perfevere*,

WIL. LIVINGSTON.
Haddonfield Sept. 3, 1777.

Philadelphia, September 10.
By the Supreme Executive Council of the Commonwealth of Pennfylvania.
A PROCLAMATION.

The time is at length come, in which the fate of ourfelves, our wives, children, and pofterity muft be fpeedily determined. General Howe at the head of a Britifh army, the only hope, the laft refource of our enemies, has invaded this ftate. Difmiffing his fhips, and difencumbering himfelf of his heavy artillery and baggage, he appears to have rifqued all upon the event of a movement, which muft either deliver up to plunder and devaftation, this capital of Pennfylvania, and of America, or for ever blaft the cruel defigns of our implacable foes. Bleffed be God! Providence feems to have left it to ourfelves to determine, whether we fhall triumph in victory, and reft in freedom and peace, or by tamely fubmitting, or weakly refifting, deliver ourfelves up a prey to an enemy, than whom, none more cruel and perfidious was ever fuffered to vex and deftroy any people.

View then, on the one hand, the freedom and independence, the glory and the happinefs of our rifing ftates, which are fet before us as the reward of our courage; ferioufly confider, on the other hand, the wanton ravages, the rapes, the butcheries, which have been perpetrated by thefe men in the ftate of New-Jerfey, and on the frontiers of New-York. Above all, confider the mournful profpect of feeing Americans, like the wretched inhabitants of India, ftripped of their freedom, robbed of their property, degraded beneath the brutes, and left to ftarve amidft plenty, at the will of their lordly mafters; and let us determine once for all, that we will DIE or be Free. The foe are manifeftly aiming, either by force to conquer, or by ftratagem and ftolen marches, to elude the vigilance of our brave commander. Declining a battle with our countrymen, they have attempted to fteal upon us with furprize. They have been hitherto defeated, but numbers are abfolutely neceffary to watch them on every quarter at once. The neighbouring ftates are hurrying forward their militia, and we hope, that by rifing as one man, and fetting the foe at a diftance from his fleet, we fhall fpeedily inclofe him like a lion in the toils.

The

The Council, therefore, moſt earneſtly beſeech and intreat all perſons whatſoever, to exert themſelves without delay, to ſeize this precious opportunity of cruſhing the foe now in the bowels of our country, by marching forth inſtantly under their reſpective officers to the aſſiſtance of our great General, that he may be able to environ and demoliſh the only Britiſh army that remains formidable in America, or in the world. Animated with the hope that Heaven, as before it has done, in all times of difficulty and danger, will again crown our righteous efforts with ſucceſs, we look forward to the proſpect of ſeeing our inſulting foes cut off from all means of eſcape; and by the goodneſs of the Almighty, the Lord of Hoſts and God of battles, wholly delivered into our hands.

Thomas Wharton, jun. Preſident.
T. Matlack, Secretary.
God ſave the people!

London Gazette Extraordinary.
Friday, January 9, 1778.
Admiralty-Office, January 8, 1778.

The following is an extract of a letter received laſt night by the Eagle Packet from the Vice Admiral Lord Viſcount Howe, Commander in Chief of his Majeſty's ſhips and veſſels in North America, to Mr. Stephens, dated on board his Majeſty's ſhip the Eagle, in the Delaware, the 23d of November, 1777.

Eagle, Delaware, November 23, 1777.

Sir,

The General adviſing me of his intention to ſend a packet immediately to England, I avail myſelf of the opportunity to acquaint you, for the information of the Lords Commiſſioners of the Admiralty, reſpecting the progreſs of the military ſervices in which the ſhips of war have been concerned, ſince the date of my laſt letter of the 25th of October.

I mentioned in that letter the preparations making for the attack meditated on the works the rebels had conſtructed on either ſhore, for preventing an open communication by water with the army at Philadelphia, on which it was obvious to them that the farther operations of the campaign would greatly depend.

The wind ſtill continuing to prevent the Vigilant from paſſing to the rear of the enemy's works on Fort Iſland, by the only channel practicable for that purpoſe, the opportunity was taken by the King's forces, and by the enemy with equal aſſiduity, to ſtrengthen the preparations judged expedient on either part for the propoſed attack.

The officers and ſeamen of the ſhips of war and tranſports were employed in the mean time, with unremitting fatigue and perſeverance, to convey proviſions, artillery, and ſtores, to the Schuylkill, between Fort-Iſland and the Pennſylvania ſhore, 6 twenty-four-pounders from the Eagle, and 4 thirty-two-pounders from the Somerſet, tranſported in the ſame manner, with the requiſite proportions of ammunition, were mounted in the batteries erected by the General's appointment on Province-Iſland.

The wind becoming favourable the 15th inſtant, the firſt occaſion was taken for ordering the ſhips upon the intended ſervice.

The Somerſet and Iſis were appointed to proceed up the Eaſtern channel of the river, to act againſt the fort in the front. The Roebuck, Pearl, and Liverpool, with the Cornwallis galley, and ſome ſmaller armed veſſels, againſt a battery with heavy artillery which the rebels had lately opened on a point above, and near to Manto-creek, in a ſituation to rake the ſhips anchored to fire upon the fort, and more advantageouſly choſen, as the ſhoalneſs of

Rrr 2 the

the water did not admit ships to approach within a defirable diftance of the work.

The Vigilant, with a hulk mounting 3 eighteen-pounders, commanded by Lieutenant Botham of the Eagle, proceeded at the fame time through the channel round Hog Ifland, and anchored on that fide the fort, according to the intention pointed out for co-operating with the batteries on the Pennfylvania fhore.

The Ifis, being as well placed in the Eaftern channel as the circumftances of the navigation would permit, rendered very effential fervice againft the fort and gallies, much to the perfonal honour of Capt. Cornwallis, and credit of the difcipline in his fhip. The Roebuck and other frigates ftationed againft the battery were equally well conducted.

Greater caution being neceffary in placing the Somerfet, that fhip could not be carried as far up the channel as the Ifis was advanced.

The impreffion made by the batteries on Province Ifland (before very confiderable) being united with the well-directed efforts from the Vigilant and Hulk, foon filenced the artillery of the fort; and farther preparations being in progrefs for opening the eftocade and forcing the works next morning, the enemy fet fire to and evacuated the fort during the night.

The numbers of the enemy killed and wounded appeared to have been very confiderable. Thofe in the different fhips, as ftated in the annexed return, were much lefs than could be fuppofed, particularly of the Ifis and Roebuck, which were ftruck many times from the gallies and works.

As a farther evidence to their Lordfhips of the meritorious conduct of the feveral officers therein named, I have added the General's concurring fentiments fignified to me on the occafion. Captain Duncan remained feveral weeks with the army, to fu-

perintend the different nautic fervices and preparations before-mentioned.

A detachment from the army under the command of Lord Cornwallis, having been landed the 18th at Billingport, (where a poft had been fome time before eftablifhed) for attacking the redoubt at Red-Bank, the enemy abandoned and blew up the work. They had paffed feveral of their gallies unperceived above the town of Philadelphia, in the night of the 19th, which proved very favourable for the purpofe; and attempted to do the fame with the reft of the gallies, and other water force, the following night: but being feafonably difcovered, they were oppofed with fo much effect, by Lieutenant Watt of the Roebuck, (ordered by Captain Hammond, before my arrival, to take his ftation in the Delaware prize, near the town) that, not more than three or four of the former appeared to have efcaped: and being otherwife unable to prevent the capture of the reft of their armed-craft, (confifting of two zebecques, the two floating-batteries, and feveral fhips, befides fire veffels, amounting to about feventeen in number) they were quitted and burnt. Lieutenant Watt having teftified great propriety and fpirit on this occafion, I have continued him in the command of the Delaware, retained as an armed fhip in the fervice, to remain near the town of Philadelphia, where fuch additional naval force is paticularly requifite.

A more accurate infpection of the obftructions to the navigation of the river adjacent to Fort Ifland, becoming impracticable under the circumftances before-ment oned, two channels were difcovered through which the tranfports, containing the provifions, ftores, and other neceffaries for the army, might proceed to Philadelphia. They were ordered up the river accordingly, to be afterwards
secured

fecured at the wharfs of the town, for the approaching winter months.

The unfortunate event of Lieutenant-general Burgoyne's operations with the Northern army terminating, as I am advifed by the Commander in Chief, with the furrender of thofe troops agreeable to the tenor of a convention executed the 16th of laft October, has rendered a fuitable provifion neceffary to be made for their conveyance to Europe. A proper number of tranfports has been appropriated for that occafion. But as it would be fcarce practicable at this feafon of the year for light tranfports to gain the port of Bofton, where the embarkation is conditioned to take place, tranfports have been ordered under convoy of the Raifonable to Rhode-Ifland; that if the propofed alteration is adopted, and the troops can be embarked at that port, they may be fooner releafed.

The following are copies of the papers referred to in the aforementioned extract:

Return of the number of men killed and wounded on board the different fhips employed in the attack of the works of the enemy on Fort Ifland, their armed craft, and other defences erected to obftruct the paffage of the River Delaware, on the 15th day of November, 1777.

Somerfet. 5 Seamen wounded.
Ifis. 3 Seamen wounded.
Roebuck. 3 Seamen killed, 7 ditto wounded.
Liverpoole. None.
Pearl. 1 Mafter killed, 3 feamen wounded.
Vigilant. 1 Midfhipman, 1 feamen, killed; lent from the Eagle.
Cornwallis Galley. 1 Second Mafter and Pilot wounded.
Sloop commanded by Lieutenant Botham. None.

Total killed —	6
—— wounded —	19
	——
	25

Philadelphia, November 17, 1777.
My Lord,

I cannot too highly acknowledge the fignal fervices the army has received from the perfeverance and activity of the officers and feamen under your Lordfhip's command, fince the King's troops entered Philadelphia; and I fhall be happy, by your Lordfhip's affiftance, to have my fentiments of them made as acceptable, and generally known as poffible.

But my thanks are more particularly due to Captain Duncan for his unwearied attention and judgment on all occafions; and to Captain Henry and Lieutenant Botham for the gallantry they difplayed on the 15th inftant, in the reduction of the enemy's work on Mud Ifland; which I requeft your Lordfhip will be pleafed to communicate to thofe gentlemen in the moft diftinguifhed manner.

In thefe acknowledgments I beg to include the Captains and crews of the fhips in the Eaftern channel, contributing to the fuccefs of the attack, more immediately affifted by the well directed fire of the Ifis.

I have the honour to be, &c. &c.
(Signed)   W. HOWE.
To *Vifcount* HOWE, &c. &c. &c.

Whitehall, January 8, 1778.
The following is copy and extract of two letters from the honourable General Sir William Howe to Lord George Germain:

Philadelphia, November 28, 1777.
My Lord,

From a variety of difficulties attending the conftruction of additional batteries, in a morafs, againft the fort upon Mud Ifland, and in tranfportation of the guns and ftores, they were not opened againft the enemy's defences until the 10th inftant. On the 15th, the wind proving fair, the Vigilant armed fhip, carrying 16 twenty-four pounders, and a hulk with three twenty-four pounders, got up to the fort through the channel between Province and Hog Ifland; thefe, ticle, ... by several ships of war in the .... channel, as well .. by the batteries on shore, did such execution upon the fort and collateral block house, that the enemy, dreading an inc.... assault, evacuated the .... in the night between the 15th and 16th, and it was possessed the .... at day-break by the grenadiers of the guards. Much commendation is .... to Brigadier-general Cleaveland, to the officers and men of the corps of artillery, and to the troops in general employed upon this service, attended with great fatigue.

The enemy's fire upon the ships of war, the Vigilant and hulk, from two floating batteries, seventeen gallies and armed vessels, and from a battery on the Jersey shore, was exceedingly heavy; but the gallantry displayed by the naval commanders, their officers and seamen, on this occasion, frustrated all their efforts, and contributed principally to the reduction of the enemy's works. Permit me at the same time to report to your Lordship, that the perseverance of the officers and seamen employed in bringing up stores from the fleet, under the conduct of Captain Duncan, of the Eagle, demand my highest acknowledgments; and that the services they rendered were most essential, and borne with the utmost chearfulness.

I have the honour to inclose a return, No. 1, of the cannon, and stores found in the fort. The enemy's loss during the siege is computed to have been 400 killed and wounded. The loss to the King's troops was only seven killed and five wounded.

On the 18th at night, Lord Cornwallis marched with a corps from camp, and passed the Delaware on the 19th from Chester to Billing's-fort, where he was joined by Major-general Sir Thomas Wilson, with a corps that arrived a few days before from New-York under his command,

having with him Brigadier-general Leslie and Pattison.

As soon as the necessary preparations were made, his Lordship pursued his march to attack the enemy intrenched at Red bank. Upon his approach the rebels evacuated the post, and retired to Mount Holly, where they joined a corps of observation, detached from the main army of the rebels, encamped at White Marsh. His Lordship found in the enemy's works, cannon, ammunition, and stores, as per return, No. 2. The intrenchments being demolished, his corps returned by Gloucester on the 27th, and joined the army in this camp.

The enemy's shipping having no longer any protection, and not finding it adviseable to attempt the passage of the river, the channel being commanded by the batteries of the town, and the Delaware frigate, they were quitted without being dismantled; and burnt on the night between the 20th and 21st; but the gallies of a smaller draught of water, by keeping close along the Jersey shore, escaped, from the great breadth of the river.

A forward movement against the enemy will immediately take place, and hope will be attended with the success that is due to the spirit and activity of his Majesty's troops.

The passage of the river, by the reduction of the two places aforementioned, has been sufficiently opened to bring up frigates and transports; but the removal of the chevaux de frise is postponed to a more favourable season.

Major-general Sir Thomas Spencer Wilson having represented the very critical situation of his private concerns in England, has my leave to return, and has taken charge of my dispatches to your Lordship, by the Eagle Packet.

With the most perfect respect,

I have the honour to be, &c.

W. HOWE.

Returns

Returns of ordnance and stores found in Mud Island Fort, taken from the rebels by the King's troops the 16th of November, 1777.

IRON ORDNANCE.

On travelling carriages. 1 Thirty-two-pounder; 1 twenty-four-pounder; 7 eighteen-pounders, 2 unserviceable; 1 twelve-pounder; 2 four-pounders.

On garrison carriages. 14 Eight-pounders, 1 unserviceable; sunk with a scow, of sorts, 10.

SHOT.

Round loose. 1475 Twenty-four-pounders; 843 eighteen-pounders; 165 twelve-pounders; 1100 eight-pounders; 16 four-pounders.

Barr. 6 Thirty-two-pounders; 4 twenty-four-pounders; 169 eighteen-pounders.

Grape quilted. 12 Thirty-two-pounders; 84 eighteen-pounders; 20 twelve-pounders; 110 eight-pounders; 8 four-pounders:

Fixed with powder for twelve-pounders. 1 Case; 9 grape.

Small iron for case. 4 cwt.

Cartridges paper filled. 65 Eight-pounders.

Sponges of sorts, 36.

Ladles ditto, 9.

Wad-hooks, 15.

Aprons of lead, 9.

Linstocks, 6

Budge barrels, 2.

SAMUEL CLEAVELAND, Brigadier-general commanding *Philadelphia,* [the Royal Artillery. *Nov.* 18, 1777.

Return of the artillery and military stores found in the Fort of Red Bank, the 22d of November, 1777.

6 Eighteen-pounders, 1 unserviceable; 3 eighteen-pounders, mounted on truck carriages, 2 unserviceable; 2 six-pounders, mounted on ditto, spiked and unserviceable; 1 four-pounder, mounted on ditto, unserviceable; 1 four-pounder, mounted on ditto, with elevating screw, spiked; 3 four-pounders, mounted on ditto, spiked; 1 three-pounder on ditto, spiked and unserviceable; 8 howitzer swivels; 4 howitzer ditto, carried off by a naval Captain; 3 swivels; 1 travelling carriage for eighteen-pounder; 5 trucks carriages for ditto; 1 travelling carriage for nine-pounders; 4 ditto for six-pounders; three limbers for ditto.

SHOT.

Round. 536 Twenty-four-pounders; 318 eighteen-pounders; 156 twelve-pounders; 51 nine-pounders; 23 six-pounders; 1301 four-pounders; 173 three-pounders; 20 one-pounders; 32 half-pounders.

Barr. 7 Twenty-four-pounders; 25 twelve-pounders; 50 nine-pounders; 65 three-pounders.

Grape quilted. 14 Twelve-pounders; 54 six-pounders; 28 four-pounders.

Grape in bags, 24.

Box of different natures, 1.

Round shot fixed to wood bottoms. 5 Twelve-pounders; 6 six-pounders; 6 four-pounders; 16 three-pounders.

Hand grenades, 18.

Wad-hooks. 1 Thirty-two-pounder; 1 six-pounder.

Sponges. 1 Six-pounder; 2 four-pounders.

Aprons of lead, 4.

Drag ropes, 3,

Traversing handspike, 1.

Pikes, 93.

Intrenching tools, 30.

Boxes with ball cartridges, 9.

Cask with musquet balls, 1.

JAMES PATTISON, Brigadier-general, Commander of the Royal Artillery in North-America.

Camp at Woodbury,

Nov. 23, 1777.

Extract of a letter from General Sir WILLIAM HOWE *to Lord* GEORGE GERMAIN, *dated Philadelphia, the* 19th *of November,* 1777.

The last accounts I have received from Rhode Island, mention a descent which the enemy threatened upon that place about the 30th of October, and

of

of confiderable preparations they had made with that defign; but the difpofition of the Admiral and Major-general Pigot to oppofe them, together with the fpirited behaviour of the inhabitants, who affociated for the defence of Newport, induced them to defift and feparate.

[It was obferved by moft people, that the intelligence contained in the above Gazette, was very unworthy of publifhing as an *Extraordinary Gazette*. And even the intelligence, fuch as it is, is given *imperfectly*. There is in it an extract of a letter from Rhode Ifland, but not a word from New-York. It is of more importance to know the *ftate* of New-York, than Rhode Ifland. Minifters will not deny they have advices from New-York; but they will not publifh them, becaufe they are *difagreeable*. New-York is furrounded by the enemy, and General Clinton defires to be *recalled*. Not a word is mentioned of the fkirmifh on Province Ifland, in which the King's troops were worfted; and for which, two officers of the King's army have been tried by a Court-martial, and broke.]

Whitehall, Jan. 18, 1778.
The following letter from the Hon. General Sir William Howe to Lord George Germain, one of his Majefty's principal Secretaries of State, was this morning received by the Earl Cornwallis, who arrived from Philadelphia in the Brilliant armed fhip:
Philadelphia, December 13, 1777.
My Lord,
Lord Cornwallis having applied for leave of abfence to attend his private bufinefs in Europe, I take this opportunity of fending my difpatches by his Lordfhip in the Brilliant armed fhip.
Since my laft, the enemy being joined by upwards of four thoufand men, with cannon, from the Nor-

thern army, affembled their whole force in a ftrong camp at White-marfh, covered in part by Sandy Run, fourteen miles diftant from hence, with their right to Wiffahi-chon-creek.

Upon a prefumption that a forward move might tempt the enemy, after receiving fuch reinforcement, to give battle for the recovery of this place, or that a vulnerable part might be found to admit of an attack upon their camp, the army marched on the night of the 4th inftant, the van commanded by Lieutenant-general Earl Cornwallis, the main body by Lieutenant-general Knyphaufen, and on the next morning took poft upon Chefnut-hill in front of the enemy's right. The enemy foon after detached a corps of 1000 men to attack the light infantry pofted in front under the command of Lieutenant-colonel Abercromby; the confequences of which was, that upon the firft onfet of the 2d battalion of light infantry, and part of the 1ft, they were inftantly defeated, with the lofs of between 30 and 40 men killed and wounded, and a Brigadier made prifoner.

Not judging it advifeable to attack the enemy's right, the army, having remained in the fame pofition during the 6th, marched at one o'clock in the morning of the 7th, the van and main body commanded as before, to take poft on Edge-hill, one mile diftant from the enemy's left. A corps of one thoufand men, compofed of riflemen and other troops from the enemy's Northern army, were found by the van-guard pofted on this hill with cannon. Lord Cornwallis immediately attacked with the 1ft light infantry, fupported by the 33d regiment, and defeated this body, with a confiderable lofs of officers and men, their cannon narrowly efcaping. The thicknefs of the wood where the rebels were pofted, concealing them from the view of the light infantry, occafioned eccafioned the lofs of one officer killed, three wounded, and between 20 and 30 men killed and wounded, from their firft fire

Major-general Grey with his brigade, light infantry of the guards, Queen's rangers, Heffian and Anfpach chaffeurs, took poft upon the left, in front of the enemy's centre. A detachment to harrafs this corps was immediately routed by the General's advanced guard, compofed of his light troops, with a lofs to the enemy of fifty killed and wounded.

Your Lordfhip will fee, by the inclofed return, the lofs fuftained by the King's troops in the above-mentioned attacks

The enemy's camp being as ftrong on their centre and left as upon the right, their feeming determination to hold this pofition, and unwilling to expofe the troops longer to the weather in this inclement feafon, without tents or baggage of any kind for officers or men, I returned on the 8th to this place. The rear guard, under the command of Lord Cornwallis, quitted Edge-hill on the right, about four o'clock in the afternoon, without the fmalleft appearance of the enemy; and Major-general Grey retiring from his poft at the fame time, without the leaft moleftation, the army arrived in this camp at nine o'clock in the evening.

On the 11th, at day-break, Lord Cornwallis, with Major-general Grant under his command, paffed the Schuylkill with a ftrong corps, and the waggons of the army, to collect forage for the winter fupply, which his Lordfhip accomplifhed, and returned yefterday evening.

The enemy having quitted their camp at White-marfh fome hours before Lord Cornwallis marched from hence, his Lordfhip met the head of their army at a bridge they had thrown over the Schuylkill, near to Matfon's-ford, about three miles below Swedes-ford, and fifteen miles diftant from hence. Over this bridge the enemy had paffed 800 men, who were immediately difperfed by his Lordfhip's advanced troops, obliging part of them to re-crofs it, which occafioned fuch an alarm to their army, that they broke the bridge; and his Lordfhip proceeded to forage without meeting with any interruption.

The enemy's intention feems to be, to take their winter quarters at Carlifle, York, and Lancafter, and probably they may have a corps at Reading, and another at Burlington in Jerfey.

The 71ft regiment, and regiment of Mirbach, are immediately to embark, to reinforce Sir Henry Clinton at New-York, upon his reprefentation of a want of troops for the defence of that poft; and I propofe to put the army immediately into winter quarters in this town, where there is fufficient room.

Major-general Daniel Jones is arrived at New-York, and orders will be fent to him to join this part of the army.

With the moft perfect refpect,

I have the honour to be, &c.

W. Howe.

Return of the killed, wounded, and miffing, in the different fkirmifhes, from the 4th to the 8th of December, 1777.

1ft Battalion of light infantry. 1 Lieutenant, 2 Serjeants, 11 rank and file, killed; 2 Lieutenants, 1 Serjeant, 25 rank and file, wounded; 1 rank and file, miffing.

Guards. 1 Rank and file, killed; 1 rank and file, wounded; 4 rank and file, miffing.

4th Regiment. 2 Rank and file, killed; 1 Lieutenant, 3 Serjeants, 9 rank and file, wounded.

7th Regiment. 1 Rank and file, miffing.

15th Regiment. 2 Rank and file, miffing.

17th Regiment. 3 Rank and file, miffing.

23d Regiment. 3 Rank and file, *miffing.*

26th Regiment. 2 Rank and file, *miffing.*

28th Regiment. 2 Rank and file, *wounded*; 2 rank and file, *miffing.*

33d Regiment. 3 Rank and file, *wounded.*

37th Regiment. 3 Rank and file, *miffing.*

46th Regiment. 1 Rank and file, *miffing.*

49th Regiment. 5 Rank and file, *miffing.*

Queen's American Rangers. 1 Rank and file, *killed*; 1 rank and file, *wounded*; 5 rank and file, *miffing.*

Heffian Yegers. 1 Rank and file, *killed*; 9 rank and file, *wounded.*

Royal Artillery. 3 Rank and file, *wounded*; 1 rank and file, *miffing.*

Total. 1 Lieutenant, 2 Serjeants, 16 rank and file, *killed*; 3 Lieutenants, 4 Serjeants, 53 rank and file, *wounded*; 33 rank and file, *miffing.*

Names of Officers killed and wounded. *1ft Light infantry.* Lieutenant Pennyfeather, 15th regiment, *killed*; Lieutenant French, 22d regiment, Lieutenant Ankettell, 17th regiment, *wounded.*

4th Regiment. Lieutenant Weft, *wounded.*

(Signed) W. HOWE.
[*London Gazette.*]

' *Burlington, (N. Jersey) Dec. 24.*
Head-quarters, on Schuylkill, Dec. 17.

GENERAL ORDERS.

The Commander in Chief, with the highest fatisfaction, expreffes his thanks to the officers and foldiers for the fortitude and patience with which they have fuftained the fatigues of the campaign.

Although in fome inftances we have unfortunately failed, yet upon the whole, Heaven has fmiled upon our arms, and crowned them with fignal fuccefs; and we may on the beft grounds conclude, that by a fpirited continuance in the meafures ne-ceffary for our defence, we fhall finally obtain the end of our warfare, *Independence, Liberty,* and *Peace.* Thefe are bleffings worth contending for at a every hazard; but we hazard nothing—the power of America alone, duly exerted, would have nothing to dread from the force of Britain. Yet we ftand not wholly upon our own ground, France yields us every aid we afk; and there are reafons to believe the period is not very diftant when fhe will take a more active part, by declaring war againft the british crown. Every motive, therefore, irrefiftibly urges us, nay commands us to a firm and manly perfeverance in our oppofition to our cruel oppreffors—to flight difficulty, endure hardfhips, and condemn every danger.

The General ardently wifhes it were now in his power to conduct the troops into the beft winter quarters: but where are thefe to be found? Should we retire to the interior parts of the ftate, we fhould find them crowded with virtuous citizens, who, facrificing their All, have left Philadelphia and fled hither for protection; —to their diftreffes, humanity forbids us to add. This is not all!— We fhould leave a vaft extent of fertile country to be defpoiled and ravaged by the enemy, from which they would draw vaft fupplies, and where many of our firm friends would be expofed to all the miferies of an infulting and wanton depredation.—A train of evils might be enumerated, but thefe will fuffice. Thefe confiderations make it indifpenfibly neceffary for the army to take fuch a pofition as will enable it moft effectually to prevent diftrefs, and give the moft extenfive fecurity; and in that pofition we muft make ourfelves the beft fhelter in our power. With alacrity and diligence, huts may be erected that will be warm and dry. In thefe the troops will be compact, more fecure againft furprizes, than if a divided ftate, and at hand to protect the country. Thefe

cogent

cogent reasons have determined the General to take post in the neighbourhood of this camp, and influenced by them, he persuades himself that the officers and soldiers, with one heart and one mind, will resolve to surmount every difficulty with a fortitude and patience becoming their profession, and the sacred cause in which they are engaged. He himself will share the hardships and partake of every inconvenience.——

The legislature of New-Jersey, at their last sitting at Prince-town, appointed the honourable John Wetherspoon, Abraham Clark, Jonathan Elmer, Nathaniel Scudder and Elias Boudinot, Esqrs. delegates to represent this state in Congress.

Boston, December 11.

The following gentlemen are chosen by the General Assembly of this state, as delegates to serve in the Continental Congress, the ensuing year, viz. Hon. John Hancock, Esq. Samuel Adams, Esq. John Adams, Esq. Robert T. Paine, Esq. Eldridge Gerry, Esq. Francis Dana, Esq. James Lovell, Esq.

The Speech of his Excellency Governor CLINTON, *to the Assembly of the State of New-York, at the opening of the Session, in Kingston, on Wednesday the 10th of December.*

Gentlemen of the Senate and General Assembly,

The invasion of the state, on the nothern and western frontiers, and the prospect of an attack by General Howe, on the fortresses on the Highlands, obliged me to prorogue the legislature, and to deny myself the pleasure of seeing our free and happy constitution, so early organized as I could have wished. This I was the more readily led to do, as well from the busy season of the year, as the confidence, which the people justly reposed in the abilities, and integrity of the gentlemen, in whom the administration of government was then vested.

At present, by the kind interposition of Providence, the cloud which hung over us, seems in a great measure dispelled, and we have reason to expect a happy issue to this campaign.

The good conduct, and bravery of the garrison of Fort Schuyler, seconded by the intrepidity of the late gallant General Herkemer, and the militia of Tryon county, have entirely frustrated the designs of the enemy upon that part of the state, and obliged them, after the loss of a great part of their army, with the most of their baggage and artillery, disgracefully to abandon their enterprise.

The complete victory gained near Bennington, by the valour of the militia of New Hampshire, Massachusetts-Bay, and the North-Eastern counties of this state, together with a small body of Continental troops, we have reason to hope, will secure our northern frontiers. I have however, thought proper, in order to strenghten the troops commanded by Major General Gates, to repress the incursions of the savages, to embody part of the militia, and march them to the northward. I have also made a further draught for the protection of the exposed inhabitants of the county of Westchester, and for the defence of the posts in the Highlands, which I have the pleasure of assuring you, are in so respectable a state of defence, as to promise us security against any attack on that quarter. This, together with the several obstructions in Hudson's river, has probably induced General Howe to alter his original plan, and to adopt another, which from the vigilance of his Excellency General Washington, and the spirit of the southern militia, we have every reason to hope, will prove equally abortive, notwithstanding the possession of Philadelphia.

Gentlemen of the Senate and General Assembly,

As the security of every free state must, under God, depend upon its in-

ternal

ternal ftrength, I take this early opportunity to recommend to you, as a matter of the utmoft importance, a fpeedy revifion of the militia laws, which having been drawn at the commencement of this controverfy, are, from an alteration in circumftances, become inapplicable to our prefent fituation.

The ftate of our finances likewife claims your ferious attention. The want of an organized government, has hitherto rendered it impoffible to make any provifion for finking the money, which the war obliged us to iffue, and we have thus accumulated a debt, which, if neglected, will not only prove burthenfome to the ftate, but ftrike the credit of our currency, which it behoves us fo much to fupport.

You will eafily perceive, Gentlemen, from the long fufpenfion of law, and the diforder incident thereto, the neceffity of making proper provifion for the fupport of government, on the vigour and dignity of which the tranquility of the ftate will in a great meafure depend.

As the conftitution has not prefcribed the particular mode, in which elections are to be conducted, you will turn your attention to fome law for that very neceffary purpofe.

Without detaining you any longer at this time, I fhall, Gentlemen, in the courfe of the feffion, take occafion to lay before you, fuch other matters, as I conceive the neceffities of the State require.

Gentlemen,

The late convention having, in their plan of government, manifefted the moft fcrupulous attention to the freedom and happinefs of the people, and by marking the line between the executive, legiflative, and judicial powers, wifely provided for the fecurity of each, it becomes our duty to fecond their endeavours: and as our conduct will, in fome meafure, be a rule for thofe who are hereafter entrufted with the adminiftration of government, let us remain within the feveral departments in which the conftitution has placed us, and thereby preferve the fame inviolate, and repay the truft repofed in us, by our conftituents, when they made us the guardians of their rights.

I do not urge this, Gentlemen, becaufe I conceive the caution neceffary to you, but to fhew the important light in which I fee this object, and to convince you (however unequal I may find myfelf to the tafk) that it fhall always be my ftrenuous endeavour, on the one hand, to retain and exercife for the advantage of the people, the power with which they have invefted me; on the other, carefully to avoid the invafion of thofe rights, which the conftitution has placed in other perfons.

GEO. CLINTON.
Kingfton, Dec. 10, 1777.

By order of his Excellency Sir HENRY CLINTON, *Knight of the moft honourable Order of the Bath, &c.*

Whereas a Proclamation, iffued from this office, bearing date the 15th inftant, giving notice to fuch inhabitants of Long-Ifland and Staten-Ifland, as were in want of falt, to cure the neceffary provifions for their family's ufe, the enfuing winter, that upon their producing to the fuperintendant of this port, or his deputies, a certificate from the Juftice of Peace next to their place of refidence, that they *were proper perfons to be trufted,* would be allowed to carry, from New-York, any quantity of falt, not exceeding *three bufhels for a family.* And whereas it appears, that the mode pointed out by the faid Proclamation, for obtaining certificates, is inadequate to the purpofes thereby intended; publik notice is therefore hereby given, that fuch of the inhabitants of Long-Ifland, &c. as fhall hereafter apply, at this office, for the faid quantity of three bufhels of falt, muft produce a certificate from the Commanding

Commanding Officer of the King's troops, on Long-Island, or from a Field Officer of the militia of the county in which they reside, *that they are proper persons to be trusted*, and that such of the inhabitants of Staten-Island, as shall hereafter apply for the same quantity of salt, must produce at this office, a like certificate from General Campbell or General Skinner: and in order that due attention may be paid to this Proclamation, authority is hereby granted to any person or persons, *to seize all such salt as they may discover, on board any vessel or craft, or that may be transporting by land, through any parts of Long-Island or Staten-Island*, unless accompanied with a permission from this office: which salt so seized shall be the sole property of the person or persons seizing the same.

ANDREW ELLIOT, Superintendant.
Superintendant's Office,
 Nov. 18, 1777.

By *Major-general* JAMES ROBERTSON, *Commandant of New-York*,
PROCLAMATION.

In order that the poorer inhabitants of this city may receive some supplies of wood at a reasonable price, I have appointed John Thompson, Esq. of Brooklyn, to employ a number of persons to cut wood on Long-Island for that purpose, and bring it down to the wharf nearest to where the said wood is cut: therefore such persons as shall produce proper recommendations, will obtain orders from me to receive a proportion of the said wood, on their paying to the said John Thompson, the charges of cutting and carting the said wood, with an addition of four shillings per cord for his trouble in this service.

JAMES ROBERTSON, M. G.
And Commandant of New-York.

The following is copied from the
LEYDEN GAZETTE:
We have been requested on the part of the Commissioners from the Congress, at Paris, to insert the following letter addressed to all Captains and commanders of ships of war, or other armed vessels belonging to the United States of America:

" Gentlemen,

" Complaints having been brought to us of violences offered by American vessels, armed in neutral nations, in seizing vessels belonging to their subjects and carrying their flag, and in taking those of the enemy while they were under the protection of the coasts of neutral countries, contrary to the usage and custom of civilized nations; these presents are to request you not to commit any such violations, contrary to the right of nations, but to conform yourselves to the express powers in your commissions, which is to limit yourselves to the capture of such vessels at such times as they shall not be under the protection of a port, river, or neutral coast, and confine yourselves only to seizing such ships as shall have on board soldiers, ammunition, provisions, or other contraband merchandizes, destined for the British armies, and vessels employed against the United States. In all other cases you will respect the rights of neutrality as you would yourselves expect protection, and treat all neutral vessels with the greatest regard and friendship, for the honour of your country and that of yourselves.

" We are, Gentlemen,
 " Your most humble servants,
 " BENJAMIN FRANKLIN,
 " SILAS DEANE,
 " ARTHUR LEE,
Commissioners of the Congress.
At Paris, Nov. 21, 1777.

The following is an authentic COPY *of the* INSTRUCTIONS *given by* CONGRESS *to the American Plenipotentiaries sent to the several Courts of Europe.*

In Congress, Dec. 30, 1776.
Resolved,
That Commissioners be sent to the
Courts

Courts of Vienna, France, Spain, Pruffia, and the Grand Duke of Tufcany.

That the feveral Commiffioners of the United States be inftructed to affure the refpective Courts, that notwithftanding the artful and infidious endeavours of the Court of Great Britain, to reprefent the Congrefs and Inhabitants of thefe States to the European powers, as having a difpofition again to fubmit to the Sovereignty of the Crown of Great Britain, it is their determination, at all events, to maintain their Independence.

That the Commiffioners be refpectively directed to ufe every means in their power, to procure the affiftance of the Emperor of Germany, and of their moft Chriftian, Catholick, and Pruffian Majefties, for preventing Ruffian, German, and other foreign troops, from being fent to North America for hoftile purpofes againft the United States, and for obtaining a recall of thofe already fent.

That his Moft Chriftian Majefty be induced, if poffible, to affift the United States in the prefent war with Great Britain, by attacking the Electorate of Hanover, or any part of the dominions of Great Britain in Europe, the Eaft or Weft Indies.

That the Commiffioners be further empowered to ftipulate with the Court of France, that all the trade between the United States, and the Weft India Iflands, fhall be carried on by veffels either belonging to the fubjects of his Moft Chriftian Majefty, or thefe States, each having liberty to carry on fuch trade.

That the Commiffioners be likewife inftructed to affure his Moft Chriftian Majefty, that fhould his forces be employed in conjunction with the United States, to exclude his Britannick Majefty from any fhare in the Cod Fifhery of America, by reducing the Iflands of Newfoundland and Cape Breton; and that fhips of war be furnifhed, when required, by the United States, to reduce Nova Scotia, the Fifhery fhall be enjoyed equally, and in common, by the fubjects of his Moft Chriftian Majefty, provided the Province of Nova Scotia, Ifland of Cape Breton, and the remaining part of Newfoundland, be annexed to the territory and government of the United States.

That fhould the propofals, made as above, be infufficient to produce the propofed Declaration of War, and the Commiffioners are convinced and that it cannot otherwife be accomplifhed, they muft affure his Moft Chriftian Majefty, that fuch of the Britifh Weft India Iflands, as in the courfe of the war, fhall be reduced by the united force of France and thefe States, fhall be yielded an abfolute property to his Moft Chriftian Majefty. The United States engage, on timely notice, to furnifh at the expence of the faid States, and deliver at fome convenient port or ports, in the faid State, provifions for carrying an expedition againft the faid Iflands, to the amount of two millions of dollars, and fix frigates, mounting not lefs than twenty-four guns each, manned and fitted for fea; and to render any other affiftance which may be in their power, as becomes good allies.

That the Commiffioners for the Courts of France and Spain confult together, and prepare a Treaty of Commerce and Alliance, as nearly as may be, fimilar to the firft propofed to the Court of France, and not inconfiftent therewith, nor difagreeable to his Moft Chriftian Majefty, to be propofed to the Court of Spain; adding thereto,

That if his Catholick Majefty will join with the United States in a war with Great Britain, they will affift in reducing to the poffeffion of Spain, the Town and Harbour of Penfacola,

Penſacola, provided the citizens and inhabitants of the United States ſhall have the free and uninterrupted navigation of the Miſſiſippi, and the uſe of the Harbour of Penſacola ; and will, provided it ſhall be true that his Portugueſe Majeſty has inſulingly expelled the veſſels of theſe States from his ports, or has confiſcated ſuch veſſels, declare war againſt the ſaid King, if that meaſure ſhall be agreeable to, and ſupported by the Courts of France and Spain.

That the Commiſſioners for the Court of Berlin conſult with the Commiſſioners at the Court of France, and prepare ſuch Treaty or Treaties of Friendſhip and Commerce to be propoſed to the King of Pruſſia, as ſhall not be diſagreeable to their Moſt Chriſtian and Catholick Majeſties.

Extract of the Minutes,
CHARLES THOMPSON,
Secretary of the Congreſs.
By Order of the Congreſs,
JOHN HANCOCK, Preſident.

The following is an authentic copy of the letter which was ſent to Lord Lord North, by the Plenipotentiaries of the United States of America :

To the Right Hon. Lord NORTH, *Firſt Lord of the Treaſury, Chancellor of the Exchequer, and Principle Miniſter of the King of Great Britain.*

" My Lord,

" From motives of duty and an earneſt deſire of mitigating the calamities of war, we propoſed, near a year ſince, to the King of Great Britain's Ambaſſador here, an exchange of priſoners in Europe. The anſwer we received muſt have been made known to your Lordſhip, and the world will judge of its decency. It would have been honourable for that

nobie Lord, and happy for thouſands, who have ſince ſuffered unneceſſarily, if he had conſidered that moderation is a mark of wiſdom, and humanity an ornament to the higheſt ſtation. Theſe are the ſentiments at leaſt which have governed the Congreſs and people of the United States. They have wiſhed that this war, into which they entered with reluctance, might be diſtinguiſhed by the humanity with which it was conducted ; and that compaſſion might heal the wounds that were inflicted. The records of Congreſs, my Lord, were filled with proofs of tender care and attention, not only to the wants, but to the comfort and accommodation of their priſoners.

" We have wiſhed in vain to find ſuch inſtances in the acts of Britiſh governments, for unhappily all we have ſeen on this ſubject, is the public declaration of the governors and general who was choſen to commence this war that the American officers and ſoldiers ſhould be treated with equal indignity, and all devoted, without diſtinction, to the moſt ignominious fate, in terms too low for us to repeat. We have never heard of this proceeding, having been cenſured by the government from which he derived his authority. Neither has the invitation to the Indian ſavages, at a public treaty, to drink the blood and feaſt upon the body of thoſe whom you call your ſubjects, been ever diſavowed.

" It is an univerſal complaint, that the practices of thoſe in authority under you have been conformable to the principles of theſe public acts.

" Colonel Parker, a gentleman of rank, was thrown into a common gaol in Boſton, covered over with wounds, where he periſhed unpitied, for want of the common comforts which his ſituation and humanity required.

" Colonel Ethan Allen was dragged

ged in chains, from Canada to England, from England to Ireland, from Ireland to Carolina, and from thence to New-York; at a time when the officers taken from you, in the same expedition, were treated not only with lenity, but every possible indulgence.

"The barbarous treatment of Mr. Lovel, in Boston, has no parallel. Of the prisoners made in Fort Washington, two thirds of them perished by the unexampled cruelty and rigours of their captivity. Even in England, the severities which the American prisoners suffer, are, according to the testimony of every one we have seen, of the most grievous kind. Stripes have been inflicted on some, to make them commit the deepest of all crimes, the fighting against the liberties of their country. Numbers are now groaning in bondage in Africa and India, to which they were compelled by menaces of an immediate ignominious death; as contrary to every rule of war among civilized nations, as to every dictate of humanity.

"It is with the greatest regret we mention these cruelties. For the honour of humanity, we hope they will not be committed again. Your Lordship must know, that it is in the power of those we have the honour to represent, to make ample retaliation upon the numerous prisoners of all ranks in their possession; and we warn and beseech you not to render it their indispensable duty. Upwards of five hundred British seamen have been generously treated, set at liberty by our cruzers in these seas, and sent at the public expence to their country. We trust, you will think yourselves bound to dismiss, an equal number of seamen taken in the service of the United States.

"We also desire, that a person appointed by us, may have permission to furnish the subjects of the United States, who are in your prisons, with the necessaries they may want from time to time; and that a general cartel may be immediately settled, by which the unfortunate on both sides may be relieved as soon as possible from the miseries of imprisonment.

"We must beg a speedy answer, that we may transmit, without delay, the determination of your court to our constituents.

"We have the honor to be with the highest respect, my Lord,

"Your Lordship's most obedient,
"And most humble servants,
"Benjamin Franklin.
"Silas Deane.
"Arthur Lee.
"Commissioners Plenipotentiary from the Independent and United States of America."

Passi, near Paris,
Dec. 12, 1777.

The answer received from government the 3d of January, 1778, on the subject of the American prisoners, is to the following effect:

"His majesty's servants do not approve of the proposal of inspectors. They understand the establishment of the prisoners to be what is usual and proper in such cases; if there has been any neglect, they have given strict orders to have it rectified, and they will always be ready to redress any complaints that shall be made. The prisoners shall be permitted to receive, under proper regulations, any charitable donations, in their favor. Besides this, government are disposed, and have it in their intentions, as opportunity shall offer, to exchange them in America against British prisoners there. If any complaints are made through the hands of Mr. H —— y, or through any other proper channel, they will be taken into consideration, according to the case, and redressed."

Whitehall, March 17, 1778.

Copy of a letter from General Sir WILLIAM HOWE *to Lord* GEORGE GERMAIN, *one of his Majesty's principal Secretaries of State, dated at Philadelphia, the 19th of January, 1778.*

My Lord,

The present appearance of the weather encouraging me to hope the river will be sufficiently open in a few days to admit of a packet sailing, I have prepared my dispatches to this date, and shall send them off without waiting for the receipt of those from your Lordship by the Lord Hyde packet, which I am informed by Sir Henry Clinton arrived at New-York on the 1st instant, and were detained upon a supposition that the navigation of this river would not be open for a ship of force, and not thinking it adviseable, to trust them in the packet, or in the armed vessel bringing the advice.

There has not any thing more material happened since the departure of Lord Cornwallis, who I requested to be the bearer of my last dispatches, than the passing a considerable detachment of the army across the Schuylkill on the 22d of December, to take post on the heights of Derby, in order to cover the collecting and transporting by water, as well as by land, a large quantity of forage which that country afforded. About 1000 tons were brought in, a quantity judged to be nearly sufficient for the winter consumption; and the detachment returned on the 28th of December, without any further attempts from the enemy to retard the progress of the foragers, than from small parties skulking, as is their custom, to seize upon the straggling soldiers:—one of these parties, consisting of two officers and thirty men, were decoyed by two dragoons of the 17th regiment into an ambuscade, and made prisoners.

On the 30th and 31st of December the troops went into winter quarters in this town, where they are well accommodated.

The enemy's army, excepting a detachment of 1200 men at Wilmington, is hutted in the woods near Valley Forge upon the Schuylkill, 26 miles from hence, and in a very strong position.

Colonel Harcourt, who will have the honour of presenting these dispatches, has my leave to go to England upon his private affairs, to whom I beg leave to refer your Lordship for the fullest information that may be required.

I have the honour to be, &c.

W. HOWE.

List of Ships taken by the AMERICANS.

Ships Names and Masters.	From and to	
Active, Mauger,	Newfoundland to a market.	
Adventure, Foot,	Yarmouth to Cumberland.	
Adventure, Rawlinson,	Ireland to New-York,	retaken.
Ainslie,	Halifax to Quebec.	
Alexander, Welley,	Halifax to Jamaica.	
Amelia, Tyrie,	Senegal to Kingston,	with 70 slaves.
Amherst, Lorain,	Honduras to London.	
Amity's Regard,	West-Indies to New-York.	
Anne, Wilson,	Newfoundland to Jamaica,	retaken.
Ariadne, Traser,	West-Indies to Halifax,	retaken.
Aurora, Stewart,	Liverpool to New-York.	
Betsey, Booth,	Africa to the West-Indies,	with 170 slaves.
Betsey, Grant,	Halifax to Quebec.	
Betsey, Gamblet,	West-Indies to New-York.	

Betsey,

Ships Names and Masters.	From and to	
Betsey, Keagh,	Honduras to Jamaica.	
Betty, Dawson,	Liverpool to Dominica.	
Black Prince, Cooke,	Senegal to Dominica,	with 215 slaves.
Britannia, Wood,	Newfoundland to a market,	discharged.
Brothers,	Madeira to New-York,	retaken.
Canadian, Barcinth,	From Isle du Madame,	retaken.
Charlotte, Stephens,	Ireland to the West-Indies,	retaken.
Charlotte, Urban,	West-Indies to St. Augustine's.	
Charming Elizabeth,	West-Indies to New-York.	
Charming Peggy,	Jamaica to New-York,	250 hhds. rum.
Clifton, Collins,	Africa to the West-Indies,	with 300 slaves.
Concord, Mason,	New-York to the West-Indies.	
Constant, Betsey,	Leeward Islands to Halifax,	100 pun. of rum.
Count of Provence, Sheal,	West-Indies to London,	retaken.
Darly, Rimmer,	Senegal to Dominica,	full of slaves.
Dispatch, Le Geyts,	Newfoundland to a market.	
Dolphin, Polberg,	On the Banks of Newfoundland.	
Dolphin, Sewell,	London to the Bay of Honduras.	
Dorothy, Muns,	New-York to Jamaica,	retaken.
Emp. of Germany, Hawkins,	Corke to Bourdeaux.	
Endeavour, Hagget,	Liverpool to New-York.	
Fair Lady, Taylor,	Gold Coast to Jamaica,	with 270 slaves.
Fame, Coats,	St. Augustine's to London.	
Fanny, Gladwin,	Mississippi to London.	
Fanny, a snow,	Grenadoes to New-York.	
Flora, Wallace,	Leeward Islands to St. Augustine's.	
Flora, Robinson,	Newfoundland to a market.	
Fly, Bray,	London to Senegal.	
Fly, Burden,	Ditto to West-Indies.	
Fortune, Kenyan,	Ditto to Cadiz.	
Fox, a King's ship,	Halifax to London,	retaken.
General Howe privateer,	cruizing near Martinico, fitted out at Grenada.	
General Howe, Underwood,	Jamaica to New-York,	retaken.
General Keppel, Masters,	for England.	
George, Baker,	On the Banks of Newfoundland.	
George, Ellworthy,	Newfoundland to a market.	
George, Wheaton,	Bay Chaleurs to a market.	
George, Bullfinch,	Malaga to London.	
Gloucester, Lawson,	Newfoundland to West-Indies.	
Good Intent, Desper,	Newfoundland to Dominica.	
Gunton, Jones,	Yarmouth to America.	
Harriet, Hayman,	West-Indies to Liverpool.	
Hawke, Best,	Newfoundland to a market.	
Hazard,	Corke to Jamaica,	
Hope, Butler,	Newfoundland to a market.	
Hope, a schooner,	In the Delaware.	
Howe, Baine,	Pensacola to Greenock.	
Howe, Underwood,	———— ————,	retaken.
Jamaica Packet, Humphreys,	Grenada to London.	
James, Pierpoint,	Tobago to Halifax.	

[To be continued]

INDEX

I N D E X

To the FIFTH VOLUME of the REMEMBRANCER.

I owe,

INDEX.

INDEX.

I N D E X.

F I N I S.